Datsun 200SX Automotive Repair Manual

AF807614

by Rik Paul
and John H Haynes Member of the Guild of Motoring Writers

Models covered

Datsun 200SX Sport Luxury and Deluxe models;
Hardtop and Hatchback, with 2.0 or 2.2 liter NAPS-Z engine.
1980 thru 1983

ISBN 1 85010 356 9

Printed in England *(12M1 — 647)*

Haynes Publishing Group
Sparkford Nr Yeovil
Somerset BA22 7JJ England

Haynes Publications, Inc
861 Lawrence Drive
Newbury Park
California 91320 USA

Library of Congress

Catalog card number

86-82656

Acknowledgements

Thanks are due to the Nissan Motor Company for their assistance with technical information and supply of certain illustrations.

The Champion Spark Plug Company supplied the illustrations showing the various spark plug conditions. The bodywork repair photographs used in this manual were provided by Lloyd's Industries Limited who supply 'Turtle Wax', 'Dupli-Color Holts', and other Holts range products.

About this manual

Its aim

The aim of this manual is to help you get the best value from your car. It can do so in several ways. It can help you decide what work must be done (even should you choose to get it done by a garage), provide information on routine maintenance and servicing, and give a logical course of action and diagnosis when random faults occur. However, it is hoped that you will use the Manual by tackling the work yourself. On simpler jobs it may be quicker than booking the car into a garage, and going there twice, to leave and collect it. Perhaps most important, a lot of money can be saved by avoiding the costs the garage must charge to cover its labor and overheads.

The manual has drawings and descritions to show the function of the various components so that their layout can be understood. Then the tasks are described and photographed in a step-by-step sequence so that even a novice can do the work.

Its arrangement

The manual is divided into twelve Chapters, each covering a logical sub-division of the vehicle. The Chapters are each divided into Sections, numbered with single figures, e.g. 5; and the Sections into photographs (or sub-sections), with decimal numbers following on from the Section they are in, e.g. 5.1, 5.2, 5.3 etc.

It is freely illustrated, especially in those parts where there is a detailed sequence of operations to be carried out. There are two forms of illustration; figures and photographs. The figures are numbered in sequence with decimal numbers, according to their position in the Chapters; e.g. Fig. 6.4 is the 4th drawing/illustration in Chapter 6. Photographs are numbered (either individually or in related groups) the same as the Section or sub-section of the text where the operation they show is described.

There is an alphabetical index at the back of the manual as well as a contents list at the front.

References to the left or right of the vehicle are in the sense of a person in a seat facing forward.

While every care is taken to ensure that the information given in this manual is correct, no liability can be accepted by the authors or publishers for loss, damage or injury caused by any errors in, or omissions from, the information given.

Introduction to the Datsun 200SX

Although the 200SX was originally introduced in 1977, the car received a major redesign for the 1980 model year.

Besides new styling for the exterior and interior, the new version also features a larger chassis, the advanced-design NAPS-Z (Nissan Anti-Pollution System) engine, electronic fuel injection, as well as numerous other changes and improvements.

While still maintaining the slot in the Datsun line-up one step below the 280ZX, the new 200SX has been upgraded to appeal more to the moderate luxury/sport interests.

Two body styles are available; the 2-door hardtop and the 2-door hatchback. In addition, either model can be obtained in the standard Deluxe version or in the more luxurious Sport/Luxury (SL) version. Numerous comfort and convenience options are also available with either package.

The NAPS-Z engine is available with either a 5-speed manual transmission or 3-speed automatic transmission.

Mechanically, the 200SX is a straightforward, reliable car, which is not overly difficult to work due to the fact that most of its components are used on other tried and tested Datsun models.

Further information on the 200SX's various systems and components, as well as complete specifications, can be found in the appropriate individual chapters.

Contents

	Page
Acknowledgements	2
About this manual	2
Introduction to the Datsun 200SX	2
Vehicle identification numbers	6
Buying parts	8
Maintenance techniques, tools and working facilities	8
Automotive chemicals and lubricants	12
Jacking and towing	13
Booster battery (jump) starting	14
Safety first!	15
Troubleshooting	16
Chapter 1 Tune-up and routine maintenance	25
Chapter 2 Engine	48
Chapter 3 Cooling, heating and air conditioning systems	71
Chapter 4 Fuel and exhaust systems	79
Chapter 5 Engine electrical systems	98
Chapter 6 Emissions control systems	110
Chapter 7 Part A: Manual Transmission	122
Chapter 7 Part B: Automatic Transmission	132
Chapter 8 Driveline	136
Chapter 9 Braking system	146
Chapter 10 Chassis electrical system	161
Chapter 11 Suspension and steering systems	202
Chapter 12 Bodywork	224
Chapter 13 Supplement: Revisions and information on 1982 and 1983 models	241
Conversion factors	252
Index	253

Datsun 200SX SL two-door hatchback

Datsun 200SX SL two-door hardtop

Vehicle identification numbers

Modifications are a continuing and unpublicized process in vehicle manufacture. Since spare parts manuals and lists are compiled on a numerical basis, the individual vehicle numbers are essential to identify correctly the component required.

Vehicle identification Number (VIN):
This very important identification number is located on a plate attached to the left top of the dashboard and can be easily seen while looking through the windshield from the outside of the car (photo). The VIN also appears on the Vehicle Certificate of Title and Registration. It gives such valuable information as where and when the vehicle was manufactured, the model year of manufacture and the body style.

Vehicle identification plate:
This plate, which is attached to the right side of the firewall, contains the car type, engine capacity, maximum horsepower, wheelbase, engine type and car chassis serial number (photo).

Vehicle serial number
The vehicle chassis serial number, in addition to being found on the vehicle identification plate, is also stamped on the firewall adjacent to the identification plate (photo).

Engine serial number:
The engine serial number is stamped on the left side of the cylinder block, directly below the two middle spark plugs and above the engine oil dipstick.

Manual transmission serial number:
The serial number for the manual transmission is stamped onto the top of the transmission's clutch housing.

Automatic transmission serial number:
The serial number for the automatic transmission is located on the right side of the transmission case.

Color code label:
A sticker with the color code of the car's paint is located on the top right side of the radiator support. This number is useful for matching the color and type of paint for repair work.

Emission control information label:
This label is located on the right underside of the hood. Information contained on this label includes the types of emissions systems used on the car and basic tune-up specs.

Vacuum hose routing diagram:
This label is located in the middle of the underside of the hood, and identifies and shows the routing of the various vacuum lines used in the engine compartment.

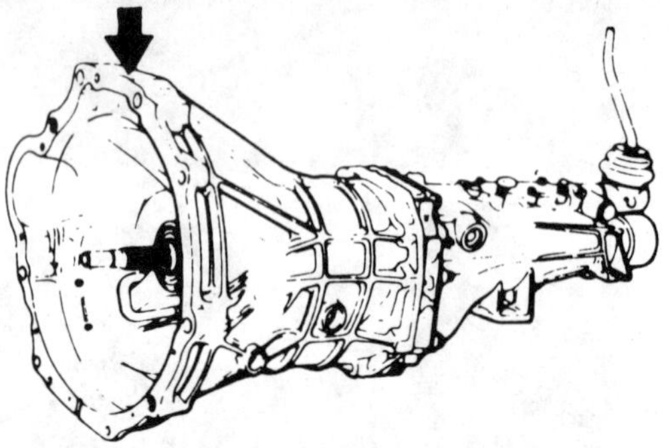

Fig. 0.2 Location of the manual transmission serial number

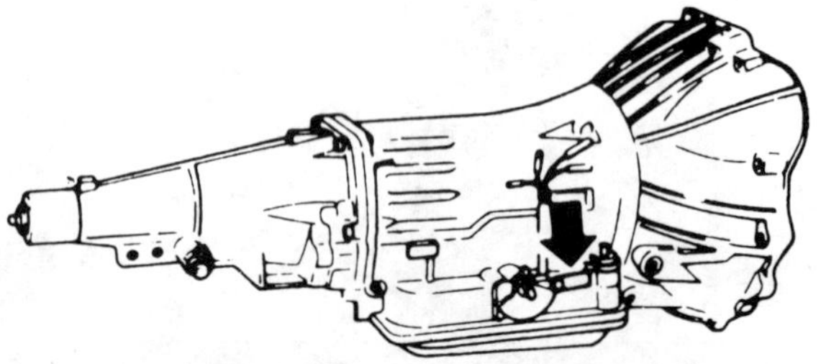

Fig. 0.3 Location of the automatic transmission serial number

VIN (Vehicle Identification Number) location

Both the vehicle identification plate and the chassis serial number are located on the right side of the firewall in the engine compartment

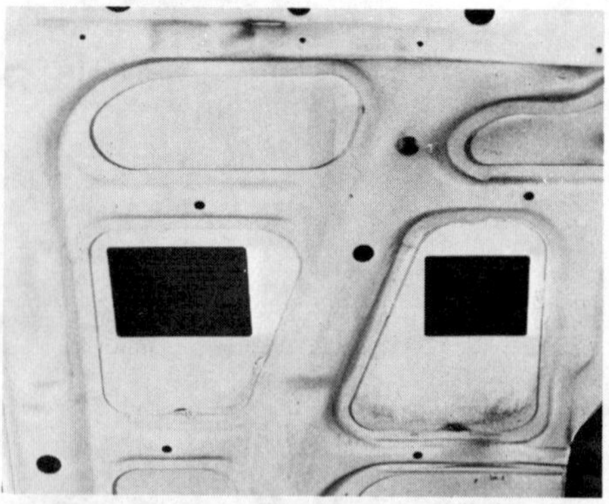

Both the emission control information label and the vacuum hose routing diagram are located on the underside of the hood

Destination	Class	Model		Engine	Transmission	Differential carrier	Wheel Size.........Offset mm (in.)	Tire size
US	Hardtop	California	PLS110FEV	Z20E	FS5W71B	H165B	5J-14............25 (0.98)	185/ 70-SR14
			PLS110AEV		3N71B			
	Hatchback		KPLS110FEV		FS5W71B			
			KPLS110AEV		3N71B			
	Hardtop	Non-California	PLS110FEU		FS5W71B		*1 5-1/2 JJ-14....25 (0.98)	185/ 70-SR14
			PLS110AEU		3N71B			
	Hatchback		KPLS110FEU		FS5W71B			
			KPLS110AEU		3N71B			
Canada	Hardtop		PLS110FEN		FS5W71B		*2 4-T x 16........35 (1.38)	T135/ 70D16*2
			PLS110AEN		3N71B			
	Hatchback		KPLS110FEN		FS5W71B			
			KPLS110AEN		3N71B			

***1 – Aluminum wheel (Option)**
***2 – Spare tire**

Prefix and suffix designations:

K P L

- K – Hatchback
- □ – Hardtop
- P – Z20 engine
- L – Left drive

F E U C L R P S T

- T – Sun roof (glass)
- S – Sport Luxury model
- P – Power Steering
- R – Sunroof (steel)
- L – Rear window wiper
- C – Air conditioner
- U – Non-California model for US
- V – California model
- N – Canada model
- E – EFI
- F – Manual Transmission
- A – Automatic transmission

□ means no indication

Fig. 0.1 Datsun 200SX model variations and vehicle identification code chart

Buying parts

Once you've found all the identification numbers, record them for reference when buying parts. Since the manufacturers change specifications, parts and vendors (who subcontract various components on the vehicle), providing the I.D. numbers is about the only way to be reasonably sure that you are buying parts for your particular vehicle. Still, that isn't absolute.

Whenever possible, take the worn part down to the parts house or dealer so that direct comparison with the new or rebuilt unit can be made. Along the trail from the manufacturer to parts shelf there are a dozen places that the part can end up with the wrong number or be listed incorrectly.

The two places to purchase new parts for your vehicle, the parts house and the dealer, differ in the type of parts that they carry. While the dealer can obtain virtually every part for your vehicle, the parts house is usually limited to normal high-wear items such as: shocks, tune-up parts, various engine gaskets, V-belts, water pumps, clutches, brake parts etc. Rarely will a parts house that specializes in foreign or domestic parts have body or interior parts, large suspension components, engine blocks, transmission gears or cases. It's always best to call the parts house and ask first, because many times you'll end up going to the vehicle dealer.

Used parts can be obtained for roughly half the price of new parts, but you don't always know what you're getting. Once again, take your worn part to the wrecking yard for direct comparisons.

Whether new, used or rebuilt, the best course is to buy from someone who specializes in your vehicle.

Maintenance techniques, tools and working facilities

There are a number of techniques involved in maintenance and repair that will be referred to throughout this manual. Application of these techniques will enable the home mechanic to be more efficient, better organised and capable of performing the various tasks properly, which will ensure that the repair job is thorough and complete.

Fastening systems

Fasteners, basically, are nuts, bolts, pins or clamps used to hold two or more parts together. There are a few things to keep in mind when working with fasteners. Almost all of them use a locking device of some type, either a lock washer, lock nut, a key or thread adhesive. All threaded fasteners should be clean, straight, have undamaged threads and undamaged corners on the hex head where the wrench fits. Develop the habit of replacing all damaged nuts and bolts with new ones.

Rusted nuts and bolts should be treated with a rust penetrating fluid. Some mechanics use turpentine in a spout type oil can, a procedure which works quite well. After applying the rust penetrant, let it "work" for a few minutes before trying to loosen the nut or bolt. Badly rusted fasteners may have to be chiseled off or removed with a special nut breaker, available at tool stores.

Flat washers and lock washers, when removed from an assembly should always be replaced exactly as removed. Replace any damaged washers with new ones. Always use a flat washer between a lock washer and any soft metal surface (such as aluminium) or thin sheet metal. Special lock nuts can only be used once or twice before they lose their locking ability and must be replaced.

If a bolt or stud breaks off in an assemblly, it can be drilled out and removed with a special tool called an E-Z out. Most automotive machine shops can perform this task, as well as others (such as the repair of threaded holes that have been stripped out).

Torqueing sequences and procedures

When threaded fasteners are tightened down, they are tightened to a specific torque value (torque is basically a twisting force). Over tightening the fastener can weaken it and cause it to break while under tightening can cause it to eventually come loose. Each bolt depending on the material it's made of and the diameter of its shank, has a specified torque value. The size and strength of a bolt is determined by the job it must do. Small bolts are generally used in light duty applications, while larger ones are used for heavy duty requirements.

Throughout this manual, references are made to specific torque values for fasteners in various components or assemblies. Be sure to follow the torque recommendations closely.

Fasteners laid out in a pattern on an assembly (i.e. cylinder head bolts, oil pan bolts, differential cover bolts, etc.) must be loosened and torqued in a sequence to avoid warping the assembly. Initially, the bolts/nuts should go on finger tight only. Next, they should be tightened one full turn each, in a criss-cross or diagonal pattern. After each one has been tightened one full turn, return to the first one tightened and tighten them all one half turn, following the same pattern. Then tighten each of them one quarter turn at a time until each fastener has been torqued to the proper value. To loosen and remove an assembly, the procedure would be reversed.

Disassembly sequence

Component disassembly should be done with care and purpose to help ensure that the parts go back together properly with nothing left over. Always keep track of the sequence in which parts are removed. Make note of special characteristics or markings on parts that can be installed more than one way (such as a grooved thrust washer on a shaft). It is a good idea to lay the disassembled parts out on a clean surface in the order that they were removed.

When removing fasteners from an assembly, keep track of which ones belong in which location. Sometimes threading a bolt back in a part, or putting the washers and nut back on a stud, can prevent mixups later. If nuts and bolts cannot be returned to their original locations, they should be kept in a compartmented box or a series of small boxes. A cupcake or muffin tin is ideal for this purpose, since each cavity can hold the bolts and nuts from a particular area (i.e. oil pan bolts, valve cover bolts, engine mount bolts, etc.). A pan of this type is especially helpful when working on assemblies with very small parts (such as the carburetor, alternator, valve train or interior dash and trim pieces). The cavities can be marked with paint or tape to identify the contents.

Whenever wiring looms, harnesses or connectors are separated, it's a good idea to identify them with numbered pieces of masking tape so that they can easily be reconnected.

Gasket sealing surfaces

Throughout any vehicle, gaskets are used to seal the mating surfaces between two parts and keep lubricants, fluids, vacuum or pressure contained in an assembly.

Many times these gaskets are coated with a liquid or paste type gasket sealing compound before assembly. Age, heat and pressure can sometimes cause the two parts to stick together so tightly that they are very difficult to separate. Often the assembly can be loosened by striking it with a soft-faced hammer near the mating surfaces. A regular hammer can be used if a block of wood is placed between the hammer and the part. Do not hammer on cast parts or parts that could be easily damaged. With any particularly stubborn part, always recheck to see that every fastener has been removed.

Avoid using a screwdriver or bar to pry apart an assembly, as they can easily mar the gasket sealing surfaces of the parts (which must remain smooth). If prying is absolutely necessary, use an old broom handle, but keep in mind that extra clean-up will be necessary if the wood splinters.

After the parts are separated, the old gasket must be carefully scraped off and the gasket surfaces cleaned. Stubborn gasket material can be soaked with rust penetrant or treated with a special chemical to soften it so that it can be easily scraped off. A scraper can be fashioned from a piece of copper tubing by flattening and sharpening one end. Copper is recommended because it is usually softer than the surfaces to be scraped, which reduces the chance of gouging the part. Some gaskets can be removed with a wire brush, but regardless of the method used, the mating surfaces must be left clean and smooth. If for some reason the gasket surface is gouged, then a gasket sealer thick enough to fill scratches will have to be used upon reassembly of the components. For most applications, a non-drying (or semi-drying) gasket sealer should be used.

Hose removal tips

Hose removal precautions closely parallel gasket removal precautions. Avoid scratching or gouging the surface that the hose mates against or the connection may leak. Because of various chemical reactions, the rubber in hoses can bond itself to the metal spigot that the hose fits over. To remove a hose, first loosen the hose clamps that secure it to the spigot. Then, with slip joint pliers, grab the hose at the clamp and rotate it around the spigot. Work it back and forth until it is completely free, then pull it off (silicone or other lubricants will ease removal if they can be applied between the hose and the spigot). Apply the same lubricant to the inside of the hose and the outside of the spigot to simplify installation.

If a hose clamp is broken or damaged, do not re-use it. Do not reuse hoses that are cracked, split or torn.

Tools

A selection of good tools is a basic requirement for anyone who plans to maintain annd repair his or her own vehicle. For the owner who has few tools, if any, the initial investment might seem high, but when compared to the spiraling costs of routine maintenance and repair, it is a wise one.

To help the owner decide which tools are needed to perform the tasks detailed in this manual, the following tool lists are offered: *Maintenance and minor repair, Repair and overhaul* and *Special.* The newcomer to practical mechanics should start off with the *Maintenance and minor repair* tool kit, which is adequate for the simpler jobs performed on a vehicle. Then, as his confidence and experience grow, he can tackle more difficult tasks, buying additional tools as they are needed. Eventually the basic kit will be built into the *Repair and overhaul* tool set. Over a period of time, the experienced do-it-yourselfer will assemble a tool set complete enough for most repair and overhaul procedures and will add tools from the *Special* category when he feels the expense is justified by the frequency of use.

Maintenance and minor repair tool kit

The tools in this list should be considered the minimum for performance of routine maintenance, servicing and minor repair work. We recommend the purchase of combination wrenches (box end and open end combined in one wrench); while more expensive than open-ended ones, they offer the advantages of both types of wrench.

Combination wrench set ($\frac{1}{4}$ in to 1 in or 6 mm to 19 mm)
Adjustable wrench – 8 in
Spark plug wrench (with rubber insert)
Spark plug gap adjusting tool
Feeler gauge set
Brake bleeder wrench
Standard screwdriver ($\frac{5}{16}$ in x 6 in)
Phillips screwdriver (2 x 6 in)
Combination pliers – 6 in
Hacksaw and assortment of blades
Tire pressure gauge
Grease gun
Oil can
Fine emery cloth
Wire brush
Battery post and cable cleaning tool
Oil filter wrench
Funnel (medium size)
Safety goggles
Jack stands (2)
Drain pan

Note: if basic tune-ups are going to be a part of routine maintenance, it will be necessary to purchase a good quality stroboscopic timing light and a combination tachometer/dwell meter. Although they are included in the list of *Special* tools, they are mentioned here because they are absolutely necessary for tuning most vehicles properly.

Repair and overhaul tool set

These tools are essential for anyone who plans to perform major repairs and are in addition to those in the *Maintenance and minor repair tool kit.* Included is a comprehensive set of sockets which, though expensive, will be found invaluable because of their versatility (especially when various extensions and drives are available). We recommend the $\frac{1}{2}$ in drive over the $\frac{3}{8}$ in drive. Although the larger drive is bulky and more expensive, it has the capability of accepting a very wide range of large sockets (ideally, the mechanic would have a $\frac{3}{8}$ in drive set and a $\frac{1}{2}$ in drive set).

Socket set(s)
Reversible ratchet
Extension – 10 in
Universal joint
Torque wrench (same size drive as sockets)
Ball pein hammer – 8 oz
Soft-faced hammer (plastic/rubber)
Standard screwdriver ($\frac{1}{4}$ in x 6 in)
Standard screwdriver (stubby – $\frac{5}{16}$ in)
Phillips screwdriver (No 3 x 8 in)
Phillips screwdriver (stubby – No 2)
Pliers – vise grip
Pliers – lineman's
Pliers – needle nose
Pliers – circlip (internal and external)
Cold chisel – $\frac{1}{2}$ in
Scriber
Scraper (made from flattened copper tubing)
Center punch
Pin punches ($\frac{1}{16}$, $\frac{1}{8}$, $\frac{3}{16}$ in)
Steel rule/straight edge – 12 in
Allen wrench set ($\frac{1}{8}$ to $\frac{3}{8}$ in or 4 mm to 10 mm)
A selection of files
Wire brush (large)
Jack stands (second set)
Jack (scissor or hydraulic type)

Note: Another tool which is often useful is an electric drill motor with a chuck capacity of $\frac{3}{8}$ in (and a set of good quality drill bits).

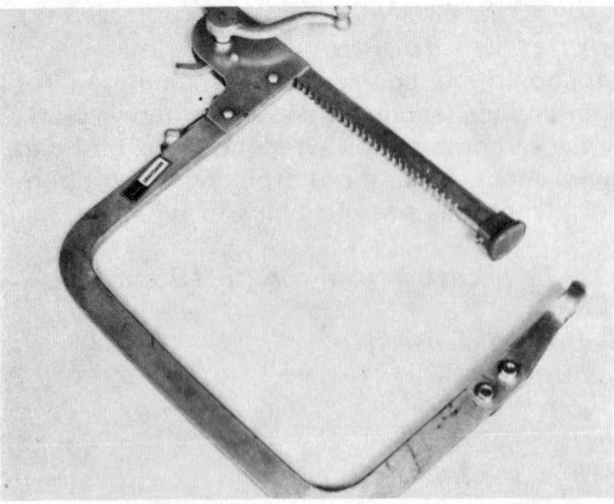

Valve spring compressor

Piston ring compressor

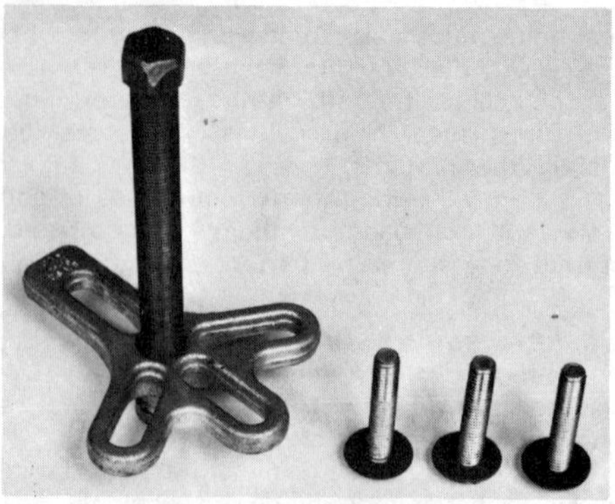

Universal hub puller

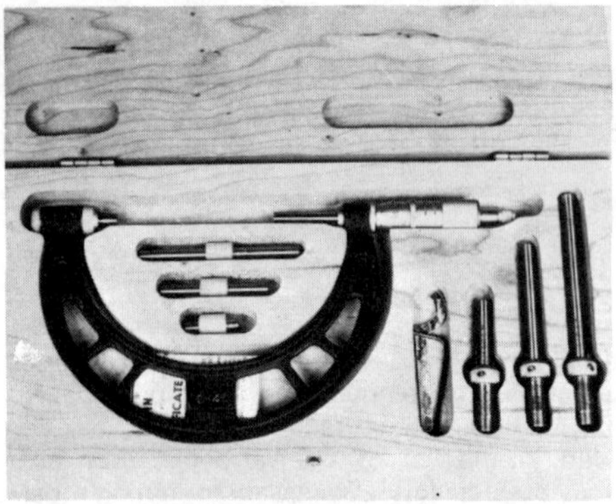

Micrometer set

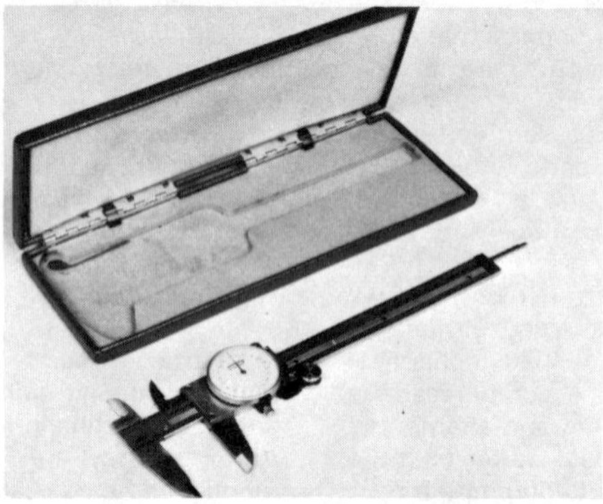

Vernier caliper

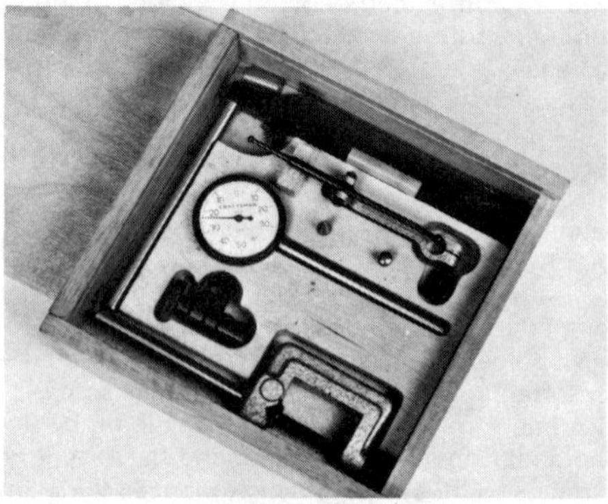

Dial gauge set

Special tools

The tools in this list include those which are not used regularly, are expensive to buy, or which need to be used in accordance with their manufacturer's instructions. Unless these tools will be used frequently, it is not very economical to purchase many of them. A consideration would be to split the cost and use between yourself and a friend or friends. In addition, most of these tools can be obtained from a tool rental shop on a temporary basis.

This list contains only those tools and instruments widely available to the public, and not those special tools produced by vehicle manufacturers for distribution to dealer service departments. Occasionally, references to the manufacturer's special tools are included in the text of this manual. Generally, an alternative method of doing the job without the special tool is offered. However, sometimes there is no alternative to their use. Where this is the case, and the tool cannot be purchased or borrowed, the work should be turned over to the dealer, a repair shop or an automotive machine shop.

Valve spring compressor
Piston ring compressor
Cylinder ridge reamer
Cylinder surfacing hone
Balljoint separator
Universal hub/bearing puller
Impact screwdriver
Micrometer(s) and/or dial calipers
Dial indicator set
Stroboscopic timing light
Tachometer/dwell meter
Universal electrical multi-meter
Cylinder compression gauge
Cable hoist
Floor jack

Buying tools

For the do-it-yourselfer who is just starting to get involved in vehicle maintenance and repair, there are a couple of options available when purchasing tools. If maintenance and minor repair is the extent of the work to be done, the purchase of individual tools is satisfactory. If, on the other hand, extensive work is planned, it would be a good idea to purchase a modest tool set from one of the large retail chain stores. A set can usually be bought at a substantial savings over the individual tool prices (and they often come with a tool box). As additional tools are needed, add-on sets, individual tools and a larger tool box can be purchased to expand the tool selection. Building a tool set gradually allows the cost of the tools to be spread over a longer period of time and gives the mechanic the freedom to choose only those tools that will actually be used.

Tool stores will often be the only source of some of the special tools that are needed, but regardless of where tools are bought, try to avoid cheap ones (especially when buying screwdrivers and sockets) because they won't last very long. The expense involved in replacing cheap tools will eventually be greater than the initial cost of quality tools.

Care and maintenance of tools

Good tools are expensive, so it makes sense to treat them with respect. Keep them in a clean and usable condition and store them properly when not in use. Always wipe off any dirt, grease or metal chips before putting them away. Never leave tools lying around in the work area. Upon completion of a job, always check closely under the hood for tools that may have been left there (so they don't get lost during a test drive).

Some tools, such as screwdrivers, pliers, wrenches and sockets, can be hung on a panel mounted on the garage or workshop wall, while others should be kept in a tool box or tray. Measuring instruments, gauges, meters, etc. must be carefully stored where they cannot be damaged by weather or impact from other tools.

When tools are used with care and stored properly, they will last a very long time. Even with the best of care, tools will wear out if used frequently. When a tool is damaged or worn out, replace it; subsequent jobs will be safer and more enjoyable if you do.

For those who desire to learn more about tools and their used, a book entitled *How to Choose and Use Car Tools* is available from the publishers of this manual.

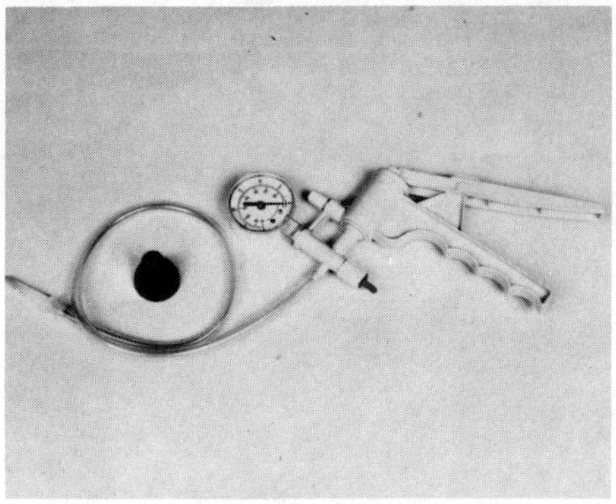
Vacuum tester

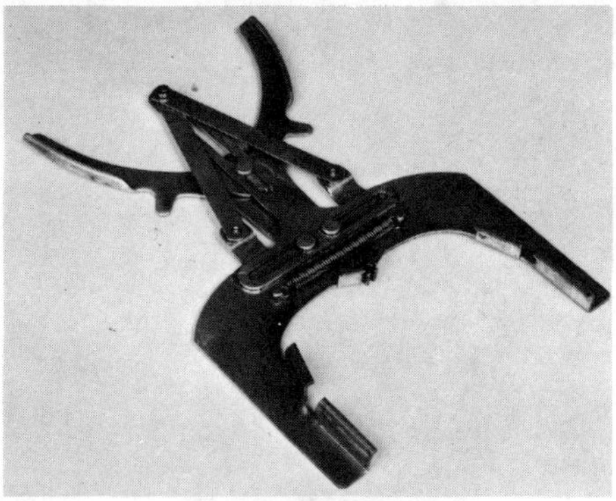
Piston ring expander

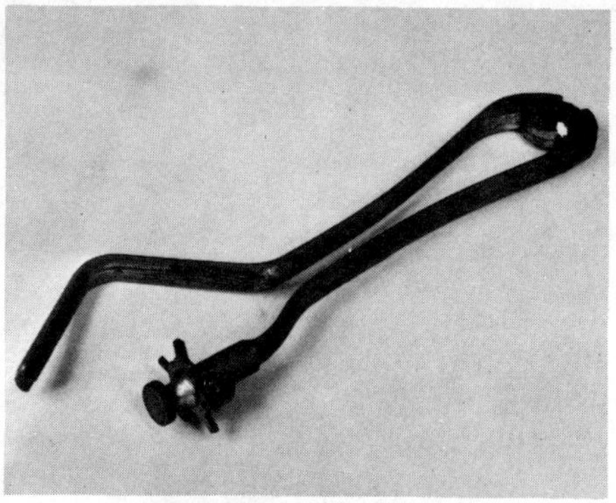
Piston ring groove cleaner

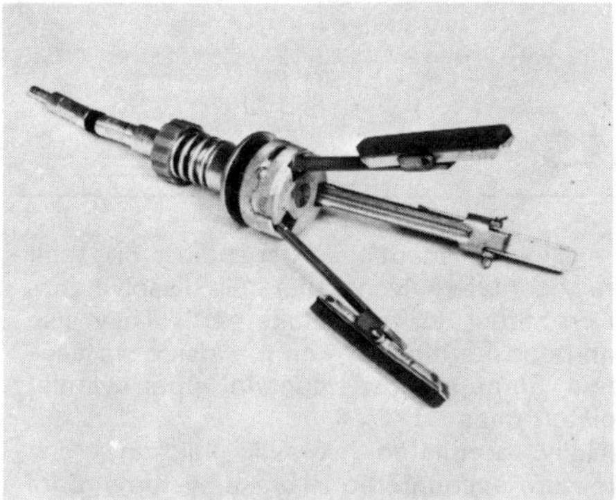
Cylinder hone

Cylinder ridge reamer

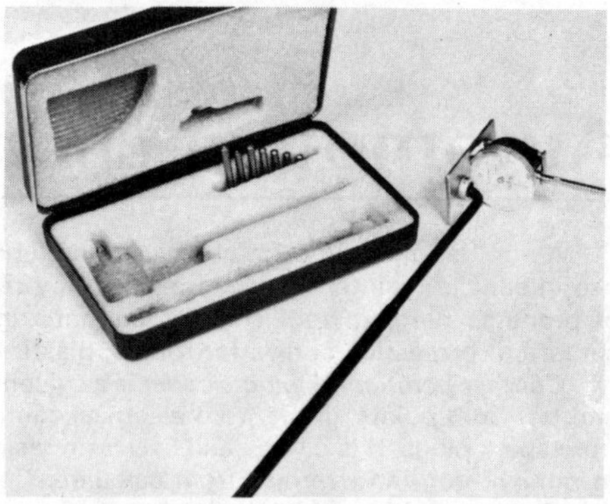
Cylinder bore taper gauge set

Working facilities

Not to be overlooked when discussing tools is the workshop. If anything more than routine maintenance is to be carried out, some sort of suitable work area is essential.

It is understood, and appreciated, that many home mechanics do not have a good workshop or garage available, and end up removing an engine or doing major repairs outside (it is recommended that the overhaul or repair be completed under the cover of a roof).

A clean, flat workbench or table of suitable working height is an absolute necessity. The workshop should be equipped with a vise that has a jaw opening of at least 4 inches.

As mentioned previously, some clean, dry storage space is also required for tools, as well as the lubricants, fluids, cleaning solvents, etc. which soon become necessary.

Sometimes waste oil and fluids, drained from the engine or transmission during normal maintenance or repairs, present a disposal problem. To avoid pouring oil on the ground or into the sewage system, simply pour the used fluids into large containers, seal them with caps and place them in a normal trash receptacle. Plastic jugs (such as old anti-freeze containers) are ideal for this purpose.

Always keep a supply of old newspapers and clean rags available. Old towels are excellent for mopping up spills. Many home mechanics use rolls of paper towels for most work because they are readily available and disposable. To keep the area under the vehicle clean, a large cardboard box can be cut open and flattened to protect the garage or shop floor.

Whenever working over a painted surface (such as when leaning over a fender to service something under the hood), always cover it with an old blanket or bedspread to protect the finish. Vinyl covered pads, made especially for this purpose, are available at auto parts stores.

Automotive chemicals and lubricants

A number of automotive chemicals and lubricants are available for use in vehicle maintenance and repair. They represent a wide variety of products ranging from cleaning solvents and degreasers to lubricants and protective sprays for rubber, plastic and vinyl.

Contact point/spark plug cleaner is a solvent used to clean oily film and dirt from points, grime from electrical connectors and oil deposits from spark plugs. It is oil free and leaves no residue. It can also be used to remove gum and varnish from carburetor jets and other orifices.

Carburetor cleaner is similar to contact point/spark plug cleaner but it is usually has a stronger solvent and may leave a slight oily residue. It is not recommended for cleaning electrical components or connections.

Brake system cleaner is used to remove grease or brake fluid from brake system components (where clean surfaces are absolutely necessary and petroleum-based solvents cannot be used); it also leaves no residue.

Silicone based lubricants are used to protect rubber parts such as hoses, weatherstripping and grommets, and are used as lubricants for hinges and locks.

Multi-purpose grease is an all purpose lubricant used whever grease is more practical than a liquid lubricant such as oil. Some multi-purpose grease is colored white and specially formulated to be more resistant to water than ordinary grease.

Bearing grease/wheel bearing grease is a heavy grease used where increased loads ,and friction are encountered (i.e. wheel bearings, universal joints, etc.).

High temperature wheel bearing grease is designed to withstand the extreme temperatures encountered by wheel bearings in disc brake equipped vehicles. It usually contains molybdenum disulfide, which is a 'dry' type lubricant.

Gear oil (sometimes called gear lube) is a specially designed oil used in differentials, manual transmissions and manual gearboxes, as well as other areas where high friction, high temperature lubrication is required. It is available in a number of viscosities (weights) for various applications.

Motor oil, of course, is the lubricant specially formulated for use in the engine. It normally contains a wide variety of additives to prevent corrosion and reduce foaming and wear. Motor oil comes in various weights (viscosity ratings) of from 5 to 80. The recommended weight of the oil depends on the seasonal temperature and the demands on the engine. Light oil is used in cold climates and under light load conditions; heavy oil is used in hot climates and where high loads are encountered. Multi-viscosity oils are designed to have characteristics of both light and heavy oils and are available in a number of weights from 5W-20 to 20W-50.

Oil additives range from viscosity index improvers to slick chemical treatments that purportedle reduce friction. It should be noted that most oil manufacturers caution against using additives with their oils.

Gas additives perform several functions, depending on their chemical makeup. They usally contain solvents that help dissolve gum and varnish that build up on carburetor and intake parts. They also serve to break down carbon deposits that form on the inside surfaces of the combustion chambers. Some additives contain upper cylinder lubricants for valves and piston rings.

Brake fluid is a specially formulated hydraulic fluid that can withstand the heat and pressure encountered in brake systems. Care must be taken that this fluid does not come in contact with painted surfaces or plastics. An opened container should always be resealed to prevent contamination by water or dirt.

Undercoating is a petroleum-based tar-like substance that is designed to protect metal surfaces on the under-side of a vehicle from corrosion. It also acts as a sound deadening agent by insulating the bottom of the vehicle.

Weatherstrip cement is used to bond weatherstripping around doors, windows and trunk lids. It is sometimes used to attach trim pieces as well.

Degreasers are heavy duty solvents used to remove grease and grime that accumulates on engine and chassis components. They can be sprayed or brushed on and, depending on the type, are rinsed with either water or solvent.

Solvents are used alone or in combination with degreasers to clean parts and assemblies during repair and overhaul. The home mechanic should use only solvents that are non-flammable and that do not produce irritating fumes.

Gasket sealing compounds may be used in conjunction with gaskets, to improve their sealing capabilities, or alone, to seal metal-to-metal joints. Many gaskets can withstand extreme heat, some are impervious to gasoline and lubricants, while others are capable of filling and sealing large cavities. Depending on the intended use, gasket sealers either dry hard or stay relatively soft and pliable. They are usually applied by hand, with a brush, or are sprayed on the gasket sealing surfaces.

Thread cement is an adhesive locking compound that prevents threaded fasteners from loosening because of vibration. It is available in a variety of types for different applications.

Moisture dispersants are usually sprays that can be used to dry out electrical components such as the distributor, fuse block and wiring connectors. Some types can also be used as treatment for rubber and as a lubricant for hinges,cables and locks.

Waxes and polishes are used to help protect painted and plated surfaces from the weather. Different types of paint may require the use of different types of wax or polish. Some polishes utilize a chemical or abrasive cleaner to help remove the top layer of oxidized (dull) paint in older vehicles. In recent years, many non-wax polishes (that contain a wide variety of chemicals such as polymers and silicones) have been introduced. These non-wax polishes are usally easier to apply and last longer than conventional waxes and polishes.

Jacking and towing

Jacking

The jack supplied with the car should be used only for changing a wheel due to a roadside flat or for raising the car enough to allow jack stands to be placed under the car to support its weight. Under no circumstances should repair work be done under the car while it is supported by this jack, nor should the engine be started or run while this jack is being used.

The 200SX comes equipped with a scissors-type jack, which is designed to lift one corner of the car by being used at the points shown in the accompanying illustration.

The car should be on level ground with the transmission in "Park" (automatic) or "Reverse" (manual). The parking brake should be firmly set. Blocking the front and rear of the wheel on the same side as the one being lifted will further prevent the car from rolling.

Remove the jack from the trunk and assemble it. Place the jack under the appropriate jacking point, turn it clockwise and slowly raise it so that it engages in the notch formed in the rocker panel. The base of the jack should still be sitting flat on the ground.

Operate the jack with a slow, smooth motion, and be attentive to any shifting in the weight of the car.

Raise the vehicle just enough so either the wheel and tire to be changes just clears the ground, or so jack stands can be placed into position under the car. If jack stands are being used, rotate the jack lever counterclockwise to lower it until the weight of the car is off the jack.

To remove the jack stands, the jack must be used once more to lift the vehicle so the stands can be removed from under the car. Then the car can be lowered to the ground and the jack removed.

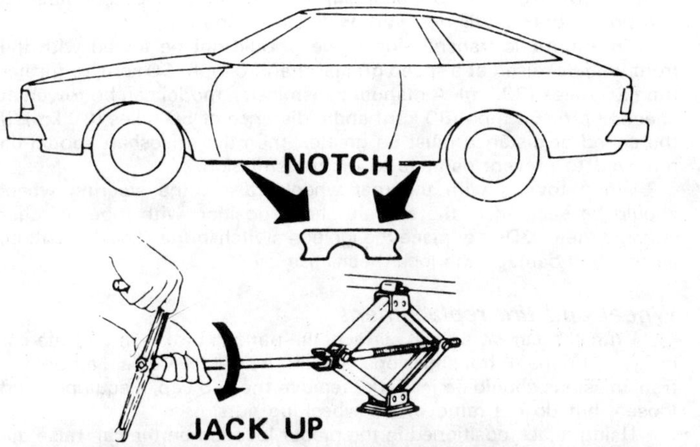

The scissors-type jack supplied with the 200SX should be securely engaged in the rocker panel notch during use

Towing

The car can be towed while rolling on its own wheels, providing that the transmission, axles, steering system and power train are in good condition. If any of these components are damaged, a dolly must be used.

Safety is a major consideration when towing, and all applicable

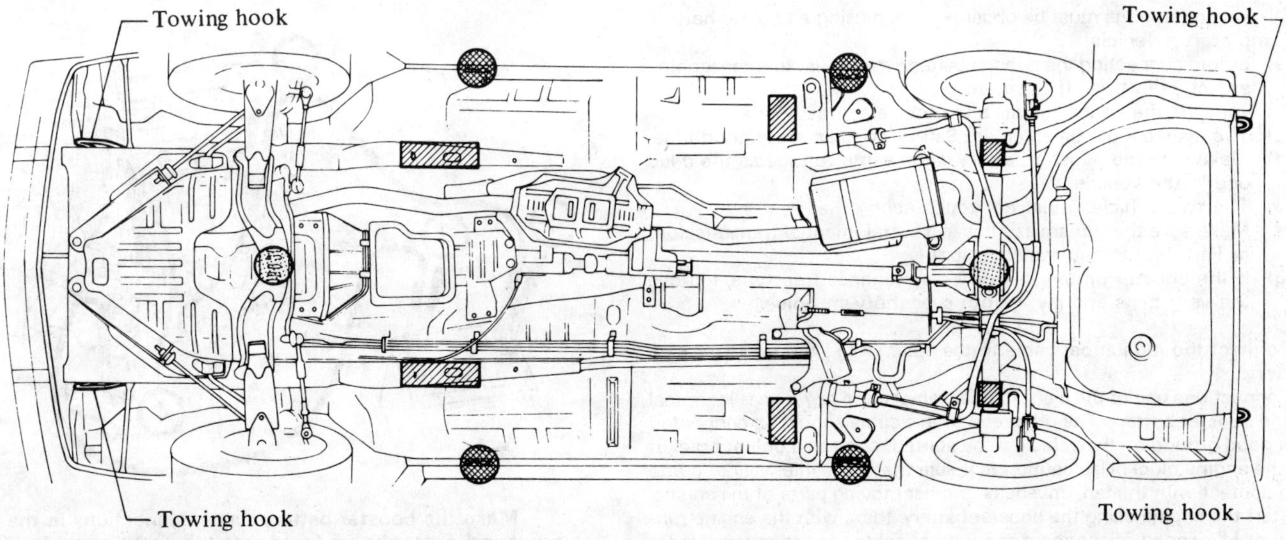

: Jack-up point for pantograph jack

: Jack-up point for garage jack

: Supportable point for safety stand

Recommended jacking and support points for the 200SX

state and local laws should be obeyed. A safety chain system must be used for all towing.

Towing equipment should be securely attached to the main structural members of the car and not to the bumper or brackets. The tow hooks, located under the front and rear bumpers should be used only in emergency situations, such as pulling the car from mud, snow, a ditch, etc. Do not apply force to these hooks in a sideward direction.

While towing, the parking brake should be fully released and the transmission should be in Neutral. The steering must be unlocked (ignition switch in the Off position). Remember that power steering and power brakes will not work with the engine off.

An automatic transmission model should not be towed with the front wheels raised at a speed greater than 20 mph (30 kph), or further than 20 miles (30 km). A manual transmission model can be towed at speeds up to 50 mph (80 kph) and a distance of 50 miles (80 km). If the speed or distance must be greater, then the driveshaft should be removed to prevent damage to the transmission.

When towing with the rear wheels raised, the steering wheel should be secured in the straight-ahead position with rope or other suitable means. Do not place the ignition switch in the "Lock" position, as this will damage the lock mechanism.

Wheel and tire replacement

With the car on a level surface, the parking brake on and the car in gear (manual transmissions should be in 'Reverse'; automatic transmissions should be in 'Park') remove the hub cap, if equipped and loosen, but do not remove, the wheel lug nuts.

Using a jack positioned in the proper location on the car, raise the car just enough so that the tire clears the ground surface.

Remove the lug nuts.

Remove the wheel and tire.

If a flat tire is being replaced, ensure that there's adequate ground clearance for the new inflated tire, then mount the wheel and tire on the wheel studs.

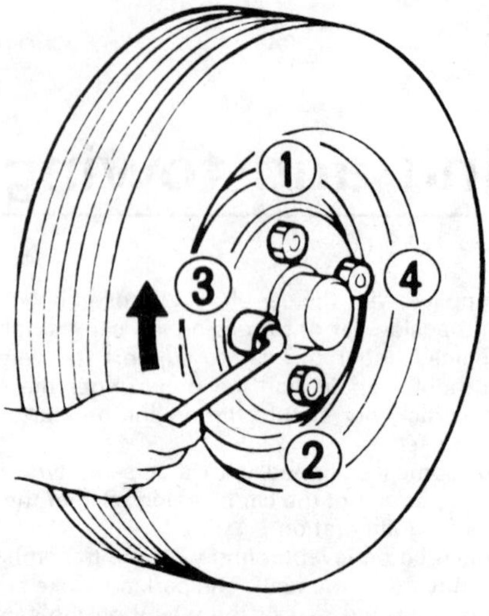

The wheel lug nuts should be tightened in the diagonal pattern shown

Apply a light coat of spray lubricant or light oil to the wheel stud threads and install the lug nuts. On steel wheels, be sure the cone-shaped end faces the wheel.

Lower the car until the tire contacts the ground and the wheel studs are centered in their wheel holes.

Tighten the lug nuts evenly in a cross-pattern, and torque to specs.

Lower the car completely and remove the jack.

Replace the hub cap, if so equipped.

Booster battery (jump) starting

Certain precautions must be observed when using a booster battery to jump start a vehicle.

a) Before connecting the booster battery, make sure that the ignition switch is in the Off position.
b) Turn off the lights, heater and other electrical loads.
c) The eyes should be shielded. Safety goggles are a good idea.
d) Make sure the booster battery is the same voltage as the dead one in the vehicle.
e) The two vehicles must not touch each other.
f) Make sure the transmission is in Neutral (manual transmission) or Park (automatic transmission).
g) If the booster battery is not a maintenance-free type, remove the vent caps and lay a cloth over the vent holes.

Connect the red jumper cable to the *positive* (+) terminals of each battery.

Connect one end of the black jumper cable to the *negative* (–) terminal of the booster battery. The other end of this cable should be connected to a good ground on the vehicle to be started, such as a bolt or bracket on the engine block. Use caution to insure that the cable will not come into contact with the fan, drivebelts or other moving parts of the engine.

Start the engine using the booster battery, then, with the engine running at idle speed, disconnect the jumper cables in the reverse order of connection.

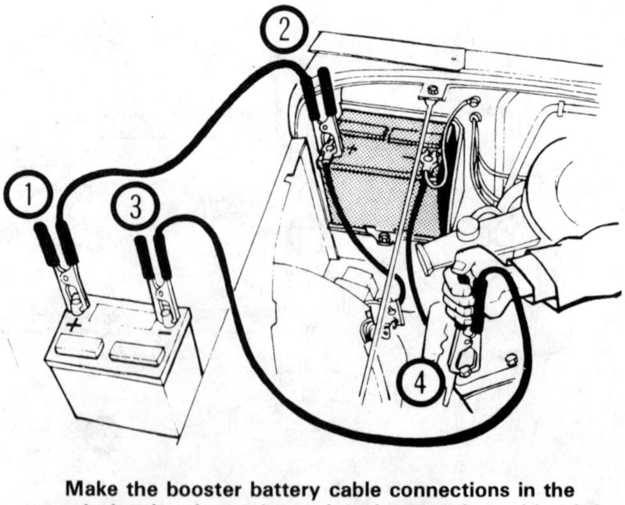

Make the booster battery cable connections in the numerical order shown (note that the negative cable of the booster battery is not attached to the negative terminal of the dead battery)

Safety first!

Regardless of how enthusiastic you may be about getting on with the job at hand, take the time to ensure that your safety is not jeopardized. A moment's lack of attention can result in an accident, as can failure to observe certain simple safety precautions. The possibility of an accident will always exist, and the following points should not be considered a comprehensive list of all dangers. Rather, they are intended to make you aware of the risks and to encourage a safety conscious approach to all work you carry out on your vehicle.

Essential DOs and DON'Ts

DON'T rely on a jack when working under the vehicle. Always use approved jackstands to support the weight of the vehicle and place them under the recommended lift or support points.
DON'T attempt to loosen extremely tight fasteners (i.e. wheel lug nuts) while the vehicle is on a jack — it may fall.
DON'T start the engine without first making sure that the transmission is in Neutral (or Park where applicable) and the parking brake is set.
DON'T remove the radiator cap from a hot cooling system — let it cool or cover it with a cloth and release the pressure gradually.
DON'T attempt to drain the engine oil until you are sure it has cooled to the point that it will not burn you.
DON'T touch any part of the engine or exhaust system until it has cooled sufficiently to avoid burns.
DON'T siphon toxic liquids such as gasoline, antifreeze and brake fluid by mouth, or allow them to remain on your skin.
DON'T inhale brake lining dust — it is potentially hazardous (see *Asbestos* below)
DON'T allow spilled oil or grease to remain on the floor — wipe it up before someone slips on it.
DON'T use loose fitting wrenches or other tools which may slip and cause injury.
DON'T push on wrenches when loosening or tightening nuts or bolts. Always try to pull the wrench toward you. If the situation calls for pushing the wrench away, push with an open hand to avoid scraped knuckles if the wrench should slip.
DON'T attempt to lift a heavy component alone — get someone to help you.
DON'T rush or take unsafe shortcuts to finish a job.
DON'T allow children or animals in or around the vehicle while you are working on it.
DO wear eye protection when using power tools such as a drill, sander, bench grinder, etc. and when working under a vehicle.
DO keep loose clothing and long hair well out of the way of moving parts.
DO make sure that any hoist used has a safe working load rating adequate for the job.
DO get someone to check on you periodically when working alone on a vehicle.
DO carry out work in a logical sequence and make sure that everything is correctly assembled and tightened.
DO keep chemicals and fluids tightly capped and out of the reach of children and pets.
DO remember that your vehicle's safety affects that of yourself and others. If in doubt on any point, get professional advice.

Asbestos

Certain friction, insulating, sealing, and other products — such as brake linings, brake bands, clutch linings, torque converters, gaskets, etc. — contain asbestos. *Extreme care must be taken to avoid inhalation of dust from such products since it is hazardous to health.* If in doubt, assume that they *do* contain asbestos.

Fire

Remember at all times that gasoline is highly flammable. Never smoke or have any kind of open flame around when working on a vehicle. But the risk does not end there. A spark caused by an electrical short circuit, by two metal surfaces contacting each other, or even by static electricity built up in your body under certain conditions, can ignite gasoline vapors, which in a confined space are highly explosive. Do not, under any circumstances, use gasoline for cleaning parts. Use an approved safety solvent.

Always disconnect the battery ground (–) cable *at the battery* before working on any part of the fuel system or electrical system. Never risk spilling fuel on a hot engine or exhaust component.

It is strongly recommended that a fire extinguisher suitable for use on fuel and electrical fires be kept handy in the garage or workshop at all times. Never try to extinguish a fuel or electrical fire with water.

Fumes

Certain fumes are highly toxic and can quickly cause unconsciousness and even death if inhaled to any extent. Gasoline vapor falls into this category, as do the vapors from some cleaning solvents. Any draining or pouring of such volatile fluids should be done in a well ventilated area.

When using cleaning fluids and solvents, read the instructions on the container carefully. Never use materials from unmarked containers.

Never run the engine in an enclosed space, such as a garage. Exhaust fumes contain carbon monoxide, which is extremely poisonous. If you need to run the engine, always do so in the open air, or at least have the rear of the vehicle outside the work area.

If you are fortunate enough to have the use of an inspection pit, never drain or pour gasoline and never run the engine while the vehicle is over the pit. The fumes, being heavier than air, will concentrate in the pit with possibly lethal results.

The battery

Never create a spark or allow a bare light bulb near the battery. The battery normally gives off a certain amount of hydrogen gas, which is highly explosive.

Always disconnect the battery ground (–) cable *at the battery* before working on the fuel or electrical systems.

If possible, loosen the filler caps or cover when charging the battery from an external source. Do not charge at an excessive rate or the battery may burst.

Take care when adding water and when carrying a battery. The electrolyte, even when diluted, is very corrosive and should not be allowed to contact clothing or skin.

Always wear eye protection when cleaning the battery to prevent the caustic deposits from entering your eyes.

Household current

When using an electric power tool, inspection light, etc., which operates on household current, always make sure that the tool is correctly connected to its plug and that, where necessary, it is properly grounded. Do not use such items in damp conditions and, again, do not create a spark or apply excessive heat in the vicinity of fuel or fuel vapor.

Secondary ignition system voltage

A severe electric shock can result from touching certain parts of the ignition system (such as the spark plug wires) when the engine is running or being cranked, particularly if components are damp or the insulation is defective. In the case of an electronic ignition system, the secondary system voltage is much higher and could prove fatal.

Troubleshooting

Contents

Symptom **Applicable Section**

Engine and performance
Battery will not hold a charge 11
Engine backfires 18
Engine diesels (continues to run) after switching off 21
Engine hard to start when cold 4
Engine hard to start when hot 5
Engine lacks power 17
Engine 'lopes' while idling or idles erratically 8
Engine misses at idle speed 9
Engine misses throughout driving speed range 14
Engine rotates but will not start 2
Engine stalls 16
Engine starts but stops immediately 7
Engine surges while holding accelerator steady 19
Engine will not rotate when attempting to start 1
Excessive fuel consumption 24
Excessively high idle speed 10
Excessive oil consumption 23
Fuel odor 25
Hesitation or stumble on acceleration 15
Ignition light fails to come on when key is turned 13
Ignition light fails to go out 12
Low oil pressure 22
Miscellaneous engine noises 26
Pinging or knocking engine sounds on hard acceleration or uphill 20
Starter motor noisy or excessively rough in engagement 6
Starter motor operates without rotating engine 3

Engine cooling system
Abnormal coolant loss 31
Corrosion 33
External coolant leakage 29
Internal coolant leakage 30
Overcooling 28
Poor coolant circulation 32

Clutch
Clutch pedal stays on floor when disengaged 39
Clutch slips (engine speed increases with no increase in road speed) 35
Fails to release (pedal pressed to the floor – shift lever does not move freely in and out of reverse) 34
Grabbing (chattering) on takeup 36
Squeal or rumble with clutch fully disengaged (pedal depressed) 38
Squeal or rumble with clutch fully engaged (pedal releaed) 37

Manual transmission
Difficulty in engaging gears 45
Fluid leakage 44
Noise occurs while shifting gears 46
Noisy in all gears 41
Noisy in Neutral with engine running 40
Noisy in one particular gear 42
Slips out of gear 43

Automatic transmission
Engine will start in gears other than 'P' (Park) or 'N' (Neutral) 50
Fluid leakage 47
General shift mechanism problems 48
Transmission slips, shifts rough, is noisy or has no drive in forward or reverse 51
Transmission will not downshift with the accelerator pedal pressed to the floor 49

Driveshaft
Knock or clunk when transmission is under initial load (just after transmission is put into gear) 53
Leakage of fluid at front of driveshaft 52
Metallic grating sound consistent with road speed 54
Scraping noise 56
Vibration 55
Whining or whistling noise 57

Rear axle and differential
Knocking sound during starting or gear shifting 59
Noise – same when in drive as when vehicle is coasting 58
Noise while turning 60
Oil leakage 62
Vibration 61

Brakes
Brake pedal feels spongy when depressed 66
Brake pedal pulsates during brake application 69
Brakes drag (indicated by sluggish engine performance or wheels being very hot after driving) 70
Excessive brake pedal travel 65
Excessive effort required to stop vehicle 67
Noise (high-pitched squeak) 64
Pedal travels to floor with little resistance 68
Rear brakes lock up under heavy brake application (indicated by a skidding effect) 72
Rear brakes lock up under light brake application (indicated by a skidding effect) 71
Vehicle pulls to one side under braking 63

Suspension and steering
Car pulls to one side 73
Excessively stiff steering 77
Excessive pitching and/or rolling around corners or during braking 75
Excessive play in steering 78
Excessive tire wear (not specific to one area) 84
Excessive tire wear on inside edge 86
Excessive tire wear on outside edge 85
Lack of power assistance (with power steering system) 79
Miscellaneous noises 83
Noisy power steering pump 82
Shimmy, shake or vibration 74
Steering effort not the same in both directions (power system) .. 81
Steering wheel fails to return to straight-ahead position 80
Tire tread worn in one place 87
Wandering or general instability 76

This section provides an easy-reference guide to the more common faults which may occur during the operation of your Datsun. These faults and their probable causes are grouped under their respective systems e.g. Engine, Cooling System, etc., and also refer to the Chapter and/or Section which deals with the problem.

Remember that successful fault diagnosis is not a mysterious 'black art' practiced only by professional mechanics, it's simply the result of a bit of knowledge combined with an intelligent, systematic approach to the problem. Always work by a process of elimination starting with the simplest solution and working through to the most complex – and never overlook the obvious. Even the most thorough and organized motorists have been known to forget to fill the gas tank or have left the car lights on overnight, so don't assume that you are above such oversights.

Finally, always get clear in your mind why a fault has occurred and take steps to ensure that it doesn't happen again. If the electrical system fails owing to a poor connection, check all other connections in the system to make sure that they don't fail as well; if a particular fuse continues to blow, find out why – don't just go on replacing fuses. Remember, failure of a small component can often be indicative of potential failure or incorrect functioning of a more important component or system.

Engine and performance

1 Engine will not rotate when attempting to start

1 Battery terminal connections loose or corroded. Check the cable terminals at the battery; tighten or clean corrosion as necessary.
2 Battery discharged or faulty. If the cable connectors are clean and tight on the battery posts, turn the key to the 'On' position and switch on the headlights and/or windshield wipers. If these fail to function, the battery is discharged.
3 Automatic transmission not fully engaged in 'Park' (P) or neutral (N).
4 Broken, loose or disconnected wiring in the starting circuit. Inspect all wiring and connectors at the battery, starter solenoid and ignition switch (on steering column).
5 Starter motor pinion jammed on flywheel ring gear. If manual transmission, place gearshift in gear and rock the car to manually turn the engine. Remove starter (Chapter 5) and inspect pinion and flywheel (Chapter 2) at earliest convenience.
6 Starter solenoid faulty (Chapter 5).
7 Starter motor faulty (Chapter 5).
8 Ignition switch faulty (Chapter 10).

2 Engine rotates but will not start

1 Fuel tank empty.
2 Battery discharged (engine rotates slowly). Check the operation of electrical components as described in previous Section.
3 Battery terminal connections loose or corroded. See previous Section.
4 Fuel not reaching injectors. Check for clogged fuel filter or lines, or defective fuel pump. Also make sure the tank vent lines are not clogged. (Chapter 4).
5 EFI system not operating properly. Check the relay, control unit, exhaust gas sensor and wiring harness for loose connections or damage (Chapter 4).
6 Faulty distributor components. Check the cap and rotor (Chapter 1.
7 Low cylinder compression (test compression as described in Chapter 1).
8 Valve clearances not properly adjusted (Chapter 1).
9 Water in fuel. Drain and fill with new fuel.
10 Defective cylinder head temperature sensor (Chapter 4).
11 Air leak. Check intake manifold, engine oil dipstick, oil cap, PCV valve and air flow meter hoses.
12 Excessive moisture on, or damage to ignition components (Chapter 5).
13 Worn, faulty or incorrectly adjusted spark plugs (Chapter 1).
14 Broken, loose or disconnected wiring in the starting circuit (see previous Section).
15 Distributor loose, thus changing ignition timing. Turn the distributor body as necessary to start the engine, then set ignition timing as soon as possible (Chapter 1).
16 Broken, loose or disconnected wires at the ignition coil, or faulty coil (Chapter 5).

3 Starter motor operates without rotating engine

1 Starter pinion sticking. Remove the starter (Chapter 5) and inspect.
2 Starter pinion or engine flywheel teeth worn or broken. Remove the inspection cover on the left side of the engine and inspect.

4 Engine hard to start when cold

1 Battery discharged or low.Check as described in Section 1.
2 Fuel not reaching the injector system. Check the fuel filter, lines and fuel pump (Chapter 4).
3 Faulty EFI system (Chapter 4).

5 Engine hard to start when hot

1 Air filter in need of replacement.
2 Fuel not reaching EFI system (see Section 4). Check particularly for a vapor lock situation, brought about by clogged fuel tank vent lines.

6 Starter motor noisy or excessively rough in engagement

1 Pinion or flywheel gear teeth worn or broken. Remove the inspection cover on the left side of the engine and inspect.
2 Starter motor retaining bolts loose or missing.

7 Engine starts but stops immediately

1 Loose or faulty electrical connections at distributor, coil or generator.
2 Vacuum leak at the gasket surfaces of the intake manifold. Check that all mounting bolts are tightened to specifications and all vacuum hoses connected to the manifold are positioned properly and are in good condition.
3 Fuel not reaching EFI system (see Section 4).
4 EFI system not working properly. Check the relay, control unit, injectors and air regulator (Chapter 4).

8 Engine 'lopes' while idling or idles erratically

1 Vacuum leakage. Check mounting bolts at the intake manifold for tightness. Check that all vacuum hoses are connected and are in good condition. Use a stethescope or a length of fuel line hose held against your ear to listen for vacuum leaks while the engine is running. A hissing sound will be heard. A soapy water solution will also detect leaks. Check the intake manifold gasket surfaces.
2 Leaking EGR valve or plugged PCV valve (see Chapter 6).
3 Air cleaner clogged and in need of replacement (Chapter 1).
4 Fuel pump not delivering sufficient fuel (Section 4).
5 Leaking head gasket. If this is suspected, perform a cylinder compression check (Chapter 1).
6 Timing chain or gears worn and in need of replacements (Chapter 2).
7 Camshaft lobes worn, necessitating the removal of the camshaft for inspection (Chapter 2).
8 Valve clearance out of adjustment (Chapter 1).
9 Ignition timing out of adjustment (Chapter 1).
10 Ignition system not operating properly (Chapter 5).
11 EFI system not operating properly (Chapter 4).
12 Damaged exhaust gas sensor (Chapter 1).

9 Engine misses at idle speed

1 Spark plugs faulty or not gapped properly (Chpter 1).
2 Faulty spark plug wires (Chapter 1).
3 Excessive moisture and/or damage on distributor components (Chapter 1).
4 Shorts in ignition, coil or spark plug wires.
5 Sticking or faulty emissions systems (see Chapter 6).
6 Clogged fuel filter and/or foreign matter in fuel. Remove the fuel filter (Chapter 1) and inspect.
7 Vacuum leaks at intake manifold or at hose connections. Check as described in Section 8.
8 Incorrect idle speed (Chapter 1) or idle mixture (Chapter 4).
9 Incorrect ignition timing (Chapter 1).
10 Uneven or low cylinder compression. Remove plugs and use compression tester as per manufacturer's instructions (Chapter 1).

10 Excessively high idle speed

1 Defective air regulator (Chapter 4).
2 Throttle valve opened excessively at idle (Chapter 4).
3 Idle speed incorrectly adjusted (Chapter 1).
4 Defective Vacuum Control Valve (VCV) (Chapter 6).
5 Valve clearances incorrectly adjusted (Chapter 1).

11 Battery will not hold a charge

1 Generator drive belt defective or not adjusted properly (Chapter 1).
2 Battery terminals loose or corroded (Chapter 1).
3 Generator not charging properly (Chapter 5).
4 Loose, broken or faulty wiring in the charging circuit (Chapter 5).
5 Short in vehicle circuitry causing a continual drain on battery (Chapter 10).
6 Battery defective internally.
7 Faulty regulator (Chapter 5).

12 Ignition light fails to go out

1 Fault in generator or charging circuit (Chapter 5).
2 Generator drive belt defective or not properly adjusted (Chapter 1).

13 Ignition light fails to come on when key is turned

1 Ignition light bulb faulty (Chapter 10).
2 Generator faulty (Chapter 5).
3 Fault in the printed circuit, dash wiring or bulb holder (Chapter 10).

14 Engine misses throughout driving speed range

1 Fuel filter clogged and/or impurities in the fuel system. Check fuel filter (Chapter 1) or clean system (Chapter 4).
2 Faulty or incorrectly gapped spark plugs (Chapter 1).
3 Incorrectly set ignition timing (Chapter 1).
4 Cracked distributor cap, disconnected distributor wires, or damage to the distributor components (Chapter 1).
5 Leaking spark plug wires (Chapter 1).
6 Emissions system components faulty (Chapter 6).
7 Low or uneven cylinder compression pressures. Remove spark plugs and test compression with gauge (Chapter 1).
8 Weak or faulty ignition coil (Chpter 5).
9 Weak or faulty ignition system (Chapter 5).
10 Vacuum leaks at intake manifold or vacuum hoses (see Section 8).
11 Loose EFI harness connections (Chapter 4).
12 Leaky EGR valve (Chapter 6).
13 Defective EFI control unit (Chapter 4).

15 Hesitation or stumble on acceleration

1 Ignition timing incorrectly set (Chapter 1).
2 Ignition system not operating properly (Chapter 5).
3 Air flow meter not operating properly. Check for smooth movement of the flap (Chapter 4).
4 Intake air leakage. Check at the PCV valve, VC valve, engine oil dipstick, oil cap, intake manifold and air flow meter hoses (refer to Section 8).
5 Mixture ratio feedback system not operating properly (Chapter 6).
6 Low fuel pressure. Check for proper operation of the fuel pump, and for blockage in the fuel filter and lines (Chapter 4).
7 EFI system not operating correctly (Chapter 4).

16 Engine stalls

1 Idle speed incorrectly set (Chapter 1).
2 Fuel filter clogged and/or water and impurities in the fuel system (Chapter 1).
3 EFI system not operating properly (Chapter 4).
4 Distributor components damp, or damage to distributor cap, rotor etc. (Chapter 1).
5 Emissions system components faulty (Chapter 6).
6 Faulty or incorrectly gapped spark plugs. (Chapter 1). Also check spark plug wires (Chapter 1).
7 Vacuum leak at the intake manifold or vacuum hoses. Check as described in Section 8.
8 Valve lash incorrectly set (Chapter 1).
9 Defective exhaust gas sensor (Chapter 1).

17 Engine lacks power

1 Incorrect ignition timing (Chapter 1).
2 Excessive play in distributor shaft. At the same time check for faulty distributor cap, wires, etc. (Chapter 1).
3 Faulty or incorrectly gapped spark plugs (Chapter 1).
4 Air cleaner needs replacing (Chapter 1).
5 Weak coil or condensor (Chapter 5).
6 Faulty coil (Chapter 5).
7 Brakes binding (Chapters 1 and 9).
8 Automatic transmission fluid level incorrect, causing slippage (Chapter 1).
9 Manual transmission clutch slipping (Chapter 8).
10 Fuel filter clogged and/or impurities in the fuel system (Chapter 1 and 4).
11 EGR system not functioning properly (Chapter 6).
12 Use of sub-standard fuel. Fill tank with proper octane fuel.
13 Low or uneven cylinder compression pressures. Test with compression tester, which will also detect leaking valves and/or blown head gasket (Chapter 1).
14 EFI system not operating properly. Check for seized injector, loose harness connectors, defective throttle valve switch, defective air flow meter, or if the throttle valve is not opening all the way (Chapter 4).
15 Intake air leak. Check around the intake manifold, the engine oil dipstick, oil cap, air intake air flow meter hoses, and PCV valve (refer to Section 8).

18 Engine backfires

1 EGR system not functioning properly (Chapter 6).
2 Ignition timing incorrect (Chapter 1).
3 EFI system not operating properly (Chapter 4).
4 Mixture ratio feedback system not operating properly (Chapter 6).
5 Vacuum leak (refer to Section 8).
6 Valve clearances not correctly adjusted (Chapter 1).
7 Damaged valve springs or sticking valves (Chapter 2).
8 Intake air leak. (see Section 15).

19 Engine surges while holding accelerator steady

1 Air flow meter not functioning properly. Check for smooth movement of the flap (Chapter 4).
2 Intake air leak (see previous Section).

3 Fuel pump not working properly (Chapter 4).
4 Mixture ratio feedback system not operating properly (Chapter 6).
5 EFI system not operating properly (Chapter 4).

20 Pinging or knocking engine sounds on hard acceleration or uphill

1 Incorrect grade of fuel. Fill tank with fuel of the proper octane rating.
2 Ignition timing incorrect (Chapter 1).
3 Carbon build-up in combustion chambers. Remove cylinder head and have chambers cleaned (Chapter 2).
4 Improper spark plugs (Chapter 1).

21 Engine diesels (continues to run) after switching off

1 Idle speed too fast (Chapter 1).
2 Ignition timing incorrectly adjusted (Chapter 1).
3 Incorrect heat range of spark plugs (Chaapter 1).
4 Intake air leak. (see Section 15).
5 Carbon build-up in combustion chamber. Remove the cylinder head and have chambers cleaned (Chapter 2).
6 Valves sticking (Chapter 2).
7 Damaged cylinder head temperature sensor (Chapter 4).
8 Valve clearance incorrctly adjusted (Chapter 1).
9 EGR system not operating properly (Chapter 6).
10 EFI system not operating properly. Check the control unit, the air flow meter and for loose harness connections (Chapter 4).
11 Check for causes of overheating (Section 27).

22 Low oil pressure

1 Improper grade of oil.
2 Oil pump regulator valve not operating properly (Chapter 2).
3 Oil pump worn or damaged (Chapter 2).
4 Engine overheating (refer to Section 28).
5 Clogged oil filter (Chapter 1).
6 Clogged oil strainer (Chapter 2).
7 Oil pressure gauge not working properly (Chapter 2).

23 Excessive oil consumption

1 Loose oil drain plug.
2 Loose or damaged oil pan gasket (Chapter 2).
3 Loose or damaged timing chain cover gasket (Chapter 2).
4 Front or rear crankshaft oil seal leaking (Chapter 2).
5 Loose or damaged rocker cover gasket (Chapter 2).
6 Oil filter not tightened all the way (Chapter 1).
7 Loose or damaged oil pressure switch (Chapter 2).
8 Pistons and cylinders excessively worn (Chapter 2).
9 Pistons rings not positioned correctly on pistons (Chapter 2).
10 Worn or damaged piston rings (Chapter 2).
11 Intake and/or exhaust valve oil seals in need of replacement (Chapter 2).
12 Worn valve stems. Valves in need of replacement (Chapter 2).

24 Excessive fuel consumption (see also insufficient power)

1 Dirty or clogged air filter element (Chapter 1).
2 Incorrectly set ignition timing (Chapter 1).
3 Incorrectly set idle speed (Chapter 1).
4 Low tire pressure or incorrect tire size (Chapter 11).
5 Fuel leakage. Check all connections, lines and components in the fuel system (Chapter 4).
6 EFI system not operating properly (Chapter 4).

25 Fuel odor

1 Fuel leakage. Check all connections, lines and components of the fuel system (Chapter 4).
2 Fuel tank overfilled. Fill only to automatic shut-off.
3 Charcoal canister filter in Evaporative Emissions Control system in need of replacement (Chapter 6).
4 Vapor leaks from Evaporative Emissions Control system lines (Chapter 6).

26 Miscellaneous engine noises

1 *A strong dull noise that becomes more rapid as the engine accelerates* indicates worn or damaged crankshaft bearings or an unevenly worn crankshaft. To pinpoint the troublespot, remove the spark plug wire from one plug at a time and crank the engine over. If the noise stops, the cylinder with the removed plug wire indicates the problem area. Replace the bearing and/or service or replace the crankshaft (Chapter 2).
2 *A similar (yet slightly higher pitched) noise* to the crankshaft knocking described in the previous paragraph, that becomes more rapid as the engine accelerates, indicates worn or damaged connecting rod bearings (Chapter 2). The procedure for locating the problem cylinder is the same as described in paragraph 1.
3 *An overlapping metallic noise that increases in the intensity as the engine speed increases, yet diminishes as the engine warms up* indicates abnormal piston and cylinder wear (Chpter 2). To locate the problem cylinder, use the procedure described in paragraph 1.
4 *A rapid clicking noise that becomes faster as the engine accelerates* indicates a worn piston pin or piston pin hole. This sound will happen each time the piston hits the highest and lowest points of its stroke (Chapter 2). The procedure for locating the problem piston is described in paragraph 1.
5 *A metallic noise coming from the water pump* indicates worn or damaged water pump bearings or pump. Replace the water pump with a new one (Chapter 3).
6 *A rapid tapping sound or clicking sound that becomes faster as the engine speed increases* indicates "valve tapping" or improperly adjusted valve clearances. This can be identified by holding one end of a plastic hose to your ear and placing the other end at different spots along the length of the rocker cover. The point where the sound is loudest indicates the problem valve. Adjust the valve clearance (Chapter 1).
7 *A steady metallic rattling or rapping sound coming from the area of the timing chain cover* indicates a worn, damaged or out-of-adjustment timing chain. Service or replace the chain and related components (Chapter 2).

Engine cooling system

27 Overheating

1 Insufficient coolant in system (Chapter 1).
2 Fan belt defective or not adjusted properly (Chapter 1).
3 Radiator core blocked or radiator grille dirty and restricted (Chapter 3).
4 Thermostat faulty (Chapter 3).
5 Fan not functioning properly (Chapter 3).
6 Radiator cap not maintaining proper pressure. Have cap pressure tested by gas station or repair shop.
7 Ignition timing incorrect (Chapter 1).
8 Defective water pump (Chapter 3).
9 Improper grade of engine oil.
10 Inaccurate temperature gauge (Chapter 10).

28 Overcooling

1 Thermostat faulty (Chapter 3).
2 Inaccurate temperature gauge (Chapter 10).

29 External coolant leakage

1 Deteriorated or damaged hoses. Loose clamps at hose connections (Chapter 1).

2 Water pump seals defective. If this is the case, water will drip from the 'weep' hole in the water pump body (Chapter 3).
3 Leakage from radiator core or header tank. This will require the radiator to be professionally repaired (see Chapter 3 for removal procedures).
4 Engine drain plugs or water jacket freeze plugs leaking (see Chapters 1 and 2).
5 Leak from water temperature gauge connections (Chapter 2).
6 Leak from damaged gaskets or small cracks (Chapter 2).
7 Damaged head gasket. This can be verified by checking the condition of the engine oil as noted in Section 31.

30 Internal coolant leakage

Note: *Internal coolant leaks can usually be detected by examining the oil. Check the dipstick and inside of valve cover for water deposits and an oil consistency like that of a milkshake.*
1 Faulty cylinder head gasket. Have the system pressure-tested professionally or remove the cylinder heads (Chapter 2) and inspect.
2 Cracked cylinder bore or cylinder head. Dismantle engine and inspect (chapter 2).
3 Loose cylinder head bolts (tighten as described in Chapter 2).

31 Abnormal loss

1 Overfilling system (Chapter 1).
2 Coolant boiling away due to overheating (see causes in Section 15).
3 Internal or external leakage (see Sections 22 and 23).
4 Faulty radiator cap. Have the cap pressure-tested.

32 Poor coolant circulation

1 Inoperative water pump. A quick test is to pinch the top radiator hose closed with your hand while the engine is idling, then let loose. You should feel a surge of coolant if the pump is working properly (Chapter 3).
2 Restriction in cooling system. Drain, flush and refill the system (Chapter 1). If it appears necessary, remove the radiator (Chapter 3) and have it reverse-flushed or professionally cleaned.
3 Loose water pump drive belt (Chapter 3).
4 Thermostat sticking (Chapter 3).
5 Insufficient coolant (Chapter 1).

33 Corrosion

1 Excessive impurities in the water. Soft, clean water is recommended. Distilled or rainwater is satisfactory.
2 Insufficient antifreeze solution. (Refer to Chapter 1 or 3 for the proper ratio of water to antifreeze).
3 Infrequent flushing and draining of system. Regular flushing of the cooling system should be carried out at the specified intervals as described in *Routine Maintenance Schedule (Chapter 1).*

Clutch

Note: *All service information on the clutch is contained in Chapter 8, unless otherwise noted.*

34 Fails to release (pedal pressed to the floor – shift lever does not move freely in and out of reverse

1 Clutch face wet with oil. Remove clutch disc and inspect.
2 Clutch disc warped, bent or excessively damaged.
3 Diaphragm spring fatigued. Remove clutch cover/pressure plate assembly and inspect.
4 Leakage of fluid from clutch hydraulic system. Inspect master cylinder, operating cylinder and connecting lines.
5 Air in clutch hydraulic system. Bleed the system.
6 Insufficient pedal stroke. Check and adjust as necessary.
7 Piston cup in operating cylinder deformed or damaged.
8 Lack of grease on pilot bushing.

35 Clutch slips (engine speed increases with no increase in road speed)

1 Worn or oil soaked clutch disc facing.
2 Clutch disc not seated in. It may take 30 or 40 normal starts for a new disc to seat.
3 Diaphragm spring weak or damaged. Remove clutch cover/pressure plate assembly and inspect.
4 Flywheel warped (Chapter 2).
5 Debris in master cylinder preventing the piston from returning to its normal position.
6 Clutch hydraulic line damaged.

36 Grabbing (chattering) on take-up

1 Oil on clutch disc facings. Remove disc and inspect. Correct any leakage source.
2 Worn or loose engine or transmission mounts. These units may move slightly when clutch is released. Inspect mounts and bolts.
3 Worn splines on clutch gear. Remove clutch components and inspect.
4 Warped pressure plate or flywheel. Remove clutch components and inspect.
5 Diaphragm spring fatigued. Remove clutch cover/pressure plate assembly and inspect.
6 Clutch disc facing hardened or warped.
7 Clutch disc rivets loose.

37 Squeal or rumble with clutch fully engaged (pedal released)

1 Improper pedal adjustment. Adjust pedal free play.
2 Release bearing binding on transmission bearing retainer. Remove clutch components and check bearing. Remove any burrs or nicks, clean and relubricate before reinstallation.
3 Pilot bushing worn or damaged.
4 Clutch disc rivets loose.
5 Clutch disc cracked.
6 Fatigued clutch disc torsion springs. Replace clutch disc.

38 Squeal or rumble with clutch fully disengaged (pedal depressed)

1 Worn, faulty or broken release bearing.
2 Worn or broken pressure place diaphragm finger.

39 Clutch pedal stays on floor when disengaged

1 Bind in linkage or release bearing Inspect linkage or remove clutch components as necessary.
2 Linkage springs being over-extended. Adjust linkage for proper lash. Make sure proper pedal stop (bumper) is installed.

Manual transmission

Note: *All service information on the manual transmission is contained within Chapter 7, unless otherwise noted.*

40 Noisy in Neutral with engine running

1 Input shaft bearing worn.
2 Damaged main drive gear bearing.
3 Insufficient transmission oil (Chapter 1).
4 Transmission oil in poor condition. Drain and fill with proper grade oil. Check old oil for water or debris (Chapter 1).

5 Noise can be caused by variations in engine torque. Change the idle speed and see if noise disappears.

41 Noisy in all gears

1 Either of the above causes, and/or:
2 Worn or damaged output gear bearings or shaft.

42 Noisy in one particular gear

1 Worn, damaged or chipped gear teeth for that particular gear.
2 Worn or damaged synchronizer for that particular gear.

43 Slips out of gear

1 Transmission loose on clutch housing.
2 Stiff shift lever seal.
3 Shift linkage binding.
4 Broken or loose input gear bearing retainer.
5 Dirt between clutch lever and engine housing.
6 Worn linkage.
7 Damaged or worn check balls, fork rod ball grooves or check springs.
8 Worn mainshaft or countershaft bearings.
9 Loose engine mounts (Chapter 2).
10 Excessive gear end play.
11 Wear in synchronizer units.

44 Fluid leakage

1 Excessive amount of lubricant in transmission (see Chapter 1 for correct checking procedures. Drain lubricant as required).
2 Side cover loose or gasket damaged.
3 Rear oil seal or speedometer oil seal in need of replacement.
4 To pinpoint a leak, first remove all built-up dirt and grime from around the transmission. Degreasing agents and/or steam cleaning will achieve this. With the underside clean, drive the car at low speeds so the air flow will not blow the leak far from its source. Raise the car and determine where the leak is coming from.

45 Difficulty in engaging gears

1 Clutch not releasing fully.
2 Loose or damaged shift linkage. Make a thorough inspection, replacing parts as necessary.
3 Insufficient transmission oil (Chapter 1).
4 Transmission oil in poor condition. Drain and fill with proper grade of oil. Check oil for water or debris (Chapter 1).
5 Worn or damaged striking rod.
6 Sticking or jamming gears.

46 Noise occurs while shifting gears

1 Check for proper operation of the clutch (Chapter 8).
2 Faulty synchromesh assemblies. Measure baulk ring-to-gear clearance. Also, check for wear or damage to baulk rings or any parts of the synchromesh assemblies.

Automatic transmission

Note: *Due to the complexity of the automatic transmission, it is difficult for the home mechanic to properly diagnose and service this component. For problems other than the following, the vehicle should be taken to a reputable mechanic.*

47 Fluid leakage

1 Automatic transmission fluid is a deep red color, and fluid leaks should not be confused with engine oil which can easily be blown by air flow to the transmission.
2 To pinpoint a leak, first remove all built-up dirt and grime from around the transmission. Degreasing agents and/or steam cleaning will achieve this. With the underside clean, drive the car at low speeds so the air flow will not blow the leak from its source. Raise the car and determine where the leak is coming from. Common areas of leakage are:

a) Fluid pan: tighten mounting bolts and/or replace pan gasket as necessary (Chapter 1).
b) Rear extension: tighten bolts and/or replace oil seal as necessary (Chapter 8).
c) Filler pipe: replace the rubber oil seal where pipe enters transmission case.
d) Transmission oil lines: tighten connectors where lines enter transmission case and/or replace lines.
e) Vent pipe: transmission over-filled and/or water in fluid (see checking procedures, Chapter 1).
f) Speedometer connector: replace the O-ring where speedometer cable enters transmission case.

48 General shift mechanism problems

1 Section 2 in Chapter 7 deals with checking and adjusting the shift linkage on automatic transmissions. Common problems which may be attributed to maladjusted linkage are:

a) Engine starting in gears other than 'P' (Park) or 'N' (Neutral).
b) Indicator on quadrant pointing to a gear other than the one actually being used.
c) Vehicle will not hold firm when in 'P' (Park) position.

49 Transmission will not downshift with accelerator pedal pressed to the floor

1 Section 4 in Chapter 7 deals with adjusting the kickdown switch to enable the transmission to downshift properly.

50 Engine will start in gears other than 'P' (Park) or 'N' (Neutral)

1 Section 3 in Chapter 7 deals with adjusting the neutral start switch used with automatic transmissions.

51 Transmission slips, shifts rough, is noisy or has no drive in forward or reverse gears

1 There are many probable causes for the above problems, but the home mechanic should concern himself only with one possibility; fluid level.
2 Before taking the vehicle to a specialist, check the level of the fluid and condition of the fluid as described in Chapter 1. Correct fluid level as necessary or change the fluid and filter if needed. If problem persists, have a professional diagnose the probable cause.

Driveshaft

52 Leakage of fluid at front of driveshaft

1 Defective transmission rear oil seal. See Chapter 7 for replacing procedures. While this is done, check the splined yoke for burrs or a rough condition which may be damaging the seal. If found, these can be dressed with crocus cloth or a fine dressing stone.

53 Knock or clunk when transmission is under initial load (just after transmission is put into gear)

1 Loose or disconnected rear suspension components. Check all mounting bolts and bushings (Chapters 1 and 11).
2 Loose driveshaft bolts. Inspect all bolts and nuts and tighten to

torque specifications (Chapter 8).
3 Worn or damaged universal joint bearings. Replace driveshaft (Chapter 8).
4 Worn sleeve yoke and mainshaft spline (Chapter 8).
5 Defective center bearing or insulator (Chapter 8).

54 Metallic grating sound consistent with road speed

1 Pronounced wear in the universal joint bearings. Replace driveshaft (Chapter 8).

55 Vibration

Note: *Before it can be assumed that the driveshaft is at fault, make sure the tires are perfectly balanced and perform the following test.*
1 Install a tachometer inside the car to monitor engine speed as the car is driven. Drive the car and note the engine speed at which the vibration (roughness) is most pronounced. Now shift the transmission to a different gear and bring the engine speed to the same point.
2 If the vibration occurs at the same engine speed (rpm) regardless of which gear the transmission is in, the driveshaft is NOT at fault since the driveshaft speed varies.
3 If the vibration decreases or is eliminated when the transmission is in a different gear at the same engine speed, refer to the following probable causes.
4 Bent or dented driveshaft. Inspect and replace as necessary (Chapter 8).
5 Undercoating or built-up dirt, etc. on the driveshaft. Clean the shaft thoroughly and test.
6 Worn universal joint bearings. Replace the driveshaft (Chapter 8).
7 Driveshaft and/or companion flange out of balance. Check for missing weights on the shaft. Remove driveshaft (Chapter 8) and reinstall 180° from original position. Retest. Have driveshaft professionally balanced if problem persists.
8 Loose installation of the driveshaft (Chapter 8).
9 Defective center bearing (Chapter 8).
10 Worn transmission rear bushing (Chapter 7).

56 Scraping noise

1 Check that the dust cover on the sleeve yoke is not rubbing on the transmission rear extension (Chapter 8).

57 Whining or whistling noise

1 Defective center bearing (Chapter 8).

Rear axle and differential

58 Noise – same when in drive as when vehicle is coasting

1 Road noise. No corrective procedures available.
2 Tire noise. Inspect tires and tire pressures (Chapter 1).
3 Front wheel bearings loose, worn or damaged (Chapter 1).
4 Insufficient differential oil (Chapter 1).
5 Defective differential (Chapter 8).

59 Knocking sound during starting or gear shifting

1 Defective or incorrectly adjusted differential (Chapter 8).

60 Noise while turning

1 Defective differential (Chapter 8).

61 Vibration

1 See probable causes under 'Driveshaft'. Proceed under the guidelines listed for the driveshaft. If the problem persists, check the rear wheel bearings by raising the rear of the car and spinning the wheels by hand. Listen for evidence of rough (noisy) bearings. Remove and inspect (Chapter 8).

62 Oil leakage

1 Pinion oil seal damaged (Chapter 8).
2 Axle shaft oil seals damaged (Chapter 8).
3 Differential inspection cover leaking. Tighten mounting bolts or replace the gasket as required (Chapter 8).
4 Loose filler or drain plug on differential (Chapter 1).
5 Clogged or damaged breather on differential (Chapter 8).

Brakes

Note: *Before assuming a brake problem exists, check: that the tires are in good condition and are inflated properly (Chapter 1); the front end alignment is correct (Chapter 11); and thaat the vehicle is not loaded with weight in an unequal manner. All service procedures for the braking system are described in Chapter 9, unless otherwise noted.*

63 Vehicle pulls to one side under braking

1 Defective, damaged or oil-contaminated disc pad on one side. Inspect as described in Chapter 1. Refer to Chapter 9 if replacement is required.
2 Excessive wear of brake pad material or disc on one side. Inspect and correct as necessary.
3 Loose or disconnected front suspension components. Inspect and tighten all bolts to specifications (Chapter 1).
4 Defective caliper assembly. Remove caliper and inspect for stuck piston or damage.
5 Disc pad-to-rotor adjustment needed. Inspect automatic adjusting mechanism for proper operation.
6 Scored or out-of-round rotor.
7 Loose caliper mounting.
8 Incorrect adjustment of wheel bearings.

64 Noise (high-pitched squeak)

1 Front brake pads worn out. This noise comes from the wear sensor rubbing against the disc. Replace pads with new ones immediately.
2 Glazed or contaminated pads.
3 Dirty or scored rotor.
4 Bent support plate.

65 Excessive brake pedal travel

1 Partial brake system failure. Inspect entire system (Chapter 1) and correct as required.
2 Insufficient fluid in master cylinder. Check (Chapter 1) and add fluid and bleed system if necessary.
3 Air in system. Bleed system.
4 Excessive lateral play of discs.
5 Brakes out of adjustment. Inspect the operation of the automatic adjusters.
6 Defective check valve. Replace valve and bleed system.

66 Brake pedal feels spongy when depressed

1 Air in hydraulic lines. Bleed the brake system.
2 Faulty flexible hoses. Inspect all system hoses and lines. Replace parts as necessary.
3 Master cylinder mountings insecure. Inspect master cylinder bolts (nuts) and torque-tighten to specifications.

4 Master cylinder faulty.
5 Incorrect pad-to-rotor clearance. Check operation of automatic adjusters.
6 Defective check valve. Replace valve and bleed system.
7 Clogged reservoir cap vent hole.
8 Deformed rubber brake lines.
9 Soft or swollen caliper seals.
10 Poor quality brake fluid. Bleed entire system and fill with new approved fluid.

67 Excessive effort required to stop vehicle

1 Power brake booster not operating properly.
2 Excessively worn pads. Inspect and replace if necessary.
3 One or more caliper pistons seized or sticking. Inspect and rebuild as required.
4 Brake pads contaminated with oil or grease. Inspect and replace as required.
5 New pads fitted and not yet 'bedded in'. It will take a while for the new material to seat against the rotor.
6 Worn or damaged master cylinder or caliper assemblies. Check particularly for frozen pistons.
7 Also see causes listed under Section 66.

68 Pedal travels to floor with little resistance

1 Little or no fluid in the master cylinder reservoir caused by: leaking caliper piston(s); loose, damaged or disconnected brake lines. Inspect entire system and correct as necessary.

69 Brake pedal pulsates during brake application

1 Wheel bearings not adjusted properly or in need of replacement (Chapter 1).
2 Caliper not sliding properly due to improper installation or obstructions. Remove and inspect.
3 Rotor not within specifications. Remove the rotor and check for excessive lateral run-out and parallelism. Have the rotor professionally machined or replace it with a new one. Also check that all rotors are the same thickness.

70 Brakes drag (indicated by sluggish engine performance or wheels being very hot after driving)

1 Output rod adjustment too long at the brake pedal.
2 Obstructed master cylinder compensator. Disassemble master cylinder and clean.
3 Master cylinder piston seized in bore. Overhaul master cylinder.
4 Caliper assembly in need of overhaul.
5 Brake pads need replacing.
6 Piston cups in master cylinder or caliper assembly deformed. Overhaul master cylinder.
7 Rotor not within specs. (Section 69).
8 Parking brake assembly will not release.
9 Clogged brake lines.
10 Wheel bearings out of adjustment (Chapter 8).
11 Brake pedal height improperly adjusted.

71 Rear brakes lock up under light brake application (indicated by a skidding effect)

1 Tire pressures too high.
2 Tires excessively worn (Chapter 11).
3 Defective NP valve.

72 Rear brakes lock up under heavy brake application (indicated by a skidding effect)

1 Tire pressures too high.
2 Tires excessively worn (Chapter 11).
3 Front brake pads contaminated with oil, mud or water. Clean or replace the pads.
4 Front brake pads excessively worn.
5 Poor front braking effect caused by defective master cylinder or caliper assembly.

Suspension and steering

Note: *All service procedures for the suspension and steering systems are described in Chapter 11, unless otherwise noted.*

73 Car pulls to one side

1 Tire pressures uneven (Chapter 1).
2 Defective tire (Chapter 1).
3 Excessive wear in suspension or steering components (Chapter 1).
4 Front end in need of alignment.
5 Front brakes dragging. Inspect braking system as described in Section 70.
6 Wheel bearings improperly adjusted (Chapter4).
7 Wheel lug nuts not tight.

74 Shimmy, shake or vibration

1 Tire or wheel out of balance or out of round. Have professionally balanced.
2 Loose, worn or out of adjustment wheel bearings (Chpter 1).
3 Shock absorbers and/or suspension components worn or damaged.
4 Wheel lug nuts not tight.
5 Incorrect tire pressures.
6 Excessively worn or damaged tire.
7 Loosely mounted steering gear housing.
8 Steering gear improperly adjusted.
9 Loose, worn or damaged steering components.

75 Excessive pitching and/or rolling around corners or during braking

1 Defective shock absorbers. replace as a set.
2 Broken or weak coil springs and/or suspension components.
3 Worn or damaged stabilizer bar or bushings.
4 Worn or damaged rear links or bushings.

76 Wandering or general instability

1 Improper tire pressures.
2 Worn or damaged transverse link or tension rod bushings.
3 Incorrect front end alignment.
4 Worn or damaged steering linkage or transverse link.
5 Improperly adjusted steering gear.
6 Out of balance wheels.
7 Loose wheel lug nuts.
8 Worn or damaged rear link bushings.
9 Worn rear shock absorbers.
10 Fatigued or damaged rear coil springs.

77 Excessively stiff steering

1 Lack of lubricant in power steering fluid reservoir (Chapter 1).
2 Incorrect tire pressures (Chapter 1).
3 Lack of lubrication at ball joints (Chapter 1).
4 Front end out of alignment.
5 Steering gear out of adjustment or lacking lubrication.
6 Improperly adjusted wheel bearings.
7 Defective strut assembly mounting bearing.
8 Interference of steering column with turn signal switch.
9 Tire pressures too low.

10 Worn or damaged balljoints.
11 Worn or damaged steering linkage.
12 See also Section 79.

78 Excessive play in steering

1 Loose wheel bearings (Chapter 1).
2 Excessive wear in suspension or steering components (Chapter 1).
3 Steering gear improperly adjusted.
4 Incorrect front end alignment.

79 Lack of power assistance (with power steering systems)

1 Steering pump drive belt faulty or not adjusted properly (Chapter 1).
2 Fluid level low (Chapter 1).
3 Hoses or pipes restricting the flow. Inspect and replace parts as necessary.
4 Air in power steering system. Bleed system.
5 Defective power steering pump.

80 Steering wheel fails to return to straight-ahead position

1 Incorrect front end alignment.
2 Tire pressures too low.
3 Steering gears improperly engaged.
4 Steering column out of alignment.
5 Worn or damaged balljoint.
6 Worn or damaged steering linkage.
7 Improperly lubricated idler arm.
8 Insufficient oil in steering gear.
9 Lack of fluid in power steering pump.

81 Steering effort not the same in both directions (power system)

1 Fluid leakage from steering gear.
2 Clogged fluid passage in steering gear.

82 Noisy power steering pump

1 Insufficient oil in pump.
2 Clogged hoses or oil filter in pump.
3 Loose pulley.
4 Improperly adjusted drive belt. (Chapter 1).
5 Defective pump.

83 Miscellaneous noises

1 Improper tire pressures.
2 Insufficiently lubricated balljoint or steering linkage.
3 Loose or worn steering gear, steering linkage or suspension components.
4 Defective shock absorber.
5 Defective wheel bearing.
6 Worn or damaged transverse link or tension rod bushing.
7 Damaged coil spring.
8 Loose wheel lug nuts.
9 Worn or damaged rear link bushings.
10 Worn or damaged rear shock absorber mounting bushing.
11 Incorrect rear axle endplay adjustment.
12 See also causes of noises at the rear axle and driveshaft.

84 Excessive tire wear (not specific to one area)

1 Incorrect tire pressures.
2 Tires out of balance. Have professionally balanced.
3 Wheels damaged. Inspect and replace as necessary.
4 Suspension or steering components excessively worn (Chapter 1).

85 Excessive tire wear on outside edge

1 Inflation pressures not correct.
2 Excessive speed on turns.
3 Front-end alignment incorrect (excessive toe-in). Have professionally aligned.
4 Suspension arm bent or twisted.

86 Excessive tire wear on inside edge

1 Inflation pressures incorrect.
2 Front-end alignment incorrect (toe-out). Have professionally aligned.
3 Loose or damaged steering components (Chapter 1).

87 Tire tread worn in one place

1 Tires out of balance. Balance tires professionally.
2 Damaged or buckled wheel. Inspect and replace if necessary.
3 Defective tire.

Chapter 1 Tune-up and routine maintenance

Refer to Chapter 13 for Specifications and information related to 1982 and 1983 models

Contents

Accelerator linkage check and pedal adjustment	22
Air filter replacement	12
Air induction valve filter replacement	20
Automatic transmission fluid change	34
Battery maintenance and servicing	8
Brakes check	27
Chassis lubrication	26
Clutch pedal adjustments	23
Cooling system check and servicing	21
Cylinder compression testing	16
Differential fluid change	35
Distributor check	13
Drivebelt check and adjustment	11
Driveshaft inspection	30
EEC (Evaporative Emissions Control) filter replacement	32
Engine oil and filter change	7
Exhaust gas sensor servicing	33
Exhaust system check	29
Fluid levels check	4
Fuel filter replacement	18
Fuel system check	31
Idle speed adjustment	14
Ignition timing	15
Introduction	1
PCV valve replacement	19
Parking brake adjustment	24
Routine maintenance intervals	2
Spark plug wires check	10
Spark plugs replacement	9
Suspension and steering check	28
Tire and tire pressure checks	5
Tire rotation	6
Tune-up – general information	3
Valve clearance adjustment	17
Wheel bearings check	25

Specifications

Note: *Additional specifications and torque settings can be found in each individual Chapter.*

Quick reference capacities

	US	Liters	Imperial
Engine oil			
With oil filter	$4\frac{5}{8}$ qt	4.4	$3\frac{7}{8}$ qt
Without oil filter	$4\frac{1}{8}$ qt	3.9	$3\frac{3}{8}$ qt
Fuel tank			
Hardtop	14 gal	53	$11\frac{5}{8}$ gal
Hatchback	$15\frac{7}{8}$ gal	60	$13\frac{1}{4}$ gal
Coolant			
Including heater	10 qt	9.5	$8\frac{3}{8}$ qt
Excluding heater	$9\frac{1}{4}$ qt	8.8	$7\frac{3}{4}$ qt
Transmission			
Manual	$4\frac{1}{4}$ pt	2.0	$3\frac{1}{2}$ pt
Automatic	$5\frac{7}{8}$ qt	5.5	$4\frac{7}{8}$ qt
Power steering system	$1\frac{1}{4}$ qt	1.2	$1\frac{1}{8}$ qt
Steering gear	$\frac{5}{8}$ pt	0.28	$\frac{1}{2}$ pt
Differential	$2\frac{3}{8}$ pt	1.1	2 pt
Windshield washer tank	$2\frac{1}{8}$ qt	2.0	$1\frac{3}{4}$ qt
Rear window washer tank	$1\frac{1}{8}$ qt	1.0	$\frac{7}{8}$ qt

Recommended fluids and lubricants

Engine oil*	
–30°F to 20°F	SAE 5W-20 SAE 5W-30
0°F to 60°F	SAE 10W SAE 5W-30 SAE 10W-30 SAE 10W-40
20°F to 100°F	SAE 20W SAE 10W-30 SAE 10W-40 SAE 20W-40 SAE 20W-50

**All engine lubricants should be labeled API SE*

Automatic transmission fluid	DEXRON type
Manual transmission oil	API GL-4 SAE 140W (above 50°F) SAE 90W (between 30° and 100°F) SAE 85W (between 10° and 85°F) SAE 80W-90 (below 100°F) SAE 80W (below 85°F) SAE 75W (below 50°F)
Steering gear oil	API GL-4 (refer to manual transmission oil for correct weight)
Differential oil	API GL-5 (refer to manual transmission oil for correct weight)
Power steering fluid	DEXRON type
Brake fluid	DOT 3
Clutch fluid	DOT 3 brake fluid
Coolant	Mixture of good quality ethylene glycol based antifreeze and water, in at least a 50/50 ratio (but not to exceed 70/30 ratio of antifreeze to water)
Windshield washer solvent	Good quality solvent intended for this use (in freezing temperatures, a windshield washer antifreeze/solvent should be used with water to prevent the system from freezing)
Parking brake cables	Chassis grease
Chassis lubrication	Chassis grease
Hood and door hinges	Engine oil
Hood latch assembly	
Pivots and spring anchor	Engine oil
Release pawl	Chassis grease
Key lock cylinders	WD-40 spray lubricant or equivalent

General engine data

Spark plugs	
US models (standard)	BP6ES
Canada models and US models (option)	BPR6ES
Spark plug gap	0.8 - 0.9 mm (0.031 - 0.035 in)
Valve clearance	**Intake**
Hot	0.30 mm (0.012 in)
Cold	0.21 mm (0.008 in)
	Exhaust
Hot	0.30 mm (0.012 in)
Cold	0.23 mm (0.009 in)
Ignition timing	
Manual transmission	
1980 California models	6° BTDC at 700 rpm
1980 49-States and Canada models	8° BTDC at 700 rpm
1981 US models	6° BTDC at 750 rpm
1981 Canada models	8° BTDC at 750 rpm
Automatic transmission	
1980 California and all 1981 US models	6° BTDC at 700 rpm
1980 49-States and all Canada models	8° BTDC at 700 rpm
Idle mixture adjustment (CO %)	
1980 California and all 1981 US models	Preset and sealed at factory
1980 49-States and all Canada models	1.3 ± 1.0%
Cylinder compression pressure	
Standard	171 psi (12.0 kg/cm^2)
Minimum	128 psi (9.0 kg/cm^2)

General chassis and body data

Brake pad wear limit	0.08 in (2 mm)
Clutch pedal	
Height	6.61 to 6.85 in (168 to 174 mm)
Free play	0.04 to 0.20 in (1 to 5 mm)
Parking brake adjustment	
Number of notches	7 to 8
Lever stroke (measured at center of handle)	3.50 to 4.00 in (90 to 100 mm)
Tire pressures (with tires cold)	
185/70SR14 (standard)	26 psi
T135/70D16 (spare tire)	60 psi

Torque specifications

	ft-lb	m-kg
Spark plugs	12	1.7
Oil pan drain plug	18	2.5
Rocker arm nut	14	1.9
Manual transmission drain plug	22	3.0
Manual transmission filler plug	22	3.0
Differential drain plug	60	8.0
Differential filler plug	60	8.0
Wheel lug nuts	65	9.0

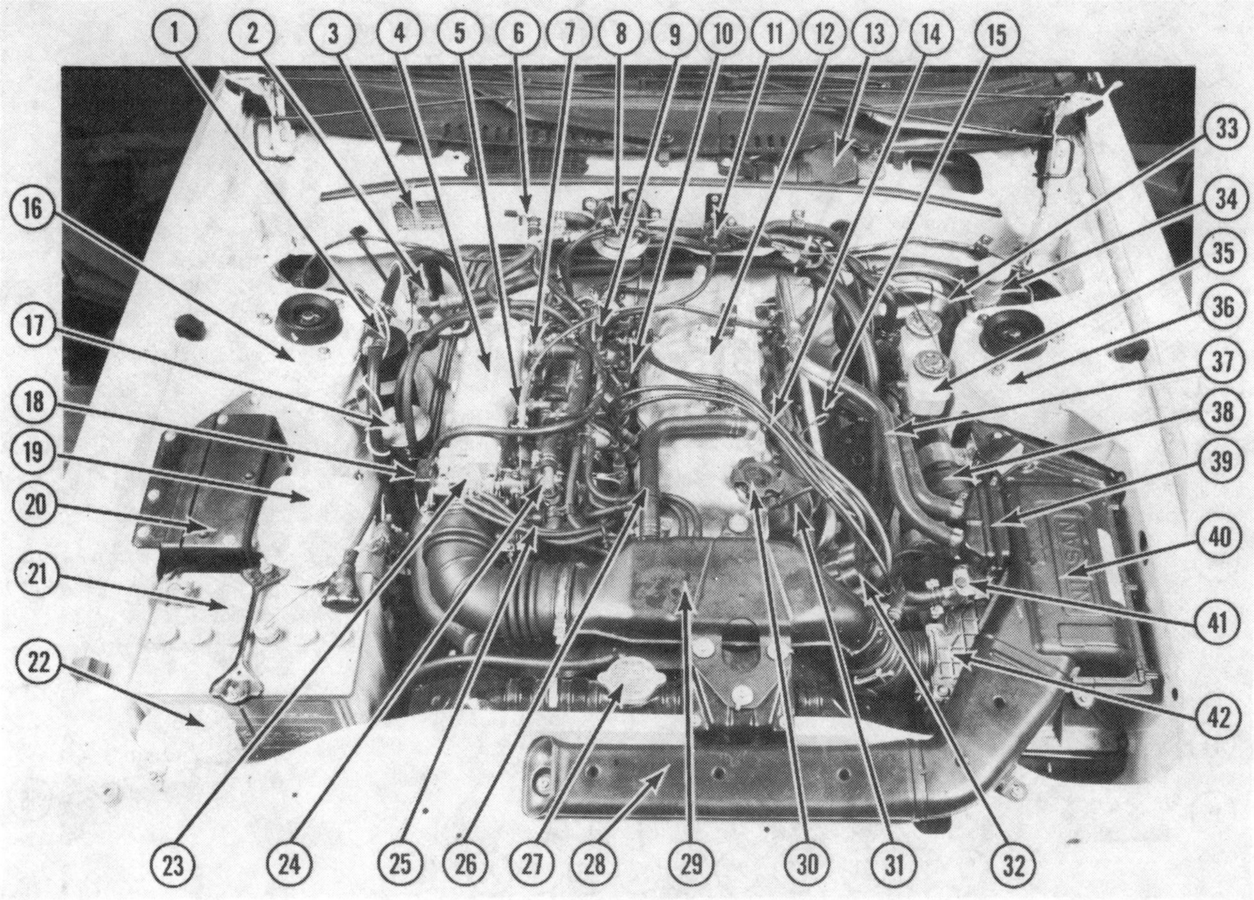

Typical view of the engine compartment

1 *A/C receiver drier and sight glass*
2 *A/C expansion and suction throttle valves*
3 *Vehicle identification plate*
4 *Intake manifold*
5 *Throttle cable adjusting nuts*
6 *Brake booster check valve*
7 *Vacuum control valve*
8 *VVT or BPT valve*
9 *Fuel pipe assembly*
10 *Injectors*
11 *EFI vacuum switch*
12 *Rocker arm cover*
13 *Windshield wiper motor*
14 *Spark plug wires*
15 *Engine oil dipstick*
16 *Right shock well*
17 *Fuel filter*
18 *Throttle valve switch*
19 *Windshield washer reservoir*
20 *Relay bracket*
21 *Battery*
22 *Coolant reservoir*
23 *Throttle chamber*
24 *Air regulator*
25 *Vacuum lines*
26 *PCV vent hose*
27 *Radiator*
28 *Inlet air duct*
29 *Air pipe*
30 *Engine oil filler cap*
31 *Exhaust manifold*
32 *Distributor*
33 *Brake vacuum booster*
34 *Clutch master cylinder*
35 *Brake master cylinder*
36 *Left shock well*
37 *Air induction lines*
38 *Ignition coil*
39 *Air induction valve case*
40 *Air cleaner*
41 *AIS unit*
42 *Air flow meter*

1 Introduction

This Chapter was designed to help the home mechanic maintain his (or her) car for peak performance, economy, safety and longevity.

On the following pages you will find a maintenance schedule along with Sections which deal specifically with each item on the schedule. Included are visual checks, adjustments and item replacements. Location of the various components mentioned can be aided by refering to the engine compartment and other overall photos included.

Servicing your car using the time/mileage maintenance schedule and the sequenced Sections will give you a planned program of maintenance. Keep in mind that it is a full plan, and maintaining only a few items at the specified intervals will not give you the sarne results.

You will find as you service your car that many of the procedures can, and should, be grouped together due to the nature of the job at hand. Examples of this are as follows:

If the car is fully raised for a chassis lubrication, for example, this is the ideal time for the following checks: manual transmission fluid, differential fluid, exhaust system, suspension, steering and the fuel system.

If the tires and wheels are removed, as during a routine tire rotation, go ahead and check the brakes and wheel bearings at the same time.

If you must borrow or rent a torque wrench, you will do best to service the spark plugs, repack (or replace) the wheel bearings and check any other critical bolts for proper torque all in the same day to save time and money.

The first step of this or any maintenance plan is to prepare yourself before the actual work begins. Read through the appropriate Sections for all work that is to be performed before you begin. Gather together all necessary parts and tools. If it appears you could have a problem during a particular job, don't hesitate to ask advice from your local parts man or dealer service department.

2 Routine maintenance intervals

Note: *The pre-drive inspection outlined in the owner's manual covers checks and maintenance that should be carried out on a daily or pre-drive basis. It is condensed and included here to remind you of its importance. Always perform the pre-drive inspection at every maintenance interval (in addition to the procedures listed).* The following intervals are recommended by the manufacturer, not the publishers of this manual. It may be wise, in many cases, to perform the maintenance at shorter intervals.

Before driving

Check the engine oil level (Sec 4)

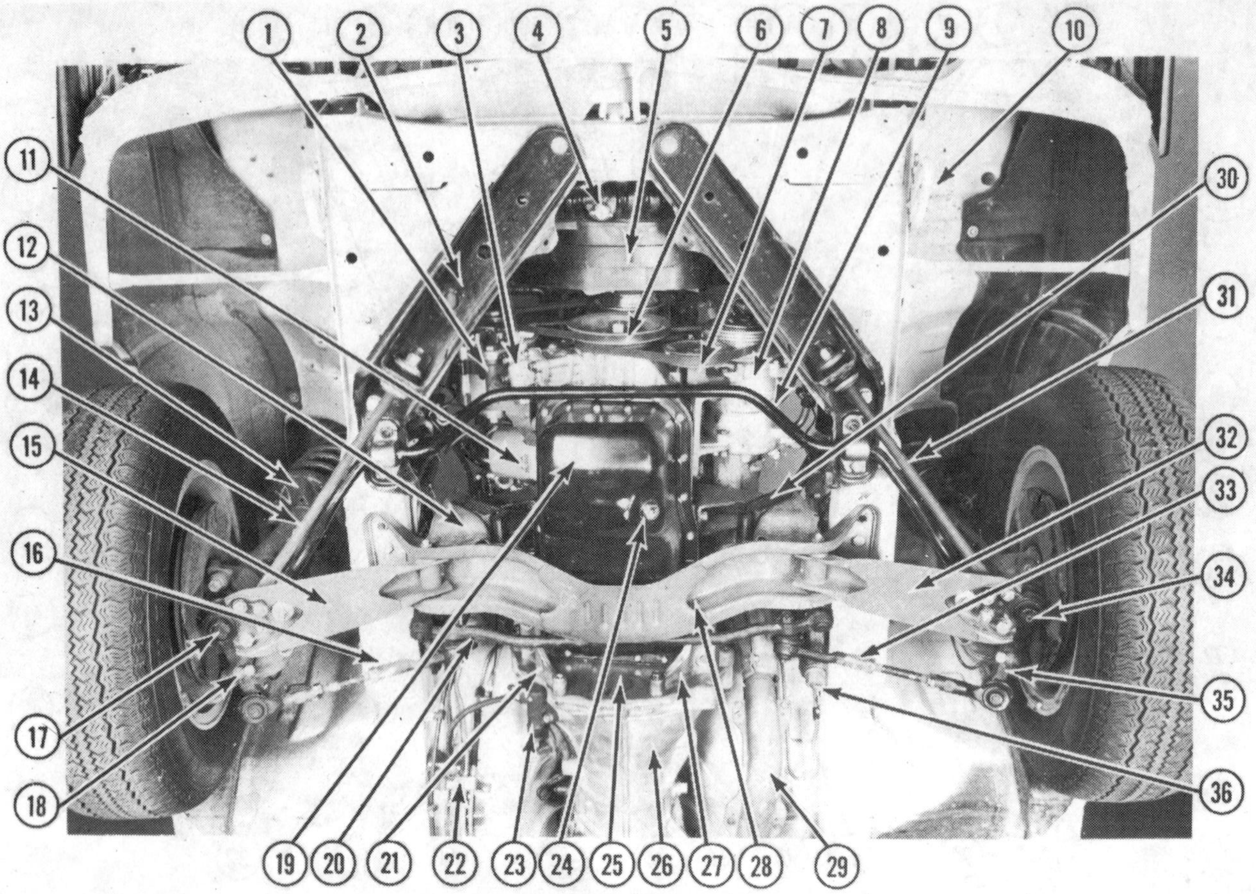

Typical view of the engine compartment underside

1 Alternator
2 Tension rod bracket
3 Oil pump
4 Radiator drain plug
5 Fan shroud
6 Crankshaft pulley
7 Drivebelt idler pulley
8 A/C compressor
9 Front stabilizer bar
10 Tow hook
11 Oil filter
12 Right engine mount
13 Right spring and strut assembly
14 Right tension rod
15 Right transverse link
16 Right tie rod
17 Right balljoint
18 Right steering knuckle
19 Oil pan
20 Steering linkage cross rod
21 Right engine gusset
22 Fuel feed and return lines
23 Clutch operating cylinder
24 Engine oil drain plug
25 Rear plate
26 Transmission
27 Left engine gusset
28 Crossmember
29 Front exhaust pipe
30 Left engine mount
31 Left tension rod
32 Left transverse link
33 Left tie rod
34 Left balljoint
35 Left steering knuckle
36 Steering gear arm

Check the engine coolant level (Sec 4)
Check the tires and tire pressures (Sec 5)
Check the automatic transmission fluid level (Sec 4)
Check the windshield washer fluid level (Sec 4)
Check the power steering fluid level, if equipped (Sec 4)

At the first 1000 miles

Check the drive belts (Sec 11)
Check the intake and exhaust valve adjustments (Sec 17)
Check and adjust the idle speed (Sec 14)
Check and adjust the mixture ratio (Canada and 1980 49-State models only) (should be done by Datsun dealer)
Inspect the steering gear box (Sec 28)
Inspect the suspension system (Sec 28)
Inspect the drive shaft (Sec 30)

Every 7500 miles or 6 months – whichever comes first

Change the engine oil and filter (Sec 7)
Check all fluid levels (Sec 4)

Every 15 000 miles or 12 months – whichever comes first

Check the drive belts (Sec 11)
Check the intake and exhaust valve adjustments (Sec 17)
Check the idle speed (Sec 14)
Check the mixture ratio (Canada models only and 1980 49-State models only) (should be done by Datsun dealer)
Check and adjust the ignition timing (Sec 15)
Replace the PCV valve (Sec 19)
Inspect the brakes (Sec 27)
Replace the brake fluid (Sec 27)
Check the steering and suspension components (Sec 28)
Lubricate the chassis components (Sec 26)
Check the fuel system components (Sec 31)
Check the exhaust system (Sec 29)
Check the drive shaft (Sec 30)
Rotate the tires (Sec 6)
Lubricate the body components (Sec 26)
Check the clutch pedal adjustments (Sec 23)
Check the parking brake adjustment (Sec 24)
Replace the fuel filter (Sec 18)
Check and adjust the throttle linkage (Sec 22)
Change the automatic transmission fluid if the car is driven under abnormal conditions (Sec 34)

Every 30 000 miles or 24 months – whichever comes first

Replace the air cleaner filter (Sec 12)
Check the vapor lines (should be done by Datsun dealer)
Inspect and service the cooling system (Sec 21)
Replace the spark plugs (Sec 9)
Check the spark plug wires (Sec 10)

Typical view of rear underside of car

1 Fuel pump and damper bracket
2 Fuel feed and return lines
3 Parking brake adjuster
4 Drive shaft
5 Rear universal joint
6 Muffler
7 Hydraulic brake line
8 Right lower link
9 Right coil spring
10 Right upper link
11 Right parking brake cable
12 Fuel filler hose
13 Parking brake equalizer
14 Differential
15 Differential drain plug
16 Fuel tank
17 Rear stabilizer bar
18 Rear axle
19 Left parking brake cable
20 Exhaust tail pipe
21 Left lower link
22 Left upper link
23 Left coil spring

Check the exhaust gas sensor (1981 US models only) (Sec 33)
Replace the air induction valve filter (1980 US models only) (Sec 20)
Inspect the brake booster vacuum hoses and check valve (Sec 27)
Check the front wheel bearings (Sec 25)
Change differential gear oil if a trailer is frequently towed (Sec 35)
Replace the charcoal canister (EEC) filter (Sec 32)
Service the catalytic converter (Sec 29)
Change the automatic transmission fluid (Sec 34)

3 Tune-up – general information

The term "Tune-up" is loosely used for any general operation that puts the engine back in its proper running condition. A tune-up is not a specific operation, but rather a combination of individual operations, such as replacing the spark plugs, adjusting the idle speed, setting the ignition timing, etc.

If, from the time the car is new, the routine maintenance schedule (Section 2) is followed closely and frequent checks are made of fluid levels and high wear items, as suggested throughout this manual, the engine will be kept in a relatively good running condition and the need for additional tune-ups will be minimized.

More likely than not, however, there will be times when the engine is running poorly due to lack of regular maintenance. This is even more likely if a used car is bought which has not received regular and frequent maintenance checks. In such cases an engine tune-up will be needed outside of the regular routine maintenance intervals.

The following series of operations are those most often needed to bring a generally poor running engine back into a proper state of tune.

Minor tune-up

Clean, inspect and test battery (Sec 8)
Check all engine fluids (Sec 4)
Check and adjust drive belts (Sec 11)
Replace spark plugs (Sec 9)
Test cylinder compression (Sec 16)
Inspect distributor cap and rotor (Sec 13)
Inspect spark plug and coil wires (Sec 10)
Replace air filter (Sec 12)
Check and adjust idle speed (Sec 14)
Check and adjust ignition timing (Sec 15)
Replace fuel filter (Sec 18)
Replace air induction valve filter (Sec 20)
Replace PCV valve (Sec 19)
Adjust valve clearances (Sec 17)
Check and service cooling system (Sec 21)

Major tune-up (the above operations combined with those listed below)

Check vacuum advance system (Chapter 6, Spark Timing Control System)
Check EGR system (Chapter 6)
Test alternator and voltage regulator (Chapter 5)
Test ignition system (Chapter 5)
Test charging system (Chapter 5)
Check fuel system (Sec 31 and Chapter 4)

4 Fluid levels check

1 There are a number of components on a vehicle which rely on the use of fluids to perform their job. Through the normal operation of the car, these fluids are used up and must be replenished before damage occurs. See the Recommended Lubricants Specifications for the specific fluid to be used when adding is required. When checking fluid levels, it is important that the car is on a level surface.

Engine oil

2 The engine oil level is checked with a dipstick which is located at the side of the engine block. This dipstick travels through a tube and into the oil pan at the bottom of the engine (photo).
3 The oil level should be checked preferably before the car has been driven, or about 15 minutes after the engine has been shut off. If the oil is checked immediately after driving the car, some of the oil will remain in the upper engine components, thus giving an inaccurate reading on the dipstick.
4 Pull the dipstick from its tube and wipe all the oil from the end with a clean rag. Insert the clean dipstick all the way back into the oil pan and pull it out again. Observe the oil at the end of the dipstick. At its highest point, the level should be between the 'L' and 'H' marks.
5 It takes approximately 1 quart of oil to raise the level from the 'L' mark to the 'H' mark on the dipstick. Do not allow the level to drop below the 'L' mark, as this may cause engine damage due to oil starvation. On the other hand, do not overfill the engine by adding oil above the 'H' mark, as this may result in oil-fouled spark plugs, oil leaks or oil seal failures.
6 Oil is added to the engine after removing a twist-off cap located on the rocker arm cover. An oil can spout or funnel will reduce spills as the oil is poured in.
7 Checking the oil level can also be a step toward preventative maintenance. If you find the oil level dropping abnormally, this is an indication of oil leakage or internal engine wear which should be corrected. If there are water droplets in the oil, or it is milky-looking, this also indicates component failure, and the engine should be checked immediately. The condition of the oil can also be checked along with the level. With the dipstick removed from the engine, take your thumb and index finger and wipe the oil up the dipstick, looking for small dirt particles or engine filings which will cling to the dipstick. This is an indication that the oil should be drained and fresh oil added (Section 7).

Engine coolant

8 Most vehicles are equipped with a pressurized coolant recovery system which makes coolant level checks very easy. A white coolant reservoir is connected by a hose to the radiator cap (photo). As the engine heats up during operation, coolant is forced from the radiator, through the connecting tube and into the reservoir. As the engine cools, this coolant is automatically drawn back into the radiator to keep the level correct.
9 The coolant level should be checked when the engine is cold. Merely observe the level of fluid in the reservoir, which should be between the 'MAX' and 'MIN' marks on the side of the reservoir. If the system is completely cooled, also check the level in the radiator by removing the cap.
10 Under no circumstances should the radiator cap be removed while the system is hot, as escaping steam could cause serious injury. Wait until the engine has completely cooled, then wrap a thick cloth around the cap and turn it to its first stop. If any steam escapes from the cap, allow the engine to cool further. Then remove the cap and check the level in the radiator. It should be 2 - 3 inches below the bottom of the filler neck.
11 If only a small amount of coolant is required to bring the system up to the proper level, regular water can be used. However, to maintain the proper antifreeze/water mixture in the system, both should be mixed together to replenish a low level. High-quality antifreeze offering protection to −20° should be mixed with water in the proportion specified on the container. Do not allow antifreeze to come in contact with your skin or painted surfaces of the car. Flush contacted areas immediately with plenty of water.

4.2 The engine oil dipstick is located on the left side of the engine

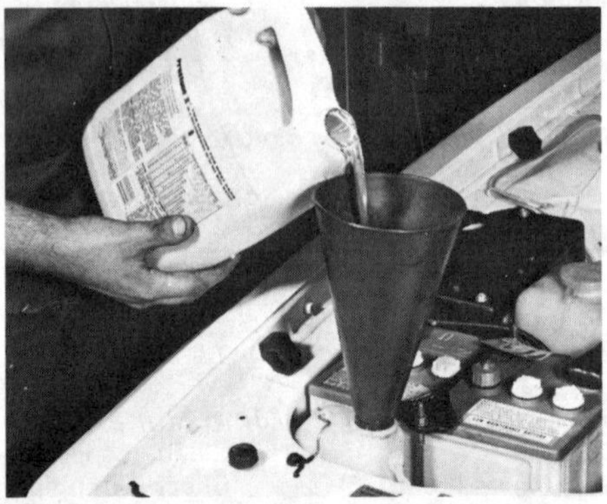

4.8 The radiator reservoir tank is located directly in front of the battery

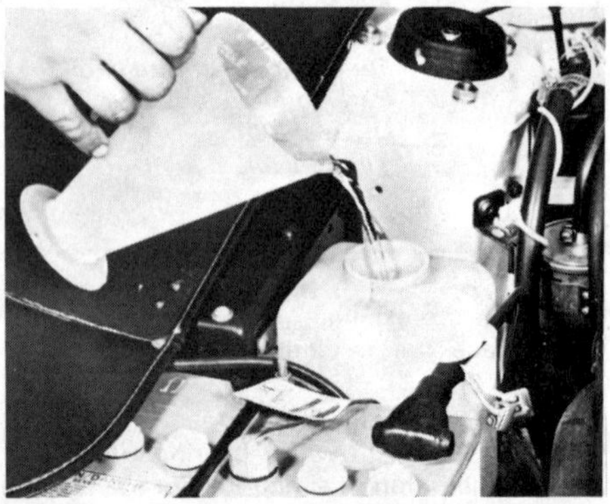

4.15 The windshield washer reservoir is behind the battery and attached to the relay bracket

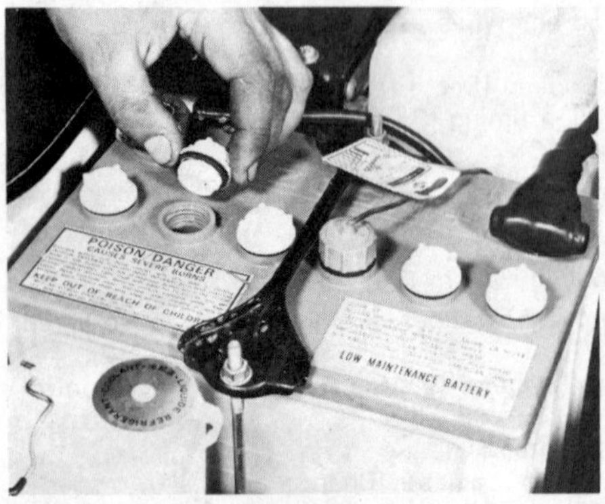

4.18 Even if equipped with a battery fluid warning light, the rest of the battery cells should be checked periodically

4.26 The brake master cylinder cap is removed by depressing the outer ring and twisting counterclockwise

4.32 The clutch master cylinder is located behind the left shock well at the firewall

12 Coolant should be added to the reservoir after removing the cap at the top of the reservoir.
13 As the coolant level is checked, observe the condition of the coolant. It should be relatively clear. If the fluid is brown or a rust color, this is an indication that the system should be drained, flushed and refilled.
14 If the cooling system requires repeated additions to keep the proper level, have the pressure radiator cap checked for proper sealing ability. Also check for leaks in the system (cracked hoses, loose hose connections, leaking gaskets, etc).

Windshield washer

15 The fluid for the windshield washer system is located in a plastic reservoir directly in back of the battery (photo). The level inside the reservoir should be maintained near the top of the reservoir.
16 An approved washer solvent should be added through the plastic cap whenever replenishing is required. Do not use plain water alone in this system, especially in cold climates where the water could freeze.

Battery

Note: *There are certain precautions to be taken when working on or near the battery: a) Never expose a battery to open flame or sparks which could ignite the hydrogen gas given off by the battery; b) Wear protective clothing and eye protection to reduce the possibility of the corrosive sulfuric acid solution inside the battery harming you (if the fluid is splashed or spilled, flush the contacted area immediately with plenty of water); c) Remove all metal jewelry which could contact the positive terminal and another grounded metal source, thus causing a short circuit; d) Always keep batteries and battery acid out of the reach of children.*
17 Vehicles equipped with maintenance-free batteries require no maintenance as the battery case is sealed and has no removal caps for adding water.
18 If equipped with a conventional battery, the caps on the top of the battery should be removed periodically to check for a low water level (photo). This check will be more critical during the warm summer months.
19 Remove each of the caps and add distilled water to bring the level of each cell to the split ring in the filler opening.
20 At the same time the battery water level is checked, the overall condition of the battery and its related components should be inspected. If corrosion is found on the cable ends or battery terminals, remove the cables and clean away all corrosion using a baking soda/water solution or a wire brush cleaning tool designed for this purpose.

Brake master cylinder

21 The brake master cylinder is located on the left side of the engine compartment, and has two separate reservoirs each with its own cap.
22 To check the level of the brake fluid, simply note how high the fluid is in relation to the MAX and MIN marks on the side of each reservoir.
23 Some models are equipped with brake fluid warning lights in the dash which indicate when the brake fluid in the master cylinder is too low.
24 If the brake fluid is significantly below the MAX mark, or if the brake fluid warning light comes on, additional fluid should be added to the reservoir.
25 Before removing the cap, use a rag to clean off all dirt, grease, etc. from around the cap area. If any foreign matter enters the master cylinder with the cap removed, blockage in the brake system lines can occur. Also make sure all painted surfaces around the master cylinder are covered, as brake fluid will ruin paintwork.
26 Remove the cap and lift it out of the reservoir (photo).
27 Carefully pour the specified brake fluid into the master cylinder. Be careful not to spill the fluid on painted surfaces. Be sure the specified fluid is used, as mixing different types of brake fluid can cause damage to the system. See *Recommended Lubricants* in the front of this Chapter or your owner's manual.
28 At this time the fluid and master cylinder can be inspected for contamination. Normally, the braking system will not need periodic draining and refilling, but if rust deposits, dirt particles or water droplets are seen in the fluid, the system should be dismantled, drained and refilled with fresh fluid.
29 Reinstall the master cylinder cap. Make sure it is properly seated to prevent fluid leakage and/or system pressure loss.
30 The brake fluid in the master cylinder will drop slightly as the brake pads at each wheel wear down during normal operation. If the master cylinder requires repeated replenishing to keep it at the proper level, this is an indication of leakage in the brake system which should be corrected immediately. Check all brake lines and their connections, along with the booster (see Chapter 9 for more information).
31 If upon checking the master cylinder fluid level you discover that one or both reservoirs is below the MIN mark or totally empty, the braking system should be bled (Chapter 9). When the fluid level gets low, air can enter the system and should be removed by bleeding the brakes.

Clutch fluid

32 To check the level of the brake fluid in the clutch master cylinder, simply note how high the fluid is in relation to the MAX and MIN marks on the side of the reservoir.
33 If the clutch fluid is significantly below the MAX mark, additional fluid should be added to the reservoir.
34 Before removing the cap, use a rag to clean all dirt, grease, etc. from around the cap area. If any foreign matter enters the master cylinder with the cap removed, blockage in the clutch system lines can occur. Also make sure all painted surfaces around the master cylinder are covered, as the fluid will ruin paintwork.
35 Remove the cap by twisting it counterclockwise, and lifting it off the reservoir.
36 Carefully pour the specified brake fluid into the master cylinder (photo). Be careful not to spill the fluid on painted surfaces. Be sure the specified fluid is used, as mixing different types can cause damage to the system. See Recommended Lubricants in the front of this Chapter or your owner's manual.
37 At this time the fluid and master cylinder can be inspected for contamination. Normally, the clutch system will not need periodic draining and refilling, but if rust deposits, dirt particles or water droplets are seen in the fluid, the system should be dismantled, drained and refilled with fresh fluid.
38 Reinstall the master cylinder cap. Make sure it is properly seated to prevent fluid leakage and/or system pressure loss.
39 If the master cylinder requires repeated replenishing to keep it at the proper level, this is an indication of leakage in the clutch system which should be corrected immediately. Check all clutch lines and their connections. (See Chapter 8 for more information).
40 If upon checking the master cylinder fluid level you discover that one or both reservoirs is below the MIN mark or totally empty, the clutch system should be bled (Chapter 8).

Manual transmission

41 Manual shift transmissions do not have a dipstick. The fluid level is checked by removing a plug in the side of the transmission case (photo). Locate this plug and use a rag to clean the plug and the area around it.
42 With the vehicle components cold, remove the plug. If fluid immediately starts leaking out, thread the plug back into the transmission because the fluid level is alright. If there is no fluid leakage, completely remove the plug and place your little finger inside the hole. The fluid level should be just at the bottom of the plug hole.
43 If the transmission needs more fluid, use a syringe to squeeze the appropriate lubricant into the plug hole to bring the fluid up to the proper level.
44 Thread the plug back into the transmission and tighten it securely. Drive the car and check for leaks around the plug.

Automatic transmission

45 The fluid inside the transmission must be at normal operating temperature to get an accurate reading on the dipstick. This is done by driving the car for several miles, making frequent starts and stops to allow the transmission to shift through all gears.
46 Park the car on a level surface, place the selector lever in Park and leave the engine running at an idle.
47 Remove the transmission dipstick (located on the right side, near the rear of the engine) and wipe all the fluid from the end of the dipstick with a clean rag.
48 Push the dipstick back into the transmission until the cap seats firmly on the dipstick tube. Now remove the dipstick again and observe the fluid on the end. The highest point of fluid should be between the

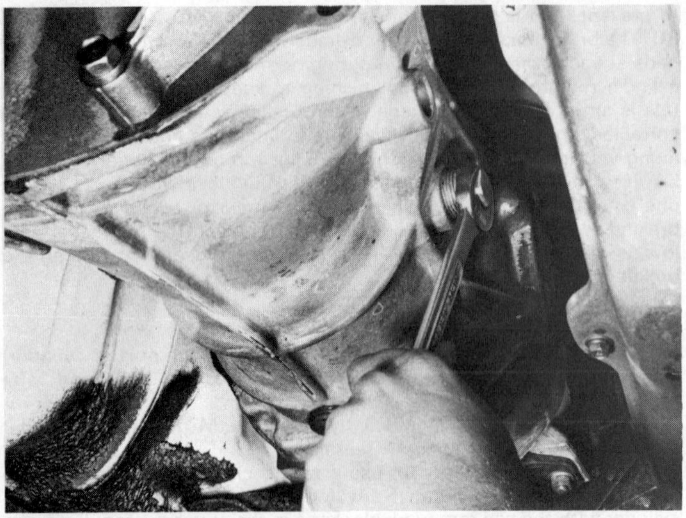

4.41 The manual transmission filler plug must be removed to both check the level and add oil

4.53 The differential filler plug is located on the rear of the rear axle housing

'H' mark and $\frac{1}{4}$ inch below the 'H' mark.

49 If the fluid level is at or below the 'L' mark on the dipstick, add sufficient fluid to raise the level to the 'H' mark. Fluid should be added directly into the dipstick guide tube, using a funnel to prevent spills.

50 It is important that the transmission not be overfilled. Under no circumstances should the fluid level be above the 'H' mark on the dipstick, as this could cause internal damage to the transmission. The best way to prevent overfilling is to add fluid a little at a time, driving the car and checking the level between additions.

51 Use only transmission fluid of the DEXRON type as specified in *Recommended Lubricants* at the front of this Chapter.

52 The condition of the fluid should also be checked along with the level. If the fluid at the end of the dipstick is a dark reddish-brown color, or if the fluid has a 'burnt' smell, the transmission fluid should be changed. If you are in doubt about the condition of the fluid, purchase some new fluid and compare the two for color and smell.

Differential

53 Like the manual transmission the rear axle has an inspection and fill plug which must be removed to check the fluid level (photo).

54 Remove the plug from the differential. Use your little finger to reach inside the rear axle housing to feel the level of the fluid. It should be at the bottom of the plug hole.

55 If this is not the case, add the proper lubricant into the rear axle carrier through the plug hole. A syringe or a small funnel can be used for this.

56 Tighten the plug securely and check for leaks after the first few miles of driving.

Power steering

57 Unlike manual steering, the power steering system relies on fluid which may, over a period of time, require replenishing.

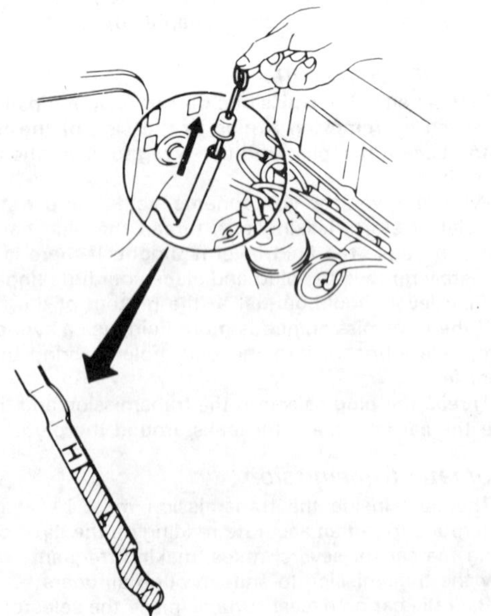

Fig. 1.1 The automatic transmission fluid should be filled only to the 'H' mark on the dipstick; no higher (Sec 4)

Fig. 1.2 The power steering fluid can be checked either hot or cold, and should be within the appropriate area on the dipstick (Sec 4)

58 The reservoir for the power steering pump is mounted to the right shock well.
59 The power steering fluid level can be checked either after the car has been driven, with the fluid at operating temperature, or with the engine and fluid cold. Either way, the front wheels should be pointed straight ahead.
60 With the engine shut off, use a rag to clean the reservoir cap and the areas around the cap. This will help to prevent foreign material from falling into the reservoir when the cap is removed.
61 Twist off the reservoir cap which has a built-in dipstick attached to it. Pull off the cap and clean the fluid at the bottom of the dipstick with a clean rag. Now reinstall the dipstick/cap assembly to get a fluid level reading. Remove the dipstick/cap and observe the fluid level. It should be within the 'hot' range marked on the dipstick if the fluid is hot, or within the 'cold' range if the fluid is cold.
62 If additional fluid is required, pour the specified lubricant directly into the reservoir using a funnel to prevent spills.
63 If the reservoir requires frequent fluid additions, all power steering hoses, hose connections, the power steering pump and the steering box should carefully checked for leaks.

5 Tire and tire pressure checks

1 Periodically inspecting the tires can not only prevent you from being stranded with a flat tire, but can also give you clues as to possible problems with the steering and suspension systems before major damage occurs.
2 Proper tire inflation adds miles to the lifespan of the tires, allows the car to achieve maximum miles-per-gallon figures, and helps the overall riding comfort of the car.
3 When inspecting the tire, first check the wear on the tread. Irregularities in the tread pattern (cupping, flat spots, more wear on one side than the other) are indications of front end alignment and/or balance problems. If any of these conditions are found you would do best to take the car to a competent repair shop which can correct the problem. See Chapter 11 for more information.
4 Also check the tread area for cuts or punctures. Many times a nail or tack will imbed itself into the tire tread and yet the tire will hold its air pressure for a short time. In most cases, a repair shop or gas station can repair the punctured tire.
5 It is also important to check the sidewalls of the tire, both inside and outside. Check for the rubber being deteriorated, cut or punctured. Also inspect the inboard side of the tire for signs of brake fluid leakage, which indicates that a thorough brake inspection is needed immediately (Section 27).
6 Incorrect tire pressure cannot be determined merely by looking at the tire. This is especially true for radial tires. A tire pressure gauge must be used. If you do not already have a reliable gauge, it is a good idea to purchase one and keep it in the glove box. Built-in pressure gauges at gas stations are often unreliable. If you are in doubt as to the accuracy of your gauge, many repair shops have 'master' pressure gauges which you can use for comparison purposes.

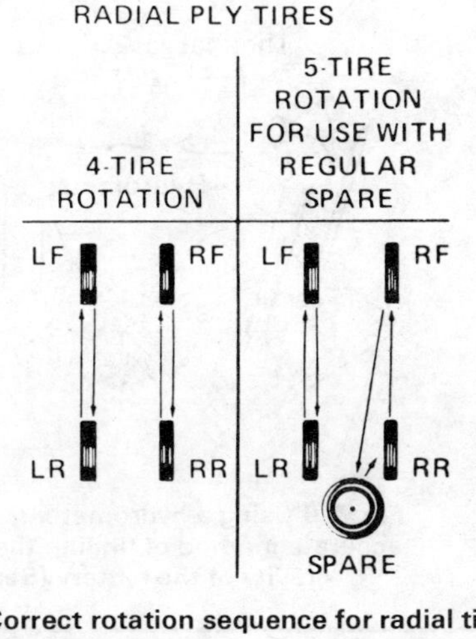

Fig. 1.3 Correct rotation sequence for radial tires (Sec 6)

7 Always check tire inflation when the tires are cold. Cold, in this case, means that the car has not been driven more than one mile after sitting for three hours or more. It is normal for the pressure to increase 4 to 8 pounds or more when the tires are hot.
8 Unscrew the valve cap protruding from the wheel or hubcap and firmly press the gauge onto the valve stem. Observe the reading on the gauge and check this figure against the recommended tire pressure listed on the tire placard. This tire placard is usually found attached to the inside of the glove box door.
9 Check all tires and add air as necessary to bring all tires up to the recommended pressure levels. Do not forget the spare tire. Be sure to reinstall the valve caps, which will keep dirt and moisture out of the valve stem mechanism.

6 Tire rotation

1 The tires should be rotated at the specified intervals and whenever uneven wear is noticed. Since the car will be raised and the tires removed anyway, this is a good time to check the brakes (Section 27) and/or repack the wheel bearings (Section 25). Read over these Sections if this is to be done at the same time.
2 The location for each tire in the rotation sequence depends on the type of tire used on your car. Tire type can be determined by reading the raised printing on the sidewall of the tire. The accompanying figure shows the rotation sequence for each type of tire.
3 Radial tires, used on this car, tend to wear faster in the shoulder area than other tire designs. This is especially so for the front tires. Therefore, in order to obtain the maximum life from the tires, they should be rotated every 15 000-miles interval, as shown in the Routine Maintenance schedule.
4 Rotating the tires simply means that the rear tires are removed from the rear axle and remounted on the front axle. At the same time, the front tires are likewise transferred to the rear axle.
5 It is important with radial tires that the tires be kept on the same side of the car during rotation. For example, the right rear tire should be remounted in the right front position, while the right front tire is remounted in the right rear position. The same goes for the left side.
6 See the information at the front of this manual for the proper procedures to follow in raising the car and changing a tire; however, if the brakes are to be checked do not apply the parking brake as stated. Make sure the tires are blocked to prevent the car from rolling.
7 Preferably, the entire car should be raised at the same time. This can be done on a hoist or by jacking up each corner of the car and then lowering the car onto jack stands placed under the frame rails. Always use four jack stands and make sure the car is firmly supported all around.
8 After rotation, check and adjust the tire pressures as necessary and be sure to check wheel nut tightness.

7 Engine oil and filter change

1 Frequent oil changes may be the best form of preventative maintenance available for the home mechanic. When engine oil gets old, it gets diluted and contaminated, which ultimately leads to premature parts wear.
2 Although some sources recommend oil filter changes every other oil change, we feel that the minimal cost of an oil filter and the relative ease with which it is installed dictate that a new filter be used whenever the oil is changed.
3 The tools necessary for a normal oil and filter change are: a wrench to fit the drain plug at the bottom of the oil pan; an oil filter wrench to remove the old filter; a container with at least a 6 quart capacity to drain the old oil into; and a funnel or oil can spout to help pour fresh oil into the engine.
4 In addition, you should have plenty of clean rags and newspapers handy to mop up any spills. Access to the underside of the car is greatly improved if the car can be lifted on a hoist, driven onto ramps or supported by jack stands. Do not work under a car which is supported only by a bumper, hydraulic or scissors-type jack.
5 If this is your first change on the car, it is a good idea to crawl underneath and familiarize yourself with the locations of the oil drain plug and the oil filter. Since the engine and exhaust components will be warm during the actual work, it is best to figure out any potential

problems before the car and its accessories are hot.

6 Allow the car to warm up to normal operating temperature. If the new oil or any tools are needed, use this warm-up time to gather everything necessary for the job. The correct type of oil to buy for your application can be found in Recommended Lubricants in the front of this Chapter.

7 With the engine oil warm (warm engine oil will drain better and more built-up sludge will be removed with the oil), raise the vehicle for access beneath. Make sure the car is firmly supported.

8 Move all necessary tools, rags and newspapers under the car. Position the drain pan under the drain plug. Keep in mind that the oil will initially flow from the pan with some force, so place the pan accordingly.

9 Being careful not to touch any of the hot exhaust pipe components, use the wrench to remove the drain plug near the bottom of the oil pan (photo). Depending on how hot the oil has become, you may want to wear gloves while unscrewing the plug the final few turns.

10 Allow the old oil to drain into the pan. It may be necessary to remove the pan farther under the engine as the oil flow reduces to a trickle.

11 After all the oil has drained, clean the drain plug thoroughly with a clean rag. Small metal filings may cling to this plug which could immediately contaminate your new oil.

12 Clean the area around the drain plug opening and reinstall the drain plug. Tighten the plug securely with your wrench. If a torque wrench is available, the torque setting is 20 ft-lb.

13 Move the drain pan into position under the oil filter.

14 Now use the filter wrench to loosen the oil filter. Chain or metal band-type filter wrenches may distort the filter canister, but don't worry too much about this as the filter will be discarded anyway.

15 If the filter is on so tight it cannot be loosened, or is inaccessible with a filter wrench, as a last resort you can punch a metal bar or long screwdriver directly through the bottom of the canister and use this as a T-bar to turn the filter. If this must be done, be prepared for oil to spurt out of the canister as it is punctured.

16 Completely unscrew the old filter. Be careful, it is full of oil. Empty the old oil inside the filter into the drain pan.

17 Compare the old filter with the new one to make sure they are of the same type.

18 Use a clean rag to remove all oil, dirt and sludge from the area where the oil filter mounts to the engine. Check the old filter to make sure the rubber gasket is not stuck to the engine mounting surface. If this gasket is stuck to the engine (use a flashlight if necessary), remove it.

19 Open one of the cans of new oil and fill the new filter with fresh oil. Also smear a light coat of this fresh oil onto the rubber gasket of the new oil filter.

20 Screw the new filter to the engine following the tightening directions printed on the filter canister or packing box. Most filter manufacturers recommend against using a filter wrench due to possible overtightening or damage to the canister.

21 Remove all tools, rags, etc from under the car, being careful not to spill the oil in the drain pan. Lower the car off its support devices.

22 Move to the engine compartment and locate the oil filler cap on the rocker arm cover.

23 If an oil can spout is used, push the spout into the top of the oil can and pour the fresh oil through the filler opening. A funnel placed into the opening may also be used.

24 Pour about 3 quarts of fresh oil into the engine. Wait a few minutes to allow the oil to drain to the pan, then check the level on the oil dipstick (see Section 2 if necessary). If the oil level is at or near the lower 'L' mark, start the engine and allow the new oil to circulate.

25 Run the engine for only about a minute and then shut it off. Immediately look under the car and check for leaks at the oil pan drain plug and around the oil filter. If either is leaking, tighten with a bit more force.

26 With the new oil circulated and the filter now completely full, recheck the level on the dipstick and add enough oil to bring the level to the 'H' mark on the dipstick.

27 During the first few trips after an oil change, make a point to check for leaks, and also check the oil level.

28 The old oil drained from the engine cannot be reused in its present state and should be disposed of. Oil reclamation centers, auto repair shops and gas stations will normally accept the oil which can be refined and used again. After the oil has cooled, it can be drained into a suitable container (capped plastic jugs, topped bottles, milk cartons, etc) for transport to one of these disposal sites.

8 Battery maintenance and servicing

General maintenance and testing

1 Most models are equipped with a conventional battery, in which the electrolyte level should be checked every week. This is done by removing all 6 caps and seeing how high the fluid level is in each cell. Refer to the accompanying figure for the proper level.

2 If the car is equipped with a battery level warning light the fluid level should still be checked visually on a regular basis to make sure all cells are remaining even.

3 On some models a sealed maintenance-free battery is used. As opposed to conventional batteries, it has no vent plugs in the top, and is completely sealed except for a small vent hole. Because of its sealed design this battery never needs water added, which greatly decreases the normal maintenance of it.

4 A temperature-compensated hydrometer is built into the top of maintenance-free batteries, which gives an indication of the electrolyte level and the battery's state of charge. If a blue indicator is seen in the indicator window on top of the battery, then the battery is properly charged. If the indicator is transparent, then the battery's charge is low and requires charging.

5 Periodically clean the top and sides of the battery, removing all dirt and moisture. This helps prevent corrosion and ensures that the battery does not become partially discharged by leakage through dampness and dirt.

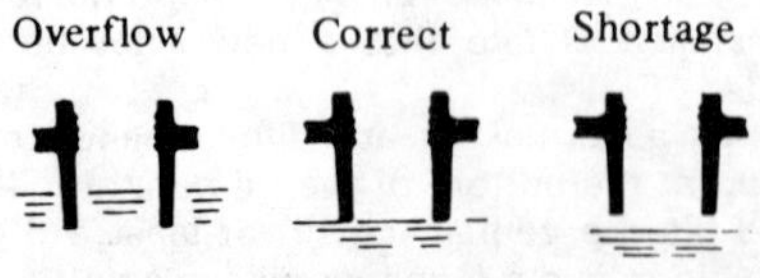

Fig. 1.4 The correct level for the battery electrolyte is just to the bottom of the filler hole rings (Sec 8)

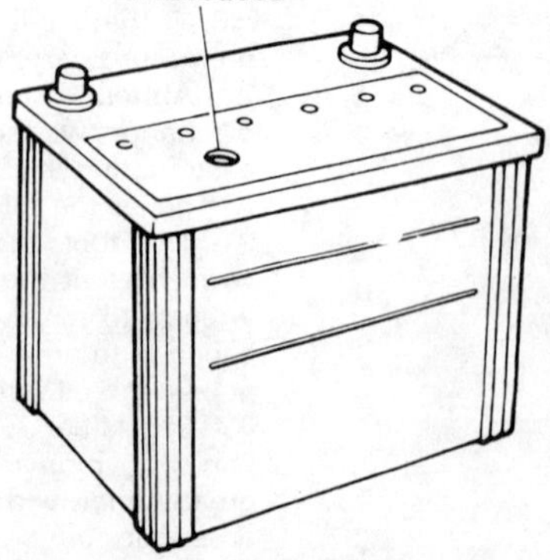

Fig. 1.5 The maintenance-free type battery has a built-in indicator on top to show the state of charge (Sec 8)

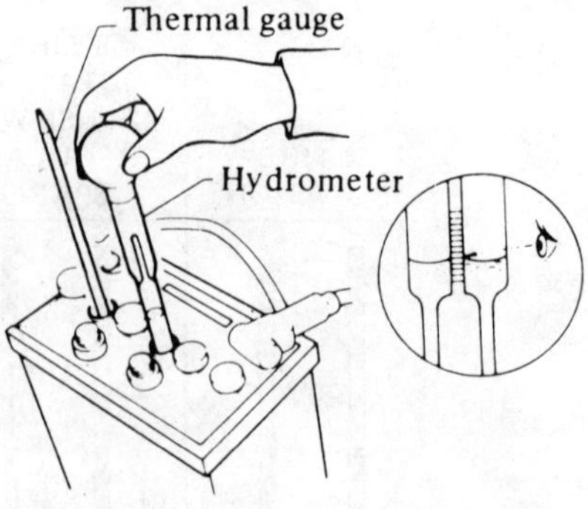

Fig. 1.6 Using a hydrometer is the most accurate method of finding the specific gravity of the battery (Sec 8)

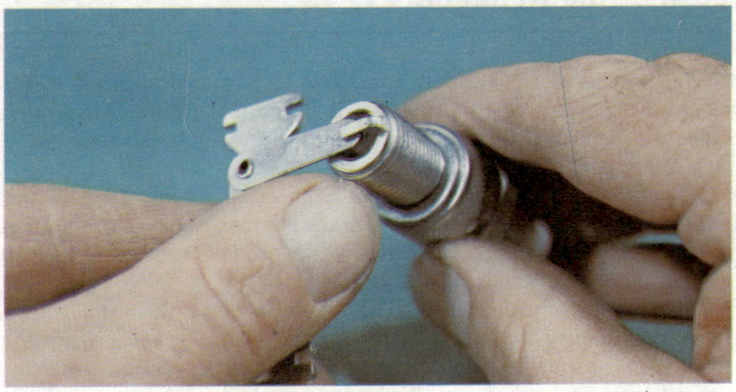

Measuring plug gap. A feeler gauge of the correct size (see ignition system specifications) should have a slight 'drag' when slid between the electrodes. Adjust gap if necessary

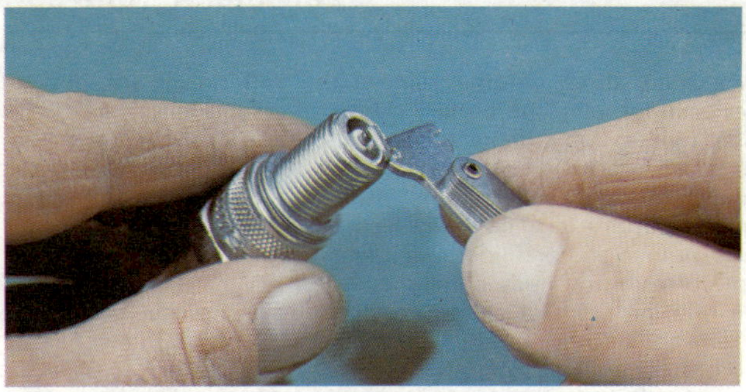

Adjusting plug gap. The plug gap is adjusted by bending the ground electrode inwards, or outwards, as necessary until the correct clearance is obtained. Note the use of the correct tool

Normal. Gray brown deposits, lightly coated core nose. Gap increasing by around 0.001 in (0.025 mm) per 1000 miles (1600 km). Plugs ideally suited to engine, and engine in good condition

Carbon fouling. Dry, black, sooty deposits. Will cause weak spark and eventually misfire. Fault: over-rich fuel mixture. Check: carburetor mixture settings, float level and jet sizes; choke operation and cleanliness of air filter. Plugs can be re-used after cleaning

Oil fouling. Wet, oily deposits. Will cause weak spark and eventually misfire. Fault: worn bores/piston rings or valve guides; sometimes occurs (temporarily) during running-in period. Plugs can be re-used after thorough cleaning

Overheating. Electrodes have glazed appearance, core nose very white – few deposits. Fault: plug overheating. Check: plug value, ignition timing, fuel octane rating (too low) and fuel mixture (too weak). Discard plugs and cure fault immediately

Electrode damage. Electrodes burned away; core nose has burned, glazed appearance. Fault: pre-ignition. Check: as for 'Overheating' but may be more severe. Discard plugs and remedy fault before piston or valve damage occurs

Split core nose (may appear initially as a crack). Damage is self-evident, but cracks will only show after cleaning. Fault: pre-ignition or wrong gap-setting technique. Check: ignition timing, cooling system, fuel octane rating (too low) and fuel mixture (too weak). Discard plugs, rectify fault immediately

6 Once every three months, remove the battery and inspect the battery securing bolts, the battery clamp plate, and battery leads for corrosion (white fluffy deposits on the metal which are brittle to touch). If any corrosion is found, clean off the deposits with an ammonia or baking soda solution. After cleaning, smear petroleum jelly on the battery terminals and lead connectors. Application of a zinc-base primer and/or underbody paint will help to prevent recurrence of corrosion on body panel metal.
7 The freezing point of electrolyte depends on its specific gravity. Since freezing can ruin a battery, it should be kept in a fully charged state to protect against freezing.
8 If topping-up the battery becomes excessive and the case has been inspected for cracks that could cause leakage, but none are found, the battery is being over-charged and the alternator will have to be tested and if necessary serviced as described in Chapter 5.
9 If any doubt exists about the state of charge of a battery, a hydrometer should be used to test it by withdrawing a little electrolyte from each cell in turn.
10 The specific gravity of the electrolyte at the temperature of 80°F (26.7°C) will be approximately 1.270 for a fully charged battery. For every 10°F (5.5°C) that the electrolyte temperature is above that stated, add 0.04 to the specific gravity or subtract 0.04 if the temperature is below that stated.
11 A specific gravity reading of 1.240 with an electrolyte temperature of 80°F (26.7°C) indicates a half-charged battery.

INDICATED SPECIFIC GRAVITY	ACTUAL SPECIFIC GRAVITY										
1.300	1.280	1.284	1.288	1.292	1.296	1.300	1.304	1.308	1.312	1.316	1.320
1.280	1.260	1.264	1.268	1.272	1.276	1.280	1.284	1.288	1.292	1.296	1.300
1.260	1.240	1.244	1.248	1.252	1.256	1.260	1.264	1.268	1.272	1.276	1.280
1.240	1.220	1.224	1.228	1.232	1.236	1.240	1.244	1.248	1.252	1.256	1.260
1.220	1.200	1.204	1.208	1.212	1.216	1.220	1.224	1.288	1.232	1.236	1.240
1.200	1.180	1.184	1.188	1.192	1.196	1.200	1.204	1.208	1.212	1.216	1.220
1.180	1.160	1.164	1.168	1.172	1.176	1.180	1.184	1.188	1.192	1.196	1.200
1.160	1.140	1.144	1.148	1.152	1.156	1.160	1.164	1.168	1.172	1.176	1.180
1.140	1.120	1.124	1.128	1.132	1.136	1.140	1.144	1.148	1.152	1.156	1.160
1.120	1.100	1.104	1.108	1.112	1.116	1.120	1.124	1.128	1.132	1.136	1.140
1.100	1.080	1.084	1.088	1.092	1.096	1.100	1.104	1.108	1.112	1.116	1.120
	−1°C 30°F	4°C 40°F	10°C 50°F	16°C 60°F	21°C 70°F	27°C 80°F	32°C 90°F	38°C 100°F	43°C 110°F	49°C 120°F	54°C 130°F
	ELECTROLYTE TEMPERATURE										

Fig. 1.7 Battery specific gravity temperature correction chart (Sec 8)

12 Some of the common causes of battery failure are:

a) *Accessories, especially headlights, left on overnight or for several hours.*
b) *Slow average driving speeds for short intervals.*
c) *The electrical load of the car being more than the generator output. This is especially common when several high-draw accessories are being used simultaneously, such as radios/stereos, air-conditioning, window defoggers, light systems, etc.*
d) *Charging system faults, such as electrical shorts, slipping belt, defective alternator or faulty voltage regulator.*
e) *Battery neglect, such as loose or corroded terminals or loose battery hold-down clamp.*

Battery charging

13 In winter when heavy demand is placed upon the battery, such as when starting from cold, and much electrical equipment is continually in use, it's a good idea to occasionally have the battery fully charged from an external source.
14 When charging the battery the negative cable should be disconnected. Also the charger leads should be connected to the battery **before** the charger is plugged in or turned on. If the leads are connected to the battery terminals after the charger is on, a spark could occur which could ignite the battery gases.
15 The battery should be charged at a low rate of about 4 to 6 amps, and should be left on for at least a couple of hours. Alternatively, a trickle charger charging at the rate of 1.5 amps can be safely used overnight.
16 Special rapid 'boost' charges which are claimed to restore the power of the battery in 1 to 2 hours are most dangerous, as they can cause serious damage to the battery plates. This type of charge should only be used in a 'crisis' situation.
17 The battery should be left on the charger only until the specific gravity of the battery is brought up to a normal level (paragraphs 9 - 11). On maintenance-free batteries, continue to charge only until the blue indicator is seen in the indicator window. Do not overcharge the battery. **Note**: *Some 'automatic' battery chargers will automatically shut off after the battery is fully charged, making it unnecessary to keep a close watch on the state of charge.*
18 When disconnecting the charger, once again turn the charger off or unplug it **before** disconnecting the charger leads from the battery.

Emergency jump starting

Note: *When jump starting the battery, be sure that the voltage of the booster battery does not exceed 12 volts. Jumping from a higher voltage battery can cause damage to the EFI control unit and other electrical components.*

19 Apply the parking brake and place the transmission in 'Park' if automatic, or 'Neutral' if manual.
20 Remove any rings, watches, or other jewelry.
21 Do not allow any battery acid to contact eyes, skin, clothing or painted surfaces. Flush any contacted area immediately with water.
22 Hook up one end of the positive jumper cable to the positive terminal of the booster battery and the other end to the positive terminal of the discharged battery. Do not permit the vehicles to touch each other. Be sure that the positive jumper cable does not contact any metal part of either car, as this will create a short circuit.
23 Hook up one end of the negative jumper cable to the negative terminal of the booster battery and the other end to a solid engine ground at least 18 inches (450 mm) from the discharged battery. Do not connect the cable directly to the negative terminal of the dead battery.
24 Start the engine of the car that is providing the boost and turn off all electrical accessories.
25 Start the engine of the car with the discharged battery.
26 Reverse these directions exactly when removing the jumper cables. The negative cable must be removed from the engine that was jump-started first.

Battery removal and installation

27 The battery is located at the front right side of the engine compartment, and is held in place by a hold-down clamp across the top of the battery case.
28 As hydrogen gas is produced by the battery, keep open flames or lighted cigarettes away from the battery at all times.
29 Always keep the battery in the upright position. Any spilled electrolyte from the vent hole should be immediately flushed with large quantities of water. Wear eye protection when working with a battery to prevent serious eye damage from splashed fluid.
30 Always disconnect the negative (–) battery cable first, followed by the positive (+) cable.
31 If equipped with a battery fluid warning light, disconnect the wiring lead running to one of the battery vent caps.
32 Loosen the 2 clamp nuts until the hooked bottom ends of the clamp rods can be disengaged from the battery support bracket. Then lift off the entire clamp assembly.
33 Carefully lift the battery from its tray and out of the engine compartment.
34 Installation is a reversal of removal; however, make sure that the hold-down clamp is securely tightened. Do not over-tighten, however, as this may damage the battery case. The battery posts and cable ends should be cleaned prior to connection.

9 Spark plugs replacement

1 Properly functioning spark plugs are a necessity if the engine is to perform properly. At the intervals specified in the Routine Maintenance

schedule, the spark plugs should be replaced with new ones.

2 There are 8 spark plugs used on the Z20E engine, 4 are located on either side of the cylinder head.

3 In most cases the tools necessary for a spark plug replacement job are a plug wrench or spark plug socket which fits onto a ratchet wrench and a spark plug feeler gauge to check and adjust the spark plug gap. Special spark plug wire removal tools are also available for separating the wire boot from the spark plug.

4 The best policy to follow when replacing spark plugs is to purchase the new spark plugs beforehand, adjust them to the proper gap and then replace each plug one at a time.

5 When buying the new spark plugs it is important to replace the old plugs with new ones of the same heat range and type. A series of numbers and letters are stamped on the plug to help identify each variation. The correct type of plug for your Datsun engine can be found in the Specifications at the beginning of this Chapter, but should be checked with the information found in the factory owner's manual. If differences exist between these sources, purchase the type specified by the factory.

6 With the new spark plugs at hand, allow the engine to thoroughly cool before attempting the removal. During this cooling time, each of the new spark plugs can be inspected for defects and the gap can be checked.

7 The spark plug gap is of considerable importance. If it is too large or too small the size of the spark and its efficiency will be seriously impaired. The gap is checked by inserting the proper thickness gauge between the electrodes at the tip of the plug. The gap between these electrodes should be the same as that given in the specifications. The gauge wire or blade should just touch each of the electrodes. If the gap is incorrect, use the notched adjuster on the gauge to bend the curved side electrode slightly until the proper gap is achieved. The center electrode should never be bent as this may crack the insulation and cause plug failure, or worse.

8 Also, at this time check for cracks in the spark plug body, indicating the spark plug should be replaced with a new one. If the side electrode is not exactly over the center one, use the notched adjuster to align the two.

9 Cover the fenders of the car to prevent damage to exterior paint.

10 With the engine cool, remove the spark plug wire from one spark plug. Do this by grabbing the boot at the end of the wire, not the wire itself. Sometimes it is necessary to use a twisting motion while the boot and plug wire is pulled free. Using a plug wire removal tool is the easiest and safest method.

11 If compressed air is available, use this to blow any dirt or foreign material away from the spark plug area. A common bicycle pump will also work. The idea here is to eliminate the possibility of foreign material falling into the engine cylinder as the spark plug is replaced.

12 Now place the spark plug wrench or socket over the plug and remove it from the engine by turning in a counterclockwise motion.

13 The condition and appearance of the spark plugs will tell much about the condition and tune of the engine. If the insulator nose of the spark plug is clean and white with no deposits, this is indicative of a weak mixture, or too hot a plug (a hot plug transfers heat away from the electrode slowly – a cold plug transfers it away quickly).

14 If the tip and insulator nose is covered with hard, black-looking deposits, then this is indicative that the mixture is too rich. Should the plug be black and oily, then it is likely that the engine is fairly worn, as well as the mixture being too rich.

15 If the insulator nose is covered with light tan to greyish brown deposits, then the mixture is correct and it is likely that the engine is in good condition.

16 If there are any traces of long, brown, tapering stains on the outside of the white portion of the plug, then the plug will have to be replaced with a new one, as this shows that there is a faulty joint between the plug body and the insulator, and compression is being allowed to leak away.

17 Compare the spark plug with those shown on page *35* to get an indication of the overall running condition of the engine.

18 Insert one of the new plugs into the engine, tightening it as much as possible by hand. The spark plug should screw easily into the engine. If it doesn't, change the angle of the spark plug slightly, as chances are the threads are not matched (cross-threaded).

19 Firmly tighten the spark plug with the wrench or socket. It is best to use a torque wrench for this to assure that the plug is seated correctly. The correct torque figure is shown in the Specifications.

20 Before pushing the spark plug wire onto the end of the plug, inspect it following the procedures outlined in Section 10.

21 Install the plug wire to the new spark plug.

10 Spark plug wires check

1 The spark plug wires should be checked at the recommended intervals or whenever new spark plugs are installed.

2 The wires should be inspected one at a time to prevent mixing up the order which is essential for proper engine operation.

3 Disconnect the plug wire from the spark plug. A removal tool can be used for this, or you can grab the rubber boot, twist slightly and then pull the wire free. Do not pull on the wire itself, only on the rubber boot.

4 Inspect inside the boot for corrosion which will look like a white, crusty powder. Some models use a conductive white grease which should not be mistaken for corrosion.

5 Now push the wire and boot back onto the end of the spark plug. It should be a tight fit on the plug end. If not, remove the wire and use a pair of pliers to carefully crimp the metal connector inside the wire

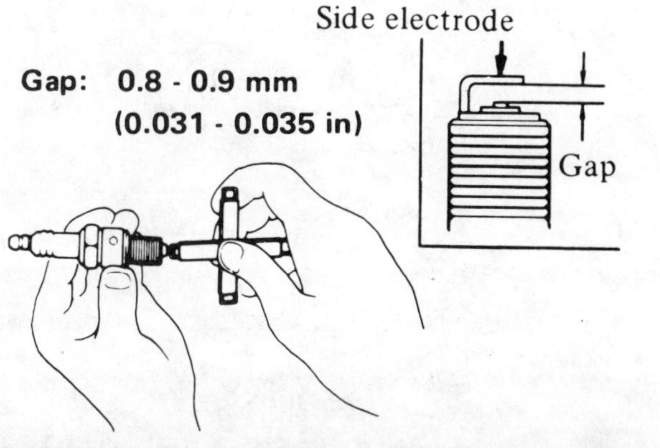

Fig. 1.8 To adjust the gap of the spark plug, the side electrode is bent until it is the proper distance from the center electrode (Sec 9)

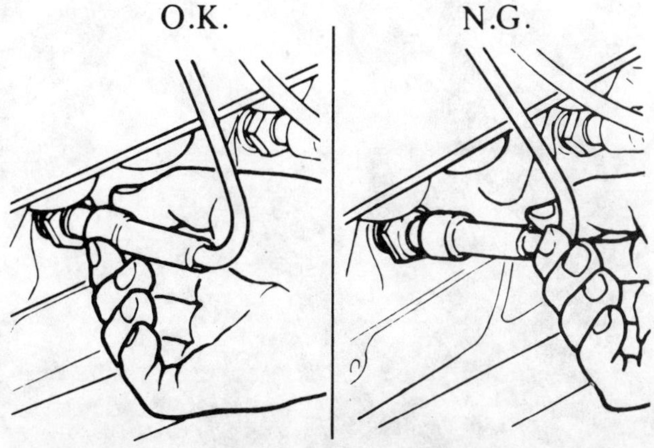

Fig. 1.9 When disconnecting the wires from the spark plugs, always pull the wire boot, not the wire itself (Sec 10)

boot until the fit is secure.

6 Now using a clean rag, clean the wire its entire length. Remove all built-up dirt and grease. As this is done, inspect for burns, cracks or any other form of damage. Bend the wires in several places to ensure the conductive inside wire has not hardened.

7 Disconnect the wire at the distributor (again, pulling and twisting only on the rubber boot). Check for corrosion and a tight fit in the same manner as the spark plug end.

8 Reinstall the wire boot onto the top of the distributor.

9 Check the remaining spark plug wires in same way, making sure they are securely fastened at the distributor and spark plug.

10 A visual check of the spark plug wires can also be made. In a darkened garage (make sure there is ventilation), start the engine and observe each plug wire. Be careful not to come into contact with any moving engine parts. If there is a break or fault in the wire, you will be able to see arcing or a small spark at the damaged area.

11 If it is decided the spark plug wires are in need of replacement, purchase a new set for your specific engine model. Wire sets can be purchased which are pre-cut to the proper size and with the rubber boots already installed. Remove and replace each wire individually to prevent mix-ups in the firing sequence.

11 Drivebelt check and adjustment

1 The drivebelts, or V-belts as they are sometimes called, at the front of the engine play an important role in the overall operation of the car and its components. Due to their function and material make-up, the belts are prone to failure after a period of time and should be inspected and adjusted periodically to prevent major engine damage.

2 The number of belts used on a particular car depends on the accessories installed. Drivebelts are used to turn: the alternator, power steering pump; water pump; fan; and air conditioning compressor. (One belt is used to turn both the alternator and water pump/fan).

3 With the engine off, open the hood and locate the various belts at the front of the engine. Using your fingers (and a flashlight if necessary), move along the belts checking for cracks or separation. Also check for fraying and for glazing which gives the belt a shiny appearance. Both sides of the belts should be inspected, which means you will have to twist the belt to check the underside.

4 The tension of each belt is checked by pushing on the belt at a distance halfway between the pulleys. Push firmly with your thumb and see how much the belt moves downward (deflects), (photo). A rule of thumb, so to speak, is that if the distance (pulley center to pulley center) is between 7 inches and 11 inches the belt should deflect $\frac{1}{4}$ inch. If the belt is longer and travels between pulleys spaced 12 inches to 16 inches apart, the belt should deflect $\frac{1}{2}$ in.

5 If it is found necessary to adjust the belt tension of one of the belts, either to make it tighter or looser, refer to the appropriate procedure below.

11.4 Checking drivebelt tension

Alternator/water pump belt

6 Loosen both the upper alternator adjusting bolt and the lower alternator mounting bolt.

7 Pivot the alternator either away from the engine or toward the engine until the proper belt tension is obtained. It may be necessary to use some sort of pry bar to move the alternator. If this is done to gain the proper leverage, be very careful not to damage either the alternator or the part be pried against.

8 While holding the alternator in that position, retighten the 2 bolts. Then recheck the belt tension to make sure it is still correct.

Air conditioning compressor belt and power steering belt

9 Both of the belts that turn these components use idler pulleys to control the tension (Fig. 1.10). There are two ways to adjust the tension, depending on the type of idler pulley used.

10 On one type, the idler pulley lock nut, at the center of the pulley, must first be loosened. Then turn the idler pulley adjusting bolt either clockwise or counterclockwise, until the proper belt tension is obtained. Retighten the idler pulley lock nut.

11 With the other type of idler pulley, the lock bolt is the bolt used to attach the pulley to its bracket. While holding the pulley with an open-end wrench, loosen the lock bolt (photo). Then, using either the open

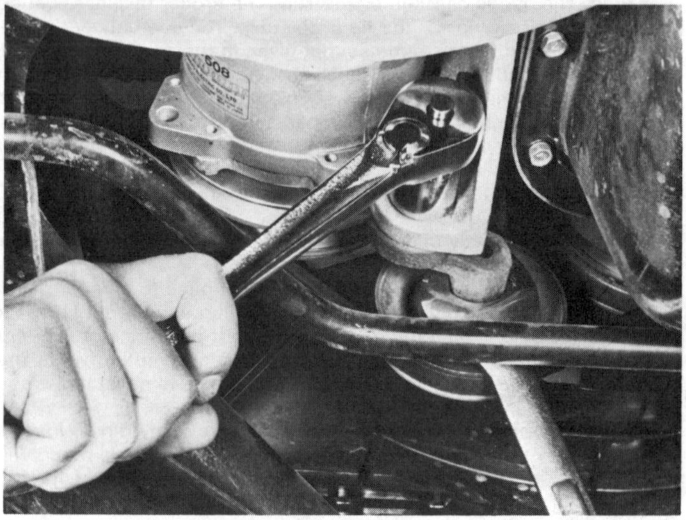

11.11 Some types of drive belt idler pulleys are adjusted by loosening the locking bolt in the rear and pivoting it

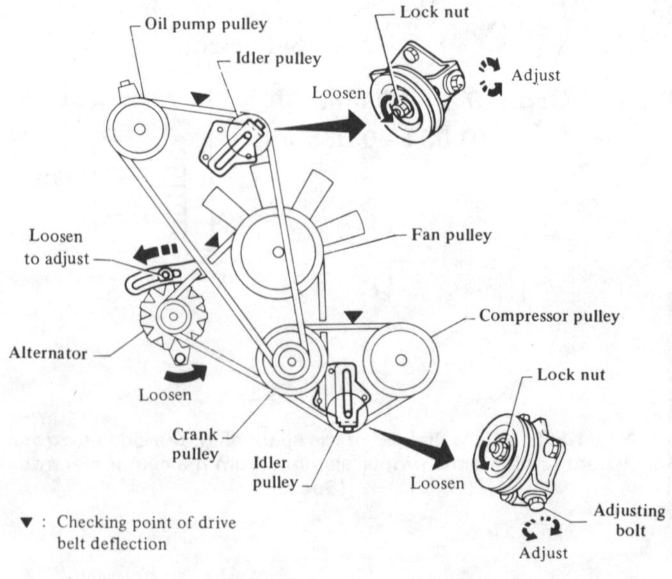

Fig. 1.10 Adjustment methods for the engine drivebelts (Sec 11)

end wrench or a pry bar, move the idler pulley in the required direction to produce the correct belt tension. While holding it in this position, retighten the lock bolt.

12 With either pulley, after retightening the lock nut or bolt, recheck the belt tension to make sure it is still correct.

12 Air filter replacement

1 At the specific intervals, the air filter should be replaced with a new one. A thorough program of preventive maintenance would also call for the filter to be inspected periodically between changes, especially if the car is often driven in dusty conditions.

2 The air filter is located inside the air cleaner housing at the left front of the engine compartment. It is mounted to the top of the air flow meter.

3 Remove the 2 screws that hold the inlet air duct to the radiator support and lift it off, while simultaneously disengaging it from the air cleaner.

4 Disconnect the air induction hose(s) from the metal pipe(s) (photo).

5 Remove the screw that retains the I.A.S. unit to the air cleaner housing, and lift the unit off.

6 Remove the remaining 2 screws that retain the air cleaner lid, and lift the lid up (photo).

7 Lift the air filter out of the housing. If it is covered with dirt or soot, it should be replaced.

8 Wipe the inside of the air cleaner housing with a rag.

9 Place the old filter (if in good condition) or the new filter (if replacement is necessary) into the air cleaner housing. Be sure the side marked 'UP' faces upward (the side with the rubber grommet should be down) (photo).

10 Reinstall the top plate of the air cleaner in the reverse order it was removed.

13 Distributor check

1 Although the breakerless distributor used on this car requires much less maintenance than conventional distributors, periodic inspections should be performed at the intervals specified in the routine maintenance schedule and whenever any work is performed on the distributor.

2 Remove the distributor cap by first disconnecting the ignition coil wire(s) from the coil(s), and then unsnapping the spring clips that hold the cap to the distributor body.

3 Place the cap, with the spark plug and coil wires still attached, out of the way. Use a length of wire or tape to secure it, if necessary.

4 Remove the rotor, which is now visible at the top of the distributor shaft. On models with one ignition coil, the rotor simply pulls off the shaft. On models with two ignition coils, the rotor is retained to the shaft by a single screw in its side. Place the rotor in a safe place where it cannot be damaged.

5 Visually inspect the various distributor components for any obvious signs of wear or damage. If dirt or oil has built up in the distributor, remove it by using a contact cleaner or other electrical parts solvent.

6 Check the wire connections at the IC unit (the component that has 2 or 3 wires running to it) to make sure they are clean and tight. Also check the wires to make sure they are not cracked or broken.

7 While the distributor cap is off, check the air gap as described in Chapter 5.

8 Before installing the rotor, inspect it for cracks or damage. Carefully check the condition of the metal contact at the top of the rotor for excessive burning or pitting. If in doubt as to its quality, replace it with a new one.

9 Before installing the distributor cap, inspect it for cracks or damage. Closely examine the contacts on the inside of the cap for excessive corrosion or damage (photo). Slight scoring is normal. Again, if in doubt as to the quality of the cap, replace it with a new one as described in Chapter 5.

12.4 Separate the air induction hoses from their metal tubes to give clearance for operations on the left side

12.6 Locations of the 3 air cleaner top mounting screws

12.9 Installing the air filter

13.9 If the distributor cap or rotor terminals are corroded or damaged, they should be replaced

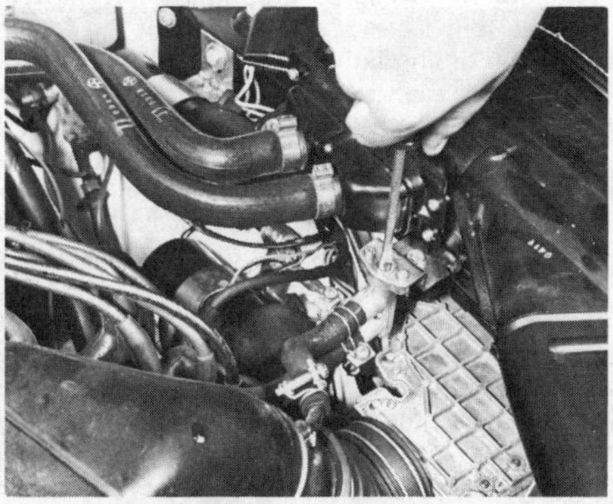

14.10 The idle adjusting screw is located in the I.A.S. unit attached to the air cleaner housing

15.2 To see the timing marks with the timing light, both the pulley notch and timing plate should be marked with paint or chalk

14 Idle speed adjustment

1 Engine idle speed is the speed at which the engine operates when no accelerator pedal pressure is applied. This speed is critical to the performance of the engine itself, as well as many engine sub-systems.
2 A hand-held tachometer must be used when adjusting idle speed to get an accurate reading. The exact hook-up for these meters varies with the manufacturer, so follow the particular directions included.
3 Set the parking brake and block the wheels. Be sure the car is in neutral (manual transmission) or park (automatic transmission).
4 If equipped with an air conditioner, be sure it is turned off.
5 Start the engine and allow it to reach normal operating temperature.
6 Open the hood and run the engine at about 2000 rpm for about 2 minutes. Then allow it to idle again.
7 *1980 49-state models only:* disconnect the air induction hose(s) from the metal pipe(s), and securely plug the pipe(s).
8 *1980 49-state models and all Canada models:* race the engine 2 or 3 times and then allow it to idle again for about a minute.
9 If the car has an automatic transmission, have an assistant shift to Drive while keeping the brake pedal firmly depressed. If it has a manual transmission, it can remain in neutral.
10 Now check the engine idle speed with the tachometer and compare it with the Specifications at the beginning of this Chapter.
11 If the idle speed is not correct, turn the idle speed adjusting screw (clockwise for slower, counterclockwise for faster) until the idle speed is correctly set (photo).
12 Automatic transmissions can now be shifted back to Park and the engine turned off.

15 Ignition timing

1 The proper ignition timing setting for your car is printed on the tune-up decal located on the underside of the hood. It can also be found in the Specifications section at the beginning of this Chapter. If there are any discrepancies between these specs, the tune-up decal should be given preference.
2 Locate the timing mark plate located alongside the crankshaft pulley (photo). The 'O' mark is Top Dead Center (TDC). To locate which mark the notch in the pulley must line up with to achieve correct timing, count back from the 'O' mark the number of degrees BTDC (Before Top Dead Center) as noted in the Specifications. Each mark on the timing plate equals 5 degrees. Thus if your vehicle specifications call for 6° BTDC, you should make a mark with fine paint or chalk just before the 5 mark on the timing plate.
3 Now locate the timing notch in the pulley and mark it with a dab of paint or chalk so it will be visible under the strobe light. To locate the notch it may be necessary to have an assistant temporarily turn the ignition off and on in short bursts to bring the notch into a position where it can be cleaned and marked. **Note:** *Stay clear of all moving engine components if the engine is turned in this manner.*
4 Connect a tachometer according to the manufacturer's instructions and check that the idle speed is correct. If not, adjust it as described in Section 14.
5 Allow the engine to reach normal operating temperature. Be sure the air conditioner, if equipped, is off.
6 With the ignition off, connect the pick-up lead of the timing light to the number one spark plug wire. This is the wire leading to the spark plug on the right (intake manifold) side of the engine, closest to the front of the car. Use either a jumper lead between the wire and plug or an inductive-type pick-up. Do not pierce the wire or attempt to insert a wire between the boot and the wire. Connect the timing light power leads according to the manufacturer's instructions.
7 Check that the wiring for the timing light is clear of all moving engine components, then start the engine.
8 Point the flashing timing light at the timing marks, again being careful not to come in contact with moving parts. The marks you made should appear stationary. If the marks are in alignment, the timing is correct. If the marks are not aligned, turn off the engine.
9 Loosen the adjusting screws at the base of the distributor (indicated by the long slots they are mated with) just until the distributor can be rotated.
10 Now start the engine and slowly rotate the distributor either left or right until the timing marks coincide.
11 Shut off the engine and tighten the distributor adjusting screws, being careful not to move the distributor.
12 Restart the engine and recheck the timing to make sure the marks are still in alignment.
13 Disconnect the timing light.
14 Race the engine 2 or 3 times and then allow it to run at idle. Recheck the idle speed with the tachometer. If it has changed from its correct setting, readjust it.
15 Drive the car and listen for 'pinging' noises. These will be most noticeable when the engine is hot and under load (climbing a hill, accelerating from a stop). If you hear engine pinging, the ignition timing is too far advanced (Before Top Dead Center). Reconnect the timing light and turn the distributor to move the mark 1° or 2° in the retard direction. Road test the car again for proper operation.
16 To keep 'pinging' at a minimum, yet still allow you to operate the car at the specified timing setting, it is advisable to use gasoline of the same octane at all times. Switching fuel brands and octane levels can decrease performance and economy, and possibly damage the engine.

16 Cylinder compression testing

1 The purpose of testing the cylinder compression is to check the condition of the sealing components within the combustion chamber. Specifically, this test reveals excessive wear of the piston rings, cylinder walls or valves.
2 The only special tool needed for this test is a compression tester. These are available in two main types; one that screws into the spark plug hole, and a type that is simply held tightly in the spark plug hole. The screw-in types are usually more expensive, but are more accurate and easier to use.
3 Before beginning, check that the battery is fully charged and the engine oil is properly filled.
4 Start the engine and allow it to idle until it reaches normal operating temperature. Then turn it off.
5 Remove all 4 spark plugs from one side of the cylinder head. Do not remove the plugs from the other side.
6 Disconnect the wiring connectors from all 4 injectors.
7 Have an assistant depress the accelerator pedal all the way so the throttle valve is fully open.
8 Insert the compression tester into the first spark plug hole and have your assistant crank the engine over several times. Watch the gauge of the compression tester carefully and note the highest reading obtained.
9 Jot this reading down on a piece of paper. Then repeat the test on the other 3 cylinders.
10 A compression reading of around 171 psi (12.0 kg/cm^2) indicates that compression is normal. Readings slightly below this are acceptable as long as all cylinders are relatively even. No cylinder should have a reading less than 80% of the highest reading obtained.
11 If one or more cylinders are significantly lower than the others, or if readings of below 128 psi (9.0 kg/cm^2) are obtained, then too much compression is being lost and servicing is required.
12 To help pinpoint the source of the problem, squirt a small amount of engine oil into the cylinder(s) giving the low readings, and retest the compression as before.

a) If the reading was higher after adding the oil, then the piston rings or cylinder walls are probably worn.
b) If the reading remained low, then the valves are either sticking or are not seating properly.

13 If cylinder compression is abnormally low in two adjacent cylinders, and adding oil does not help improve the compression, then the head gasket is probably damaged between these two cylinders. This could also be the cause for oil or water entering the combustion chamber.
14 If the compression tests show too much compression in the cylinders, then there could be excessive carbon build-up in the combustion chamber, which would also be a cause for hard starting when the engine is warm.

17 Valve clearance adjustment

1 Although the valves can be adjusted with the engine cold, it is

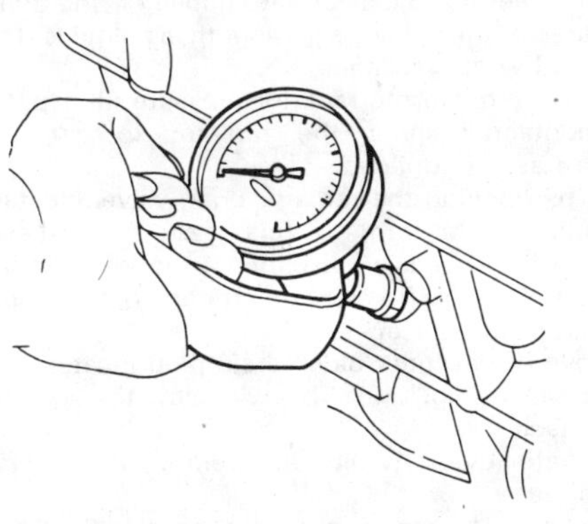

Fig. 1.11 Testing the cylinder compression with a compression gauge can pinpoint faulty rings or valves (Sec 16)

Fig. 1.12 Valve clearance is measured by inserting a feeler gauge between the rocker arm screw and the valve (Sec 17)

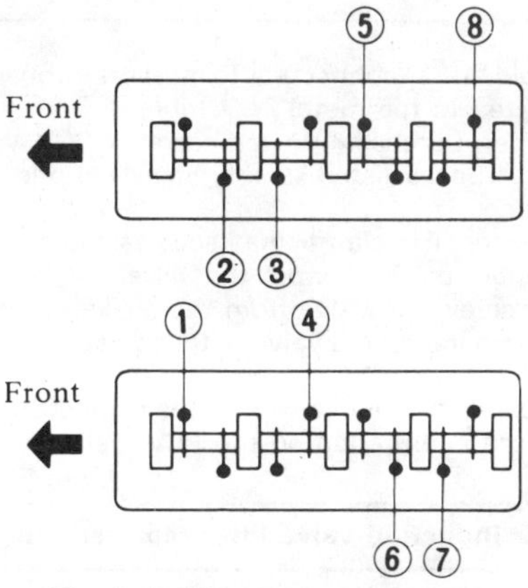

Fig. 1.13 When the number one camshaft lobe is pointing downward, the valves shown (lower) can be adjusted. The valves shown (upper) can be adjusted when the number one camshaft lobe is pointing upward (Sec 17)

better to adjust them with the engine hot. If they are adjusted cold, they should be rechecked once the engine has warmed up, and readjusted if necessary to conform to the hot engine Specifications.
2 Start the engine and allow it to reach normal operating temperature. Then turn the engine off.
3 Remove the rocker arm cover as described in Chapter 2.
4 Rotate the camshaft so that the number 1 cam lobe points directly down. This can be done by using a wrench and socket on the crankshaft pulley bolt, at the front of the engine, and turning the crankshaft counterclockwise. Removing the spark plugs makes this easier. Another method is to use the ignition key to operate the starter to short bursts. If this is done the ignition coil wire(s) should be disconnected from the distributor cap and grounded on the engine to prevent the car from firing.
5 The valve clearance is measured by inserting the proper feeler gauge between the end of the valve stem and the rocker arm screw (see accompanying figure). It should move with a slight drag when slid back and forth.
6 If the gap is either too large or too small, loosen the rocker arm nut and turn the rocker arm screw to obtain the correct gap.
7 Once the gap has been set, hold the rocker arm screw in position with the screwdriver and retighten the rocker arm nut.
8 Recheck the valve clearance. Sometimes it will change slightly when the rocker arm nut is tightened. If this is the case, readjust it until it is correct.
9 With the camshaft in this position, the number 1, 4, 6, and 7 valves can be adjusted using the procedure just described.
10 Now rotate the camshaft until the number 1 cam lobe is pointing straight up. In this position the number 2, 3, 5 and 8 valves can be adjusted in the same manner.
11 After all valves have been adjusted, reinstall the rocker arm cover.

18 Fuel filter replacement

1 The fuel filter is a metal canister-like object attached by a bracket to the right shock well, and is specially designed for the high fuel pressures of the Datsun Electronic Fuel Injection system. Be sure to replace it with an equivalent fuel filter.
2 Before disconnecting the fuel lines from the filter, the pressure in the fuel system must be reduced to prevent dangerous spraying. This is done in the following manner:

a) Locate the fuel pump relay-2 attached to the engine compartment relay bracket (photo). The relay bracket must be disconnected from the body in order to gain access to the relays.
b) Start the engine and allow it to idle.
c) With the engine running, disconnect the wiring connector leading to the fuel pump relay-2. **Note:** *Wires to this relay are light green, blue, blue/white stripe and black/white stripe. If necessary, see Section 8, Chapter 2.*
d) Wait for the engine to stall, then crank the engine over 2 or 3 times.
e) Turn the ignition switch off and reconnect the wiring connector to the fuel pump relay-2. Remount the relay bracket.

3 Disconnect both fuel lines from the fuel filter, and lift the filter out of its bracket (photo).
4 When connecting the fuel lines to the new filter, use hose clamps and position them so they are 3 mm (0.12 in) from the end of the hose.

19 PCV valve replacement

1 The PCV valve is located on the left rear underside of the intake

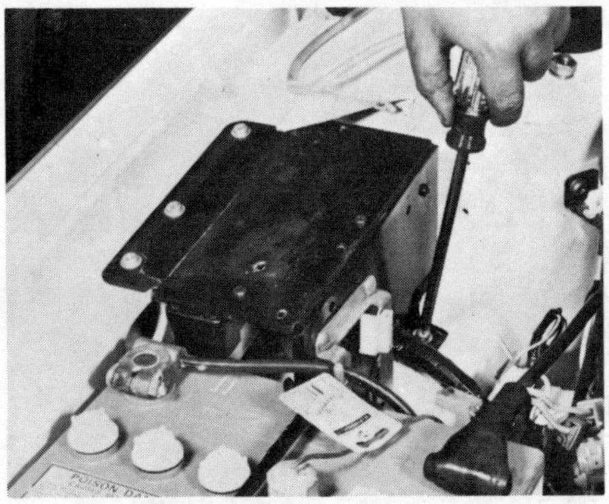

18.2 Removing the relay bracket

18.3 Removing the fuel filter

20.1 Removing the air induction valve case from the air cleaner housing

manifold. It is connected to a short rubber hose, which is in turn connected to the metal PCV tube.
2 When purchasing a replacement PCV valve, make sure it is the proper type as listed in the Specifications at the beginning of this Chapter.
3 Loosen the clamp that secures the hose to the PCV valve and disconnect the hose from the valve.
4 Unscrew the valve from the intake manifold.
5 Compare the old valve with the new one to make sure they are the same.
6 Screw the new valve into the manifold and connect the hose to it.
7 More information on the PCV system can be found in Chapter 6.

20 Air induction valve filter replacement

1 Remove the 4 screws that retain the air induction valve case to the air filter housing, and lift the case free (photo).
2 Pry the old filter from the air filter housing.
3 Press the new filter into position, and reinstall the valve case.

21 Cooling system check and servicing

1 Many major engine failures can be attributed to a faulty cooling system. If equipped with an automatic transmission, the cooling system also plays an integral role in automatic longevity.
2 The cooling system should be checked with the engine cold. Do this before the car is driven for the day or after it has been shut off for one or two hours.
3 Remove the radiator cap and thoroughly clean the cap (inside and out) with clean water. Also clean the filler neck on the radiator. All traces of corrosion should be removed.
4 Carefully check the upper and lower radiator hoses along with the smaller diameter heater hoses. Inspect their entire length, replacing any hose which is cracked, swollen or shows signs of deterioration. Cracks may become more apparent if the hose is squeezed.
5 Also check that all hose connections are tight. A leak in the cooling system will usually show up as white or rust-colored deposits on the areas adjoining the leak.
6 Use compressed air or a soft brush to remove bugs, leaves, etc, from the front of the radiator or air conditioning condensor. Be careful not to damage or cut yourself on the sharp cooling fins.
7 Finally, have the cap and system tested for proper pressure. If you do not have a pressure tester, most gas stations and repair shops will do this for a minimal charge.
8 At the same time the cooling system is checked, as per the maintenance schedule, it should also be drained, flushed and refilled. This is to replenish the antifreeze mixture and prevent rust and corrosion which can impair the performance of the cooling system and ultimately cause engine damage.
9 As antifreeze is a poisonous solution, take care not to spill any of the cooling mixture on the vehicle's paint or your own skin. If this happens, rinse immediately with plenty of clear water. Also, it is advisable to consult your local authorities about the dumping of antifreeze before draining the cooling system. In many areas reclamation centers have been set up to collect automobile oil and drained antifreeze/water mixtures rather than allowing these liquids to be added to the sewage and water facilities.
10 With the engine cold, remove the radiator pressure fill cap.
11 Move a large container under the radiator to catch the water/antifreeze mixture as it is drained.
12 Drain the radiator by opening the radiator drain valve, located in the center of the radiator's bottom). If this drain has excessive corrosion and cannot be turned easily, disconnect the lower radiator hose to allow the coolant to drain. Be careful that none of the solution is splashed on your skin or in your eyes.
13 If accessible, remove the cylinder block drain plug located at the left rear of the cylinder block (Fig.1.14). This will allow the coolant to drain from the engine itself.
14 Disconnect the radiator overflow pipe and remove the reservoir. Flush it out with clean water.
15 Place a cold water hose (a common garden hose is fine) in the radiator filler neck at the top of the radiator and flush the system until the water runs clear at all drain points.
16 In severe cases of contamination or clogging of the radiator, remove it (see Chapter 3) and reverse-flush it. This involves simply inserting the cold pressure hose in the bottom radiator outlet to allow the clear water to run against the normal flow, draining through the top. A radiator repair shop should be consulted if further cleaning or repair is necessary.
17 Where the coolant is regularly drained and the system refilled with the correct antifreeze/inhibitor mixture there should be no need to employ chemical cleaners or descalers.
18 To refill the system, reconnect the radiator hoses and install the drain plug securely in the engine. Special thread sealing tape (available at auto parts stores) should be used on the drain plug going into the engine block. Install the expansion reservoir and the overflow hose.
19 Fill the radiator to the base of the filler neck and then add more coolant to the expansion reservoir so that it reaches the 'MIN' mark.
20 Run the engine until normal operating temperature is reached, and with the engine idling, add coolant up to the correct level (see Section 4), then install the radiator cap. Install the reservoir cap.
21 Always refill the system with a mixture of high-quality antifreeze and water in at least a 50/50 proportion. The antifreeze should not exceed a 70/30 ratio with the water, however.
22 Keep a close watch on the coolant level and the various cooling hoses during the first few miles or driving. Tighten the hose clamps and/or add more coolant mixture as necessary.

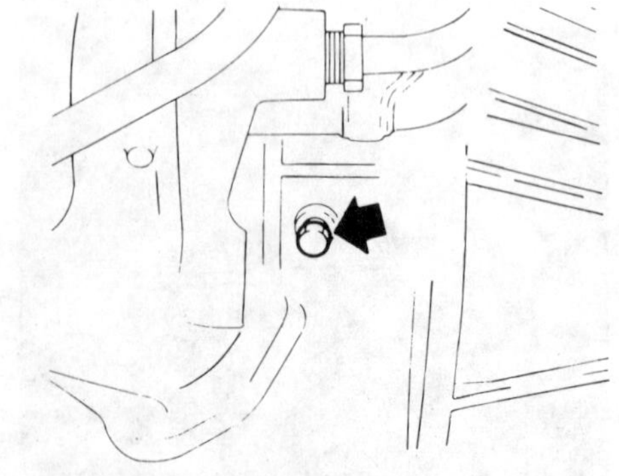

Fig. 1.14 Coolant can be drained from the engine by removing the cylinder block drain plug at the left rear of the block (Sec 21)

22.5 Adjusting the throttle cable adjusting nuts

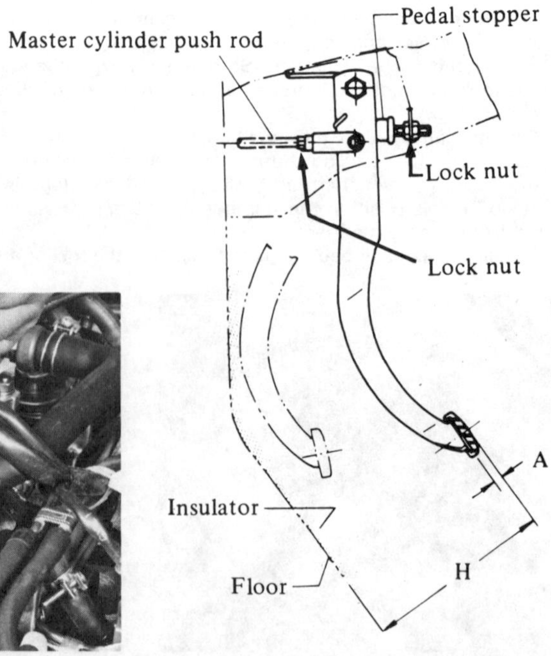

Fig. 1.15 The clutch pedal should be periodically adjusted for correct height and free play (Sec 23)

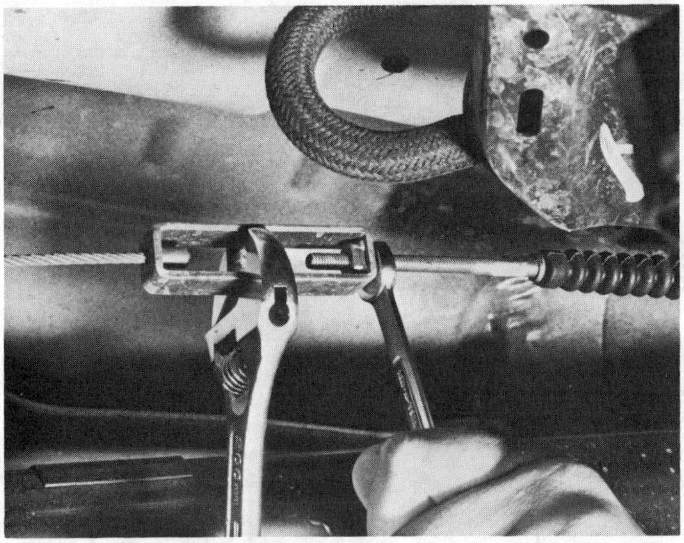

24.5 The parking brake adjuster is located on the underside of the car on the right of the driveshaft

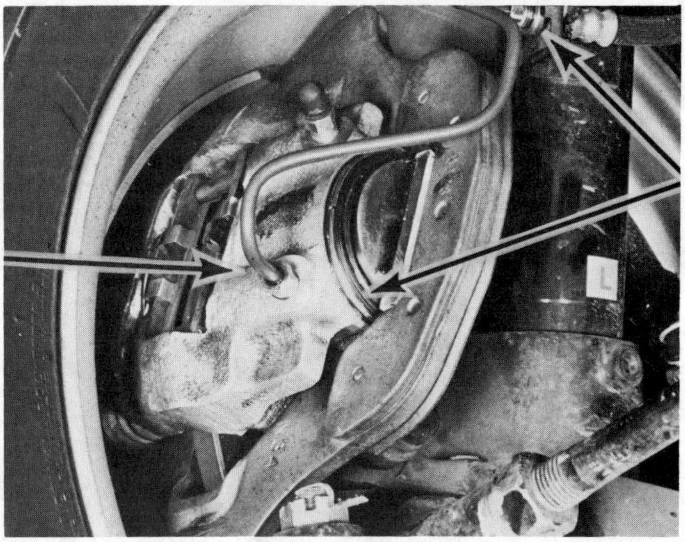

27.7 The disc brake caliper assemblies should be regularly checked for leaking fluid at the brake lines and piston seals

22 Accelerator linkage check and pedal adjustment

1 With the engine off, depress the accelerator pedal several times to make sure that the cable linkage is operating smoothly, without jamming or dragging. Also check that the pedal is returning to its original position when released.
2 Open the hood, and then disconnect the rubber boot that runs between the air pipe and the throttle chamber.
3 Have an assistant fully depress the accelerator pedal several times, and look into the throttle chamber to make sure the throttle valve is opening fully when the pedal is depressed and is closing fully when the pedal is released.
4 Finally check the free play of the accelerator pedal. This is the distance the pedal can be depressed before it begins pulling on the accelerator cable. The free play should not be over 2 mm (0.08 in).
5 If the free play is greater than this, loosen the accelerator cable adjusting nuts on the left side of the intake manifold and slide the cable housing in its bracket until the correct pedal free play is obtained (photo). Then retighten the cable adjusting nuts.

23 Clutch pedal adjustments

1 If equipped with a manual transmission, it is important to have the clutch pedal height and free play correctly adjusted.
2 The height of the clutch pedal is the distance the pedal sits away from the floor (measurement 'H' in Fig. 1.15). This distance should be between 168 and 174 mm (6.61 and 6.85 in). If the pedal height is not within this range, loosen the locknut on the pedal stopper located in the bracket just forward of the clutch pedal, and turn the stopper in or out until the pedal height is correctly adjusted. Retighten the locknut.
3 The free play is the pedal slack, or the distance the pedal can be depressed before it begins to have any effect on the clutch (measurement 'A' in Fig. 1.15). This distance should be 1 - 5 mm (0.04 - 0.20 in). If it is not, loosen the locknut on the clutch master cylinder pushrod, to which the clutch pedal is attached. Turn the pushrod until the free play is correctly adjusted, and then retighten the locknut.

24 Parking brake adjustment

1 The parking brake does not need routine maintenance but the cable may stretch over a period of time necessitating adjustment. Also, the parking brake should be checked for proper adjustment whenever the rear brake cables have been disconnected.
2 While sitting in the driver's seat, pull up on the parking brake lever with heavy pulling force. When correctly adjusted the lever should move upward 7 or 8 ratchet clicks. The adjustment can be checked also by measuring the distance the lever moves upward. The proper adjustment is $3\frac{1}{2}$ to 4 inches (90 to 100 mm), measured at the center of the handle. If the movement of the lever is shorter or longer than these Specifications, the parking brake needs adjustment.
3 Raise the rear of the car and support it on jackstands.
4 Loosen the locknut at the parking brake cable adjuster.
5 Turn the adjuster until the parking brake lever, when pulled, moves the proper distance (photo).
6 Retighten the adjuster locknut.
7 Before lowering the car to the ground, check that both rear wheels turn freely with the parking brake released, and that there is no brake drag in either direction.

25 Wheel bearings check

1 In most cases, the front wheel bearings will not need servicing until the brake pads are changed. However, these bearings should be checked whenever the front wheels are raised for any reason.
2 With the vehicle securely supported on jack stands, spin the wheel and check for noise, rolling resistance or free play. Now grab the top of the tire with one hand and the bottom of the tire with the other. Move the tire in and out on the spindle. If it moves more than 0.005 in, the bearings should be checked, and replaced if necessary. Refer to Chapter 11 for the proper procedure.

26 Chassis lubrication

1 A grease gun and a cartridge filled with the proper grease (see Recommended Lubricants) are the only equipment necessary to lubricate the balljoints and tie rods.
2 The balljoint grease fitting is located on the underside of each balljoint, while the tie rod fitting is located on the bottom of the joint between the tie rod and the steering knuckle.
3 For easier access under the car, raise the vehicle with a jack and place jack stands under the frame. Make sure the car is firmly supported by the stands.
4 Before you do any greasing, force a little of the grease out of the nozzle to remove any dirt from the end of the gun. Wipe the nozzle clean with a rag.
5 Wipe the grease fitting nipple clean and push the nozzle firmly over the fitting nipple. (Some models have a plug installed in place of a grease fitting. A proper fitting will have to be bought and installed.) Squeeze the trigger on the grease gun to force grease into the component. Both the balljoints and tie rods should be lubricated until the rubber reservoir is firm to the touch. Do not pump too much grease into these fittings as this could rupture the reservoir. If the grease seeps out around the grease gun nozzle, the nipple is clogged or the nozzle is not fully seated around the fitting nipple. Resecure the gun nozzle to the fitting and try again. If necessary, replace the fitting.
6 Wipe any excess grease from the components and the grease fitting.
7 While you are under the car, clean and lubricate the brake cable

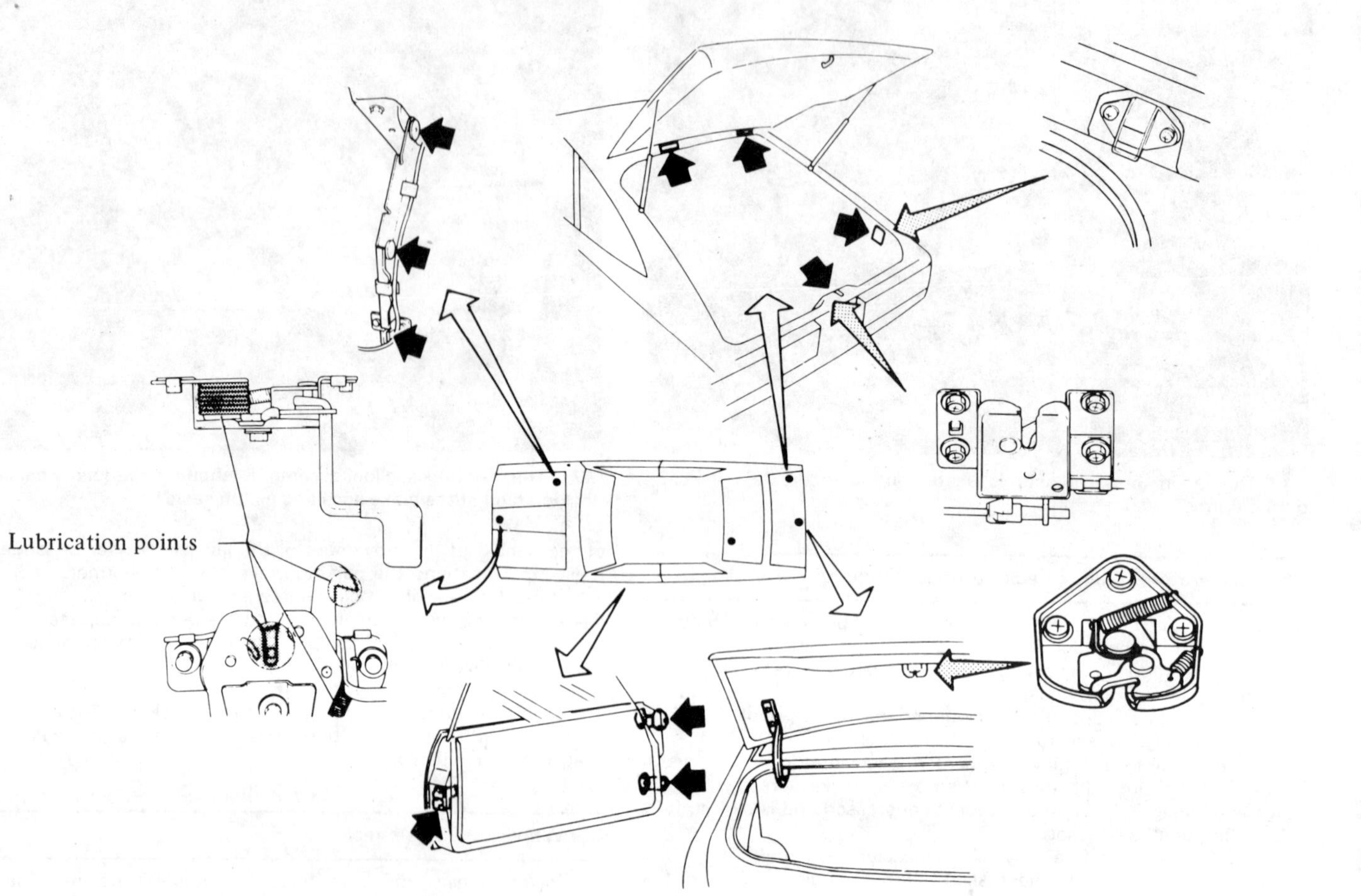

Fig. 1.16 Lubrication points on the 200SX body (hardtop and hatchback) (Sec 26)

along with its cable guides and levers. This can be done by smearing some of the chassis grease onto the cable and its related parts with your fingers.

8 Lower the car to the ground for the remaining body lubrication process.

9 Open the hood and smear a little chassis grease on the hood latch mechanism. Have an assistant pull the release knob from inside the car as you lubricate the cable at the latch.

10 Lubricate all the hinges (door, hood, trunk) with a few drops of light engine oil to keep them in proper working order.

11 Finally, the key lock cylinders can be lubricated with spray-on graphite, which is available at auto parts stores.

27 Brakes check

1 The brakes should be inspected every time the wheels are removed or whenever a fault is suspected. Indication of a potential braking system fault are: the car pulls to one side when brake pedal is depressed; noises coming from the brakes when they are applied; excessive brake pedal travel; pulsating pedal; and leakage of fluid, usually seen on the inside of the tire or wheel.

Disc brake inspection

2 The thickness of the lining on the disc pads should be checked on a regular basis as damage can occur if the linings become excessively worn. All four pads on each axle (two on each wheel) should be replaced at the same time. Also, do not mix different types of replacement pads. All should be manufactured from the same material to give uniform performance.

3 To perform an inspection of the disc pad linings, first remove the wheel. Now visible is the disc brake caliper which contains the pads. There is an outer pad and an inner pad. Both should be removed as described in Chapter 9.

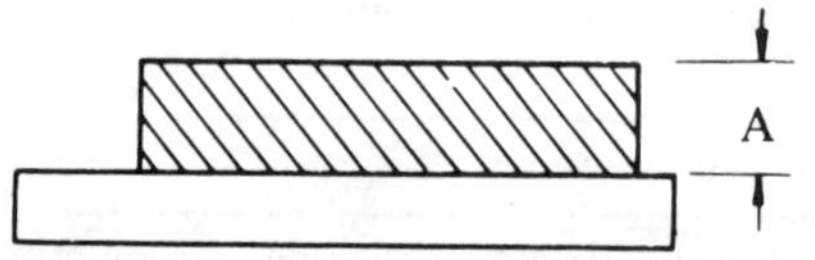

Fig. 1.17 When inspecting the disc brakes, the lining on the pad should be measured to determine the amount of wear (Sec 27)

4 Measure the thickness of the lining material (see accompanying figure). If it is thinner than 2 mm (0.08 in), the pads should be replaced.

5 Even if the pads are not worn down to their limit, check that their surfaces are not glazed or deeply scored. If so, they should be replaced.

6 While checking the pad linings, also inspect the rotor surface for scoring or 'hot spots' indicated by small discolored blemishes. Light scoring is acceptable but if the damage is excessive the rotor should be resurfaced or replaced.

7 Before installing the wheels, check for any leakage around the brake hose connections leading to the caliper (photo) or damage (cracking, splitting, etc) to the brake hose. Replace the hose or fittings as necessary, referring to Chapter 9.

8 Finally, open the hood and check the hydraulic lines running from the master cylinder for any leakage. Also, check the vacuum lines running to the power brake booster to be sure they are not hardened or cracked, and are tight on their connections.

28 Suspension and steering check

1 Whenever the front of the car is raised for service it is a good idea to visually check the suspension and steering components for wear.

2 Indication of a fault in these systems are: excessive play in the steering wheel before the front wheels react; excessive sway around corners or body movement over rough roads, and binding at some point as the steering wheel is turned.
3 Before the car is raised for inspection, test the shock absorbers by pushing downwards to rock the car at each corner. If you push the car down and it does not come back to a level position within one or two bounces, the shocks are worn and need to be replaced. As this is done, check for squeaks and strange noises from the suspension components. Information on shock absorber and suspension components can be found in Chapter 11.
4 Now raise the front end of the car and support it firmly with jack stands. Because of the work to be done, make sure the car cannot fall from the stands.
5 Crawl under the car and check for loose bolts, broken or disconnected parts and deteriorated rubber bushings on all suspension and steering components. Look for grease or fluid leaking from around the steering gear assembly. Check the power steering hoses and their connections for leaks.
6 The balljoint seals should, likewise, be checked at this time. After cleaning around the balljoints, inspect the seals for wear, cracking or damage, and replace if necessary as described in Chapter 11.
7 Grip the top and bottom of the wheel and try to rock it. It will not take any great effort to be able to feel any play in the wheel bearing. If this play is very noticeable it would be as well to adjust it straight away as it could confuse further examinations. It is also possible that during this check, play may be discovered in the lower suspension balljoint (at the foot of the suspension strut). If this is the case the balljoint will need renewal.
8 Next grip each side of the wheel and try rocking it laterally. Steady pressure will, of course, turn the steering but an alternated back and forward pressure will reveal any loose joint. If some play is felt it would be easier to get assistance from someone, so that while one person rocks the wheel from side to side, the other can look at the joints and bushes on the track-rods and connections. Excluding the steering box itself there are eight places where the play may occur. The two outer balljoints on the two outer track-rods are the most likely, followed by the two inner joints on the same rods, where they join to the center rod. Any play in these means renewal of the balljoint. Next are the two swivel bushes, one at each end of the center track-rod. Finally check the steering box Pitman arm balljoint and the one on the idler arm which supports the center track-rod on the side opposite the steering box. This unit is bolted to the side of the frame member and any play calls for renewal of the bushes.
9 To check the steering box, first make sure that the bolts holding the steering box to the side-frame member are tight. Then get another person to help examine the mechanism. One should look at, or get hold of, the Pitman arm at the bottom of the steering box while the other turns the steering wheel a little way from side-to-side. The amount of lost motion between the steering wheel and the Pitman arm indicates the degree of wear somewhere in the steering box mechanism. This check should be carried out with the wheels first of all in the straight-ahead position and then at nearly full lock on each side. If the play only occurs noticeably in the straight-ahead position then the wear is most probably in the worm and/or nut. If it occurs at all positions of the steering, then the wear is probably in the sector shaft bearing. Oil leaks from the unit are another indication of such wear. In either case the steering box will need removal for closer examination and repair.

29 Exhaust system check

1 With the exhaust system cold (at least three hours after being driven), check the complete exhaust system from its starting point at the engine to the end of the tailpipe. This is best done on a hoist where full access is available.
2 Check the pipes and their connections for signs of leakage and/or corrosion indicating a potential failure. Check that all brackets and hangers are in good condition and are tight.
3 At the same time, inspect the underside of the body for holes, corrosion, open seams, etc. which may allow exhaust gases to enter the trunk or passenger compartment. Seal all body openings with silicone or body putty.
4 Rattles and other driving noises can often be traced to the exhaust system, especially the mounts and hangers. Try to move the pipes, muffler and catalytic converter. If the components can come into contact with the body or driveline parts, secure the exhaust system with new mountings.
5 This is also an ideal time to check the running condition of the engine by inspecting the very end of the tailpipe. The exhaust deposits here are an indication of engine tune. If the pipe is black and sooty or bright white deposits are found here, the engine is in need of a thorough tune-up.

30 Driveshaft inspection

1 Raise the rear of the car and support it securely on jack stands. The transmission should be in Neutral.
2 Slide under the car and visually inspect the condition of the driveshaft. Look for any dents or cracks in the tubing. If any are found the driveshaft must be replaced (Chapter 8).
3 Check for any oil leakage at the front or rear of the driveshaft. Leakage where the driveshaft enters the transmission indicates a defective rear transmission seal. Leakage where the driveshaft enters the differential indicates a defective pinion seal. For these operations refer to Chapters 7 and 8 respectively.
4 While still under the car, have an assistant turn the rear wheel so the driveshaft will rotate. As it does, check that the universal joints are operating properly without binding, noise or looseness. Also listen for any noise from the center bearing, indicating that it is worn or damaged. Refer to Chapter 8 to correct any problems.
5 The universal joints can also be checked with the driveshaft motionless, by gripping your hands on either side of the joint and attempting to twist the joint. Any movement at all in the joint is a sign of considerable wear. Lifting up on the shaft will also indicate movement in the universal joints.
6 Finally check the driveshaft mounting bolts at both ends to make sure they are tight.

31 Fuel system check

There are certain precautions to take when inspecting or servicing the fuel system components. Work in a well ventilated area and do not allow open flames (cigarettes, appliance pilot lights, etc) to get near the work area. Mop up spills immediately and do not store fuel-soaked rags where they could ignite.
Caution: *The fuel system is under considerable pressure. Prior to*

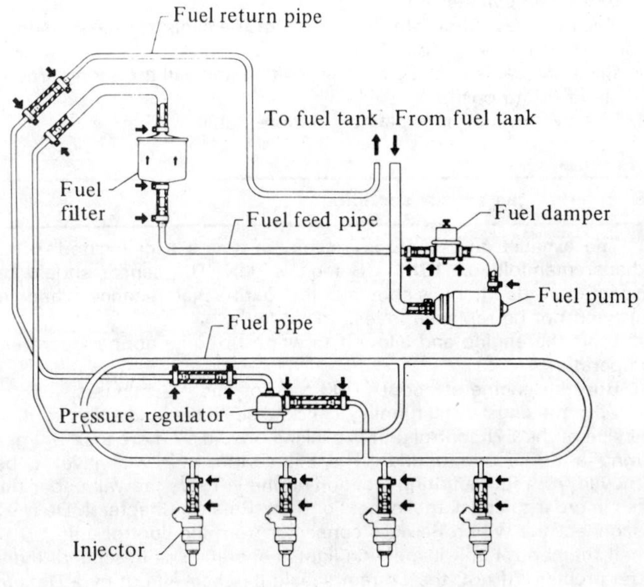

Fig. 1.18 When inspecting the fuel system, check carefully for leaks at the points where metal lines and rubber hoses join (Sec 31)

disconnecting any fuel lines, the pressure in the system must be reduced. For this procedure refer to Section 18. Plug all disconnected fuel lines immediately after disconnection to prevent the tank from emptying itself.

1 The fuel system is most easily checked with the car raised on a hoist where the components under the car are readily visible and accessible.

2 If the smell of gasoline is noticed while driving, or after the car has sat in the sun, the system should be thoroughly inspected immediately.

3 Remove the gas filler cap and check for damage, corrosion and a proper sealing imprint on the gasket. Replace the cap with a new one if necessary.

4 With the car raised, inspect the gas tank and filler neck for punctures, cracks or any damage. The connection between the filler neck and the tank is especially critical. Sometimes a rubber filler neck will leak due to loose clamps or deteriorated rubber; problems a home mechanic can usually rectify.

5 Do not under any circumstances try to repair a fuel tank yourself (except rubber components) unless you have considerable experience. A welding torch or any open flame can easily cause the fuel vapors to explode if the proper precautions are not taken.

6 Carefully check all rubber hoses and metal lines leading away from the fuel tank. Check for loose connections, deteriorated hose, crimped lines or damage of any kind. Follow these lines up to the front of the car, carefully inspecting them all the way. Repair or replace damaged sections as necessary.

7 If a fuel odor is still evident after the inspection, refer to Chapter 6; *Evaporative Emission Control System.*

32 EEC (Evaporative Emissions Control) filter replacement

1 The function of the EEC system is to draw fuel vapors from the fuel tank, store them in a charcoal canister and then burn these fumes during normal engine operation.

2 The filter at the bottom of the charcoal canister should be replaced at the specified intervals. If, however, a fuel odor is detected, the canister, filter and system hoses should immediately be inspected for fault (Chapter 6).

3 To replace the filter, locate the canister at the front of the engine, on the left side of the radiator. It has 3 hoses running out of the top of it.

4 The canister is held to the body only by a spring, secured around the outside of the canister body. The canister is removed by simply lifting it out of its mounting position and free of the spring.

5 Turn the canister upside-down and pull the old filter from the bottom of the canister (photo).

6 Push the new filter into the bottom of the canister, making sure it is seated all the way around.

7 Place the canister back into the position and pull the spring around it to hold it into position.

8 The EEC system is explained in more detail in Chapter 6.

33 Exhaust gas sensor servicing

1 The exhaust gas sensor is a screw-in type sensor located in the exhaust manifold on 1981 US models only. The sensor should be inspected at the intervals shown in the routine maintenance schedule, but need not be replaced unless found faulty.

2 Start the engine and allow it to warm up to its normal operating temperature.

3 Run the engine at about 2000 rpm for about 2 minutes.

4 With the engine still running, check to see if the inspection light on the side of the EFI control unit is blinking on and off more than 3 times during a 10-second period. (The EFI control unit will have to be removed from its mounting location on the left side firewall under the dash in order to check the inspection light. Refer to Chapter 4. Do NOT disconnect the wiring harness connector from the control unit.

5 If the control unit inspection light is operating as described, there is no problem. If not, the system should be checked out by a Datsun dealer.

6 If the exhaust gas sensor needs to be replaced, it may be difficult to remove when the engine is cold, so the operation is best done with the engine at operating temperature.

32.5 The EEC filter is located on the underside of the charcoal canister

- *a) Remove the wiring connector from the sensor.*
- *b) Apply a penetrating oil to the threads of the exhaust gas sensor and allow it to soak in for about 5 minutes.*
- *c) Carefully unscrew the sensor and remove it. Be careful that you do not damage the threads in the exhaust manifold while removing the sensor.*
- *d) Coat the threads of the new sensor completely with an anti-seize compound and install it.*
- *e) Carefully torque the sensor to Specifications.*
- *f) Reconnect the wiring connector to the sensor.*

7 Whether the exhaust gas sensor has been inspected and/or replaced or not, at 30 000 miles the exhaust gas sensor warning lamp will come on to indicate that the sensor should be inspected and serviced if necessary. Therefore, after inspecting the exhaust gas sensor, disconnect the warning lamp harness connector located under the right side of the instrument panel, so that it will not remain on.

34 Automatic transmission fluid change

1 At the specified time intervals, the transmission fluid should be changed. The routine maintenance chart calls for an automatic transmission fluid change only once every 30 000 miles. This interval should be shortened to every 15 000 miles if the car is normally driven under one or more of the following conditions: heavy city traffic; where the outside temperature normally reaches 90°F or higher; in very hilly or mountain areas; or if a trailer is frequently pulled.

2 Since there is no drain plug, the transmission oil pan must be removed from the bottom of the transmission to drain the fluid. Before doing any draining, purchase the specified transmission fluid (see Recommended Lubricants in the front of this Chapter) and an oil pan gasket.

3 Other tools necessary for this job include: jack stands to support the vehicle in a raised position; wrench to remove the oil pan bolts; standard screwdriver; drain pan capable of holding at least 8 pints; newspapers and clean rags.

4 The fluid should be drained immediately after the car has been driven. This will remove any built-up sediment better than if the fluid were cold. Because of this, it may be wise to wear protective gloves (fluid temperature can exceed 350° in a hot transmission).

5 After the car has been driven to warm up the fluid, raise the vehicle and place it on jack stands for access underneath.

6 Move the necessary equipment under the car, being careful not to touch any of the hot exhaust components.

7 Place the drain pan under the transmission oil pan and remove the oil pan bolts along the rear and sides of the pan. Loosen, but do not remove, the bolts at the front of the pan.

8 Carefully pry the pan downward at the rear, allowing the hot fluid to drain into the drain pan. If necessary, use a screwdriver to break the gasket seal at the rear of the pan; however, do not damage the pan or

35.2 The differential drain plug can be removed using a $\frac{1}{2}$-in ratchet wrench extension with no socket

transmission in the process.

9 Support the pan and remove the remaining bolts at the front of the pan. Lower the pan and drain the remaining fluid into the drain receptacle. As this is done, check the fluid for metal filings which may be an indication of internal failure.

10 Thoroughly clean the transmission oil pan with solvent. Inspect for metal filings or foreign matter. Dry with compressed air if available. It is important that all remaining gasket material be removed from the oil pan mounting flange. Use a gasket scraper or putty knife for this.

11 Apply a bead of gasket sealant around the oil pan mounting surface, with the sealant to the inside of the bolt holes. Press the new gasket into place on the pan, making sure all bolt holes line up.

12 Lift the pan up to the bottom of the transmission and install the mounting bolts. Tighten the bolts in a diagonal fashion, working around the pan. Using a torque wrench, tighten the bolts to specifications.

13 Lower the car off its jack stands.

14 Open the hood and remove the transmission fluid dipstick from its guide tube.

15 It is best to add a little fluid at a time, continually checking the level with the dipstick. Allow the fluid time to drain into the pan. Add fluid until the level just registers on the end of the dipstick. In most cases, a good starting point will be 4 to 5 pints added to the transmission through the filler tube (use a funnel to prevent spills).

16 With the selector lever in Park, apply the parking brake and start the engine without depressing the accelerator pedal (if possible). Do not race the engine at a high speed; run at slow idle only.

17 Depress the brake pedal and shift the transmission through each gear. Place the selector back into Park and check the level on the dipstick (with the engine still idling). Look under the car for leaks around the transmission oil pan mating surface.

18 Add more fluid through the dipstick tube until the level on the dipstick is $\frac{1}{4}$ inch below the lower mark on the dipstick. Do not allow the fluid level to go above this point, as the transmission would then be overfull, necessitating the removal of the pan to drain the excess fluid.

19 Push the dipstick firmly back into its tube and drive the car to reach normal operating temperature (15 miles of highway driving or its equivalent in the city). Park the car on a level surface and check the fluid level on the dipstick with the engine idling and the transmission in Park. The level should now be at the upper mark on the dipstick. If not, add more fluid as necessary to bring the level up to this point. Again, do not overfill.

35 Differential oil change

1 Move a drain pan (at least 5 pint capacity), rags, newspapers and a $\frac{1}{2}$ in drive ratchet wrench with extension under the rear of the car.

2 With the drain pan under the differential, use the wrench and extension to loosen the differential drain plug (photo).

3 Once loosened, carefully unscrew it with your fingers until you can remove it from the differential case.

4 Allow all of the oil to drain into the pan. Then replace the drain plug, torqueing it to specs.

5 Now remove the differential inspection plug on the rear of the differential housing. Using a hand pump, syringe or funnel fill the differential with the correct amount and grade of oil (see Specifications), until the level is just at the bottom of the inspection plug hole.

6 Now reinstall the inspection plug, torqueing it to Specifications.

Chapter 2 Engine

Refer to Chapter 13 for Specifications and information related to 1982 and 1983 models

Contents

Bearings (main and rod) – checking clearances 38
Camshaft – inspection and servicing 6
Camshaft – removal and installation 5
Crankshaft – removal 30
Crankshaft and bearings – inspection and servicing 31
Crankshaft and main bearings – installation 36
Cylinder block – inspection 32
Cylinder head – assembly 15
Cylinder head – cleaning 12
Cylinder head – disassembly 11
Cylinder head – inspection 13
Cylinder head – installation 16
Cylinder head – removal 10
Engine – installation 39
Engine – rebuilding alternatives 33
Engine – removal 26
Engine mounts – replacement 25
Engine overhaul – general assembly information 34
Engine overhaul – general disassembly information 27
Engine start-up (following overhaul) 40
Exhaust manifold – removal and installation 9
Flywheel – removal and installation 22
Front cover and timing gear – removal and installation 19
Front oil seal – replacement 20
General information 1
Intake manifold – removal and installation 8
Oil pan – removal and installation 21
Oil pump – overhaul 18
Oil pump – removal and installation 17
Pilot bushing – replacement 24
Pistons and connecting rods – cleaning and inspection 29
Pistons and piston rings – assembly 35
Pistons, connecting rods and bearings – installation 37
Pistons, connecting rods and bearings – removal 28
Rear oil seal – replacement 23
Rocker arm cover – removal and installation 2
Valve rocker assembly – disassembly and reassembly 4
Valve rocker assembly – removal and installation 3
Valves and valve seats – inspection and servicing 14
Valves spring and seal – removal and installation (cylinder head in car) 7

Specifications

General

Engine model	Z20E
Type	In-line four-cylinder with overhead cam
Firing order	1–3–4–2
Displacement	1952 cc

Cylinder head

Surface warp limit	0.004 in (0.1 mm)

Camshaft

Outer diameter of camshaft journal	1.2967 to 1.2974 in (32.935 to 32.955 mm)
Endplay	0.008 in (0.2 mm)
Cam lobe height	1.5148 to 1.5168 in (38.477 to 38.527 mm)
Cam lobe wear limit	0.0098 in (0.25 mm)
Camshaft bend (total indicator reading at center journal	0.0039 in (0.10 mm)
Inner diameter of bearing	1.2992 to 1.3002 in (33.000 to 33.025 mm)
Journal-to-bearing clearance	0.0018 to 0.0035 in (0.045 to 0.090 mm)

Valves

Valve head diameter	
Intake	1.654 to 1.661 in (42.0 to 42.2 mm)
Exhaust	1.496 to 1.504 in (38.0 to 38.2 mm)
Valve length	
Intake	4.835 to 4.846 in (122.8 to 123.1 mm)
Exhaust	4.866 to 4.878 in (123.6 to 123.9 mm)

Valves, continued

Valve stem diameter	
Intake	0.3136 to 0.3142 in (7.965 to 7.980 mm)
Exhaust	0.3128 to 0.3134 (7.945 to 7.960 mm)
Valve face angle	45°30′
Valve head margin	
Intake (standard)	0.067 in (1.7 mm)
Intake wear limit	0.020 in (0.5 mm)
Exhaust (standard)	0.059 in (1.5 mm)
Exhaust wear limit	0.020 in (0.5 mm)
Grinding of valve stem end limit	0.020 in (0.5 mm)
Valve spring free height	
Outer spring	1.9594 in (49.77 mm)
Inner spring	1.7362 in (44.10 mm)
Valve spring assembled height	
Outer spring (standard)	1.575 in @ 50.7 lb (40.0 mm @ 23.0 kg)
Outer spring wear limit	1.575 in @ 42.6 lb (40.0 mm @ 19.3 kg)
Inner spring (standard)	1.378 in @ 24.3 lb (35.0 mm @ 11.0 kg)
Inner spring wear limit	1.378 in @ 19.6 lb (35.0 mm @ 8.9 kg)
Out-of square limit	
Outer spring	0.087 in (2.2 mm)
Inner spring	0.075 in (1.9 mm)
Rocker arm-to-rocker shaft clearance	0.0003 to 0.0019 in (0.007 – 0.049 mm)
Valve guide diameter	
Outer	0.4733 to 0.4738 in (12.023 to 12.034 mm)
Inner	0.3150 to 0.3157 in (8.000 to 8.018 mm)
Stem-to-guide clearance	
Intake	0.0008 to 0.0021 in (0.020 to 0.053 mm)
Exhaust	0.0016 to 0.0029 in (0.040 to 0.073 mm)
Stem end deflection limit	0.008 in (0.2 mm)
Valve seat	
Contacting face angle	45°
Contacting width	
Intake	0.071 to 0.094 in (1.8 to 2.4 mm)
Exhaust	0.059 to 0.075 in (1.5 to 1.9 mm)
Outer diameter (standard)	
Intake	1.7755 to 1.7761 in (45.097 to 45.113 mm)
Exhaust	1.5779 to 1.5786 in (40.080 to 40.096 mm)

Cylinder block

Surface warp limit	0.004 in (0.1 mm)
Inner diameter of cylinder bore	3.3465 to 3.3484 in (85.000 to 85.050 mm)
Cylinder bore cut-of-round (standard)	less than 0.0006 in (0.015 mm)
Cylinder bore taper (standard)	less than 0.0006 in (0.015 mm)
Piston-to-cylinder clearance	0.0010 to 0.0018 in (0.025 to 0.045 mm)

Pistons

Diameter	
Standard	3.3459 to 3.3478 in (84.985 to 85.035 mm)
1st oversize	3.3648 to 3.3667 in (85.465 to 85.515 mm)
2nd oversize	3.3844 to 3.3864 in (85.965 to 86.015 mm)
Piston ring gap	
Top ring	0.0098 to 0.0157 in (0.25 to 0.40 mm)
Second ring	0.0059 to 0.0118 in (0.15 to 0.30 mm)
Oil ring	0.0118 to 0.0354 in (0.30 to 0.90 mm)
Piston ring side clearance	
Top ring	0.0016 to 0.0029 in (0.040 to 0.073 mm)
Second ring	0.0012 to 0.0025 in (0.030 to 0.063 mm)

Connecting rod and bearing

Connecting rod big endplay	0.008 to 0.012 in (0.2 to 0.3 mm)	
Connecting rod bearing sizes	**Bearing thickness**	**Crankpin diameter**
Standard	0.0588 to 0.0593 in (1.493 to 1.506 mm)	1.9670 to 1.9675 in (49.961 to 49.974 mm)
0.0098 in (0.25 mm) Undersize	0.0637 to 0.0642 in (1.618 to 1.631 mm)	1.9571 to 1.9576 in (49.711 to 49.724 mm)
0.0197 in (0.50 mm) Undersize	0.0686 to 0.0691 in (1.743 to 1.756 mm)	1.9473 to 1.9478 in (49.9461 to 49.474 mm)
0.0295 in (0.75 mm) Undersize	0.0735 to 0.0741 in (1.868 to 1.881 mm)	1.9374 to 1.9379 in (49.211 to 49.224 mm)
Connecting rod bearing clearance		
Standard	0.0010 to 0.0022 in (0.025 to 0.055 mm)	
Maximum	0.0047 in (0.12 mm)	

Crankshaft and main bearings

Crank journal diameter	2.1631 to 2.1636 in (54.942 to 54.955 mm)	
Crankpin diameter	1.9670 to 1.9675 in (49.961 to 49.974 mm)	
Journal and pin taper and out-of-round		
Standard	less than 0.0004 in (0.01 mm)	
Maximum	0.0012 in (0.03 mm)	
Crankshaft free endplay		
Standard	0.0020 to 0.0071 in (0.05 to 0.18 mm)	
Maximum	0.012 in (0.3 mm)	
Main bearing clearance		
Standard	0.0008 to 0.0024 in (0.020 to 0.062 mm)	
Maximum	0.0047 in (0.12 mm)	
Main bearing sizes	**Bearing thickness**	**Crank journal diameter**
Standard	0.0717 to 0.0722 in (1.822 to 1.835 mm)	2.1631 to 2.1636 in (54.942 to 54.955 mm)
0.0098 in (0.25 mm) Undersize	0.0767 to 0.0772 in (1.947 to 1.960 mm)	2.1532 to 2.1537 in (54.692 to 54.705 mm)
0.0197 in (0.50 mm) Undersize	0.0816 to 0.0821 in (2.072 to 2.085 mm)	2.1434 to 2.1439 in (54.442 to 54.455 mm)
0.0295 in (0.75 mm) Undersize	0.0865 to 0.0870 in (2.197 to 2.210 mm)	2.1335 to 2.1341 in (54.192 to 54.205 mm)
0.0394 in (1.00 mm) Undersize	0.0914 to 0.0919 in (2.322 to 2.335 mm)	2.1237 to 2.1242 in (53.942 to 53.955 mm)

Flywheel maximum runout

0.0059 in (0.15 mm)

Oil pump

Type	Trochoid
Rotor tip clearance	
Standard	less than 0.0047 in (0.12 mm)
Wear limit	0.0079 in (0.20 mm)
Outer rotor-to-body clearance	
Standard	0.0059 to 0.0083 in (0.15 to 0.21 mm)
Wear limit	0.0197 in (0.50 mm)
Rotor side clearance	
Standard	0.0016 to 0.0031 in (0.04 to 0.08 mm)
Wear limit	0.0079 in (0.20 mm)

Torque specifications

	ft-lb	m-kg
Front cover bolts		
Small	5	0.7
Large	10	1.3
Chain guide bolts	6	0.8
Chain tensioner bolts	6	0.8
Water pump bolts		
Small	5	0.7
Large	10	1.3
Crankshaft pulley bolt	102	14.0
Intake manifold bolts and nut	15	1.9
Alternator bracket bolts	36	5.0
Alternator adjusting bolt	18	2.5
Engine mounting bracket bolts	25	3.5
Exhaust manifold bolts and nuts	14	1.9
EGR tube nut	29	3.0
A/C compressor bracket bolts	36	5.0
Cylinder head bolts	55	7.5
Valve rocker assembly bolts	14	2.0
Camshaft sprocket bolt	102	14.0
Spark plugs	12	1.7
Rocker arm nuts	14	1.9
Main bearing cap bolts	36	5.0
Connecting rod big end nut	36	5.0
Oil pan bolts	6	0.8
Oil pan drain plug	18	2.5
Gusset-to-cylinder block bolts	37	5.2
Flywheel bolts	109	15.0
Clutch cover bolts	14	1.9
Torque converter bolts	32	4.5
Transmission-to-cylinder block bolts	38	5.2
Transmission-to-gusset bolts	37	5.2
Oil pump bolts	10	1.3
Engine support bracket-to-insulator	27	3.7
Exhaust manifold-to-exhaust pipe	16	2.3

1 General information

The Z20E 'NAPS-Z' engine in the 200SX is the four-cylinder in-line type, with valve operation by means of an overhead camshaft.

The cast iron cylinder block contains the four bores and acts as a rigid support for the five bearing crankshaft. The machined cylinder bores are surrounded by water jackets to dissipate heat and control operating temperature.

The cylinder head is of aluminium and incorporates wedge type combustion chambers. Two spark plugs are used with each cylinder to burn the fuel/air mixture with greater efficiency.

Two valves per cylinder are mounted at a slight angle in the cylinder head and are actuated by a pivot type rocker arm in direct contact with the cam mechanism. Double springs are fitted to each valve.

The camshaft is driven by a roller chain from the front of the crankshaft. Chain tension is controlled by a tensioner which is operated by oil and spring pressure. The rubber shoe type tensioner controls vibration and tension of the chain.

The pistons are of a special aluminium casting with struts to control thermal expansion. There are two compression and one oil control ring. The piston pin is a hollow steel shaft which is fully floating in the piston and a press fit in the connecting rod small-end. The pistons are attached to the crankshaft via forged steel connecting rods.

The distributor, which is mounted on the left-hand side of the cylinder block, is driven by a helical gear mounted on the front of the crankshaft. The oil pump, which is mounted low down on the right-hand side of the cylinder block, is on a common center-line to the distributor and is driven by the same helical gear.

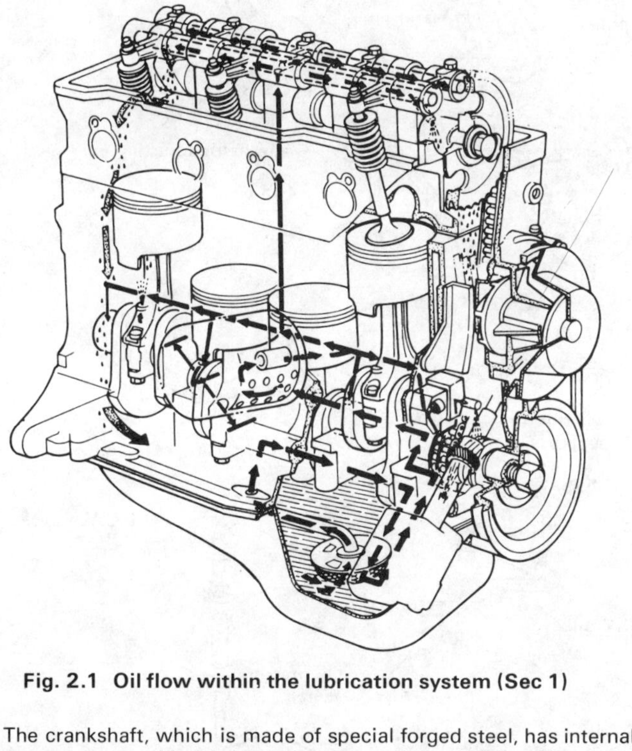

Fig. 2.1 Oil flow within the lubrication system (Sec 1)

The crankshaft, which is made of special forged steel, has internal oil passages to provide lubrication to the main and big-end bearings. Oil is delivered, via the filter and pressure relief valve, to the main oil gallery from which it passes to the main bearing journals and then to the connecting-rod bearing journals through drillings in the crankshaft. Oil spillage from the connecting rod big-ends, as well as a jet hole drilled through the connecting rod into the big-ends, provides splash lubrication for the pistons and connecting rod small ends. At the top of the engine, galleries drilled in the camshaft supports provide oil for the five bearings, while a pipe that runs along the length of the camshaft, delivers oil to each cam pad surface, to provide lubrication for the rocker arm and pivot.

Whenever engine work is required, there are some basic steps which the home mechanic should perform before any work is begun. These preliminary steps will help prevent delays during the operation. They are as follows:

Read through the appropriate sections in this manual to get an understanding of the processes involved, tools necessary and replacement parts which will be needed

Contact your local Datsun dealer or automotive parts store to check on replacement parts availability and cost. In many cases, a decision must be made beforehand whether to simply remove the faulty component and replace it with a new or rebuilt unit or to overhaul the existing part

If the vehicle is equipped with air-conditioning, it is imperative that a qualified specialist depressurize the system if this is required to perform the necessary engine repair work. The home mechanic should never disconnect any of the air-conditioning system while it is still pressurized, as this can cause serious personal injury as well as possibly damage the air-conditioning system. Ascertain if depressurization is necessary while the vehicle is still operational

2 Rocker arm cover – removal and installation

1 Remove the rubber hose from the rocker arm cover breather tube.
2 Remove the spark plug wires from all 8 spark plugs and position them out of the way.
3 Loosen the throttle cable adjusting screws and disconnect the cable from the throttle lever. Then remove the throttle cable clamp from the rocker cover and position the throttle cable out of the way.
4 Remove the 8 rocker arm cover mounting bolts.
5 Remove the rocker arm cover. To break the gasket seal it may be necessary to tap the cover with your hand or a rubber mallet. Do not pry on the cover.
6 Prior to installation clean all dirt, oil and old gasket material from the sealing surfaces of the cover and cylinder head with a degreaser.
7 Place a continuous bead of silicone sealant around the sealing lip of the cover. Be sure to apply the sealant to the inside of the mounting bolt holes.
8 Place the gasket into position on top of the cylinder head then place the rocker arm cover on the head. While the sealant is still wet, install the mounting bolts and torque them to specifications.
9 Complete the installation by reversing the sequence of the removal procedure.

3 Valve rocker assembly – removal and installation

1 Remove the rocker arm cover as described in Section 2.
2 The valve rocker assembly is held to the cylinder head by 10 mounting bolts. These bolts should be loosened a quarter of a turn at a time working inward from both ends (photo). Loosen these bolts until they are free of the cylinder head but do not remove them from the valve rocker assembly.
3 Once all mounting bolts are loosened, lift the valve rocker assembly from the cylinder head (photo).
4 If the valve rocker assembly needs to be disassembled, refer to Section 4. If the valve rocker assembly is not to be disassembled be sure not to remove the 4 bolts at either end of the assembly, as the assembly will come apart if these bolts are removed.
5 When installing the valve rocker assembly, first tighten the bolts until they are finger tight, then again working inward from both ends, tighten the bolts a quarter of a turn at a time until they are all torqued to specifications. **Note:** *Since some of the valves are in the open position on the rocker assembly, be sure that the corresponding pistons are not at the top of their stroke, as this will interfere with the installation of the valve rocker assembly.*

4 Valve rocker assembly – disassembly and reassembly

1 If not previously done, remove all of the valve rocker assembly mounting bolts except the 4 on either end.
2 While holding the assembly together carefully remove the 2 bolts from one end of the assembly and allow the springs to expand.
3 Remove the components from the assembly noting the order in which they are installed. Do not mix up the rocker arms, they should

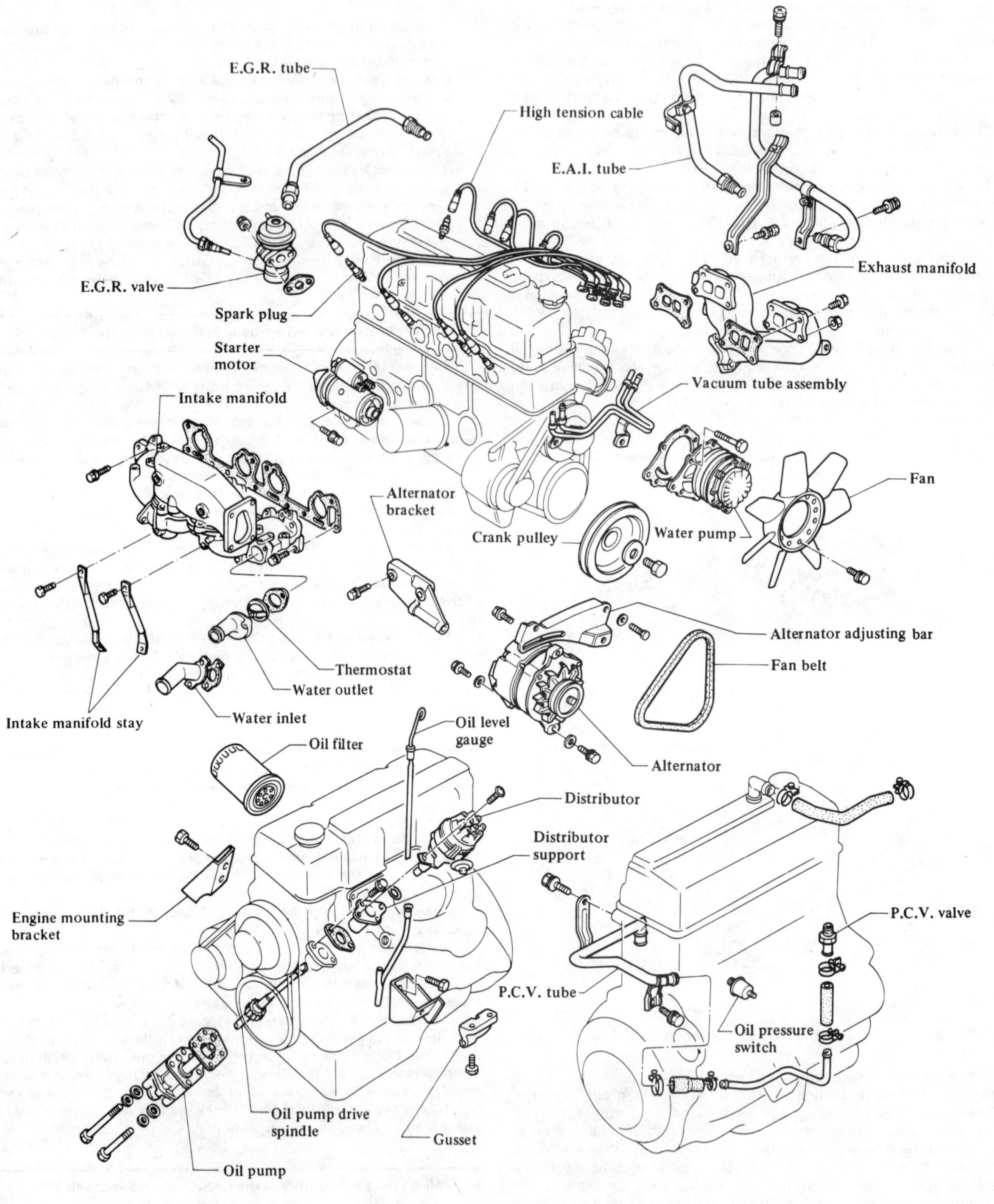

Fig. 2.2 External engine components

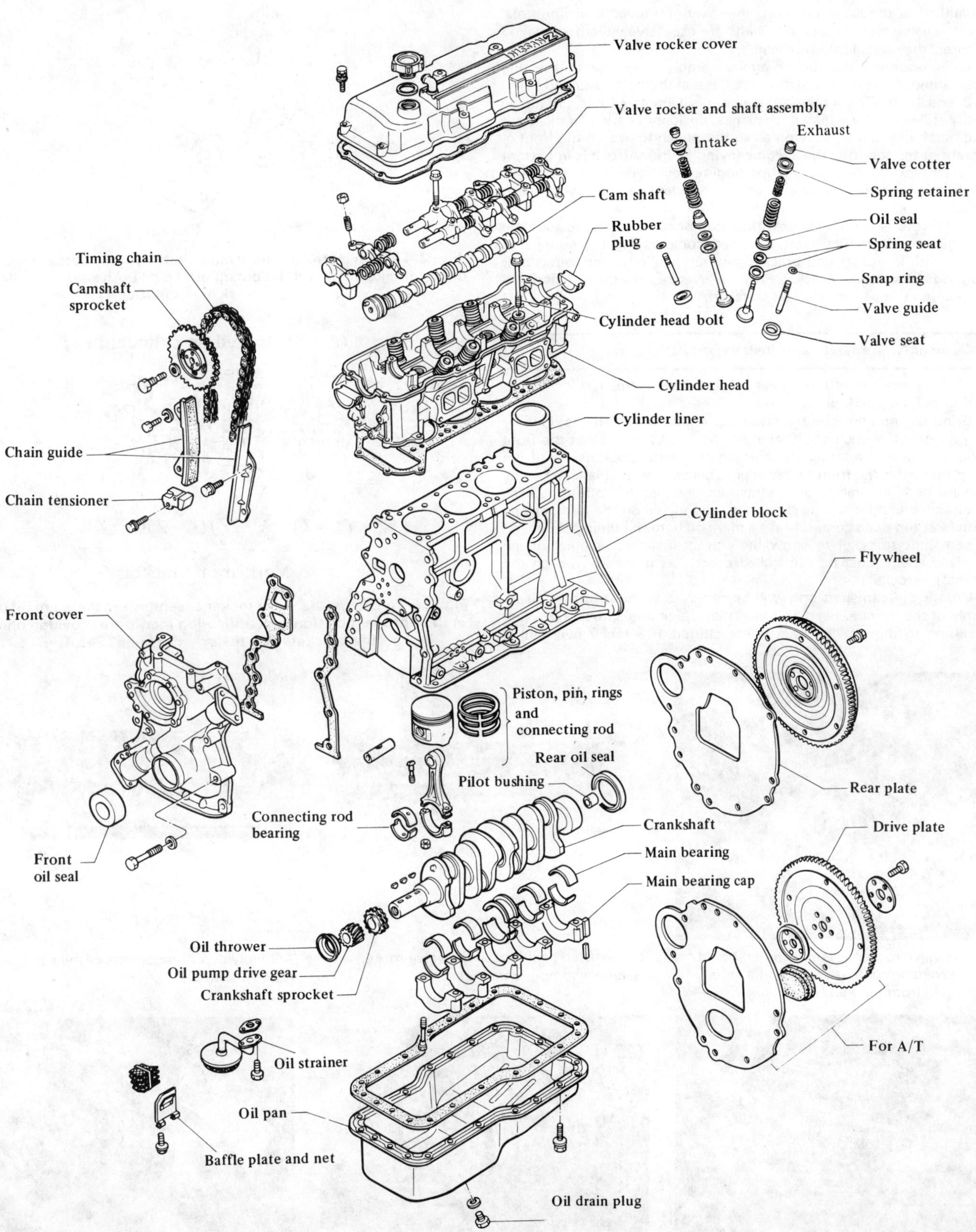

Fig. 2.3 Internal engine components

be installed in the same positions they were removed from (photo).

4 If the valve rocker assembly shafts are excessively worn, damaged or scored they should be replaced.

5 To reassemble the rocker arm assembly hold one of the end brackets and insert both shafts into it. Line up the bolt holes and insert the 2 end bolts. The intake shaft has a slit on the front surface to identify it, while the exhaust shaft has no identification mark. Both rocker shafts should be assembled so the punch marks on the front of each are at the top (See the accompanying figure). Also, it is important that the brackets are used in their original locations. To ensure this, identification marks are provided on the cylinder head, as well as each bracket.

6 Install the valve rocker assembly components onto the tubes in the order in which they were removed compressing the springs as needed until the other end bracket can be installed along with the 2 mounting bolts for that bracket. For convenience sake the remainder of the mounting bolts can also be installed.

5 Camshaft – removal and installation

1 Remove the rocker arm cover as described in Section 2.

2 Remove all spark plugs.

3 Bring the number one piston to top dead center. This is done by using a ratchet wrench and socket on the crankshaft bolt at the front of the engine and rotating the crankshaft counterclockwise until the timing marks on the front pulley align. This can be double checked by checking both the valves on the number one piston. Both the valves will be loose and be able to be shaken slightly when the number one piston is at top dead center. Make a mark on both the timing chain and the camshaft sprocket to show the correct installed position of the two. This chain must be reinstalled exactly as it is removed on the camshaft sprocket.

4 Where the camshaft only will be removed without further disassembly of the cylinder head, it is vital that the timing sprocket position in relation to the timing chain is not altered. If a major overhaul is

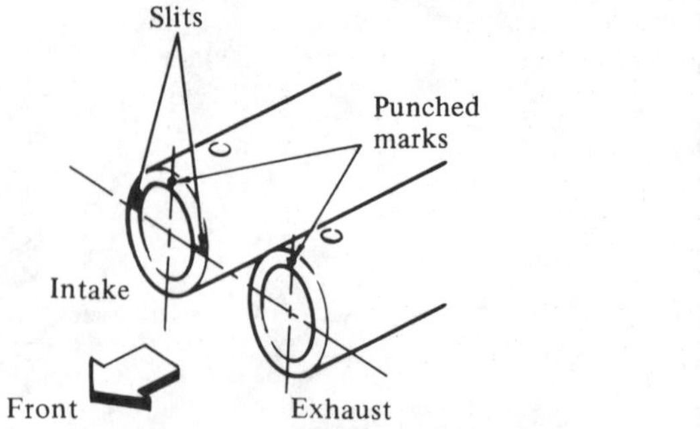

Fig. 2.4 When installed, the rocker shaft with the slits should be on the intake side, and the punch marks on both shafts should be in the 12 o'clock position (Sec 4)

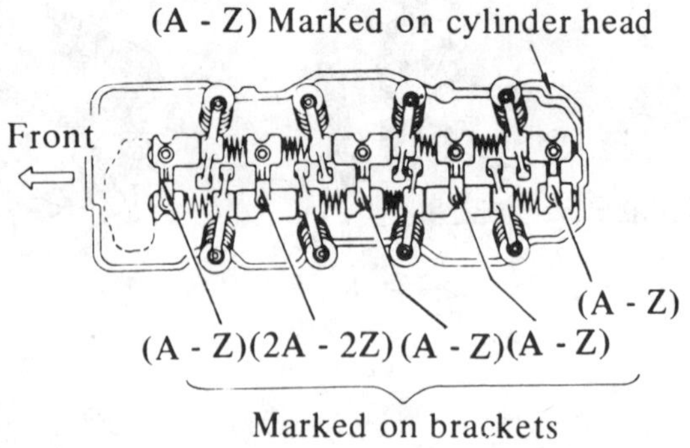

Fig. 2.5 To ensure the valve rocker assembly brackets are installed in their proper positions, identification marks are provided on both the brackets and the cylinder head (Sec 4)

3.2 The valve rocker assembly bolts should be loosened or tightened a little at a time, working in from both ends.

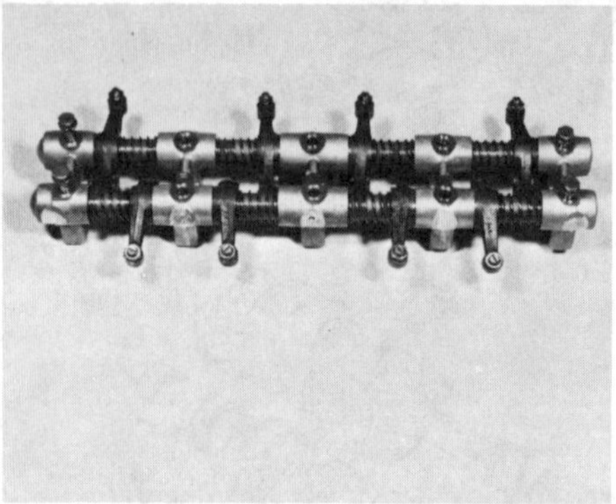

3.3 Installed positions of the valve rocker assembly components.

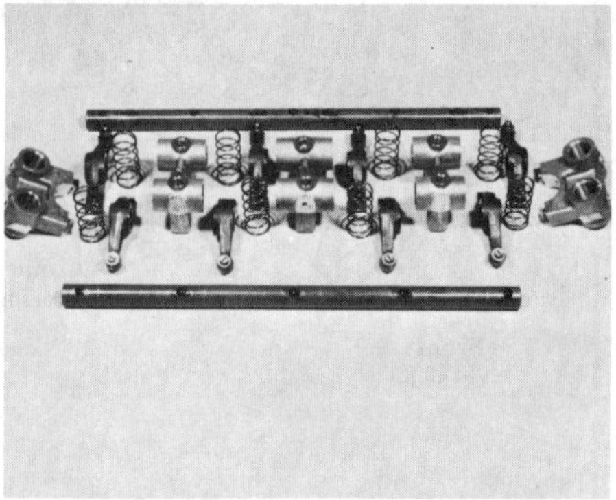

4.3 Individual components of the valve rocker assembly

5.7 While the camshaft sprocket nut is broken loose, a rod inserted through the sprocket will keep it from turning

5.9a The rubber plug in the center front of the cylinder head must be removed to withdraw the camshaft sprocket bolt

5.9b A piece of wood, cut to the dimensions listed in the text, will hold the timing chain in place while the sprocket is off

being carried out, then the retention of the timing position is not essential as this will be re-set upon installation.

5 Before removing the camshaft sprocket, cut a piece of wood until it is 10 inches long, $\frac{3}{4}$ inch thick, $1\frac{1}{2}$ inches wide at the top and approximately 1 inch at the bottom.

6 Now remove the camshaft sprocket bolt. A rod can be positioned through the camshaft to keep it from turning while the nut is broken loose (photo).

7 Insert the piece of wood into the timing case so that it wedges between the two runs of the chain. Be sure it is inserted securely. It is important that the timing chain should not be loosened or dropped into the inner cylinder as this would necessitate removal of the front cover in order to re-set the timing chain.

8 Carefully remove the camshaft sprocket from the camshaft and work the chain off of it until the sprocket can be removed (photo). The chain can be left hanging on the piece of wood (photo).

9 Remove the valve rocker assembly as described in Section 3.

10 Lift out the cam.

11 Inspection of the camshaft and cam bearings is found in Section 5.

12 When installing the camshaft, place it in its position in its lower bearing. The dowel located at the front of the camshaft should be in the 12 o'clock position.

13 Reinstall the valve rocker assembly, tightening the valve rocker assembly bolts only snugly. Temporarily tighten the 2 center bolts to 14 ft-lb (2 m-kg).

14 With the piece of wood still in place, carefully work the timing chain over the camshaft sprocket and fit the sprocket onto the end of the camshaft, with the cam dowel located in the number 2 sprocket hole. Be sure the marks made on the chain and sprocket during removal line up.

15 Carefully remove the piece of wood, and install the camshaft sprocket bolt, torquing it to specifications.

16 Tighten the valve rocker assembly bolts to their proper torque specifications.

17 Adjust the valve clearance to the 'cold' specifications as described in Chapter 1.

18 Reinstall the rocker arm cover and spark plugs.

19 Following installation, warm up the engine and readjust the valve clearances to the 'hot' specifications as described in Chapter 1.

6 Camshaft – inspection and servicing

1 Examine the bearing surfaces and the surface of the cam lobes. Surface scratches, if very shallow, can be removed by rubbing with a fine emery cloth or an oilstone. Any deep scoring will necessitate a new camshaft.

2 Mount the camshaft on V-blocks and use a dial gauge to measure lobe lift and run-out. Reject a camshaft which does not meet the specified limits.

3 Measure the journal diameters using a micrometer. Again, reject a camshaft which does not meet the specified limits.

4 Examine the condition of the bearings in the cylinder head housings and measure their diameter at two or three points internally. Where the average of these measurement exceeds the outside diameter of the respective camshaft bearing by more than 0.0039 in (0.1 mm) then the cylinder head will have to be replaced or exchanged as the bearings can only be replaced if they can be line-bored after installation.

7 Valve spring and seal – removal and installation (cylinder head in car)

Note: *Valve mechanism components must be reinstalled to their original positions. Place all removed components in a compartmented box to aid in identification.*

1 Remove the rocker arm cover as described in Section 2.

2 Remove the valve rocker assembly as described in Section 3.

3 Remove the spark plug from the cylinder being serviced.

4 There are two methods of keeping the valve in place while the valve spring is removed. If you have access to compressed air, attach an air hose adapter to your air hose and insert it into the spark plug hole. When air pressure is applied the valves will be held in place by the pressure.

5 If you do not have access to compressed air, bring the piston of that cylinder to the top dead center (TDC). Feed a long piece of $\frac{1}{4}$ in nylon cord in through the spark plug hole until it fills the combustion chamber. Be sure to leave the end of the cord hanging out of the spark plug hole so it can be removed easily.

6 Position a valve spring compressor tool over the spring. Compress the spring just enough to allow the removal of the valve spring retaining cups. Then let up on the spring.

7 Remove the valve cotter, spring retainer, inner and outer springs and oil seal. The oil seal must always be replaced whenever the spring locks have been disturbed.

8 Inspection procedures for the various valve components are detailed in Section 13.

9 Installation is the reverse of the removal procedure. **Note:** *Install both the inner and outer springs so the painted side (narrow pitch side) is toward the cylinder head. Also after installing the valve rocker assembly, adjust the valve clearances, as described in Chapter 1, to the 'cold' specifications.*

10 Following installation, warm up the engine and readjust the valve clearances to the 'hot' specifications.

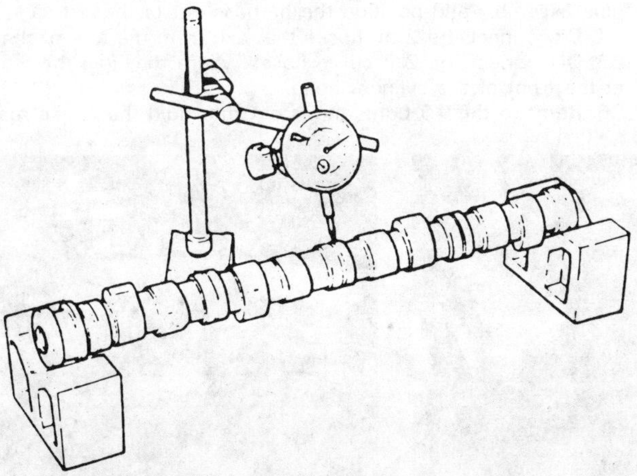

Fig. 2.6 The camshaft lobe lift and runout can be measured using a dial gauge and V-blocks (Sec 6)

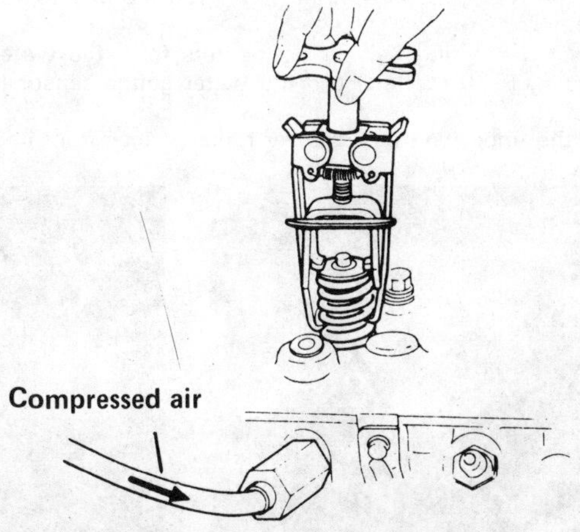

Fig. 2.7 While the valve is held in position by compressed air, a spring compressor can be used to remove the valve spring while the cylinder head is in the car (Sec 7)

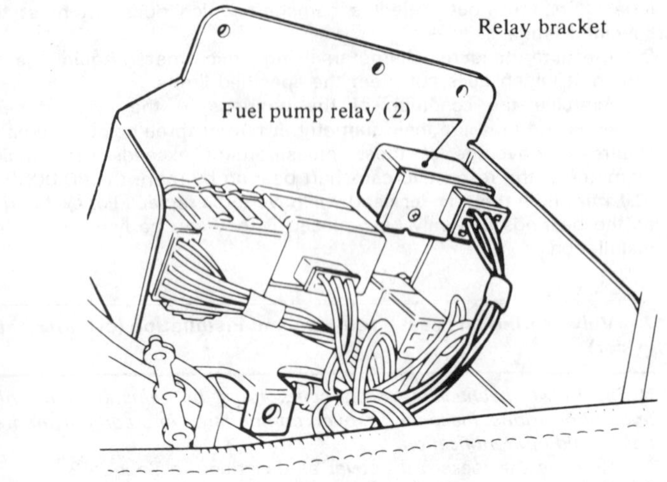

Fig. 2.8 Location of the fuel pump relay-2 on 1980 models (Sec 8)

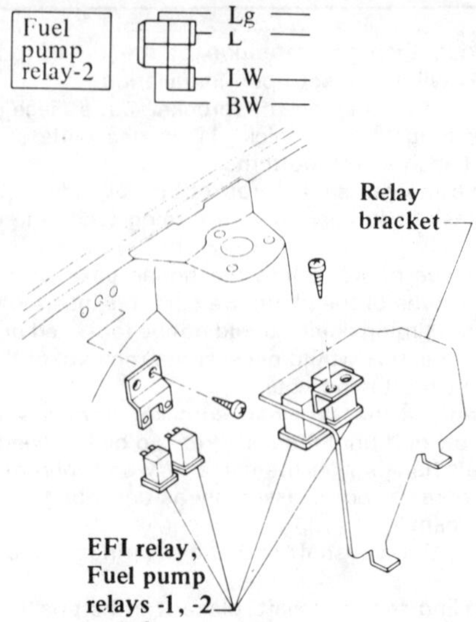

Fig. 2.9 The fuel pump relay-2 on 1981 models can be identified by its wiring harness (Sec 8)

8 Intake manifold – removal and installation

Note: *If the engine has been removed from the car disregard the following steps which do not apply.*

1 Reduce the pressure in the fuel lines to zero by using the following procedures:

- *a) Start the engine.*
- *b) Locate the fuel pump relay-2 on the relay bracket in the engine compartment, and disconnect the wiring harness connector from the relay. The relay bracket will have to be removed from the body in order to gain access to the relays.*
- *c) After the engine stalls, crank the engine over two or three times, then turn the ignition switch to 'off'.*
- *d) Reconnect the wiring harness connector to the fuel pump relay-2.*

2 Disconnect the negative battery cable.

3 Loosen the throttle cable adjusting nuts, disengage the throttle cable from the throttle lever and position it out of the way.

4 Drain the coolant system.

5 Remove the upper radiator hose.

6 Remove the rubber inlet air boot that connects the air pipe to the throttle chamber.

7 Remove the rubber hose from the fitting on the underside of the throttle chamber.

8 Disconnect the wiring harness connectors from the water temperature sensor (1980 models) and the water gauge sensor located directly below it.

9 Remove the upper end of the lower radiator hose from its fitting.

10 Disconnect the wiring connector from the throttle valve switch.

11 Disconnect the harness ground wire from the right side of the intake manifold (photo).

12 Disconnect the negative battery cable from where it is grounded on the right side of the intake manifold.

13 Disconnect the metal tube and hose fitting from the PCV valve.

14 Remove the upper bolt of the intake manifold stay and remove the vacuum line bracket from its stud. Replace the bolt in the stay loosely.

15 Remove the lower heater hose from its fitting on the intake manifold.

16 Remove all the vacuum hoses from the rear of the fuel pipe assembly and from the EGR valve.

17 Disconnect the fuel inlet hose and the fuel return hose from the fuel pipe assembly. Plug them to prevent leakage of fuel.

18 Remove the fuel hose bracket from the top of the intake manifold and position the hoses out of the way (photo).

19 Remove the EGR tube from the EGR valve. **Note:** *For access to the large nut the small vacuum line directly above it may have to be removed.*

20 Disconnect the PCV tube from the rubber fitting right below the EGR valve, and lift the tube out.

21 Disconnect the wiring connectors from the 4 injectors.

22 Disconnect the wiring connector from the air regulator.

23 Remove the tie straps that secure the wiring harness to the fuel pipe assembly and position the harness out of the way.

24 Disconnect the 2 air hoses that exit from the rear of the air pipe.

25 Disconnect the 2 vacuum hoses where they join the metal tubes at the front of the cylinder head.

26 Remove the 10 bolts and 1 nut that hold the intake manifold to

8.11 Removing the engine harness ground wire bolt located next to the negative battery cable ground bolt

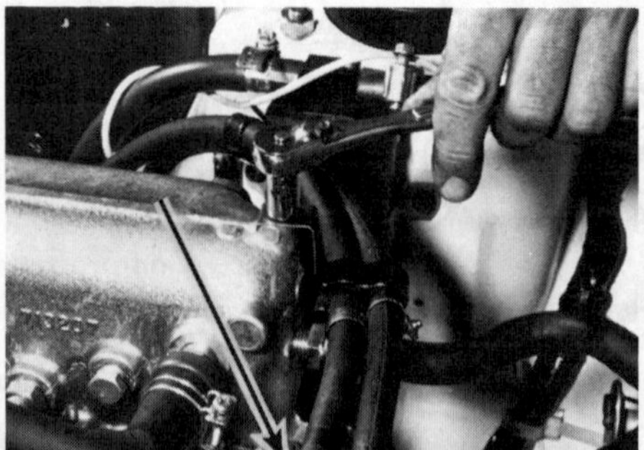

8.18 The fuel lines should be plugged to keep them from leaking and positioned out of the way (arrow)

9.10 On 1980 models, the exhaust manifold can be removed with air induction pipes still attached

the cylinder head.
27 Remove the 2 bolts from the intake manifold stays and lift the manifold out of the engine compartment with injectors, fuel pipes and related components attached.
28 If the manifold needs to be disassembled or replaced, remove the following components: throttle chamber complete with throttle vacuum switch, EGR valve, fuel pipe assembly with injectors, air regulator and hoses, thermal vacuum valve and hoses, pressure regulator, vacuum control valve and any other hoses, lines or components attached to the manifold. If the intake manifold is being replaced transfer these components to the new one. The upper and lower manifold sections can also be separated, if necessary, by removing the nuts and bolts that attach them.
29 Before installing the manifold place clean lint free rags in the engine cavity and scrupulously clean the engine block cylinder head and manifold gasket surface. All extra gasket material and sealing compound should be removed prior to installation. Remove all dirt and gasket remnants from the engine cavity.
30 Place a new intake manifold gasket into position on the manifold and loosely install the lower manifold mounting bolts and washers into the cylinder head. Be sure the chamfered side of the washers is towards the engine. Place the manifold in position against the cylinder head and install the remaining mounting bolts finger tight.
31 Tighten the manifold mounting bolts and nut evenly in relation to one another. They should be tightened a little at a time until they are torqued to specifications.
32 The remainder of the installation is the reverse of the removal procedure.
33 Fill the radiator with coolant, start the engine and check for leaks. Also check and adjust the idle speed as described in Chapter 1.

Note: *If the engine will not start for some reason, disconnect the wiring connector from the fuel pump relay-2 and crank the engine over for about 5 seconds. Then turn the ignition switch off again, and reconnect the wiring connector to the relay.*

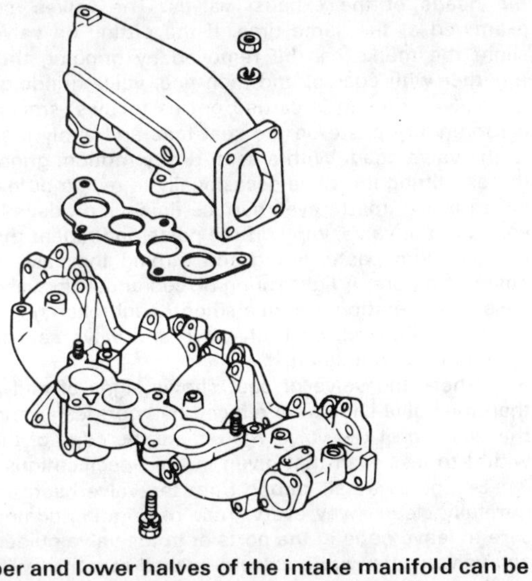

Fig. 2.10 The upper and lower halves of the intake manifold can be separated after the manifold is stripped (Sec 8)

9 Exhaust manifold – removal and installation

1 On 1980 US models, disconnect the air induction hoses from their tubes.
2 Loosen the throttle cable adjusting nuts. Disengage the cable from the throttle lever, then remove the accelerator cable guide from the rocker arm cover and position the cable out of the way.
3 Disconnect the EGR tube from the rear of the exhaust manifold.
4 Raise the front of the car and support it on jack stands.
5 Disconnect the forward exhaust pipe from the exhaust manifold.
6 Remove the dip stick.
7 Remove the spark plug wires from the exhaust side spark plugs for access to the exhaust manifold bolts.
8 On 1980 US models, remove the bolt that attaches the air induction tube bracket to the rear of the cylinder head.
9 Remove the 4 bolts and 4 nuts that retain the exhaust manifold to the cylinder head.
10 Lift out the exhaust manifold complete with air induction tubes, if equipped (photo). If the exhaust manifold needs to be replaced on 1980 US models, remove the air induction tubes from the manifold and install them in the new manifold.
11 Before installing the exhaust manifold clean the mating surfaces on the cylinder head and manifold. All excess gasket material should be removed.
12 Place a new exhaust manifold into position on the cylinder head then place the manifold into position and install the mounting bolts finger tight.
13 Tighten the manifold mounting bolts a little at a time until all of the bolts are torqued to the proper specifications. This must be done to ensure an even draw.
14 Install the remaining components. The remainder of the installation is the reverse of the removal procedure.
15 Start the engine and check for exhaust leaks between the manifold and cylinder head and between the manifold and exhaust pipe.

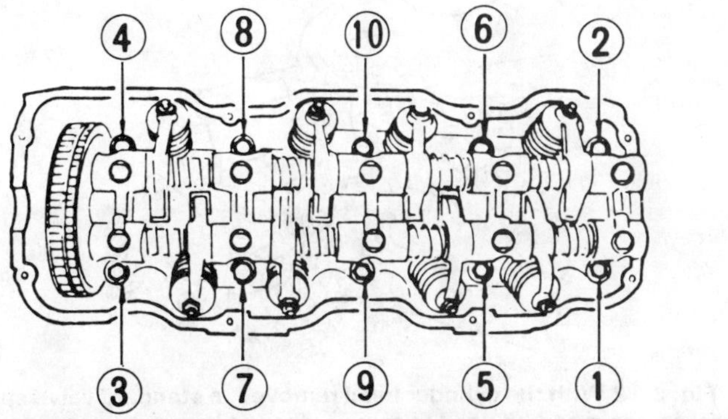

Fig. 2.11 The cylinder head bolts should be loosened evenly in the sequence shown above (Sec 10)

10 Cylinder head – removal

1 Remove the intake manifold as described in Section 8.
2 Remove the exhaust manifold as described in Section 9.
3 Remove the rocker arm cover.
4 Remove the camshaft sprocket, as described in Section 5.
5 On 1981 models, disconnect the wiring connector leading to the cylinder head temperature sensor.
6 Loosen the 10 cylinder head bolts in the sequence shown in the accompanying figure.
7 Remove the 4 bolts that attach the cylinder head to the front cover.
8 Lift the head free of the engine. If the head is stuck to the engine block do not attempt to pry it free as this may ruin the sealing surfaces. Instead use a hammer and a block of wood, tapping on the thick part of the casting. The timing chain should be left securely in place, held by the piece of wood.
9 Remove the cylinder head gasket. Place the head on a block of wood to prevent damage.
10 Refer to the following sections for inspection and installation procedures.

11 Cylinder head – disassembly

Note: *New and rebuilt cylinder heads are commonly available for Datsun engines at dealerships and auto parts stores. Due to the fact that some specialized tools are necessary for the dismantling and inspection of the heads, and replacement parts may not be readily available, it may be more practical and economical for the home mechanic to purchase a replacement head and install it referring to Section 16.*
1 Another alternative at this point is to take the cylinder head complete to a competent automotive machine shop or Datsun

dealership for the overhaul process.

2 If the complete engine is being overhauled at the same time, it may be wise to refer to Section 33 before a decision is made.

3 If it is decided to overhaul the cylinder head, read through the following Sections first to gain an understanding of the steps involved and the tools and replacement parts necessary for the job. Proceed as follows.

4 Remove the valve rocker assembly as described in Section 3. Lift off the camshaft.

5 Using a valve spring compressor (available at dealers or auto parts stores), compress each of the valve springs and remove the valve locking keys. Work on one valve at a time, removing the keys, then releasing the spring and removing the spring retainer and inner and outer spring. Place these components together on a numbered box or rack. All valve mechanism components must be kept separate so they can be returned to their original positions.

6 Remove each valve, in turn, and place in the numbered box or rack to complete the valve mechanism removal. Place the valve components in an area where they will not be able to be mixed-up.

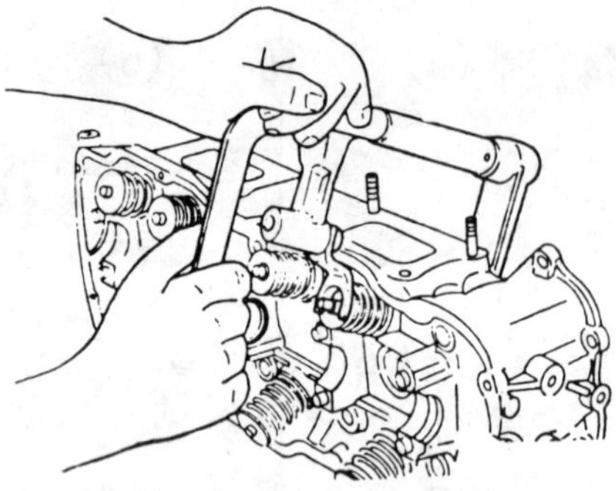

Fig. 2.12 With the cylinder head removed, a standard valve spring compressor can be used to remove the valve components (Sec 11)

12 Cylinder head – cleaning

1 Clean all carbon from the combustion chambers and valve ports. Most auto parts stores will carry this cleaning attachment which is connected to a common hand drill motor.

2 Thoroughly clean the valve guides. Again, several tools available at auto parts stores are designed for this.

3 Use parts cleaner to remove all sludge and dirt from the valve rocker assembly components and valve springs. Work on one set of components at a time, returning each set to its numbered location on your box or rack.

4 A buffing wheel should be used to remove all carbon deposits from the valves. Do not mix up the order of the valves while cleaning them.

5 Clean all carbon deposits from the head gasket mating surface. Be careful not to scratch this sealing surface.

6 Clean the threads on all cylinder head attaching bolts thoroughly.

13 Cylinder head – inspection

1 Carefully inspect the head for cracks around the exhaust ports and combustion chambers, and for external cracks in the water chamber.

2 Check the valve stem-to-bore clearance in the following fashion. Using a micrometer, check the diameter of the valve stem in three places: top, center and bottom. Exhaust valves have tapered stems and are approximately .001-in larger at the top of the stem than at the head end. Next, insert a telescope hole gauge in the valve guide bore to obtain the bore's diameter. The valve clearance can now be figured out from these measurements. If the valve stem clearance exceeds the specifications, an oversize valve must be used, and the valve guide bore must be reamed. This is a job for your dealer or machine shop. Excessive clearance will cause excessive oil consumption while insufficient clearance will result in noisy operation and may cause the valve to stick, resulting in harsh engine operation.

3 Another method of checking this clearance is as follows: one at a time, place a valve in its installed position, with the valve head slightly (about $\frac{1}{16}$-in) off its seat. Now attach a dial indicator to the head with the indicator point just touching the valve stem where it exits the cylinder head. Grab the top of the valve and move it from side to side noting the movement on the dial indicator. If the deflection is more than about 0.008 in (0.2 mm) then the guide should be replaced by a machine shop.

4 Inspect each of the valve springs and its damper. Replace any spring which is deformed, cracked or broken.

5 Check the valve spring tension using an appropriate tool. The springs are compressed to a specified height and then the tension required for this is measured. This is done without the dampers. If not within 19 lb of the specified load, the spring should be replaced with a new one.

6 The valve springs should be measured against the free lengths quoted in Specifications and renewed if they prove shorter as a result of continuous compression. In any event it is worthwhile to renew the valve springs if they have been in use for 20 000 miles or more (32 000 km).

7 Check the cylinder head for warpage. Do this by placing a straightedge across the length of the head and measuring any gaps between the straightedge and the head surface with a feeler gauge. This should be done at three points across the head gasket surface, and also in a diagonal fashion across this surface.

8 If warpage exceeds 0.004 in (0.1 mm) at any point when a straightedge which spans the entire head is used, the cylinder head should be resurfaced. Cylinder head resurfacing is a job for a professional automotive machine shop. Also note that if a cylinder head is resurfaced, the intake manifold position will be slightly altered, requiring the manifold to be resurfaced a proportionate amount.

14 Valves and valve seats – inspection and servicing

1 Examine the heads of the valves for pitting and burning, especially the heads of the exhaust valves. The valves' seatings should be examined at the same time. If the pitting on valve and seat is very slight the marks can be removed by grinding the seats and valves together with coarse, and then fine, valve grinding paste.

2 Valve grinding is carried out as follows: smear a trace of coarse carborundum paste on the seat face and apply a suction grinder tool to the valve head. With a semi-rotary motion, grind the valve head to its seat, lifting the valve occasionally to redistribute the grinding paste. When a dull, matte even surface finish is produced on both the valve seat and the valve, wipe off the paste and repeat the process with fine carborundum paste, lifting and turning the valve to redistribute the paste as before. A light spring placed under the valve head will greatly ease this operation. When a smooth, unbroken ring of light grey matte finish is produced, on both valve and valve seat faces, the grinding operation is completed.

3 Where the valve or seat shows signs of bad pitting or burning, then the valve should be refaced by your dealer and the seat recut. If the refacing of the valve will reduce the edge of the valve head (seat width) to less than that given in the Specifications, replace the valve.

4 Scrape away all carbon from the valve head and the valve stem. Carefully clean away every trace of grinding compound, taking great care to leave none in the ports or in the valve guides. Clean the valves and valve seats with a solvent-soaked rag, then with a clean rag, and finally, if an air line is available, blow the valves, valve guides and valve ports clean.

15 Cylinder head – assembly

1 Make sure all valve mechanism components are perfectly clean and free from carbon and dirt. The bare cylinder head should also be clean and free from abrasive agents which may have been used for valve grinding, reaming etc.

2 Install new oil seals and valve spring seats in the head.

3 Insert each valve in turn into its respective guide, applying a little engine oil to the stem.

4 With the aid of a spring compressor, assemble the springs (outer spring has close coils nearest cylinder head) retainers and split collets. The latter can be retained in the valve stem cut-out with a dab of thick grease.

5 Grease the camshaft bearings and place the camshaft in position

in its lower bearings. The dowel located at the front of the camshaft should be in the 12 o'clock position.
6 Reinstall the valve rocker assembly, tightening the valve rocker bolts only snugly. Temporarily tighten the 2 center bolts to 14 ft-lb (2 m-kg).

16 Cylinder head – installation

1 If not already done, thoroughly clean the gasket surface on both the cylinder heads and the engine block. Do not scratch or otherwise damage these sealing areas.
2 To get the proper torque readings, the threads of the attaching bolts must be free of dirt. This also goes for the threaded holes in the engine block. Run a tap through these holes to ensure they are clean.
3 Place the gasket in place over the engine block dowel pins.
4 Carefully lower the cylinder head onto the engine, over the dowel pins and the gaskets. Be careful not to move the gasket while doing this.
5 Coat both the threads of the cylinder head attaching bolts and the point at which the head and stem meet with a sealing compound and install each finger-tight. Do not tighten any of the bolts at this time.
6 Tighten each of the bolts, a little at a time, in the sequence shown in the accompanying figure. Continue tightening in this sequence until the proper torque reading is obtained. As a final check, work around the head in a logical front to rear sequence to make sure none of the bolts have been left out of the sequence.
7 On 1981 models, reconnect the wiring connector leading to the cylinder head temperature sensor.
8 With the piece of wood holding the timing chain still in place, carefully work the timing chain over the camshaft sprocket onto the end of the camshaft, with the cam dowel located in the number 2 sprocket hole. Be sure the marks made on the chain and sprocket during removal line up.
9 Carefully remove the piece of wood, and install the camshaft sprocket bolt, torquing it to specifications.
10 Tighten the valve rocker assembly bolts to their proper torque specifications.

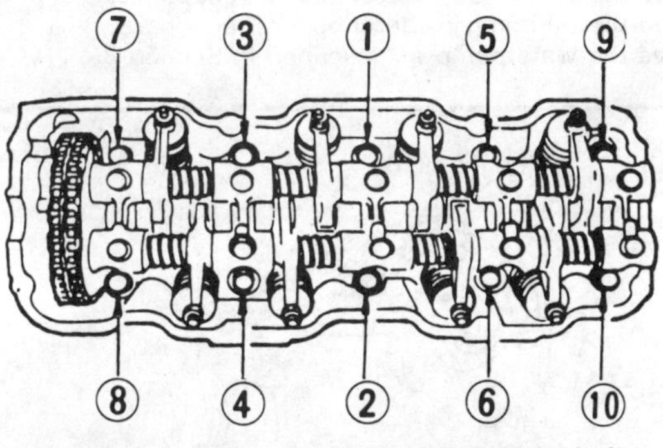

Fig. 2.13 When installing the cylinder head, the bolts should be tightened evenly in the sequence shown until they are properly torqued (Sec 16)

11 Adjust the valve clearance to the 'cold' specifications as described in Chapter 1.
12 Install the rocker arm cover, intake manifold and exhaust manifold as described in the appropriate Sections.
13 Following installation, warm up the engine and readjust the valve clearances to the 'hot' specifications as described in Chapter 1.
14 Fill the radiator with coolant, start the engine and check for leaks. Be sure to recheck the coolant level once the engine has warmed up to operating temperature. Also check and adjust the idle speed as described in Chapter 1.

17 Oil pump – removal and installation

1 Turn the crankshaft until no 1 piston is at TDC (top-dead-center). To establish this position, if the engine is in the car, remove the rocker cover and observe the position of the inlet and exhaust valves of no 1 cylinder – the camshaft lobes should be clear of both valves. Alternatively, remove no 1 spark plug and feel the compression being generated with a finger. Remove the distributor cap and check when the rotor head points to no 1 segment in the cap.
2 The engine has static timing marks on the engine front cover and crankshaft pulley. Align the notch on the crankshaft pulley with the TDC mark ('O') on the engine front cover but employ one of the methods previously described to ensure that the engine is on a compression stroke.
3 After removing the distributor cap, mark the position of the rotor in relation to the distributor body.
4 Drain the engine oil from the oil pan.
5 Unscrew and remove the bolts which secure the oil pump body to the engine front cover and withdraw the oil pump/driveshaft assembly (photo).
6 If the oil pump needs to be inspected or overhauled refer to Section 18.
7 Make sure that No. 1 piston is still at TDC.
8 Fill the pump body with engine oil to prime it and align the punch mark on the driveshaft with the oil hole below the drivegear (See accompanying figure).
9 Use a new flange gasket and insert the pump into its recess in the engine front cover.
10 Tighten the oil pump securing bolts and check that the rotor is still aligned with the mark made on the distributor body. If it is not, repeat the oil pump installation procedure.
11 Fill the engine with the proper quantity and grade of engine oil. (Refer to Chapter 1, if necessary).
12 It is recommended that the ignition timing is finally checked as described in Chapter 1.

18 Oil pump – overhaul

1 With the oil pump removed, unbolt the cover from the oil pump and extract the inner and outer rotors (photo).
2 Unscrew and remove the pressure regulator valve plug and extract the spring and valve.
3 Wash all components in clean fuel and allow to dry.

17.5 The oil pump is located on the right lower front of the engine

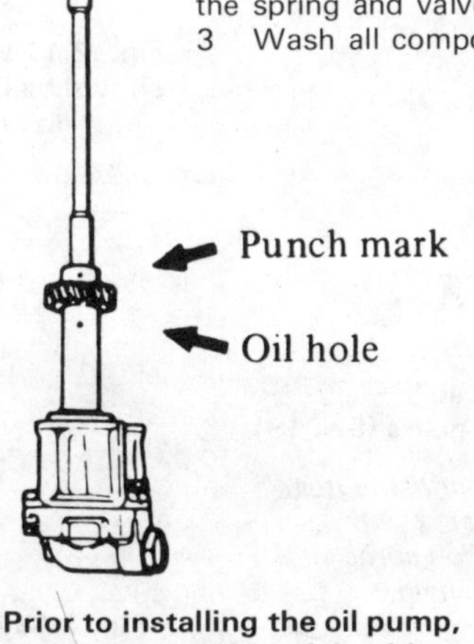

Fig. 2.14 Prior to installing the oil pump, the punch mark on the side of the drive spindle should be lined up with the pump's oil hole (Sec 17)

19.27 When installing the timing chain, the slack side chain guide should be adjusted

4 Check all components for wear or scoring and test the rotor clearances in the following manner:

(a) *using a straight edge, check the clearance between the rotor faces and the straight edge with a feeler gauge. Any difference between the two rotor faces to straight edge clearances must not exceed 0.0024 in (0.06 mm)*
(b) *check the clearance between the tops (high points) of the inner and outer rotors. This should not exceed 0.0079 in (0.20 mm)*
(c) *check the clearance between the outer rotor and the body. This should not exceed 0.0197 in (0.5 mm)*
(d) *again using the straight edge placed across the body, check the clearance between body and straight edge, this should not exceed 0.0012 in (0.03 mm). The inner and outer rotors should always be assembled in the pump body so that the dotted marks on their end faces are not visible from the cover end*

5 Where the specified clearances are exceeded, renew the components. The inner and outer rotors are only supplied as matched sets. If the oil pump body is worn or damaged, renew the complete pump assembly.

6 Check the condition of the pressure regulator valve and spring and renew if necessary.

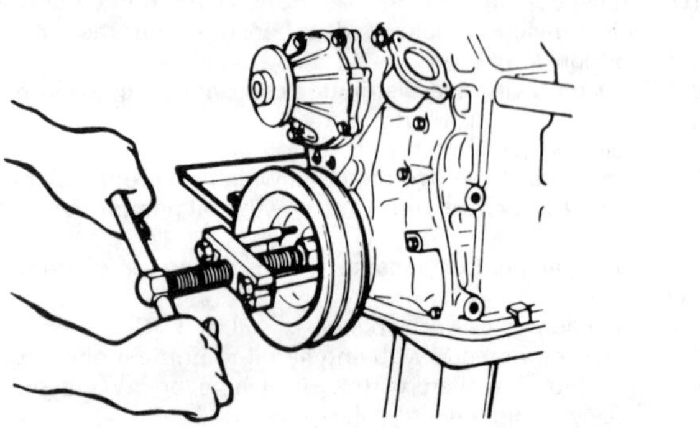

Fig. 2.15 On models equipped with air conditioning, a puller may have to be used to remove the crankshaft pulley (Sec 19)

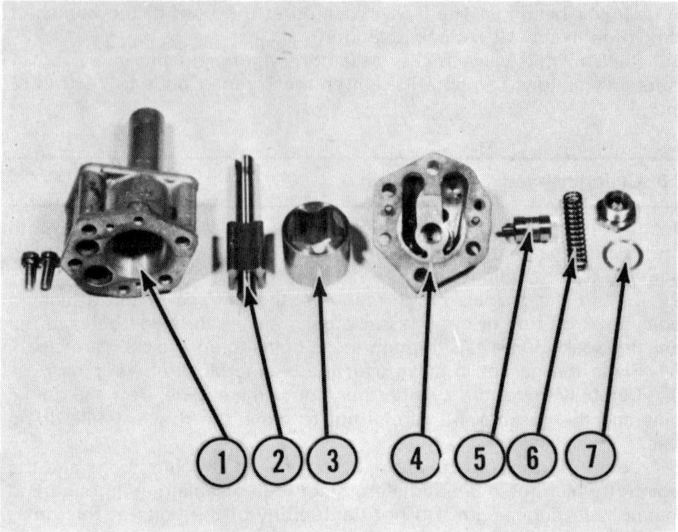

18.1 Components of the oil pump

1 *Oil pump body*
2 *Inner rotor and shaft*
3 *Outer rotor*
4 *Oil pump cover*
5 *Regulator valve*
6 *Regulator spring*
7 *Regulator cap and washer*

19 Front cover and timing gear – removal and installation

Note: *If the engine has been removed from the car, proceed to paragraph 4.*

1 Open the radiator drain plug at the center underside of the radiator and drain the engine coolant.
2 Remove the fan and radiator as described in Chapter 3.
3 Drain the engine oil from the engine.
4 Remove the distributor as described in Chapter 5.
5 Remove the oil pump as described in Section 18.
6 Remove the waterpump as described in Section 3.

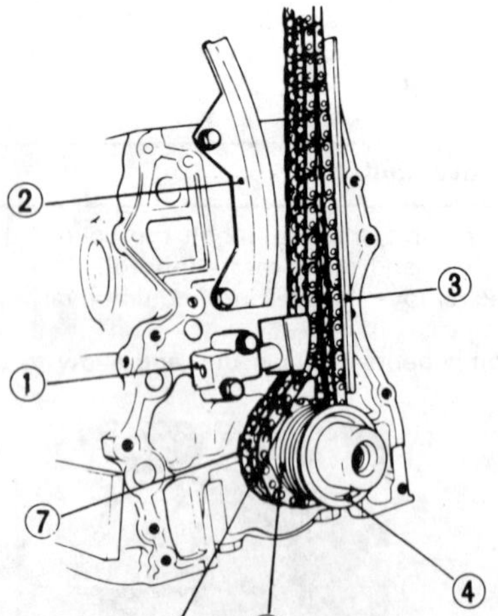

Fig. 2.16 Components comprising the timing gears (Sec 19)

1 *Chain tensioner*
2 *Chain guide (slack side)*
3 *Chain guide (tension side)*
4 *Oil thrower*
5 *Oil pump/distributor drivegear*
6 *Crankshaft sprocket*
7 *Timing chain*

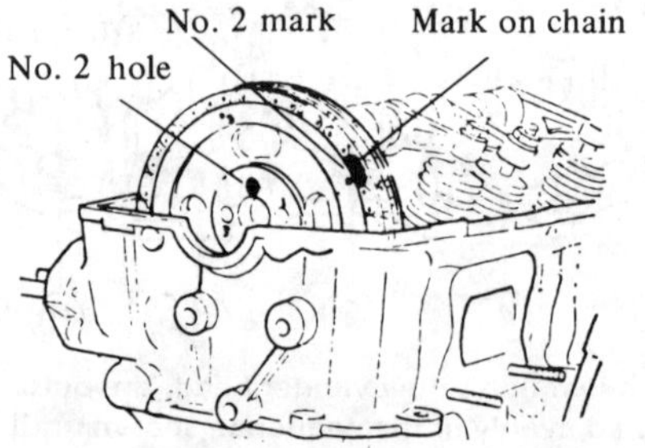

Fig. .2.17 With the number 1 piston at TDC, the camshaft dowel should be in the number 2 sprocket hole, with the chain's timing link lined with the number 2 sprocket mark (Sec 19)

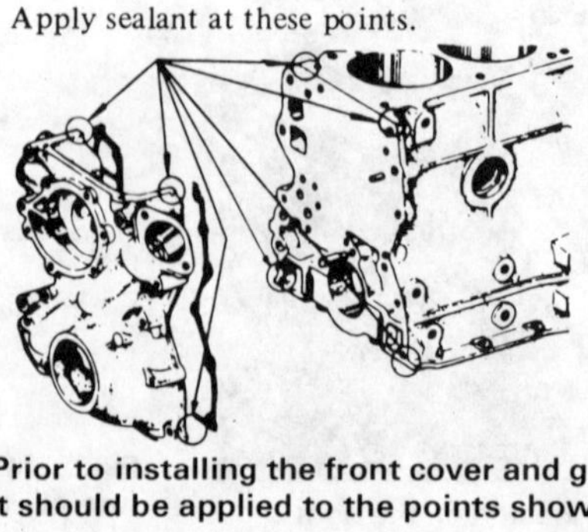

Fig. 2.18 Prior to installing the front cover and gasket, silicone sealant should be applied to the points shown (Sec 19)

20.2 The front oil seal is located in the front cover

7 Remove the upper alternator adjusting bolt. Then remove the bolts that attach the alternator adjusting arm to the front cover, and remove the adjusting arm.
8 Disconnect the hoses attached to the vacuum pipe assembly attached to the front cover. Remove the pipe assembly from the cover.
9 Since the front cover is sandwiched between the cylinder head and the oil pan, the oil pan must be removed in order to remove the front cover. Refer to Section 21 for this procedure.
10 With the oil pan removed, remove the crankshaft pulley bolt. There is considerable torque on this bolt and some means must be found to keep the engine from turning over while the bolt is broken loose. If the engine is in the car, place the transmission in its highest forward gear and apply the parking brake, then reinstall the flywheel mounting bolts into the rear end of the crankshaft. Use a long screwdriver or pry bar inserted in between these bolts to keep the crankshaft from turning.
11 Remove the crankshaft pulley.
12 Remove the mounting bolts that attach the front cover to the cylinder block and cylinder head, and lift off the front cover. If it will not come off easily, slight tapping with a soft faced hammer will help.
13 Remove the bolts that attach the chain tensioner and chain guides to the block, and lift these components off.
14 Remove the camshaft sprocket bolt, and lift off the sprocket.
15 Remove the timing chain from both the camshaft and crankshaft sprockets.
16 From the end of the crankshaft, pull off the oil thrower, the oil pump helical gear and the chain sprocket. The latter will almost certainly require the use of an extractor. Note that the three Woodruff keys are used to secure these components.
17 Examine the teeth on both the crankshaft gear and the camshaft gear wheel for wear. Each tooth forms an inverted V with the gear periphery, and if worn the side of each tooth under tension will be slightly concave in shape when compared with the other side of the tooth, i.e. one side of the inverted V will be concave when compared with the other. If any sign of wear is present the gears must be replaced.
18 Examine the links of the chain for side slackness and replace the chain if any slackness is noticeable when compared with a new chain. It is a sensible precaution to replace the chain at about 30 000 miles (48 000 km) and at lower mileage if the engine is stripped down for a major overhaul. The actual rollers on a very badly worn chain may be slightly grooved.
19 When the camshaft sprocket is bolted in position, the endplay should not exceed 0.008 in (0.2 mm) – otherwise replace it.
20 There is no adjustment to compensate for a worn timing chain. If there is any doubt at all, it is best to replace it.
21 Examine the components of the chain tensioner and guides. Replace any item which is worn or badly grooved.
22 To begin the installation, rotate the camshaft until the valves of number 1 cylinder are fully closed (equivalent to number 1 piston at TDC), then turn the crankshaft (by means of the flywheel) until number 1 piston is at TDC.
23 Bolt the two timing chain guides into position.
24 To the front of the crankshaft, fit the sprocket, oil pump/distributor drivegear and the oil thrower. Make sure that the timing marks on the sprocket are visible from the front.
25 **Do not** turn the crankshaft or camshaft until the timing chain is installed, otherwise the valves will contact the piston crowns.
26 Engage the camshaft sprocket within the upper loop of the timing chain; then engage the chain with the teeth of the crankshaft sprocket and bolt the camshaft sprocket to the camshaft ensuring that the following conditions are met:

> *a) The keyway of the crankshaft sprocket should point vertically.*
> *b) The timing marks (bright link plates) on the chain should align with those on the two sprockets and be positioned on the right side when viewed from the front.*
> *c) The locating dowel on the front of the camshaft should be in the number 2 hole of the camshaft sprocket, and the timing chain should be aligned with the number 2 timing mark.*

27 Install the chain tensioner assembly into position on the cylinder block. Then adjust the position of the chain guide above the tensioner so there is no space between the tensioner body and the tensioner plunger unit (photo).
28 Install a new front cover seal into the front cover by referring to Section 20.
29 Place the front cover gaskets into position on the cover then apply dabs of silicone sealant to the points shown in the accompanying figure.
30 Apply a small amount of lithium grease to the inside lip of the oil seal. Then place the front cover into position on the cylinder block and install the mounting bolts.
31 The remainder of the installation is the reverse of the removal procedure.

20 Front oil seal – replacement

1 Remove the front cover from the engine as described in Section 19.
2 Using a screwdriver, pry the old seal from the front cover (photo). Be careful not to damage the seal mating surface in the cover.
3 Install the new seal into the front cover with the dust seal lip toward the outside. The seal can be installed by using the appropriate oil seal installing tool, or by using a flat block of wood, large enough to cover the seal. It is important that the seal be installed evenly.
4 Reinstall the front cover.

21 Oil pan – removal and installation

Note: *If the engine has been removed from the car, proceed to paragraph 11.*
1 Drain the engine oil.
2 Raise the front of the car and support it on jackstands.
3 Disconnect the front exhaust pipe from the exhaust manifold.
4 Remove the bolts that attach the front engine mounts to the engine.
5 In order to remove the oil pan, the engine will have to be raised slightly. Because of clearance problems when the engine is raised, some parts will have to be removed or disconnected. Among these are the fan, the air induction hoses (on 1980 US models), ignition coil wires and vacuum lines leading to the engine.
6 Remove the transmission mounting bracket.
7 Attach an engine hoist to the lifting 'eyes' mounted to the engine. These are located at the corners of the cylinder head. Make sure the chain is looped properly through the engine brackets and secured with strong nuts and bolts through the chain loops. The hook on the hoist should be over the center of the engine with the lengths of chain at equal distances so the engine can be lifted straight up.
8 Lift the engine just enough to provide adequate clearance to remove the oil pan. As the engine is raised, keep a constant check on clearances around the engine, to prevent anything from binding or breaking.
9 Remove the oil pan retaining bolts and lift off the oil pan.

23.3 When installed, the lip on the rear oil seal should face outward

10 Before installing the oil pan, thoroughly clean the gasket sealing surfaces on the engine block and on the oil pan with degreaser. All sealer and gasket material must be removed.
11 Before installing the oil pan, apply a $\frac{1}{8}$-in (3 mm) diameter bead of silicone sealer around the pan's sealing flange.
12 Using a new rear oil pan seal, position the oil pan against the engine block and install the mounting bolts, torquing them to specifications.
13 Lower the engine onto the engine mount and install the retaining nuts, torquing them to specifications.
14 The remainder of the installation is the reverse of the removal procedure.
15 Fill the engine with the correct grade of oil, start the engine and check the pan for leaks.

22 Flywheel – removal and installation

1 If the engine is in the car, remove the clutch cover assembly and clutch disc as described in Chapter 8, or automatic transmission as described in Chapter 7. Bend back the tabs of the lockplates and unscrew and remove the bolts which secure the flywheel to the crankshaft rear flange.
2 If some difficulty is experienced in unscrewing the bolts due to the rotation of the crankshaft, wedge the starter ring gear by inserting a cold chisel at the starter motor aperture.
3 Lift the flywheel from the crankshaft flange.
4 Unbolt and remove the engine endplate. Now is a good time to check the cylinder block rear core plug for security and leakage.
5 If the teeth on the flywheel starter ring gear are badly worn, or if some are missing then it will be necessary to remove the ring and fit a new one, or preferably exchange the flywheel for a reconditioned unit.
6 Either split the ring with a cold chisel after making a cut with a hacksaw blade between two teeth, or use a soft headed hammer (not steel) to knock the ring off, striking it evenly and alternately at equally spaced points. Take great care not to damage the flywheel during this process.
7 Heat the new ring in an electric oven to about 200°C (392°F).
8 Hold the ring at this temperature for five minutes and then quickly fit it to the flywheel so the chamfered portion of the teeth faces the transmission side of the flywheel.
9 The ring should be tapped gently down onto its register and left to cool naturally when the contraction of the metal on cooling will ensure that it is a secure and permanent fit. Great care must be taken not to overheat the ring, indicated by its turning light metallic blue, as if this happens, the temper of the ring will be lost.
10 Where the starter ring teeth on automatic transmission models are worn or chipped then the complete flywheel should be renewed.
11 On manual transmission flywheels, inspect the clutch friction face for scoring. Light scoring may be corrected using emery cloth, but where there is deep scoring the flywheel must be replaced with a new one or clutch damage will soon occur.

26.10 Prior to removal of the engine, the air pipe assembly should be removed, complete with hoses and rubber boots

12 Before installing the flywheel, clean the mating surfaces of the flywheel and the crankshaft.
13 If removed, reinstall the rear plate.
14 To install, position the flywheel in place against the crankshaft using a new spacer, if equipped, and insert the mounting bolts, securing them only fingertight. It is a good idea to use a thread sealing agent on the bolt threads.
15 Again, while preventing the flywheel from turning, tighten the bolts a little at a time until they are all torqued to specifications.
16 Complete the remainder of the installation procedure by reversing the removal steps.

23 Rear oil seal – replacement

1 Remove the flywheel from the engine as described in Section 22.
2 Using a screwdriver, pry the old seal from the rear of the cylinder block. Be careful not to damage the seal mating surface.
3 Install the new seal into the block with the dust seal lip toward the outside (photo). The seal can be installed by using the appropriate oil seal installing tool, or by using a flat block of wood, large enough to cover the seal. One last method is to use a soft-face hammer to lightly tap around the seal, gradually tapping it down into its bore. It is important that the seal be installed evenly.
4 Reinstall the flywheel.

24 Pilot bushing – replacement

1 Remove the clutch disc and cover assembly as described in Chapter 8, or the automatic transmission as described in Chapter 7.
2 A special tool is needed to remove the pilot bushing (Fig. 2.19). This tool can be obtained from a Datsun dealer or from a well-stocked auto parts store.

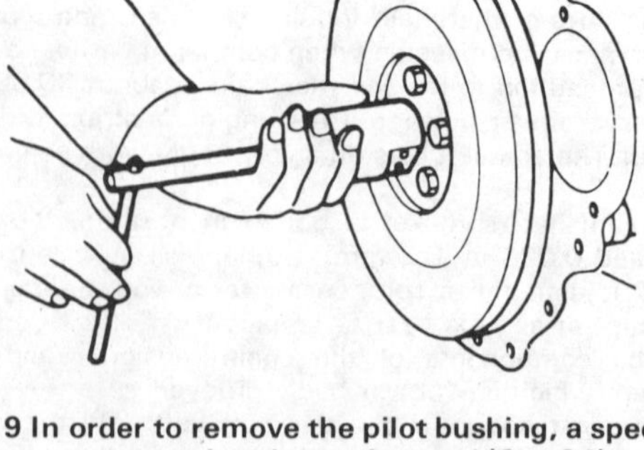

Fig. 2.19 In order to remove the pilot bushing, a special bushing removal tool must be used (Sec 24)

3 Before installing the new bushing, thoroughly clean the bushing hole.
4 Using an appropriate sized socket or piece of tubing, insert the new bushing into the hole until the outer end of the bushing is 0.157 in (4.0 mm) from the outside surface of the crankshaft flange. When installing the bushing, be careful not to damage its outer end.
5 Reinstall the clutch assembly and transmission.

25 Engine mounts – replacement

1 Engine mounts are non-adjustable and seldom require service. Periodically, they should be inspected for hardening or cracking of the rubber, or separation of the rubber from its metal backing.
2 To replace the front mounts with the engine in position in the car, support the weight of the engine with a jack and wooden block located under the oil pan.
3 Unbolt the mount from the crossmember and the cylinder block and remove.
4 Install the front mount, making sure that the projection on the insulator pad aligns with the notch in the mount bracket.
5 To replace the rear mount, support the weight of the transmission with a jack.
6 If equipped, remove the damper from the mount support.
7 Unscrew and remove the bolts which fix the insulator pad to the support.
8 Unscrew and remove the bolts which fix the mount pad to the transmission extension housing.
9 Install by reversing the removal operations.

26 Engine – removal

1 It is essential to have a good hoist, and two strong axle-stands if an inspection pit is not available. Removal will be much easier if there is someone to assist, especially during the later stages.
2 Before beginning work it is worthwhile to get all dirt cleaned off the engine at a service station equipped with steam or high pressure air and water cleaning equipment.
3 Remove the hood. Refer to Chapter 12 for the correct procedure. Set the hood in a safe place where it will not be damaged.
4 Before disconnecting any fuel lines, the pressure in the fuel system must be eliminated. This is done by following the procedure described in paragraph 1 of Section 8.
5 Disconnect the battery cables.
6 Drain the coolant from the radiator and engine block, referring to Chapter 1 if necessary.
7 Drain the engine oil.
8 Drain the oil from the transmission. Refer to Chapter 1, if necessary.
9 Remove the upper and lower radiator hoses.
10 Remove the air pipe assembly, inlet air duct and connecting boots and hoses (photo). **Note:** *Before disconnecting or removing any electrical wires, vacuum hoses, hydraulic hoses, etc., always mark them with pieces of tape to identify their installed locations.* This will eliminate possible problems and confusion in the installation procedure.
11 Loosen the accelerator cable adjusting nuts and disengage the cable from the throttle lever. Then remove the accelerator cable guide from the rocker arm cover and position the cable out of the way.
12 Label the spark plug wires as to their positions on the distributor and spark plugs. Then disconnect them and remove them from the engine compartment. Also, remove the ignition coil wire(s).
13 Disconnect the wiring connectors from the throttle valve switch, the water temperature sensor (1980 models), the temperature gauge sensor, and the cylinder head temperature sensor (1981 models).
14 Disconnect the harness ground wire and the negative battery cable from the right side of the intake manifold.
15 Disconnect the PCV tube from the PCV valve.
16 Remove the vacuum lines from the rear of the fuel pipe assembly, the rear of the intake manifold and the EGR valve.
17 Remove the fuel inlet and return hoses from the fuel pipe assembly and plug them to protect them from leaking.
18 Remove the fuel hose bracket from the top of the intake manifold and position the hoses out of the way.
19 Disconnect the wiring connectors from the injectors.
20 Disconnect the wiring connector from the air regulator.
21 Cut the tie straps, if equipped, that secure the wiring harness to the fuel pipe assembly and position the harness out of the way.
22 Disconnect the heater hoses.
23 On 1980 US models, disconnect the air induction hoses from their metal tubes.
24 Remove the air-conditioner compressor from its bracket and secure it out of the way with wire. DO NOT DISCONNECT ANY A/C LINES, without first having the system depressurized. Refer to Chapter 3, if necessary.
25 Remove the alternator as described in Chapter 5.
26 If equipped, remove the power steering pump as described in Chapter 11.
27 Remove the distributor cap.
28 Disconnect the vacuum hoses leading to the vacuum advance and the charcoal canister.
29 Remove the fan, shroud and radiator as described in Chapter 3.
30 Remove the drive belts. Refer to Chapter 1, if necessary.
31 Remove the idler pulleys.
32 Disconnect any other lines or wires running to the engine.
33 Make all necessary disconnections in preparation of removing the transmission, as described in Chapter 7. Do not yet remove the transmission mounting bracket.
34 Attach an engine hoist to the 2 lifting 'eyes' mounted to the engine. They are located at the corners of the cylinder head. Make sure the chain is looped properly through the engine brackets and secure with strong nuts and bolts through the chain loops. The hook on the hoist should be over the center of the engine with the lengths of chain at equal distances, so the engine can be lifted straight up.
35 Raise the engine just until all slack is out of the chains.
36 Remove the bolts that attach the transmission mounting bracket to the body. Then remove the bolts that attach the bracket to the transmission.
37 Remove the bolts that attach the front engine mount bracket to the engine block.
38 Carefully lift the engine straight up and then forward from the engine compartment, continually checking clearances around the

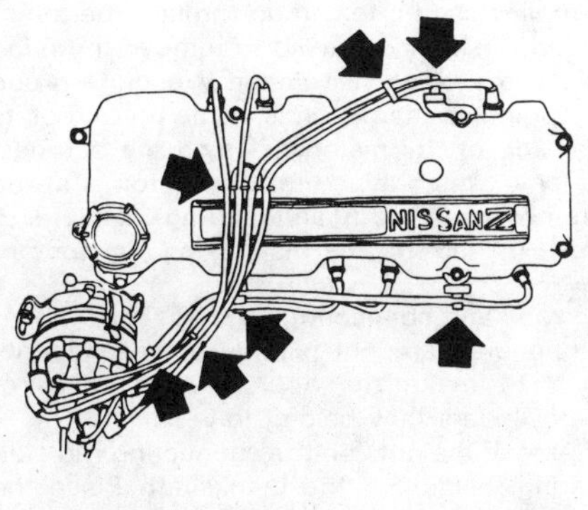

Fig. 2.20 The spark plug wires should be secured at the points shown (Sec 26)

26.38 The easiest method of removing the engine is with the transmission still attached

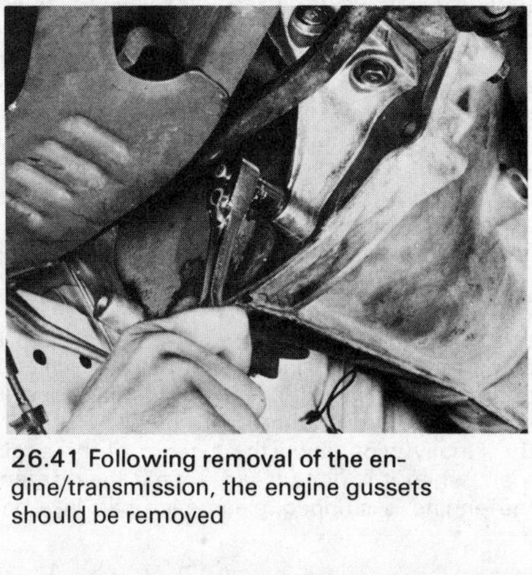

26.41 Following removal of the engine/transmission, the engine gussets should be removed

engine (photo).
39 Once the engine/transmission assembly has been removed from the car, remove the starter motor. Refer to Chapter 5, if necessary.
40 To separate the engine from an automatic transmission:

- *a) Unscrew and remove the dust cover from the lower half of the torque converter housing.*
- *b) Unscrew and remove each of the bolts which secure the torque converter to the driveplate. Access to these bolts can be gained (one at a time), by turning the engine until each bolt comes into view through the lower half of the converter housing.*
- *c) Withdraw the automatic transmission unit leaving the driveplate bolted to the crankshaft rear flange.*

41 To separate the engine from a manual transmission:

- *a) Unscrew and remove the bolts which secure the clutch bellhousing to the engine crankcase (photo).*
- *b) Withdraw the transmission in a straight line, so that its weight does not hang up on the input shaft while it is still engaged in the driven plate of the clutch mechanism.*

27 Engine overhaul – general disassembly information

1 If the engine has been removed from the car for a major overhaul, the initial operation should be to disassemble the engine into its individual components.
2 It is best to mount the engine on a dismantling stand but if one is not available, then stand the engine on a strong bench so as to be at a comfortable working height. Failing this, the engine can be stripped down on the floor.
3 Begin the disassembly operation by stripping the engine of its auxiliary accessories and related parts. This includes the following components:

Alternator and its bracket and adjusting bar
Engine mounting brackets
Clutch cover assembly and clutch disc (manual transmission) of torque converter (automatic transmission)
Drivebelt idler pulleys
Water pump
Metal vacuum tube assembly (on front cover)
Crankshaft pulley
Distributor
EGR tube at rear of engine
Exhaust manifold with air induction tubes, if equipped
Air conditioner compressor bracket, if equipped
Spark plugs
Engine oil dipstick and tube
PCV hose and tube
Power steering pump bracket, if equipped
Intake manifold assembly, including metal stays
Oil filter
Oil pressure switch
Oil pump, with drive spindle
Gussets

4 With these components removed, the general engine sub-assemblies can be removed, serviced and installed by following the operations described in the other section of this Chapter.
5 To strip the engine it is best to work from the top down. The oil pan provides a firm base on which the engine can be supported in an upright position. When the stage, where the oil pan must be removed, is reached, the engine can be turned on its side and all other work carried out with it in this position.
6 During the dismantling process the greatest care should be taken to keep the exposed parts free from dirt. As an aid to achieving this, it is a sound practice to thoroughly clean down the outside of the engine, removing all traces of oil and dirt.
7 Use a water-soluble grease solvent. This compound will make the job easier, as, after the solvent has been applied and allowed to stand for a time, a vigorous jet of water will wash off the solvent and all the grease and filth. If the dirt is thick and deeply embedded, work the solvent into it with a wire brush.
8 Finally wipe down the exterior of the engine with a rag and only then, when it is quite clean, should the dismantling process begin. As the engine is stripped, clean each part in a bath of parts cleaner.

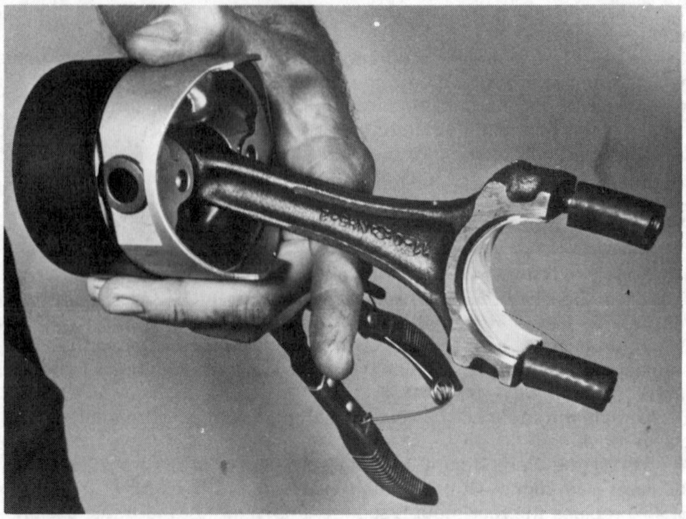

28.5 Pieces of rubber hose should be slipped over the connecting rod studs to protect the crankshaft and cylinder walls

9 Never immerse parts which have internal oilways in a solvent (such as the crankshaft), but wipe them carefully with a solvent-soaked rag. Probe the oilways with a length of wire and if an air line is available, blow the oilways through to clean them.
10 Be extremely careful using combustible cleaning agents near an open flame or inside an enclosed work area. Fumes can ignite from a lighted cigarette or a hot water heater pilot light. Wipe up any fuel or cleaner spills immediately, and do not store greasy or solvent-soaked rags where they can ignite.
11 Re-use of old engine gaskets is false economy and can give rise to oil and water leaks, if nothing worse. To avoid the possibility of trouble after the engine has been reassembled, *always* use new gaskets throughout.
12 Do not throw the old gaskets away, as it sometimes happens that an immediate replacement cannot be found and the old gasket is then very useful as a template. Hang up the old gaskets as they are removed on a suitable hook or nail.
13 Wherever possible, replace nuts, bolts and washers finger-tight from wherever they were removed. This helps avoid later loss and muddle. If they cannot be replaced, then lay them out in such a fashion that it is clear from where they came.
14 If at any time during the dismantling procedure damage is found to any of the major engine components (cylinder heads, cylinder block, crankshaft, etc), consider the possibility of purchasing new or rebuilt assemblies as described in Section 33. This decision will in most cases alter your particular rebuilding sequence, as dismantling, inspection and assembly will not be required.

28 Pistons, connecting rods and bearings – removal

1 Remove the oil pan, oil pump and cylinder heads as described previously in this Chapter.
2 Before the piston assemblies can be forced up through the top of the engine block, a ridge reamer should be used to remove the ridge and/or carbon deposits at the top of each cylinder. Working on one cylinder at a time, turn the engine so the piston is at the bottom of its stroke. Then place a rag on top of the piston to catch the cuttings. After the ridge is removed, crank the engine until the piston is at the top of the cylinder and remove the cloth and cuttings. Failure to remove this ridge may cause damage to the piston rings, pistons or cylinder walls.
3 Inspect the connecting rods and connecting rod caps for cylinder identification. If these components are not plainly marked, identify each using a small punch to make the appropriate number of indentations to identify the cylinders they belong to.
4 Working in sequence, remove the nuts on the connecting rod stud and lift the cap (with bearing inside) off the crankshaft. Place the connecting rod cap and bearing on a clean work surface marked cylinder number 1, 2, 3, etc.

28.9 Using a piston ring compressor is the easiest method of removing and installing the piston rings

31.2 A micrometer can be used to measure the journals and crankpins of the crankshaft

31.6 A feeler gauge can be used to measure the crankshaft end play at the number 3 bearing cap

5 Push a piece of rubber or plastic tubing over the connecting rod studs to completely cover the studs. This is important as these studs could easily damage the crankshaft or cylinder wall when the piston assembly is removed (photo).
6 Push the piston/connecting rod assembly out through the top of the cylinder. Place the piston with its connecting rod next to its rod cap on the sequenced work area.
7 Repeat these procedures for the remaining cylinders, turning the crankshaft as necessary to gain access to the connecting rod nuts. Reuse the rubber or plastic tubing for each assembly.
8 Remove the bearings from the connecting rods and the connecting rod caps. This is easily done with a small screwdriver. If the engine has many miles on it, it is false economy to reuse the bearings, but if they are to be reinstalled, place them in a numbered rack.
9 If a piston ring expanding tool is available, use this to remove each of the rings from the piston (photo). An alternative method is to expand the ring just enough to clear the lands of the piston body. Then place strips of tin (about $\frac{1}{4}$-in wide) under the ring at equal distances around the piston. Using a slight twisting motion, 'walk' the ring up the piston and off the top.
10 Place the rings in their 'installed' order adjacent to the piston/connecting rod on your numbered work area.
11 Separating the connecting rod from the piston requires the removal of the piston pin. This job is best left to a dealer or automotive machine shop equipped with the proper support tools and an arbor press.
12 Do not take the time to clean and inspect the piston/rod assembles at this time, as they may have to be replaced with new units depending on the condition of the cylinder block and/or crankshaft.

29 Piston and connecting rods – cleaning and inspection

1 In most cases where the engine has seen high mileage, the original pistons will have to be replaced with new ones. This is because the cylinders will have to be bored to a larger size to compensate for normal wear. If, however, the cylinder walls require only a slight finish honing, the old pistons may be reused if they are in good condition.
2 Wash the connecting rods and pistons in a cleaning solvent and dry with compressed air, if available.
3 Don't use a wire brush or any abrasive cleaning tools on any part of the piston.
4 Clean the ring grooves of the piston with a groove cleaner tool and make sure the oil ring holes and slots are clean.
5 Inspect the rods for twisting, bending, nicks or cracks. If any of the above items are found, the rod must be replaced with a new one.
6 Inspect the piston for cracked ring lands, skirts or pin bosses. Check for worn or wavy ring lands, scuffed or damaged skirts and eroded areas at the top of the piston. Replace any pistons that are damaged or show signs of excessive wear.
7 Inspect the ring grooves for nicks which may cause the rings to hang up.
8 With the piston still connected to the connecting rod, swivel the rod back and forth, noting the degree of difficulty. Compare all piston/rod assemblies. If the rods seem loose on the piston pins, and move with little or no drag, the piston pins have worn and the piston pin must be replaced.
9 If the cylinder block is in need of any machine work, even finish honing, chances are that the machinist will want the pistons on hand to check piston-to-bore clearance as the cylinder walls are cut. This measurement is critical and should be left to the machine shop.

30 Crankshaft – removal

1 Remove the engine from the car as described in Section 26 and support it on a suitable stand.
2 Remove the timing chain, oil thrower, drivegear and crankshaft sprocket from the front of the crankshaft, as described in Section 19.
3 Remove the flywheel and rear plate, as described in Section 22.
4 Remove the oil pan.
5 Remove the pistons and connecting rods from the crankshaft as described in Section 28.
6 Check that each of the main bearing caps is marked in respect of its location in the engine block. If not, use a punch to make small indentations in each cap: one indentation for the first main bearing cap, two indentations for the second cap, etc. The main bearing caps must be reinstalled in their original positions.
7 Unbolt the main bearing cap and lift each cap and its corresponding bearing off the crankshaft. A puller may be necessary to remove the center and rear main bearing cap. Place all of the main bearing caps and bearings on a work space numbered to correspond with the position of the cap in the engine block.
8 Lift the crankshaft from the engine block, being careful not to damage it in any way.
9 Remove the rear main oil seal.
10 Remove the main bearings and the main bearing caps from the block, keeping them separated as to their positions.

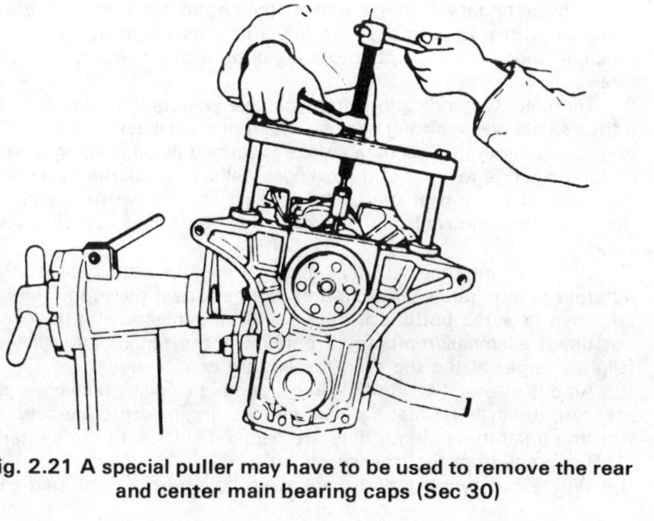

Fig. 2.21 A special puller may have to be used to remove the rear and center main bearing caps (Sec 30)

31 Crankshaft and bearings – inspection and servicing

1 Examine the crankpin and main journal surfaces for scoring, scratches or corrosion. If evident, then the crankshaft will have to be reground professionally. Check that all oil holes in the crankshaft are clear and free of burrs.
2 Using a micrometer, test each journal and crankpin at several different points for ovality (photo). If this is found to be more than 0.0004 in (0.1 mm), then the crankshaft must be reground. Undersize bearings are available to suit the recommended reground diameter, but normally your dealer will supply the correct matching bearings with the reconditioned crankshaft.
3 After a high mileage, the main bearings and the connecting rod bearings may have worn to give an excessive running clearance. The correct running clearance for the different journals is given in the Specifications. The clearance is best checked using a product such as 'Plastigage', as described in Section 38. **Note**: *Never attempt to correct excessive running clearance by filing the caps but always fit new shell bearings, having first checked the crankshaft journals and crankpins for ovality and to establish whether their diameters are of standard or reground sizes.*
4 Checking the connecting rod bearings is carried out in a similar manner to that described for the main bearings. The correct running clearance is given in the Specifications.
5 It is good practice to check the running clearance of rod and main bearings even if new bearings are installed.
6 The crankshaft endplay should be checked by forcing the crankshaft to the extreme front position, then using a feeler gauge at the front end of the center main bearing. Refer to the Specifications for the permissible clearance (photo).
7 The connecting rod side clearance should be measured with a feeler gauge between the connecting rod caps. If the side clearance is outside the specified tolerance, replace the rod assembly. This procedure is detailed in Section 38.

32 Cylinder block – inspection

1 It is important that the cylinder block be inspected carefully and as described. The cylinder block was designed to operate with exacting tolerances, and if the engine is reassembled without first properly inspecting the block, all work and cost involved in the rebuild may be for nothing.
2 Clean the cylinder block as necessary to remove built-up sludge and grime. Clean all excess gasket material from the sealing surfaces.
3 Inspect the cylinder block for cracks in the cylinder walls, water jacket, valve lifter bores and main bearing webs. Use a flashlight where necessary. In most cases, cracks will require that a new engine block be purchased.
4 The cylinder bores must be examined for taper, ovality, scoring and scratches. These checks are important for proper operation of the pistons and piston rings.
5 Scoring and scratches can usually be seen with the naked eye and felt with the fingers. If they are deep, the engine block may have to be replaced with a new one. If the imperfections are slight, a qualified machine shop should be able to hone or bore the cylinders to a larger size.
6 There are two indications for excessive wear of the cylinders. First, if the vehicle was emitting blue smoke from the exhaust system before engine dismantling. This blue smoke is caused by oil seeping past the piston rings due to wear of the cylinder walls. Second, the thickness of the ridge at the top of the cylinder (which may have been removed during piston removal) can give an indication about overall cylinder wear.
7 Using an internal-type dial gauge, measure each bore at three different points (photo). Take a measurement near the top of the bore and then near the bottom of the bore. Finally, measure at the center. Jot down all measurements to determine the taper of the cylinder (slightly larger at the top than the bottom or vice versa).
8 An out-of-round condition can be found in a similar fashion, except measure the cylinder first parallel with the engine centerline and then turn the micrometers until they are perpendicular with the centerline (180 degrees from first measurement).
9 Where the cylinder bores are worn beyond the permitted tolerances as shown in the Specifications Section, the block will have to be replaced with a new one, honed or bored.
10 A final check of the cylinder block would include an inspection for warpage. This is done with a straight edge and feeler gauges in the same manner as for the cylinder heads. The tolerances described in Section 13 also apply to the cylinder block. If warpage is slight, a machine shop can resurface the block.

33 Engine – rebuilding alternatives

1 At this point in the engine rebuilding process the home mechanic is faced with a number of options for completing the overhaul. The decision to replace the cylinder block, piston/rod assemblies and crankshaft depends on a number of factors with the number one consideration being the condition of the cylinder block. Other considerations are: cost, competent machine shop facilities, parts availability, time available to complete the project and experience.
2 Some of the rebuilding alternatives are as follows:

Individual parts – If the inspection procedures prove that the engine block and most engine components are in reusable condition, this may be the most economical alternative. The block, crankshaft and piston/rod assemblies should all be inspected carefully. Even if the block shows little wear, the camshaft bearing bores and cylinder bores should receive a finish hone; both jobs for a machine shop.

Master kit (crankshaft kit) – This rebuild package usually consists of a reground crankshaft and a matched set of pistons and connecting rods. The pistons will come already installed with new piston pins to the connecting rods. Piston rings and the necessary bearings may or may not be included in the kit. These kits are commonly available for standard cylinder bores, as well as for engine blocks which have been bored to a regular oversize.

Short block – A short block consists of a cylinder block with a crankshaft and piston/rod assemblies already installed. All new bearings are incorporated and all clearances will be within tolerances. Depending on where the short block is purchased, a guarantee may be included. The existing camshaft, valve mechanism, cylinder heads and ancillary parts can be bolted to this short block with little or no machine shop work necessary for the engine overhaul.

Long block – A long block consists of a short block plus oil pump, oil pan, cylinder head, valve cover, camshaft and valve mechanism, camshaft gear, timing chain and front cover. All components are installed with new bearings, seals and gaskets incorporated throughout. The installation of manifolds and ancillary parts is all that is necessary. Some form of guarantee is usually included with purchase.

3 Give careful though to which method is best for your situation and discuss the alternatives with local machine shop owners, parts dealers or Datsun dealership partsmen.

34 Engine overhaul – general assembly information

1 Before assembling any parts to the engine block, the block should have all necessary machine work completed and the engine block should be thoroughly cleaned. If machine work was performed, chances are that the block was hot-tanked afterwards to remove all traces of the machine cuttings.
2 The oil galleys and water passages of the block should also be thoroughly clean and free from dirt or machining leftovers. It's good practice to install new freeze plugs in the engine whenever it is stripped for a total overhaul. These plugs are difficult to replace once the engine has been assembled. These plugs are difficult to replace once the engine has been assembled and installed. If the engine was sent out for machine work and hot-tanking, it may be best to let the machine shop remove and install new plugs. If they are to be done at home, proceed as follows:

(a) Use a hammer and punch to press one side of the plug into the block.
(b) Use pliers to pry the old freeze plug out of its recess
(c) Place a suitable replacement plug into position and hammer into place until flush with the engine block. Special installation tools are available for pressing the plug into place, however a suitable sized socket will work fine.

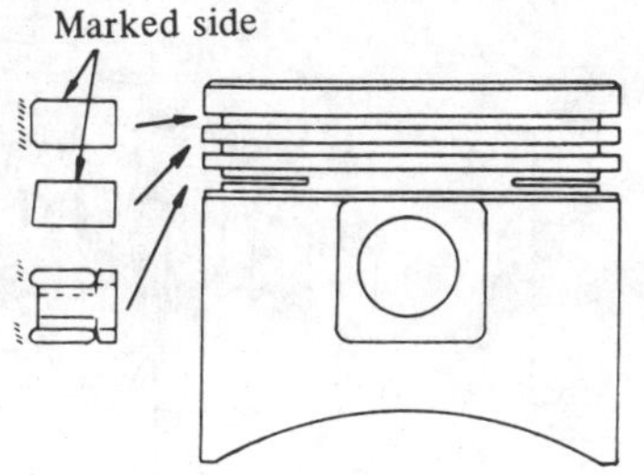

Fig. 2.22 Be sure the three piston rings are installed as shown (Sec 35)

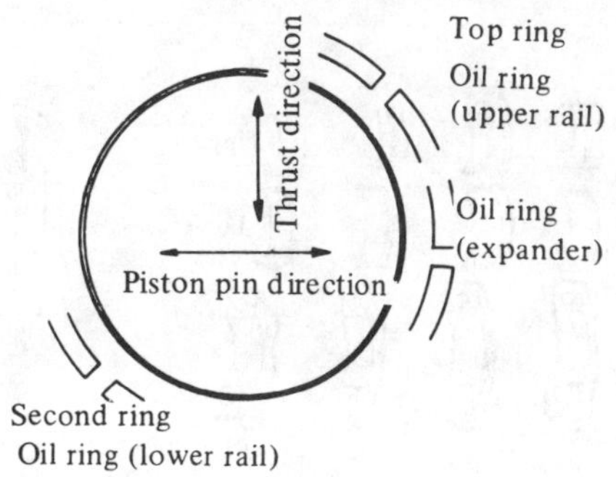

Fig. 2.23 To ensure there are not compression leaks, the gaps of the three piston rings should be positioned as shown (Sec 35)

3 Clean and examine all bolts, nuts and fasteners. Replace any that are damaged.
4 Clean and cover all engine components to keep dirt and dust away from them until they can be installed.
5 Have assembly grease and an oil can filled with engine oil handy to lubricate parts as they are installed.
6 Lay out all necessary tools and a reliable torque wrench on a clean work table for easy retrieval.
7 New gaskets and seals must be used throughout. These are commonly available together in a master rebuild gasket set.
8 In almost all cases, parts to be replaced during a major overhaul include: connecting rod bearings, main bearings, piston rings, timing chain, spark plugs and oil filter. These are in addition to any parts found damaged or excessively worn during dismantling or the various inspection processes.
9 After the crankshaft, piston/rod assemblies and the various associated bearings have been installed in the engine block, the remainder of the components (cylinder head, oil pump, camshaft, etc.,) can be installed following the installation procedures located in the various Sections of this Chapter.
10 Follow the engine disassembly sequence in the reverse order of installation, using new gaskets where necessary.

35 Pistons and piston rings – assembly

1 The piston should be attached to its appropriate connecting rod. As mentioned previously, this is a job for a professional equipped with the proper supports and an arbor press.
2 The new piston rings should be comparable in size to the piston being used.
3 The installation of the piston rings on the piston is critical to the overall performance of the rebuilt engine.
4 Measure the ring end gap of each ring before it is installed in the piston. This is done as follows:

(a) *Arrange the piston rings into sets for each piston. The set will contain a top ring, 2nd ring and a 3 piece oil control ring (2 rails and a spacer).*
(b) *Slip a top ring into the appropriate cylinder bore. Push the ring into the cylinder bore about $\frac{1}{4}$-inch below the upper limit of ring travel (a total of about 1 inch below block deck). Push the ring down into position with the top of a piston to make sure the ring is square with the cylinder wall.*
(c) *Using a feeler gauge, measure the gap between the ends of the ring (photo). If the gap is less than specified (see Specifications), remove the ring and try another top ring for fit.*
(d) *Check all top rings in the same manner and if necessary use a fine file to remove a slight amount of material from the ends of the ring(s). If inadequate end gap is used, the rings will break during operation.*
(e) *Measure the end gap of each 2nd ring and oil control ring as described above.*

5 Check the fit of each piston ring into its groove by holding the ring next to the piston and then placing the outer surface of the ring into its respective groove. Roll the ring entirely around the piston and check for any binding. If the binding is due to a distorted ring, replace the ring with a new one. Perform this check for the top and 2nd rings of each piston.
6 Install the piston rings as follows:

(a) *Study the accompanying figure thoroughly to understand exactly where each ring gap should be located in relation to*

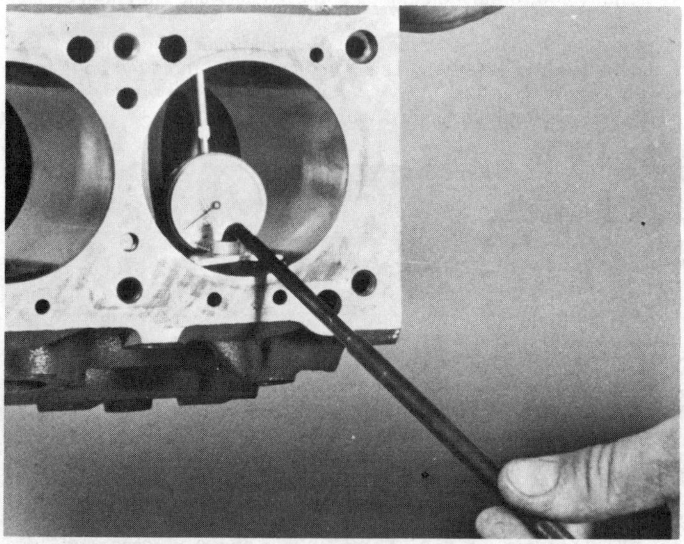

32.7 An internal-type dial gauge should be used to measure the taper and out of round dimensions of the cylinder bores

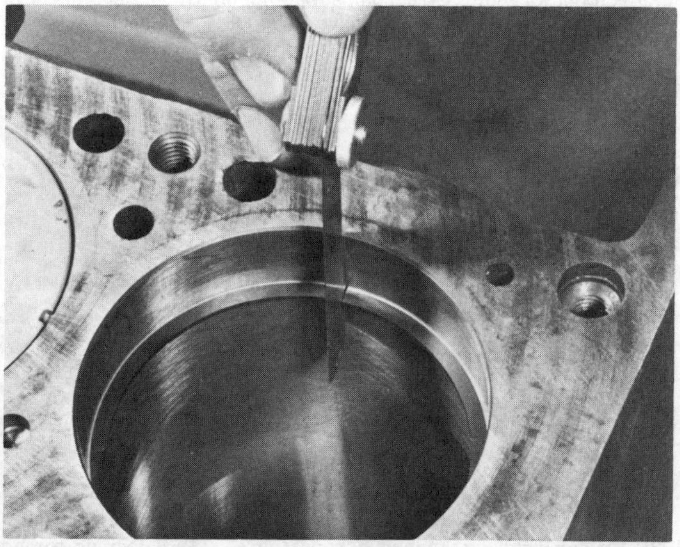

35.4 Prior to installing the piston rings, the ring end gap should be measured as shown

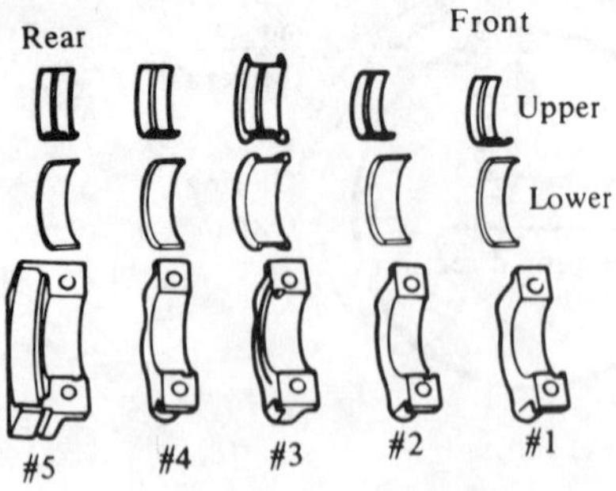

Fig. 2.24 When installing the main bearings, be sure they are positioned in their proper places, as several different types are used (Sec 36)

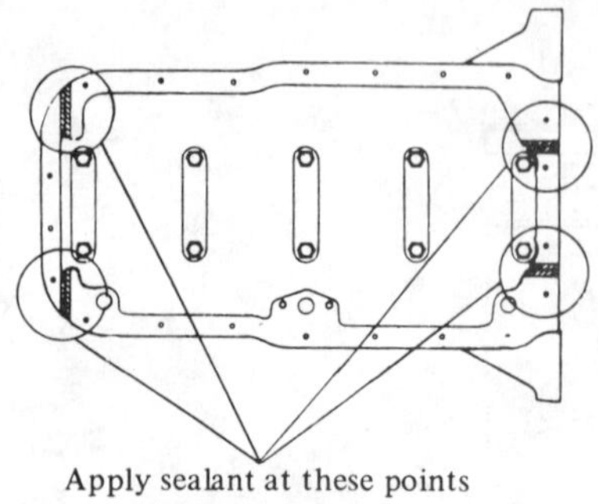

Fig. 2.25 Silicone sealant should be applied at the front cover and rear bearing cap as shown (Sec 36)

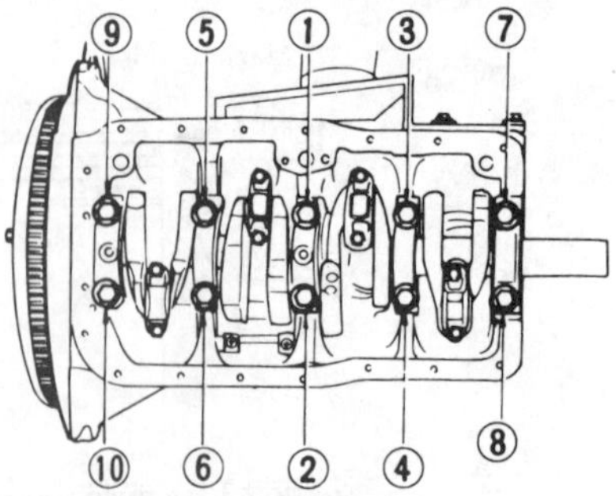

Fig. 2.26 The main bearing cap bolts should be tightened evenly in the sequence shown above (Sec 36)

the piston and other rings. The location of each ring gap is important.

(b) *If a piston ring expander tool is available, use this to install the rings. If not, small lengths of tin can be used to prevent the rings from entering the wrong groove (see Section 28 on piston ring removal).*

(c) *Install the bottom oil ring spacer in its groove and insert the anti-rotation tang in the oil hole. Hold the spacer ends butted and install the lower steel oil ring rail with the gap properly located. Install the upper steel oil ring rail and properly set its gap. Flex or squeeze the oil ring assembly to make sure it is free in the groove. If not, dress the groove with a file or replace the oil control ring assembly as necessary.*

(d) *Install the end ring and properly locate its gap.*

(e) *Install the top ring with gap properly positioned.*

(f) *Repeat the above procedures for all piston assemblies.*

7 Proper clearance of the piston rings in their grooves is very important. Clearance between the ring and its groove is checked with a blade feeler gauge, sliding the appropriately sized feeler gauge (see Specifications) between the top of the ring and the inside of the groove. Rotate the feeler blades all the way around the piston, checking for proper clearance. Replace rings or clean and dress the groove as necessary for proper clearance.

36 Crankshaft and main bearings – installation

1 Install the main bearing shells into their recesses in the crankcase, with the oil holes in correct alignment (photo). Be sure each bearing is in its proper location (see accompanying figure). Upper bearings have oil grooves, while the lower bearings are smooth. The center bearings are the only flanged ones. The number 2 and 4 bearings are the same type, while the number 1 and 5 bearings are also the same type.

2 Install the baffle plate and mesh block which are components of the crankcase ventilation system (emission control).

3 Oil the main bearing shells liberally with clean engine oil and lower the crankshaft into position in the crankcase.

4 Install each of the main bearing caps, complete with shell bearings, ensuring that they are replaced in their original locations with the arrows pointing towards the front of the engine. The center shell bearing has integral thrust segments with oil grooves.

5 The corners of the rear main bearing cap should have an application of jointing compound at the points indicated.

6 Tighten the main bearing cap bolts progressively and in the order shown to the specified torque.

7 When installation is complete, check that the crankshaft turns smoothly and the endfloat is as previously established (Section 25).

8 Apply jointing compound to the rear main bearing cap side seals and tap them into position (photo).

9 Grease the crankshaft rear oil seal and tap it into position using a piece of tubing as a drift (see Section 23).

10 Bolt on the engine rear endplate.

11 Locate the flywheel on the crankshaft rear flange and tighten the bolts to the specified torque.

37 Pistons, connecting rods and bearings – installation

1 With the pistons complete with piston rings and connecting rods, they can be installed in the engine.

2 Make sure the cylinder bores are perfectly clean. Wipe the cylinder walls several times with a light engine oil and a clean, lint-free cloth.

3 Lubricate the connecting rod bearings and install them into their appropriate rod and rod cap.

4 Lightly coat the pistons, rings and cylinder walls with light engine oil.

5 Install a length of rubber or plastic tubing over the connecting rod studs on one rod assembly. This will prevent the threaded bolts from possibly damaging the cylinder wall or crankshaft journal as the piston/rod assembly is pushed into place.

36.1 When installing the main bearings, be sure the oil holes line up with those in the block

36.8 Jointing compound should be applied to the rear main bearing cap side seals prior to installing them

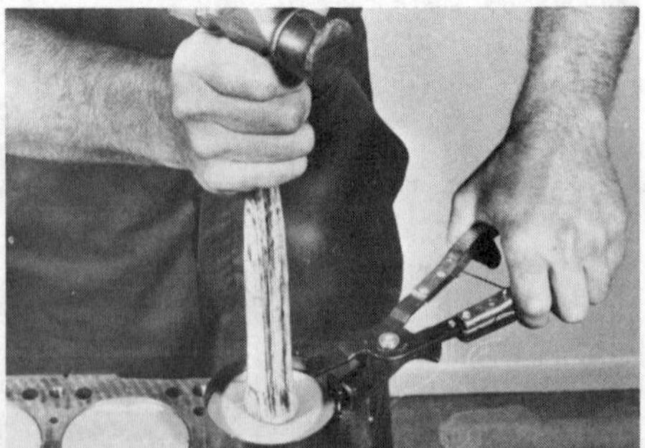

37.8 Using a piston ring compressor and tapping with a wooden hammer handle is the easiest method of installing the pistons

6 Check that all the piston ring gaps are positioned properly (see Section 35).
7 Check that the piston/rod assembly is properly positioned. Most pistons will be marked with an 'F' or a drilled-out area indicating the piston should be installed with these marks toward the front of the engine. The oil hole in the connecting rod should also be toward the right side of the engine.
8 Place a piston ring compressor around the piston, with the base of the compressor flush with the cylinder block. Tighten the compressor until the rings are flush with the piston surface and then push the piston assembly into the bore. A wooden hammer handle can be used to tap the top of the piston slightly (photo). Hold the ring compressor solidly against the cylinder block until all rings are inside the bore. Continue pushing until the connecting rod is near to its installed position.
9 Ensure that all bearing surfaces and the crankshaft journal are coated with engine oil and remove the tubing protector pieces. Install the connecting rod bearing cap (with bearing) to the connecting rod. The cylinder number on the cap should be on the same side as the number on the rod.
10 Torque the nuts to specifications.
11 Repeat this procedure for all cylinders, using the rubber or plastic tubing on each assembly to prevent damage as the pistons are pushed into place. Rotate the crankshaft as necessary to make the connecting rod nuts accessible for tightening.

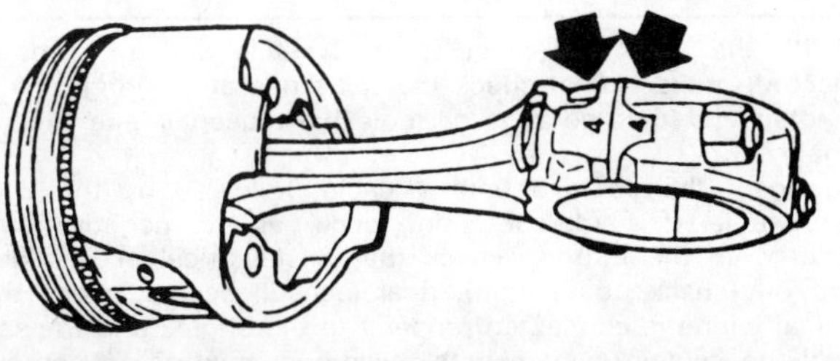

Fig. 2.27 When installed, the number on the connecting rod bearing cap should be on the same side as the number on the rod (Sec 37)

38 Bearings (main and rod) – checking clearance

Note: *There are three precautions to take when working with Plastigage. These are:*

(a) Plastigage is soluble in oil, so all oil and grease should be removed from the crankshaft and bearing surfaces while the testing is done.
(b) Do not rotate the crankshaft while the Plastigage is installed in the engine, as this may cause damage to the crankshaft or engine surfaces.
(c) Remove all traces of the Plastigage when testing is complete. Be very careful not to harm the crankshaft or bearing surfaces as the Plastigage is removed. Do not use sharp tools or abrasive cleaners; instead, remove the used Plastigage with your fingernail or a blunt wood stick.

1 Whenever an engine is overhauled the bearing clearances should be checked. This should be done for reused bearings as well as for new bearings.
2 The procedure is basically the same for both the main bearings and the connecting rod bearings.
3 With the crankshaft set into the engine block, install the main bearings into the engine block and the main bearing caps.
4 Remove all oil, grime and foreign matter from the crankshaft and bearing surfaces.
5 Place a piece of Plastigage (available at most auto supply shops) along the length of each main bearing journal on the crankshaft.
6 Install each main bearing cap and tighten the attaching bolts to specification. The arrow on each cap should face toward the front of the engine.
7 Now remove each bearing cap and measure the width of the Plastigage strip which will have flattened out when the caps were tightened. A scale is provided on the Plastigage envelope for measuring the width of the Plastigage strip, and thus, bearing clearance (see accompanying figure).

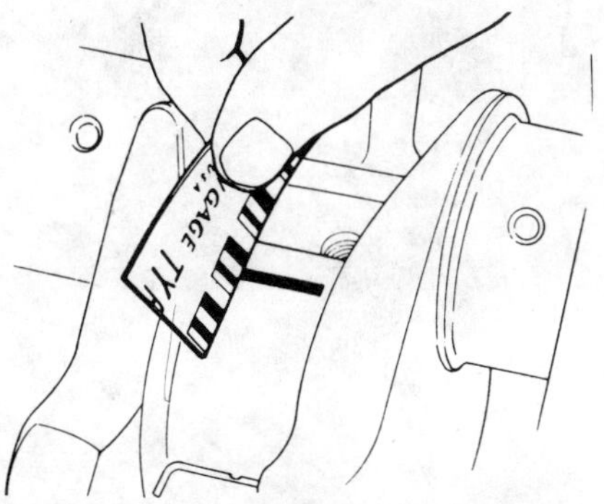

Fig. 2.28 Using Plastigage is the easiest method of measuring the main and connecting rod bearing clearances (Sec 38)

8 If the Plastigage is flattened more at the ends than in the middle, or vice versa, this is an indication of journal taper which can be checked in the Specifications Section.
9 To test for an out-of-round condition, remove all traces of the Plastigage (be careful not to damage the crankshaft or bearing surfaces) and rotate the crankshaft 90 degrees. With the crankshaft rotated to this point, use the Plastigage to check the clearances again. Compare these measurements with those taken previously to arrive at eccentricity or out of round.
10 To check connecting rod bearing clearances, install each piston/rod assembly (Section 37) and use the Plastigage as described above.
11 Connecting rod side clearance can also be checked at this time. Side clearance can be checked with the piston/rod assemblies temporarily installed for bearing clearance checking.
12 With the piston/rod assemblies installed and the bearing caps tightened to specifications, use feeler gauges to check the clearance between the sides of the connecting rods and the crankshaft.
13 If the clearance at this point is below the minimum tolerance, the rod may be machined for more clearance at this area.
14 If the clearance is too excessive, a new rod must be used or the crankshaft must be reground or replaced with a new one.
15 If the bearings have shown to be within all tolerances, they may be installed following the steps outlined in the appropriate sections.
16 If not within specifications, the bearings should be replaced with the correctly sized bearings. Upper and lower bearings should always be replaced as a unit.

39 Engine – installation

1 If the engine has been completely stripped for overhaul, it should be assembled outside of the car to the point shown in the accompanying photos.
2 Loosely bolt the left engine mounting bracket to the cylinder block.
3 If the engine has been worked on while on an engine stand, remove it from the stand and lower it onto a wooden skid or the floor.
4 If not already done, install the rear plate and flywheel.
5 If equipped with a manual transmission, install the clutch disc and cover assembly. Be sure to use a centering tool to center the clutch disc before fully tightening the cover assembly bolts. A ratchet wrench extension and a suitable sized socket will serve as a makeshift centering tool.
6 Carefully mate the transmission with the engine by reversing the separation steps described in Section 26. This is most easily done with the transmission on a rolling-type floor jack.
7 Install the starter. Refer to Chapter 5, if necessary.
8 Install the engine gussets to the engine and transmission.
9 Connect an engine hoist to the engine and lift it up. The chains should be positioned as during removal, with the engine/transmission sitting as level as possible. The fenders and radiator support should be covered with pads to protect them.
10 Carefully lower the rear of the transmission into the engine compartment. As you gradually lower it, also move the hoist rearward. Closely watch the clearances on all sides as the assembly is lowered.

39.1a State of engine assembly prior to installation in car (front view)

39.1b State of engine assembly prior to installation in car (left side view)

39.1c State of engine assembly prior to installation in car (right side view)

11 When the engine/transmission assembly is in position, loosely install the transmission support bracket to the transmission and to the body.
12 Lower the engine so that the left engine mounting bracket fits over the mounting insulator stud and loosely install the mounting nut.
13 Fit the right mounting bracket into position on its mounting insulator and bolt it to the engine block. Install the nut on the mounting stud.
14 Tighten all engine and transmission mounting bolts.
15 Disconnect the engine hoist from the engine.
16 Install the remaining components and make all connections in the reverse order of the removal procedure. Do not connect the battery yet.
17 See Section 40 for the starting-up procedure.

40 Engine start-up (following overhaul)

1 With the engine in place in the vehicle and all components connected, make a final check that all pipes and wiring have been connected and that no rags or tools have been left in the engine compartment.
2 Connect the positive battery cable, followed by the negative battery cable. If sparks or arcing occur as the negative cable is connected to the battery, check that all electrical accessories are turned off (check dome light). If arcing still occurs, check that all electrical wiring is connected properly to the engine and transaxle.
3 Fill the cooling system with the proper mixture and amount of water and antifreeze.
4 Fill the engine with the proper quantity and grade of oil.
5 Fill the transmission with the proper quantity and grade of fluid.
6 Check the tension of all drivebelts.
7 Disconnect the ignition coil wire(s) from the distributor cap and ground them on the engine.
8 Now crank the engine over for about 15 to 30 seconds. This will allow the oil pump to distribute oil and the fuel pump to start pumping fuel.
9 Now reconnect the ignition coil wire(s) to the distributor cap and start the engine. Immediately check all gauges and warning lights for proper readings, and check for leaks of coolant or oil.
10 If the engine does not start immediately, check to make sure fuel is reaching the injectors. This may take a while.
11 After allowing the engine to run for a few minutes at low speed, turn it off and recheck the oil and coolant levels.
12 Start the engine again and check the ignition timing and idle speed. Refer to Chapter 1.
13 Finally, while the engine is thoroughly warmed up, recheck the valve clearances to make sure they correspond with the hot engine specs.
14 Run the vehicle easily during the first 500 to 1000 miles (break-in period), then check the torque settings on all major engine components, particularly the cylinder heads. Tighten any bolts which may have loosened.

Chapter 3 Cooling, heating and air conditioning systems

Contents

Air conditioning compressor – removal and installation 16
Air conditioning system – checks and maintenance 15
Air conditioning system – general information 14
Antifreeze and inhibiting solutions 2
Blower unit – removal and installation 13
Condenser – removal and installation 17
Cooling system – checking and servicing 3
Cooling system – general information 1
Fan – removal and installation 7
Heater/a/c control assembly – removal and installation 11
Heater unit – removal and installation 12
Heating system – general information 10
Radiator – removal and installation 5
Reservoir tank – removal and installation 6
Thermostat – removal and installation 4
Water pump – removal and installation 9
Water pump – testing 8

Specifications

Radiator

Cap relief pressure	0.9 kg/cm² (13 psi)
Leakage test pressure	1.6 kg/cm² (23 psi)

Thermostat

Type	Wax pellet
Opening temperature	180°F (standard type) 190°F (frigid type) 170°F (tropical type)

A/C compressor

Type	swash plate
Model	SWP167
Displacement	167 cm³ (10.19 cu in)
Direction of rotation	clockwise
Drive belt type	A type

Refrigerant

Type	R-12
Capacity	0.9-1.1kg (2.0-2.4 lb)

Lubricating oil

Type	SUNISO 5GS or equivalent
Capacity	270 ml (9.1 fl oz)

Torque specifications

Torque specifications	mkg	ft-lbs
Water pump mounting bolts (small)	0.7	5.0
Water pump mounting bolts (large)	1.3	10.0
A/C compressor bracket mounting bolts	5.0	37.0
A/C compressor mounting bolts	5.0	37.0

1 Cooling system – general information

The cooling system comprises the radiator, top and bottom water hoses, water pump, cylinder and block water jackets, radiator cap with pressure relief valve and flow and return heater hoses. The thermostat is located in a recess at the front of the cylinder head. The principle of the system is that cold water in the bottom of the radiator circulates upwards through the lower radiator hose to the water pump, where the pump impeller pushes the water round the cylinder block and head through the various cast-in passages to cool the cylinder bores, combustion surfaces and valve seats. When sufficient heat has been absorbed by the cooling water, and the engine has reached an efficient working temperature, the water moves from the cylinder head past the new open thermostat into the top radiator hose and into the radiator header tank.

The water then travels down the radiator tubes when it is rapidly cooled by the in-rush of air, when the vehicle is in forward motion. A multi-bladed fan, mounted on the water pump pulley, assists this cooling action. The water, now cooled, reaches the bottom of the radiator and the cycle is repeated.

When the engine is cold the thermostat remains closed until the coolant reaches a pre-determined temperature (see the Specifications). This assists rapid warming-up.

The system is pressurized by means of a spring-loaded radiator filler cap which prevents premature boiling by increasing the boiling

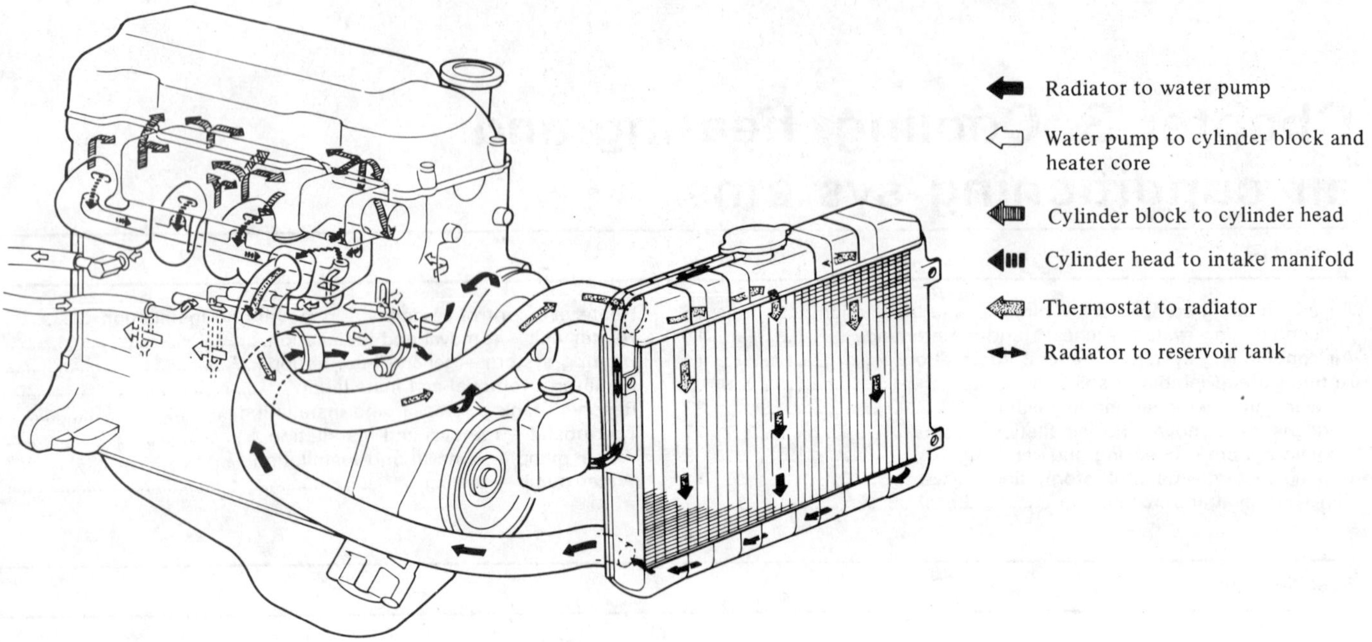

Fig. 3.1 Coolant flow within the cooling system

point of the coolant. If the coolant temperature goes above this increased boiling point, the extra pressure in the system forces the radiator cap internal spring-loaded valve off its seat and exposes the overflow pipe down which displaced coolant escapes.

It is important to check that the radiator cap is in good condition and that the spring behind the sealing washer has not weakened or corroded. Most service stations have a machine for testing that the cap operates at the specified pressure.

The coolant recovery system consists of a plastic reservoir into which the overflow coolant from the radiator flows when the engine is hot. When the engine cools and the coolant contracts, coolant is drawn back into the radiator from the reservoir and thus maintains the system at full capacity.

The coolant level should be kept between the MIN and MAX marks on the recovery bottle.

An electrosensitive capsule located in the cylinder head measures the water temperature.

The cooling system also provides the heat for the car interior heater and heats the inlet manifold.

On vehicles equipped with automatic transmission, the transmission fluid is cooled by a cooler attached to the base of the radiator.

On cars equipped with air conditioning systems, a condenser is placed ahead of the radiator and is bolted in conjunction with it.

The radiator cooling fan incorporates either a fluid coupling or a fluid/temperature controlled coupling. The latter device comprises an oil operated clutch and is a coiled bi-metallic thermostat which functions jointly to permit the fan to slip when the engine is below normal operating temperature level and does not require the supplementary air flow provided by the fan at normal running speed.

At higher engine operating temperature, the fan is locked and rotates at the speed of the water pump pulley. The fan coupling is a sealed unit and requires no periodic maintenance.

Note: *If the radiator cap has to be removed when the engine is hot, rotate the cap slowly counterclockwise to the detent and allow the residual pressure to escape. Do not press the cap down until any hissing has stopped and take extreme care that the hands are not scalded.*

2 Antifreeze and inhibiting solutions

1 It is recommended that the cooling system be filled with a water/ethylene glycol based antifreeze solution which will give protection down to at least –20°F at all times. This provides protection against corrosion and increases the coolant boiling point. When handling antifreeze, take care that it is not spilled on the vehicle paintwork, since it will invariably cause damage if not removed immediately.

2 The cooling system should be drained, flushed and refilled at least every alternate Fall. The use of antifreeze solutions for periods of longer than two years is likely to cause damage and encourage the formation of rust and scale due to the corrosion inhibitors gradually losing their efficiency.

3 Before adding antifreeze to the system, check all hose connections and check the tightness of the cylinder head bolts as such solutions are searching.

4 The exact mixture of antifreeze to water which you should use depends upon the relative weather conditions. The mixture should contain at least 50 percent antifreeze, offering protection to –34°F. Under no circumstances should the mixture contain more than 70 percent antifreeze.

3 Cooling system – checking and servicing

1 Since checking and servicing of the cooling system is included in the routine maintenance schedule for this car, these procedures are included in Chapter 1.

4 Thermostat – removal and installation

1 The thermostat is basically a restriction valve which is actuated by a heat sensitive element. It is mounted inside a housing on the right side of the engine and is designed to open and close at predetermined temperatures to allow coolant to warm up or cool the engine.

2 To remove the thermostat for replacement or testing, begin by draining the coolant until the upper level of the coolant in the radiator is below the inner grille.

3 Remove the upper radiator hose.

4 Remove the 2 bolts that retain the thermostat cover (photo).

5 Lift off the cover along with the gasket and thermostat. Note how the thermostat is positioned in its recess, as it must be replaced in this same position (photos).

6 Before installation, use a gasket scraper or putty knife to carefully

4.4 The thermostat and cover are located on the right side of the engine and connect with the upper radiator hose

4.5a The thermostat, cover and gasket are removed together

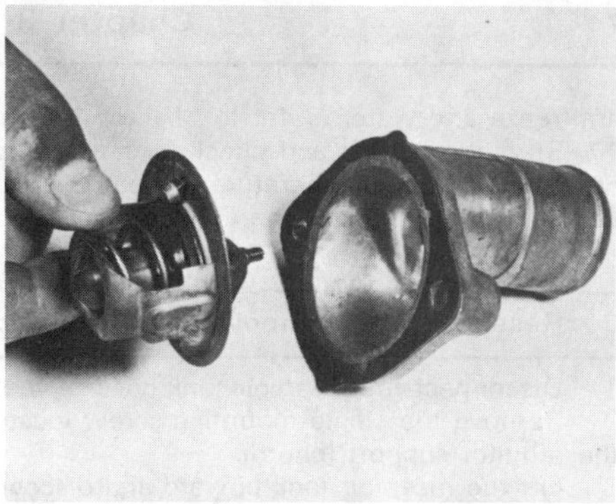

4.5b The thermostat must be installed as shown for it to operate properly

remove all traces of the old gasket on the thermostat housing and the cover.

7 Place a thin bead of silicone sealant around the sealing surface on the thermostat cover.

8 Place a new gasket in position on the cover.

9 Place the thermostat in position in the cover and carefully install the entire assembly onto the housing, torquing the bolts to specifications.

10 Reinstall the upper radiator hose.

11 Refill the radiator with the proper mixture of antifreeze and water. Refer to Chapter 1 if necessary.

12 With the radiator cap removed, start the engine and run it until the upper radiator hose becomes hot. At this point, the thermostat would be in the open position. Check the coolant level and add as necessary.

13 Reinstall the radiator cap.

5 Radiator – removal and installation

1 Open the drain valve on the under side of the radiator and drain the coolant into a container.

2 Remove the upper radiator hose.

3 Remove the lower radiator hose.

4 Remove the air cleaner inlet duct.

5 Remove the bolts and loosen all the clamps at the locations indicated by arrows in photo 5.5.

6 Remove the air duct, upper bracket and boots.

7 Remove the lower air duct bracket from the fan shroud (photo).

8 Disconnect the reservoir bottle hose from the radiator spout.

9 Remove the 4 screws that retain the shroud to the radiator and slide the shroud toward the engine.

10 If equipped with an automatic transmission, disconnect the cooler hoses from the radiator.

11 Remove the 4 screws that attach the radiator to the body.

12 Lift out the radiator.

13 With the radiator removed, it can be inspected for leaks or damage. If in need of repairs, have a professional radiator shop or dealer perform the work as special welding techniques are required.

14 Bugs and dirt can be cleaned from the radiator by using compressed air and a soft brush. Do not bend the cooling fins as this is done.

15 Installation is the reverse of the removal procedure.

16 After installation, fill the cooling system with the proper mixture of

5.5 The air duct, rubber boots and brackets must be removed in order to remove the radiator

5.7 Removing the lower air duct bracket

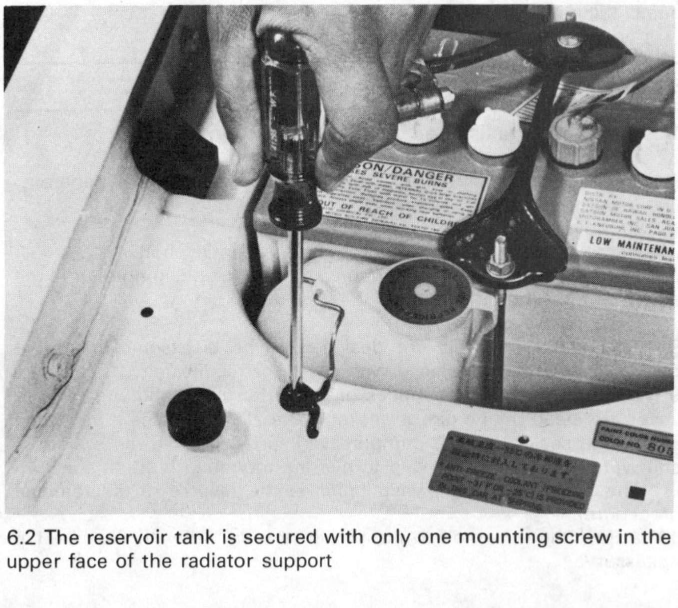

6.2 The reservoir tank is secured with only one mounting screw in the upper face of the radiator support

antifreeze and water. Refer to Chapter 1 if necessary.
17 Start the engine and check for leaks. Allow the engine to reach normal operating temperature, indicated by the upper radiator hose becoming hot. Recheck the coolant level and add more if required.

6 Reservoir tank – removal and installation

1 Disconnect the reservoir tank hose at the radiator neck (photo).
2 Remove the single mounting screw located on the upper side of the radiator support (photo).
3 Lift the reservoir tank upward and disconnect the wiring connector.
4 With your finger over the end of the hose to prevent leakage of the coolant, lift the tank from the engine compartment.
5 Drain the coolant from the tank into a container. If the tank is being replaced, disconnect the hose from the bottom of the tank.
6 Installation is the reverse of the removal procedure.
7 Refill the tank with the proper mixture of antifreeze and water. Refer to Chapter 1 if necessary.

7 Fan – removal and installation

1 Remove the radiator as described in Section 5.
2 Remove the radiator shroud.
3 Remove the 4 screws that retain the fan to the water pump and lift off the fan.
4 Installation is the reverse of the removal procedure.

8 Water pump – testing

1 A failure in the water pump can cause serious engine damage due to overloading. The pump will not be able to circulate cooled water through the engine.
2 There are three ways to check the operation of the water pump while it is still installed on the engine. If the pump is suspect, it should be replaced with a new or factory rebuilt engine.
3 With the engine warmed up to normal operating temperature, squeeze the upper radiator hose. If the water pump is working properly, a pressure surge should be felt as the hose is released.
4 Water pumps are equippped with weep or vent holes, if a failure occurs to the bladder of the pump, small amounts of water will leak from these weep holes. In most cases it will be necessary to use a flashlight from under the car to see evidence from this point in the pump body.
5 If the water pump shaft bearings fail there may be a squealing sound at the front of the engine while it is running. Shaft wear can be felt if the water pump pulley is forced up and down. Do not mistake drivebelt slippage, which also causes a squealing sound, for water pump failure.

9 Water pump – removal and installation

1 Remove the radiator as described in Section 5.
2 Remove the fan as described in Section 7.
3 Loosen the generator adjusting bolt and remove the generator water pump fan belt.
4 Remove the generator bracket (photo).
5 Remove the single large water pump mounting bolt.
6 Loosen the remaining water pump mounting bolts (photo) until the pump can be lifted off (photo).
7 Remove the gasket.
8 This water pump is not designed to be disassembled, and if defective, should be replaced with a new or rebuilt unit.
9 Be sure the sealing surfaces of the water pump and engine front cover are clean of any dirt or gasket material. Then place a thin bead of silicone sealant on the pump sealing surface. While the sealant is still wet, install the pump and torque the mounting bolts to specs.
10 The remainder of the installation is the reverse of the removal procedure.
11 Adjust the drive belt to the proper tension. Refer to Chapter 1 if necessary.

9.4 Removing the generator bracket

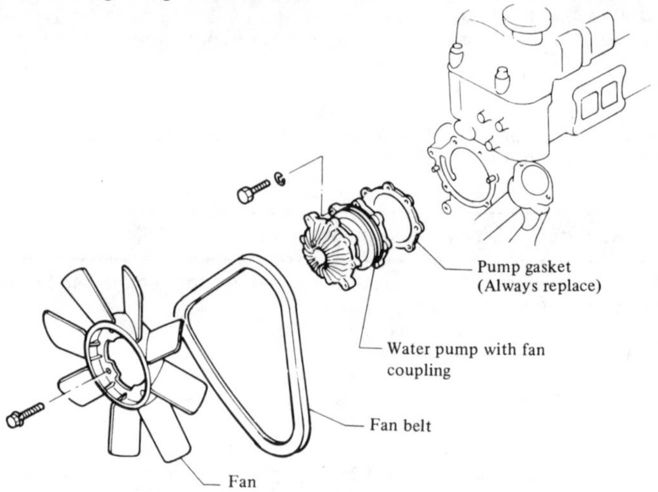

Fig. 3.2 Exploded view of the fan, fan belt and water pump (Sec 7 and 9)

12 Fill the cooling system with the proper mixture of antifreeze and water, again referring to Chapter 1 if necessary. Then start the engine and allow it to idle until it reaches normal operating temperature. This is indicated by the upper radiator hose becoming hot. Check around the water pump and radiator for any leaks.
13 Recheck the coolant level and add more if necessary.

10 Heating system – general information

The main components of the heating system include the heater unit (which contains the heater core and cable-operated valves) the blower motor, the control assembly (mounted in the dash) and the air ducts which deliver the air to the various outlet locations.

Either outside air or interior (recirculated) air (depending on the settings) is drawn into the system through the blower unit. From there the blower motor forces the air into the heater unit. The lever settings on the control assembly operate the valves in the heater unit, which determines the mix of heated and ambient air by regulating how much air is passed through the heater core. The hotter the setting the more air is passed through the core.

The air ducts carry the heated air from the heater unit to the desired location. Again, valves within the duct system regulate where in the car the air will be delivered.

The heater core is heated by engine coolant passing through it. The heater hoses carry the coolant from the engine to the heater core and then back again.

9.6a The water pump is attached by 2 large and 3 small mounting bolts

9.6b The small water pump mounting bolts need only be loosened to remove the pump

11 Heater/a/c control assembly – removal and installation

1 Refer to Chapter 10, Section 24.

12 Heater unit – removal and installation

1 Set the temperature lever on the heater control panel to the maximum bolt position.

2 Open the drain plug on the bottom of the radiator and drain the coolant.

3 Disconnect the heater hoses from the heater unit from inside the engine compartment.

4 Remove the front seats as described in Chapter 12, Section 27.

5 Remove the center console cluster as described in Chapter 10, Section 23.

6 Remove the heater/air conditioning control assembly as described in Chapter 10, Section 24.

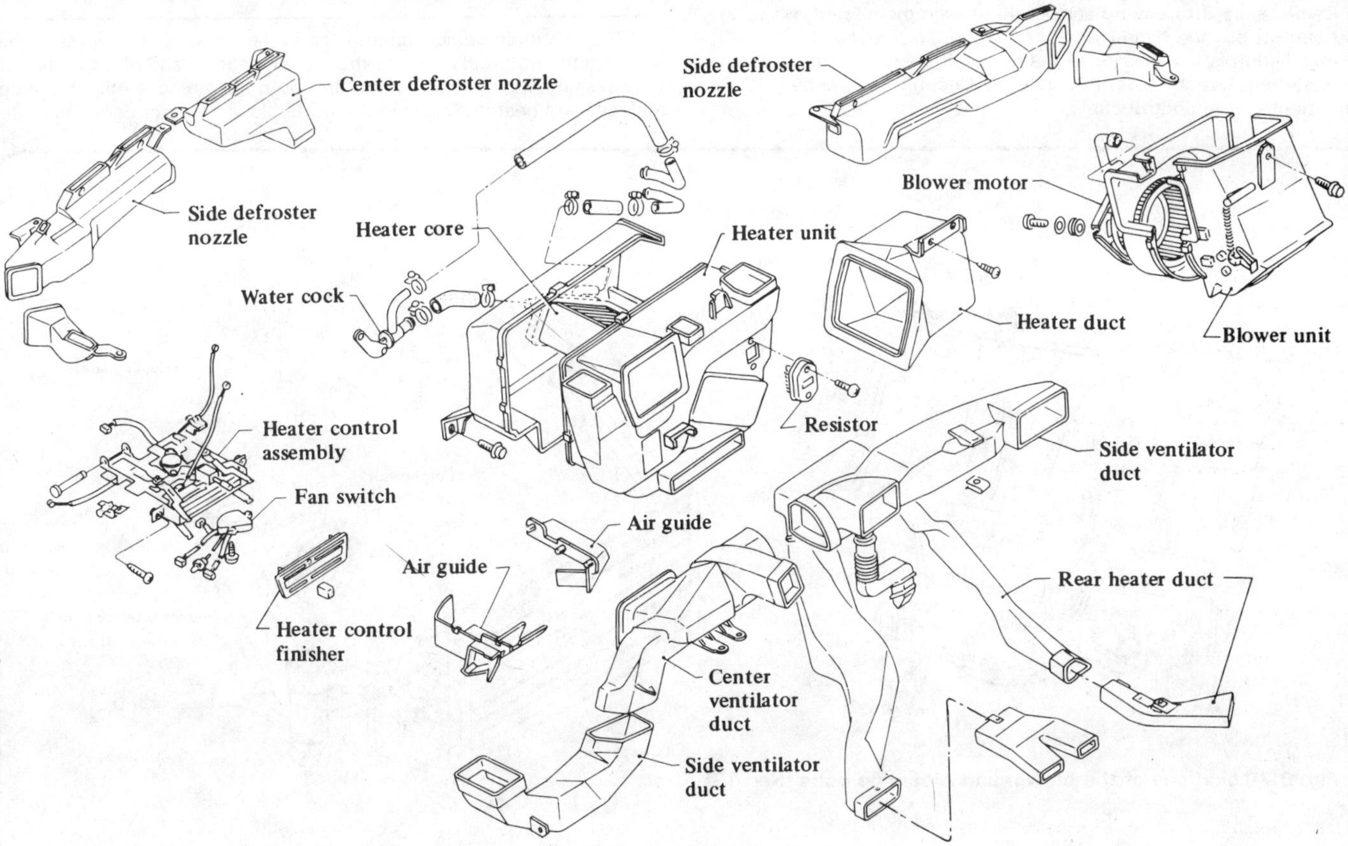

Fig. 3.3 Components of the heating system (Sec 10)

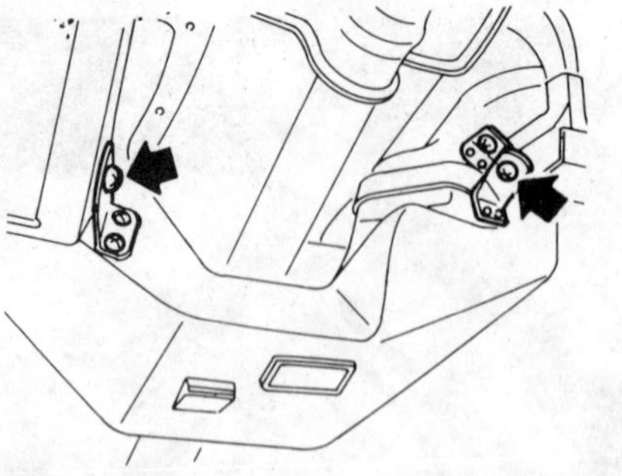

Fig. 3.4 Mounting screw locations of the left side vent ventilator duct (Sec 12)

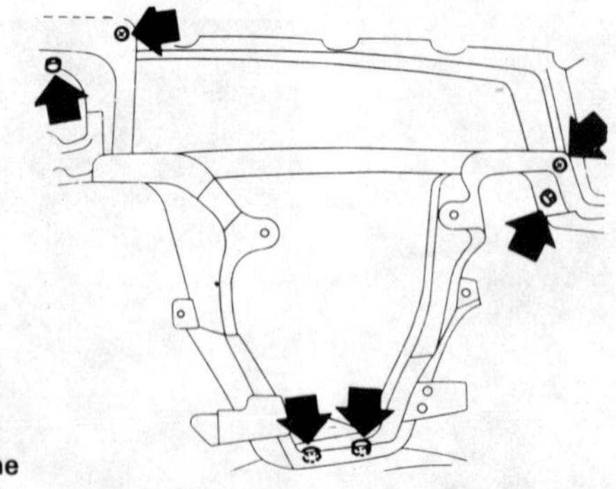

Fig. 3.5 Locations of the bolts securing the center section of the instrument panel frame (Sec 12)

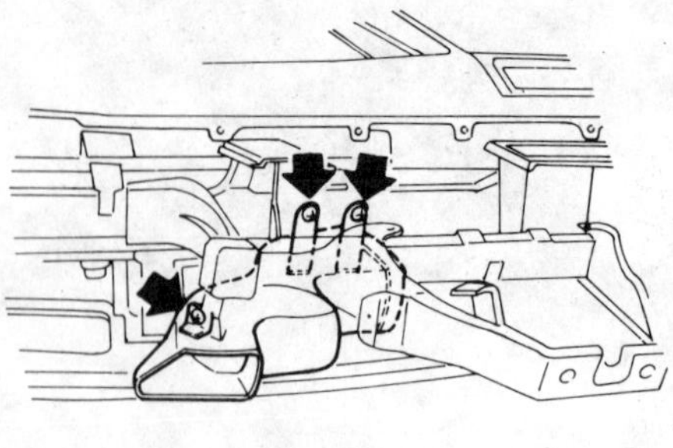

Fig. 3.6 Location of the center ventilator duct (Sec 12)

7 Remove the radio as described in Chapter 10, Section 28.
8 Remove the console box as described in Chapter 10, Section 22.
9 Remove the metal kick plates along both front doors.
10 Peel back the carpet so the rear heater ducts are fully exposed.
11 Remove the left lower instrument cover located directly below the steering column.
12 Remove the right lower panel located below the glove box.
13 Remove the side ventilator duct on the left side. See Figure 3.4.
14 Remove the center section of the instrument panel frame. It is secured by 6 mounting screws. See Figure 3.5.
15 Remove the rear heater ducts.
16 Remove the center ventilator duct. See Figure 3.6.
17 Remove the air guides located at the lower outlets of the heater unit.
18 Disconnect any wiring harness connectors leading to or mounted to the heater unit.
19 Remove the 3 mounting screws that retain the heater unit to the dash and lift out the heater unit.
20 Installation is the reverse of the removal procedure. For installing the heater/a/c control assembly, refer to Chapter 10, Section 25 for adjustment of the control cables.

13 Blower unit – removal and installation

1 Remove the 5 screws that retain the right lower dash panel to the dash. Disconnect the air duct from the rear side of the panel and lift it off.
2 Remove the end cluster lid from the right side of the dash.
3 Disconnect the intake door control cable from the blower unit.
4 Disconnect the blower unit electrical harness.
5 Remove the blower unit.
6 Installation is the reverse of the removal procedure. Following installation, adjust the intake door control cable as described in Chapter 10, Section 24.

14 Air conditioning system – general information

The air conditioning system used in the Datsum 200SX maintains proper temperature by cycling the compressor on and off according to the pressure within the system, and by maintaining a mix of cooled, ambient and heated air, using the same blower, heater core and outlet

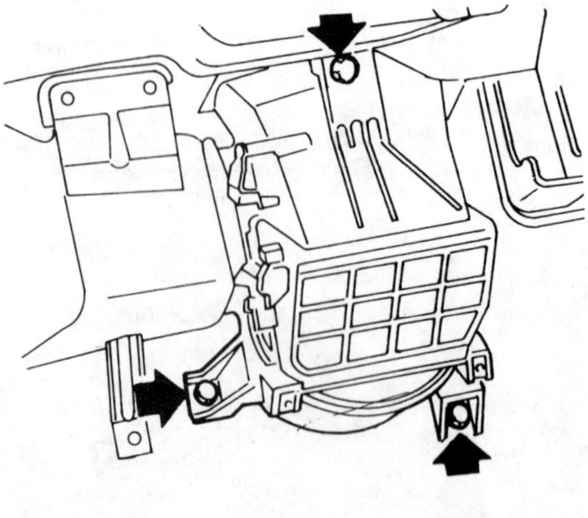

Fig. 3.7 Locations of the blower unit mounting bolts (Sec 13)

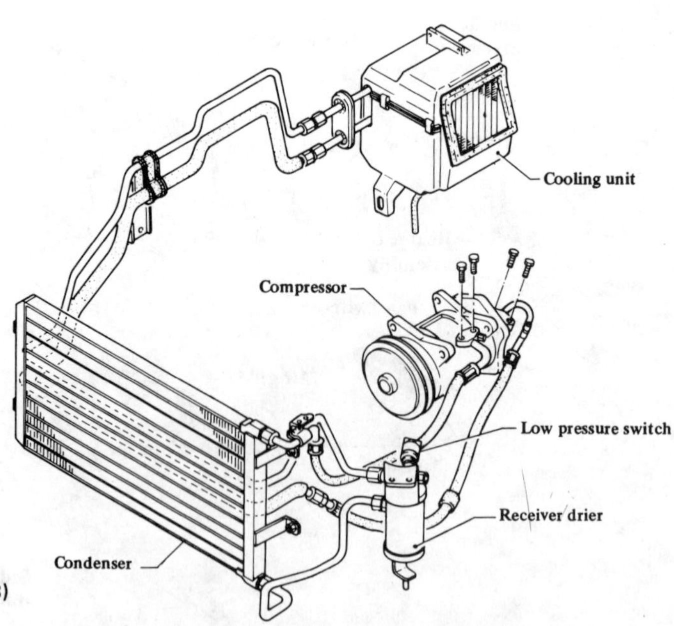

Fig. 3.8 Components of the air conditioning system (Sec 14)

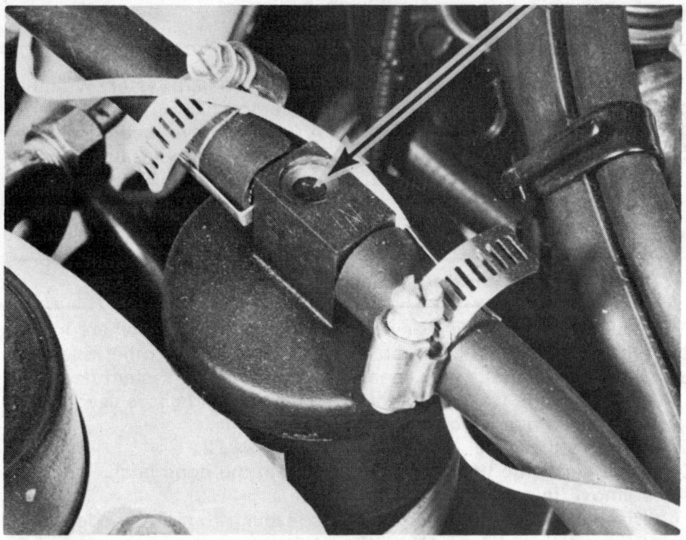

15.3a Location of the a/c system view glass (arrow) on top of the receiver drier

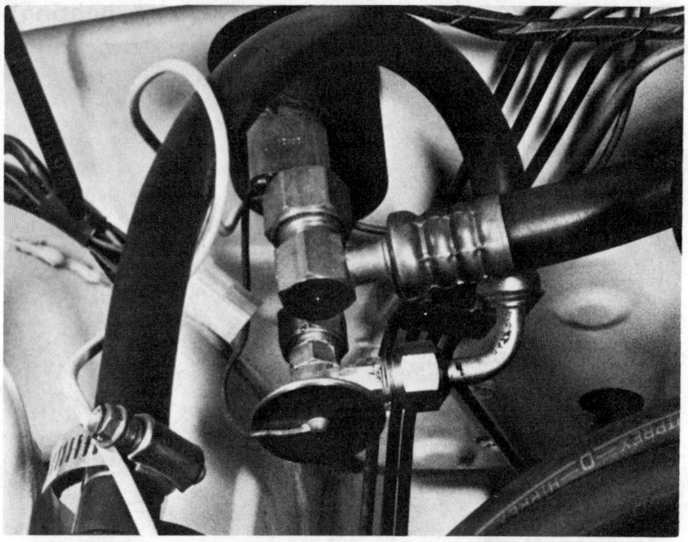

15.3b Location of the expansion and suction throttle valves at the right side fire wall

duct system that the heating system uses.

In addition, the system also is sensitive to the temperature of the air being taken in. If the intake air is below approximately 32°F, the compressor will not operate.

The main components of the system include a belt-driven compressor, a condenser (mounted in front of the radiator), a receiver, drier and an evaporator.

The system operates by air (outside or recirculated) entering the evaporator core by the action of the blower, where it receives maximum cooling if the controls are set for cooling. When the air leaves the evaporator, it enters the heater/air conditioner duct assembly and by means of a manually controlled deflector, it either passes through or bypasses the heater core in the correct proportions to provide the desired vehicle temperature.

Distribution of this air into the car is then regulated by a manually operated deflector, and is directed either to the floor vents, dash vents or defroster vents according to settings.

In view of the toxic nature of the chemicals and gases employed in the system, no part of the system should be disconnected by the home mechanic. Due to the need for the specialized evacuating and charging equipment, such work should be left to your dealer or a refrigeration specialist.

15 Air conditioner system – checks and maintenance

1 The following maintenance steps should be performed on a regular basis to ensure that the air conditioner continues to operate at peak efficiency.

a) *Check the tension of the a/c compressor drivebelt and adjust if necessary. Refer to Chapter 1, Section 11.*

b) *Visually inspect the condition of the hoses, checking for any cracking, hardening or other deterioration. Note: Do not replace without first having the system discharged.*

c) *Check that the fins of the condenser are not covered with foreign material, such as leaves or bugs. A soft brush and compressed air can be used to remove them.*

2 The a/c compressor should be run for about 10 minutes at least once every month. This is especially important to remember during the winter months because long-term non-use can cause hardening of the internal seals.

3 Due to the complexity of the air conditioning system and the special equipment required to effectively work on it, accurate trouble-shooting and repair of the system cannot be expected of the home mechanic and should be left to a professional. In any case, due to the toxic nature of the refrigerant, prior to disconnecting any part of the system, the car should be taken to a Datsun dealer or other qualified shop to have the system discharged. If the system should lose its cooling action, some causes can be diagnosed by the home mechanic. Look for other symptoms of trouble such as those in the following list. In all cases, it's a good idea to have the system serviced by a professional.

a) *If bubbles appear in the sight glass (located on top of the receiver drier this is an indication of either a small refrigerant leak or air in the refrigerant (photo). If air is in the refrigerant, the receiver drier is suspect and should be replaced.*

b) *If the view glass takes on a mist-like appearance or shows many bubbles, this indicates a large refrigerant leak. In such a case, do not operate the compresser at all until the fault has been corrected.*

c) *Sweating or frosting of the expansion valve inlet (photo) indicates that the expansion valve is clogged or defective. It should be cleaned or replaced as necessary.*

d) *Sweating or frosting of the suction line (which runs between the suction throttle valve and the compressor) indicates that the expansion valve is stuck open or defective. It should be corrected or replaced as necessary.*

e) *Frosting on the evaporator indicates a defective suction throttle valve, requiring replacement of the valve.*

f) *Frosting of the high pressure liquid line (which runs between the condenser, receiver drier and expansion valve) indicates that either the drier or the high pressure line is restricted. The line will have to be cleared or the receiver drier replaced.*

g) *The combination of bubbles in the sight glass, a very hot suction line and, possibly, overheating of the engine is an indication that either the condenser is not operating properly or the refrigerant is overcharged. Check the tensions of the fan belt and adjust if necessary (Chapter 1). Check for foreign matter covering the fins of the condenser and clean if necessary. Also check for proper operation of the cooling system. If no fault can be found in these checks, the condenser may need to be replaced.*

16 A/C compressor – removal and installation

1 Prior to disconnecting any air conditioning lines anywhere in the system the car should be taken to a Datsun dealer or other qualified automotive air conditioning repair shop to have the system depressurized. Due to the toxic nature of the chemicals and gases used in the system, this is not a job for the home mechanic.

2 Disconnect the negative battery cable.

3 There are two ways to remove the compressor from the engine compartment, each requiring the removal of other components first. One method requires the removal of the radiator and shroud (Section 5) and the other requires the removal of the ignition coil(s) (Chapter 5, Section 8) and, on 1980 US models only, the air induction hoses (Chapter 6, Section 7). At this point, decide which method you prefer and remove the appropriate components.

4 Loosen the bolt on the rear of the compressor idler pulley and move the pulley upward to loosen the A/C compressor drivebelt.

5 Remove the drivebelt from the compressor.

6 Disconnect both hoses leading to the compressor.

7 Disconnect any wires leading to the compressor.

8 Remove the 4 nuts and bolts that retain the compressor to its bracket and lift off the compressor.

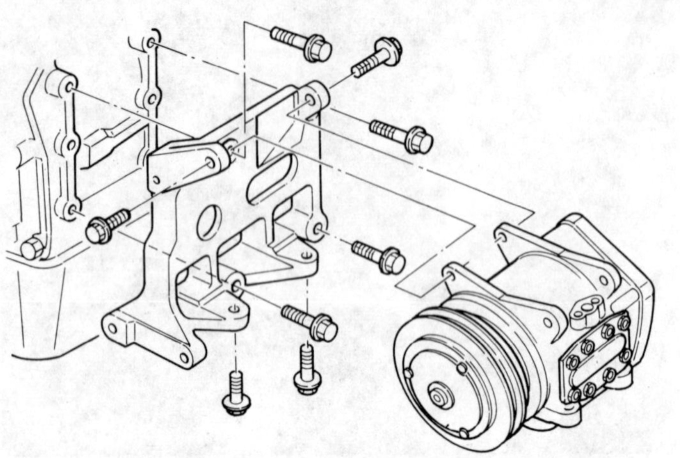

Fig. 3.9 Mounting arrangement of the a/c compressor and bracket (Sec 16)

9 Remove the compressor from the engine compartment. **Note:** *The compressor should not be left on its side or upside down for more than 10 minutes at a time, as compressor oil could enter the low pressure chambers and cause internal damage. If this should happen, the oil can be expelled from the chambers by positioning the compressor right side up and handcranking it several times.*

10 Installation is the reverse of the removal procedure. When reconnecting the hoses to the compressor be sure to use new O-rings at each connection.

11 If the radiator has been removed, refill the coolant system with the proper mixture of antifreeze and water. Refer to Chapter 1 if necessary.

12 Once the compressor and all A/C lines have been securely connected again, the car must once again be taken to a Datsun dealer or other qualified shop to have the system charged.

17 Condenser – removal and installation

1 Prior to disconnecting any air conditioning lines anywhere in the system the car should be taken to a Datsun dealer or other qualified automotive air conditioning repair shop to have the system depressurized. Due to the toxic nature of the chemicals and gases used in the system, this is not a job for the home mechanic.

2 Remove the grille as described in Chapter 12.

3 Disconnect the hood release cable from the hood latch.

4 Remove the hood latch and bracket.

5 Disconnect both rubber A/C hoses leading from the condenser.

6 Remove the clamps from the condenser that secure the lower hose to the front of the condenser and move the hose out of the way.

7 Remove the 4 screws that hold the condenser to the body and lift out the condenser.

8 If the condenser fins or air passages are clogged with foreign material, such as dirt, insects or leaves use compressed air and a soft brush to clean the condenser. If the condenser is in need of other repairs, have a professional radiator shop or Datsun dealer perform the work.

9 Installation is the reverse of the removal procedure.

10 Once all A/C lines have been securely connected again, the car must once again be taken to a Datsun dealer or other qualified shop to have the system charged.

Chapter 4 Fuel and exhaust systems

Refer to Chapter 13 for Specifications and information related to 1982 and 1983 models

Contents

Accelerator pedal – removal and installation 8
Air flow meter and air temperature sensor – removal and installation 12
Air regulator – removal and installation 18
Altitude sensor (1980 California models) – removal and installation 21
Catalytic converter – removal and installation 31
Check valve – removal and installation 27
Control unit – removal and installation 10
Dash pot (automatic transmission models) – removal, installation and adjustment 15
Dropping resistor – removal and installation 13
EFI components – general description 2
EFI components – testing 4
Exhaust gas sensor (1981 US models) – removal and installation 22
Exhaust system – general information 28
Exhaust system – inspection 29
Front exhaust pipe – removal and installation 30
Fuel filter – removal and installation 5
Fuel line – repair and replacement 6
Fuel pump and damper – removal and installation 9
Fuel system – cleaning 7
Fuel system – general information 1
Fuel system – inspection 3
Fuel tank – cleaning and purging 25
Fuel tank – removal and installation 23
Fuel tank gauge unit – removal and installation 26
IAS (Idle Adjusting Screw) unit – removal and installation 11
Injectors, pressure regulator and fuel pipe assembly – removal and installation 19
Muffler/tail pipe – removal and installation 32
Reservoir tank (hatchback) – removal and installation 24
Throttle chamber – removal and installation 16
Throttle valve switch – removal, installation and adjustment 14
Vacuum switch (1980 California models) – removal and installation 20
Water/Cylinder head temperature sensor – removal and installation 17

Specifications

Fuel pressure (measured after fuel filter)

At idling	30 psi (2.1 kg/cm^2)
Upon initial full throttle	37 psi (2.6 kg/cm^2)

Fuel pump

Cut-off discharge pressure	43-64 psi (3.0-4.5 kg/cm^2)
Design current	5.1 amps

Pressure regulator

Regulated pressure	36.3 psi (2.55 kg/cm^2)

Air regulator

Air flow quantity (at 68°F) (20°C)	671 cu ft/hr (19.0 m^3)
Heater coil resistance	25-90 ohms

Fuel injector

Coil resistance	2.35 ohms

Vacuum switch

Intake manifold vacuum when switch turns on	Approx. 6.30 inHg (160 mmHg)

Torque specifications

	ft-lb	m-kg
Throttle chamber mounting bolts	15	2.0
Exhaust gas sensor	33	4.5
Fuel tank mounting bolts	12	1.6
Reservoir tank mounting bolts	12	1.6
Exhaust manifold-to-exhaust pipe bolts	22	3.0
Catalytic converter attaching bolts	28	3.8

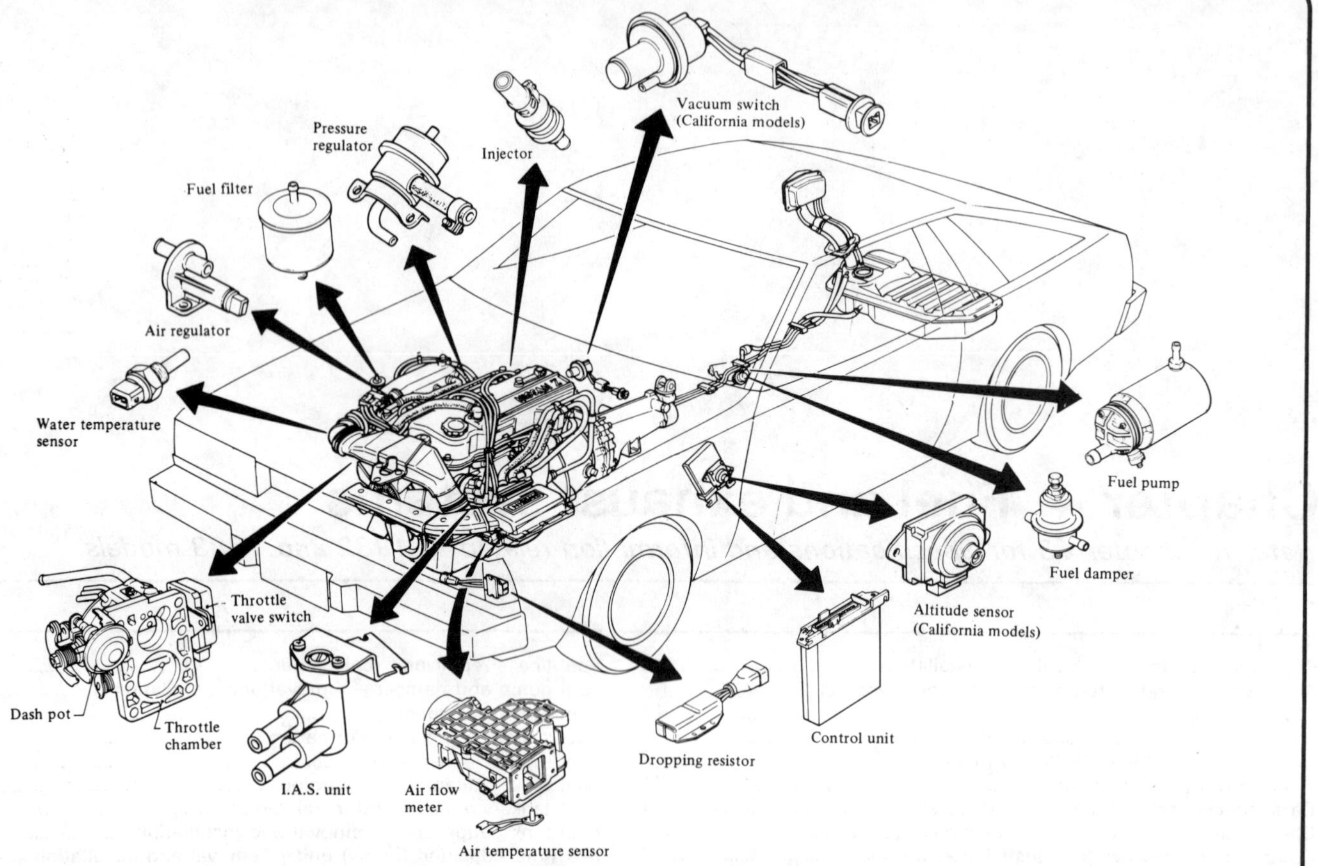

Fig. 4.1 Location of EFI system components (1980 models)

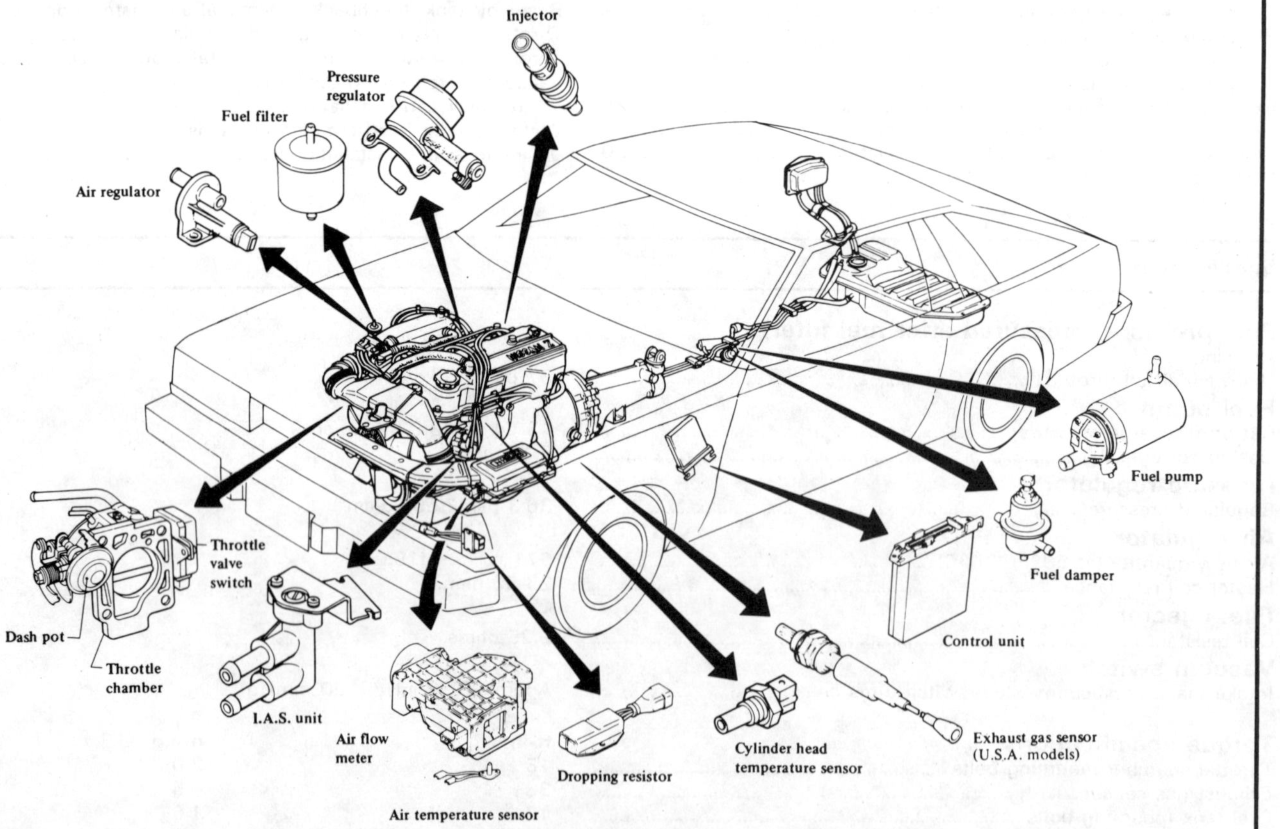

Fig. 4.2 Location of EFI system components (1981 models)

1 Fuel system – general information

The Datsun NAPS-Z engine uses an Electronic Fuel Injection (EFI) fuel system in place of the conventional carburetor-type system. Electronic fuel injection provides optimum mixture ratios at all stages of combustion, and this, together with the immediate response characteristics of the fuel injection, permits the engine to run on the weakest possible fuel/air mixture; this vastly reduces the exhaust gas toxic emission. The fuel system, as well as the exhaust system, is interrelated with and works in conjunction with the emissions control systems covered in Chapter 6. Thus, some elements that relate directly to the fuel system are covered in that Chapter.

The EFI system consists of three sub-systems: The fuel flow system, the air flow system and the electrical signaling system. The various components that make up the entire EFI system are detailed in Section 2.

Fuel from the tank is delivered under pressure from the fuel pump and, to avoid pulsation, is fed through a mechanical damper. After passing through a fuel filter and a pressure regulator, it is then injected into the intake manifold. The pressure regulator is designed to maintain a constant pressure difference between the fuel line pressure and the intake manifold vacuum. Where manifold conditions are such that the fuel pressure could be beyond that specified, the pressure regulator returns surplus fuel to the tank.

An injection of fuel occurs once every rotation of the engine. Because the injection signal comes from the control unit, all four injectors operate simultaneously and independant of the engine stroke. Each injection supplies half the amount of fuel required by the cylinder, and the length of the injection period is determined by information fed to the control unit by the various sensors included in the system.

Elements affecting the injection duration include: Engine rpm, quantity and temperature of the intake air, throttle valve opening, temperature of the engine coolant, position of the ignition switch, intake manifold vacuum pressure (1980), atmospheric pressure (1980) and amount of oxygen in the exhaust gases (1981).

Because the EFI system operates under a high fuel pressure, any slight leak can affect the system's efficiency and present a serious fire risk. Also since the intake air flow is critical to the operation of the system, even a slight air leak will cause wrong air/fuel mixtures to occur.

The electric fuel pump used in the EFI system uses three relays, located in the engine compartment relay bracket. This set-up is designed so that should the engine accidentally stop, (causing the alternator to turn off and the oil pressure to drop), the fuel pump will not operate.

The idle mixture adjusting screw on 1980 California models and all 1981 US models is pre-set at the factory and sealed with a hardened steel plug to prevent the setting from being altered. On 1980 49-state models and all Canada models, the idle mixture can be adjusted, but a CO% meter is needed to obtain the correct setting. For this reason, it is best left to a Datsun dealer or other qualified shop to do.

Note: *Certain precautions should be observed when working on the EFI system, because of its critical and sensitive components.*

a) Do not disconnect either battery cable while the engine is running

b) Prior to any operation in which a fuel line will be disconnected, the high pressure in the system must first be eliminated. This procedure is described in Section 9. Disconnect the negative battery cable to eliminate the possibility of sparks occurring while open fuel is present.

c) Prior to removing any EFI component, be sure the ignition switch is off and the negative battery cable is disconnected

d) The EFI wiring harness should be kept at least 4 inches (10 mm) away from adjacent harnesses. This includes a CB antenna feeder cable as well. This is to prevent electrical pulses in other systems from interfering with the EFI operation

e) Be sure all EFI wiring connections are tight, clean and secure as a poor connection can cause extremely high voltage surges in the ignition coil which could drain the IC circuit.

f) The accelerator should NOT be depressed prior to starting the engine. Immediately after starting, do not rev the engine unnecessarily

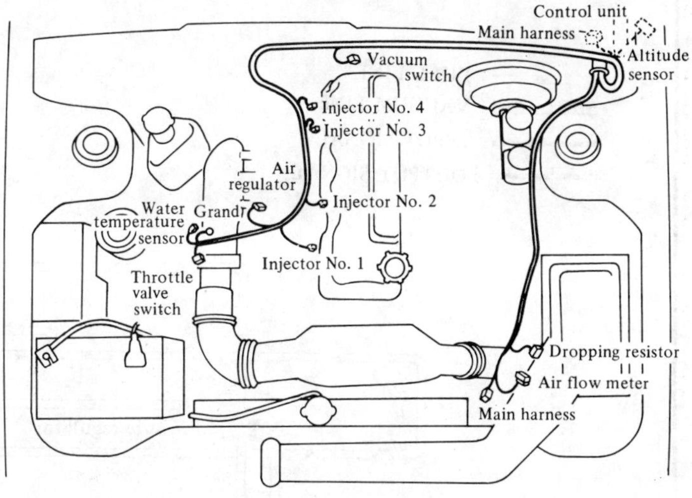

Fig. 4.3 Routing of EFI wiring harness in the engine compartment (1980 models)

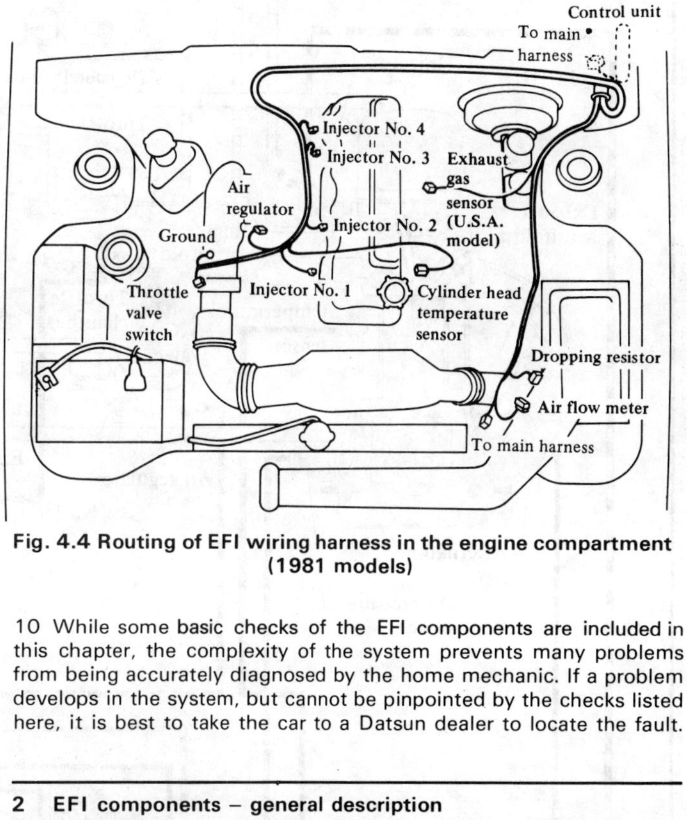

Fig. 4.4 Routing of EFI wiring harness in the engine compartment (1981 models)

10 While some basic checks of the EFI components are included in this chapter, the complexity of the system prevents many problems from being accurately diagnosed by the home mechanic. If a problem develops in the system, but cannot be pinpointed by the checks listed here, it is best to take the car to a Datsun dealer to locate the fault.

2 EFI components – general description

Control unit

The control unit is mounted on a dash panel support bracket on the driver's side of the vehicle. The essential role of this unit is to generate a pulse. Upon receiving an electrical signal from each sensor, the control unit generates a pulse whose duration (injector open time period) is controlled to provide the exact amount of fuel, according to engine characteristics at that particular time. The control unit consists mainly of three integrated circuits formed on a printed circuit board.

Airflow meter

The airflow meter measures the volume and temperature of the intake air, and sends the signal to the control unit. This is achieved by a potentiometer which is linked to the air intake flap shaft. The more air that enters the flow meter, the further the flap valve rotates, which in turn rotates the potentiometer wiper through a variable resistance coil. This increasing or decreasing resistance (dependant upon the flap

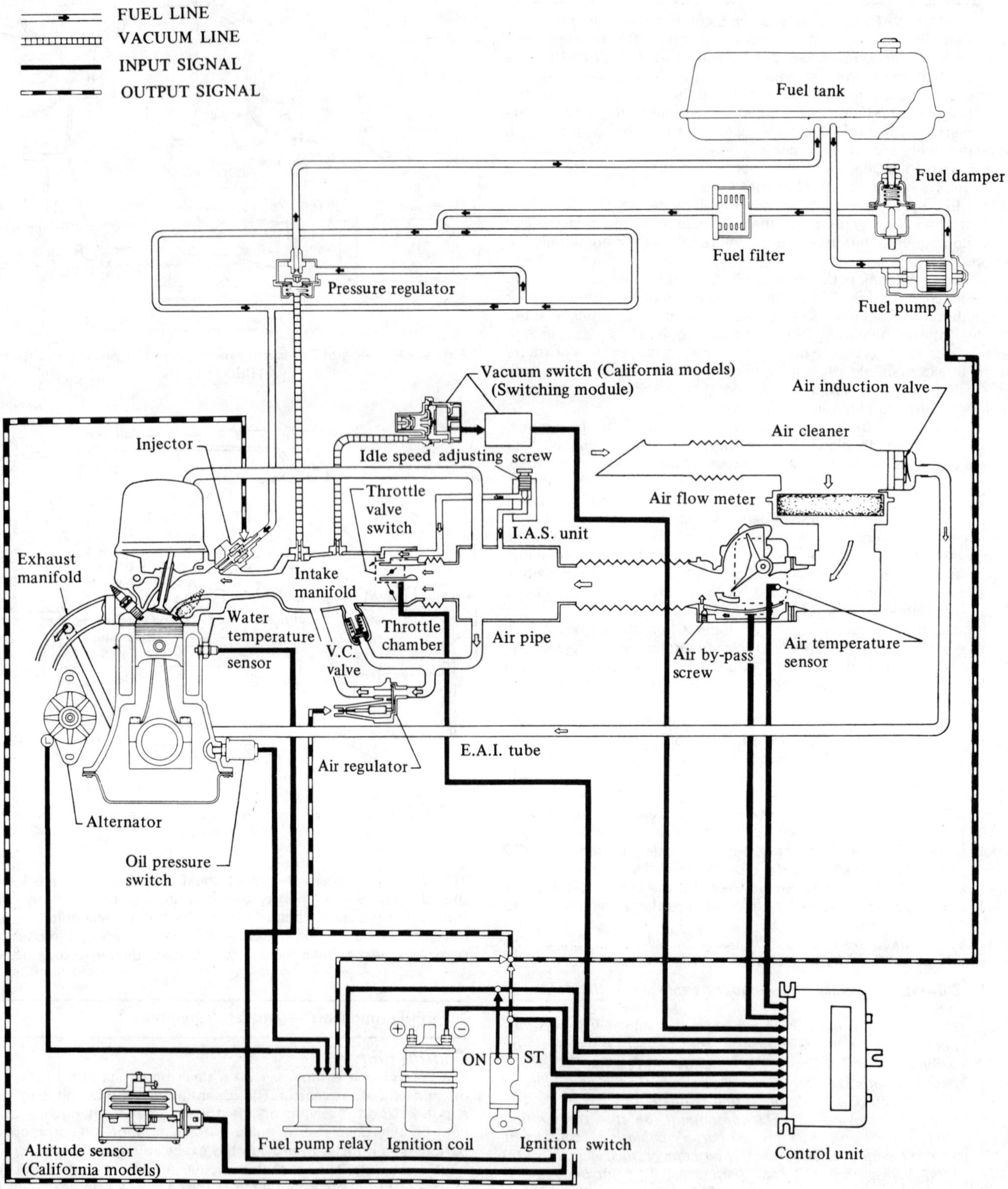

Fig. 4.5 Schematic of EFI system (1980 models)

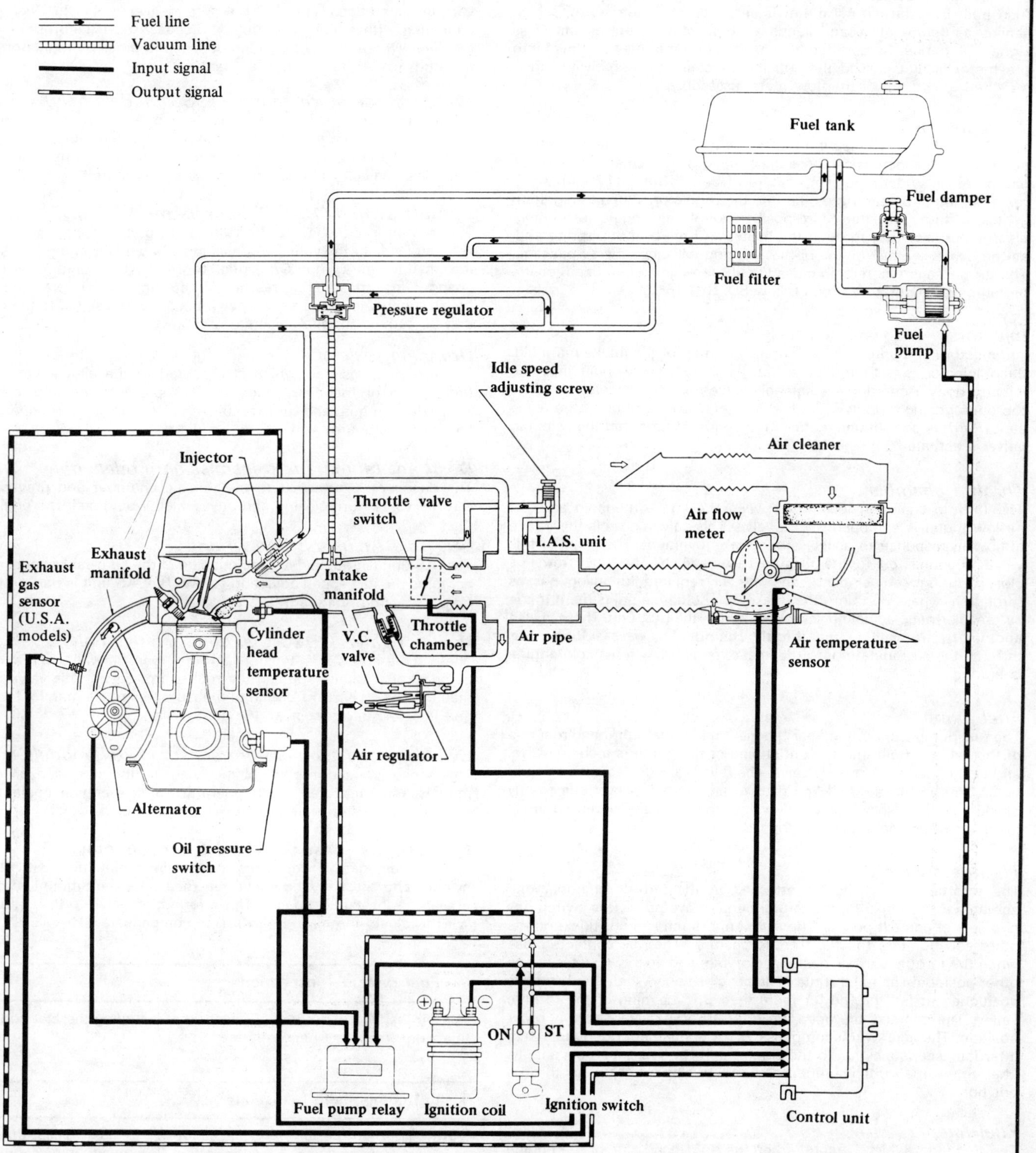

Fig. 4.6 Schematic of EFI system (1981 models)

angle) sends the signal to the control unit. In order to dampen any excessive movement of the flap, due to vacuum depressions in the intake manifold, a helical spring and compensating plate in a damper chamber are provided.

Also built into the airflow meter is an air temperature sensor which senses air temperature and sends a signal to the control unit. This signal will define the duration of the injection time. Air that flows into the meter is first passed through the air cleaner assembly which is attached to the top of the flow meter assembly.

Air regulator

The air regulator bypasses the throttle valve, to control the quantity of air required for increasing the engine idling speed when starting the engine at an underhood temperature of below 80°C (176°F). A bi-metal spring and heater are built into the regulator. When the ignition switch is turned to the *Start* position, or if the engine is running, electric current flows through the heater and the bi-metal spring and, as the heater warms up, the bi-metal spring will close the air passage. The air passage will remain closed until the engine is stopped, or the underhood temperature drops below 80°C (176°F).

Injectors

An injector is mounted on each branch portion of the intake manifold. Each injector is actuated by a small solenoid valve built into the injector body. Actuating the solenoid valve pulls the needle valve into the open position to allow the fuel to inject. The duration of the pulse sent from the control unit defines the period of time that the solenoid valve is actuated.

Throttle chamber

The throttle chamber located between the intake manifold and the airflow meter is equipped with a valve. This valve controls the intake airflow in response to accelerator pedal movement. The shaft of this valve is connected to the throttle valve switch. The valve remains closed during engine idling, and the air required for idling passes through a bypass port into the intake manifold. Idle adjustment made by the idle speed adjusting screw located in the IAS unit. There is also another bypass line in the throttle chamber to pass sufficient air through the air regulator into the intake manifold when a cold engine is started.

Fuel pump

The fuel pump is mounted near the fuel tank at the right-hand rear end of the vehicle. Built into the outlet pipe of the pump is a check valve, and at the inlet pipe, a relief valve. The relief valve is designed to open when pressure in the fuel line rises to an excessive level due to any blocking in the line. The check valve prevents any abrupt drop in pressure when the engine is stopped.

Throttle switch

The throttle valve switch is attached to the throttle chamber and actuates in response to accelerator pedal movement. This switch has two sets of contact points. One set monitors the idle position, and the other set monitors the full throttle position. The idle contacts close when the throttle valve is positioned at idle, and open when it is at any other position. The full throttle contacts close only when the throttle is positioned at full throttle (or more than 35° opening of the throttle valve). The contacts are open while the throttle valve is at any other position. The idle switch compensates for enrichment during idle and, after idle, sends a signal to the control unit to modify the fuel supply. The full throttle switch compensates for enrichment at the full throttle position.

Fuel filter

The fuel filter, which is mounted on the right-hand side of the engine compartment, ensures that only clean fuel reaches the injectors. A clogged fuel fiiter will stop the flow of fuel and cause the engine to stop. This is usually preceded by hesitation and sluggish operation.

Fuel damper

The fuel damper, which is mounted to the fuel pump at the rear of the vehicle, is designed to suppress any pulsation in fuel flow from the fuel pump.

Pressure regulator

The pressure regulator, which is mounted adjacent to the intake manifold in the fuel supply pipe, maintains a constant fuel pressure at all stages of acceleration and deceleration. Under extreme manifold vacuum conditions, the full pressure delivered by the fuel pump, combined with a high vacuum, could cause excessive pressure in the fuel line. Where such a condition occurs, the pressure regulator opens to return excess fuel to the fuel tank.

Water temperature sensor (1980 models only)

This device, which is housed in the thermostat housing, monitors any changes in the engine coolant temperature. As soon as any temperature change is sensed, a signal is sent to the control unit, where a modified injector pulse duration will be computed.

Altitude switch (1980 California models only)

This switch is attached to the instrument panel support stay, on the left-hand side of the vehicle. Consisting of a bellows and micro-switch, it transmits an *On* or *Off* signal to the control unit according to changes in atmospheric pressure. When atmospheric pressure drops below a given level the switch activates to send a signal to the control unit to reduce the fuel injected by 6%.

Dropping resistor

The dropping resistor, which is mounted to the air cleaner bracket underneath of the air cleaner housing, protects the injectors from alternator surges and effects of other electrical components by lowering the source voltage.

Dash pot (automatic transmission models only)

The dash pot is attached to the throttle chamber and prevents the throttle valve from closing abruptly, which would stall the engine.

IAS (Idle Adjusting Screw) unit

The IAS unit is attached to the right side of the air cleaner housing, and contains the idle speed adjusting screw. The IAS unit is part of the idle by-pass system for the intake air.

Vacuum valve (1980 California models only)

The vacuum valve is located on the rear firewall of the engine compartment directly behind the rocker arm cover. This valve uses a diaphragm and a micro switch to measure the intake manifold vacuum and feed the information to the control unit.

Cylinder head temperature sensor (1981 models only)

This sensor is used in place of the water temperature sensor in prior models and measures the temperature of the engine coolant. It is located on the front left side of the cylinder head.

Exhaust gas sensor (1981 US models only)

The exhaust gas sensor, which works in conjunction with the EFI system and the catalytic converter, measures the amount of oxygen present in the exhaust gases. This information is fed to the control unit which adjusts the air/fuel mixture to compensate.

3 Fuel system – inspection

1 For inspection of the fuel system (not including the Electronic Fuel Injection), refer to Chapter 1.

4 EFI components – testing

Note: *Prior to performing the following tests, unless otherwise specified, turn the ignition switch to the 'OFF' position, disconnect the negative battery cable and disconnect the wire from the 'S' terminal of the starter. Also, on 1980 California models, disconnect the wiring connector leading to the vacuum switch. On 1981 US models disconnect the wiring connector leading to the exhaust gas sensor and ground the harness connector terminal with a jumper wire.*

Fuel pump, damper and pressure regulator

1 The only tests that can be carried out on the fuel pump, are a

basic-function test and a discharge pressure check. The discharge pressure check will involve the use of a pressure gauge capable of measuring up to 40 psi accurately, and a suitable T-piece.

Basic-function check

2 To carry out the basic-function test, first disconnect the starter motor S terminal lead.
3 Turn the ignition switch to the *Start* position, where an operating sound from the rear of the vehicle should be clearly audible. If no operating sound is audible, check that the electrical wiring to the fuel pump is in order. This could involve the use of special circuit testing equipment and should be entrusted to your Datsun dealer.
4 If the fuel pump appears satisfactory in paragraph 2 proceed to check the fuel discharge pressure, as described in the following paragraphs.

Discharge pressure check

5 Release the pressure in the fuel line, as described in Section 9.
6 Connect the pressure gauge into the fuel hose immediately after the fuel filter, as shown in the accompanying figure.
7 Disconnect the wire from the 'S' terminal of the starter.
8 Seek the assistance of a second person to turn the ignition switch to the *Start* position.
9 When the ignition switch is in the *Start* position, observe the pressure reading on the pressure gauge.
10 If the reading at the pressure gauge fluctuates excessively, the fuel damper will have to be renewed.
11 If a pressure of 37 psi is not obtained, install a new pressure regulator.
12 If the reading is below 37 psi check for clogged or deformed fuel lines, and if necessary, renew the fuel pump as an assembly.
13 If all is well in the previously described checks, it does not necessarily follow that the fuel pump is serviceable. The fuel delivery pressure at full engine revolutions could possibly be below the specified figure, but to check this requires the use of a rolling road test, or alternatively, jacking-up the rear of the vehicle in order to run the vehicle in a stationary position. This operation requires the use of specially designed axle-stands, and a great deal of care must be taken while carrying out the operation. In view of this, the job is really best entrusted to your Datsun dealer.

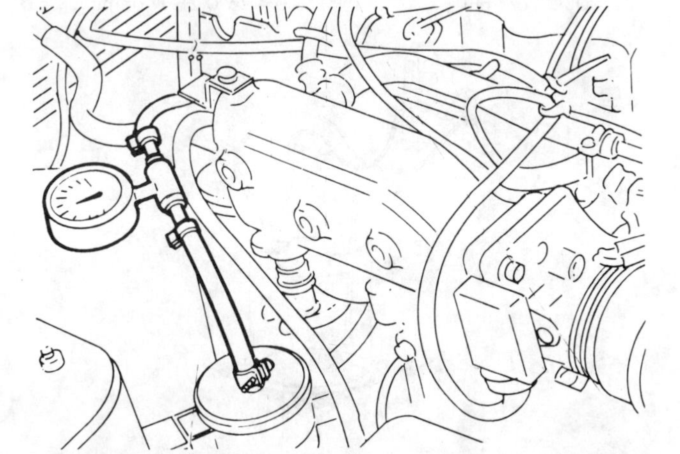

Fig. 4.7 When testing the fuel pressure, the gauge should be installed after the fuel filter as shown (Sec 4)

Control unit

14 This check employs a miniature test lamp to check whether the open-injector pulse for cranking the engine is actually applied to the injectors, should the engine fail to start. To carry out this check, the engine must be cranked at a speed of more than 80 rpm; also the battery must be known to be in good state of charge. The test lamp should be 12V-3W miniature type, with a suitable connection to its end.
15 Turn the ignition switch to the *Off* position.
16 Disconnect the harness connector of number 1 cylinder injector.
17 Now connect the test lamp to the injector harness of the number 1 cylinder.
18 Turn the ignition switch to the *Start* position to crank the engine and observe whether or not the lamp flashes. If the lamp flashes, all is well; if it doesn't, the control unit is faulty and must be renewed.
19 As a further check, if all is well at paragraph 18, disconnect the harness from the water temperature sensor or cylinder head temperature sensor and crank the engine as before. The test lamp should now be flashing a lot brighter then before. If the lamp does'nt flash brighter, the sensor is probably faulty, and should be checked as described.
20 It is emphasized that this check only proves whether or not a signal pulse is reaching the injectors. If the control unit is still under suspicion, there are numerous other circuits inside the unit that could be at fault, and it is best to have it checked professionally.

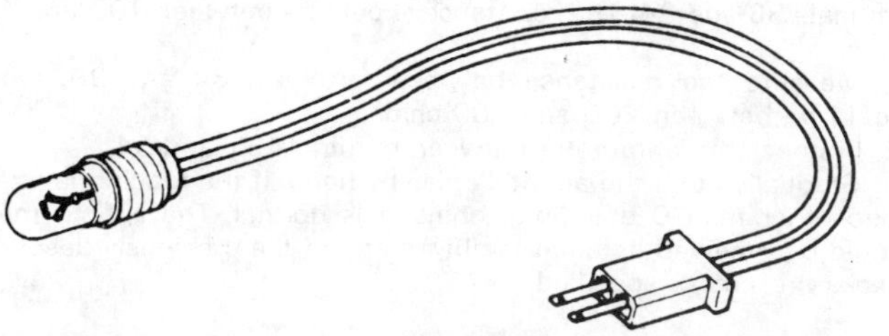

Fig. 4.8 A small 12V-3W test lamp with the proper connector is needed to test the control unit pulses going to the injectors (Sec 4)

Injectors

21 If more than one injector is suspect, the control unit should be checked as previously described.
22 To trace a single faulty injector with the engine running, use a screwdriver as a stethoscope. Attach the blade of a screwdriver to the injector and hold the handle against the ear. It should be possible to hear an operational click every time the injector operates. Compare the noise of the on the suspect injector with the other five injectors, if the noise of the operational click is noticeably less than at the other injectors, that particular injector is faulty and should be renewed.
23 If for any reason the engine will not run, disconnect the electrical connector from the cold start valve and, with the assistance of a second person operating the ignition switch to crank the engine, use the screwdriver method described in paragraph 22 to trace the faulty injector or injectors.
24 Once you have traced a possibly faulty injector, this can be proved by carrying out a continuity check. To do this, first disconnect the battery ground cable.
25 Disconnect the electrical connector from the suspect injector.
26 With the probes of an ohmmeter connected to the terminals on the injector, ensure that continuity exists. If there is no continuity, the

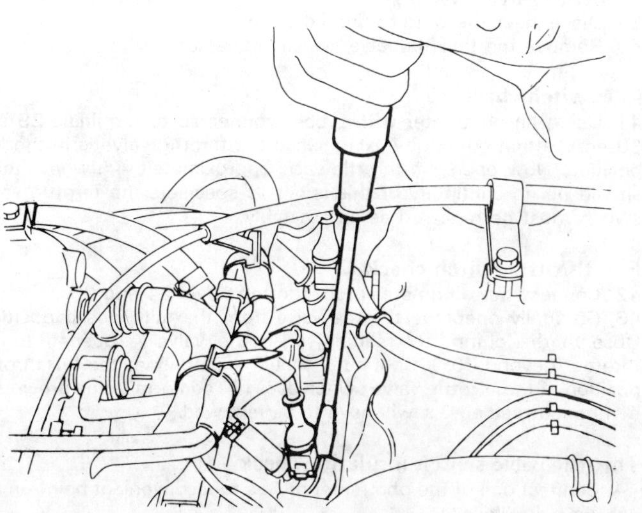

Fig. 4.9 When checking the injectors operation, a screwdriver can be used as a stethoscope by holding it between the injector and your ear (Sec 4)

solenoid coil windings could be open-circuit, or the terminal leads supplying the coil with current may be broken inside the injector. In such cases the only remedy is to renew the faulty injector.

Air flow meter and air temperature sensor

Note: *The following checks can be carried out without removing the airflow meter assembly from the vehicle.*

27 Remove the air cleaner cover and element, as described in Chapter 1.

Checking the potentiometer

28 Disconnect the battery ground cable.
29 Disconnect the harness connector from the airflow meter.
30 Now, using an ohmmeter, check the resistance between the terminals 33 and 34. The resistance should be between 100 and 400 ohms.
31 Measure the resistance between terminals 34 and 35, which should be between 200 and 500 ohms.
32 Connect the ohmmeter between terminals 32 and 34.
33 Gradually open the air intake flap by hand. If the reading is at any value other than 0 or infinite ohms, it is normal. The airflow meter should be renewed as an assembly if any of the previously described checks are not as specified.

Checking insulation resistance of the airflow meter

34 To check the insulation resistance between the airflow meter body and the potentiometer terminals, simply hold one of the ohmmeter probes in contact with the airflow meter casing and, with the other probe, touch each of the terminals (terminals 32, 33, 34 and 35). If any continuity exists, the airflow meter is faulty, and should be renewed as an assembly.

Checking the air temperature sensor

35 Connect the ohmmeter probes to terminals 25 and 34.
36 Using a normal household thermometer, measure the air temperature as near to the sensor as possible.
37 The following table gives the resistance valve over a given termparature range. The air temperature sensor is part of the airflow meter assembly and, where the resistance readings are outside the limits listed in the chart, the airflow meter must be renewed as an assembly.

Air temperature	Resistance
20°C (68°F) or above	below 2.9 K ohms
below 20°C (68°F)	2.1 K ohms or above

38 Finally, check the insulation resistance between terminal 25 and the airflow meter body. If continuity exists, the air temperature sensor is faulty; renew the air flow meter as an assembly.

Throttle valve switch

39 Disconnect the battery ground cable.
40 Remove the throttle valve switch connector.

Idle switch check

41 Using an ohmmeter with probes connected to terminals 29 and 30 ensure that continuity exists when the throttle valve is in the idle position. Now open the throttle valve approximately 4°, where there should be no continuity. If this is not as specified, the throttle valve switch must be renewed as an assembly.

Full throttle switch check

42 Connect the ohmmeter probes to terminals 24 and 30.
43 Gradually open the throttle valve from the fully closed position. Observe the ohmmeter reading when the valve is opened to full throttle (beyond 35°). Continuity should exist only at the full throttle position. If the throttle valve switch does not conform to the previously mentioned readings, it will have to be renewed.

Throttle valve switch insulation check

44 Connect one of the ohmmeter probes to a convenient point on the vehicle frame (ground).
45 With the other ohmmeter probe, touch terminals 24, 29 and 30 in turn, and observe that the ohmmeter reading is infinite at each terminal. If it is not, there's obviously a short-circuit somewhere that can only be rectified by renewing the throttle valve switch as described in Section 14.

Dropping resistor

46 Disconnect the battery ground cable.
47 Disconnect the connector from the dropping resistor.
48 Carry out the following resistance checks:

a) Between terminal 43 and terminal 41 (number 4 cylinder resistor)
b) Between terminal 43 and terminal 40 (number 3 cylinder resistor)
c) Between terminal 43 and terminal 38 (number 2 cylinder resistor)
d) Between terminal 43 and terminal 37 (number 1 cylinder resistor)

49 The resistance reading for all of the above mentioned checks should be approximately 6 ohms. If one particular terminal appears to differ from the others, the whole resistor should be renewed.

Water temperature sensor 1980 and cylinder head temperature sensor (1981)

Note: *The water temperature or cylinder head temperature sensor is designed to give a specific resistance reading over a given temperature range. It can be checked after removal from the engine compartment using containers of hot and cold water, but the procedure described is for one which is installed.*

50 Disconnect the battery ground cable.
51 Disconnect the sensor harness connector.
52 By placing a thermometer into the radiator filler neck, establish the temperature of the coolant with the engine cold.
53 Connect the probes of the ohmmeter to the terminals of the sensor. Record the resistance reading obtained and compare it with the following chart of resistance values:

Engine coolant	Resistance
−30°C (−22°F)	18.0 to 33.0 K ohms
−10°C (+14°F)	7.0 to 11.4 K ohms
20°C (68°F)	2.1 to 2.9 K ohms
50°C (122°F)	0.56 to 1.00 K ohms
80°C (176°F)	0.4 to 0.25 K ohms

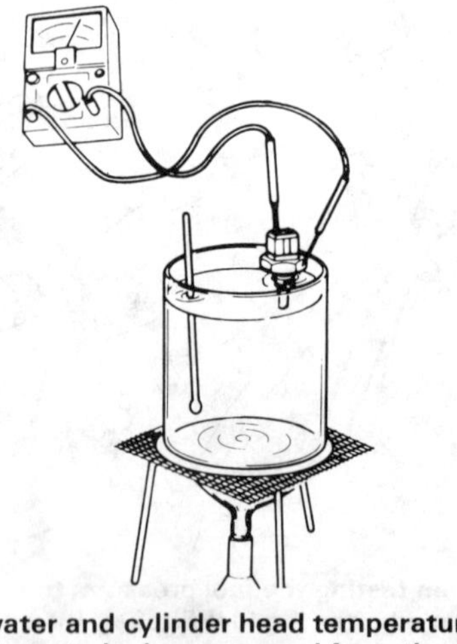

Fig. 4.10 The water and cylinder head temperature sensors are most accurately tested when removed from the car as shown (Sec 4)

54 Now reconnect the sensor harness connector and the battery ground cable. Run the engine until the normal operating temperature is reached, then repeat the operations described in the preceding paragraphs. By first carrying out a cold check, then a hot check will give a good indication of the condition of the sensor over its operating range. If the resistance readings do not come within the range specified, renew the sensor.

Air regulator

55 As an initial check, with the engine just started and running at a

very cold operating temperature, grasp the hose between the air regulator and the throttle chamber, and by squeezing it with your fingers, cut off the airflow through the hose. The engine idle should become very erratic and be noticeably reduced in idle speed.
56 As a further speed check, allow the engine to run until the normal temperature has been reached and the underhood temperature is above 80°C (176°F). Repeat the check described in the preceding paragraph, and, because the by-pass air passage should now be closed, the engine idle speed should remain constant.
57 If the air regulator still proves to be suspect after carrying out these checks, it is possible to visually check to observe whether the air regulator valve is working.
58 With the engine stationary and at a cold temperature, disconnect the hoses from each end of the air regulator.
59 By looking through the air regulator it is possible to see the by-pass port open. If all is well, reconnect the hoses and run the engine until normal operating temperature is reached.
60 Now disconnect the hoses again as described in paragraph 58. This time the by-pass port should be completely closed.
61 If the checks previously mentioned prove unsatisfactory, disconnect the electrical connector at the air regulator and, using an ohmmeter, check that there is continuity in the air regulator. If there is no continuity, or the air regulator is proved to be inoperative in the preceding checks, a replacement unit will have to be installed.

5 Fuel filter – removal and installation

1 Because replacement of the fuel filter is part of the routine maintenance schedule, refer to Chapter 1 for this procedure.

6 Fuel line – repair and replacement

Caution: *Do not disconnect any fuel lines without first eliminating the pressure from the system, as described in Section 9.*
1 The fuel injection system is designed to operate at a pressure much higher than conventional fuel systems, and any slight leakage at a fuel joint can, if left, soon become a major problem. Leaving a leaking joint is a serious fire risk and the pressure loss is certain to affect the system's efficiency. From time-to-time, check the security of all the fuel joints; check also that the rigid pipes are not kinked or bent in any way. If a rubber hose shows signs of deterioration, renew it.
2 Since the electronic fuel injection system accurately meters the intake airflow through the airflow meter, even a slight air leak will cause an improper air/fuel ratio, resulting in a faulty engine performance due to excessive wear. For this reason a thorough inspection for leaks should be made at the oil filter cap, dipstick seal, blow-by hoses, airflow meter to throttle chamber air duct etc.
3 If a section of metal fuel line needs to be replaced only brazed seamless steel should be used, as copper or aluminium tubing does not have enough duribility to withstand normal operating vibrations.
4 If only one section of a metal fuel line is damaged, it can be cut out and replaced with a piece of rubber tubing. The rubber tubing should be cut 4 inches (100 mm) longer than the section it's replacing, so that there is about 2 inches of overlap between the rubber and metal tubing at either end of the section. Hose clamps should be used to secure both ends of the repaired section.
5 If a section of metal line longer than 6 inches is being removed, use a combination of metal tubing and rubber hose so that the hose lengths will not be longer than 10 inches.
6 Never use rubber hose within 4 inches of any part of the exhaust system.

7 Fuel system – cleaning

1 With time it is likely that sediment will collect in the bottom of the fuel tank. Condensation, resulting in rust and other impurities, will usually be found in the fuel tank of any car more than 3 or 4 years old. The following procedure should be performed to eliminate foreign material or contaminated fuel from the fuel system.
2 Eliminate the pressure in the fuel lines, using the procedure described in Section 9. Then disconnect the negative battery cable.
3 Drain and remove the fuel tank as described in Section 23.
4 Remove the fuel filter as described in Chapter 1. If the filter is clogged, replace it.
5 Remove the fuel tank gauge unit from the fuel tank as described in Section 26.
6 Purge and clean the fuel tank as necessary using one of the methods described in Section 25.
7 Disconnect the fuel inlet line at the fuel pump and clean the line out by applying air pressure through it in the direction of the fuel flow.
8 Use low air pressure to clean the pipes on the tank unit.
9 Reinstall the fuel tank gauge unit.
10 Reinstall the fuel tank.
11 Connect all wires and lines except the fuel damper outlet line.
12 Connect a rubber hose to the damper outlet fitting.
13 Connect the negative battery cable.
14 Put about 6 gallons of clean fuel into the fuel tank and operate the pump by turning the engine over until about two quarts of fuel has flowed through the pump. This will clean the pump out.
15 Remove the rubber hose and reconnect the damper outlet line.
16 Check all the connections to be sure they are tight.

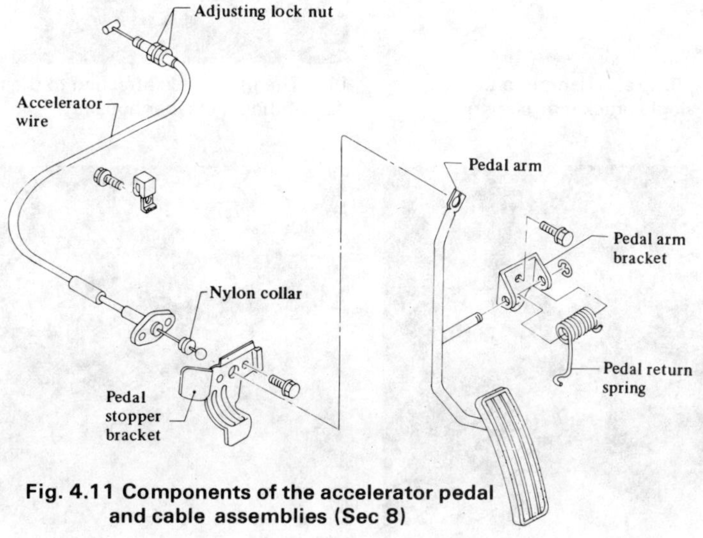

Fig. 4.11 Components of the accelerator pedal and cable assemblies (Sec 8)

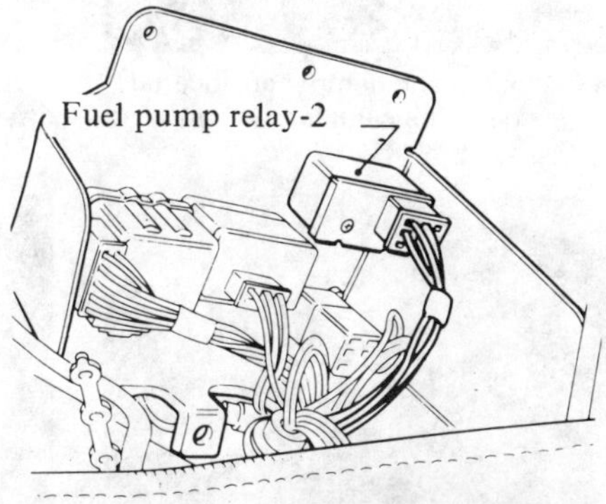

Fig. 4.12 The fuel pump relay-2 is located on the inside of the engine compartment relay bracket (1980 model shown) (Sec 9)

8 Accelerator pedal – removal and installation

1 Disengage the accelerator cable nylon collar from the upper end of the accelerator pedal by pushing it toward the end of the cable. Then disengage the cable from the pedal.
2 Remove the bolts that retain the accelerator pedal mounting bracket and lift out the the pedal.
3 Installation is the reverse of the removal procedure.
4 Following installation on automatic transmission models, check the operation of the transmission's kickdown switch, and adjust it if necessary as described in Chapter 7.

9 Fuel pump and damper – removal and installation

1 In order to prevent the fuel from being sprayed about when the fuel line is disconnected from the fuel pump, the pressure in the lines must be eliminated by using the following procedure:

a) Start the engine and allow it to idle
b) While the engine is running, disconnect the wiring harness connector from the fuel pump relay-2. This is located on the relay bracket on the right hand side of the engine compartment (see accompanying figures)
c) After the engine stalls, crank the engine over two or three times
d) Turn the ignition switch off again and reconnect the harness connector to the fuel pump relay-21. **Note:** *If the engine will not start, remove the wiring harness connector from fuel pump relay-2 and crank the engine over for about 5 seconds. Then turn the ignition switch off again*

2 Disconnect the negative battery cable.
3 Raise the rear of the car and support it on jack stands.
4 Clamp the fuel hose that runs between the fuel tank and the fuel pump to prevent spillage when the hose is disconnected.
5 Disconnect the inlet fuel line from the fuel pump and the outlet fuel line from the fuel damper. Be prepared for some fuel spillage.
6 Disconnect the 2 wires from the fuel pump noting which terminals they are attached to.
7 Remove the bolts that secure the fuel pump to the underside of the body and lift off the bracket complete with fuel pump and damper (photo).
8 To remove the fuel pump and damper from the bracket, first disconnect the fuel line that runs between the pump and damper, then remove the 2 screws that hold the upper pump retainer to the bracket. The fuel pump can now be lifted off.
9 Remove the 2 screws that hold the damper bracket to the fuel pump bracket and lift off the damper and bracket.

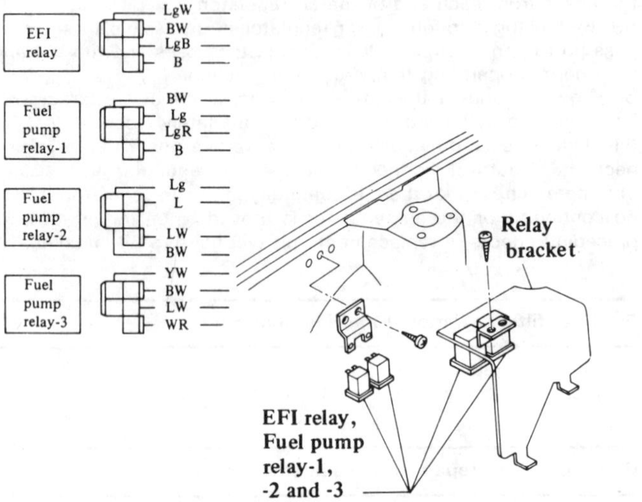

Fig. 4.13 Location and color wiring codes of the EFI and fuel pump relays (1981 models) (Sec 9).

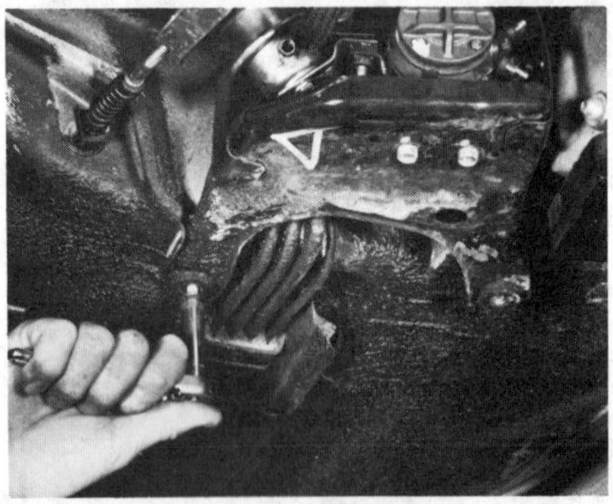

9.7a The fuel pump and damper are located on the underside of the car near the fuel tank

9.7b The fuel pump and damper are attached to a single bracket as shown

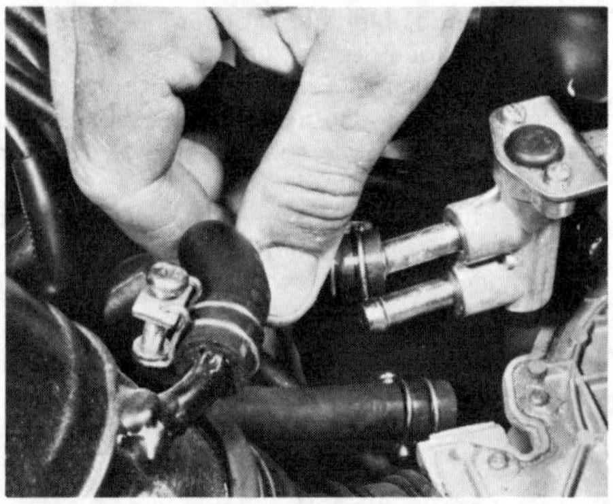

11.1 The IAS unit is attached to the right side of the air cleaner housing

12.8 The lower piece of the air cleaner housing is attached directly to the top of the air flow meter

13.4 The dropping resistor is mounted to the underside of the lower air flow meter bracket

14.2 The throttle valve switch is located on the right side of the throttle chamber

10 Installation is the reverse of the removal procedure with the following notes:

- a) *When reconnecting the high pressure outlet fuel line to the fuel damper, be sure to use a new hose clamp*
- b) *The clamp on the outlet fuel line should be approximately 3 mm from the end of the hose*
- c) *When installing the fuel lines on to the fuel damper, all fuel lines after the fuel pump are considered high pressure lines. When innstalling these, be sure that the end of the rubber hose contacts the units to which they are attached*

10 Control unit – removal and installation

1 The control unit is mounted on the left side dash panel even with the clutch and brake pedals.
2 Turn the ignition switch to the 'off' position and then disconnect the negative battery cable.
3 Remove the left finisher panel that covers the lower portion of the unit. This panel simply unsnaps.
4 Pull the lock lever on the large 35-pin wiring harness connector back and remove the connector from the control unit.
5 Remove the bolts which secure the control unit to the side panel and lift the unit out. Installation is the reverse of the removal procedure. **Note**: *When installing the 35 pin connector into the control unit be careful not to bend or break any of the terminals.*

11 IAS (Idle Adjusting Screw) unit – removal and installation

1 Disconnect the rubber hoses from the IAS unit (photo).
2 Remove the screw that retains the unit to the air filter housing and lift off the IAS unit.
3 Installation is the reverse of the removal procedure.

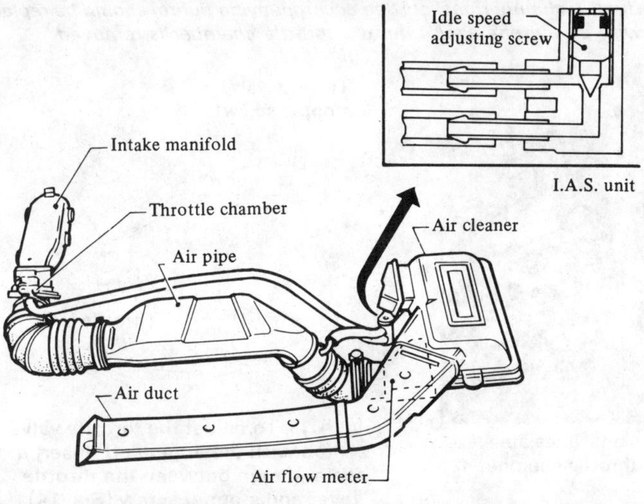

Fig. 4.14 Components of the EFI air flow system (Sec 11)

12 Air flow meter and air temperature sensor – removal and installation

Note: *The air temperature sensor is built into the air flow meter and is not designed to be removed. If the air temperature sensor is defective and needs replacement the entire air flow meter must be replaced as a unit.*
1 Remove the 2 screws that retain the inlet air duct assembly to the radiator support and lift off the duct.
2 On 1980 US models, disconnect the air induction hose or hoses leading from the air cleaner where they attach to the metal tubes.
3 Remove the screw that holds the IAS unit to the air cleaner housing and remove the unit.
4 Remove the 2 remaining screws that retain the top piece of the air cleaner housing to the bottom, and lift off the top section along with the air filter.

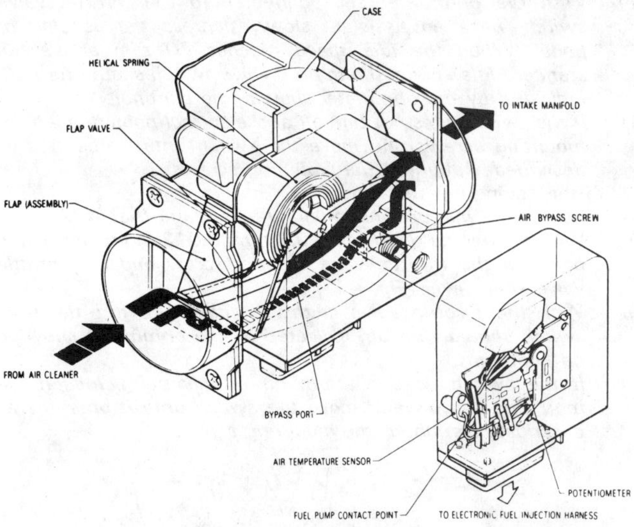

Fig. 4.15 Cutaway view of the air flow meter (Sec 12)

5 Remove the rubber boot leading from the air pipe. Disconnect it from the air flow meter.
6 Remove the 4 bolts that retain the air flow meter and lower air cleaner housing assembly to the body brackets.
7 Disconnect the wiring harness connector from the air flow meter.
8 To separate the air flow meter from the rest of the assembly first remove the brace that connects the air flow meter to the air filter lower housing (photo).
9 Remove the 10 screws that retain the air filter lower housing to the air flow meter duct.
10 Remove the 4 bolts that retain the duct to the air flow meter and separate the two.
11 Installation is the reverse of the removal procedure.

13 Dropping resistor – removal and installation

1 Disconnect the negative battery cable.
2 Remove the air flow meter assembly as described in Section 12.
3 Disconnect the wiring harness connector from the dropping resistor.
4 Remove the 2 screws that attach the resistor to the air flow meter bracket (photo) and lift off the resistor.
5 Installation is the reverse of the removal procedure.

14 Throttle valve switch – removal, installation and adjustment

1 Disconnect the negative battery cable.
2 Remove the screws that retain the throttle valve switch to the throttle chamber and pull the switch off (photo).
3 Using a small screwdriver or other tool spread the wire clip around the wiring harness connector and disconnect it from the throttle valve switch (photo).
4 Installation is the reverse of the removal procedure. **Note**: *After installation the throttle valve switch must be adjusted as described below.*
5 With the engine runnning:

- a) *Disconnect the wiring harness connector from the throttle valve switch*
- b) *Connect an ohmmeter between the number 29 and 30 terminals in the switch. (See the accompanying figure). The ohmmeter should show continuity*
- c) *Connect a tachometer according to the manufacturers instructions*
- d) *With the transmission in neutral, start the engine and check that the idle speed is correct. (Refer to Chapter 1, if necessary)*

e) *With the ohmmeter still connected to the throttle valve switch, have an assistant slowly depress the accelerator pedal. When the idle speed reaches 70 rpm above the standard idle speed, the throttle valve switch should turn off, indicated by the ohmmeter showing no continuity*

f) *If the switch does not turn off at the correct point, loosen the mounting screws and move the switch until it operates as described. Retighten the mounting screws*

6 With the engine not running:

g) *Follow the instructions in paragraphs a and b above*

h) *With the engine off, insert a 0.3 mm (0.012 in) feeler gauge between the throttle valve stopper screw and the throttle valve shaft lever (Fig. 4.17).*

i) *With the throttle valve in this position, the throttle valve switch should turn off, indicated by the ohmmeter showing no continuity*

j) *If the switch does not turn off at this point, loosen the mounting screws and move the switch until it operates as described. Retighten the mounting screws*

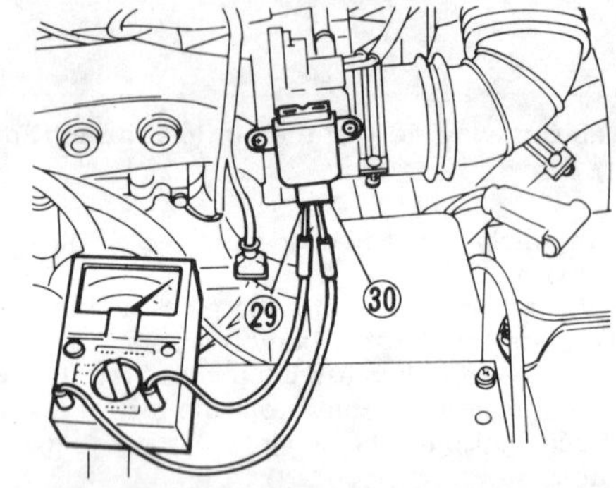

Fig. 4.16 To adjust the throttle valve switch with the engine running, connect an ohmmeter to the terminals shown (Sec 14)

15 Dash pot (automatic transmission models) – removal, installation and adjustment

1 Remove the throttle chamber as described in Section 16.
2 Remove the 2 screws thathold the dash pot assembly to the throttle chamber.
3 Installation is the reverse of the removal procedure. **Note:** *Following installation the dash pot touch speed must be adjusted as follows:*

a) *With the transmission in neutral, set the engine speed to 1500 rpm*

b) *Check that the rod end comes in contact with the adjusting screw when the rod is fully extended, or when no back pressure is present st the diaphragm*

c) *If necessary, turn the adjusting screw until contact is made as specified*

16 Throttle chamber – removal and installation

1 Disconnect the negative battery cable.
2 Remove the 3 vacuum hoses from their connectors on top of the throttle chamber (photo).
3 Remove the 2 screws that hold the throttle valve switch to the throttle chamber. Lift off the throttle valve switch and secure it out of the way.
4 Remove the rubber intake air boot from between the air pipe and the throttle chamber.
5 Remove the rubber hose from the fitting on the underside of the throttle chamber (photo).
6 Disconnect the accelerator cable from the throttle lever.
7 Using a hex wrench, remove the 4 throttle chamber mounting bolts and lift off the chamber (photo).
8 Installation is the reverse of the removal procedure. **Note**: *The throttle chamber gasket (See accompanying figure) should be replaced with a new one each time the throttle chamber is removed.*

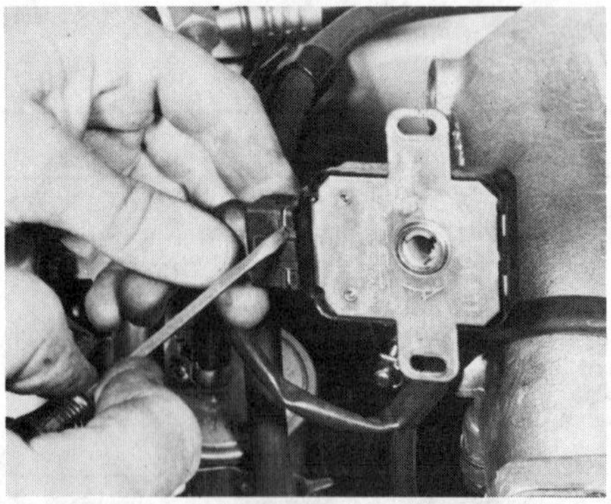

14.3 Many of the EFI wiring components use spring clips which must be pryed apart slightly to remove the connector

16.2 Three main vacuum signal lines are attached to the top of the throttle chamber

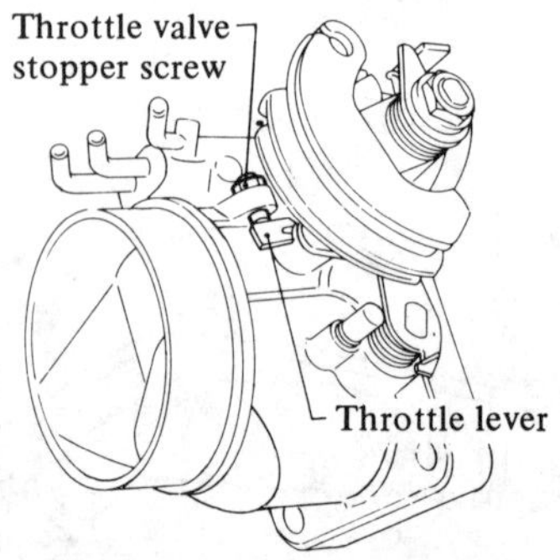

Fig. 4.17 To adjust the throttle valve switch with the engine off, insert a feeler gauge between the throttle lever and stopper screw (Sec 14)

16.5 Removing the hose attached to the lower fitting of the throttle chamber

16.7 A hex wrench is needed to remove the four throttle chamber mounting bolts

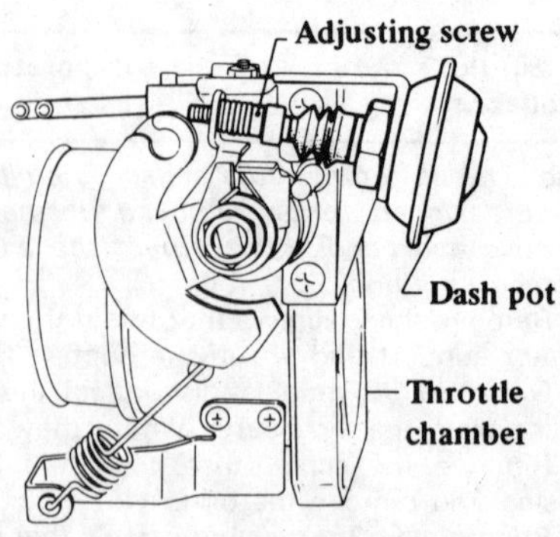

Fig. 4.18 The dash pot is mounted to the throttle chamber (Sec 15)

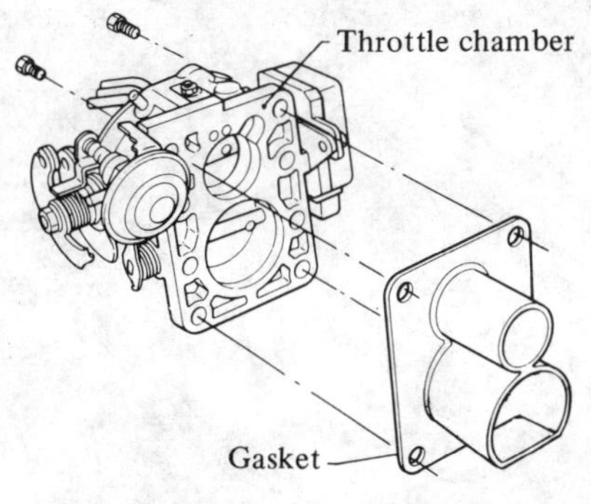

Fig. 4.19 The throttle chamber gasket should be replaced whenever the chamber is removed (Sec 16)

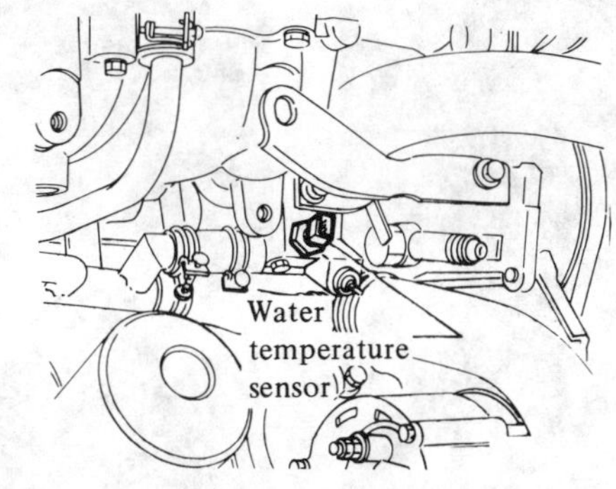

Fig. 4.20 The water temperature sensor (1980 models) is located on the right side of the engine at the thermostat (Sec 17)

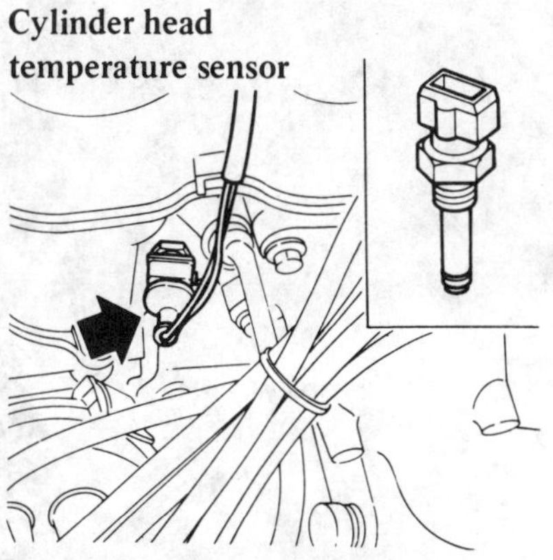

Fig. 4.21 The cylinder head temperature sensor (1981 models) is located on the left side of the engine in front of the exhaust manifold (Sec 17)

17 Water cylinder head temperature sensor – removal and installation

1 Disconnect the negative battery cable.
2 With the engine cool, remove the radiator cap and drain the coolant from the radiator.
3 For clearance on 1980 models remove the air pipe.
4 The water temperature sensor on 1980 models is located on the underside of the intake manifold directly above the rear of the alternator. The cylinder head temperature sensor in 1981 models is located at the left front of the cylinder head. Disconnect the wiring harness connector from the sensor. This connector has a wire spring clip.
5 Unscrew the sensor and remove it.
6 Prior to installing the sensor, wrap the threads with Teflon tape.
7 Installation is the reverse of the removal procedure. Be sure the copper washer is installed when installing the sensor.

18 Air regulator – removal and installation

1 Disconnect the negative battery cable.
2 Disconnect the elbow located directly above the air regulator from its rubber hose and position it out of the way.
3 Disconnect the hoses on either side of the air regulator.
4 Remove the 2 mounting screws (photo).
5 Lift up on the air regulator enough to disconnect the wiring harness from it. This connector uses a wire spring clip and must be spread by using a screwdriver.
6 Installation is the reverse of the removal procedure.

19 Injectors, pressure regulator and fuel pipe assembly – removal and installation

1 In order to prevent the fuel from being sprayed about when the fuel lines are disconnected, the pressure in the lines must be eliminated by using the following procedure:

- a) *Start the engine and allow it to idle*
- b) *While the engine is running, disconnect the wiring harness connector from the fuel pump relay-2. This is located on the relay bracket on the right hand side of the engine compartment (see accompanying figures). The relay bracket must be lifted from the body in order to gain access to the relays*
- c) *After the engine stalls, crank the engine over two or three times*

2 Disconnect the negative battery cable.
3 Loosen the accelerator cable housing adjusting nuts and disconnect the cable from the throttle lever.
4 Disconnect the rubber hose from the vacuum control valve at the rear of the intake manifold (photo). Disconnect the other end of the vacuum control hose from its fitting at the pressure regulator and remove it from the engine.
5 Remove the rubber hose from its fitting in the middle left side of the intake manifold (photo).
6 Remove the tie straps, if equipped, which secure the electrical harness to the fuel pipes.
7 Disconnect the electrical connectors from each side of the injectors and position the wiring harness out of the way.
8 Disconnect the vacuum hoses from both ends of the fuel pipe assembly noting where each is connected. If necessary mark where

18.4 The air regulator is mounted to the intake manifold to the left of the throttle chamber

19.4 The vacuum control valve is located on the rear left side of the intake manifold

19.5 Several hoses must be renewed for clearance when removing the fuel pipe assembly

19.13 Each injector is held to the intake manifold by two screws

19.14 The fuel pipe assembly, pressure regulator and all four injectors are removed from the engine as one assembly

each hose is connected so they will not be mixed up upon reinstallation.

9 Disconnect the vacuum line that leads from the pressure regulator to the intake manifold.

10 Disconnect the fuel feed hose and the fuel return hose from the fuel pipe assembly.

11 Remove the 2 bolts that hold the pressure regulator to the intake manifold.

12 Remove the 2 bolts that hold the fuel pipe assembly to the intake manifold.

13 Remove the screws that secure each of the fuel injectors (photo).

14 Lift the fuel pipe assembly out complete with injectors and pressure regulators (photo).

15 If the fuel injectors need to be removed from the fuel pipe assembly, simply loosen the clamp that retains the injector hose to the fuel pipe and pull the injector off (photo).

16 If the injector hoses are hardened, cracked or otherwise damaged, they should be replaced.

17 If the pressure regulator needs to be replaced, remove the hose that connects it to the pipe assembly.

18 Also check that the lower rubber insulators on each injector are not scratched or worn.

19 Installation is the reverse of the removal procedure with the following notes:

- a) *When inserting the injectors into the intake manifold, be sure the various components shown in the accompanying figure are installed properly; the lower rubber insulator should be free of scratches or abrasion and should be installed so it is air tight*
- b) *The fuel hoses should be installed onto the pipe fittings so that they overlap the pipes by at least 28 mm*
- c) *Turn the ignition switch off again and reconnect the harness connector to the fuel pump relay-2*
- d) *If the engine will not start, remove the wiring harness connector from the fuel pump relay-2, and crank the engine over for about 5 seconds. Then turn the ignition switch off again*

20 Vacuum switch (1980 California models) – removal and installation

1 Disconnect the negative battery cable.
2 Disconnect the vacuum hose from the switch (photo).
3 Disconnect the wiring harness connector from the vacuum switch.
4 Lift the switch out of its spring bracket.
5 Installation is the reverse of the removal procedure.

21 Altitude sensor (1980 California models) – removal and installation

1 The altitude sensor is located in the left side dash panel behind the control unit.

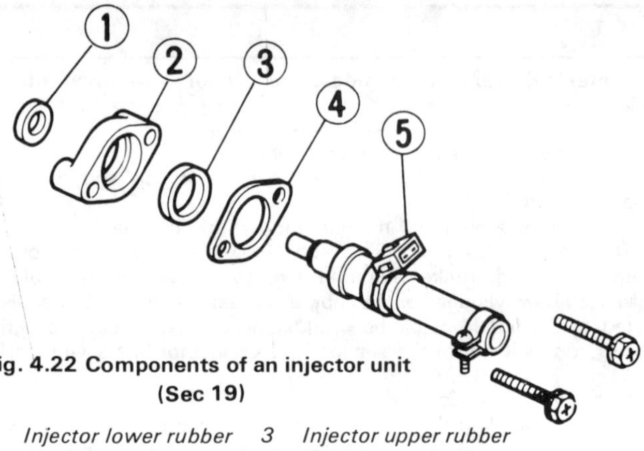

Fig. 4.22 Components of an injector unit (Sec 19)

1 *Injector lower rubber insulator*
2 *Injector lower holder*
3 *Injector upper rubber insulator*
4 *Injector upper holder*
5 *Injector*

2 Disconnect the negative battery cable.
3 Remove the control unit as described in Section 10.
4 Remove the 2 bolts that hold the altitude sensor to the side panel.
5 Disconnect the wiring harness connector from the altitude sensor.
6 Installation is the reverse of the removal procedure.

22 Exhaust gas sensor (1981 US models) – removal and installation

1 Disconnect the negative battery cable.

2 The exhaust gas sensor is located in the exhaust downpipe. Disconnect the wiring harness connector from the sensor.

3 Unscrew the sensor and remove it from the exhaust pipe.

4 Installation is the reverse of the removal procedure. **Note:** *Be sure the sensor is torqued to specifications and that there is no leakage of exhaust gas once installed.*

23 Fuel tank – removal and installation

Note: *Any repairs to the fuel or filler neck should be carried out by a professional who has experience in this critical and potentially dangerous work.*

Caution: *While performing any work on the fuel tank it is advisable to have a CO_2 fire extinguisher on hand and to wear safety glasses. All precautions should be taken to keep any kind of combustion (lighted cigarettes, etc.) or sparks away from the area of the tank and drained fuel.*

1 Disconnect the negative battery cable.

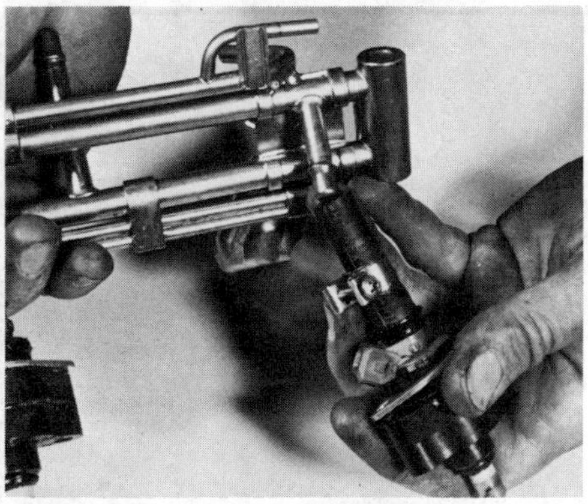

19.15 The injectors can be removed from the fuel pipe assembly by loosening the clamp as shown

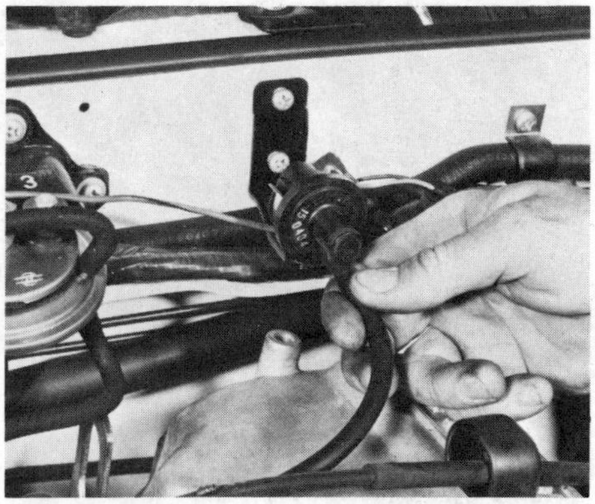

20.2 The vacuum valve (1980 California models) is located on the rear firewall behind the rocker arm cover

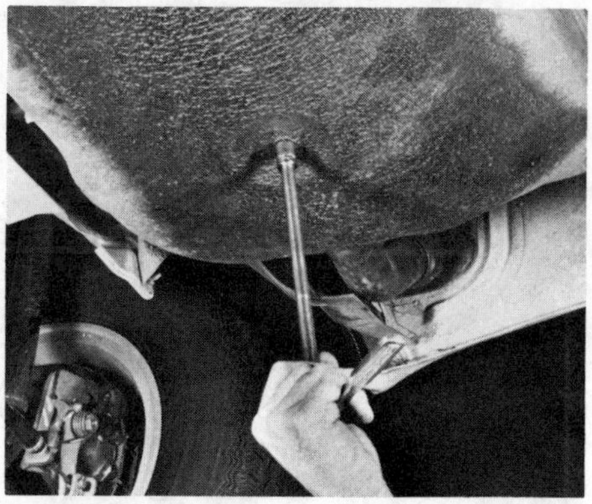

23.2 The fuel tank can be drained by removing the drain plug in the center of the tank

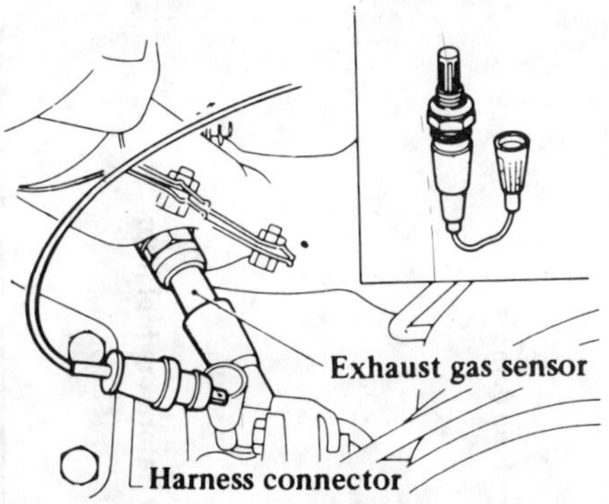

Fig. 4.23 The exhaust gas sensor (1981 US models) is located in the front exhaust pipe (Sec 22)

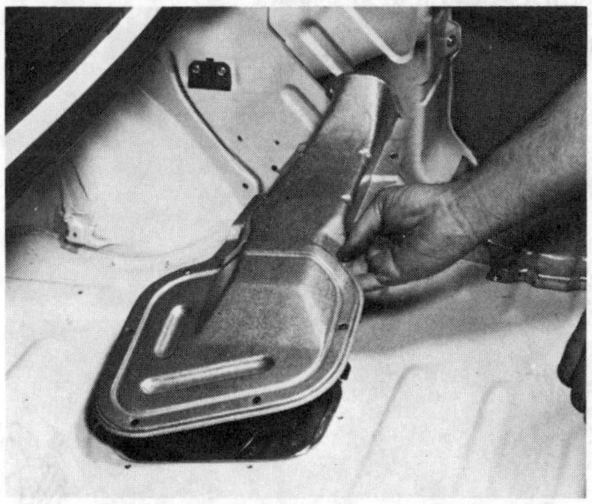

23.4 Metal shields are used to enclose the fuel system components in the trunk or rear hatchback compartment

23.10 On hardtop models, a metal shield is used to protect the fuel filler hose

2 Remove the drain plug from the bottom of the fuel tank (photo) and drain the fuel into a suitable container.
3 Open the trunk or hatchback door and remove the trim piece that allows access to the connections at the top of the fuel tank.
4 Remove the metal shield that covers the fuel tank connections (photo).
5 Disconnect the wiring harness connector that leads to the fuel tank gauge unit (See accompanying figure).
6 Disconnect the fuel tank ventilation hose from its fitting on the top of the fuel tank.
7 Disconnect the 2 evaporation hoses from their fittings.
8 On hatchbacks, disconnect the fuel filler hose.
9 Raise the rear of the car and support it on jack stands.
10 On hardtops, remove the bolt and 2 screws that secure the fuel filler hose shield and lift off the shield. (photo).
11 Disconnect the fuel filler hose from the fuel tank.
12 Disconnect the fuel outlet hose, fuel return hose and evaporation hose from their metal fuel lines directly above the rear axle (see accompanying figure).
13 While the fuel tank is supported, remove the bolts which secure it in place and carefully lower and remove the tank.
14 Before installing the tank make sure that all traces of dirt and corrosion are cleaned from it. A coat of rust preventative paint is recommended. If the tank is rusted internally however, it should be replaced with a new one.
15 Installation is the reverse of the removal procedure.

24 Reservoir tank (hatchback) – removal and installation

1 Remove the negative battery cable.
2 Open the hatchback door and remove the trim panels that will

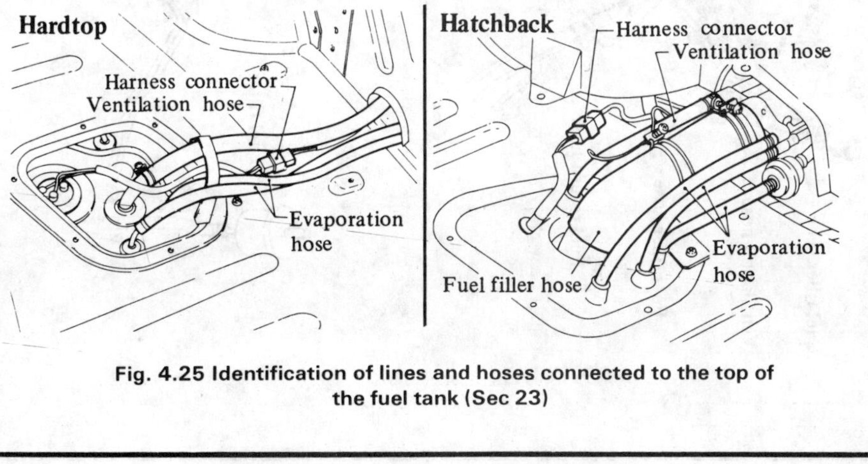

Fig. 4.25 Identification of lines and hoses connected to the top of the fuel tank (Sec 23)

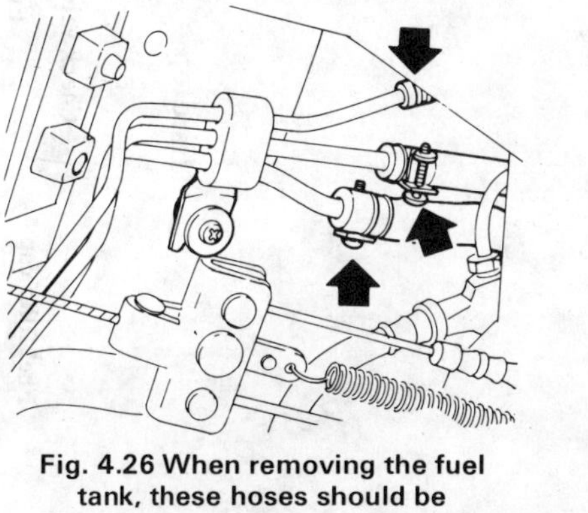

Fig. 4.26 When removing the fuel tank, these hoses should be disconnected where they meet the metal lines above the rear axle (Sec 23)

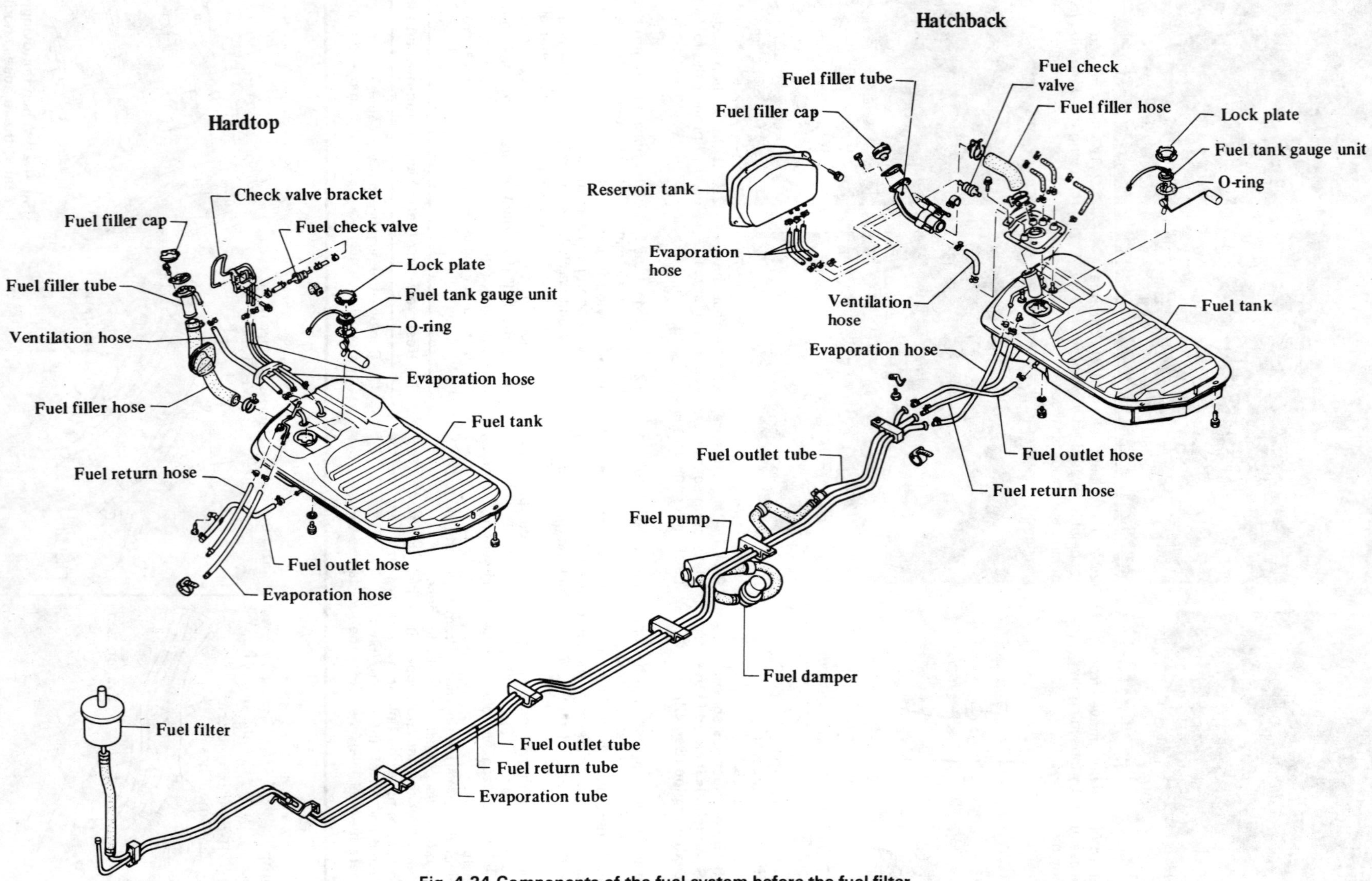

Fig. 4.24 Components of the fuel system before the fuel filter

allow access to the reservoir tank.
3 Remove the right speaker.
4 Remove the side lower finisher (See accompanying figure).
5 Remove the metal shield that protects the reservoir tank.
6 Remove the evaporation hoses from the reservoir tank.
7 Remove the bolts that secure the reservoir tank to the body and lift the tank out.
8 The same precautions apply to the reservoir tank as were noted under fuel tank removal in Section 23.
9 Installation is the reverse of the removal procedure.

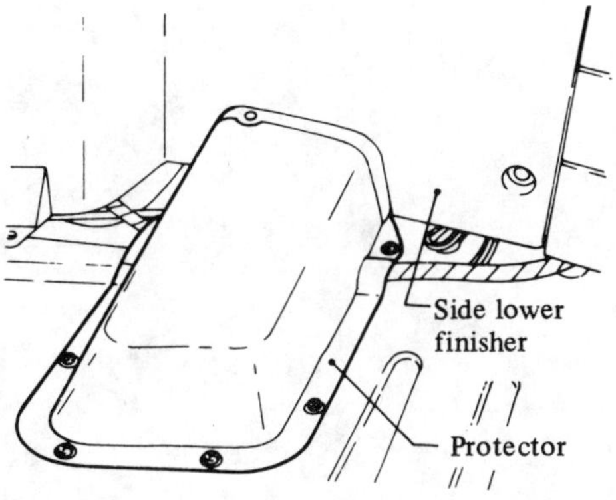

Fig. 4.27 On hatchback models, the side lower finisher and protector must be removed to reach the reservoir tank (Sec 24)

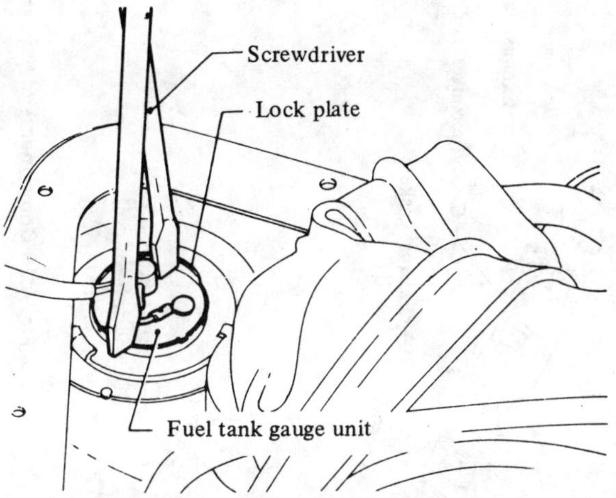

Fig. 4.28 Two screwdrivers can be used as shown to twist off the fuel tank gauge unit lock plate (Sec 26)

25 Fuel tank – cleaning and purging

1 Drain and remove the fuel tank as described in Section 23.
2 Remove he fuel tank gauge unit as decribed in Section 26.
3 Turn the tank over and empty out any remaining fuel.
4 If repair work needs to be done to the fuel tank that does not involve any heat or flame, the tank can be satisfactorily cleaned by running hot water into it and letting it overflow out the top for at least five minutes. **This method, however, does not remove gas vapors.**
5 If repair work involving heat or flame is necessary, have it done by an experienced professional. The following, more thorough procedures should be used to remove all fuel and vapors from the tank.
6 Fill the tank completely with tap water, agitate vigorously and drain.
7 Add a gasoline emulsifying agent to the tank according to the manufacturer's instructions, refill with water, agitate approximately 10 minutes and drain.
8 Flush to overflowing once again with water for several minutes and drain.
9 The tank is now ready for repair work.
10 Under no circumstances perform repair work involving heat or flame without first carrying out the above procedures.

26 Fuel tank gauge unit – removal and installation

Caution: *While performing any work on the fuel tank it is advisable to have a CO_2 fire extinguisher on hand and to wear safety glasses. All precautions should be taken to keep any kind of combustion (lighted cigarettes, etc.) or sparks away from the area of the tank.*
1 Disconnect the **negative** battery cable.
2 Open the trunk or hatchback door and remove the trim piece that allows access to the connections at the top of the fuel tank.
3 Remove the metal shield that covers the fuel tank connections.
4 Disconnect the wiring connector leading to the fuel tank gauge unit.
5 Remove the rubber grommet.
6 Using two screwdrivers as shown in the accompanying figure, turn the gauge unit lock plate counterclockwise until the gauge unit can be lifted from the tank.
7 Installation is the reverse of the removal procedure.

27 Check valve – removal and installation

1 Remove the trunk or hatchback finishing panels on the right side, giving access to the check valve (photo).
2 Disconnect the check valve from its hoses and remove it.
3 Installation is the reverse of the removal procedure.

28 Exhaust system – general information

The exhaust system consists of the muffler, catalytic converter and

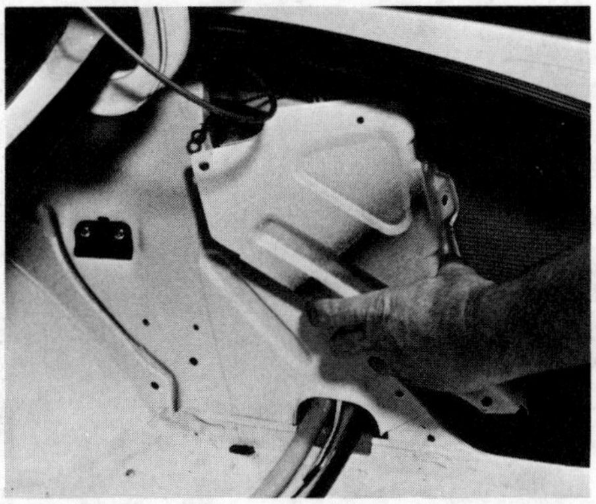

27.1 On hardtop models, remove inside right trunk trim to reach fuel check valve

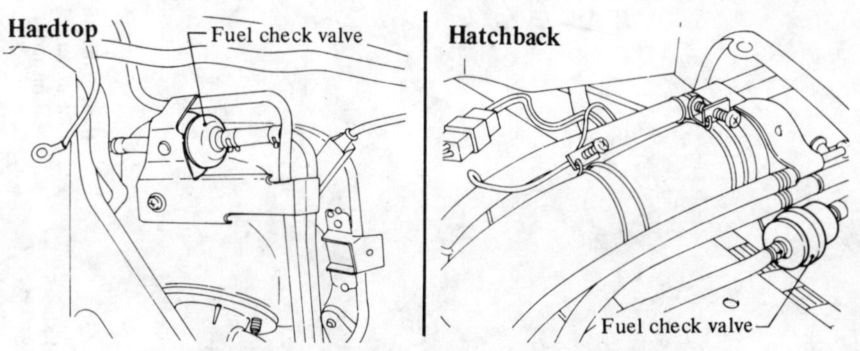

Fig. 4.29 The fuel check valve is located on the right side of the trunk (hardtop) or rear compartment (hatchback) (Sec 27)

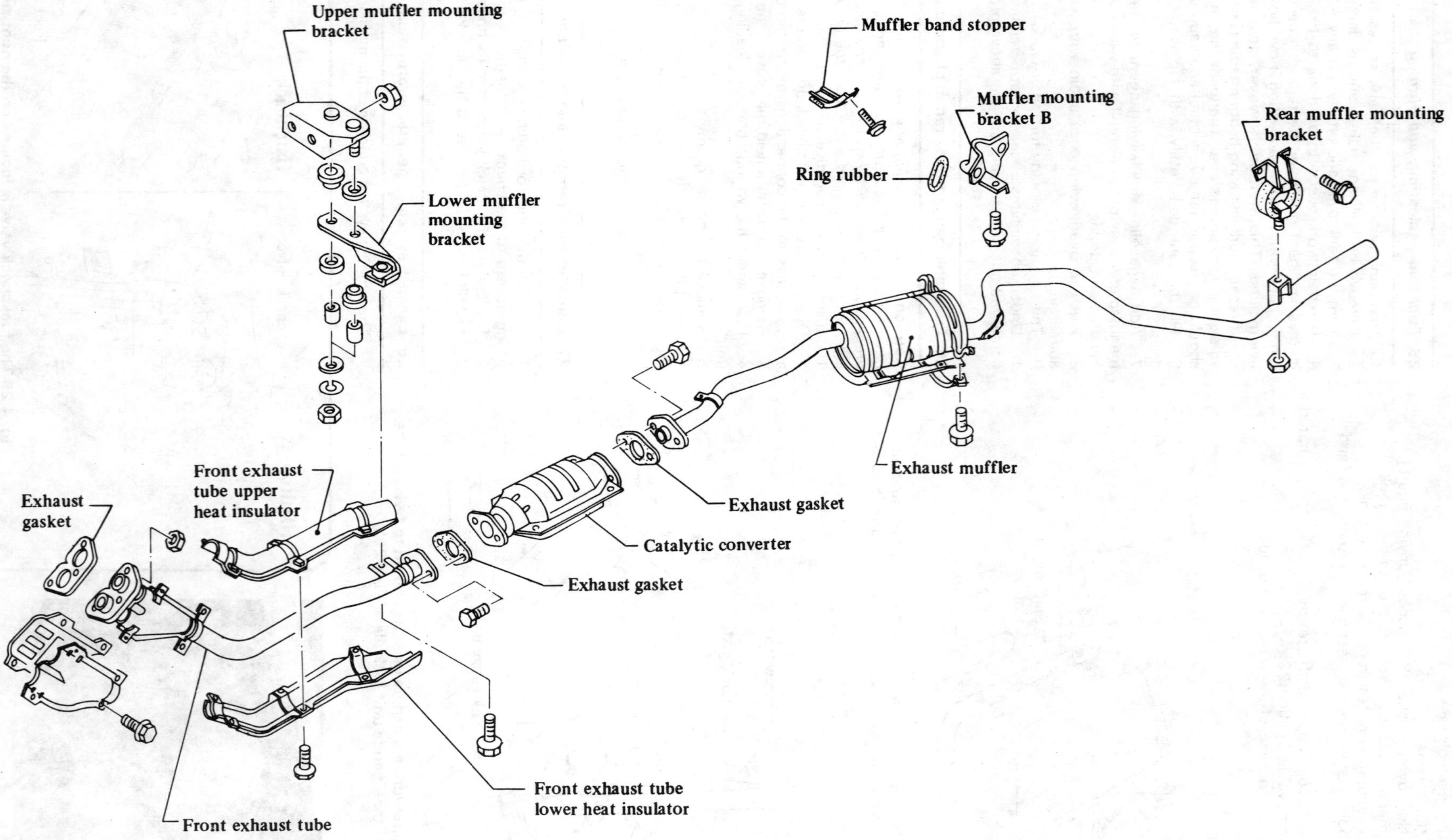

Fig. 4.30 Components of the exhaust system

exhaust pipes and includes three main pieces: the front exhaust pipe which attaches to the exhaust manifold, the catalytic converter and the intermediate pipe-muffler-tailpipe assembly.

The catalytic converter is attached to both front exhaust pipe and the intermediate pipe by mounting bolts. The muffler, on the other hand, is welded to the intermediate pipe and the tailpipe.

The interior of the catalytic converter is a honeycomb-like design that is coated with platinum and rhodium. When these elements interact with the hydrocarbon (HC), carbon manoxide (CO) and oxides of nitrogen (NOx) in the exhaust, it causes reactions to occur that convert the CO to CO_2 (carbon dioxide), the HC to CO and H_2O (water), and reduces the NOx.

In 1980 models, the catalytic converter is aided in this process by the Air Induction System, while in 1981 US models, the Mixture Ratio Feedback System is designed to keep the fuel/air mixture at the optimum ratio for the conversions to take place. Both of these systems are described in Chapter 6.

Since lead and phosphorus additives in gasoline can poison the converter's catalytic elements, thus rendering it ineffective in altering the gases' toxic elements, only unleaded fuel should be used in the vehicle.

Periodic maintenance of the converter is not required but it has limited working life after which it must be replaced. This is usually at intervals of around 30 000 miles (48 000 km).

In order to accurately test the functioning of the converter, a CO test is needed. For this reason, we recommend you take the car to a Datsun dealer or other qualified shop to have the converter tested.

If, through physical damage, the use of leaded fuels or because its active elements have been depleted, the catalytic converter is rendered ineffective, it must be replaced as a unit. For the replacement procedure refer to Section 31.

It should be noted that since the internal chemical conversions occur between the 600° and 1200°F, the converter operates at a very high temperature. Before performing any work on or near the converter, be sure it has cooled sufficiently to avoid serious burns.

When replacing any exhaust system parts, be sure you allow enough clearance from all points on the underbody to avoid overheating the floor pan and possibly damaging the interior carpet and insulation.

The entire exhaust system is attached to the body with mounting brackets and mounting rubbers. If any one of the parts are improperly installed, excessive noise and vibration will be transmitted to the body.

Regular inspection of the exhaust system should be made to keep it at maximum efficiency. Look for any damage or mispositioned parts, open seams, holes, loose conections, excessive corrosion or other defects which could allow exhaust fumes to seep into the car.

29 Exhaust system – inspection

1 Because inspection of the exhaust system is part of the routine maintenance schedule, refer to Chapter 1 for this procedure.

30 Front exhaust pipe – removal and installation

1 Raise the front of the car and support it on jack stands.
2 Remove the lower catalytic converter shield.
3 Using a piece of thick wire, secure the catalytic converter to the underside of the car.
4 Remove the lower muffler mounting bracket.
5 Loosen, but do not remove the 2 bolts attaching the front exhaust pipe to the catalytic converter. If the bolts are corroded and cannot be easily broken loose, penetrating oil and tapping with a plastic-head hammer may help.
6 Remove the bolts that attach the front exhaust pipe to the exhaust manifold. Again, penetrating oil and tapping may be necessary.
7 Now, while supporting the front exhaust pipe, remove the 2 bolts holding the pipe to the converter, and lift out the pipe.
8 Installation is the reverse of the removal procedure. **Note:** *Be sure to use new gaskets between the front exhaust pipe and the exhaust manifold, and the front exhaust pipe and the catalytic converter. Also, before installing the bolts that attach these parts, apply an anti-sieze compound to the threads.*

31 Catalytic converter – removal and installation

1 Raise the front of the car and support it on jack stands.
2 Remove the lower catalytic converter shield.
3 Using a piece of strong wire, secure the intermediate exhaust pipe to the driveshaft.
4 Remove the muffler mounting bracket.
5 While supporting the catalytic converter, break loose, but do not yet remove the 4 converter mounting bolts that attach the converter to the front and intermediate exhaust pipes. If the bolts are corroded and cannot be easily broken loose, penetrating oil and tapping with a plastic headed hammer may help.
6 While supporting the catalytic converter, remove all 4 mounting bolts, and remove the converter from the car.
7 Installation is the reverse of the removal procedure. **Note:** *Be sure to use new gaskets during installation. Also, before installing the mounting bolts, apply an anti-sieze compound to the threads.*

32 Muffler/tail pipe – removal and installation

1 The muffler is welded onto both rear intermediate pipe and the tail pipe, and the entire assembly is designed to be replaced as a unit. However, if the muffler needs replacing but the tail pipe is in good condition, a muffler shop will be able to cut off the old muffler and weld on a new one without having to replace the pipes as well. If you wish to replace the entire section as one piece, access to a hydraulic lift is needed for clearance reasons.
2 Raise the car on a hydraulic lift.
3 Remove the nut that attaches the tailpipe to the rear muffler mounting bracket.
4 Remove the 2 bolts that attach the catalytic converter to the intermediate pipe. If the bolts are corroded and cannot be easily removed, penetrating oil and tapping with a plastic headed hammer may help.
5 Disengage the muffler from the rubber rings that support it from the floor pan.
6 Remove the assembly by pulling it toward the front of the car, turning it as necessary for clearance.
7 Installation is the reverse of the removal procedure. **Note:** *Before installing the bolts that attach the converter to the intermediate pipe, apply an antisieze compound to the threads.*

Chapter 5 Engine electrical systems

Refer to Chapter 13 for information related to 1982 and 1983 models

Contents

Air-gap – adjustment ... 3
Alternator – maintenance and special precautions ... 15
Alternator – removal and installation ... 17
Charging system – general information ... 14
Charging system – testing ... 16
Distributor – installation ... 7
Distributor – removal ... 6
IC ignition unit – removal and installation ... 4
Ignition coil – removal and installation ... 8
Ignition system – general information ... 1
Ignition system – testing ... 2
Starter motor – brush replacement ... 13
Starter motor – removal and installation ... 11
Starter solenoid – removal and installation ... 12
Starting system – general information ... 9
Starting system – testing ... 10
Stator and magnet (pick-up assembly) – removal and installation ... 5

Specifications

Ignition system

Distributor

Type	
1980 California models	
Automatic transmission	D4N9-05
Manual transmission	D4N9-04
1980 49-state models (all)	D4K9-09
1980 Canada models (all)	D4K9-10
1981 US models (all):	
Automatic transmission	D4N80-13
Manual transmission	D4N80-12
1981 Canada models	
Automatic transmission	D4K9-10
Manual transmission	D4K9-14
Direction of rotation	Counterclockwise
Firing order	1-3-4-2
Air gap	0.3 to 0.5 mm (0.012 to 0.020 in)
Distributor cap carbon point length	
1980 California and all 1981 U.S. models	10 mm (0.39 in)
1980 49-state and all Canada models	12 mm (0.47 in)

Ignition coil

Type	
1980 California models	CIT-38
1981 US models (all)	CIT-46
1980 49-state and all Canada models	CIT-30
Primary voltage	12 volts
Primary resistance at 68°C (20°C)	
1980 California and all 1981 US models	1.04 to 1.27 Ohms
1980 49-state and all Canada models	0.84 to 1.02 Ohms
Secondary resistance at 68°F (20°C)	
1980 California and all 1981 US models	7.3 to 11.0
1980 49-state and all Canada models	8.2 to 12.4

Spark plugs

All spark plug information is contained in the Chapter 1 specifications.

Starting system

Starter motor

Type	
US models with automatic transmission	S114-180F
US models with manual transmission	
1980	S114-229E
1981	S114-229F
Canada models (all):	
1980	S114-255A
1981	S114-304
Terminal voltage (no load)	
US models	11.5 Volts
Canada models	11 Volts
Current (no load)	
US models	less than 60 Amps
Canada models	less than 100 Amps
Speed (no load)	
US models with automatic transmission	over 6000 rpm
US models with manual transmission	over 7000 rpm
Canada models (all)	over 3900 rpm
Minimum brush length	
US models	12 mm (0.47 in)
Canada models	11 mm (0.43 in)

Charging system

Alternator

Type	
1980 models	LR160-47
1981 models	LR 160-78
Nominal rating	12 Volts/60 Amps
Hot output current	
1980 models	Over 45 Amps at 2500 rpm Over 60 Amps at 5000 rpm
1981 models	Over 50 Amps at 2500 rpm Over 60 Amps at 5000 rpm
Regulated output voltage	14.4 to 15.0 Volts
Minimum brush length	
1980 models	7.5 mm (0.29 in)
1981 models	7.0 mm (0.28 in)

1 Ignition system – general information

In order that the engine can run correctly it is necessary for an electrical spark to ignite the fuel/air mixture in the combustion chamber at exactly the right moment in relation to engine speed and load. The ignition system is based on feeding low tension (LT) voltage from the battery to the coil where it is converted to high tension (HT) voltage. The high tension voltage is powerful enough to jump the spark plug gap in the cylinders many times a second under high compression pressures, providing that the system is in good condition and that all adjustments are correct.

The ignition system is divided into two circuits; the low tension circuit and the high tension circuit.

The low tension (sometimes known as the primary) circuit consists of the ignition switch, ignition and accessory relay, the primary windings of the ignition coil(s), the transistorized IC ignition unit, the pick-up assembly in the distributor and all connecting wires.

The high tension circuit consists of the high tension or secondary windings of the ignition coil(s) the heavy ignition lead from the center of the coil to the center of the distributor cap, the rotor, the spark plug leads and spark plugs.

The distributor used in this system is a pulse-triggered, transistor-controlled, inductive discharge unit in which the contact points of a conventional distributor are replaced by a control module and magnetic pick-up assembly.

The system functions in the following manner. Low tension voltage fed to the coils is changed into high tension voltage by the magnetic pick-up in the distributor. When the ignition switch is turned on, current flows through the primary circuit. A reluctor on the distributor shaft is aligned with the magnetic stator element of the pick-up assembly within the distributor housing, and as it turns it induces a low voltage in the pick-up coil. When the teeth on the reluctor and the magnets in the stator line up, a signal passes to the IC ignition unit which opens the coil's primary circuit. When the primary circuit is opened by the transistor unit, the magnetic field built up in the primary winding collapses and induces a very high voltage in the secondary winding. The high voltage current then flows from the coil, along the heavy ignition lead, to the carbon brush in the distributor cap. From the carbon brush, current flows to the distributor rotor which distributes the current to one of the terminals in the distributor cap. The spark occurs while the high tension voltage jumps across the spark plug gap. This process is repeated for each power stroke of the engine.

The system features a longer spark duration and the dwell period automatically increases with engine speed. This is desirable for fitting the leaner mixtures provided by the emissions control systems.

The IU ignition unit used in U.S. models is located inside the distributor, while the IU unit used in Canada models is attached to the outside of the distributor housing.

Because the Z20E Datsun engine used in U.S. models uses two sets of spark plugs for each cylinder, the ignition system utilizes two ignition coils. Both are located on the left side of the engine compartment, directly behind the air cleaner housing. The upper coil works in conjunction with the exhaust plugs, while the lower one works with the intake plugs. Canada models use a conventional set-up with 1 spark plug per cylinder and 1 ignition coil.

The distributor used on all models is equipped with both mechanical and vacuum advanced mechanisms. The mechanical governor mechanism compresses two weights which move out from the distributor shaft due to centrifugal force as the engine speed increases. The weights are held in position by two light springs, and it is the tension of the springs which is largely responsible for the correct spark advancement.

The vacuum control consists of a diaphragm, one side of which is connected via a small-bore tube to a vacuum source, and the other side to the magnetic pick-up assembly. Vacuum in the intake manifold which varies with engine speed and throttle opening, causes the diaphragm to move, which, in turn, moves the magnetic pick-up assembly, thus advancing or retarding the spark. The distributor vacuum advance is controlled by the Spark Timing Control System, and is explained in detail in Chapter 6.

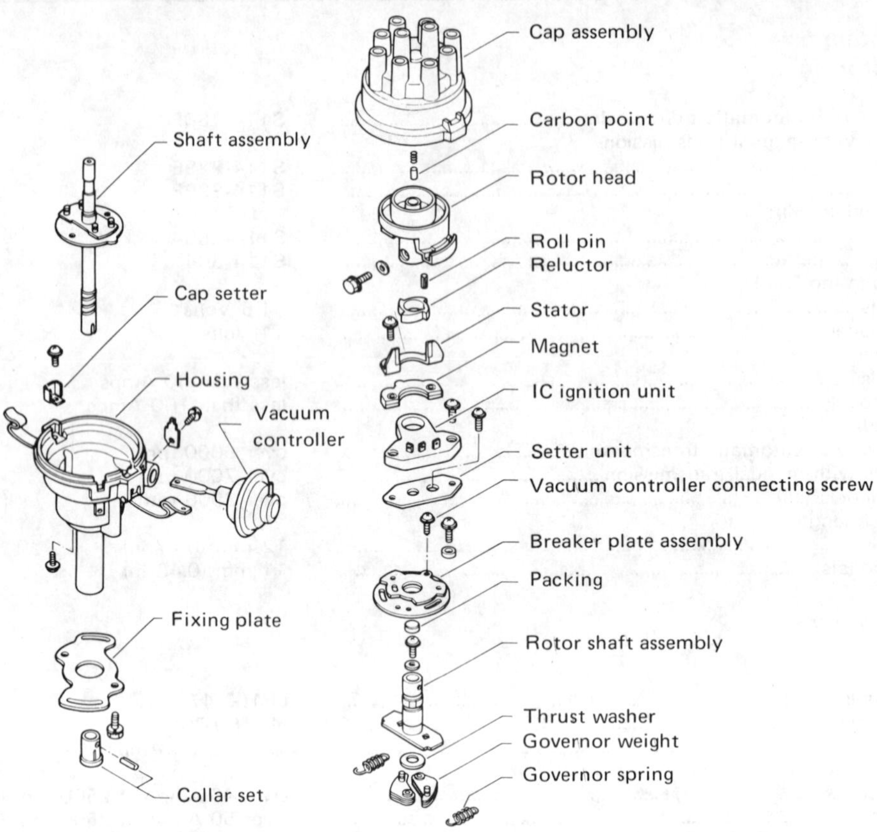

Fig. 5.1 Exploded view of the distributor (1980 California models and all 1981 U.S. models)

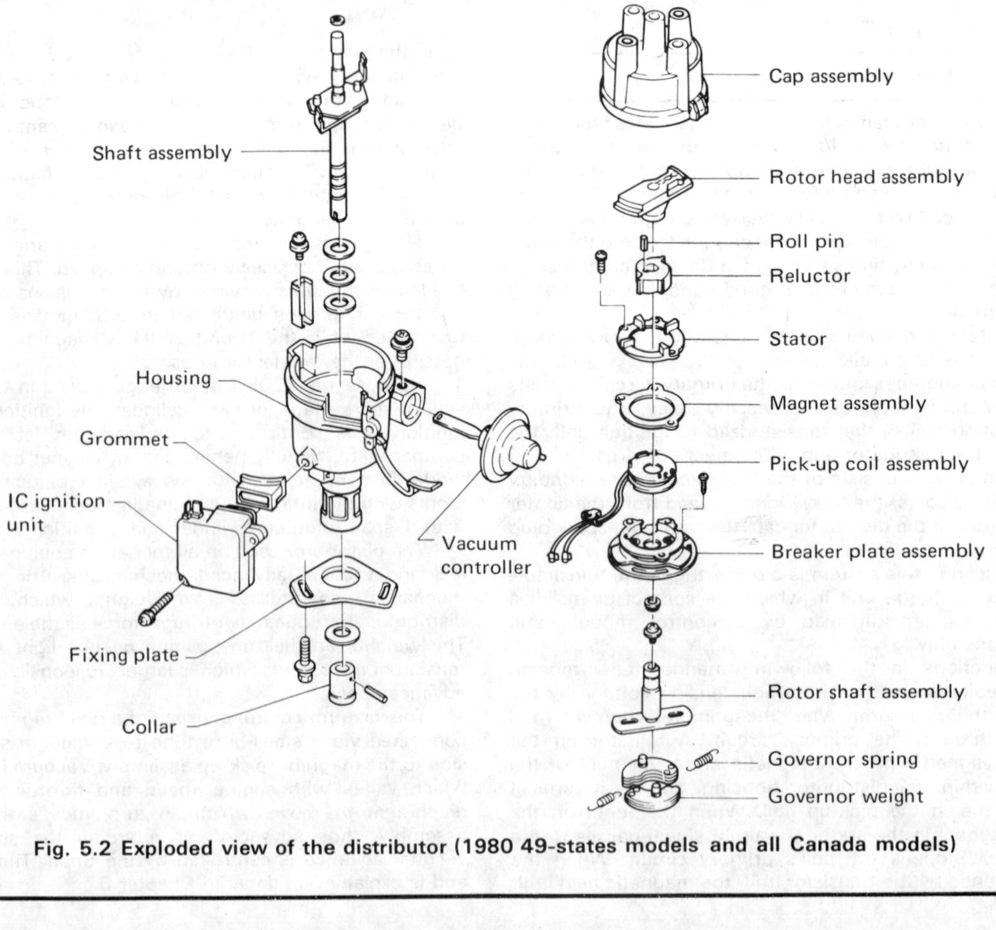

Fig. 5.2 Exploded view of the distributor (1980 49-states models and all Canada models)

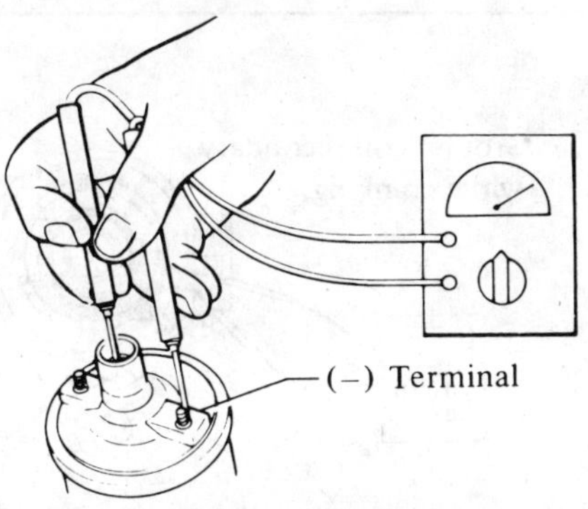

Fig. 5.3 Proper ohmmeter connections for checking the secondary circuit of the ignition coil (Sec 2)

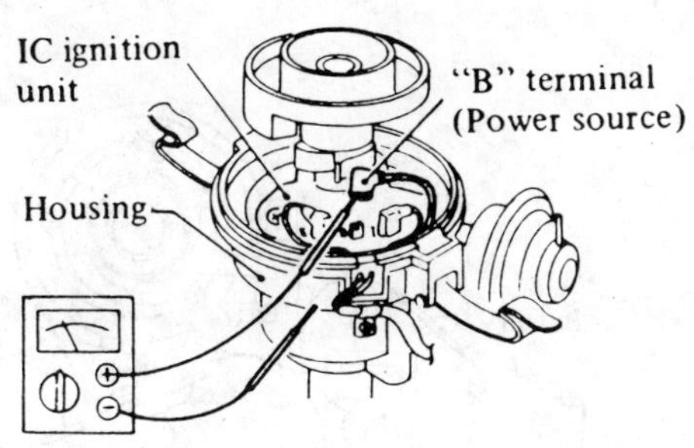

Fig. 5.4 Proper voltmeter connections for checking the power supply circuit (dual ignition systems) (Sec 2)

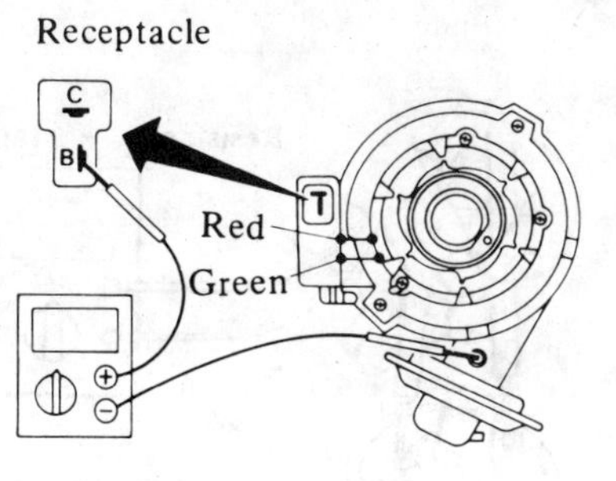

Fig. 5.5 Proper voltmeter connections for checking the power supply circuits (single ignition systems) (Sec 2)

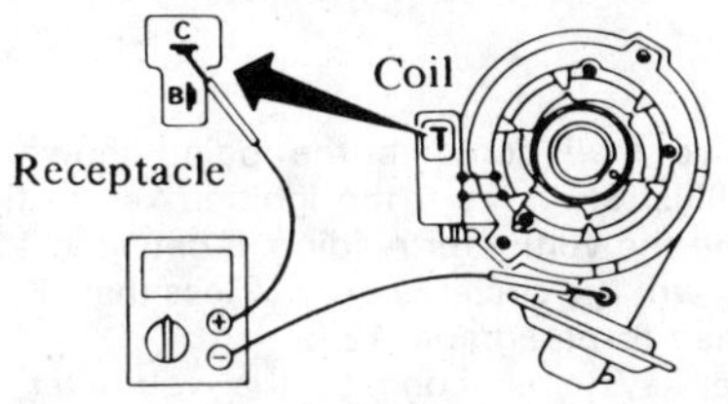

Fig. 5.6 Proper voltmeter connections for checking the ignition primary circuit (single ignition systems) (Sec 2)

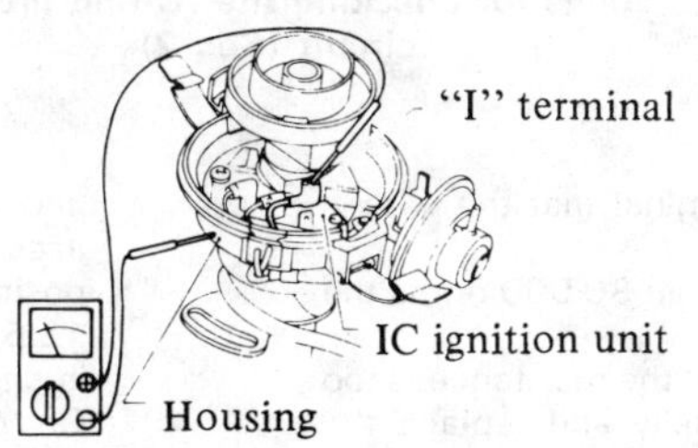

Fig. 5.7 Proper voltmeter connections for checking the ignition primary circuit (dual ignition systems – step one) (Sec 2)

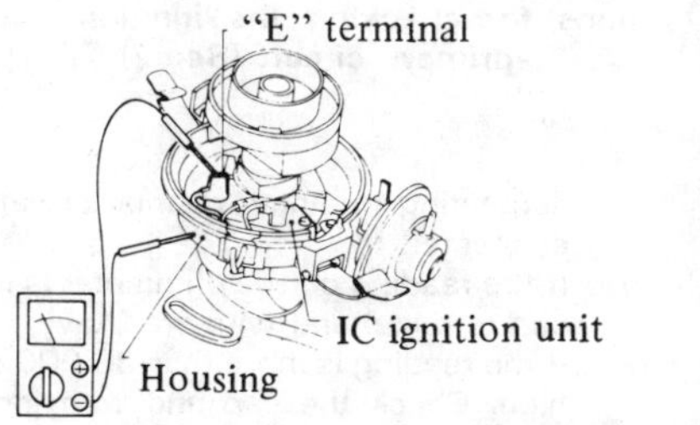

Fig. 5.8 Proper voltmeter connections for checking the ignition primary circuit (dual ignition systems – step two) (Sec 2)

Caution: *Because of the higher voltage generated by this electronic ignition system, extreme caution should be taken whenever an operation is performed involving ignition components. This not only includes the distributor, coil, control module and ignition wires, but related items are connected to the system as well, such as the plug connections, tachometer and any testing equipment. Consequently, before any work is performed such as replacing ignition components or even connecting testing equipment, the ignition should be turned off or the battery ground cable disconnected.*

Note: *Never disconnect any of the ignition HT leads when the engine is running, or the transistor ignition unit will be permanently damaged.*

2 Ignition system – testing

Caution: *Never touch your bare hand to any high tension cables or parts while the engine is running or being cranked. Even insulated parts can cause a shock if they are moist. It is recommended that you wear dry, insulated gloves or wrap the part in dry cloth before handling.*

1 If the car will turn over but will not start, the first check of the ignition system should be to visually inspect the condition of the spark plugs, spark plug wires, distributor cap and rotor as described in Chapter 1.

2 If these are all in good condition, and the plug wires are secure in their connections, the next check should be to see if current is flowing through the high tension circuit, thus sparking the plugs.

a) Turn the ignition switch to the 'OFF' position.
b) Disconnect the EFI fusible link connector located near the positive battery terminal (refer to Chapter 10).
c) Disconnect the wiring connector leading to the cold start valve.
d) Disconnect the ignition coil wire from the distributor cap and hold it approximately $\frac{3}{16}$ to $\frac{1}{4}$ inch (4 to 5 mm) from a clean metal area of the engine (note paragraph 1). Have an assistant crank the engine over and check if a spark occurs between the coil wire and the engine. In systems with two ignition coils check both coil wires in this manner.
e) If a spark occurs, the ignition system is okay, and the problem lies in another system. If no spark occurs, or occurs intermittently, proceed with further ignition system tests.

3 In order to accurately diagnose problems in the Datsun system, a voltmeter which measures in the 0 to 20 volts DC and 0 to 10 volts AC ranges, and an ohmmeter which measures in the 0 to 1000 ohms and 0 to 5000 ohms ranges are needed.

4 If it is possible to start the engine, do so and let it run about 5 to 15 minutes with the hood closed to bring all components to normal operating temperature.

5 *Checking the battery voltage with no load.*

a) With the ignition key in the 'OFF' position, connect a voltmeter so its positive lead is on the positive battery terminal and its negative lead is on the negative battery terminal.
b) Note the reading on the voltmeter. If the reading is between 11.5 volts and 12.5 volts, the battery is okay and you should proceed to paragraph 6.
c) If the reading is below 11.5 volts, the battery is insufficiently charged. It should be brought to a full charge either by running the engine or by using a battery charger. If the car has been used on a regular basis and there is no obvious cause for the battery to be discharged (such as leaving the lights on), then the condition of the battery, charging system and starting system should be checked out as described in this chapter or Chapter 1.

6 *Checking the battery voltage while the engine is cranking.*

a) Leave the voltmeter connected to the battery as in the last paragraph.
b) Disconnect the ignition coil wire(s) from the distributor cap and ground it to the engine.
c) Have an assistant crank the engine over for about 15 seconds and note the reading on the voltmeter.
d) If the voltage is more than 9.6 volts, the battery is okay and you should proceed to paragraph 7. If the voltage was below 9.6 volts the battery is insufficiently charged. Refer to paragraph 5.

7 *Checking the distributor cap and secondary winding.*

a) Disconnect the spark plug wires from the plugs.
b) Disconnect the ignition coil wire(s) from the coil(s).
c) Remove the distributor cap, with spark plug and coil wires still attached.
d) Connect an ohmmeter so that one lead is inserted in the spark plug end of one of the plug wires and the other lead is

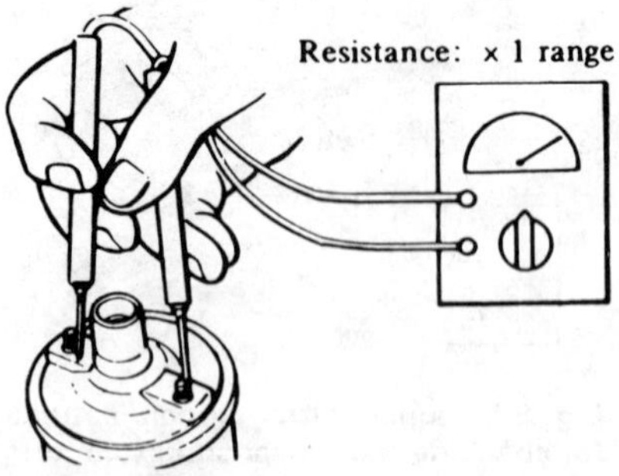

Fig. 5.9 Proper ohmmeter connections for checking the ignition coil primary circuit (Sec 2)

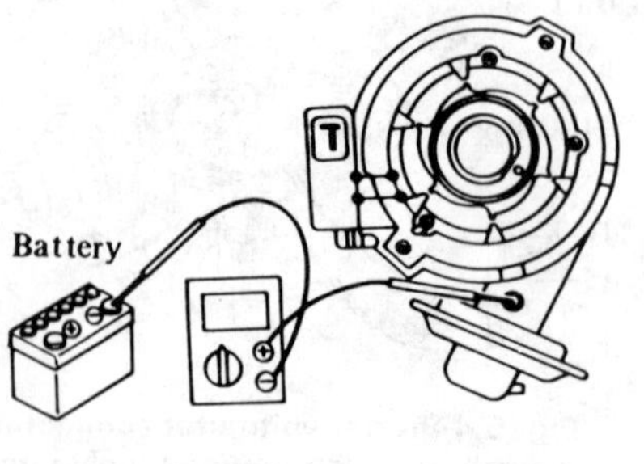

Fig. 5.10 Proper voltmeter connections for checking the IC unit ground circuit (Sec 2)

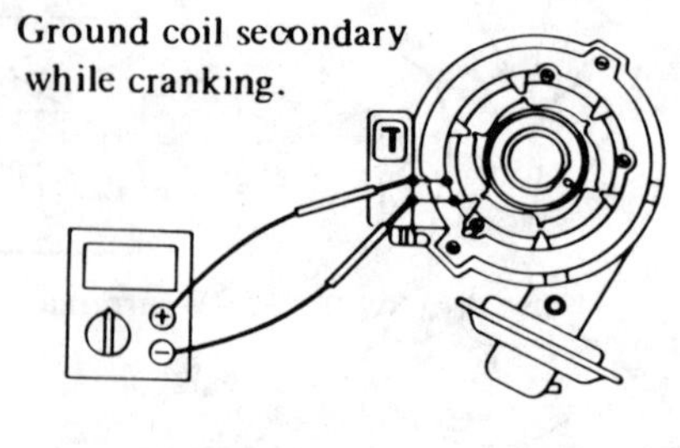

Fig. 5.11 Proper voltmeter connections for checking the pick-up coil resistance (single ignition systems) (Sec 2)

contacting the inner distributor cap terminal that the wire is connected to.

e) If the reading on the ohmmeter is less than 30 000 ohms the cap terminal and wire are okay.

f) If the reading is more than 30 000 ohms, the resistance is too high. Check the cap and wire individually and replace the appropriate part.

g) Repeat this test on each of the spark plug and coil wires.

8 *Checking the ignition coil secondary circuit.*

a) With the ignition key in the 'OFF' position, connect the ohmmeter so that one lead is contacting the center high tension wire connector and the other lead is contacting the negative coil terminal.

b) If the reading is between 7300 and 11 000 ohms on dual ignition systems (1980 California models and all 1981 U.S. models) or between 8200 and 12 400 ohms on single ignition systems, (1980 49 States models and all Canada models), the secondary coil windings are okay.

c) If the ohmmeter reading is not within these specs, replace the ignition coil (on systems with dual ignition coils be sure to test each coil).

9 *Checking the power supply circuit at the distributor.*

a) On dual ignition systems, connect the positive lead of the voltmeter to the 'B' terminal on the IC ignition unit in the distributor (when performing this or any of the following tests, it is not necessary to disconnect the wiring connector when hooking up the voltmeter or ohmmeter, providing they have probes that can be inserted into the rear of the connector).

b) Ground the negative voltmeter lead to the outside of the distributor body.

c) On single ignition systems, connect the positive voltmeter lead to the 'B' connection. Ground the negative voltmeter lead to the point shown in the accompanying illustration.

d) Turn the ignition key to the 'ON' position and note the voltmeter reading.

e) If the reading is between 11.5 and 12.5 volts, the power supply circuit is okay. If the reading is below 11.5 volts, inspect the wiring between the ignition switch and the IC unit for damage, or loose or dirty connections.

10 *Checking the power supply circuit while the engine is being cranked.*

a) Ground the coil wire(s) to the engine.

b) Connect the voltmeter as in paragraph 9.

c) Have an assistant crank the engine over for about 15 seconds and note the reading on the voltmeter.

d) If the reading is less than 1 volt below the battery cranking voltage (measure in paragraph 6) and is greater than 8.6 volts, the circuit is okay.

e) If the reading is more than 1 volt below the battery cranking voltage and/or is below 8.6 volts, inspect the wiring between the ignition switch and the IC unit for damage, or loose or dirty connections.

11 *Checking the ignition primary circuit.*

a) On single ignition systems, connect the voltmeter so the positive lead is connected to the 'C' terminal on the IC unit, and the negative lead contacts the point shown in the accompanying illustration. Turn the ignition key to the 'ON' position and note the voltmeter reading. If between 11.5 and 12.5 volts is shown, the circuit is okay. If less than 11.5 volts is shown, proceed to paragraph 12.

b) On dual ignition systems, connect the voltmeter so the positive lead contacts the 'I' terminal on the IC unit, and the negative lead contacts the outside of the distributor body. Turn the ignition key to the 'ON' position and note the voltmeter reading. If less than 11.5 volts is shown, proceed to paragraph 12. If between 11.5 and 12.5 volts is shown, reconnect the positive voltmeter lead to the 'E' terminal on the IC unit and, with the ignition key still 'ON', take another voltmeter reading. If between 11.5 and 12.5 volts is shown again, the circuit is okay. If less than 11.5 volts is shown on this reading, proceed to paragraph 12.

12 *Checking the ignition coil primary circuit.*

a) With the ignition key in the 'OFF' position and the ignition coil wire removed from the coil, connect an ohmmeter (set in the Ix range) between the positive and negative terminals on the ignition coil.

b) If the ohmmeter reading is between 1.04 and 1.27 ohms (dual ignition systems) or between 0.84 and 1.02 ohms (single ignition systems) the coil is okay, and the ignition switch and the wiring running between the ignition switch, the coil and the IC unit should be checked for damage, or loose or dirty connections.

c) If the ohmmeter reading is not within these specs, the ignition coil should be replaced.

d) In dual ignition systems, be sure to test both ignition coils.

13 *Checking the IC unit ground circuit.*

a) Remove the ignition coil wire(s) from the distributor cap and ground it to the engine.

b) Connect a voltmeter so its negative lead is connected to the negative battery terminal, and the positive lead is connected to the point shown in the accompanying illustration.

c) Have an assistant crank the engine over for about 15 seconds, and note the voltmeter reading.

d) If more than 0.5 volts is shown, check the grounding of the distributor, the wiring between the battery and the chassis ground and the negative battery cable connection.

e) If the reading shows 0.5 volts or less on dual ignition systems, the IC unit should be replaced.

f) If 0.5 volts or less is shown in single ignition systems, further checks are still needed. Proceed to paragraph 14.

14 *Checking the pick-up coil resistance.*

a) For this check the engine should be at normal operating temperature.

b) With the ignition switch in the 'OFF' position, connect an ohmmeter (set in the 100x range) as shown in the accompanying illustration and note the reading.

c) If approximately 400 ohms is shown, the pick-up coil resistance is okay.

d) If the reading is substantially above or below 400 ohms, inspect the pick-up coil and its wiring for damage, or loose or

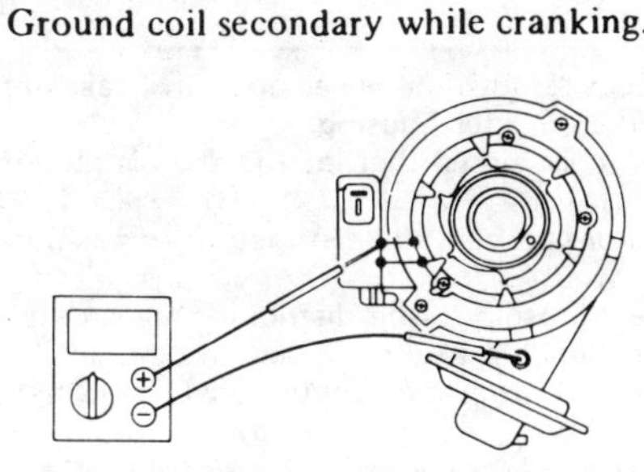

Fig. 5.12 Proper voltmeter connections for checking the pick-up coil output (single ignition systems) (Sec 2)

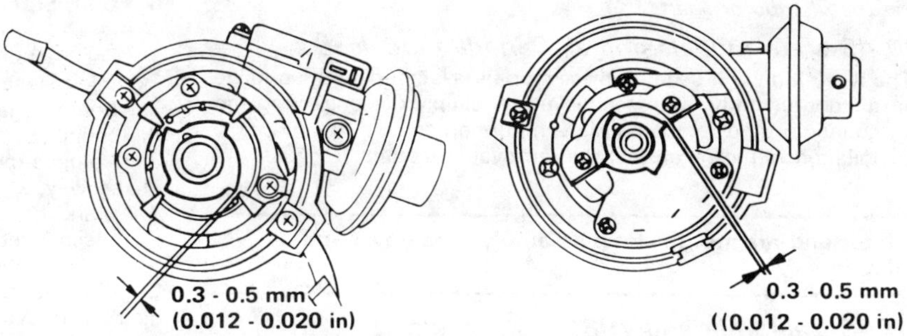

Fig. 5.13 The air gap is the distance between the reluctor teeth and the stator magnets (right: 1980 California models and all 1981 US models; left: 1980 49-states models and all Canada models) (Sec 3)

dirty connections.

15 *Checking the pick-up coil output.*

a) The engine should still be at normal operating temperature.
b) Connect a voltmeter (set on the low AC volt scale) between the points shown in the accompanying illustration.
c) Have an assistant crank the engine over for about 15 seconds, and observe the movement of the voltmeter needle.
d) If the needle is steady, check the physical condition of the pick-up coil and reluctor for damage. Also check the wiring between the pick-up coil and the IC unit for damage, or loose or dirty connections.
e) If the needle wavers while the engine is being cranked, and there is still no spark being produced, replace the IC unit.

3 Air gap – adjustment

Note: *To ensure that the ignition system functions correctly, the air-gap (distance between the pick-up coil and reluctor) must be maintained as specified. To do this, proceed as follows:*

1 Disengage the two spring retaining clips and remove the cap from the distributor.
2 Remove the rotor from the end of the distributor shaft.
3 Position one of the raised segments of the reluctor directly opposite the pole piece protruding from the pick-up coil. This is best carried out by removing the spark plugs (to relieve compression) and rotating the engine by pulling on the alternator drivebelt. Another method is to turn the crankshaft by using a ratchet wrench on the crankshaft bolt at the front of the engine.
4 Using feeler gauges, measure the gap between the pole and the reluctor segment which should be 0.3 to 0.5 mm (0.012 to 0.020 in). If the air-gap requires adjustment, loosen the pick-up coil retaining screws and move the coil in the required direction.
5 When the correct air-gap has been obtained, tighten the pick-up coil retaining screws; install the rotor and the distributor cap, ensuring that the cap is correctly positioned.
6 The pick-up can be removed by removing the two retaining screws and disconnecting the primary leads at the terminal block below the air cleaner.

4 IC ignition unit – removal and installation

1980 California models and all 1981 U.S. models

1 Remove both the ignition coil wire(s) from the coil.
2 Remove the distributor cap from the distributor and secure it out of the way. **Note:** *For extra clearance you may want to remove the air induction system hoses and valve case from the air cleaner housing.*
3 Remove the bolt on the side of the rotor and remove the rotor from the distributor shaft.
4 Using two screwdrivers pry off the reluctor from the distributor shaft (be careful not to damage the teeth) (photo).
5 Remove the 3 wires from the IC ignition unit (photo).
6 Remove the 2 screws that retain the IC ignition unit to the distributor and lift it out.
7 Installation is the reverse of the removal procedure.
Note: *The reluctor can be installed simply by pressing it back on the*

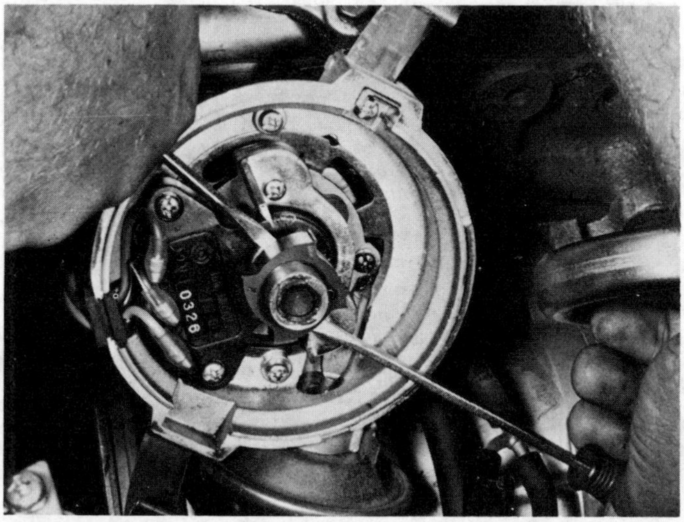

4.4 The reluctor is best removed from the distributor shaft by using two screwdrivers to pry up as shown

4.5 The IC unit (internal type) has three wire connections and is attached to the distributor by two screws

distributor shaft. The pin in the reluctor should be lined up with the flat spot in the distributor shaft.

1980 49-state models and all Canada models

8 The IC ignition unit used on these models is located on the outside of the distributor body, and is removed by simply disconnecting the wiring connector and removing the 2 mounting screws.
9 Installation is the reverse of the removal procedure.

5 Stator and magnet (pick-up assembly) – removal and installation

All 1980 California and 1981 US models

1 Remove the ignition coil wires from the distributor cap.
2 Remove the distributor cap from the distributor and secure it out of the way. **Note:** *For extra clearance you may want to remove the air induction system hoses and valve case from the air cleaner housing.*
3 Remove the bolt on the side of the rotor and remove the rotor from the distributor shaft.
4 Using 2 screwdrivers positioned on either side of the reluctor, pry the reluctor off of the distributor shaft. Be careful not to damage the teeth of the reluctor.
5 Remove the screws that retain the stator and magnet to the breaker plate and lift them off.
6 Installation is the reverse of the removal procedure.
Note: *the reluctor can be installed simply by pressing it back on the distributor shaft, but be sure the pin in the reluctor is lined up with the float side of the distributor shaft.*
Also, before tightening the stator, check and adjust the air gap as described in Section 3.

All 1980 49 States models and '80 and '81 Canada models

7 Disconnect the ignition coil wire from the top of the distributor cap.
8 Remove the distributor cap from the distributor and position it out of the way.
9 Pull off the rotor from the distributor shaft.
10 Using 2 screwdrivers on either side of the reluctor carefully pry the reluctor from the distributor shaft. Be careful not to damage the teeth on the reluctor.
11 Remove the screws that retain the stator and magnet to the distributor breaker plate and lift them off.
12 Disconnect the distributor wiring harness and lift out the pick-up coil assembly.
13 Installation is the reverse of the removal procedure with tne following notes: When installing the reluctor, be sure the pin is lined up with the flat side of the distributor shaft. Also, before tightening the stator, check and adjust the air gap as described in Section 3.

6 Distributor – removal

1 For clearance purposes remove the hoses and valve case of the air induction system from the air filter housing.
2 Remove the ignition coil wire(s) that lead to the distributor from the coil(s).
3 Remove the distributor cap from the distributor and position it out of the way.
4 Mark the rotor in relationship to the distributor housing (photo).
5 Disconnect the wires leading to the IC ignition unit.
6 Remove the vacuum line from the vacuum advance canister.
7 Remove the 2 distributor mounting screws and lift out the distributor. **Note:** *Be sure not to loosen the distributor adjusting screws (photo).*

7 Distributor – installation

If the engine was not rotated after removal

1 Position the rotor in the location it was in when the distributor was removed.
2 Lower the distributor down into the engine. To mesh the groove in the bottom of the distributor shaft with the drive spindle (which turns the distributor shaft), it may be necessary to turn the rotors slightly.
3 With the base of the distributor all the way down against the engine block and the mounting screw holes lined up, the rotor should be pointing to the mark made on the distributor housing during removal. If the rotor is not in alignment with the mark, repeat the previous steps.
4 Install the 2 distributor mounting screws and tighten them securely.
5 Connect the vacuum line to the vacuum advance canister.
6 Reconnect the wires to the IC unit.
7 Reinstall the distributor cap and connect the ignition coil wire(s).
8 Check the ignition timing as described in Chapter 1.

If the engine was rotated after removal

9 Turn the crankshaft by applying a wrench to the crankshaft pulley bolt at the front of the engine until the number 1 piston is at Top-Dead-Center (TDC). This can be ascertained by removing the number 1 spark plug and inserting a dial gauge in the plug hole. If you are careful not to scratch the cylinder, you can also use a length of stiff wire to feel the piston come to the top of the cylinder. One other method is to use a flashlight and watch the piston through the hole.
10 Since the number 1 and 4 pistons are both at the top of their stroke at the same time, be sure the number 1 piston is at TDC by checking that the timing marks at the front pulley are correctly lined up. If this is not the case, rotate the number 1 piston one more revolution.

6.4 Prior to removing the distributor the relationship of the rotor to the distributor body should be marked for ease of installation

6.7 To remove the distributor, only the two attaching bolts (arrows), need be unscrewed (do not loosen the adjusting bolts marked with white paint)

11 Temporarily install the distributor cap onto the distributor. Note where the number 1 spark plug terminal inside the cap is located in relation to the distributor body, and make a mark on the outside of the body at this point.
12 Remove the distributor cap again. Rotate the rotor until it is aligned with the mark. In this position it should be firing the number one spark plug.
13 Proceed with installation as detailed in paragraphs 2 through 8. Disregard the rotor mark references is paragraph 3.

8 Ignition coil – removal and installation

1 Remove the coil wire leading from the distributor.
2 Remove the dust boot.
3 Peel back the rubber dust caps from the coil terminals and remove the nuts and wires from the coil.
4 Remove the 2 screws that hold the coil bracket to the body and lift off the coil.
5 If the coil needs to be removed from its bracket loosen the bracket screws until the bracket is loose enough for the coil to be pulled out.
6 Installation is the reverse of the removal procedure.

9 Starting system – general information

The function of the starting system is to crank the engine. This system is composed of a starting motor, solenoid and battery. The battery supplies the electrical energy to the solenoid, which then completes the circuit to the starting motor which does the actual work of cranking the engine.

Models sold in the U.S. use a non-reduction gear type of starter motor. On this starter, the solenoid is mounted on top of the starter motor. When the ignition switch is operated, the solenoid's gearshift lever moves the starter drive pinion gear into engagement with the teeth on the flywheel. As the solenoid reaches the end of its stroke and with the pinion by now partially engaged with the flywheel ring gear associated with inertia type starter motors.

Models sold in Canada are equipped with a reduction gear type of starter. This starter operates in a similar manner to the type described above except that in order to combat extremely low temperatures, increased rotating torque is provided through a reduction gear located between the armature and pinion gear.

An overrunning clutch is fitted to both types of starter motor to transmit the driving torque and to prevent the armature from overrunning when the engine fires and starts.

The solenoid and starting motor are mounted together at the rear right side of the engine. No periodic lubrication or maintenance is required to the starting system components.

The electrical circuitry of the vehicle is attanged so that the starter motor can only be operated on automatic transmission models when the lever is at 'P' or 'N'.

Never operate the starter motor for more than 30 seconds at a time without pausing to allow it to cool for at least two minutes. Excessive cranking can cause overheating, which can seriously damage the starter.

10 Starting system – testing

1 If the starter motor does not rotate at all when the switch is operated on an automatic transmission model, check that the shifter is in the 'N' or 'P' position.
2 Check that the battery is well charged and all cables, both at the battery and starter solenoid terminals, are secure.
3 If the motor can be heard spinning but the engine is not being cranked, then the overrunning clutch in the starter motor is slipping and the assembly must be removed from the engine and replaced.
4 Often when the starter fails to operate, a click can be heard coming from the starter solenoid when the ignition switch is turned to the 'start' position. If this is heard, proceed to paragraph 12. If even this click is not heard, disconnect the ignition wire (usually black and yellow) from the starter solenoid.
5 Connect a test light between this lead and the negative battery terminal.
6 Have an assistant turn the key, and note whether the test light comes on or not. If the light comes on, proceed to paragraph 12.
7 If the test light did not come on, connect a voltmeter (set on the low scale) between the positive battery terminal and the bayonet connector at the solenoid. The black and yellow wire should be connected.
8 Disconnect the ignition coil wire(s) from the distributor cap and ground it to the engine, so the car will not start.
9 Have an assistant attempt to crank the engine over and note the reading on the voltmeter. If less than 1.5 volts is shown, there is an open circuit in the starter, and it should be replaced with a new or rebuilt unit.
10 If the voltmeter shows more than 1.5 volts, connect a jumper wire between the positive battery terminal and the 'S' terminal on the solenoid.
11 Again, turn the ignition switch to the 'start' position and listen for a clock from the solenoid. If there still is no click and the starter does not turn, both the solenoid and starter are defective and should be replaced. If a click is heard and the starter turns, then there is an open circuit in the ignition switch, inhibitor switch or relay (on automatic transmission models) or in the wires or connectors.
12 If a click was heard when the ignition switch was turned to the 'start' position in paragraph 4, or if the starter turned at all, then the starter current should be tested. Disconnect the positive battery cable at the starter.
13 Connect an ammeter (set in the 500A range) between this cable and its terminal on the starter.
14 Remove the ignition coil wire(s) from the distributor cap to keep the engine from starting.
15 Have an assistant attempt to crank the engine and note the reading on the ammeter and the speed at which the starter turns.
16 If the ammeter reading was less than 150 amps and the starter speed was normal, the starter is okay and the problem lies elsewhere.
17 If the reading was less than 150 amps but the starter motor speed was slow, proceed to paragraph 22.
18 If the ammeter reading was more than 150 amps, reinstall the ignition coil wire into the distributor cap.
19 Have an assistant start the engine, but hold the key in the 'start' position so that the starter motor doesn't stop operating. Note the ammeter reading. (Do not allow the starter motor to turn for more than 30 seconds at a time).
20 If the ammeter reading is less than 60 amps and the starter turns fast, then the problem is a mechanical one such as a tight engine. Check that the engine oil is not too thick, and for other causes of resistance within the engine.
21 If the ammeter reading was over 60 amps, the starter is shorted and must be replaced with a new one.
22 If the ammeter reading in paragraph 15 was less than 150 amps, but the starter turned slowly, test for a voltage drop in the starter positive circuit.
23 Connect a voltmeter (set on the low scale) so the positive lead is on the positive battery post (or cable) and the negative lead is connected to the 'M' solenoid terminal (this is the terminal with the braided copper strap leading to the starter motor).
24 Remove the ignition coil wire(s) from the distributor cap and ground them on the engine.
25 Have an assistant attempt to crank the engine over and note the reading on the voltmeter. If less than 1 volt is shown, proceed to paragraph 28.
26 If more than 1 volt is shown, connect the negative voltmeter lead to the B solenoid terminal (this is the terminal which connects to the battery).
27 Again, have an assistant crank the engine and note the reading on the voltmeter. If more than 1 volt is shown, then the problem is a bad connection between the battery and the starter solenoid. Check the positive battery cable for looseness or corrosion. If the reading indicated less than 1 volt, then the solenoid is defective and should be replaced.
28 If the voltmeter test in paragraph 25 showed less than 1 volt, test for a voltage drop in the starter ground circuit.
29 Connect the negative lead of the voltmeter (set on the low scale) to the negative battery terminal, and hold the positive voltmeter lead to the starter housing. Be sure to make a good connection.
30 Have an assistant crank the engine and note the voltmeter reading. If the reading shows more than 0.5 volts, then there is a bad

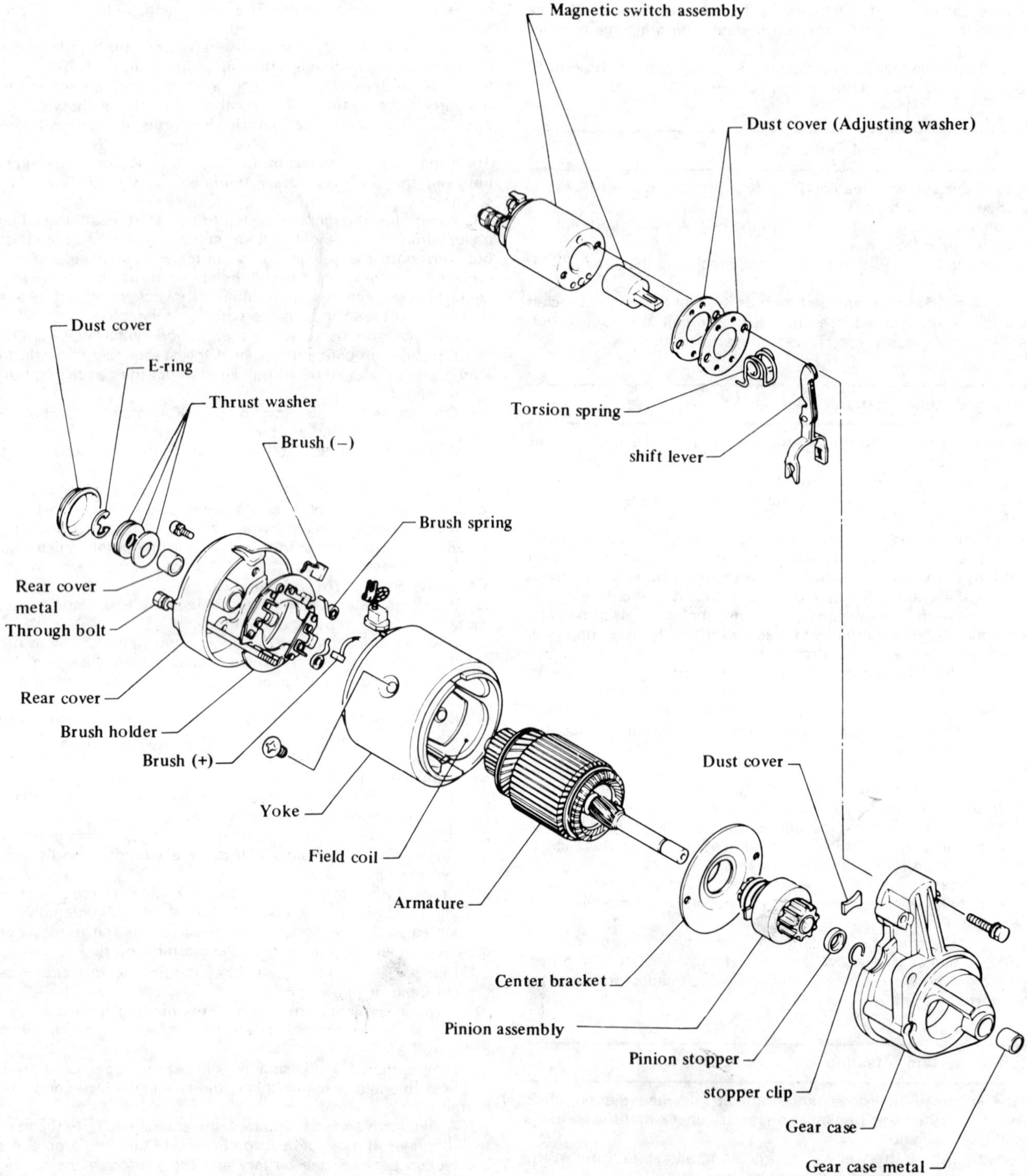

Fig. 5.14 Exploded view of the starter motor and solenoid (non-reduction gear type)

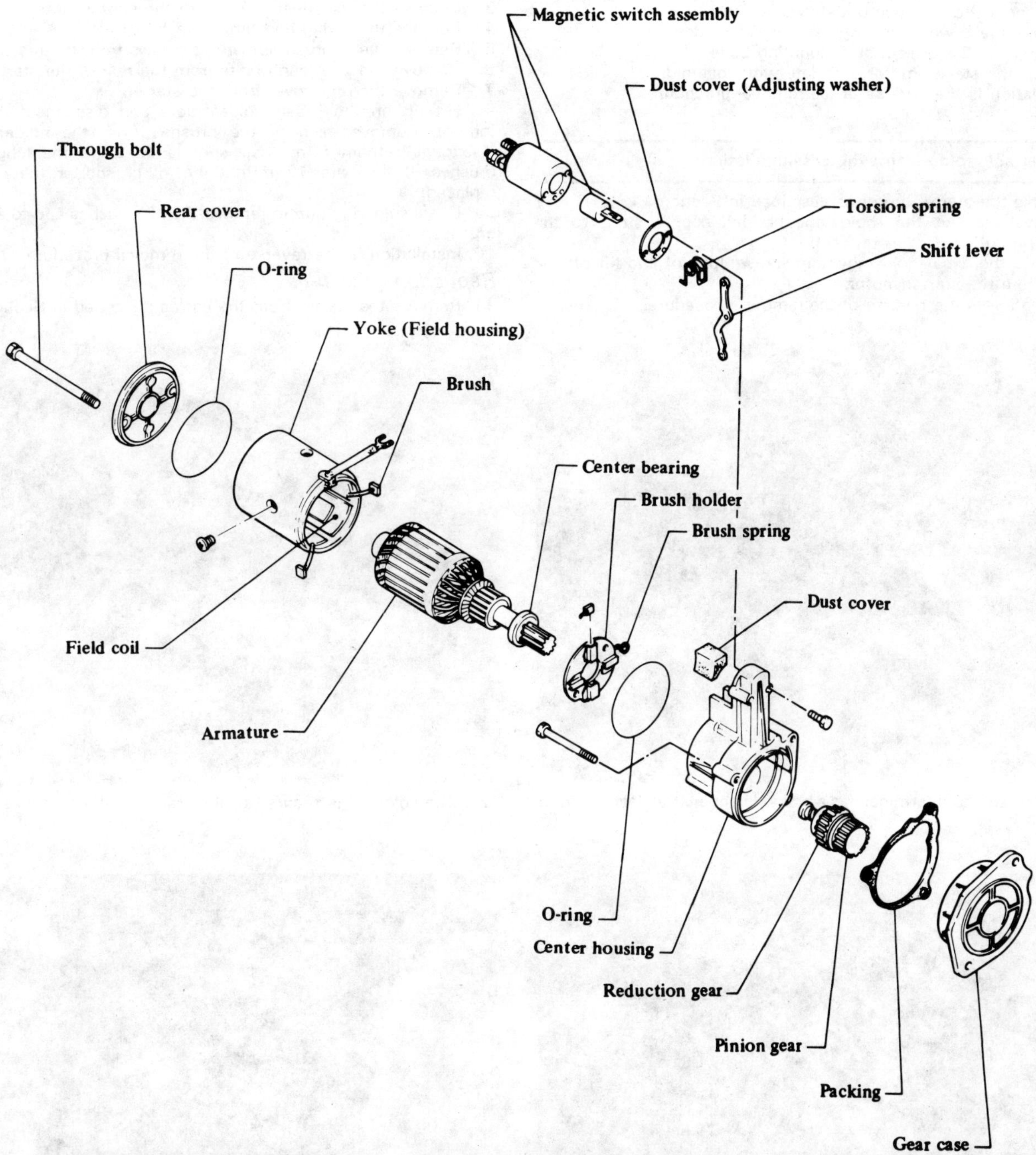

Fig. 5.15 Exploded view of the starter motor and solenoid (reduction gear type)

ground connection. Check the negative battery cable for looseness or corrosion. Also check the starter motor ground connections and the tightness of the starter motor mounting bolts.
31 If the voltmeter reading shows less than 0.5 volts, proceed to paragraph 7 and follow the procedure outlined there.

11 Starter motor – removal and installation

1 Disconnect the negative battery cable.
2 Remove the 2 wires from the starter solenoid.
3 Remove the 2 starter motor mounting bolts.
4 Lift out the starter motor complete with solenoid.
5 Installation is the reverse of the removal procedure.

12 Starter solenoid – removal and installation

1 Remove the starter motor as described in Section 11.
2 Remove the nut that holds the braided copper strap to the solenoid (photo).
3 Remove the 2 solenoid mounting screws (photo) and lift off the solenoid from the starter motor.
4 Installation is the reverse of the removal procedure.

Note: *During installation be sure to engage the solenoid plunger with the starter motor shift lever (photo).*

13 Starter motor – brush replacement

Non-reduction gear type

1 Remove the starter motor as described in Section 11.
2 Remove the starter solenoid as described in Section 12.
3 Remove the rear dust cover from the starter motor.
4 Remove the E-ring and thrust washer.
5 Remove the 2 brush holder set screws from the rear plate.
6 Remove the 2 through bolts from the rear of the starter.
7 Remove the rear cover from the starter.
8 Lift up on the brush holder plate and disconnect the springs (photo). Remove each of the brushes from the holder plate by disengaging them from their springs. Measure the length of the brushes. If they are 12 mm (0.47 in) or shorter they should be replaced.
9 Use a soldering gun to remove the old brushes and to attach new brushes.
10 Installation is the reverse of the removal procedure.

Reduction gear type

11 Remove the starter from the car as described in Section 11.

12.2 The 'M' solenoid terminal has a braided copper strap leading from the starter

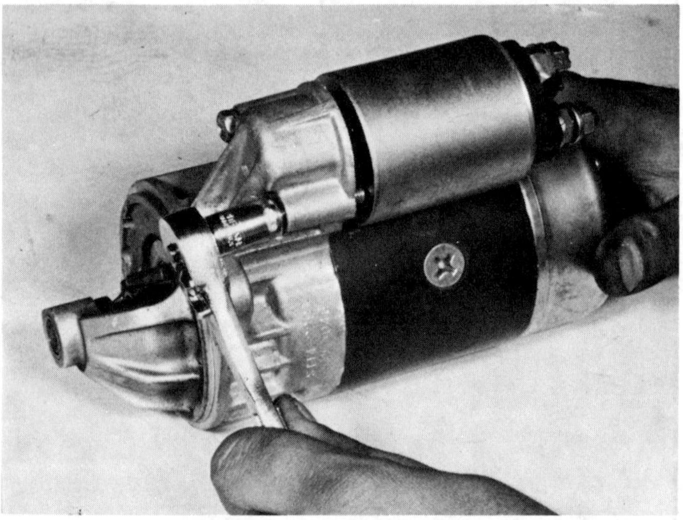

12.3 The solenoid is secured to the starter motor by two screws

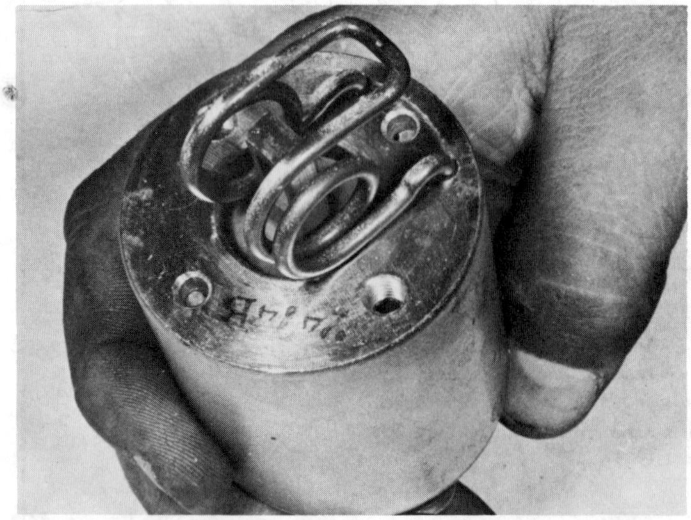

12.4 The solenoid should be assembled as shown prior to installation (during installation the solenoid plunger should be engaged with the starter motor shift lever)

13.9 The starter motor brushes (non-reduction gear type) are retained to the brush holder by springs, and to the yoke by solder

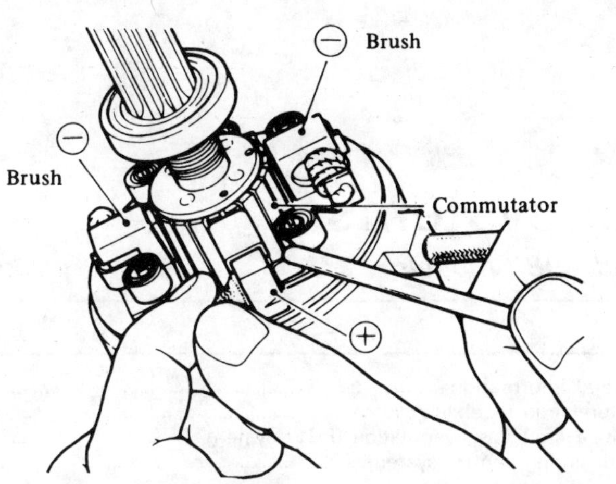

Fig. 5.16 The starter motor brushes can be removed from the brush holder by holding the brush spring aside and sliding it out (Sec 13)

12 Remove the solenoid as described in Section 12.
13 Remove the through bolts by unscrewing them and drawing them out through the rear.
14 Remove the rear cover from the starter motor. Be careful not to damage the O-ring.
15 Remove the yoke, armature and brush holder as an assembly from the center housing. Be careful not to knock the brushes, commutator or coil against any adjacent part.
16 Lift up the brush springs and remove the brushes from the brush holder.
17 Measure the length of the brushes. If they are 11 mm (0.43 in) or shorter they should be replaced.
18 Use a soldering gun to remove the brushes from the yoke and solder new brushes on.
19 Reassembly of the starter motor is the reverse of the disassembly procedure.

14 Charging system – general information

The charging system is made up of the alternator, voltage regulator and the battery. These components work together to supply electrical power for the engine ignition, lights, radio, etc.

The alternator is turned by a drivebelt at the front of the engine. Thus, when the engine is operating, voltage is generated by the internal components of the alternator to be sent to the battery for storage.

The alternator uses a solid-state regulator that is mounted inside the alternator housing. The purpose of this voltage regulator is to limit the alternator voltage to a pre-set value. This prevents power surges, circuit overloads, etc., during peak voltage output. The regulator voltage setting cannot be adjusted.

The charging system does not ordinarily require periodic maintenance. The drivebelts, electrical wiring and connections should, however, be inspected during normal line-ups (see Section 15).

15 Alternator – maintenance and special precautions

1 Alternator maintenance consists of occasionally wiping away any dirt or oil which may have collected.
2 Check the tension of the driving belt (refer to Chapter 1).
3 No lubrication is required as alternator bearings are grease sealed for the life of the unit.
4 Take extreme care when making circuit connections to a vehicle fitted with an alternator and observe the following. When making connections to the alternator from a battery always match correct polarity. Before using electric-arc welding equipment to repair any part of the vehicle, disconnect the connector from the alternator and disconnect the positive battery terminal. Never start the car with a battery charger connected. Always disconnect both battery leads before using a mains charger, if boosting from another battery, always connect in parallel using heavy cable.

16 Charging system – testing

1 Where a faulty alternator is suspected, first ensure that the battery is fully charged. If necessary, have it charged from an outside source. Refer to Chapter 1.
2 Visually inspect all wires and connections to make sure they are clean, tight and in good condition.
3 A 30-volt voltmeter is necessary to accurately test the charging system.
4 Turn the ignition switch to the 'ON' position, and check that the alternator warning light in the instrument cluster illuminates. If it does, proceed to paragraph 7.
5 If the warning light did not come on, check that the warning light bulb is not burned out. Refer to Chapter 10.
6 If the warning light bulb is in good condition and no faults can be found in the connections between the alternator and the warning light, a defective alternator or regulator is indicated. In either case, the alternator should be replaced with a new or rebuilt unit.
7 If the warning light does come on with the ignition switch in the 'ON' position, start the engine and allow it to idle. The light should go out. If it remains on, even dimly or as a flicker, a faulty alternator is indicated. Replace it with a new or rebuilt unit.
8 Slowly increase the engine speed to 1500 rpm and maintain it at that speed.
9 Turn the main headlights on and again check the alternator warning light. If it remains off, proceed to paragraph 11.
10 If the warning light comes on dimly, lower the engine speed to its normal idle speed. Connect the voltmeter between the B and L terminals and measure the voltage. If more than 0.5 volts is shown the alternator needs replacing. If less than 0.5 volts is shown, the unit is okay.
11 If the warning light emained off when the lights were turned on, maintain the engine speed at 1500 rpm and measure the voltage at the B terminal. Be sure the S terminal is correctly connected.
12 If more than 15.5 volts is shown the IC regulator is defective. Replace the alternator.
13 If the voltage reading is between 13 and 15 volts, lower the engine speed once again to its normal level.
14 Turn the headlights on and again check the alternator warning light in the dash. It should remain off. If the light comes on, a defective alternator is indicated and it should be replaced.

17 Alternator – removal and installation

1 Disconnect the negative battery cable.
2 For clearance, raise the front of the car and support it on jackstands.
3 Remove all wires from the rear of the alternator. Be sure to label them as to their locations.
4 Loosen the upper drivebelt adjusting bolt and move the alternator torward the engine until the drivebelt can be removed from the alternator pulley.
5 Remove the adjusting bolt and the 2 alternator mounting bolts located at the bottom of the alternator.
6 Remove the alternator from the car. There is minimal clearance for removing the alternator and it must be worked out between the fan shroud, oil pump and tension rod bracket.
8 Installation is the reverse of the removal procedure.

Chapter 6 Emissions control systems

Refer to Chapter 13 for information related to 1982 and 1983 models

Contents

Air induction system (AIS) 7
Deceleration control system 6
Evaporative emission control system 4
Exhaust gas recirculation (EGR) system 3
General information 1
Mixture ratio feedback system 8
Positive crankcase ventilation (PCV) system 2
Spark timing control system 5

Specifications

Torque specifications

	ft-lb	m-kg
Thermal vacuum valves	16 or less	2.2 or less
EAI tube attaching nuts	25 to 33	3.5 to 4.5
EGR tube attaching nut	25 to 33	3.5 to 4.5
BPT valve mounting screws	2.7 to 3.7	0.38 to 0.51
VVT valve mounting screws	2.7 to 3.7	0.38 to 0.51

1 General information

As smog standards have become more stringent, the emissions control systems developed to meet these requirements have not only become increasingly more diverse and complex, but are now designed as integral parts of the operation of the engine. Where once the anti-pollution devices used were installed as peripheral "add-on" components, the present systems work closely with such other systems as the fuel, ignition and exhaust systems, and in some cases even control vital engine operations.

Because of this close integration of systems, disconnecting or not maintaining the emissions control systems, besides being illegal, can adversely affect engine performance and life, as well as fuel economy.

This is not to say that the emissions systems are particularly difficult for the home mechanic to maintain and service. You can perform general operational checks, and do most (if not all) of the regular maintenance easily and quickly at home with common tune-up and hand tools.

While the end result from the various emissions systems is to reduce the output of pollutants into the air (namely hydrocarbons [HC], carbon monoxide [CO], and oxides of nitrogen [NOx]), the various systems function independently toward this goal. This is the way in which this Chapter is divided. Information on the catalytic converter system can be found in Chapter 4.

5 If the routing of the vacuum hoses as shown in the figures within this Chapter differs in any way from the Vacuum Hose Routing Diagram, located on the underside of the hood, the information on the diagram should take precedence over these figures.

2 Positive crankcase ventilation (PCV) system

General description

1 The positive crankcase ventilation, or PCV, as it is more commonly called, reduces hydrocarbon emissions by circulating fresh air through the crankcase. This air combines with blow-by gases, or gases blown past the piston rings during compression, and the combination is then sucked into the intake manifold to be reburned by the engine.

2 This process is achieved by using one air pipe running from the air duct to the rocker arm cover, a one-way PCV valve located on the right side of the intake manifold and a second air pipe running from the crankcase to the PCV valve.

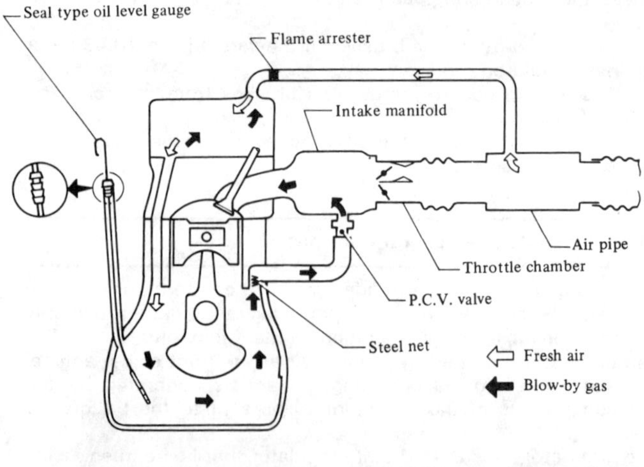

Fig. 6.1 Diagram of the 1980 PCV system (Sec 2)

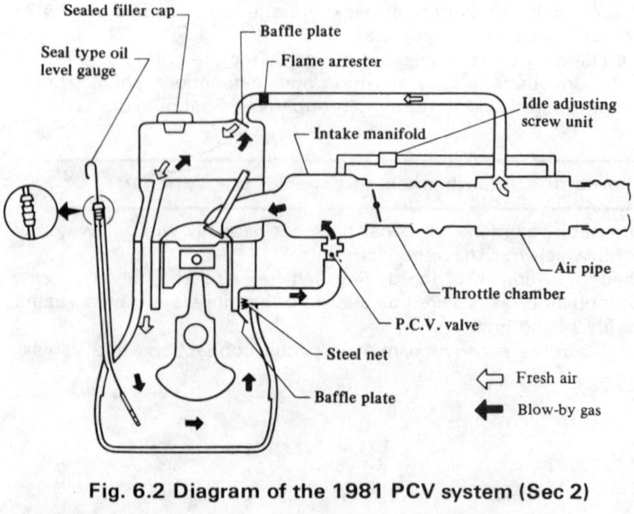

Fig. 6.2 Diagram of the 1981 PCV system (Sec 2)

3 During partial throttle operation of the engine the vacuum created in the intake manifold is great enough to suck the gases from the crankcase, through the PCV valve and into the manifold. The PCV valve allows the gases to enter the manifold, but will not allow them to pass in the other direction.
4 The ventilating air is drawn into the rocker arm cover from the air pipe, and then into the crankcase.
5 Under full-throttle operation, the vacuum in the intake manifold is not great enough to suck the gases in. Under this condition the blow-by gases flow backwards into the rocker arm cover, through the air tube and into the air pipe, where it is carried into the intake manifold in the normal air intake flow.

Checking crankcase ventilation system

6 The PCV system can be checked for proper operation quickly and easily. This system should be checked regularly as carbon and gunk deposited by the blow-by gases will eventually clog the PCV valve and/or system hoses. When the flow of the PCV system is reduced or stopped, common symptoms are rough idling or a reduced engine speed at idle.
7 To check for proper vacuum in the system, disconnect the rubber air hose where it exits the air pipe (photo).
8 With the engine idling, place your thumb lightly over the end of the hose. You should feel a slight pull of vacuum. The suction may be heard as your thumb is released. This will indicate that air is being drawn all the way through the system. If a vacuum is felt, the system is functioning properly.
9 If there is very little vacuum or none at all, at the end of the hose, the system is clogged and must be inspected further.
10 With the engine still idling, disconnect the vent tube from the PCV valve (photo). Now place your finger over the end of the valve and feel for a suction. You should feel a relatively strong vacuum at this point. This indicates that the valve is good.
11 If no vacuum is felt at the PCV valve, remove the valve from the intake manifold (photo). Shake it and listen for a clicking sound. That is the rattle of the valve's check needle. If the valve does not click freely, replace it.
12 If a strong vacuum is felt at the PCV valve, yet there is still no vacuum during the test described in paragraph 8, then one of the system's vent tubes is probably clogged. Both should be removed and blown out with compressed air.
13 If, after cleaning the vent tubes, there is still no suction at the air pipe, there is a blockage in an internal passage. This requires disassembly of the engine to correct.
14 When purchasing a new PCV valve, make sure it is the proper one. See the specifications in Chapter 1. An incorrect PCV valve may pull too much or too little vacuum, possibly causing damage to the engine.

3 Exhaust gas recirculation (EGR) system

General description – overview (all models)

1 This system is used to reduce oxides of nitrogen (NOx) emitted from the exhaust. Formation of these pollutants takes place at very high temperatures; consequently, it occurs during the peak temperature period of the combustion process. To reduce peak temperatures, and thus the formation of NOx, a small amount of exhaust gas is taken from the exhaust system and recirculated in the combustion cycle.
2 Four different EGR systems are used in the 1980 and 1981 models. In 1980, one system was used in the 49-state models, while a slightly different system was used in California models. In 1981, both of these systems were replaced by a new and simpler system that was used in all US models. The EGR system used in the Canada models is different from any of the US systems, but remains constant both years.
3 In addition, within each system various EGR valves are used according to the transmission used and the altitude the car is expected to be operated at. For replacement, the EGR valve can be identified by the part number stamped on the recessed portion at the top of the valve.
4 Because a malfunctioning EGR system can severely affect the performance of the engine, it is important to understand how each system works in order to accurately troubleshoot it. Common engine problems associated with the EGR system are: rough idling or stalling when at an idle, rough engine performance upon light throttle application and stalling on deceleration.

General description – 1981 US models

5 The EGR system used in all 1981 US models is a very simple system that incorporates an EGR valve and one thermal vacuum valve (TVV).
6 The heart of any EGR system is the EGR valve, which controls the flow of exhaust gases into the intake manifold for reburning. Under normal conditions the EGR valve is closed, which prevents the passage of exhaust gases into the intake manifold. The bi-metal type TVV is incorporated into the system to control the opening of the valve so that it will open only at the optimum time.
7 The direct vacuum signal that opens the valves comes from the throttle chamber venturi at the throttle valve. This vacuum signal is only great enough to open the EGR valve during mid-range throttle positions. At idle and at full throttle, the vacuum signal lessens and the EGR valve will close again.
8 The TVV is placed into the vacuum signal line between the throttle chamber and the EGR valve, and is designed so that it will not allow the vacuum signal to reach the EGR valve until the engine coolant temperature reaches 95°F(35°C), or normal operating temperature. This prevents the EGR system from leaning out the rich gas/air mixture needed during cold engine operation.
9 The EGR valve in this system, then, will not operate at all until the coolant reaches 95°F or higher, and then only at mid-range throttle positions.

General description – 1980 and 1981 Canada models

10 The system used in all 1980 and 1981 Canada models is similar to the system just described but also incorporates a back-pressure transducer (BPT) valve as another control for the opening of the EGR valve.
11 The thermal vacuum valve (TVV) used in this system is designed so that it will not let the vacuum signal from the throttle chamber pass until the coolant temperature has reached at least 104°F (40°C).
12 The BPT valve is tapped into the vacuum signal line after the TVV,

2.7 Disconnecting the PCV rubber vent hose from the air pipe

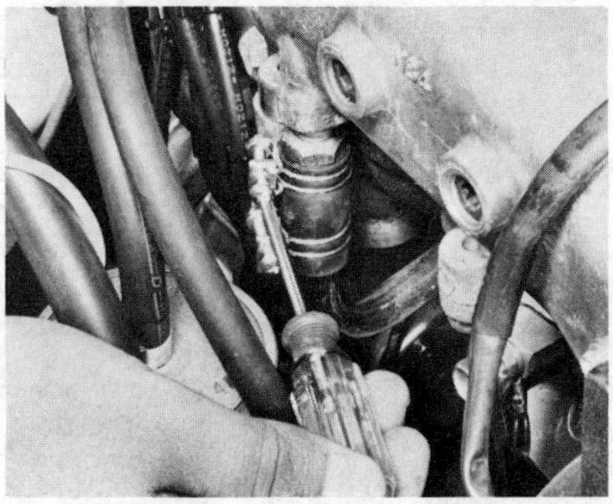

2.10 The vent tube must be removed from the valve for testing the PCV valve

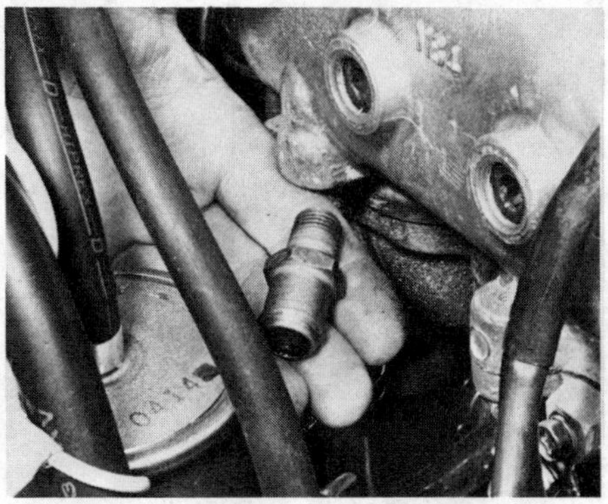

2.11 If a clicking sound can be heard when the PCV valve is shaken, then the valve is good

and allows an air bleed to take place in the line until it is closed. This air bleed, when present, keeps the vacuum pressure low, thus preventing the EGR valve from opening.

13 The BPT valve is also connected by an air line to the lower portion of the EGR valve, which opens it up to the exhaust pressure coming from the exhaust manifold. When this pressure reaches a predetermined point, it will overcome the spring-loaded diaphragm in the BPT valve, and close off the valve. The closing of the valve stops the air bleed in the signal line, and thus allows the vacuum signal to reach and open the EGR valve.

14 The conditions, then, for the EGR valve to open in this system are: 1) the engine coolant must be 104°C or higher, 2) the gas pressure in the exhaust manfiold must be great enough to close the BPT valve, and 3) the throttle must be in a mid-range position.

General description – 1980 49-state models

15 The EGR system used in1980 49-state models is similar to the Canada system with a couple of principal differences. Two thermal vacuum valves (TVV), each calibrated at a different temperature setting are tapped into the vacuum signal line. Also, a venturi vacuum

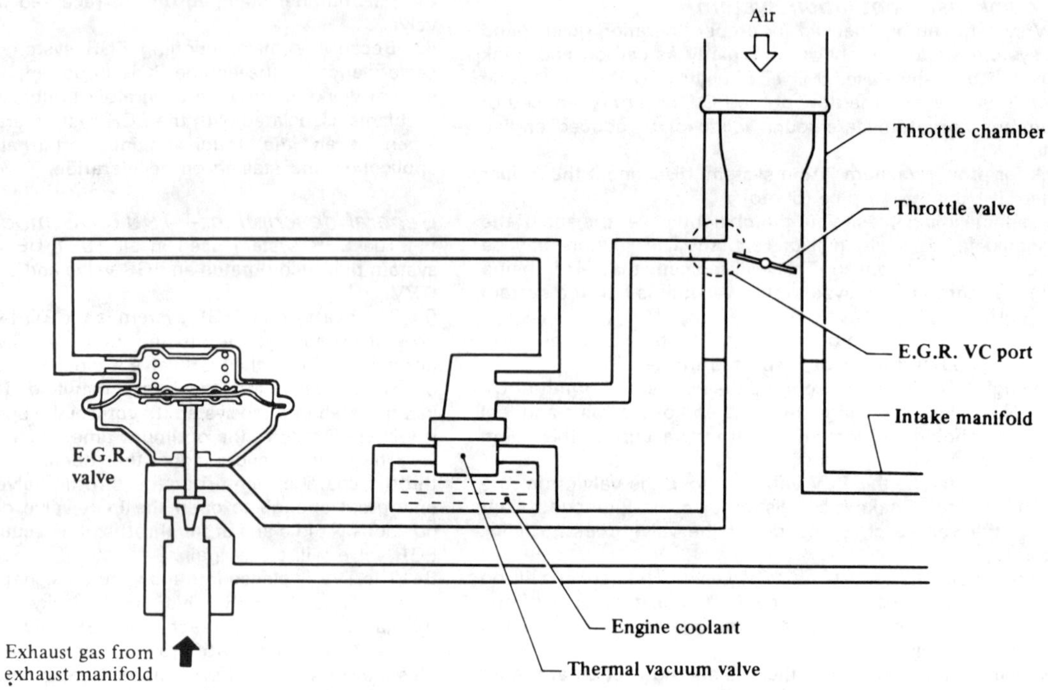

Fig. 6.3 Diagram of the EGR system for 1981 US cars (Sec 3)

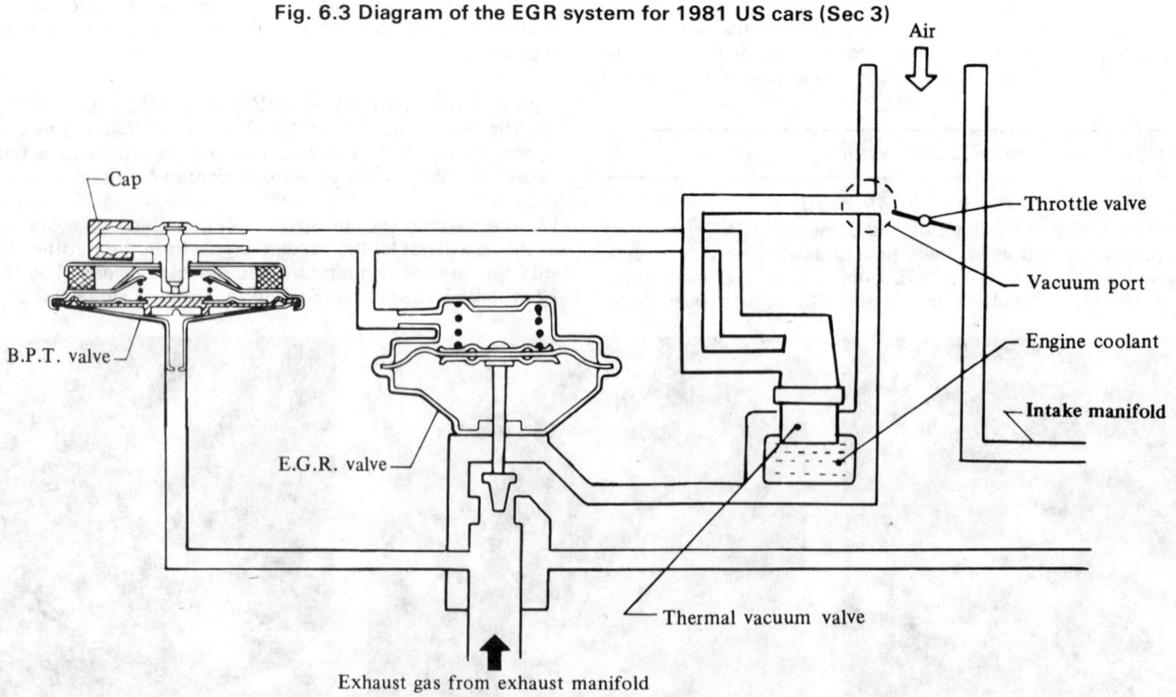

Fig. 6.4 Diagram of the EGR system for all Canada models (Sec 3)

transducer (VVT) valve is used in place of the BPT valve. This system uses a fairly complex set of controls to control the opening of the EGR valve.

16 Both of the TVVs (one is located on top and the other on the underside of the intake manifold) are designed to permit air bleeds in the vacuum signal line and therefore must be closed before the EGR valve can open. The upper TVV (Type-A1) is calibrated to stay open until the engine coolant reaches 140°F (60°C). At this point the valve's wax sensor will expand and seal off the air leak. The lower TVV (Type-A3), on the other hand, is calibrated to stay closed until the coolant temperature exceeds 203°F (95°C). Therefore both valves will be closed at the same time only while the engine coolant is between 140° and 203°F.

17 The VVT valve also permits an air bleed through it, and therefore must be closed before the EGR valve can open. The VVT valve can be closed by either one of two ways. One method, as with the BPT valve in the Canada system, is if the exhaust gas back-pressure becomes great enough, this pressure will cause the valve to close. The VVT

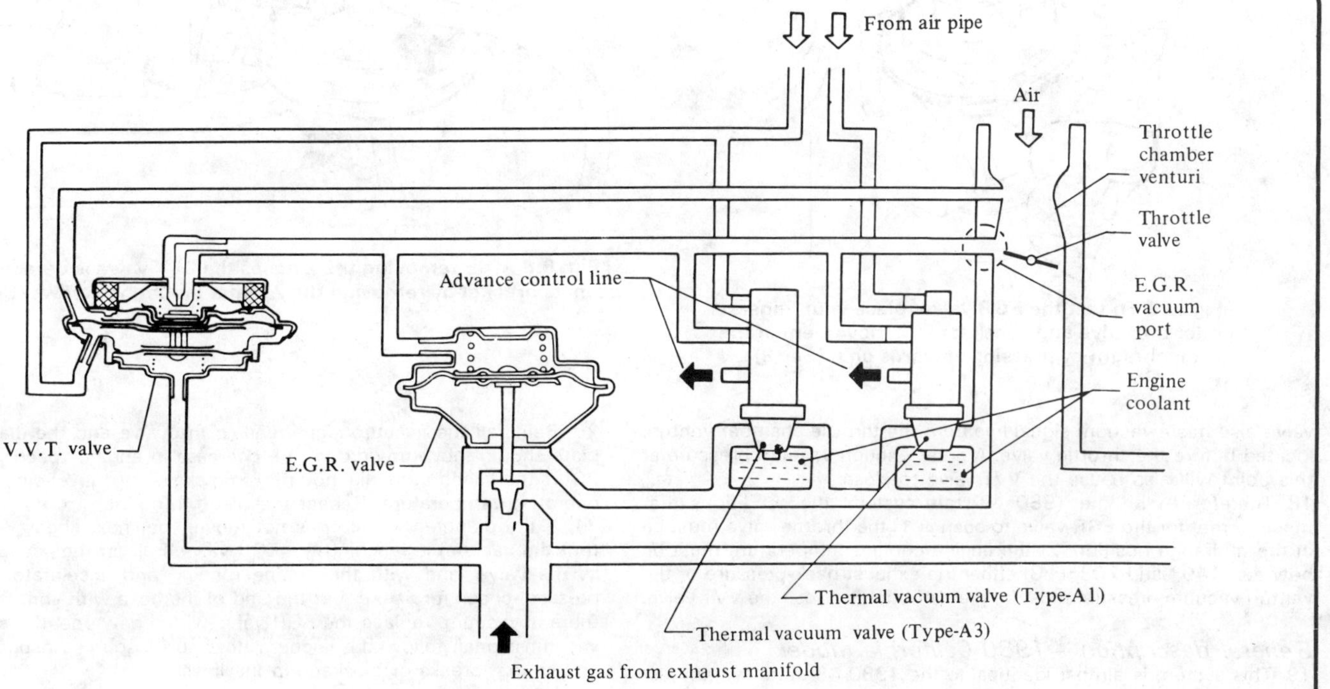

Fig. 6.5 Diagram of the EGR system for 1980 49-state models (Sec 3)

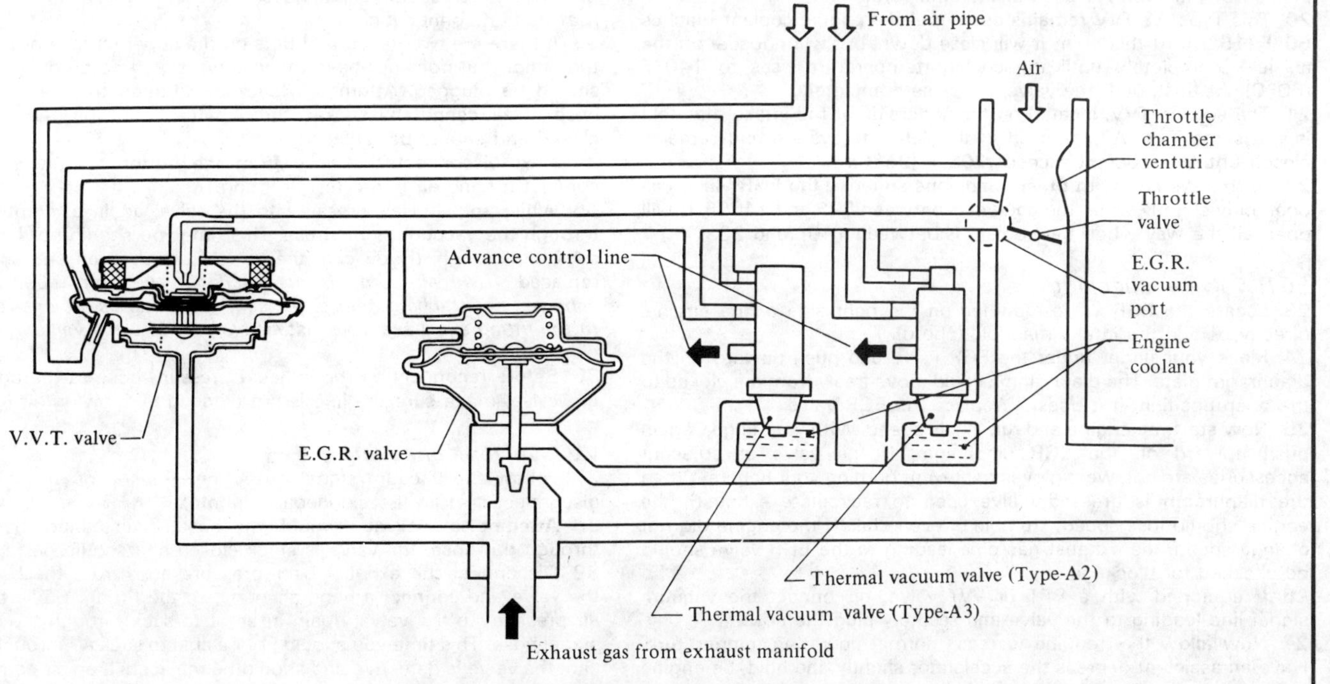

Fig. 6.6 Diagram of the EGR system for 1980 California models (Sec 3)

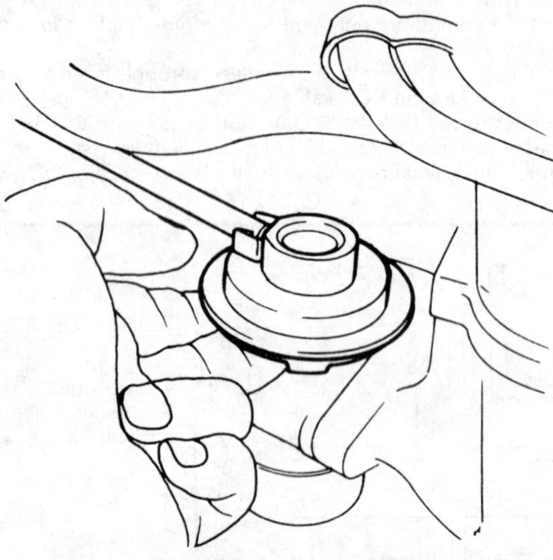

Fig. 6.7 To test the EGR valve, place your fingers under the valve and check for free movement of the diaphragm by pressing upwards on it (Sec 3)

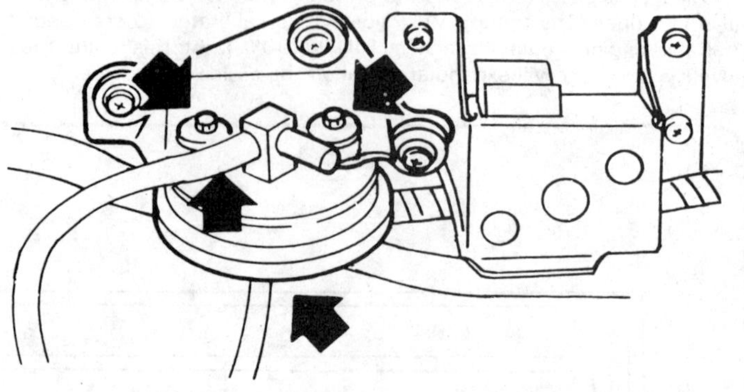

Fig. 6.8 After removing the 2 hoses the BPT valve is detached from its bracket by removing the 2 upper mounting screws (Sec 3)

valve also has a vacuum signal line from the throttle chamber venturi, located before the throttle valve. A great enough vacuum pressure at this point will also cause the VVT valve to close.

18 Therefore, with the 1980 49-state system, the conditions that must be met for the EGR valve to open is 1) the throttle valve must be in the midrange position, 2) the engine coolant temperature must be between 140° and 203°F, 3) either the exhaust back-pressure or the venturi vacuum pressure must be great enough to close the VVT valve.

General description – 1980 California model

19 This system is almost identical to the 1980 49-state system just described. The only component difference is that a Type-A2 thermal vacuum valve (TVV) is used on the top upper intake manifold position instead of the Type-A1 used in the other system.

20 This Type-A2 TVV remains open until the engine coolant reaches 50°F (15°C). At this point it will close down, but will not seal off the air leak completely until the coolant temperature rises to 140°F (60°C). At this point, the valve will close completely.

21 The second TVV, located on the underside of the intake manifold is the same Type-A3, as used in the 49-state system and remains closed until the coolant exceeds 203°F (95°C).

22 In this system, with other conditions suitable, the EGR valve will open only slightly while the coolant is between 59° and 140°F. It will open all the way when the coolant is between 140° and 203°F.

EGR valve – checking

23 Locate the EGR valve mounted on the right side of the engine, directly behind the intake manifold (photo).

24 Place your finger under the EGR valve and push upward on the diaphragm plate. The diaphragm should move freely from the closed to the open position. If it doesn't, replace the EGR valve.

25 Now start the engine and run at idle speed. With your finger, again push upward on the EGR diaphragm. If the valve or adjacent accessories are hot, wear gloves to prevent burning your fingers. When the diaphragm is pressed (valve open to recirculate exhaust), the engine should lose speed, stumble or even stall. If the engine did not change speed, the exhaust gas pipe leading to the EGR valve should be checked for blockage.

26 If equipped with a BPT or VVT valve, disconnect the vacuum signal line leading to the valve and securely plug the hose.

27 Now allow then engine to reach normal operating temperature. Have an assistant depress the accelerator slightly and hold the engine speed constant above idle.

28 Pull off the vacuum signal line at the EGR valve and check that the diaphragm plate moves downward, accompanied by an increase in engine speed.

29 Reinstall the vacuum signal line to the valve and the diaphragm plate should move upward with a decrease in engine speed.

30 If the diaphragm did not move, make sure the engine was at operating temperature. Repeat the test if in doubt.

31 If the diaphragm still does not move, your next check would be that the vacuum is reaching the EGR valve. Pull off the vacuum hose at the valve, and with the engine running and accelerator slightly pressed, check for vacuum at the end of the hose with your thumb. If there is vacuum, replace the EGR valve with a new one. If there is no vacuum signal, follow the vacuum hose to its source, inspecting for any cracks, breaks or blockage in the lines.

BPT valve – checking

32 Follow the vacuum signal hose from the BPT valve and disconnect it at its first connection.

33 If there are two vacuum outlets on the upper surface of the valve, the outlet that does not have the vacuum signal hose connected to it should be plugged. Attempt to suck air through the vacuum signal hose. If air cannot be sucked through the hose, the valve is stuck closed and should be replaced.

34 Next disconnect the hose from the bottom of the valve and connect a hand air pump to the fitting.

35 While applying air pressure to the valve, again attempt to suck through the vacuum signal hose. This time you should not be able to suck air through. If you can, the valve is stuck open and should be replaced. *If an air pump is not available, the same effect can be achieved by attaching a hose, the same diameter as the one removed, to the fitting and have an assistant blow air into the valve in order to close it.*

36 Before reconnecting the exhaust pressure hose to the bottom of the valve, make sure the line is not clogged by blowing air into it.

VVT valve – checking

37 Follow the vacuum signal hose from the top of the valve, and disconnect it at its first connection (photo).

38 Attempt to suck air through the hose. If air cannot be sucked through the hose, the valve is stuck closed and should be replaced.

39 Disconnect the exhaust back-pressure hose from the bottom of the valve and connect a hand air pump to the fitting. While applying air pressure to the valve, again attempt to suck through the vacuum signal hose. This time you should not be able to suck air through. If you can, the valve is defective and should be replaced. If an air pump is not available, the same effect can be achieved by connecting a hose, the same diameter as the one removed, to the fitting and having an assistant blow into it to close the valve.

40 Before reconnecting the exhaust pressure hose to the bottom of

3.23 The EGR valve is mounted to the rear of the intake manifold on the right side of the engine

3.37 The VVT valve is mounted to the rear of the engine compartment, right behind the EGR valve

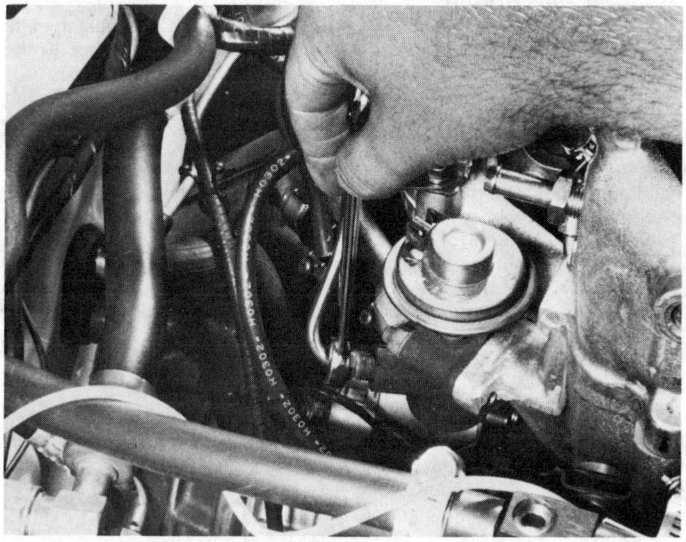

3.52 Disconnecting the metal back-pressure signal tube that connects the EGR valve to the BPT/VVT valve

3.53 Removing the bolt that secures the back-pressure signal line to the intake manifold

the valve, make sure the line is not clogged by blowing air into it.
41 Next, disconnect the venturi vacuum hose from the top left side of the valve, and connect a vacuum pump to the fitting. While applying vacuum pressure to the valve, once again attempt to suck air through the vacuum signal hose. If you are able to draw air through, the valve is stuck open and should be replaced.
42 Before reconnecting the venturi vacuum hose, make sure it is not clogged by blowing air through it. Then follow it along its entire length checking that there are no cracks, or other leaks.
43 Finally, follow the air vent hose from the bottom left side of the valve and disconnect it at its first connection. Attempt to suck air through the hose. If you are able to, then one of the diaphragms is leaking and the valve should be replaced.
44 Reconnect the hose to the connection you removed it from. Now disconnect it from the valve itself, and check that the line is not clogged by blowing air through it.

Thermal vacuum valve (TVV) – checking

45 To check for proper functioning of the thermal vacuum valve on 1981 US models and Canada models for both 1980 and 1981, start with a cold engine. Disconnect the vacuum signal hose from the EGR valve. On Canada models, disconnect the vacuum signal hose from the BPT valve and plug it. Now start the engine and, with your thumb, feel if any vacuum is coming through the line. If vacuum is reaching the valve immediately after starting the engine, the TVV should be replaced.
46 Now wait for the engine to reach normal operating temperature and, again, feel for vacuum at the end of the hose. If no vacuum is reaching the EGR valve, first check that the hoses are not clogged. Then, if all lines are clear, replace the TVV.
47 The easiest method of testing the thermal vacuum valve located on the upper side of the intake manifold on 1980 49-state and California models is as follows: with the engine cold, follow the hose from the middle fitting of the valve to where it "T"s into the vacuum signal line, and disconnect it at the "T". Attempt to suck air through each hose. While the engine is cold, the valve should be open which means you should be able to draw air through it. If this is not the case, check first that the hose is clear. If that is not the problem, then replace the faulty valve.
48 Next, start the engine and allow it to reach normal operating temperature. Again, attempt to suck air through the hose. At this point, you should not be able to draw air through it. If this is not the case, replace the faulty valve.
49 The thermal vacuum valve located on the underside of the intake manifold on 1980 49-state and California models will not close until after the coolant temperature reaches 203°F. Therefore, it is not practical to test it on the car. Allow the car to cool down enough so the lower TVV can be removed from the car, complete with the hoses attached to it. Once removed, attempt to suck air through the vacuum signal hose leading from the middle fitting. While the valve is cold, it should be closed, preventing you from drawing air through it. If air can be drawn through it, replace the valve.

50 Plug the hose leading from the lower fitting. Now put the valve in a pan and submerge it in water. Do not let the water get into the hoses or the inside of the valve. Heat the water until its temperature is above 203°F. Now attempt to suck air through the hose leading from the middle fitting. At this point the valve should be open, and you should be able to suck air through it. If you cannot draw air through it, and the hose is not clogged, replace the valve.

EGR valve – removal and installation

51 For clearance, reposition any hoses that will be in the way of working on and removing the EGR valve. If hoses are disconnected, be sure to label them and their fittings for proper reconnection.
52 If equipped, unscrew the nut that connects the exhaust back pressure line to the EGR valve (photo).
53 If equipped, remove the screw that secures the back-pressure line bracket in position (photo), and move the back-pressure line away from the EGR valve.
54 Remove the vacuum signal hose from the top of the EGR valve.
55 Unscrew the large nut that retains the exhaust gas tube to the EGR valve.
56 Remove the 2 EGR valve mounting nuts.
57 Lift up on the exhaust gas tube until there is enough clearance to remove the EGR valve and pull the valve off of its studs.
58 Clean the mating surfaces of the EGR valve and the intake manifold, removing all traces of old gasket material.
59 Installation is the reverse of the removal procedure. **Note:** *Be sure to use a new gasket when installing the EGR valve.*

VVT valve – removal and installation

60 Disconnect all hoses from the VVT valve. Be sure to label them as to their location.
61 Remove the 2 screws that hold the valve to its bracket, then lower the valve from the bracket and remove it from the engine compartment.
62 Installation is the reverse of the removal procedure. **Note:** *If replacing the VVT valve be sure the new valve has the same type number stamped on it as the old one.*

BPT valve – removal and installation

63 Disconnect the vacuum signal hose from the top of the BPT valve.
64 Remove the screws that hold the valve to its bracket, and lift off the valve.
65 Disconnect the exhaust back-pressure hose from the bottom of the valve, and remove the valve from the engine compartment.
66 Installation is the reverse of the removal procedure. **Note:** *If replacing the valve, be sure the new valve has the same type number stamped on it as the old one.*

Thermal vacuum switch – replacement

67 Drain the engine coolant.
68 Disconnect the vacuum hoses from the switch, noting their positions for reassembly.
69 Using a suitable wrench, remove the switch.
70 When installing the switch, apply thread sealer to the threads, being careful not to allow the sealant to touch the bottom sensor.
71 Install the switch and tighten it to specifications.

4 Evaporative emission control system

General description

1 The evaporative emissions control system (EEC) is designed to prevent the release of hydrocarbons in the form of fuel vapor to the outside air.
2 This is achieved by venting the vapor in the fuel tank to a canister filled with activated charcoal, where the vapor is stored when the engine isn't running.
3 On top of this canister is a purge control valve with two hoses leading from it. The thicker hose is the purge hose, and runs directly to the intake manifold while the smaller hose is the vacuum signal line. Inside the purge control valve, are two holes. One, a very small hole, is called the constant purge orifice and is always open to the intake manifold. The second hole, a larger one directly in the center of the valve, is the main purge orifice and is normally covered by the valve's diaphragm.

Fig. 6.9 Diagram of a typical Evaporative Emission Control System (Sec 4)

4 When the engine is started fresh air is drawn into the canister through an opening in the bottom. This fresh air picks up the stored vapors and carries them to the intake manifold. At idle, there is enough vacuum coming through the constant purge line to draw in a small amount of this air/vapor mixture through the constant purge orifice. The purge control valve, however, remains closed. As the engine speed increases, the manifold vacuum becomes great enough to open the diaphragm of the purge control valve, which allows the air/vapor mixture to be drawn in greater quantity to the intake manifold.
5 The operation of this system depends on maintaining a sealed fuel system. Therefore, a positive sealing gas cap is used which, under normal conditions, provides only a small vent to the outside air, and will open fully only if vacuum pressure within the fuel tank becomes too great.
6 A fuel check valve is located in the vent line between the fuel tank and the canister. When the engine is off, this valve allows the fuel vapor to bleed off into the canister when the pressure in the fuel tank reaches a certain level. When the engine is running, this valve allows outside air to be drawn into the tank from the canister. This effectively vents the tank so the fuel being drawn out for burning doesn't eventually cause a vacuum in the tank and produce vapor lock.
7 In addition, a vapor/liquid separator is used on hatchback models to prevent liquid fuel from being drawn into the canister.
8 Other than the periodic replacement of the canister air filter detailed in Chapter 1, Section 32, the EEC system normally requires no periodic attention.

Checking

9 One symptom that the EEC system is not operating properly is an abnormally strong smell of gasoline around the car. Another symptom is if a vapor lock condition should occur while the engine is operating, causing the engine to stop running.
10 Begin the inspection of the system by checking the vent and vacuum lines for leaks or deterioration. Also check that the air filter in the bottom of the canister is clean. If not, replace it as described in Chapter 1.
11 To check for fuel vapor leakage at the purge control valve, follow the rubber hose leading from the valve outlet fitting to where it enters a Y-fitting, and disconnect the hose from the Y-fitting. Attempt to lightly suck air through the hose. If you are able to suck air through the hose, then remove the top cover from the purge control valve and check for a dislocated or cracked diaphragm. If the valve is defective, a diaphragm kit can be bought and installed to correct the problem.
12 To check the constant purge orifice, follow the constant purge line down to where it connects with a metal tube and disconnect the hose from the tube. Blow air into the hose to ensure that the hose and orifice are clear. If air cannot be blown through, remove the purge control valve and clear the constant purge orifice and hose if necessary.
13 Inspect the fuel tank filler cap. Wipe the valve housing clean on the underside of the cap. Suck the valve gently and a slight resistance should be felt. Suck harder and note that as the valve clicks, any resistance should disappear. Failure to operate in this way will mean a new cap must be fitted.
14 Finally test the fuel check valve (Fig. 6.12). Disconnect the valve and blow into the valve from the fuel tank side. A severe resistance should be felt with a proportion of air passing out of the opposite side. Now blow into the valve from the engine side. No resistance should be felt.

Purge control valve – diaphragm replacement

15 Purchase a diaphragm kit.
16 Remove the 3 hoses from their fittings on top of the canister.
17 Release the retaining spring around the body of the canister and life the canister out of the engine compartment.
18 Pry off the top cover of the purge control valve.
19 Remove the diaphragm from the inside of the top cover.
20 Install a new diaphragm into the top cover, making sure the edge of the diaphragm is located in its groove all the way around the cover.
21 Replace the diaphragm spring and retainer with new ones supplied with the diaphragm kit.
22 With the new spring and retainer in place, snap the valve cover back onto the canister.
23 Reinstall the canister.
24 Reconnect the 3 hoses, making sure they are in the proper locations.

5 Spark timing control system

1 The spark timing control system, used only on US cars, is designed to control the distributor vacuum advance under varying conditions, in order to help reduce HC and NOx emissions, as well as to assure stable idling and good fuel economy.
2 Although the basic function of the system is the same in both the 1980 and 1981 models, the design of the system was greatly changed from one year to the next. For that reason we will present them here as two totally separate systems.

General description – 1980 models

3 The spark timing control system used in 1980 model cars is a relatively simple system that uses thermal vacuum valves (TVVs) to control the actuation of the distributor vacuum advance.
4 The TVVs are the same two used in the EGR system (Section 2, 1980 49-state and California models). One is located on the upper front of the intake manifold, and the other is located in the lower rear of the intake manifold. These TVVs are tapped into a vacuum signal line running between the throttle valve and the distributor. Since the TVVs allow an air bleed in the vacuum signal line when open, both valves must be closed before they will allow the vacuum signal to reach the distributor.
5 The opening and closing of the valves is determined by the temperature of the engine coolant. The upper TVV (Type-A1 in 49-state models; Type-A2 in California models) is calibrated to be closed until the coolant temperature reaches 59°F (15°C). At this point it will stay open between 59° and 140°F (60°C). Above 140°F it will close again. The lower TVV (Type-A3 is calibrated to remain closed until

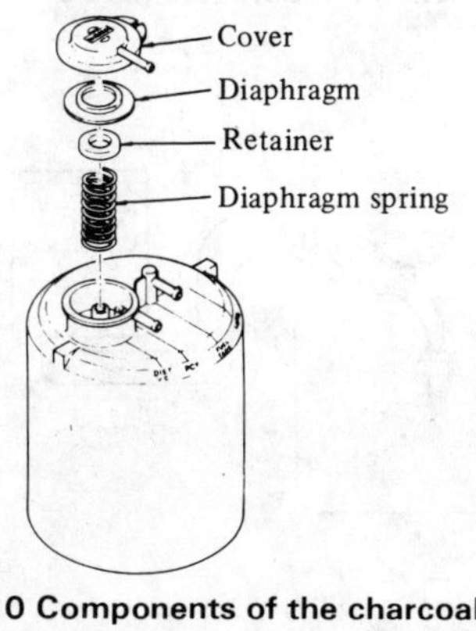

Fig. 6.10 Components of the charcoal canister's purge control valve (Sec 4)

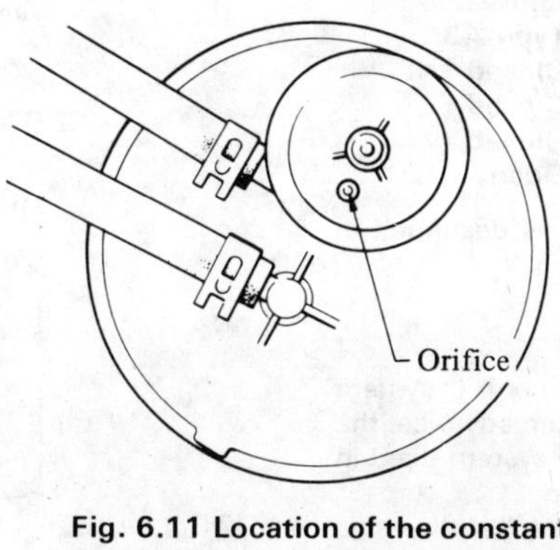

Fig. 6.11 Location of the constant purge orifice under the purge control valve (Sec 4)

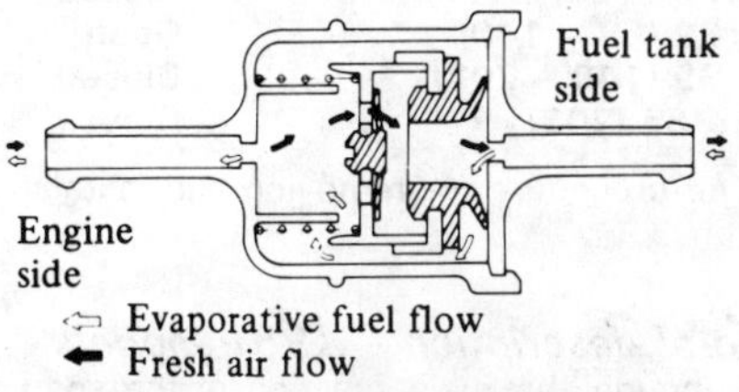

Fig. 6.12 When testing the fuel check valve, blowing air through from the fuel tank side should be difficult, while from the engine side it should be easier (Sec 4)

coolant temperature exceeds 203°F (95°C). Therefore, the only temperature ranges in which both valves are closed at the same time, and thus allow the vacuum signal to be passed to the distributor, are below 59°F and between 140° amd 203°F, which is the normal operating temperature of the car.

6 In addition, since the vacuum signal is taken from the throttle valve, at idle the vacuum pressure is not great enough to advance the distributor, so the spark timing control system does not operate at all at idle.

Checking – 1980 models

7 Begin any check of this system by inspecting all lines and hoses, making sure they are properly connected and there are no leaks or cracks.

8 Next the advance mechanism inside the distributor should be checked to be sure it is operating correctly. To do this, first remove the distributor cap so that the rotation of the timing plate can be observed. Next disconnect the vacuum line from the distributor, and connect a vacuum pump to the fitting. Apply vacuum pressure to the distributor and watch that the timing plate rotates inside. If the timing plate does not rotate, then there is a fault with the advance mechanism which must be corrected (refer to Chapter 5). If a vacuum pump is not handy, the same effect can be achieved by attaching a long rubber hose (the same diameter as the vacuum hose removed) to the fitting and sucking through it.

9 Reconnect the vacuum line to the distributor and reinstall the distributor cap.

10 Hook up a timing light according to the manufacturer's instructions. With the engine cold, start the engine and have an assistant apply throttle to keep the engine running at about 2000 rpm. Immediately check the spark timing with the timing light. The needle in the coolant temperature gauge should be on the "C". If the outside temperature is below 59°F, the system should be actuated and the timing should be advanced from its normal setting (Chapter 1 Specifications).

11 Continue to run the engine at around 2000 rpm and observe the spark timing while the engine warms up. You may wish to adjust the idle speed screw to maintain this engine speed. If the outside temperature was below 59°F, the timing should retard as the engine begins to warm up.

12 By the time the engine approaches normal operating temperature (the needle in the middle of the gauge), the spark timing should have advanced again. If this sequence does not take place, the TVVs are suspect.

13 The most accurate method of testing the TVVs is to remove them from the car and test them individually using the basic method described for testing the lower EGR thermal vacuum valves (Section 3). By drawing on the hose attached to the lowest fitting, you should be able to suck air through it when the valve is open, but not when it's closed. If either valve fails to operate as expected, it should be replaced. **Note:** *when testing be sure to plug the hose connected to the EGR outlet fitting (middle fitting on Type-A1 and A3, and the top fitting on Type-A2).*

Thermal vacuum valve calibration

Water temperature °C (°F)	Thermal vacuum valve Type-A1,A2	Type-A3
Below 15 (59)	Closed	Closed
15 – 60 (59 – 140)	Open	Closed
60 – 95 (140 – 203)	Closed	Closed
Above 95 (203)	Closed	Open

14 The procedure for removing and installing TVVs is described in Section 3.

General description – 1981 models

15 Although the main function of the spark timing control system used in 1981 models is to control the distributor vacuum advance, the method of achieving this is entirely different from the system used in 1980 models.

16 With this system, a vacuum signal line runs from the throttle valve to the distributor vacuum advance mechanism. Tapped into this line is a vacuum switching valve. When this valve is open it allows an air bleed through it, thus nullifying the vacuum signal coming from the throttle valve, and preventing it from reaching the distributor. When the vacuum switching valve is closed, it seals off the air bleed and allows the vacuum signal to affect the advance mechanism.

17 The opening and closing of the vacuum switching valve is controlled electrically by two other switches; a water temperature switch and either a neutral switch or inhibitor switch, depending upon transmission type.

18 The water temperature switch which is located at the radiator is calibrated so that it will open, or allow current to pass through to the vacuum switching valve when coolant temperature is below 50°F

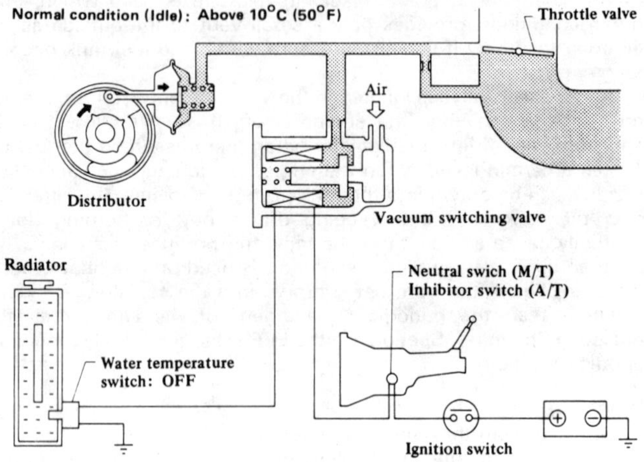

Fig. 6.13 Diagram of the 1981 Spark Timing Control System when actuated (Sec 5)

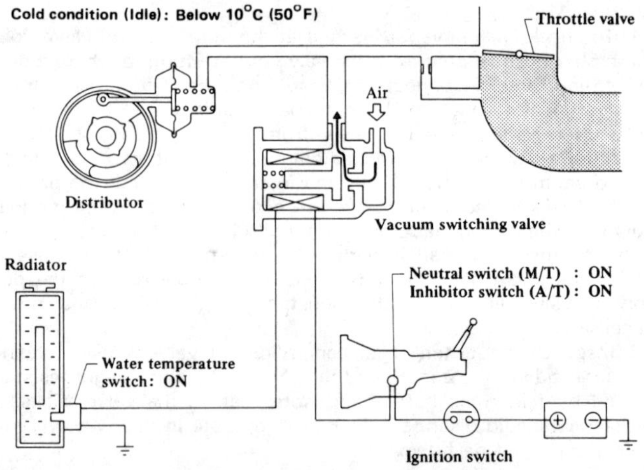

Fig. 6.14 Diagram of the 1981 Spark Timing Control System when not actuated (Sec 5)

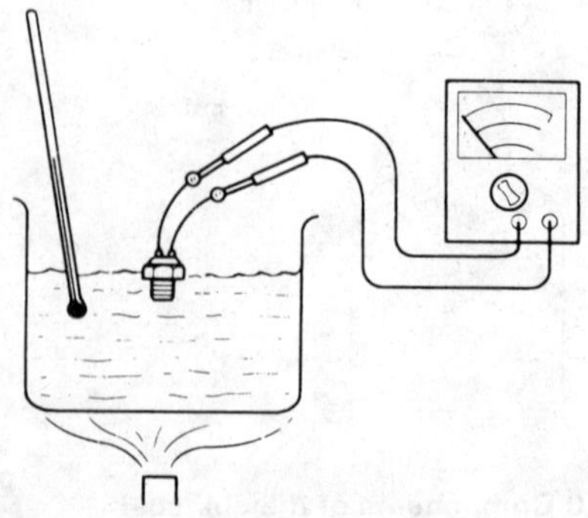

Fig. 6.15 To test the water temperature switch, connect a continuity tester to its wires and submerge it in water (Sec 5)

19 A neutral switch is used with manual transmission models and is located on the left side of the transmission. The inhibitor switch is used with automatic transmission models, and is also located on the left side. The neutral switch is on, (permitting current to pass through it) only when the gears are in the neutral position. The inhibitor switch is on only when the gears are in either the Neutral or Park positions.
20 The vacuum switching valve is designed so that as long as one of the two switches is off, it will be actuated. Only when both the water temperature switch and the neutral/inhibitor switch are both on at the same time will current reach the vacuum switching valve and de-actuate the system. Therefore, the only time that the vacuum switching valve is preventing the vacuum signal from reaching the distributor, is when the coolant temperature is below 50°F and the transmission gears are in Neutral (manual) or Neutral or Park (automatic).

Checking – 1981 models

21 Begin any inspection of the system by examining all hoses and wires to make sure they are properly connected and are in good condition.
22 Next, the vacuum advance mechanism inside the distributor should be checked as described in paragraphs 8 and 9.
23 With the engine cold, hook up a timing light according to the manufacturer's instructions.
24 Place the transmission in the neutral (manual), or N or P (automatic) position.
25 If the outside temperature is above 50°F, remove the water temperature switch from the radiator, leaving the switch connected to its wires. Immediately plug the radiator opening to prevent leakage of coolant. Now submerge the switch in a small container of water that has been chilled to below 50°F. *If the outside temperature is below 50°F, this step can be ignored.*
26 Start the engine, and immediately check the spark timing with the timing light. The timing mark should be in its normal position (Chapter 1 Specifications).
27 Have an assistant momentarily move the shift lever to another position other than neutral (manual) or Neutral or Park (automatic). **CAUTION**: *Be sure the emergency brake is on and the wheels are secured chocked to prevent the car from moving. Also keep the brake pedal fully depressed.* The spark timing should advance when the shifter is moved to the new position.
28 Reinstall the water temperature switch in the radiator.
29 Allow the engine to reach normal operating temperature and check the spark timing again. It should still be in the advanced position.
30 Once more, have an assistant run through the gears, while you observe the spark timing. It should not change from the advanced position.
31 If the spark timing is not being advanced or retarded as described above, the components of the system should be checked individually to locate the problem.
32 Remove the water temperature switch from the radiator and plug the radiator opening to prevent coolant leakage. Connect a continuity tester to the switch's wires, and dip the switch in a container of water at a temperature below 50°F. The tester should show continuity. Slowly heat the water. When the temperature rises above 50°F, the tester should show no continuity. If the switch does not perform as described, it should be replaced.
33 Locate the neutral switch on a manual transmission, or the inhibitor switch on an automatic transmission. Disconnect the wires leading from it, and connect a continuity tester to them. With the engine off, have an assistant shift the gear selector through the entire range of gears. The neutral switch should show continuity only when the transmission is on Neutral. The inhibitor switch should show continuity only when the transmission is in park (P) or neutral (N). If this is not the case, the switch should be replaced.
34 The easiest method of testing the vacuum switching valve is first to disconnect the wires. Next remove the hose from the valve that "T"s into the vacuum signal line. Follow the hose that leads from the valve's air inlet fitting and disconnect it at its first connection. Attempt to blow air through this hose. If you are able to, the valve is defective. Now connect jumper wires to the wires leading from the valve, and run them directly to the battery. After the valve is connected directly to the battery, again try to blow air through the air inlet hose. This time you should be able to blow air easily through it. If not, replace the valve.

6 Decelerating control system

General description

1 The decleration control system is designed to prevent backfiring in the exhaust system and excessive oil consumption during deceleration.
2 The only operating component in the system is a vacuum control valve (VCV) located at the rear left side of the intake manifold. When, during deceleration, the vacuum in the intake manifold reaches a specified pressure, the VCV will open, admitting outside air to enter the intake manifold, thus reducing the vacuum pressure.

Vacuum control valve (VCV) – checking

3 To check the operation of the vacuum control valve. Disconnect the opposite end of the rubber hose running from the VCV, from its fitting directly above the air regulator.
4 Place your finger over the end of the hose (photo). There should be no air being drawn in through the hose at this time. If there is, then the valve is stuck open and should be replaced.
5 Next have an assistant rev the engine to about 4000 rpm for a few moments, and then quickly let off the throttle. You should feel air being drawn into the hose immediately following the let-up on the throttle.
6 If no air was being drawn in during the moments of deceleration,

6.4 The vacuum control valve is tested by feeling for suction at the end of the rubber hose

6.9 To remove the vacuum control valve, use a wrench on the flats, as shown, to unscrew it from the intake manifold

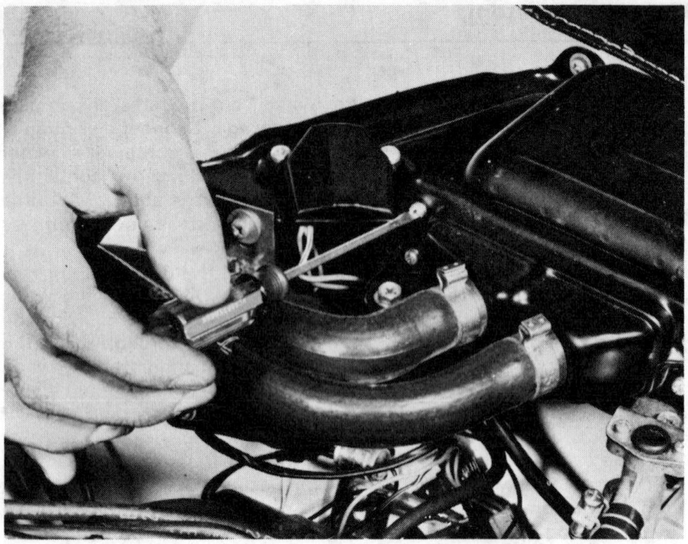

7.8 The AIS valve case is attached to the air filter housing by 4 screws

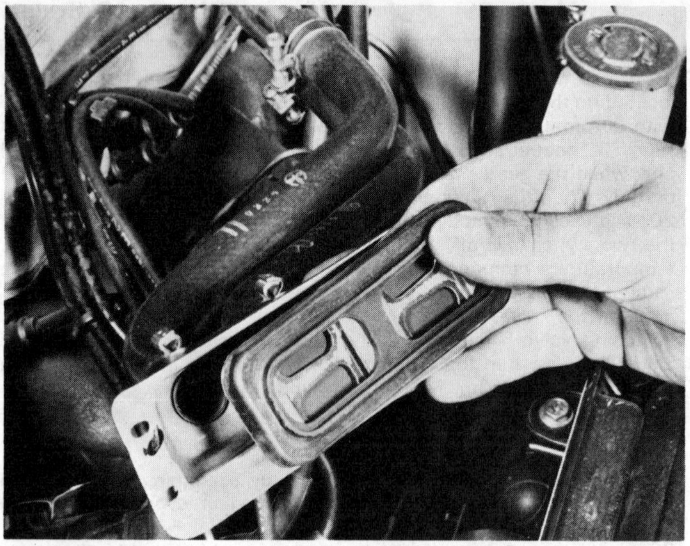

7.9 When installing the reed valve into the valve case, be sure it opens away from the air filter housing

check that the hose is not clogged or leaking. If the hose is okay, then the VCV should be replaced.

7 **Note**: *This method of testing the VCV is not accurate at an altitude of 2300 to 4000 feet (700 to 1200 meters) and above, due to the fact that intake manifold vacuum often will not reach the necessary pressure to open the VCV.*

Vacuum control valve (VCV) – removal and installation

8 Disconnect the rubber hose from the VCV.

9 Unscrew the VCV from the intake manifold (photo).

10 Prior to installation, wrap the threads of the VCV with teflon tape.

11 Screw the VCV into the intake manifold and reconnect the rubber hose to it.

7 Air induction system (AIS)

General description

1 The purpose of the AIS system is to reduce hydrocarbons in the exhaust by drawing fresh air directly into the exhaust manifold. The fresh, oxygen-rich air helps combust the unburned hydrocarbons before they are expelled as exhaust. Only 1980 models are equipped with this system.

2 The components of this simple system include an air filter and a one-way reed valve, both of which are located in a case attached to the air cleaner, and one or two (depending upon model) EAI tubes connecting the valve case with the exhaust manifold. California model

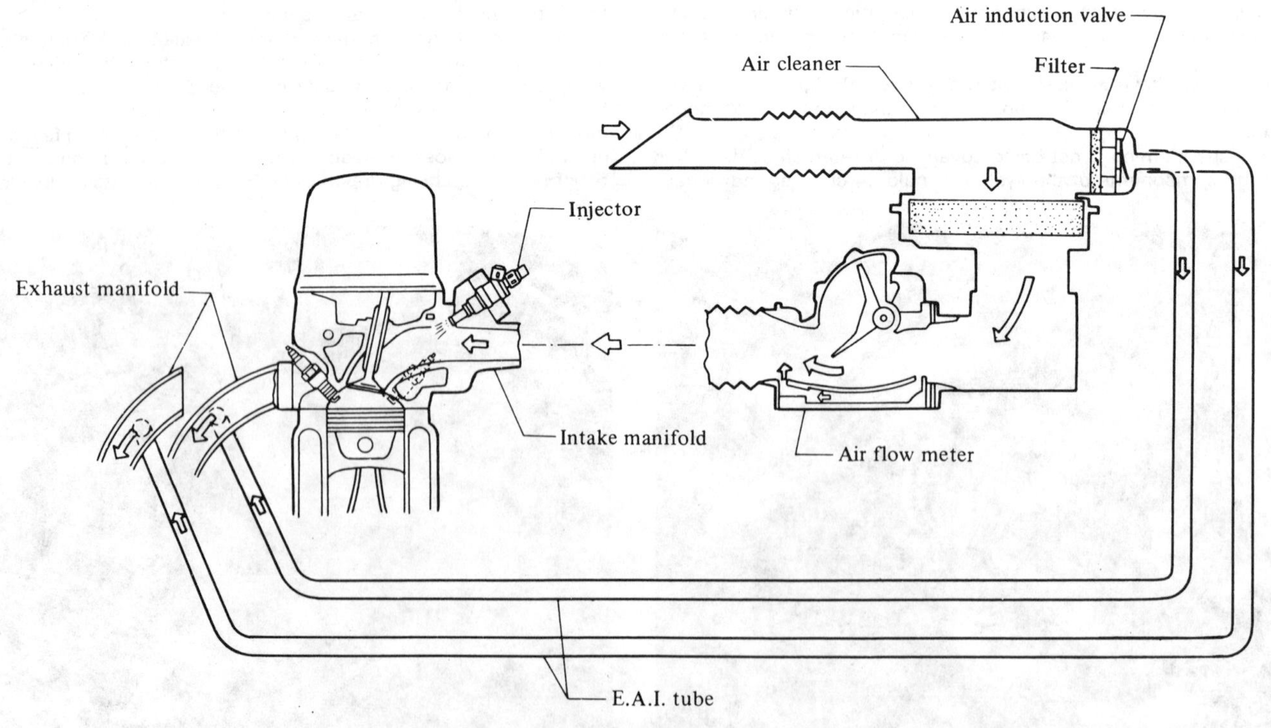

Fig. 6.16 Typical Air Induction System (Type A shown) (Sec 7)

cars use a Type A system which incorporates two air tubes leading to the exhaust manifold. The Type B system used by 49-state models only uses one air tube.

3 The opening and closing of the exhaust valves creates vacuum pulses which draw in fresh air through the filter and valve assembly. The reed valve only admits air to be drawn into the manifold, and prevents exhaust back-pressure from forcing the gases back out.

Checking

4 The simplicity of the system makes it a very reliable one which seldom causes problems. Periodic checks should be made, however, of the condition of the components to be sure there are no leaks or cracks in the system.

5 Two simple functional tests can be performed to ensure that the system is operating properly. Disconnect the rubber hose(s) from the metal EAI tube(s). For the first test, attempt to suck air through the rubber hose, and then attempt to blow air through the hose. The reed valve should allow you to suck air through the hose but prevent you from blowing it back through. If you are able to blow air through the hose then the valve is defective and should be replaced. If you are not able to suck air in, then check for a clogged air filter or hose. If this is not the case, then replace the valve.

6 For the second test, start the engine and allow it to idle. With the engine idling hold your hand over the open end of the metal EAI tube(s). There should be a steady stream of air being sucked into it. Have an assistant apply throttle and as the engine gains speed the suction should increase. If this does not happen, either there are leaks or blockage in the tubes.

Air induction valve filter – replacement

7 Refer to Chapter 1, Section 20.

Air induction valve – removal and installation

8 Remove the 4 screws that attach the valve case to the air filter housing (photo).

9 Lift the case away from the air filter housing and pry out the reed valve from the case (photo).

10 Installation if the reverse of the removal procedure. **Note**: *Be sure the filter valve opens away from the filter when installed.*

Air induction valve case – removal and installation

11 The rubber hose(s) are clamped to the valve case. Only if the valve case or hose(s) need to be replaced separate from the other, cut the clamp(s) that secure the two together, and separate them.

12 Remove the 4 screws that attach the valve case to the air filter housing.

13 Disconnect the rubber hose(s) from the metal air tube(s).

14 Pry the reed valve out of the valve case if necessary.

15 Installation is the reverse of the removal procedure. **Note**: *If the rubber hose(s) has been removed from the valve case, hose clamps should be used to secure them together.*

EAI tubes – removal and installation

16 Disconnect the rubber hose(s) from the EAI.tube(s).

17 Unscrew the nut that attaches each tube to the exhaust manifold. Due to the high temperature in this area, these nuts may be difficult to loosen. Penetrating oil applied to the threads of these nuts may help.

18 Remove the bolts that attach the EAI tube brackets to the engine and lift the tubes off. The brackets can be removed from the tubes if necessary by loosening the retaining screws and sliding the brackets off.

19 Before installing, apply a coat of anti-seize compound to the threads of the large end nuts.

20 Installation is the reverse of the removal procedure.

8 Mixture ratio feedback system

General description

1 The mixture ratio feedback system was introduced in the 1981 models in order to increase the efficiency of the catalytic converter (described in Chapter 4), by monitoring and adjusting the fuel/air mixture ratio being burned.

2 The principal components of this system are an exhaust gas sensor located in the front exhaust pipe and an electronic control unit which is tied into the fuel injection system.

3 The operation of the catalytic converter is most efficient at a specific mixture ratio. The exhaust gas sensor measures the amount of oxygen present in the exhaust and relays this information to the electronic control unit. The control unit then adjusts the injection pulse width to obtain the optimum mixture ratio.

4 Due to the complexity of this system and its relationship with the fuel injection system, it is difficult for the home mechanic to properly diagnose and troubleshoot it. One simple check that can be made though is to look at the small inspection light on the side of the electronic control unit. The unit may have to be removed from its mounting position under the dash for checking. While the engine is operating, the light should blink on and off at least 3 times every 10 seconds. If this is not happening, or if there are other indications that the system is malfunctioning, take the car to a Datsun dealer or other qualified mechanic to have the system checked out.

Chapter 7 Part A: Manual transmission

Contents

General information 1
Overhaul 4
Removal and installation 3
Rear oil seal – replacement 2

Specifications

Model	FS5W71B	
Number of speeds	5 forward, 1 reverse	
Synchromesh type	Warner	
Gear ratios		
1st	3.321	
2nd	2.077	
3rd	1.308	
4th	1.000	
5th	0.833	
Reverse	3.382	
Speedometer gear ratio	19/6	
Oil capacity	$4\frac{1}{4}$ pt (2.0 liters) ($3\frac{1}{2}$ Imp pt)	
Gear endplay (mm)	**in**	**mm**
1st main gear	0.0106 to 0.0134	(0.27 to 0.34)
2nd main gear	0.0047 to 0.0075	(0.12 to 0.19)
3rd main gear	0.0051 to 0.0146	(0.13 to 0.37)
5th main gear	0.0039 to 0.0067	(0.10 to 0.17)
Rev. idler gear	0.0020 to 0.0197	(0.05 to 0.50)
Baulk ring/gear clearance (mm)		
All except overdrive (5th) gear		
Standard	0.0472 to 0.0630	(1.20 to 1.60)
Wear limit	0.031 (0.08)	
Overdrive (5th) gear		
Standard	0.0394 to 0.0551	(1.00 to 1.40)
Wear limit	0.020 (0.5)	
Snap-ring sizes (mm)		
Main drive gear bearing	0.0681	(1.73)
	0.0709	(1.80)
	0.0736	(1.87)
	0.0764	(1.94)
	0.0791	(2.01)
	0.0819	(2.08)
Mainshaft front	0.055	(1.4)
	0.059	(1.5)
	0.063	(1.6)
Mainshaft rear end bearing	0.043	(1.1)
	0.047	(1.2)
	0.047	(1.3)
	0.051	(1.3)
	0.055	(1.4)
Counter drive gear	0.055	(1.4)
	0.059	(1.5)
	0.063	(1.6)
Torque specifications	**ft-lb**	**m-kg**
Transmission-to-engine bolts	37	5.2
Clutch operating cylinder mounting bolts	26	3.6
Transmission mounting bracket-to-body bolts	27	3.7
Rear mounting insulator attaching bolts	27	3.7
Gusset attaching bolts	22	3.1
Rear extension attaching bolts	13	1.8

Torque specifications, continued

	ft-lb	m-kg
Starter motor mounting bolts	25	3.5
Bearing retainer-to-adapter plate bolts	15	2.0
Mainshaft lock nut	112	15.5
Counter gear lock nut	83	11.5
Front cover attaching bolts	14	1.9
Filler plug	22	3.0
Drain plug	22	3.0
Ball pin	20	2.8
Striking lever lock nut	7.6	1.0
Check ball plug	16	2.2
Electrical switches	18	2.5

1 General information

The manual transmission is of the five-forward speed and one reverse type, with synchromesh on all forward gears. The forward gears are of a helical gear formation, and the reverse gear a sliding mesh type using spur gears.

The main driveshaft gear is meshed with the counter drivegear. The forward speed gears on the countershaft are in constant mesh with the main gears. Each of the main gears rides on the mainshaft on needle roller bearings, rotating freely.

When the gearchange lever is operated, the relevant coupling sleeve is caused to slide on the synchronizer hub and engages its inner teeth, with the outer teeth formed on the mainshaft gear. The synchronizer hub is splined to the mainshaft so enabling the parts to rotate in unison. Moving the gearchange lever to the reverse gear position moves the mainshaft reverse gear into engagement with the reverse idler gear.

The gear selector mechanism is controlled from a floor-mounted lever. Movement of the lever is transferred through a striking rod to dogs on the ends of the selector rods, and then through the medium of shift forks which are permanently engaged in the grooves of the synchro unit sleeves.

The transmission used in the 1980 and 1981 models are identical, with the exception of the design of the overdrive gear synchronizer assemblies.

2 Rear oil seal – replacement

1 Remove the driveshaft as described in Chapter 8.

2 Being careful not to damage the output shaft of transmission housing, use a screwdriver to pry out the old seal (photo).

3 Apply a coat of gear oil to the lips of the new seal and drive it into place using an appropriate sized socket.

4 Reinstall the driveshaft.

3 Manual transmission – removal and installation

1 Disconnect the negative battery cable.

2 Working inside the car, remove the shifter access panel from the console box.

3 Remove the insulator from the hole in the floorpan.

4 Place the shifter in the neutral position. Then remove the E-ring

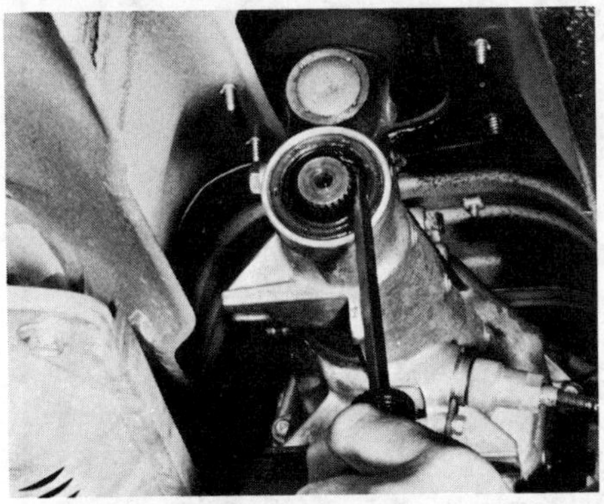

2.2 The rear oil seal can be removed with the transmission still in the car

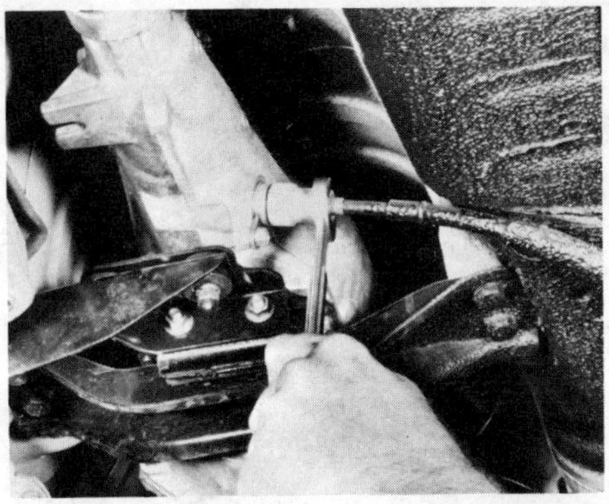

3.8 Location of the speedometer connection on the manual transmission

3.12 The exhaust pipe support bracket is bolted to the transmission mounting insulator

3.15 The bolts attaching the support bracket to the transmission should be removed before removing the bracket

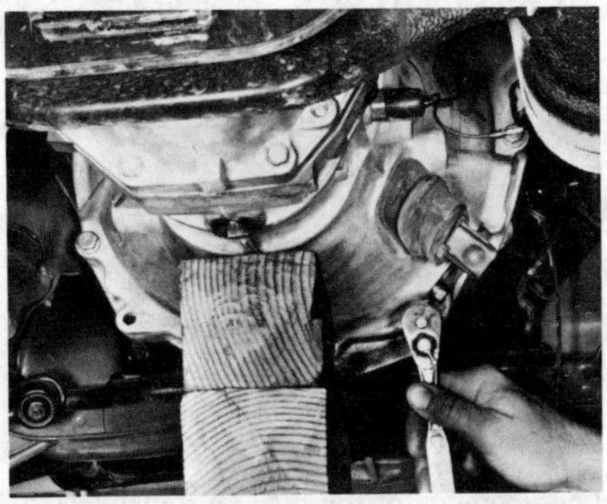

3.17 The transmission should be well supported prior to removing the clutch housing-to-engine bolts

4.4 All electrical switches can be simply unscrewed from the transmission

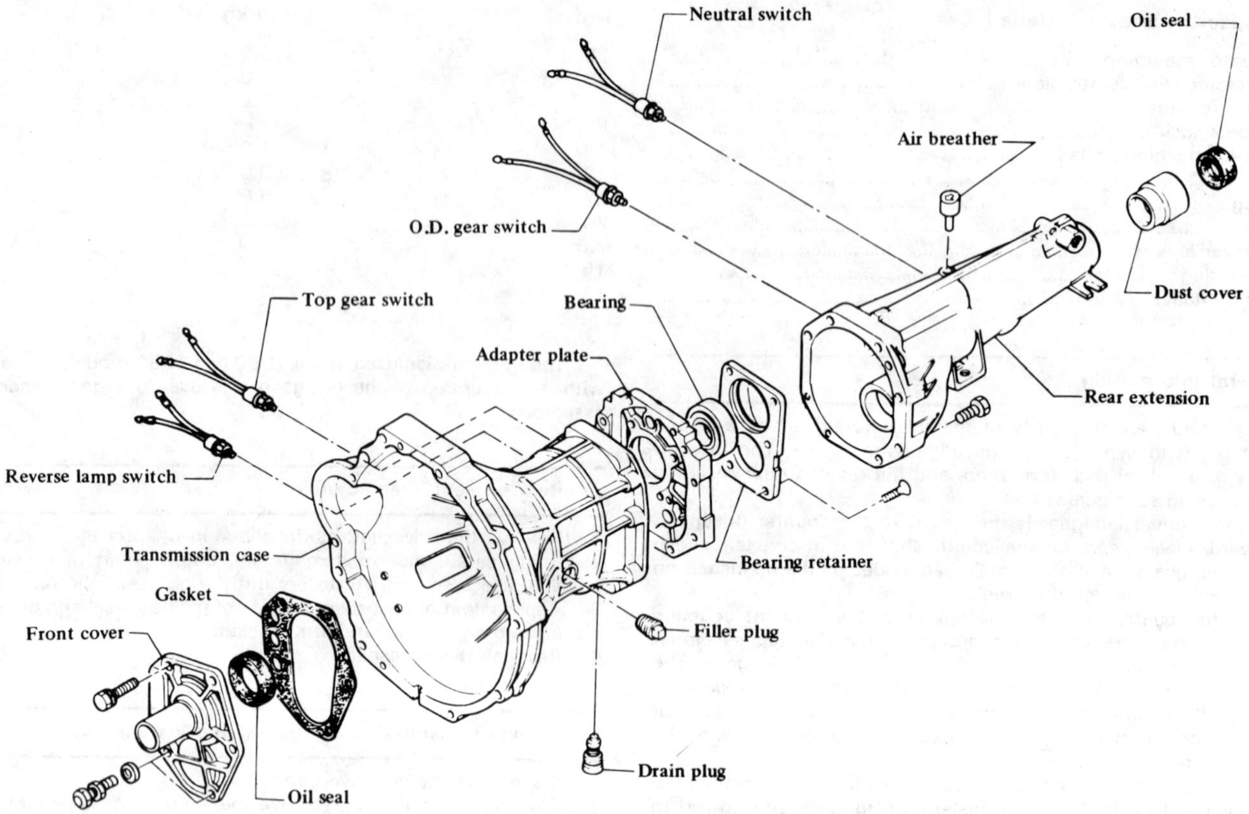

Fig. 7.1 External components of the manual transmission (1980 models)

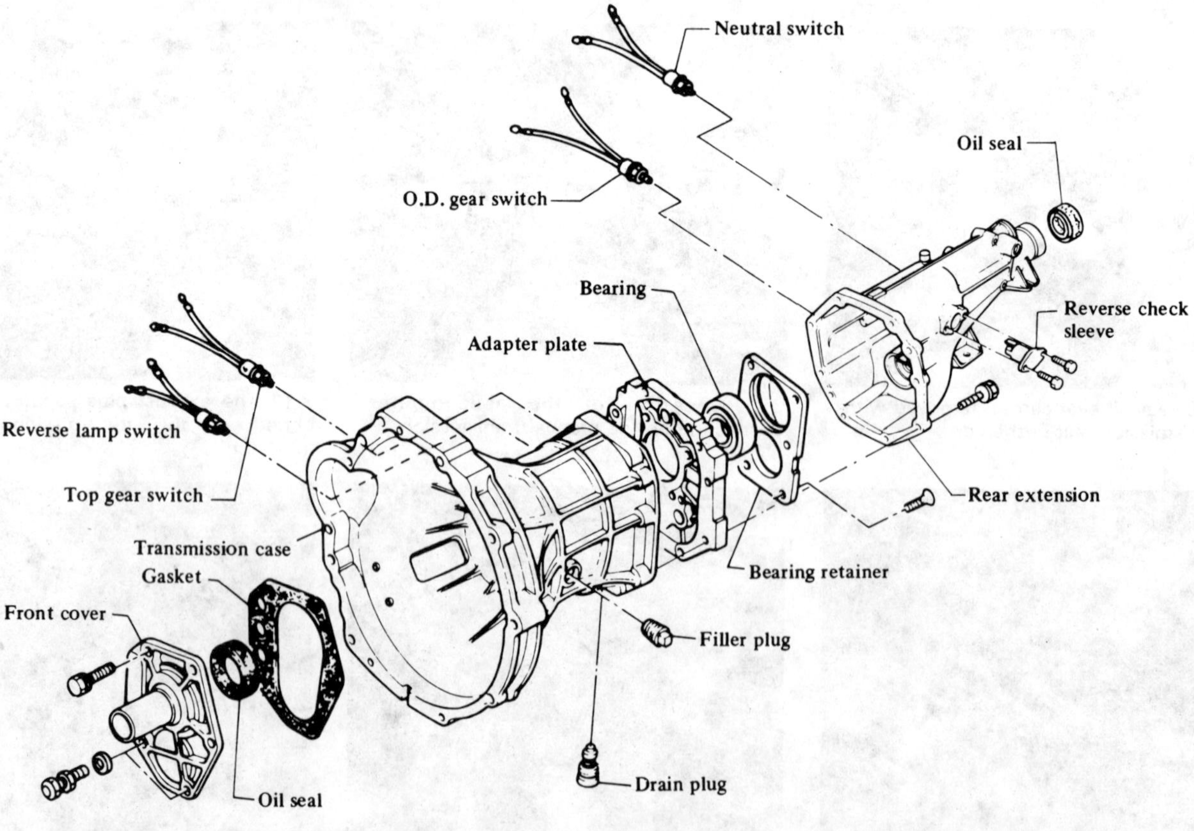

Fig. 7.2 External components of the manual transmission (1981 models)

and pin, and lift out the shifter.
5 Disconnect the exhaust downpipe from the engine and wire it out of the way.
6 Jack up the car and safely support its weight on suitable blocks or stands. Be sure the car is high enough that the transmission can be slid out from underneath when removed.
7 Disconnect the wires from the back-up light switch, the top gear switch, the neutral switch and/or the overdrive switch, as equipped.
8 Disconnect the speedometer cable (photo).
9 Drain the oil from the transmission.
10 Remove the driveshaft, as described in Chapter 8. As this is done, plug up or cover over the opening at the rear of the transmission to prevent leakage of oil.
11 Unbolt and remove the clutch operating cylinder and tie it back out of the way. There is no need to disconnect the hydraulic line. (Further information can be found in Chapter 8).
12 Remove the exhaust pipe support bracket from the transmission mount (photo).
13 Support the engine under the oil pan using a suitable jack and a block of wood as an insulator.

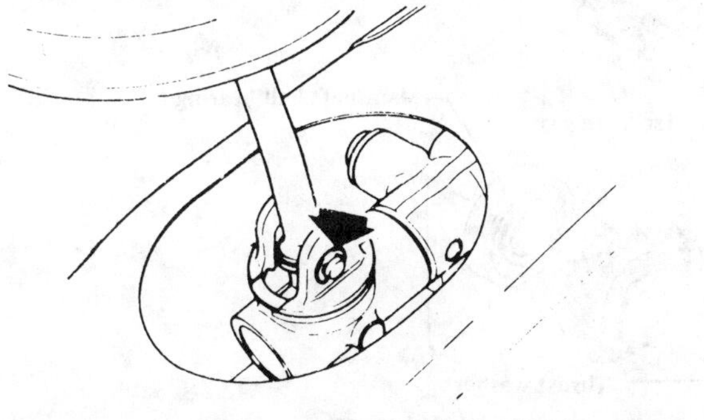

Fig. 7.3 Location of the shift lever retaining pin (arrow) (Sec 3)

14 Place a second jack under the transmission.
15 Undo and remove the transmission mounting insulator securing nuts and the mounting-to-bodyframe bolts (photos).
16 Remove the starter motor from the bellhousing.
17 Unscrew and remove the bolts which secure the clutch bellhousing to the engine crankcase (photo).
18 Lower each of the two jacks simultaneously, until the transmission can be withdrawn to the rear and removed from beneath the vehicle. Do not allow the weight of the transmission to hang upon the input shaft while it is engaged with the splines of the clutch driven plate.
19 For details on repairing or overhauling a manual transmission, refer to Section 4.
20 Installation is a reversal of removal but smear a trace of grease on the input shaft splines and check if the clutch mechanism has been centralized as described in Chapter 8.
21 Check the clutch pedal free-travel and adjust if necessary (Chapter 1) and remember to fill the transmission with the correct grade and quantity of oil.

4 Manual transmission – overhaul

Initial disassembly

1 With the transmission removed, thoroughly clean the external faces.
2 Remove the rubber dust boot from the withdrawal lever aperture in the clutch bellhousing.
3 Remove the release bearing and hub together with the withdrawal lever (Chapter 8).
4 Remove the reverse lamp switch, neutral switch, top gear switch, and/or overdrive (overdrive) gear switch, as equipped (photo).
5 Remove the screw that retains the speedometer gear to the rear extension housing and lift out the gear (photo).
6 Pry off the E-ring from the stopper guide pin and drive out the pin (photo).
7 Remove the return spring plug, and lift out the return spring and plunger (photo).

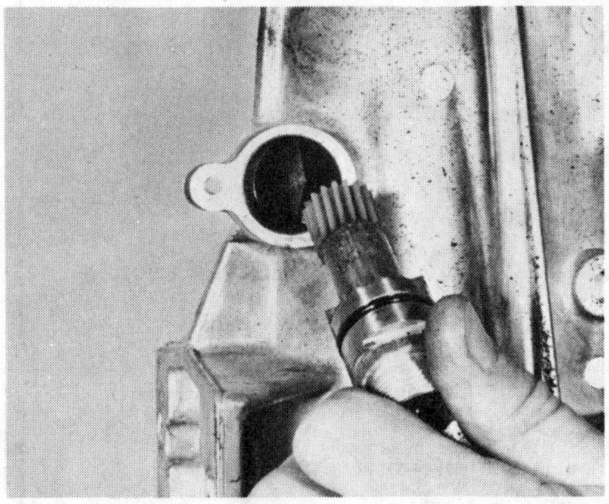

4.5 The O-ring on the speedometer pinion should be replaced during servicing

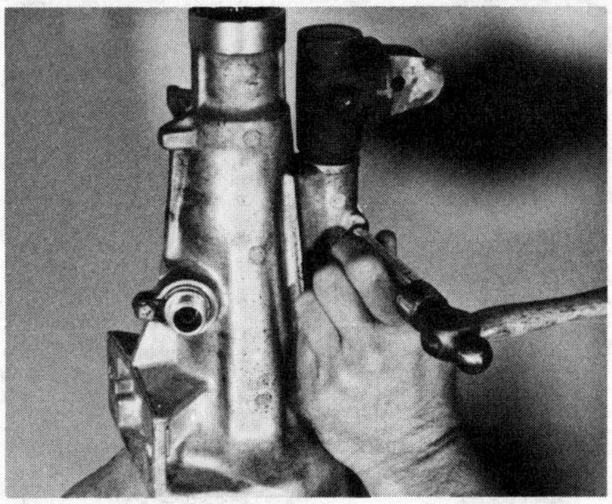

4.6 The stopper guide pin can be driven out with a punch

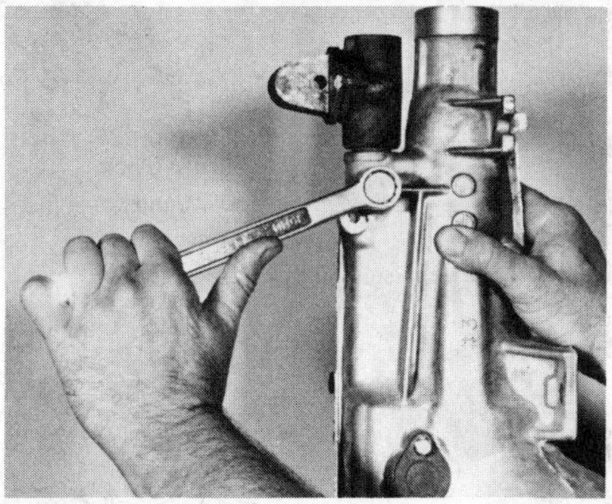

4.7 Location of the return spring plug

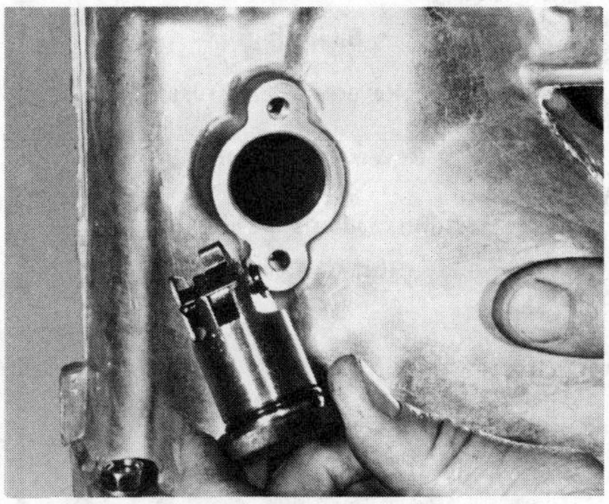

4.8 The reverse check sleeve is retained by 2 screws

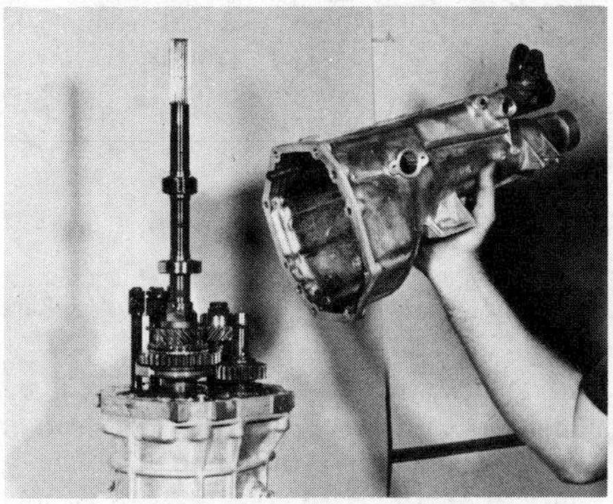

4.9 The rear extension housing can be tapped free of the transmission using a rubber-headed hammer

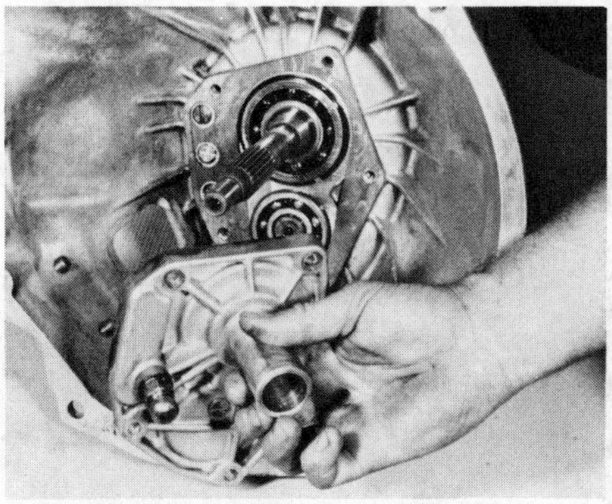

4.10a The front cover is held to the clutch housing by 6 screws

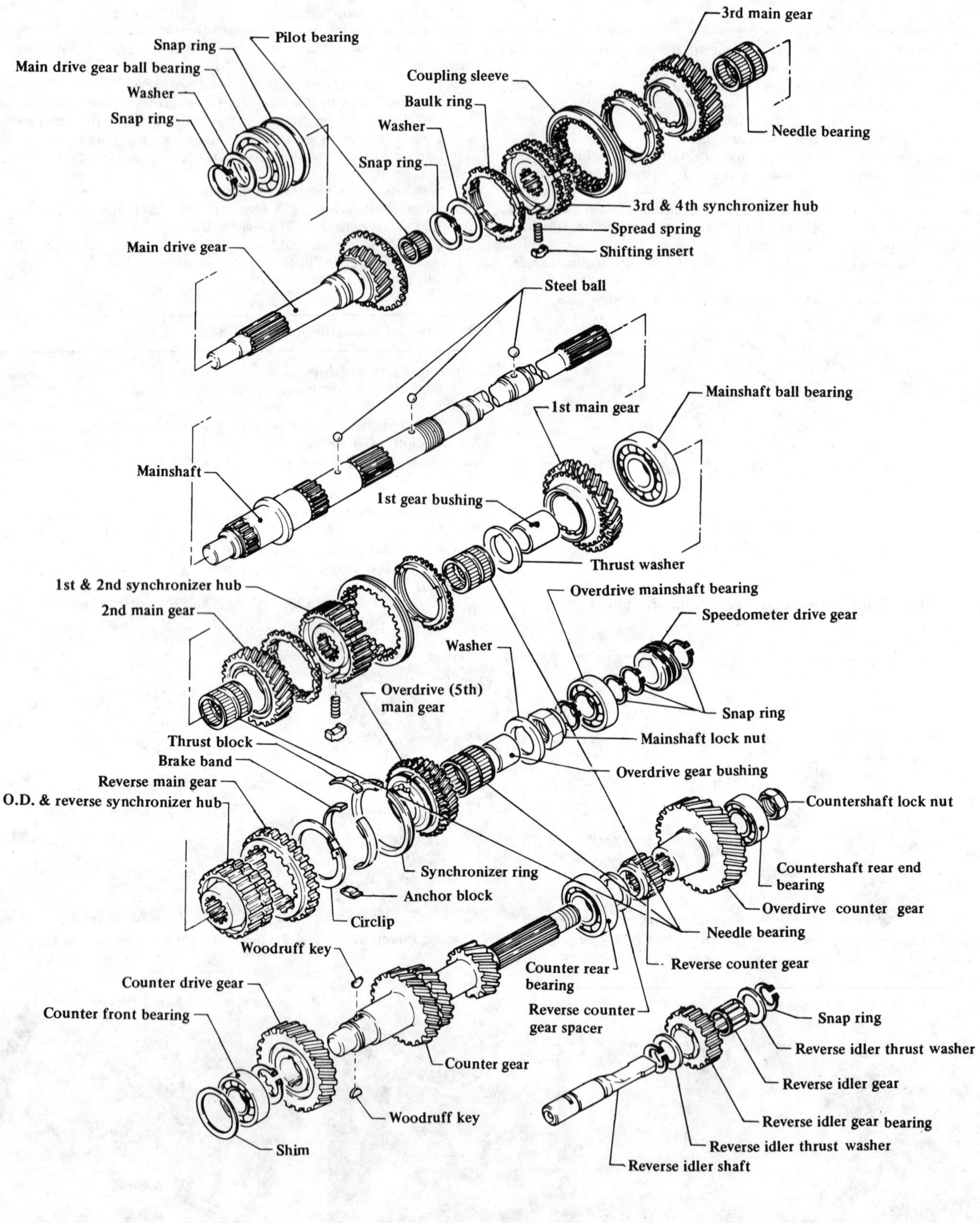

Fig. 7.4 Exploded view of the gears and shafts of the manual transmission (1980 models)

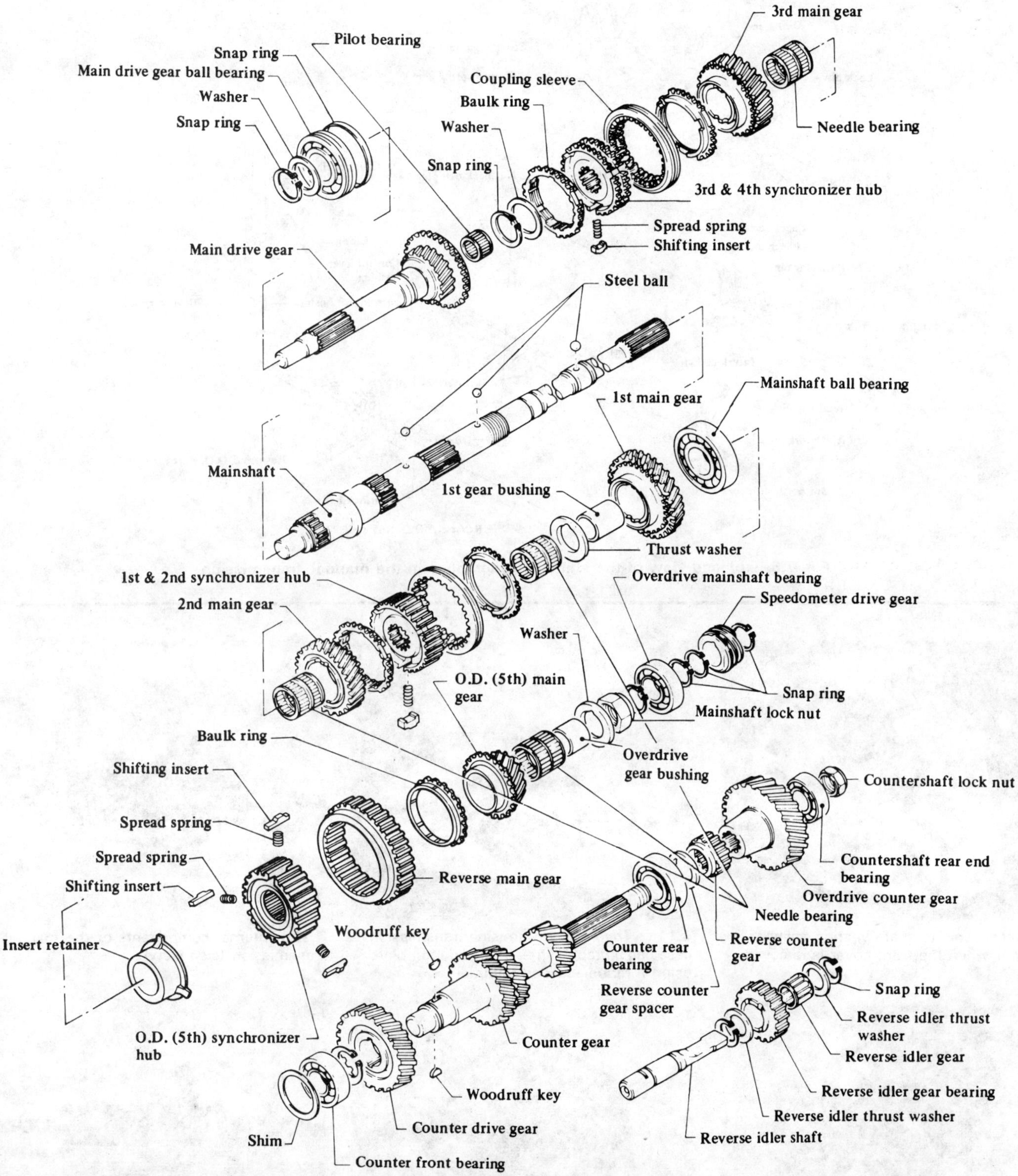

Fig. 7.5 Exploded view of the gears and shafts of the manual transmission (1981 models)

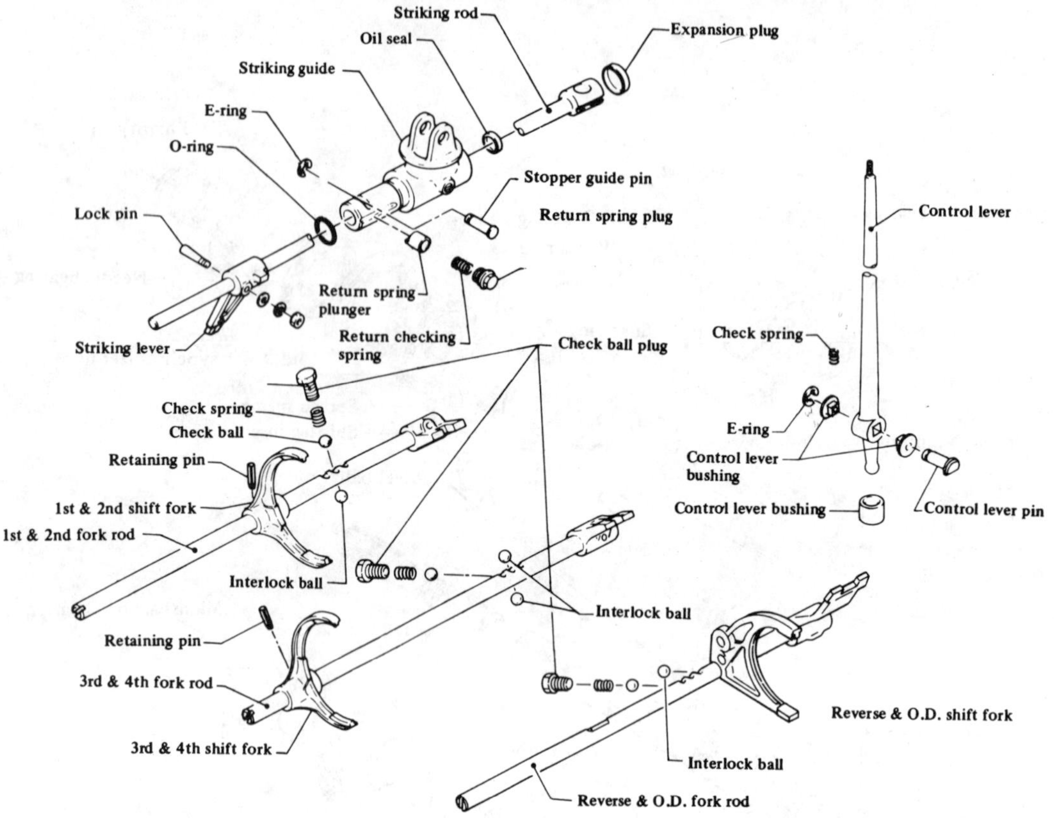

Fig. 7.6 Exploded view of the shift rod assemblies in the manual transmission

4.10b The countershaft bearing shim will drop out when the front cover is removed

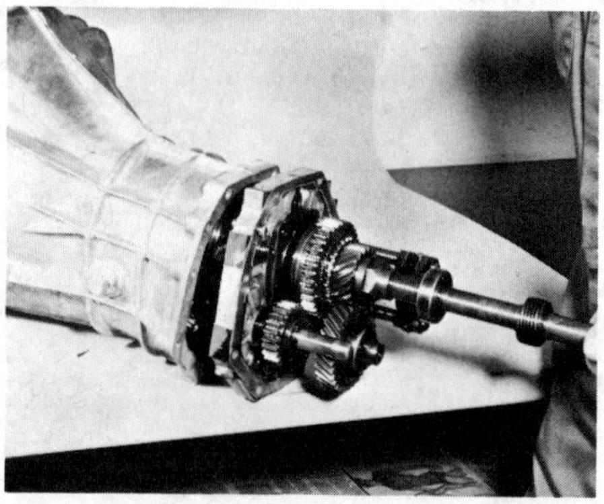

4.11a The clutch housing/transmission case can be tapped free of the adapter plate using a rubber-headed hammer

4.11b Internal components of the manual transmission (side view)

4.11c Internal components of the manual transmission (front view)

4.11d Internal components of the manual transmission (rear view)

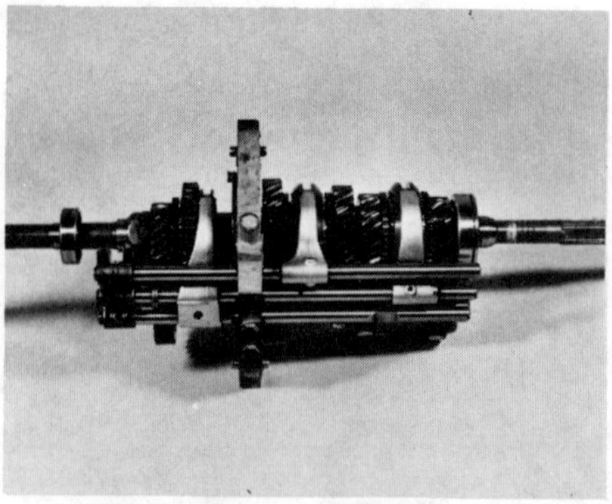

4.13 Installed arrangements of the shift rods and forks

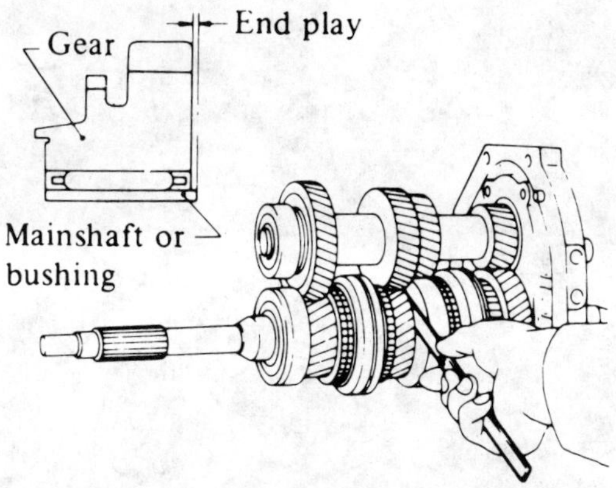

Fig. 7.7 Gear endplay should be measured both before and after disassembling the transmission, to check for wear and proper installation (Sec 4)

8 Remove the 2 screws that retain the reverse check cover to the housing and lift out the reverse check sleeve (photo).
9 Unscrew the securing bolts, and drive the rear extension housing from the main transmission casing, using a soft mallet.
10 Unscrew and remove the front cover retaining bolts: remove the front cover and extract the countershaft bearing shim and the input shaft bearing snap-ring (photos).
11 Drive off the one-piece bellhousing/transmission casing from the adaptor plate (photos).
12 Make up a suitable plate and bolt it to the transmission adaptor plate and then secure the support plate in a vise.
13 Drive out the securing pins from each of the shift forks, using a suitable thin drift (photo).
14 Unscrew and remove the three detent ballplugs.
15 Withdraw the selector rods from the adaptor plate.
16 Catch the shift forks, and extract the balls and springs as the selector rods are withdrawn. The four smaller balls are the interlock balls.
17 At this point, inspect the gears and shafts for any wear, chipping or cracking.
18 Also, use a feeler gauge between each mainshaft gear to determine the amount of gear end play that exists. The standard end gear play should be as follows:

1st gear – 0.0106 to 0.0134 in (0.27 to 0.34 mm)
2nd gear – 0.0047 to 0.0075 in (0.12 to 0.19 mm)
3rd gear – 0.0051 to 0.0146 in (0.13 to 0.37 mm)
Overdrive (5th) gear – 0.0039 to 0.0067 in (0.10 to 0.17 mm)
Reverse idler gear 0.0020 to 0.0197 in (0.05 to 0.50 mm)

19 If the gear endplay is not within specs, or if the gears or shafts show signs of wear or damage, the gear assemblies should be disassembled and the defective parts replaced.
20 Lock the gears and using a suitable two legged extractor, draw the front bearing from the countershaft.
21 Extract the now explosed snap-ring from the countershaft.
22 Withdraw the countershaft gear together with the input shaft. Take care not to drop the needle roller bearing which is located on the front of the mainshaft.
23 Extract the snap-ring from the front end of the mainshaft, followed by the thrust washer.
24 Withdraw 3rd/4th synchronizer unit, followed by 3rd gear.
25 Both the mainshaft nut and the countershaft nuts are staked to prevent them from loosening. Use a hammer and punch to drive out the staking.
26 Remove the countershaft nut. Once removed, this nut should not be reused.
27 Use a gear puller to remove the countershaft overdrive gear and bearing.
28 Remove the reverse counter gear and spacer.
29 Remove the snap-ring from the reverse idler shaft and remove the reverse idler gear.
30 Remove the snap-ring that retains the speedometer gear to the mainshaft, and remove the speedometer gear and steel ball.
31 Remove the other 2 snap-rings from behind the speedometer gear and withdraw the overdrive mainshaft bearing.
32 Drive out the staking on the mainshaft nut and remove it. Once removed, this nut should not be reused.
33 Remove the thrust washer, overdrive gear bushing, needle bearing, overdrive gear, reverse main gear, overdrive synchronizer assembly and insert retainer (1981 only).
34 Drive the mainshaft and countershaft assemblies simultaneously from the adaptor plate, using a soft-faced mallet.

Mainshaft

35 Carefully examine the gearwheels and shaft splines for chipping of the teeth or wear and then dismantle the gear train into its component parts, renewing any worn or damaged items.
36 Examine the shaft itself for scoring or grooving, also the splines for twist, taper or general wear.
37 Examine the synchromesh units for cracks or wear or general slackness in the assembly and renew if evident, particularly if there has been a history of noisy gearchange or where the syncromesh can be easily 'beaten'.
38 Press the baulk ring tight against the synchromesh cone and measure the gap between the two components. If it is less than specified, renew the components (refer to specifications and accompanying figure).
39 When reassembling the synchromesh unit ensure that the ends of the snap-ring on opposite sides of the units do not engage in the same slot.

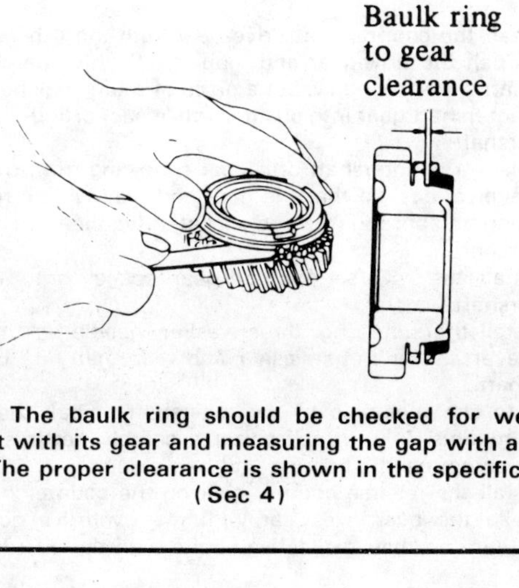

Fig. 7.8 The baulk ring should be checked for wear by mating it with its gear and measuring the gap with a feeler gauge. The proper clearance is shown in the specifications (Sec 4)

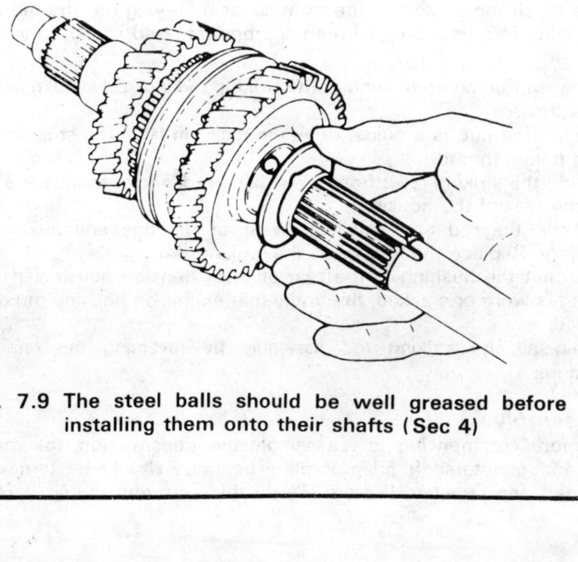

Fig. 7.9 The steel balls should be well greased before installing them onto their shafts (Sec 4)

4.54 The front oil seal is located in the front cover and can be pried out with a screwdriver

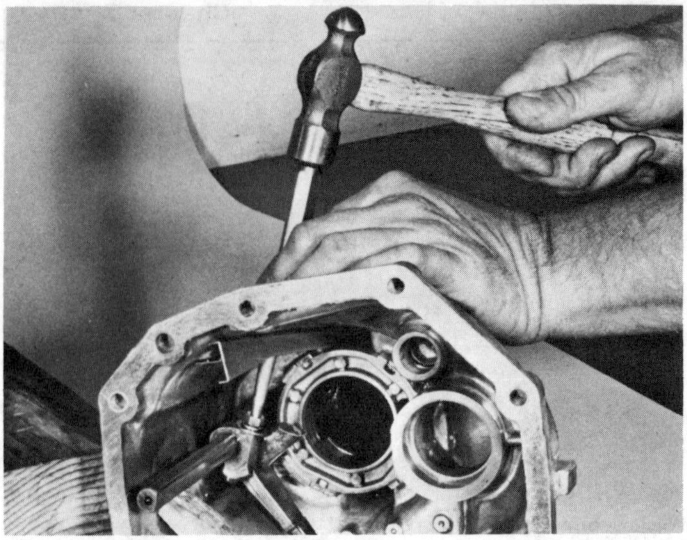

4.56 Use a punch to drive the striking rod lock pin from the striking lever

40 Commence assembly of the mainshaft by installing the 2nd gear needle bearing, 2nd gearwheel, the baulk ring followed by the 1st/2nd synchromesh unit, noting carefully the direction of installing the latter.
41 Now install the 1st gear baulk ring, needle bearing, steel ball, thrust washer, bushing and 1st gear. Be sure the steel ball is well greased when installed.

Countershaft

42 The countershaft front bearing was removed at the time of dismantling the transmission into major units.
43 The countershaft rear bearing was left in position in the adapter plate.
44 Withdraw the countershaft drive gear and extract the two Woodruff keys.
45 Check all components for wear, especially the gear teeth and shaft splines for chipping. Reinstall the Woodruff keys and the snap-ring.
46 Reassembly is a reversal of dismantling.

Input shaft (main drive gear)

47 Remove the snap-ring and spacer.
48 Withdraw the bearing using a two-legged extractor or a press. Once removed (by means of its outer track), discard the bearing.
49 Press the new bearing onto the shaft, applying pressure to the center track only.
50 Reinstall the washer.
51 Several thicknesses of snap-rings are available for the main input shaft bearing, as listed in the specifications. Choose a size that will eliminate bearing endplay.

Oil seals

52 Pry out the oil seal from the rear extension and drive in a new one, with the seal lips facing inwards.
53 Reinstall the speedometer pinion sleeve O-ring seal.
54 Reinstall the oil seal in the front cover by prying out the old one and driving in a new one, with an appropriate sized socket (photo).

Rear extension housing

55 Loosen the nut on the end of the striking rod lock pin, until it is half off the threads.
56 Using the nut as a guide, drive the lock pin from the striking rod with a punch (photo).
57 Slide the striking lever from the striking rod, and withdraw the rod from the rear of the housing.
58 Check the rod and lever for wear or damage and replace if necessary. Replace the O-ring on the striking rod.
59 Inspect the bushing in the rear of the extension housing. If this bushing is worn or cracked, the entire rear extension housing must be replaced.
60 Reinstall the striking rod assembly by reversing the removal procedure.

Reassembly

61 Before commencing to reassemble the transmission, the mainshaft and countershaft adaptor plate bearings should be removed, examined and renewed if worn. To do this, unscrew the six screws which retain the bearing retainer plate to the adapter plate. The use of an impact driver will probably be required for this operation.
62 With the bearing retainer plate removed, press the mainshaft and countershaft bearings from the adaptor plate. Apply pressure only to the outer tracks of the bearings.
63 Check the bearings for wear by first washing them in clean gasoline and drying in air from a tire pump. Spin them with the fingers, and if they are noisy or slack in operation, reinstall them.
64 Check that the dowel pin and oil trough are correctly positioned on the adapter plate.
65 Tap the mainshaft bearing lightly and squarely into position in the adapter plate.
66 Drive the reverse idler shaft into the adapter plate so that ⅔rds of its length is projecting rearwards. Ensure that the cutout in the shaft is positioned to receive the edge of the bearing retainer plate.
67 Install the bearing retainer plate and tighten the screws to the specified torque.
68 Stake each screw in two places to prevent them from loosening.
69 Tap the countershaft rear bearing into position in the adapter plate.
70 Press the mainshaft assembly into position in the bearing in the adapter plate. Support the rear of the bearing center track during this operation.
71 Press the countershaft assembly into position in the bearing in the adapter plate. Again support the rear of the bearing center track during this operation.
72 Install the needle bearing, 3rd gear, baulk ring and the 3rd/4th synchromesh unit to the front of the mainshaft.
73 Install the thrustwasher, and then choose a snap ring from the sizes listed in the specifications that will minimize endplay.
74 Insert the needle pilot bearing in its recess at the end of the input shaft.
75 Mesh the countershaft drive-gear with the 4th gear on the input shaft. Push the drivegear and input shaft onto the countershaft and mainshaft simultaneously, but a piece of tubing will be needed to drive the countershaft gear into position while supporting the rear end of the countershaft.
76 Select a countershaft drivegear snap-ring from the sizes listed in the specifications, so that the gear end play will be minimized.
77 Using an appropriate sized socket, drive the front bearing onto the countershaft.
78 Install the reverse counter gear spacer onto the rear of the countershaft.
79 Install the snap-ring, thrustwasher, needle bearing, reverse idler gear, reverse idler thrustwasher and rear snap-ring onto the reverse idler shaft.
80 Onto the rear side of the mainshaft, install the insert retainer (1981 models only), synchronizer assembly, reverse gear, overdrive gear bushing, needle bearing and baulk ring.
81 Install the reverse counter gear on the countershaft.
82 Mesh the overdrive gear with the overdrive counter gear and install them on their respective shafts with the overdrive gear on the

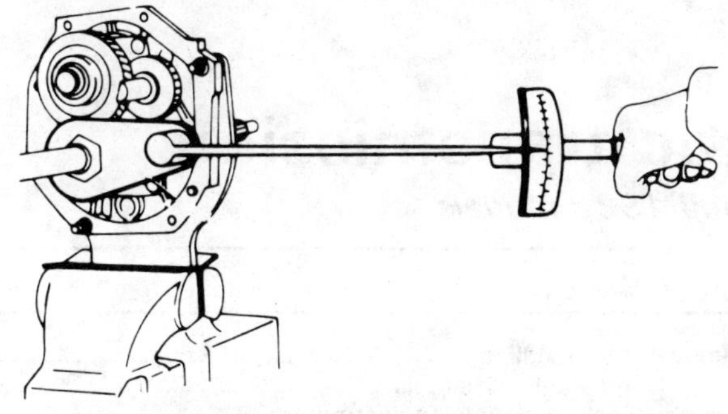

Fig. 7.10 The mainshaft locknut should be torqued to specs using a torque wrench and adapter as shown (Sec 4)

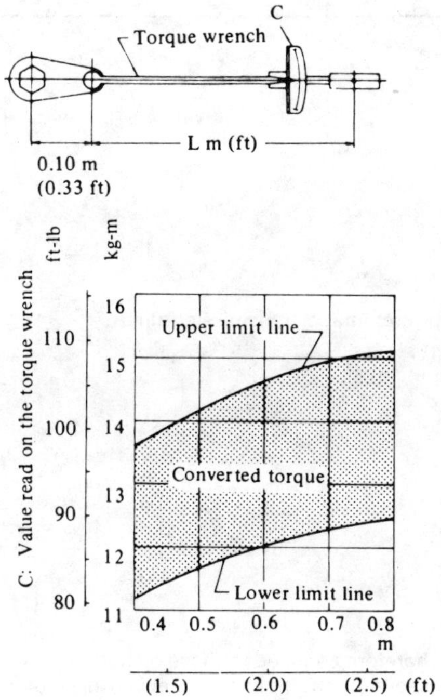

Fig. 7.11 When tightening the mainshaft locknut, the true torque can be found by matching the torque reading on the wrench with the chart above (Sec 4)

mainshaft and the overdrive counter gear on the countershaft.

83 Apply grease to the steel ball and install it and the thrustwasher onto the rear of the mainshaft.

84 Install a new lock nut onto the rear of the mainshaft and torque it to specs. **Note:** *In order to accurately tighten the nut to its torque specs, a wrench adaptor should be used as shown in the accompanying figure. Used with the adapter, the torque reading on the wrench will not be accurate and should be converted to the correct torque by referring to the chart shown.*

85 Install the countershaft rear end bearing onto the countershaft.

86 Install the countershaft lock nut and torque it to specs.

87 Use a hammer and punch to stake both the mainshaft and countershaft lock nuts so they engage the grooves in their respective shafts.

88 Once again measure the gear endplay, as described in paragraph 18.

89 Fit a snap-ring onto the mainshaft and then install the overdrive mainshaft bearing.

90 Choke a snap-ring from the sizes listed in the specifications to eliminate endplay of the mainshaft rear bearing.

91 Install the next snap-ring, then grease the steel ball and install the ball and the speedometer drive gear onto the mainshaft. Finally install the last snap-ring.

92 Locate the 1st/2nd shift fork onto the 1st/2nd synchronizer unit, (the long end of the shift fork must be towards the countershaft). Now locate the 3rd/4th shift fork onto the 3rd/4th synchronizer unit, (the long end of the shift fork must be the opposite side to the 1st/2nd shift fork).

93 Locate the overdrive reverse shift fork onto the overdrive synchronizer so that the upper rod hole is in line with the 3rd/4th shift fork.

94 Slide the 1st/2nd selector rod through the adapter plate and into the 1st/2nd shift fork; align the hole in the rod with the hole in the fork and drive in a new retaining pin.

95 Align the notch in the 1st/2nd selector rod with the detent (check) ball bore, then install the detent (check) ball, spring and screw in the detent ball plug. Apply a little thread sealant to the detent ball plug.

96 Now invert the adapter plate assembly (hold the 3rd/4th and O.D./reverse shift forks in position) so that the check ball plug assembled at paragraph 95, is lowermost. Drop two interlock balls into the 3rd/4th detent ball plug hole and, using a suitable thin probe, push them up against the 1st/2nd selector rod (if the adapter plate is correctly positioned, the interlock balls will drop into position). Slide the 3rd/4th selector rod through the upper hole of the OD/reverse shift fork and the adapter plate, ensuring that the interlock balls are held between this selector rod and the 1st/2nd selector rod, and into the 3rd/4th shift fork. Align the holes in the shift fork and selector rod, and drive in a new retaining pin. Now install a detent ball, spring and detent ball plug (with thread sealant applied) to the 3rd/4th detent ball plug bore. Ensure that the notch in the 3rd/4th selector rod is aligned with the detent ball plug bore before assembling the detent ball.

97 Drop two interlock balls into the remaining detent ball plug bore, ensuring that they locate against the 3rd/4th selector rod. Slide the overdrive/reverse selector rod through the overdrive reverse shift fork and into the adapter plate. Ensure that the two interlock balls are held in position between the 3rd/4th selector rod and the overdrive/reverse selector rod, sliding the overdrive/reverse selector rod into the adaptor plate until the notch in the selector rod aligns with the detent ball plug bore. Insert the detent ball, spring and detent ball plug as before. Drive in a new retaining pin to retain the overdrive/reverse shift fork to the overdrive/reverse selector rod.

98 Finally, tighten the three detent ball plugs to the specified torque.

99 Thoroughly oil the enitre assembly and check to see that the selector rods operate correctly and smoothly.

100 Clean the mating faces of the adapter plate and the transmission casing and apply gasket sealant to both surfaces.

101 Tap the transmission casing into position on the adapter plate using a soft faced mallet, taking particular care that it engages correctly with the input shaft bearing and countershaft front bearing.

102 Fit the outer snap-ring to the input shaft bearing.

103 Clean the mating faces of the adapter plate and rear extension housing and apply gasket sealant.

104 Arrange the shift forks in their neutral mode and then lower the rear extension housing onto the adapter plate so that the striking lever engages correctly with the selector rods.

105 Fit the bolts which secure the sections of the transmission together and tighten them to the specified torque.

106 Measure the amount by which the countershaft front bearing protrudes from the transmission casing front face. Use feeler blades for this and then select the appropriate shims after reference to the following table:

Measurement	*Shim (thickness)*
0.1150/0.1185 in (2.92/3.01 mm)	*0.0236 in (0.6 mm)*
0.1189/0.1124 in (3.02/3.11 mm)	*0.0197 in (0.5 mm)*
0.1228/0.1264 in (3.21/3.31 mm)	*0.0157 in (0.4 mm)*
0.1268/0.1303 in (3.22/3.31 mm)	*0.0118 in (0.3 mm)*
0.1307/0.1343 in (3.32/3.41 mm)	*0.0079 in (0.2 mm)*
0.1346/0.1382 in (3.42/3.51 mm)	*0.0039 in (0.1 mm)*

107 Stick the shim in position using a dab of thick grease, then fit the front cover to the transmission casing (within the clutch bellhousing) complete with a new gasket and taking care not to damage the oil seal as it passes over the input shaft splines.

108 Tighten the securing bolts to the specified torque, making sure that the bolt threads are coated with gasket sealant to prevent oil seepage.

109 Complete the reassembly by reversing the steps described in paragraphs 1 through 8 of this section.

Chapter 7 Part B: Automatic transmission

Refer to Chapter 13 for information related to 1982 and 1983 models

Contents

General information 5
Inhibitor switch 7
Kickdown switch – adjustment 8
Rear oil seal – replacement 10
Removal and installation 11
Shift linkage – adjustment 6
Vacuum diaphragm rod – adjustment 9

Specifications

Model	3N71B	
Stall torque ratio	2.0:1	
Gear ratios:		
1st	2.458	
2nd	1.458	
3rd	1.000	
Reverse	2.182	
Recommended fluid	Dexron-type automatic transmission fluid	
Fluid capacity	$5\frac{7}{8}$ qt (5.5 liters)	
Torque specifications	**ft-lb**	**m-kg**
Torque converter-to-flywheel bolts	33	4.5
Converter housing-to-engine-bolts	33	4.5
Oil pan mounting bolts	4.3	0.6
Inhibitor switch mounting bolts	4.3	0.6
Shift linkage lock nut	25	3.5
Oil cooler pipe-to-connections	29	4.0

5 General information

The automatic transmission unit is the type JATCO 3N71B.

The unit provides three forward ratios and one reverse. Changing of the forward gear ratios is completely automatic in relation to the vehicle speed and engine torque output and is dependent upon the vacuum pressure in the manifold and the vehicle road speed to actuate the gear change mechanism at the precise time.

The transmission has six selector positions:

P – Parking position which locks the output shaft to the interior wall of the transmission housing. This is a safety device for use when the vehicle is parked on an incline. The engine may be started with 'P' selected and this position should always be selected when adjusting the engine while it is running. Never attempt to select 'P' when the vehicle is in motion.

R – Reverse gear.

N – Neutral. Select this position to start the engine or when idling in traffic for long periods.

D – Drive, for all normal motoring conditions.

2 – Locks the transmission in second gear for wet road conditions or steep hill climbing or descents. The engine can be over-revved in this position.

1 – The selection of this ratio above road speeds of approximately 25 mph (40 kph) will engage second gear and as the speed drops below 25 mph (40 kph) the transmission will lock into first gear. Provides maximum retardation on steep descents.

Due to the complexity of the automatic transmission unit, any internal adjustment or servicing should be left to a Datsun dealer, or other qualified transmission specialist. The information given in this Chapter is therefore confined to those operations which are considered within the scope of the home mechanic. An automatic transmission should give many tens of thousands of miles service provided normal maintenance and adjustment is carried out. When the unit finally requires major overhaul, consideration should be given to exchanging the old transmission for a factory reconditioned one, the removal and installation being well within the capabilities of the home mechanic as described later in this Chapter.

The routine maintenance chart in Chapter 1 calls for an automatic transmission fluid change once every 30 000 miles. This interval should be shortened to every 15 000 miles if the car is normally driven under one or more of the following conditions: heavy city traffic, where the outside temperature normally reaches 90°F or higher; in very hilly or mountainous areas; or if a trailer is frequently pulled. Refer to Chapter 1 for the proper procedures for checking and changing the automatic transmission fluid and filter.

The automatic transmission uses an oil cooler, located at the radiator, to prevent excessive temperatures from developing inside the transmission. Should the oil cooler need flushing or other servicing, take it to a dealer or other radiator specialist.

If rough shifting or other malfunctions occur in the automatic transmission, check the following items first before assuming the fault lies within the transmission itself: the fluid level, the kickdown switch adjustment, manual shift linkage adjustment and engine tune. All of these elements can adversely affect the performance of the transmission.

Periodically clean the outside of the transmission housing as the accumulation of dirt and oil is liable to cause overheating of the unit under extreme conditions.

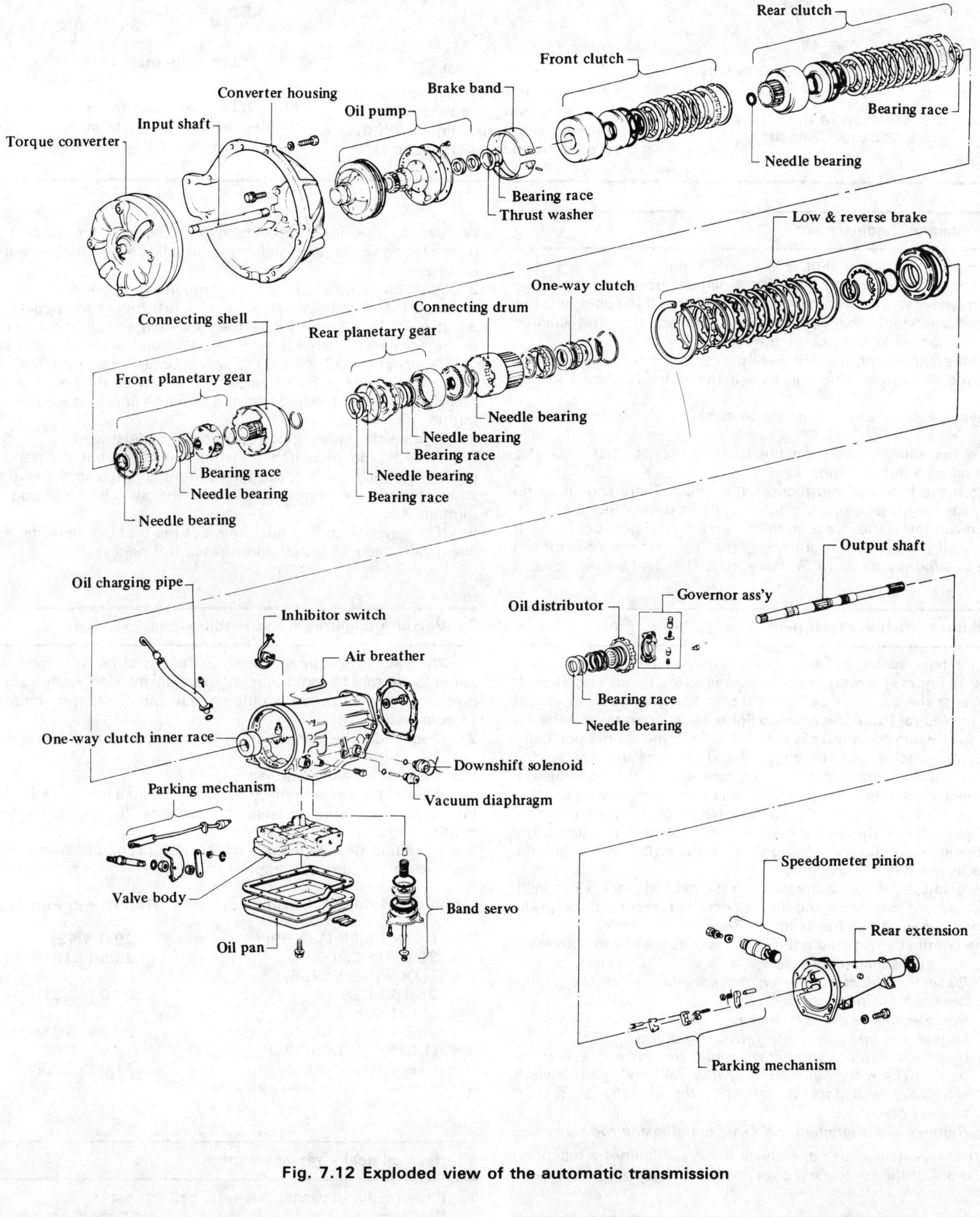

Fig. 7.12 Exploded view of the automatic transmission

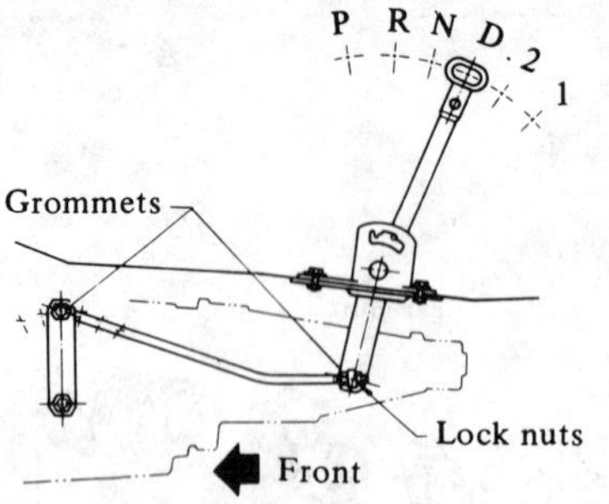

Fig. 7.13 Location of the selector rod locknut (Sec 6)

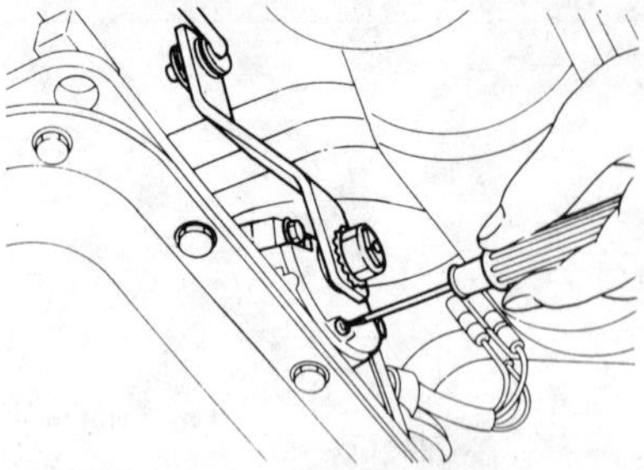

Fig. 7.14 The inhibitor switch is adjusted by removing the screw shown and aligning the screw hole with the rotor hole underneath (Sec 7)

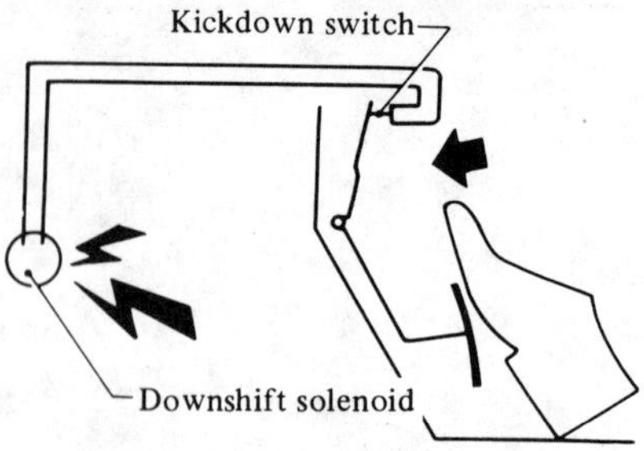

Fig. 7.15 The kickdown switch is located at the upper post of the accelerator pedal (Sec 8)

6 Shift linkage – adjustment

1 To check the manual shift linkage adjustment, move the shifter through the entire range of gears. You should be able to feel the detents in each gear. If these detents are not felt or if the pointer is not properly aligned with the correct gear selection, the shift linkage should be adjusted in the following manner.
2 With the engine off, place the shift lever in the drive (D) gear.
3 Working underneath the car, loosen the locknuts shown in Fig. 7.13.
4 Move the shift lever so that it is correctly aligned with the D position.
5 Move the selector lever on the transmission so that it is also correctly aligned in the D position.
6 Tighten the locknuts and recheck the levers. There should be no tendency for the selector rod to push or pull one rod against the other.
7 Again run the shifter through the entire range of gear positions. If there are still problems, the grommets that connect the selector rod with the levers may be worn or damaged and should be replaced.

7 Inhibitor switch – adjustment

1 The inhibitor switch peforms two functions. It provides current to the back-up lights when the transmission is in the reverse position. It also prevents the car from being started in any gear position except Park (P) or Neutral (N). If the back-up lights fail to operate, or if the car will not start when the shifter is in the middle of the P or N positions, the inhibitor switch should be checked and, if necessary, adjusted.
2 Locate the inhibitor switch on the right side of the transmission and connect a continuity tester to the black and yellow wires.
3 With the engine off, but the ignition switch on, have an assistant run the gear shifter through the entire range of gear positions. The tester should show current passing through the switch only when the shifter is in the P or N positions.
4 Now connect the continuity tester to the red and black wires. With this arrangement the tester should show current passing through the switch only when the shifter is in the Reverse (R) position.
5 If the continuity tests did not give the results described above, the switch should be adjusted as follows:

(a) Place the selector lever on the transmission in the neutral (vertical) position.
(b) Remove the screw shown in Fig. 7.14.
(c) Loosen the inhibitor switch attaching bolts.
(d) Using a thin rod or piece of wire, align the screw hole with the hole in the rotor behind the switch, by moving the switch. Holding this alignment, retighten the inhibitor switch attaching bolts.
(e) Remove the alignment rod or wire and install the screw.

6 With the switch adjusted, recheck it for continuity by repeating steps 3 and 4. If the switch still does not function properly, replace it.

8 Kickdown switch – adjustment

1 The kickdown switch, coupled with the downshift solenoid, causes the transmission to downshift when the accelerator pedal is fully depressed. This is to provide extra power when passing. If the transmission is not downshifting upon full throttle, the system should be inspected.
2 With the engine off, but the ignition on, depress the accelerator pedal all the way and listen for a click just before the pedal bottoms.
3 If no click is heard, locate the kickdown switch at the upper post of the accelerator pedal (Fig. 7. 15). Loosen the locknut and with the pedal still depressed, extend the switch until it makes contact with the post and clicks. The switch should click only as the pedal bottoms. If it clicks too soon, it will cause the transmission to downshift on part throttle.
4 Tighten the locknut, and recheck the adjustment.
5 If the kickdown switch adjustment is corrct but the transmission still will not downshift check that current is reaching the switch, and, with a continuity tester, check that the switch is passing current through it.
6 If the switch checks out okay, but the problem persists, have the downshift solenoid tested and replace it if necessary.

9 Vacuum diaphragm rod – adjustment

1 The vacuum diaphragm and the length of its rod affect the shift patterns of the transmission. If the transmission is not shifting at precisely the right points, a different vacuum diaphragm rod may have to be installed.
2 Disconnect the vacuum hose from the vacuum diaphragm on the left side of the transmission.
3 Remove the vacuum diaphragm.
4 Be sure the vacuum throttle valve is pushed into the valve body as far as possible, and measure the distance "L" in Fig. 7.16 with a depth gauge.
5 Once this measurement is taken, use the chart below to determine the correct vacuum diaphragm rod length.

Measured depth "L" mm (in)	Rod length mm (in)
Under 25.55 (1.0059)	29.0 1.42)
25.65 to 26.05 (1.0098 to 1.0256)	29.5 (1.161)
26.15 to 26.55 (1.0295 to 1.0453)	30.0 (1.181)
26.65 to 27.05 (1.0492 to 1.0650)	30.5 (1.201)
Over 27.15 (1.0689)	31.0 (1.220)

10 Rear oil seal – replacement

1 Remove the driveshaft as described in Chapter 8.
2 Being careful not to damage the output shaft or transmission housing, use a screwdriver to pry out the old seal.
3 Apply a coat of gear oil to the lips of the new seal and drive it into place using an appropriate sized socket.
4 Reinstall the driveshaft.

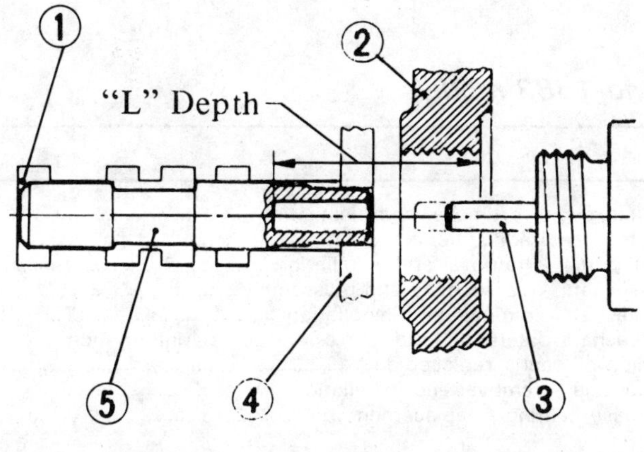

Fig. 7.16 Measurement of vacuum diaphragm rod (Sec 9)

1 *Note seated valve body*
2 *Transmission case wall*
3 *Diaphragm rod*
4 *Valve body side plate*
5 *Vacuum throttle valve*

11 Automatic transmission – removal and installation

NOTE: *Due to the complexity of the automatic transmission and the special equipment needed to service it, an automatic transmission overhaul is not practical for the home mechanic to perform. Considerable money can be saved however, by removing and installing the transmission yourself. Read through this Section to become familiar with the procedure and the tools needed for the job. The car must be raised high enough so the transmission can be lowered from the car and slid out from underneath.*

1 Prior to removal of the transmission, have the car test driven and diagnosed by a qualified transmission specialist, so that he may determine the nature and cause of the problem.

2 Removal of the engine and automatic transmission as a combined unit is described in Chapter 2 of this manual. Where it is decided to remove the transmission leaving the engine in position in the vehicle proceed as follows:

3 Disconnect the battery ground lead.

4 Drain the fluid from the transmission unit, retaining it in a clean container if required for further use.

5 Jack the car to an adequate working height and support on stands or blocks.

6 Remove the driveshaft as described in Chapter 8. As this is done, plug or cover over the opening at the rear of the transmission to prevent oil leakage.

7 Disconnect the exhaust downpipe from the engine and wire it out of the way.

8 Disconnect the wires from the starter inhibitor switch.

9 Disconnect the wire from the downshift solenoid.

10 Disconnect the vacuum pipe from the vacuum capsule which is located just forward of the downshift solenoid.

11 Separate the selector lever from the selector linkage.

12 Disconnect the speedometer drive cable from the rear extension housing.

13 Disconnect the fluid filler tube. Plug the opening.

14 Disconnect the fluid cooler tubes from the transmission casing and plug the openings.

15 Support the engine oil pan with a jack and use a block of wood to prevent damage to the surface of the oil pan.

16 Remove the cover from the lower half of the torque converter housing and drive plate in relation to each other for exact replacement.

17 Unscrew and remove the four bolts which secure the torque converter to the drive plate. Access to each of these bolts in turn is obtained by rotating the engine slowly, using a wrench on the crankshaft pulley bolt.

18 Unbolt and withdraw the starter motor.

19 Support the transmission with a jack (preferably a trolley type).

20 Remove the bolts that secure the transmission mounting bracket to the transmission.

21 Remove the transmission mounting bracket from the body.

22 Unscrew and remove the transmission-to-engine securing bolts.

23 Lower the two jacks sufficiently to allow the transmission unit to be withdrawn from below and to the rear of the vehicle. The help of an assistant will probably be required due to the weight of the unit. If an automatic transmission is in need of minor repair, take it to a GM dealer or other qualified transmission specialist. If an automatic transmission is in need of a complete overhaul, it may be more economical to replace the old transmission with a rebuilt one.

25 Installation is a reversal of removal but should the torque converter have been separated from the main assembly, ensure that the notch on the converter is correctly aligned with the corresponding one on the oil pump. To check that the torque converter has been correctly installed, the dimension A should exceed 0.846 in (21.5 mm) (Figs. 7.17 and 7.18).

26 When bolting the torque converter to the flywheel, be sure the marks made during removal are aligned. Once the converter is installed, rotate the crankshaft several times to make sure the transmission turns freely with no binding.

27 Tighten all bolts to the specified torque settings and refill the unit with the correct grade and quantity of fluid.

28 Check the operation of the inhibitor switch and the selector linkage and adjust if necessary as described in this Chapter.

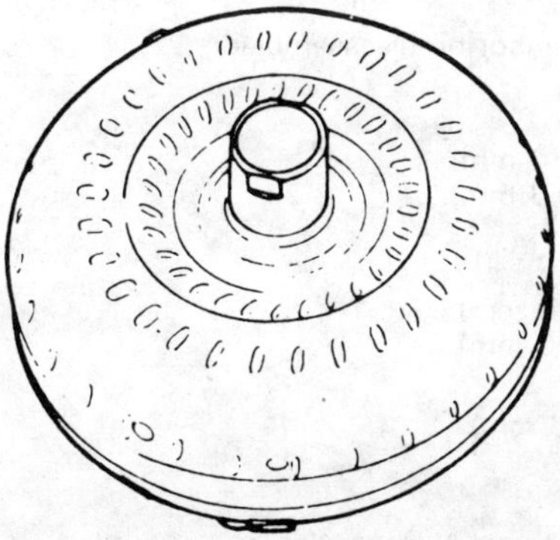

Fig. 7.17 When installing the torque converter, the notch in the converter should be aligned with the notch in the oil pump (Sec 11)

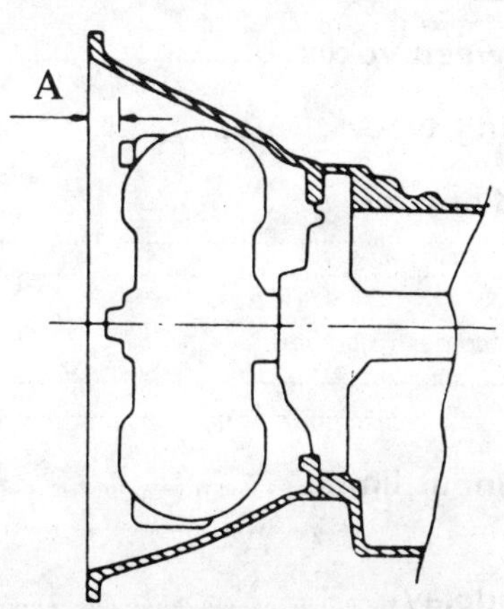

Fig. 7.18 Following torque converter installation, distance "A" above should be measured to check for proper installation (Sec 11)

Chapter 8 Driveline

Refer to Chapter 13 for information related to 1982 and 1983 models

Contents

Axleshaft, rear wheel bearing and oil seal – removal and installation ... 14
Bleeding the clutch hydraulic system ... 2
Clutch – general information ... 1
Clutch disc and pressure plate assembly – removal, inspection and installation ... 9
Clutch master cylinder – overhaul ... 6
Clutch master cylinder – removal and installation ... 5
Clutch operating cylinder – overhaul ... 8
Clutch operating cylinder – removal and installation ... 7
Clutch pedal – removal and installation ... 4
Clutch pedal adjustments ... 3
Differential – removal and installation ... 16
Driveshaft – disassembly and reassembly ... 13
Driveshaft – removal and installation ... 12
Driveshaft, differential and rear axle – general information ... 11
Pinion oil seal – replacement ... 15
Rear axle – removal and installation ... 17
Release bearing – replacement ... 10

Specifications

Clutch

Type	Single dry plate, diaphragm spring with hydraulic actuation

Clutch disc

Type	200CBL
Number of torsion springs	6
Wear limit of lining surface to rivet head	0.012 in (0.3 mm)
Runout limit	0.020 in (0.5 mm)
Distance of runout checking point from hub center	3.74 in (95 mm)
Disc diameter	7.87 in (200 mm)

Clutch cover/pressure plate assembly

Type	C200S
Diaphragm spring height	1.244 to 1.323 in (31.6 to 33.6 mm)
Maximum unevenness of spring toe height	0.020 in (0.5 mm)

Clutch pedal

Height	6.61 to 6.85 in (168 to 174 mm)
Freeplay	0.04 to 0.20 in (1 to 5 mm)

Driveshaft

Type	3S63A
Number of universal joints	3
Transmission coupling method	Sleeve type
Distance between yokes	2.48 in (63 mm)
Journal bearing type	Shell type (cannot be disassembled)
Shaft outer diameter	
1st	2.953 in (75.0 mm)
2nd	2.000 in (50.8 mm)
Shaft length (spider to spider)	
1st	12.60 in (320 mm)
2nd	28.74 in (730 mm)
Driveshaft runout limit	0.024 in (0.6 mm)

Axleshaft

Axleshaft endplay	0.0020 to 0.0157 in (0.05 to 0.40 mm)
Selection of rear axle case shim thicknesses	0.0030 in (0.075 mm) 0.0059 in (0.150 mm) 0.0089 in (0.225 mm) 0.0118 in (0.300 mm)

Differential

Type	H165B
Gear ratio	3.7 : 1
Oil capacity	$2\frac{3}{8}$ pt (1.1 liters)
Drive pinion bearing adjustment method	Collapsible spacer
Drive pinion preload (with oil seal)	6.1 – 8.7 in-lb (7 – 10 cm-kg)

Torque specifications	**ft-lb**	**m-kg**
Clutch master cylinder mounting nuts	7	1.0
Clutch tube flare nut	12	1.6
Clutch operating cylinder mounting bolts	26	3.6
Clutch cover mounting bolts	14	1.9
Drive pinion nut	160	22.0
Differential drain and filler plugs	58	8.0
Driveshaft-to-differential bolts	20	2.8
Differential mounting bolts	22	3.0
Center bearing locking nut (flange type)	200	28.0
Center bearing locking nut (nut-and-washer type)	160	22.0
Center bearing bracket mounting bolts	24	3.2
Center bearing support-to-bracket nut	7.5	1.0
Flange yoke-to-companion flange bolts	20	2.9
Baffle plate mounting nuts	18	2.5

1 Clutch – general information

The clutch is located between the engine and the transmission and its main components are the clutch disc, the pressure plate assembly and the release bearing. Other components which make up the hydraulically operated clutch system are the clutch pedal, clutch master cylinder, operating cylinder and release lever.

The clutch disc, pressure plate assembly and release bearing are mounted on the transmission input shaft. The clutch disc is sandwiched between the flywheel and the pressure plate and has a splined hub which engages and turns the input shaft. When engaged, the pressure plate is held against the clutch disc by the spring pressure of its metal fingers, and the clutch disc, in turn, is held against the engine's flywheel. The spinning of the engine is thus transmitted from the flywheel to the clutch disc and into the input shaft.

The clutch pedal is connected to the clutch master cylinder by a short pushrod. The master cylinder and hydraulic reservoir are mounted on the engine side of the bulkhead in front of the driver.

Depressing the clutch pedal moves the piston in the master cylinder forward and forces hydraulic fluid through the clutch hydraulic pipe to the operating cylinder.

The piston in the operating cylinder moves forward on the entry of the fluid and actuates the clutch release lever by means of a short pushrod.

The other end of the release lever, located inside the clutch housing is fork-shaped. This fork engages the clutch release bearing and forces the bearing against the pressure plate assembly's release fingers. When the fingers receive pressure from the release bearing they withdraw the mating surface of the pressure plate from the clutch disc which engages the clutch assembly from the engine's flywheel.

As the friction linings on the clutch disc wear, the pressure plate automatically moves closer to the disc to compensate and eliminates the necessity for adjustment.

Because access to the clutch components is difficult, any time either the engine or the transmission is removed the clutch disc, pressure plate assembly and release bearing should be carefully inspected and, if necessary, replaced. Since the clutch disc is the highest wear item, it should be replaced as a matter of course if there is any question as to its quality.

2 Bleeding the clutch hydraulic system

1 Bleeding will be required whenever the hydraulic system has been dismantled and reassembled and air has entered the system.

2 First fill the fluid reservoir with clean brake fluid which has been stored in an airtight container. Never use fluid which has drained from the system or has been bled out on a previous occasion, it may contain grit.

3 Fit a rubber or plastic bleed tube to the bleed screw on the operating cylinder and immerse the open end of the tube in a glass jar containing an inch or two of fluid.

4 Open the bleed screw about half a turn and have an assistant quickly depress the clutch pedal fully. Tighten the bleed screw and then have the clutch pedal slowly released with the foot completely removed. Repeat this sequence of operations until air bubbles are no longer seen to be ejected from the open end of the tube beneath the fluid in the jar.

5 After two or three strokes of the pedal, check that the fluid level in the reservoir has not fallen too low. Keep it well topped-up with fresh fluid otherwise air will again be drawn into the system.

6 Tighten the bleed nipple finally on a down stroke, do not overtighten it, remove the bleed tube and jar, top-up the reservoir and refit the cap.

7 If the help of an assistant is not readily available, alternative 'one-man' bleeding operations can be carried out using a bleed tube fitted with a one way valve or a pressure bleed kit both of which should be used in accordance with the manufacturer's instructions.

3 Clutch pedal adjustments

1 Because the height and free play adjustments for the clutch pedal are included in the car's routine maintenance schedule, these procedures are described in Chapter 1.

4 Clutch pedal – removal and installation

1 Remove the lower instrument cover, located directly below the steering column.

2 Disconnect the master cylinder pushrod from the pedal by prising off the snap pin and withdrawing the clevis pin.

3 Remove the stopper bolt from its bracket.

4 Pry off the E-ring from the fulcrum pin.

5 Remove the clutch pedal and the return spring.

6 Clean the parts in solvent and replace any that are damaged or excessively worn. The bushing in the pedal is press-fitted, and if it is defective, the entire pedal must be replaced.

7 Installation is the reverse of the removal procedure. **Note:** *During*

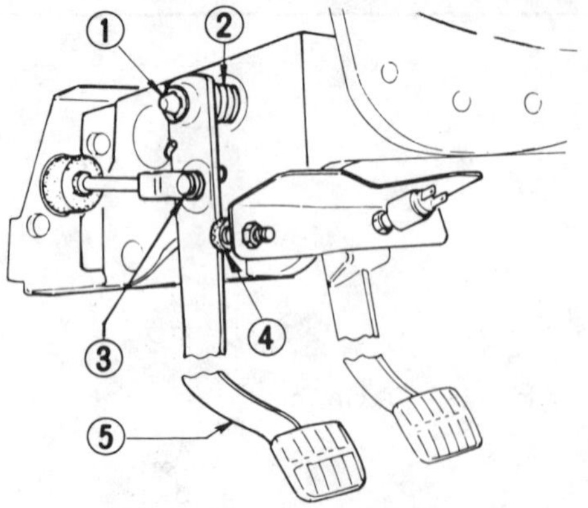

Fig. 8.1 Components of the clutch pedal assembly (Sec 4)

1 E-ring
2 Return spring
3 Clevis pin
4 Stopper bolt
5 Clutch pedal

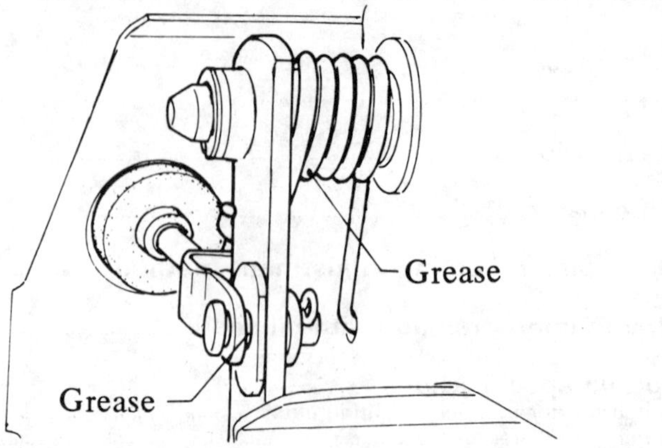

Fig. 8.2 Grease should be applied to the points shown during installation of the clutch pedal (Sec 4)

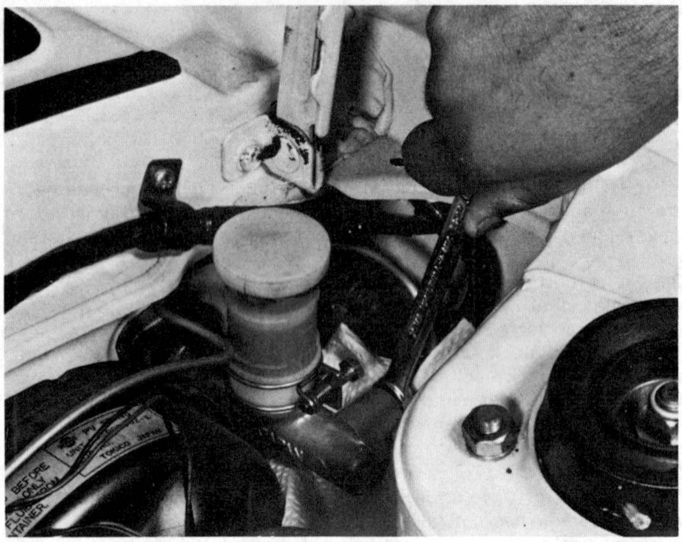

5.2 Place a rag or paper towel under the clutch master cylinder when disconnecting the fluid line

installation, apply multi-purpose grease to the pedal boss, return spring and fulcrum pin. Also, when connecting the master cylinder pushrod to the pedal, smear a little grease on the clevis pin (see accompanying figure).

8 Following installation, check the height and free play adjustments of the clutch pedal, and make adjustments as necessary as described in Chapter 1.

5 Clutch master cylinder – removal and installation

1 Disconnect the master cylinder pushrod from the pedal arm.

2 Disconnect the fluid line from the master cylinder (photo) and drain the fluid into a suitable container.

3 Remove the master cylinder flange mounting bolts and withdraw the unit from the engine compartment rear bulkhead.

4 Installation is a reversal of removal, but check the pedal height and free-play as described in Chapter 1, and bleed the hydraulic system (Section 2).

6 Clutch master cylinder – overhaul

1 Drain any fluid from the reservoir and clean away all external dirt from the cylinder.

2 Peel back the flexible rubber boot at the end of the cylinder and

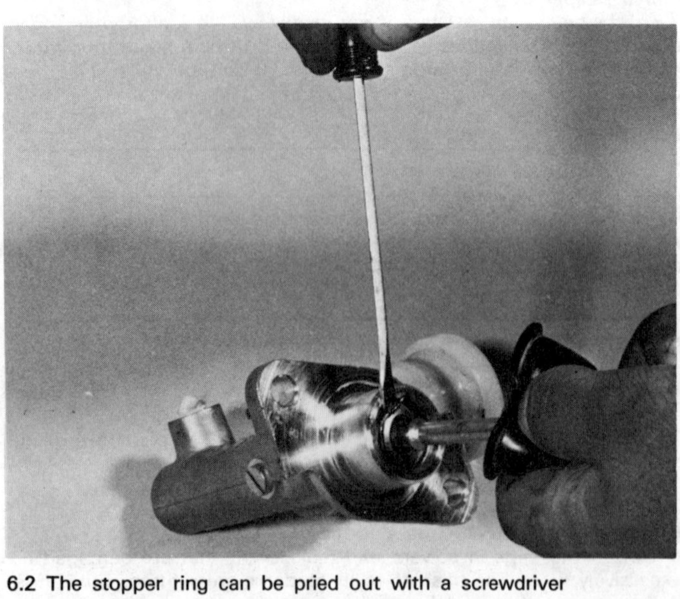

6.2 The stopper ring can be pried out with a screwdriver

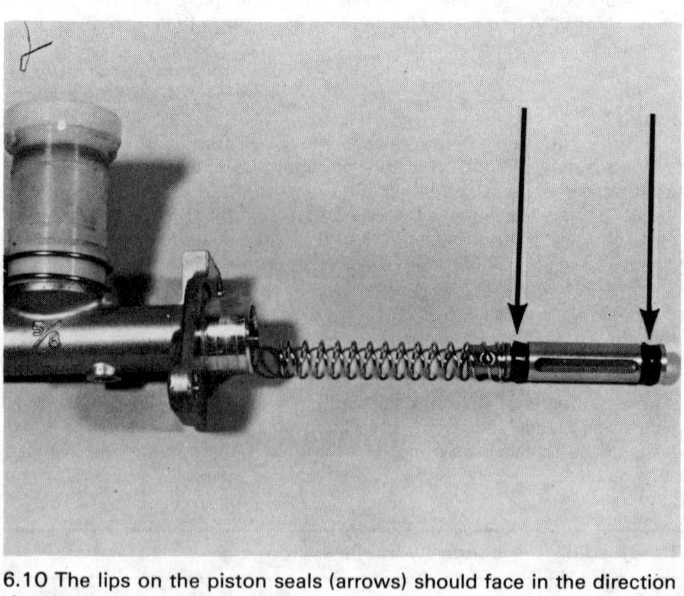

6.10 The lips on the piston seals (arrows) should face in the direction shown

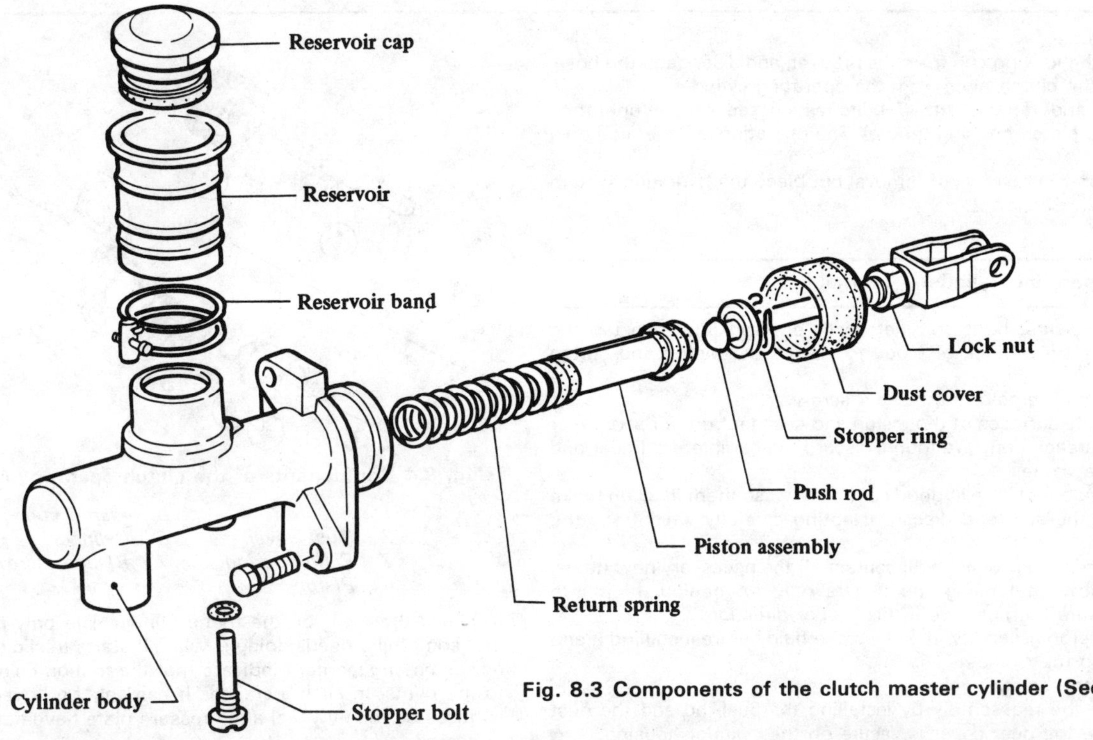

Fig. 8.3 Components of the clutch master cylinder (Sec 6)

pry out the stopper ring (photo).

3 Remove the pushrod assembly from the cylinder.

4 Use a rod to depress the piston into the cylinder and hold it depressed while you unscrew and remove the stopper bolt from the bottom of the cylinder.

5 With the stopper bolt removed, the piston and spring assembly can be removed. The piston is not designed to be disassembled.

6 Do not detach the reservoir from the cylinder body, as a new one will have to be installed if the old one is removed.

7 Examine the inner surface of the cylinder bore. If it is scored or exhibits "bright" wear areas, the entire master cylinder should be replaced.

8 If the cylinder bore is in good condition, obtain a clutch master cylinder rebuild kit, which will contain all of the necessary replacement parts.l

9 Prior to installing any parts, first dip them in brake fluid to lubricate them. **Note:** *Do not use other solvents or lubricants.*

10 If the piston seals are not already mounted on the new piston supplied in the rebuild kit, use your fingers to manipulate them into their grooves. Be sure the lips face in the proper directions (photo).

11 The installation of the parts into the cylinder is the reverse of the removal procedure.

7 Clutch operating cylinder – removal and installation

1 In order to prevent excessive loss of hydraulic fluid, when the operating cylinder hose is disconnected, remove the reservoir cap and place a piece of polythene sheeting over the open reservoir. Screw on the cap and thus create a vacuum which will stop the fluid running out of the open hose.

2 Loosen the clutch line flare nut at the bracket mounted on the

7.5 The clutch operating cylinder is located on the right side of the clutch housing

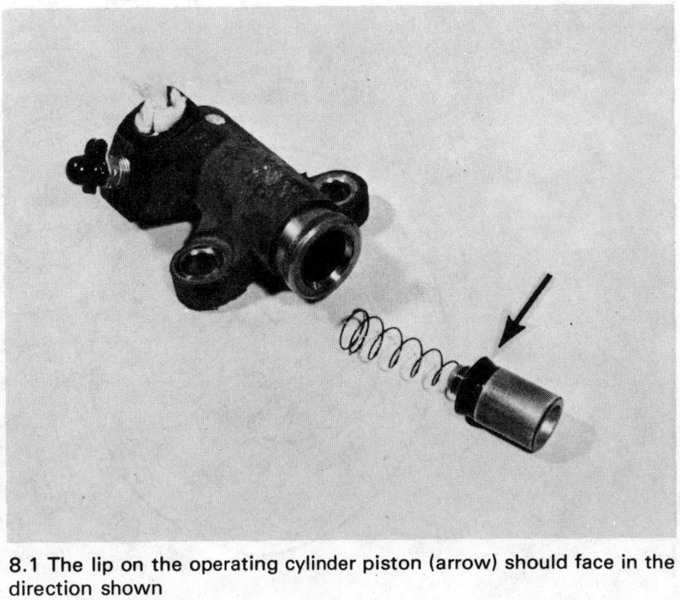

8.1 The lip on the operating cylinder piston (arrow) should face in the direction shown

body sidemember.
3 Remove the locking clip from the bracket, and disengage the hose.
4 Remove the clutch hose from the operating cylinder.
5 Unscrew and remove the 2 bolts which secure the operating cylinder to the clutch housing (photo). The operating cylinder can now be removed.
6 Installation is a reversal of removal but bleed the hydraulic system as described in Section 2.

8 Clutch operating cylinder – overhaul

1 Pull off the dust boot complete with pushrod and then tap the cylinder gently on a block of wood to extract the piston and spring (photo).
2 Unscrew and remove the bleeder screw.
3 Examine the surfaces of the piston and cylinder bore for scoring or 'bright' wear areas. If any are found, discard the complete cylinder and purchase a new one.
4 If the components are in good condition, wash them in clean brake fluid, remove the seal and discard it noting carefully which way the seal lips face.
5 Obtain a repair kit which will contain all the necessary new items.
6 Fit the new seal using the fingers only to manipulate it into position. Be sure the lips face in the proper direction.
7 Dip the piston assembly in clean brake fluid before installing it and the spring into the cylinder.
8 Reinstall the bleeder valve.
9 Complete the reassembly by installing the pushrod and the dust cover. Be sure the dust cover is secure on the cylinder housing.

9 Clutch disc and pressure plate assembly – removal, inspection and installation

1 Due to the slow-wearing qualities of the clutch, it is not easy to decide when to go to the trouble of removing the transmission in order

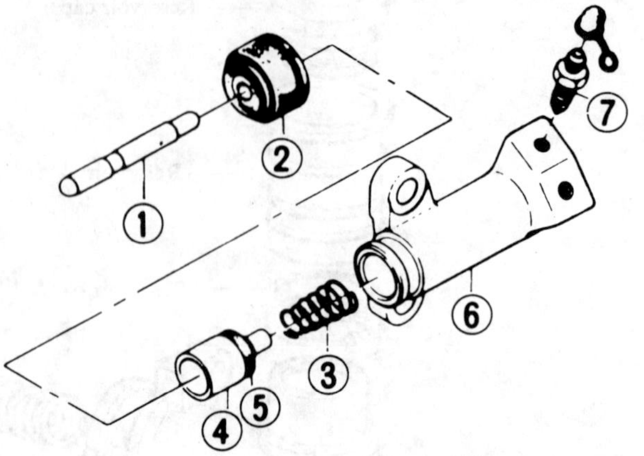

Fig. 8.4 Components of the clutch operating cylinder (Sec 8)

1 Pushrod
2 Dust cover
3 Piston spring
4 Piston
5 Piston cup
6 Cylinder
7 Bleeder screw

to check the wear on the friction lining. The only positive indication that something needs doing is when it starts to slip or when squealing noises on engagement indicate that the friction lining has worn down to the rivets. In such instances it can only be hoped that the friction surfaces on the flywheel and pressure plate have not been badly worn or scored.
2 A clutch will wear according to the way in which it is used. Much intentional slipping of the clutch while driving – rather than the correct selection of gears – will accelerate wear. It is best to assume, however, that the friction disc will need renewal at about 40 000 miles (64 000 km).
3 Because of the clutch's location between the engine and transmission the clutch cannot be worked on without removing either the engine

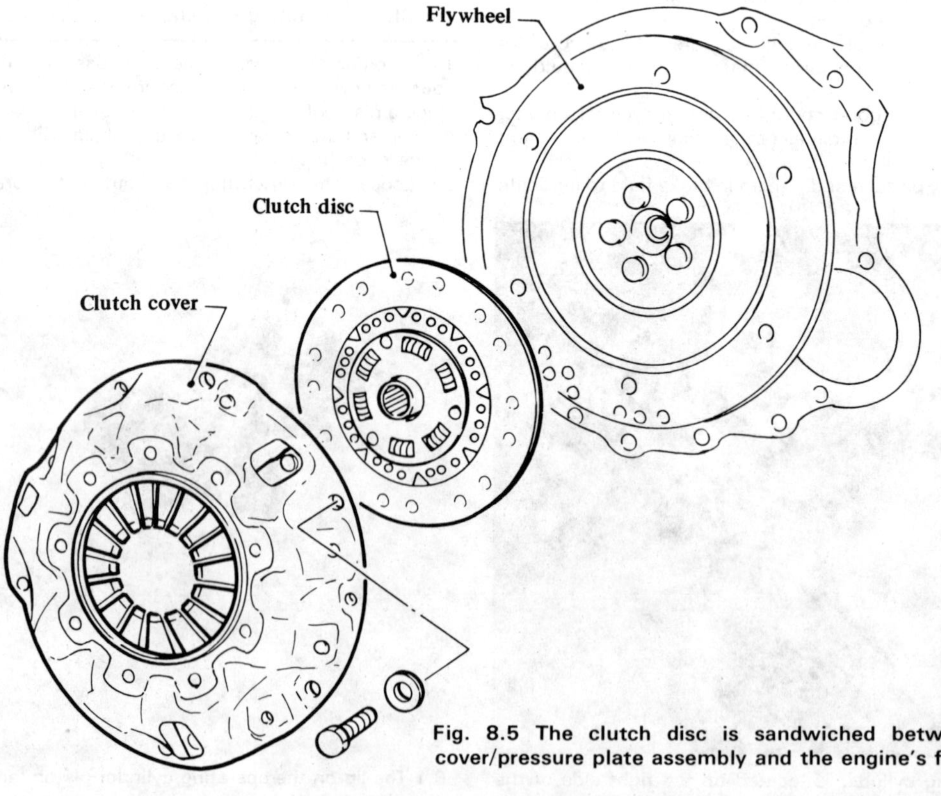

Fig. 8.5 The clutch disc is sandwiched between the clutch cover/pressure plate assembly and the engine's flywheel (Sec 9)

or transmission. If repairs which would require removal of the engine are not needed, the quickest way to gain access to the clutch is by removing the transmission, as described in Chapter 7.

4 With the transmission removed, but before removing the pressure plate assembly from the flywheel check that none of the metal fingers on the pressure plate are distorted or bent. If any damage is evident the pressure plate will need to be replaced.

5 The pressure plate need not be marked in relation to the flywheel as it can only be fitted one way due to the positioning dowels.

6 In a diagonal pattern to keep from distorting the pressure plate, loosen the attaching bolts a little at a time until the spring pressure is relieved (photo). If the flywheel begins to turn, insert a screwdriver through the starter motor opening and engage it in the teeth of the flywheel.

7 While supporting the pressure plate assembly, remove the bolts. Then remove the pressure plate and clutch disc.

8 Clean the pressure plate, flywheel mating surfaces and the bearing retainer outer surfaces of any oil and grease.

9 Examine the pressure plate surface where it contacts the clutch disc. This surface should be smooth, with no scoring, gouging or warping. Check the pressure plate cover and fingers for damage. If any fault is found with the pressure plate assembly it must be replaced as an entire unit.

10 Inspect the clutch disc for lining wear. Check for loose or broken rivets or springs. The friction plate lining surfaces should be at least $\frac{1}{32}$ in (0.8 mm) above the rivets, otherwise the disc is not worth putting back. If the lining material shows signs of breaking up or black areas where oil contamination has occurred it should also be renewed. See Section 1 paragraph 8.

11 Inspect the surface of the flywheel for rivet grooves, burnt areas or scoring (photo). If the damage is slight, the flywheel can be removed and reconditioned using a lathe. If the damage is deep, the flywheel should be replaced. Check that the ring gear teeth are not broken, cracked or seriously burned. Refer to Chapter 2 for the flywheel removal process.

12 If any traces of oil are detected on the clutch components the source should be found and eliminated. If oil is coming from the center of the flywheel, this indicates a failure of the rear oil seal (Chapter 2). Oil at the rear of the clutch assembly may indicate the need to replace the transmission input shaft seal (Chapter 7).

13 While servicing these clutch components, it's also a good idea to replace the release bearing at the same time. Refer to Section 10.

14 To install, hold the clutch disc and pressure plate together against the flywheel and insert a centering tool through the center of them. Since the transmission input shaft must pass through the center of these components, they must be properly aligned to ease the installation of the transmission. The clutch disc must be installed with the damper springs offset toward the transmission. The flywheel side should be identified as such by stamped letters in the disc.

15 Locate the clutch pressure plate so that the cover engages with the dowels and install the mounting bolts. Tighten them in steps and in a diagonal cross-pattern until they are torqued to specs.

16 Install the transmission.

10 Release bearing – replacement

1 The sealed release bearing, although designed for long life, is worth replacing at the same time as the other clutch components are being replaced or serviced.

2 Deterioration of the release bearing should be suspected when there are signs of grease leakage or the unit is noisy when spun with the fingers.

3 Remove the rubber dust boot which surrounds the withdrawal lever at the bellhousing aperture.

4 Using a screwdriver, unhook and detach the retainer spring from the ball-pin in the front transmission cover (photo).

5 Remove the withdrawal lever (photo).

6 The clutch release bearing and hub assembly can now be removed. **Note:** *Check that the release fork has not been cracked or bent. Slowly turn the front face of the release bearing, making sure it turns freely and without any noise. The release bearing is pre-lubricated and should not be washed in gasoline or any other solvent. Whenever a new clutch is installed a new release bearing should auto-*

9.6 The clutch cover mounting bolts should be unscrewed in a diagonal pattern one turn at a time.

9.11 The friction surface of the flywheel (arrow) should be smooth, with no scoring or burnt areas

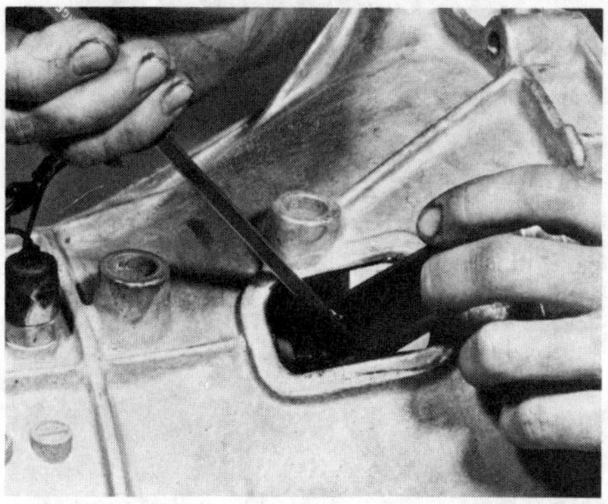

10.4 A screwdriver can be used to disengage the spring from the ball pivot

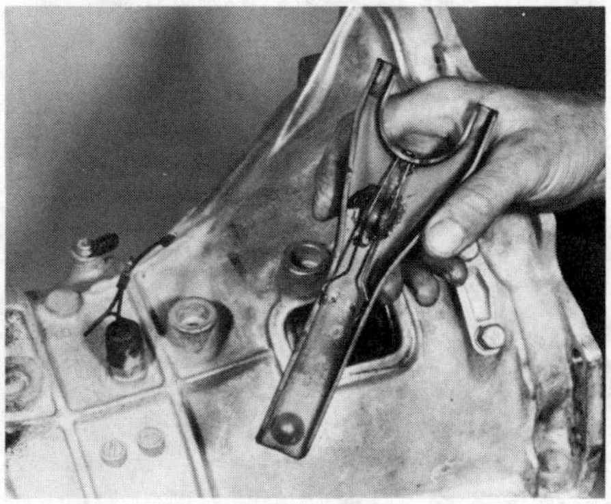

10.5 The spring is attached to the backside of the withdraw lever

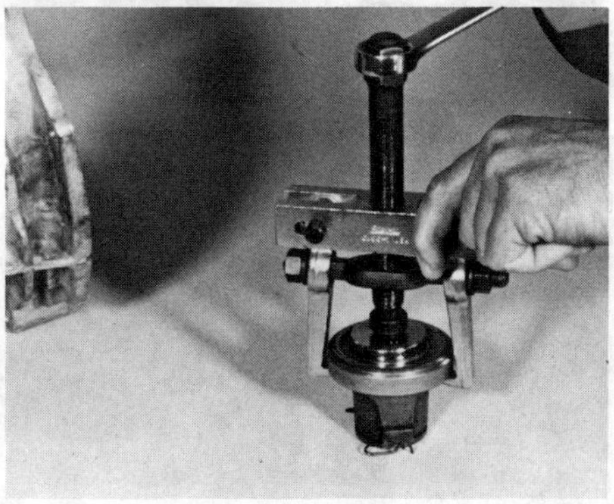

10.7 A puller can be used to separate the release bearing from its hub

12.2 The driveshaft rear flange and the pinion flange should be marked (see arrow) prior to separation

matically be used.

7 Remove the release bearing from its hub using a two or three legged puller (photo).

8 Press on the new bearing but apply pressure only to the centre track.

9 Reassembly is a reversal of dismantling but apply multi-purpose grease to the internal recess of the release bearing hub.

10 Also apply similar grease to the pivot points of the clutch withdrawal lever, the sliding surface of the bearing sleeve and the splines on the transmission main drive gear. **Note:** *Apply only a thin coat of grease to these points, as too much grease will run onto the friction plates when hot, causing damage to the clutch disc surfaces.*

11 Driveshaft, differential and rear axle – general information

1 The Datsun 200SX uses a two-piece driveshaft, which is supported by a center bearing mounted to the chassis frame. It incorporates three universal joints; one at the transmission end, one behind the center bearing and one at the axle companion flange. The universal joints are of the sealed-type; therefore no maintenance can be carried out on them.

2 The driveshaft is finely balanced during manufacture and, in the case of worn universal joints, a replacement driveshaft will have to be purchased. When removing the driveshaft to service the center bearing, the yoke-to-companion flange relationships must be maintained. This is best ensured by marking each joint before removal.

3 The rear axle is of the semi-floating type, having a "banjo" design axle housing, which is held in proper alignment with the car body by the rear suspension.

4 Mounted in the center of the rear axle ic the differential which transfers the turning force of the driveshaft to the rear axleshafts, on which the rear wheels are mounted.

5 The axleshafts are splined at their inner ends to fit into the splines in the differential wheels; outer support for the shaft is by means of the rear wheel bearing.

12 Driveshaft – removal and installation

1 Raise the rear of the car and support it on jackstands.

2 Mark the edges of the driveshaft rear flange and the differential pinion flange so that they can be realigned upon installation (photo).

3 Using a screwdriver placed through the rear universal joint to keep the shaft from turning, remove the 4 bolts that connect the rear flange with the pinion flange (photo).

4 While supporting the driveshaft, remove the 2 bolts that attach the center bearing support bracket to the body (photos).

5 Push the shaft forward slightly to disconnect the rear flanges. Then lower the shaft and carefully pull it rearward until the forward end is withdrawn from the rear of the transmission.

6 While the driveshaft is removed, the rear of the transmission should be covered or plugged to prevent loss of oil.

7 If the driveshaft needs to be disassembled, refer to Section 13.

8 Installation is the reverse of the removal procedure. **Note:** *During installation make sure the marks on the rear flanges line up.*

13 Driveshaft – disassembly and reassembly

Note: *the universal joints cannot be disassembled and, if defective, the entire section of the driveshaft that it is attached to must be replaced.*

1 Remove the heat shield from the center bearing support bracket.

2 Remove the nut that secures the 2 halves of the support bracket together, and remove them from the driveshaft.

3 Mark the relationship of the center flange to the front section of the driveshaft (photo).

4 Using a long screwdriver placed through the center universal joint to keep the shaft from turning, remove the 4 bolts that attach the center yoke flange to the companion flange.

5 Mark the companion flange in relation to the slot in the threaded shaft.

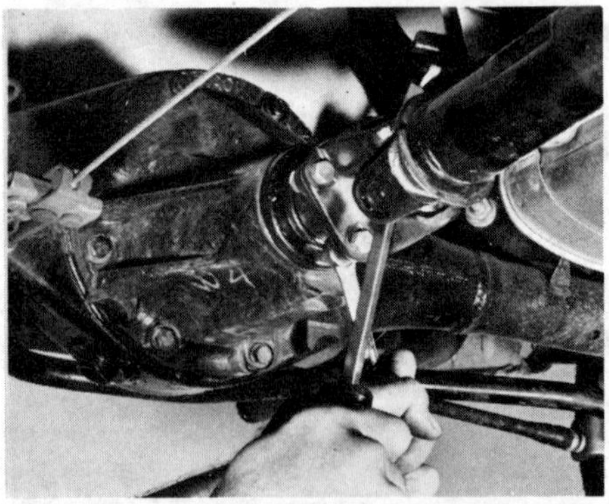

12.3 A screwdriver held through the universal joint will keep the driveshaft from turning while removing the attaching bolts

12.4 Removing the center bearing support bracket nuts

13.3 The center joint flange and the companion flange should be marked (see arrow) prior to separation

13.6 The center bearing locknut is staked to prevent it from working loose

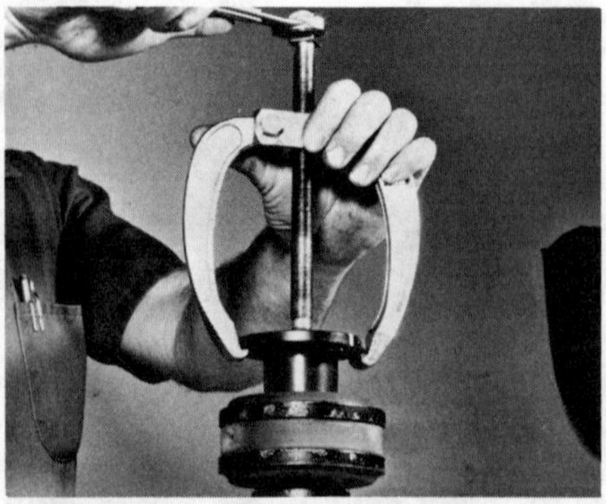

13.7 A puller is needed to separate the companion flange from the 1st shaft

13.14 The joint in the center bearing cushion should face upwards when the support bracket is installed

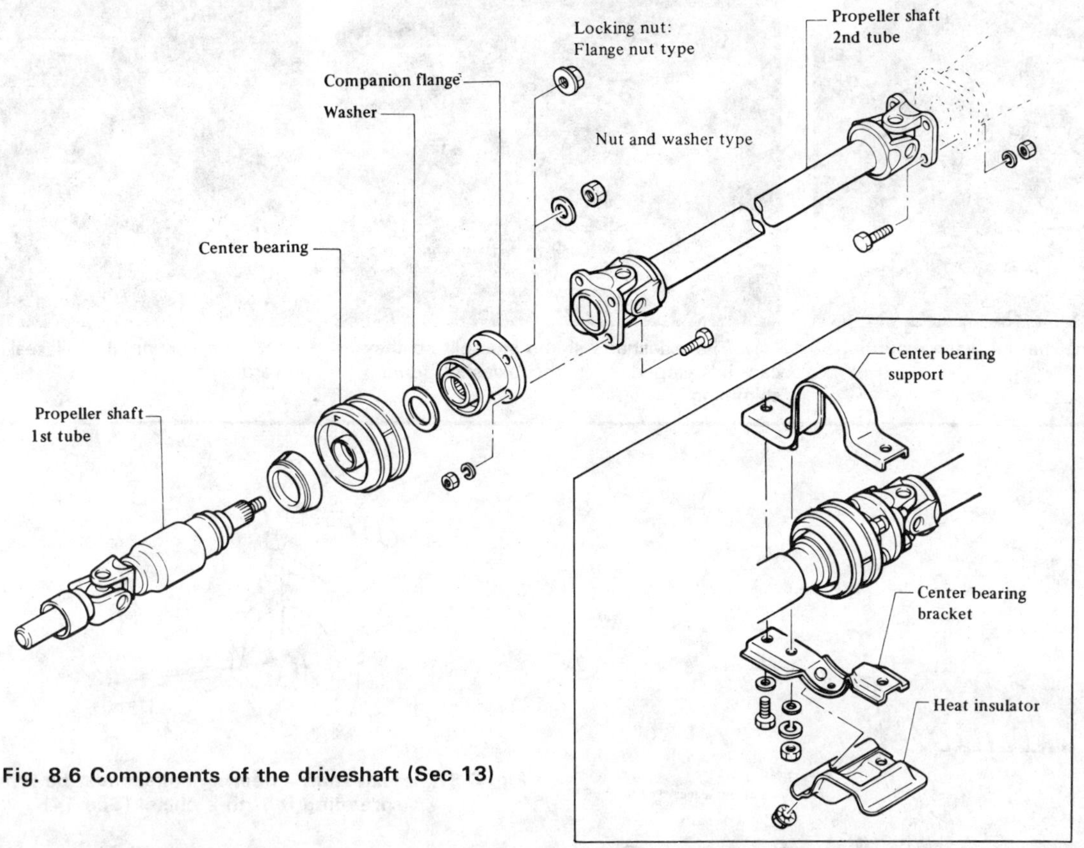

Fig. 8.6 Components of the driveshaft (Sec 13)

6 The center joint nut is staked to prevent it from working loose (photo). To remove it, first use a punch to knock the staking back out, and unscrew it from the shaft. To keep the flange from turning, either obtain a special tool designed for this purpose, or one can be made using a flat steel bar and old bolts inserted through the flange holes. The bar should be drilled to match at least 2 of the flange holes.
7 Using an appropriate puller, remove the companion flange (photo).
8 The center bearing can be removed from the front section of the driveshaft by using a hydraulic press and appropriate support plate.
9 When the new bearing is pressed onto the shaft, make sure the letter "F" is facing the front of the car.
10 Apply a coat of multi-purpose grease to the face of the center bearing and both sides of the washer, then insert the washer into the end of the center bearing.
11 Align the mark on the companion flange with the slot in the shaft and install the flange.
12 Install the locknut and torque it to specs. Stake the nut so it is engaged with the shaft's groove as before.
13 Align the marks on the companion flange and the center flange and install the attaching bolts.
14 The remainder of the reassembly is a reversal of the disassembly procedure. **Note:** *Be sure the joint in the center bearing cushion rubber is facing the upward position, when the support bracket is installed (photo).*

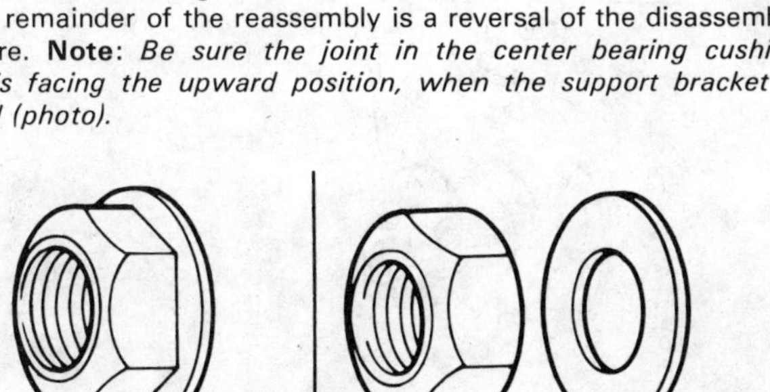

Fig. 8.7 The two types of center bearing locking nuts used on the driveshaft are the flange-type (left) and the nut-and-washer-type (right). Each has a different torque value (Sec 13)

14 Axleshaft, rear wheel bearing and oil seal – removal and installation

1 Raise the rear of the car and support it on jack stands.
2 Remove the wheel and tire.
3 Remove the brake caliper as described in Chapter 9.
4 Remove the rotor as described in Chapter 9.
5 Remove the 4 bolts that secure the baffle plate to the rear axle (photo).
6 The rear axleshaft can now be removed. If the axleshaft can not be pulled out by hand, a slide hammer can be used by attaching it to the wheel studs.
7 Remove the shim(s) from the axleshaft, if present (photo).
8 Grip the axleshaft firmly in the jaws of a vise and using a cold chisel, cut two grooves at opposite points in the collar. This will expand it (Fig. 8.9).
9 The bearing and collar can now be drawn off the shaft if a suitable puller with long extension arms is used or the axleshaft can be pressed out of the bearing and collar using a hydraulic press.
10 Prior to installation of the new bearing, if the bearing spacer has been removed, be sure it is reinstalled with the chamfer side facing the axleshaft flange.
11 When installing the new bearing to the axleshaft, make sure that the sealed side is towards the roadwheel. Pack the open side of the bearing with multipurpose grease.
12 Position the baffle plate on the shaft, then the bearing spacer and bearing, then a new collar. Pressure must be applied to the inner edge of the collar to force the bearing/collar assembly fully up against the shoulder on the axleshaft.
13 Lever out the original oil seal from the end of the axle casing and discard it (photo). Tap in the new seal so that the lips face inward and pack the space between the lips with multipurpose grease.
14 Smear the outer edge of the axleshaft bearing with grease and then pass the axleshaft into the casing. Take care not to cut the lips of the seal with the splines on the axleshaft. Hold the axleshaft horizontal, turning it slightly until its splines are felt to pick up the differential side gears then push the shaft fully home.

14.5 Removing the baffle plate mounting nuts

14.7 The axleshafts shims are split so they can be slipped over the axleshaft during shimming

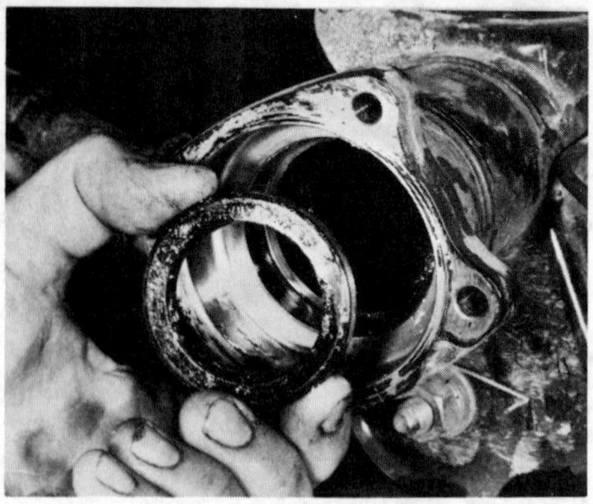

14.13 The lips on the oil seal should face inward

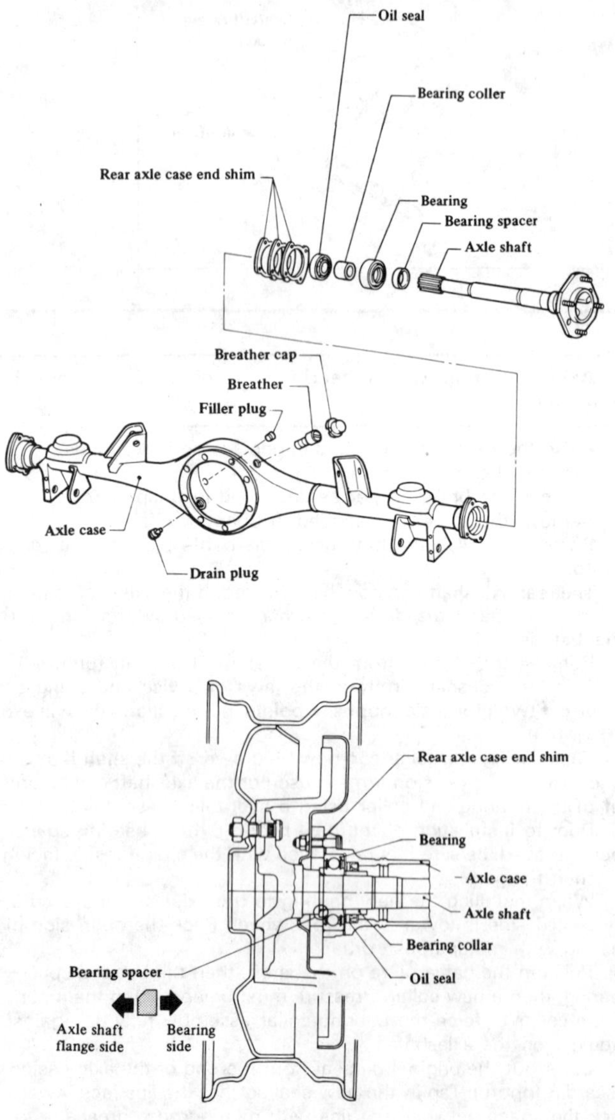

Fig. 8.8 Rear axle and axleshaft components

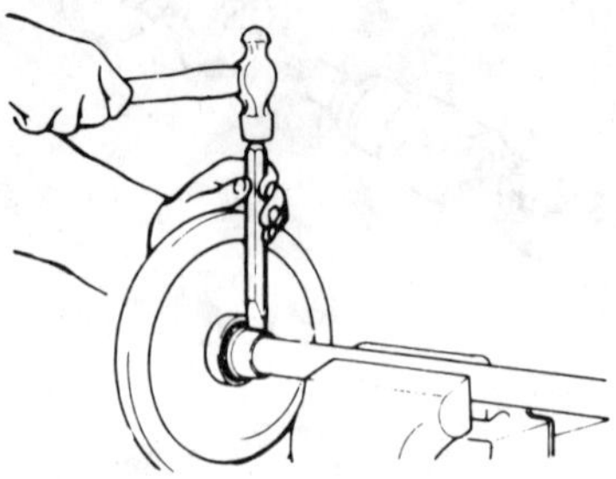

Fig. 8.9 The axleshaft's bearing collar must be removed by spreading it with a chisel (Sec 14)

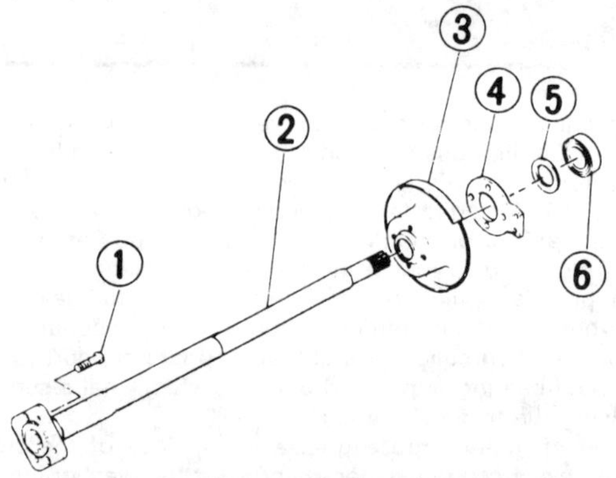

Fig. 8.10 The axleshaft components must be pressed onto the shaft in the order shown (Sec 14)

1 *Bolt*
2 *Rear axleshaft*
3 *Baffle plate*
4 *Adapter plate*
5 *Bearing spacer*
6 *Wheel bearing*

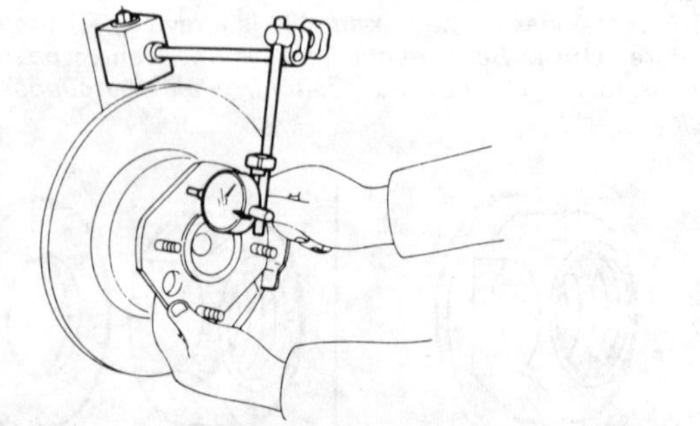

Fig. 8.11 A dial gauge should be used to measure axleshaft endplay (Sec 14)

15 Install the bolts and nuts that attach the axleshaft hub flange to the rear axle housing flange and nug them down finger tight.
16 With a feeler gauge measure the gap, if any, between the axleshaft flange and the rear axle housing flange. A shim or combination of shims will have to be selected to match this gap measurement as closely as possible. The shim sizes offered are listed in the specifications. The shims should not be over the gap measurement by more than 0.004 in (0.1 mm). To install the shims partially withdraw the axleshaft and slip the shims, into position over the shaft. The shims are split so the shaft need not be pulled all the way out.
17 Torque the flange nuts to specs.
18 Using a dial gauge as shown in the accompanying figure, measure the endplay of the axleshaft to be sure it is within the specifications.
19 The remainder of the installation is the reverse of the removal procedure.
20 Following installation, the brake system should be bled as described in Chapter 9.

15 Pinion oil seal – replacement

1 Place a suitable container beneath the differential then, remove the drain plug and allow the oil to drain from the unit. Install the drain plug.
2 Raise the rear of the vehicle to obtain access to the unit, and support the bodyframe and differential housing securely on suitable stands or blocks.
3 Disconnect the rear end of the driveshaft as described in Section 12 and move the shaft to one side.
4 Hold the pinion flange by placing two 2 in (50 mm) long bolts through two opposite holes. Bolting them up tight, undo the self-locking nut whilst holding a large screwdriver or tire lever between the two bolts as a lever.
5 Using a suitable extractor, withdraw the pinion flange from the differential unit.
6 Remove the defective oil seal by driving in one side of it and levering it out.
7 Install the new oil seal first having greased the mating surfaces of the seal and the axle housing. The lips of the oil seal must face inwards. Using a suitable socket carefully drive the new oil seal into the axle housing recess until the face of the seal is flush with the housing. Make sure that the end of the pinion is not knocked during this operation.
8 Install the pinion flange and thrust washer, and screw on the pinion nut.
9 Again holding the pinion flange still with the screwdriver or tire lever, tighten the pinion nut to specs.
10 Once the pinion nut is torqued, use the wrench to turn the pinion shaft in both directions several times to settle the bearing rollers. Then fit an inch-pound torque wrench over the pinion nut and slowly turn the pinion shaft, noting the amount of torque needed to begin the shaft rotating. This is the drive pinion preload, and should be 6.1 – 8.7 in-lb (14-30 kg- cm-kg). If the preload is below these specs, tighten the pinion nut a little at a time until the proper preload setting is obtained. **Note**: *This preload is achieved by using a collapsible spacer within the differential. If the preload is set over the recommended specs, the differential will have to be removed and the spacer replaced.*
11 The remainder of the installation is the reverse of the removal procedure.
12 Following installation, refill the differential with the proper grade and quantity of oil.

16 Differential – removal and installation

1 Raise the rear of the car and support it on jackstands.
2 Drain the oil from the differential.
3 Disconnect the rear of the driveshaft from the differential as described in Section 12, and position it out of the way.
4 Partially withdraw both axleshafts as described in Section 14, so they are disengaged from the differential.
5 Unscrew the differential housing mounting nuts evenly and in a criss-cross pattern (photo), and lift the differential out of the rear axle.
6 The overhaul of the rear axle differential unit is not within the scope of the home mechanic, due to the specialized gauges and tools which are required. Where the unit requires servicing or repair, due to wear or excessive noise, it is most economical to exchange it for a factory-reconditioned assembly.

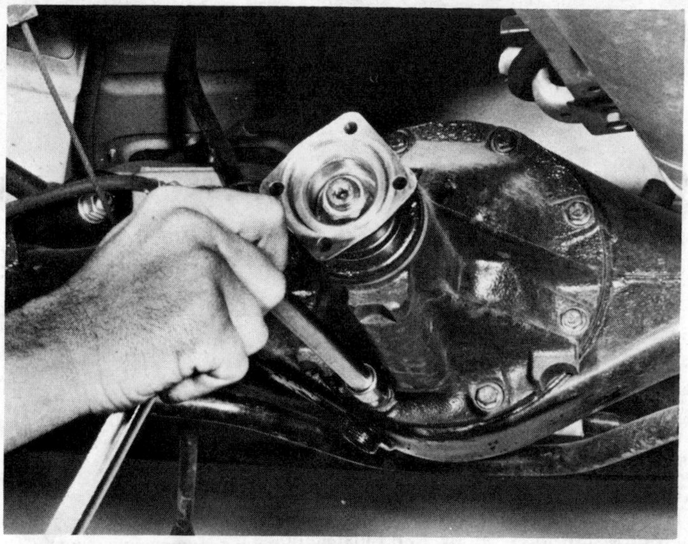

16.5 Removing the differential mounting bolts

7 Scrape all traces of old gasket from the mating surfaces of the axle casing. Position a new gasket on the axle casing having first smeared it with jointing compound.
8 Installation is the reverse of the removal procedure.
9 Following installation, fill the differential with the proper grade and quantity of oil.

17 Rear axle – removal and installation

1 Raise the rear of the car and support it under the body side members using stands.
2 Support the axle assembly on a jack placed under the differential carrier.
3 Remove the wheels and tires.
4 Disconnect the rear of the driveshaft from the differential as described in Section 12. and position it out of the way.
5 Remove the rear stabilizer bar as described in Chapter 11.
6 Disconnect the parking brake cables and brake lines from the rear brakes, as described in Chapter 9. Plug the brake lines to prevent dirt from entering them.
7 Disconnect the metal brake lines along the rear axle from the rubber brake hose leading from the front. Again, plug all lines to prevent dirt from entering them.
8 Disconnect the rear parking brake cable arrangement from the rear axle and position it out of the way.
9 Remove the lower shock absorber bolts and compress the shock bodies upward.
10 Using the jack, lower the rear axle until both rear springs can be removed.
11 Raise the axle again and disconnect both upper and lower links from the rear axle.
12 Carefully lower the axle once more and withdraw it from under the car.
13 If the rear axle housing needs to be replaced, remove the following components and transfer them to the new axle:

- Rear brake assemblies
- Axleshafts
- Metal brake lines
- Differential

14 Installation is the reverse of the removal procedure. Refer to the appropriate chapters and sections for installation of the individual components.
15 Bleed the brake system as described in Chapter 9.

Chapter 9 Braking system

Refer to Chapter 13 for Specifications and information related to 1982 and 1983 models

Contents

Bleeding the brake system ... 3
Brake light switch – removal and installation ... 20
Brakes lines – general inspection and replacement ... 4
Brake pedal – removal, installation and adjustment ... 21
Brakes – inspection ... 2
Front disc brake – pad replacement ... 5
Front disc caliper – overhaul ... 7
Front disc caliper – removal and installation ... 6
Front disc rotor – removal and installation ... 8
General information ... 1
Master cylinder – overhaul ... 14
Master cylinder – removal and installation ... 13
Parking brake – adjustment ... 17
Parking brake lever and front cable – removal and installation ... 18
Parking brake rear cables – removal and installation ... 19
Rear disc brake – pad replacement ... 9
Rear disc caliper – overhaul ... 11
Rear disc caliper – removal and installation ... 10
Rear disc rotor – removal and installation ... 12
Vacuum servo (booster) unit – general information and testing ... 15
Vacuum servo (booster unit) – removal and installation ... 16

Specifications

Front disc brake

Type	Disc-N22
Cylinder inner diameter	$2\frac{1}{8}$ in (53.98 mm)
Pad dimensions (width x thickness x length)	2.08 x 0.38 x 3.00 in (52.9 x 9.7 x 76.2 mm)
Rotor outer diameter	9.98 in (253.5 mm)

Rear disc brake

Type	Disc-AN12H
Cylinder inner diameter	1.593 in (40.46 mm)
Pad dimensions (width x thickness x length)	1.65 x 0.41 x 2.24 in (42.0 x 10.3 x 56.8 mm)
Rotor outer diameter	10.59 in (269 mm)

Pad wear limit (minimum thickness)

N22	0.079 in (2.0 mm)
AN12H	0.063 in (1.6 mm)

Rotor maximum runout

N22	0.0047 in (0.12 mm)
AN12H	0.0059 in (0.15 mm)

Rotor maximum parallelism (both types)

Rotor maximum parallelism (both types)	0.0028 in (0.07 mm)

Rotor minimum thickness

N22	0.413 in (10.5 mm)
AN12H	0.339 in (8.6 mm)

Master cylinder

Inner diameter	$\frac{7}{8}$ in (22.23 mm)
Allowable clearance between cylinder and piston (maximum)	0.0059 in (0.15 mm)

Booster (vacuum servo unit)

Type	P75
Output rod length	0.384 to 0.394 (9.75 to 10.0 mm)
Input rod length	5.12 in (130 mm)

Parking brake

Correct adjustment (number of notches)	7 to 8
Stroke	3.54 to 3.94 in (90 to 100 mm)

Brake pedal

Free play	0.04 to 0.20 in (1 to 5 mm)
Pedal height	6.10 to 6.34 in (155 to 161 mm)
Depressed pedal height (minimum)	2.36 in (60 mm)

Torque specifications

	ft-lb	m-kg
Brake tube flare nut	12	1.7
Brake hose connector	13	1.8
Air bleeder valve	6	0.8
Fulcrum pin mounting bolt	7	1.0
Booster mounting nuts	7	1.0
Booster input rod lock nut	14	2.0
Master cylinder mounting bolts	7	1.0
Front disc caliper mounting bolts	62	8.5
Front disc rotor mounting bolts	33	4.6
Rear disc caliper mounting bolts	33	4.6
NP valve mounting bolts	3	0.5

1 General information

1 The braking system in the 200SX is a split system design. It incorporates two separate circuits; one for the front brakes and one for the rear brakes. With this system if one circuit fails, the other circuit will still function.

2 The master cylinder is designed for the split system and incorporates a primary piston for one circuit and a secondary system for the other.

3 A vacuum servo unit is used which draws vacuum from the intake manifold to add power assistance to the normal brake pressure.

4 A valve regulates the fluid pressure in the brake lines so that all wheels receive equal pressure.

5 All four wheels are equipped with disc brakes. These consist of a flat, disc-like rotor which is attached to the axle and wheel. Around one section of the rotor is mounted a stationary caliper assembly which houses two hydraulically-operated disc brake pads. The inner pad is mounted to a piston facing the inner surface of the rotor, while the outer pad is mounted to a yoke and faces the outer surface of the rotor. When the brake pedal is applied, brake fluid pressure forces the piston with the inner pad against the rotor. At the same time a second piston moves the yoke inward and forces the outer pad against the rotor. The pressure and resultant friction on the rotor is what slows the wheel.

6 The rear brakes are also equipped with cable-operated parking brake mechanisms, which lock the rear pads against their rotors.

7 All four brakes adjust automatically to lining wear.

8 After completing any operation involving the dismantling of any part of the brake system always test drive the car to check for proper braking performance before resuming normal driving. When testing the brakes, perform the tests on a clean, dry, flat surface. Conditions other than these can lead to inaccurate test results. Test the brakes at various speeds with both light and heavy pedal pressure. The car should brake evenly without pulling to one side or the other. Avoid locking the brakes, as this slides the tires and diminishes braking efficiency and control.

9 Tires, car load and front end alignment are factors which also affect braking performance.

2 Brakes – inspection

1 Since inspection of the braking system is included in routine maintenance schedule, this procedure is described in Chapter 1.

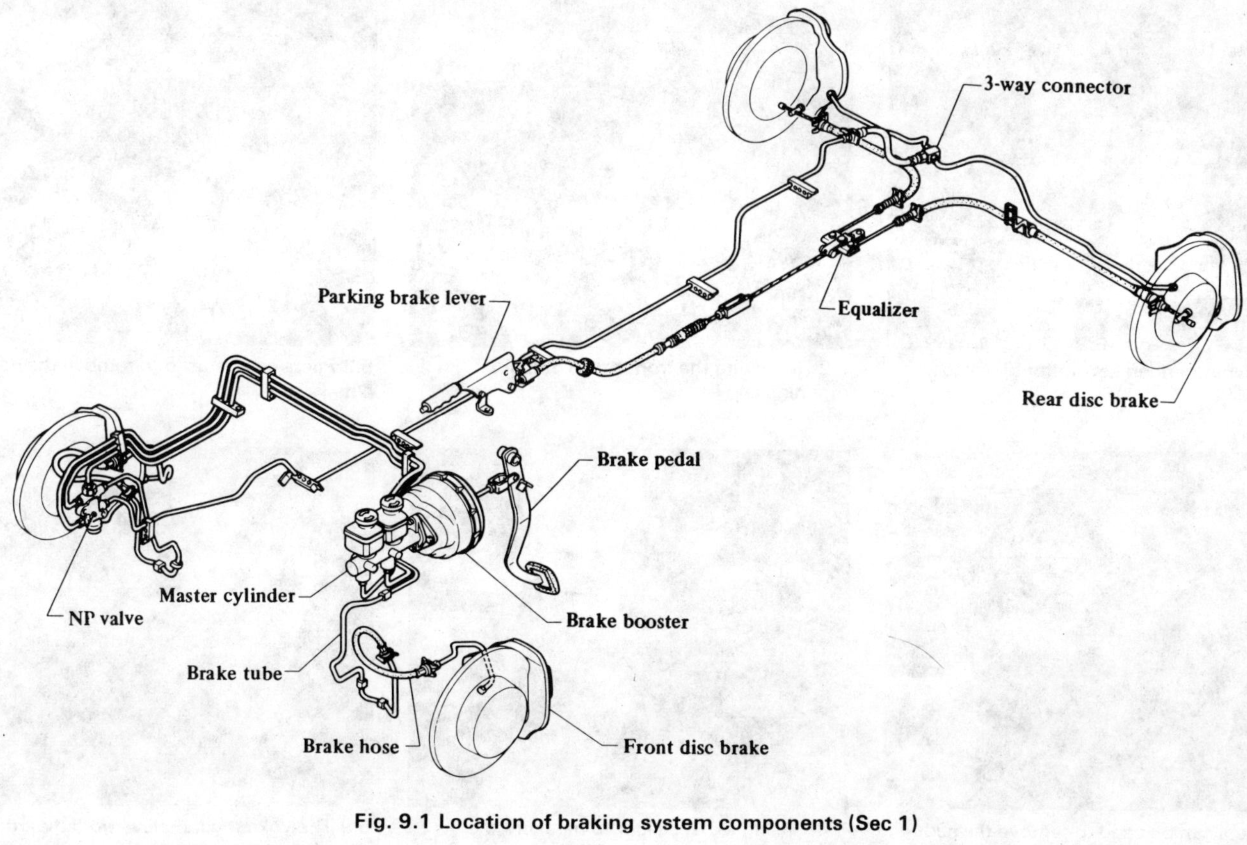

Fig. 9.1 Location of braking system components (Sec 1)

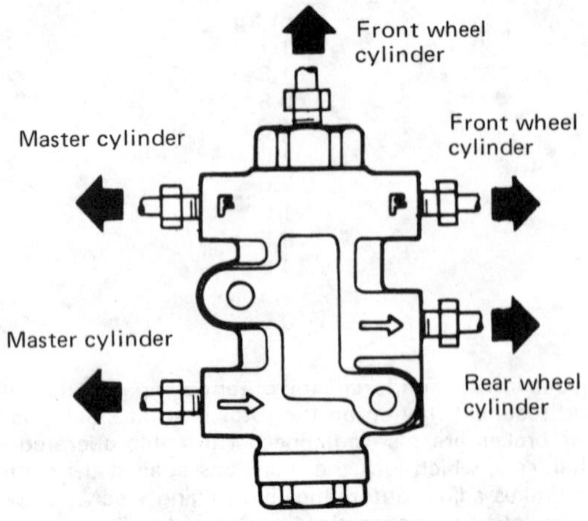

Fig. 9.2 NP valve outlet identification (Sec 1)

3 Bleeding the brake system

1 Anytime any part of the brake system is disassembled or develops a leak, or when the fluid in the master cylinder reservoir runs low, air will enter the system and cause a decrease in braking performance. To eliminate this air the brakes must be bled using the procedure described in this Section.

2 If air has entered the system because the master cylinder has been disconnected, or the master cylinder reservoir has been low or empty of fluid, or if a complete flushing of the system is needed, all four brakes should be bled. If a brake line serving only one brake is disconnected then only that brake need be bled. Likewise, if any line is disconnected anywhere in the system, the brakes served by that line must be bled.

3 Before beginning, have an assistant on hand, as well as a good supply of new brake fluid, an empty clear container such as a glass jar, a length of $\frac{3}{16}$-inch plastic, rubber or vinyl tubing to fit over the bleeder valve and a wrench to open and close the bleeder valve. The car may have to be raised and placed on jackstands for clearance.

4 If the car is equipped with power brakes, remove the vacuum reserve in the system by applying the brakes several times.

5 Check that the master cylinder reservoir is full of fluid and be sure to keep it at least half full during the entire operation. If, at any point the reservoir runs low of fluid the entire bleeding procedure must be repeated.

6 Beginning at one of the bleeder valves located on the engine side of the master cylinder, loosen the bleeder valve slightly to break it loose then tighten it to a point where it is snug but can still be loosened quickly and easily.

7 Place one end of the tubing over the bleeder valve and submerge the other end in brake fluid in the container.

8 With your assistant sitting in the driver's seat, have him pump the brakes a few times to get pressure in the system. On the last pump have him hold the pedal firmly depressed.

9 While the pedal is held depressed, open the breather valve just enough to allow a flow of fluid to leave the valve. Watch for air bubbles to exit the submerged end of the tube. When the fluid flow slows after a couple of seconds, close the valve again and have your assistant release the pedal. If he releases the pedal before the valve is closed again air can be drawn back into the system.

10 Repeat paragraphs 8 and 9 until no more air is seen in the fluid leaving the tube. Then fully tighten the bleeder valve and proceed to the other master cylinder valve, the right rear wheel, the left rear wheel, the left front wheel, and the right front wheel, in that order, and perform the same operation. Be sure to check the fluid in the master cylinder reservoir frequently (photo).

11 Do not reuse of any old brake fluid as it attracts moisture which will deteriorate the brake system components. Also do not mix different brands of brake fluid.

12 Refill the master cylinder with fluid at the end of the operation.

3.10 Recommended set-up for bleeding brakes

5.2 Removing the front brake pad pin retaining clip

5.3 Pliers can be used to remove the pad pins

5.4a Pliers can be used to remove the pads from the caliper

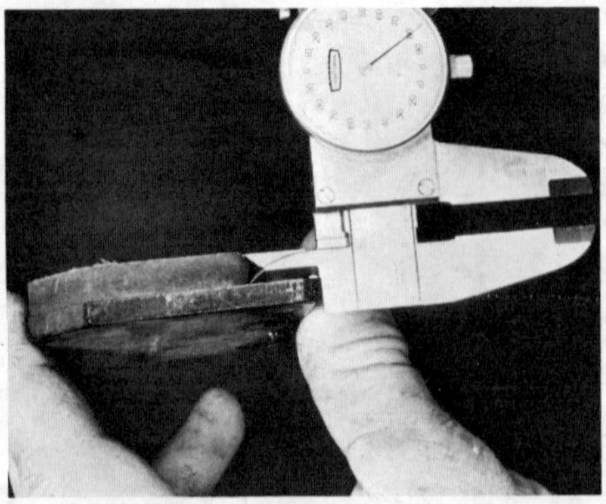

5.4b Using a dial caliper to measure the thickness of the brake pad lining

5.9 The yoke must be levered outward to install outer pad

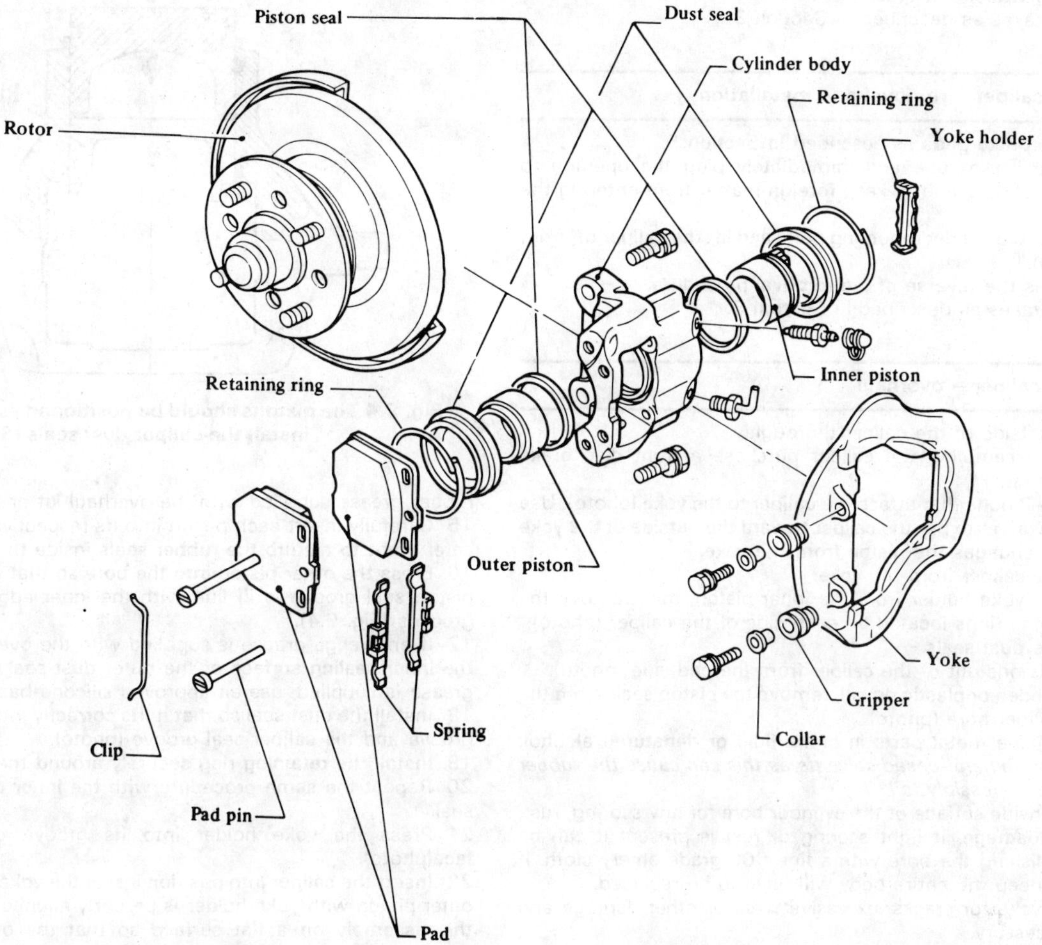

Fig. 9.3 Exploded view of the front disc brake assembly (Secs 5, 6, 7 and 8)

4 Brake lines – general inspection and replacement

1 About every six months the flexible hoses which connect the steel brake lines should be inspected for cracks, chafing of the outer cover, leaks, blisters, and other damage. These are important and vulnerable parts of the brake system and inspection should be complete. A light and mirror will prove helpful for a thorough check. If a hose exhibits any of the above conditions, replace it with a new one.
2 When it becomes necessary to replace steel lines, use only double-walled steel tubing. Never substitute copper tubing, as copper is subject to fatigue cracking and corrosion. The outside diameter of the tubing is used for sizing.
3 Some auto parts stores or brake supply houses carry various lengths of pre-fabricated brake line. Depending on the type of tubing used, these sections can either be bent by hand into the desired shape or must be bent in a tubing bender.
4 If pre-fabricated lengths are not available, obtain the recommended steel tubing and steel fitting nuts to match the line to be replaced. Determine the correct length by measuring the old brake line section and cut the new tubing to fit, leaving about $\frac{1}{2}$-inch extra for flaring the ends.
5 Install the fittings onto the cut tubing and flare the ends using an ISO flaring tool.
6 Using a tubing bender, bend the tubing to match the shape of the old brake line.
7 Tube flaring and bending can usually be done by a local auto parts store if the proper equipment mentioned in paragraphs 5 and 6 is not available.
8 When installing the brake line, leave at least 0.75 in (19 mm) clearance between the line and any moving or vibrating parts.

5 Front disc brake – pad replacement

1 Remove the wheel and tire.
2 Remove the pad clip (photo).
3 While holding the springs in position, remove the 2 pad pins. Lift off the springs (photo).
4 Remove both the inner and outer pads (photo). Measure the depth of the lining, and compare it with the specs to see if the pads need replacement (photo).
5 Place a piece of hose over the bleeder valve and place the end of the hose into a jar or other container.
6 Open the bleeder valve. Then push the outer piston in until the piston's dust seal is even with the outside edge of the dust seal retaining ring. **Caution:** *Do not push the piston in beyond this point. If the piston is pushed beyond the inside of the piston seal, the disc caliper must be removed and disassembled to remove the piston without damaging the seal.*
7 Prior to installation apply a light coat of an aerosol teflon coating (disc brake anti-squeak coating) to the back of both pads.
8 Install the inner pad.
9 Using a large screwdriver or similar lever slide the yoke outward and install the outer pad (photo).
10 Apply a light coat of grease to the pad pins.
11 While holding the springs in place, install the pad pins. Be careful

you do not get grease on the friction sides of the pads.
12 Install the pad clip.
13 Reinstall the wheel and tire.
14 Bleed the brakes as described in Section 3.

6 Front disc caliper – removal and installation

1 Remove the brake pads as described in Section 5.
2 Remove the brake tube and immediately plug the opening to prevent leakage of fluid and to keep foreign matter from entering the line (photo).
3 Remove the two caliper mounting bolts and lift the caliper off from the rotor (photo).
4 Installation is the reverse of the removal procedure.
5 Bleed the brakes as described in Section 3.

7 Front disc caliper – overhaul

1 Clean the outside of the caliper thoroughly.
2 Prior to disassembling the caliper purchase a front disc brake caliper overhaul kit.
3 Remove the 2 bolts that attach the caliper to the yoke (photo). Use a flathead screwdriver to pry the caliper toward the outside of the yoke (photo). This disengages the piston from the yoke.
4 Remove the caliper from the yoke.
5 Remove the yoke holder from the inner piston, then remove the dust seal retaining rings located on each side of the caliper (photo).
6 Remove the dust seals.
7 Push the pistons out of the caliper from the pad side (photo).
8 Using a wooden or plastic dowel, remove the piston seals from the inside of the caliper bore (photo).
9 Clean all of the metal parts in brake fluid or denatured alcohol. **Note:** *Never use mineral-based solvents as this can cause the rubber seals to swell and possibly fail.*
10 Check the inside surface of the cylinder bore for any scoring, rust, nicks or other damage. If light scoring or rust is present it can be removed by polishing the bore with a fine 600 grade emery cloth. If the damage is deep the entire body will have to be replaced.
11 Check the yoke for cracks, excessive wear or other damage and replace it if necessary.
12 Inspect the piston for scoring, rust, nicks or other damage. The sliding surface of the piston is plated and cannot be polished with emery paper. If any defects are found, the piston must be replaced. If rubber grease is supplied with the overhaul kit use it to lubricate the cylinder bore. Brake fluid can also be used for this purpose.
13 Install the 2 rubber seals into the grooves in the caliper bore. Lubricate the seals with rubber grease or brake fluid.
14 Lubricate the outer surfaces of both the pistons with either the rubber grease supplied with the overhaul kit or brake fluid.

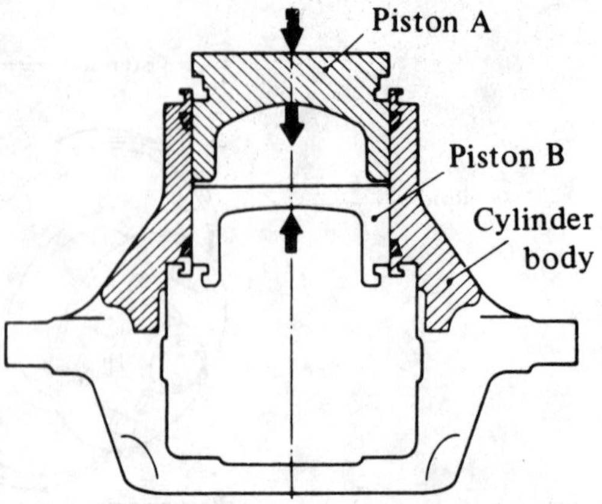

Fig. 9.4 The pistons should be positioned as shown in order to install the caliper dust seals (Sec 7)

15 Carefully insert each piston into its respective end of the bore. Be careful not to disturb the rubber seals inside the bore.
16 Press the outer piston into the bore so that the inner edge of the piston seal groove is in line with the inner edge of the caliper seal grooves (Fig. 9.4).
17 If an orange grease is supplied with the overhaul kit use it to fill the inner sealing surface of the outer dust seal (photo). If no orange grease is supplied, use an approved silicone-base grease.
18 Install the dust seal so that it fits correctly into both the piston seal groove and the caliper seal groove (photo).
19 Install the retaining ring securely around the dust seal (photo).
20 Repeat the same procedure with the inner piston and inner dust seal.
21 Press the yoke holder into its groove on the inner piston face(photo).
22 Insert the caliper into position inside the yoke making sure that the outer piston with yoke holder is properly aligned with the yoke. Place this assembly on a flat surface so that the outer piston is facing downward and apply pressure to the inner piston to press the yoke holder onto the yoke (photo). This can also be done with a hydraulic press if one is available.
23 Once the yoke holder is pressed onto the yoke, install the 2 mounting bolts that retain the yoke to the caliper housing. **Note:** *Before installing these bolts check the condition of the rubber boots and bushings, and if they are worn or otherwise damaged, replace them (photo).* Torque these bolts to specifications.

6.2 Plug the brake line openings immediately after disconnecting the line

6.3 The caliper mounting bolts are located on the rear side

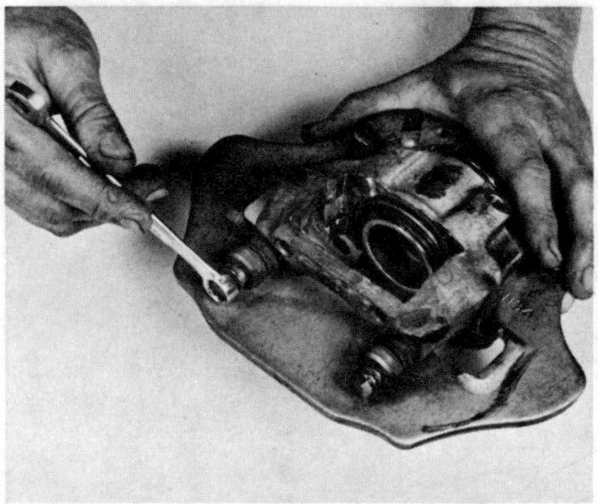

7.3a Removing the yoke-to-caliper bolts

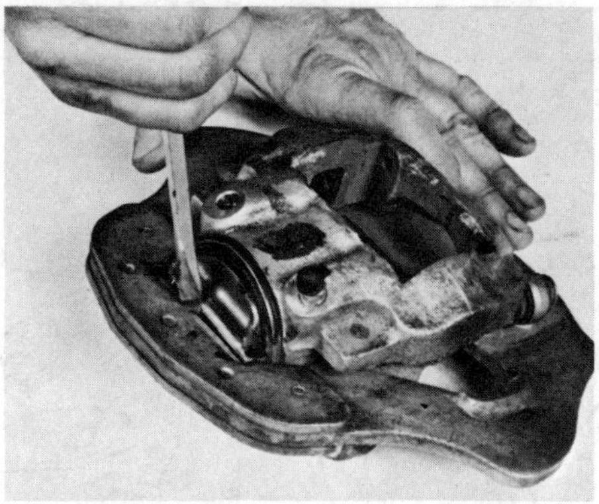

7.3b Using a screwdriver to pry the yoke holder off the yoke

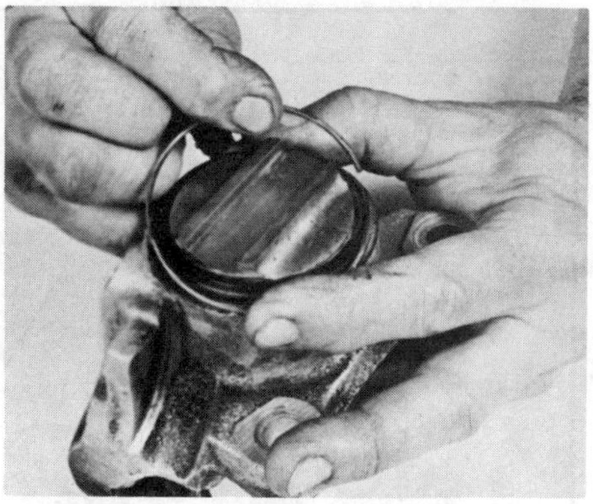

7.5a Removing the retaining ring from the inner piston dust seal

7.5b Removing the retaining ring from the outer piston dust seal

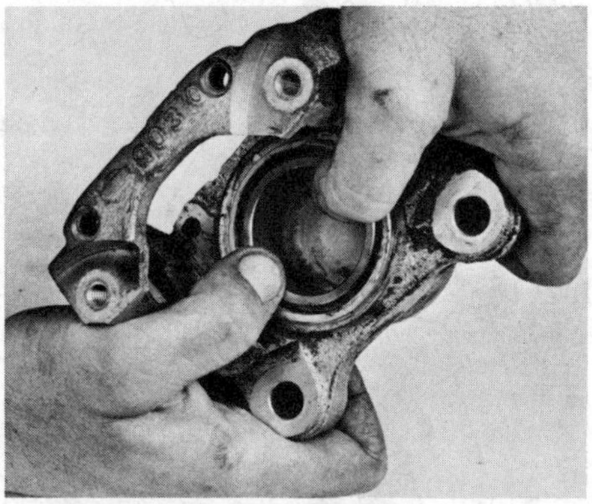

7.7 Both pistons are removed from the caliper by pushing on the outer piston

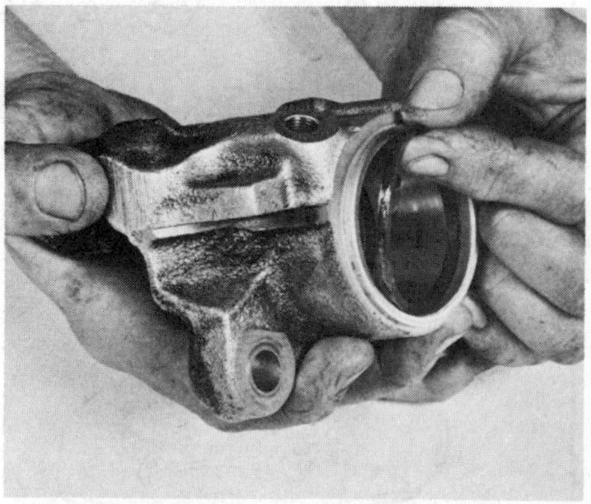

7.8 Do not use a metal tool to pry the piston seals from the caliper bore

7.17 Apply grease to the inside of the dust seals prior to installation

7.18 Installing the outer piston dust seal

7.19 Installing the retaining ring on the outer piston dust seal

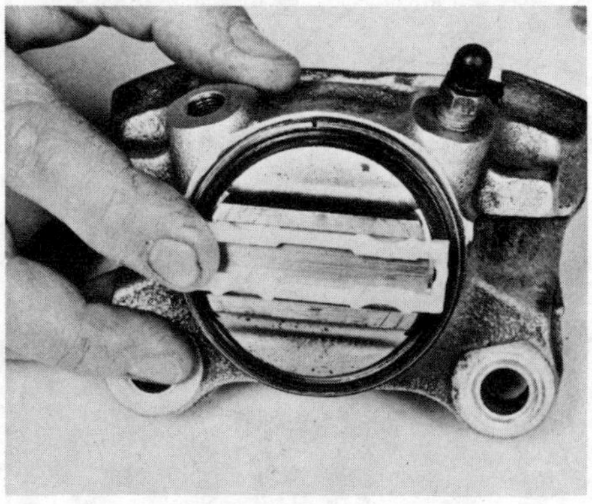

7.21 Placing the yoke holder into position on the inner piston

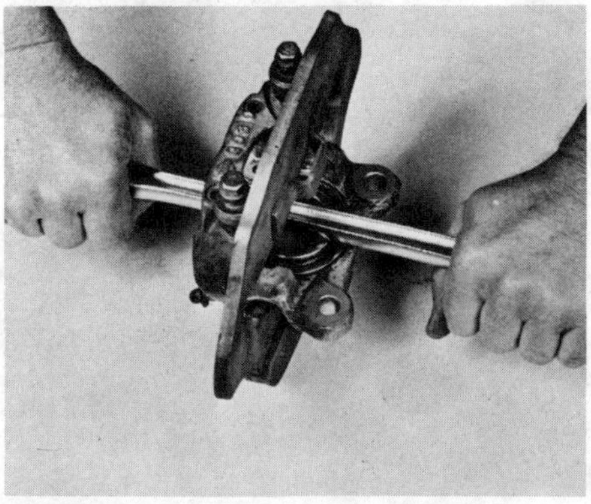

7.22 To seat the yoke holder on the yoke, downward pressure must be applied to the inner piston

7.23 Before installing the yoke-to-caliper bolts, inspect the bushings and rubber boots

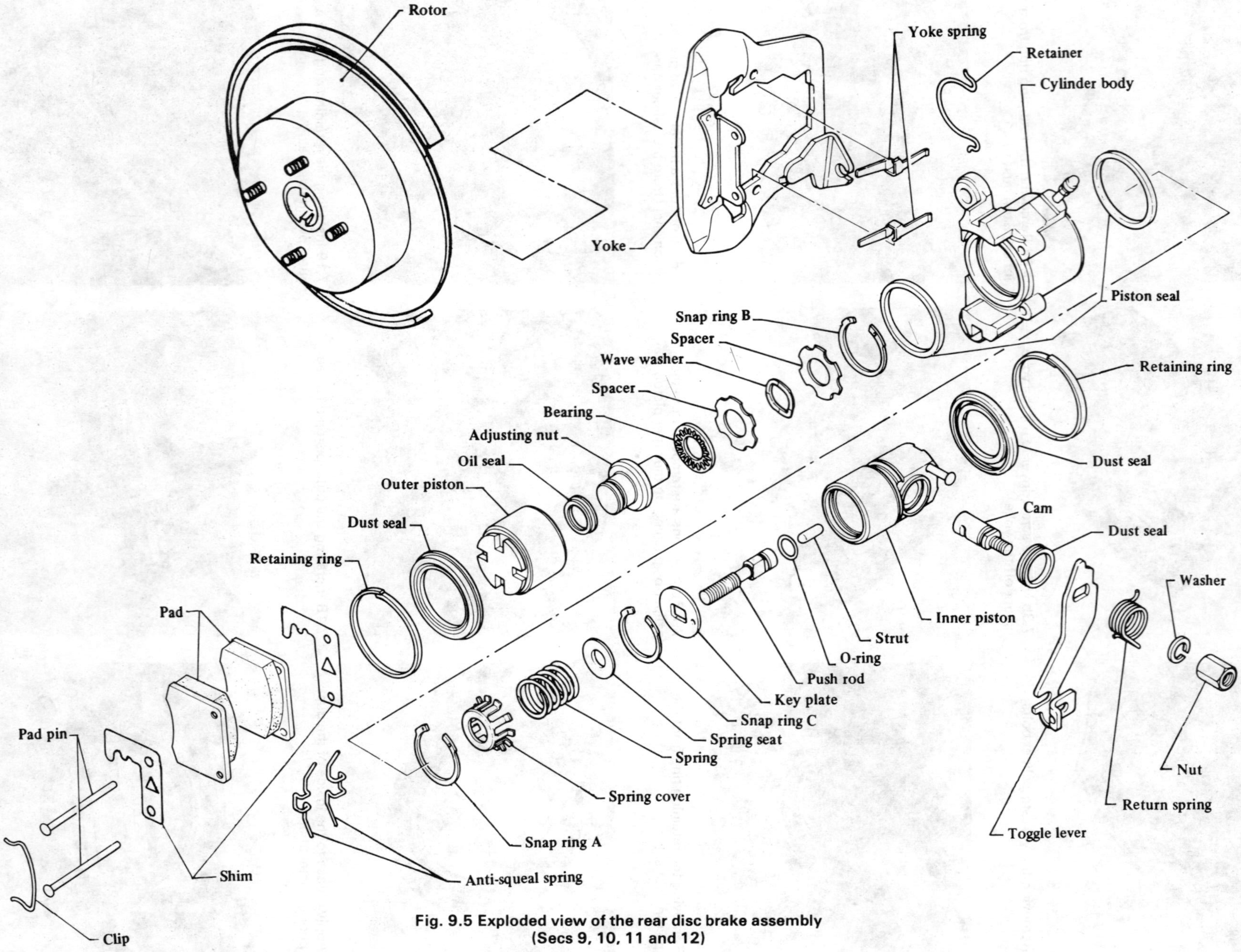

Fig. 9.5 Exploded view of the rear disc brake assembly (Secs 9, 10, 11 and 12)

8 Front disc rotor – removal and installation

1 Remove the caliper assembly as described in Section 6.
2 Use a screwdriver to pry off the hub dust cap (photo).
3 Remove the cotter pin.
4 Remove the adjusting cap.
5 Remove the wheel bearing nut and washer.
6 Remove the outer wheel bearing.
7 Remove the hub and rotor assembly.
8 If the rotor needs machining, remove only the inner wheel bearing and grease seal.
9 If the rotor needs replacing it must be separated from the hub. First, remove the bolts (photo) that secure the rotor to the hub. Then use a plastic hammer to tap along the outer edge of the hub until the hub can be removed from the rotor. Once the hub has been separated slightly, two flathead screwdrivers (one on each side) can be used to pry the two pieces apart. If the hub and rotor do not separate easily, apply penetrating oil where the two meet.
10 When installing the rotor to the hub fit it into position on the hub and loosely install the bolts.
11 Tighten the bolts in a crisscross pattern a little at a time until they are torqued to specs.
12 To complete the installation procedure refer to Chapter 11, Section 3 for re-packing the wheel bearings and installing the hub and rotor assmbly onto the shaft.

9 Rear disc brake – pad replacement

1 Remove the wheel and tire.
2 Remove the pad clip (photo).
3 While holding the anti-squeal springs in position, remove the 2 pad pins. Lift off the springs (photo).
4 Pull out both the inner and outer pads, along with their shims (photo).
5 Using a flat-head screwdriver, rotate the outer piston clockwise, to retract the piston slightly into the caliper (photo). Be careful not to damage the dust seal.
6 Prior to installing the pads, use a large screwdriver or similar lever to slide the yoke outward until there is equal clearance on both sides of the rotor to install the pads.
7 Apply a light coat of an aerosol Teflon coating (disc brake anti-squeak coating) to the back of both pad shims.
8 Position the outer piston so that one of its notches is positioned as shown in Fig. 9.6. Then install the inner pad and shim so that the protrusion on the back of the pad engages with the piston notch.
9 Install the outer pad.
10 Apply a light coat of grease to the pad pins.
11 While holding the anti-squeal springs in place, install the pad pins. Be careful you do not get grease on the friction side of the pads.
12 Install the pad clip.
13 Reinstall the wheel and tire.
14 Bleed the brakes as described in Section 3.

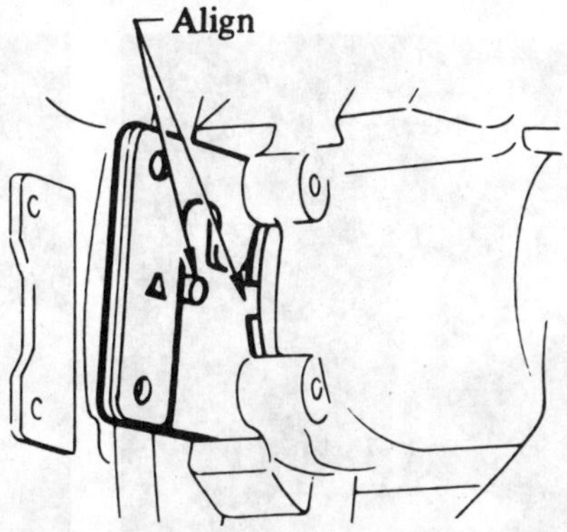

Fig. 9.6 When installing the inner rear disc pad, be sure the locating pin engages with the outer piston's notch (Sec 9)

8.2 Use a screwdriver to pry off the hub dust cap

8.9 The rotor need be removed from the hub only if it is being replaced

9.2 Removing the rear brake pad pin retaining clip

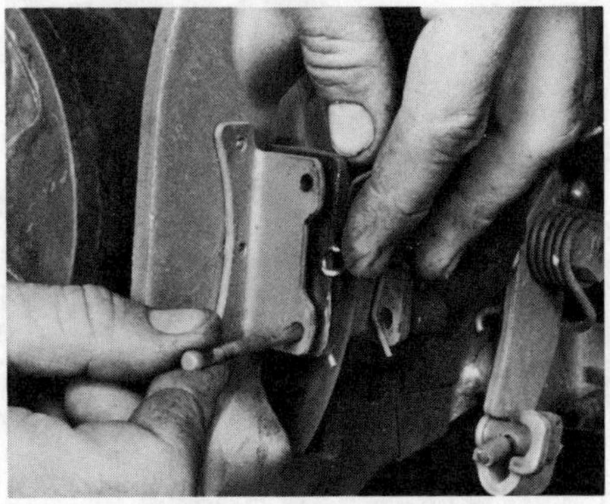

9.3 Hold the springs in place while removing the pad pins

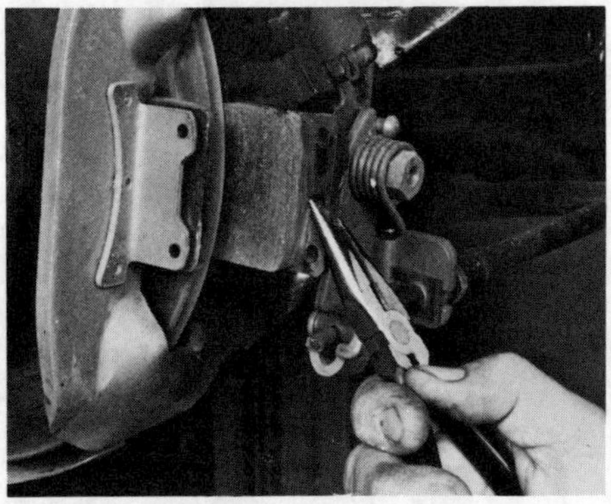

9.4 Removing the rear pads and shims

9.5 Use a screwdriver to rotate the outer piston clockwise to retract it into the caliper

10 Rear disc brake caliper – removal and installation

1 Remove the pads as described in Section 9.
2 Disconnect the brake tube from the caliper. Immediately plug the opening to prevent leakage of fluid, and to keep foreign material from entering the line.
3 Remove the retaining clip that secures the parking brake cable casing to the caliper (photo).
4 Remove the cotter pin from the cable end pin and disconnect the cable from the parking brake toggle lever.
5 Withdraw the parking brake cable housing out of the yoke bracket.
6 Remove the 2 caliper mounting bolts located on the rear of the caliper assembly.
7 Remove the caliper assembly.
8 Installation is the reverse of the removal procedure.
9 Bleed the brakes as described in Section 3.
10 Following installation, depress the brake pedal a few times to adjust the clearance between the brake pads and the rotor. Also check for any leakage of oil. Pressing on the brake pedal will automatically adjust this clearance.

11 Rear disc caliper – overhaul

1 Unclip the 2 anti-squeal clamps and remove them from the yoke (photo).
2 Separate the caliper from the yoke by pushing it outboard and remove it (photo).
3 Remove the yoke springs (photo).
4 Remove the caliper retainer clip (photo).
5 Remove the inner and outer seal retainer clips (photo).
6 Remove the outer dust seal (photo).
7 Remove the pistons from the caliper by pushing on the outer piston (photo).

10.3 Removing the locking clip that retains the rear parking brake cable to the caliper assembly

11.1 Removing the anti-squeak clamps from the yoke

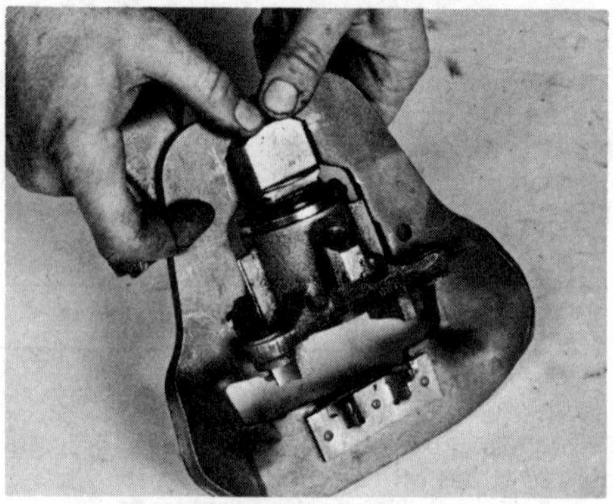
11.2 Separate the caliper from the yoke by pushing outward on the inner piston

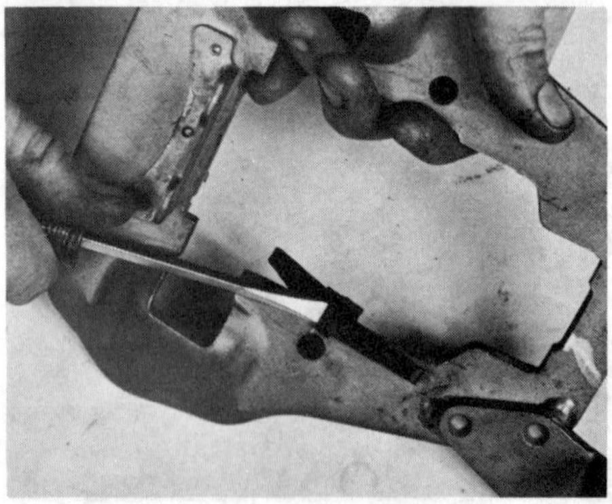
11.3 Removing the yoke springs

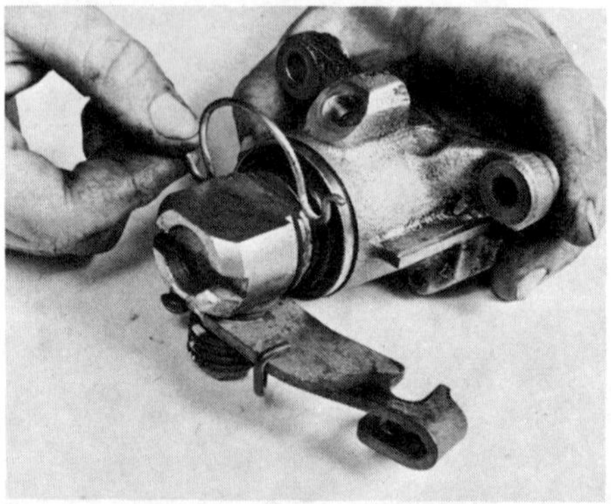
11.4 Removing the caliper retainer clip

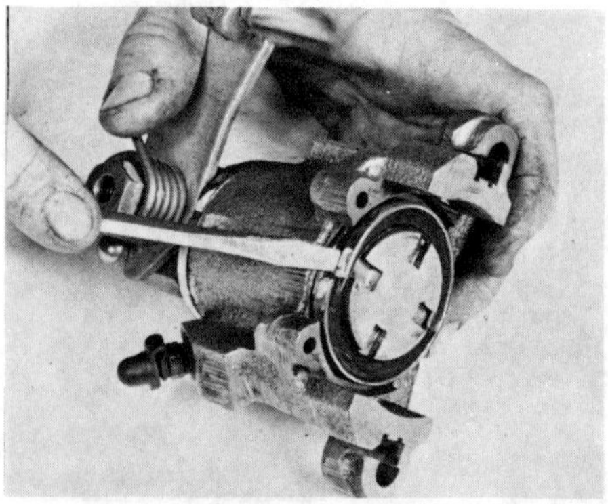
11.5 Remove the retaining rings from both piston dust seals

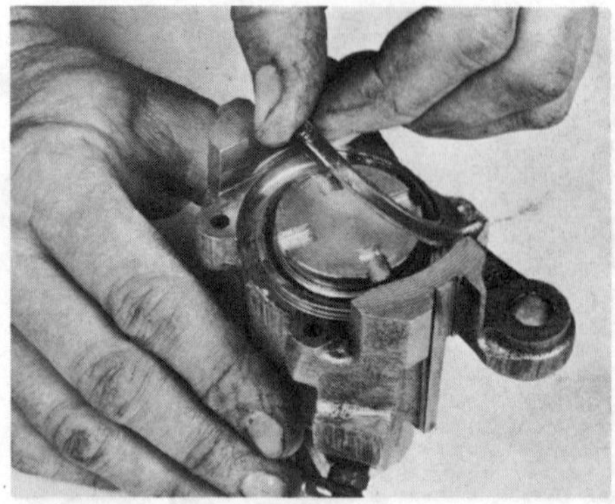
11.6 Removing the dust seal from the outer piston

11.7 Both pistons are removed from the caliper by pushing on the outer piston

11.9 The pistons are separated by turning the outer piston counterclockwise

8 Using a wooden or plastic dowel remove the 2 piston seals from the caliper bore. A metal tool is not recommended for this as it could easily scratch the bore surface.
9 Remove the outer piston assembly by unscrewing it counter-clockwise (photo).
10 Remove the snap-ring from the outer piston (photo), and lift out the piston components for inspection.
11 Remove the dust seal from the inner piston (photo).
12 Remove the outer snap-ring from the inner piston. Lift off the spring cover and spring.
13 Remove the inner snap-ring from the inner piston.
14 Turn the inner piston upside down and remove the spring seat and key plate.
15 Pull the push rod out of the piston and remove the strut and O-ring.
16 Disengage the return spring from the toggle lever (photo).
17 Remove the toggle lever and cam assembly by pulling it out of the inner piston.
18 Remove the toggle lever lip seal from the inner piston.
19 Use a screwdriver to carefully pry out the seal and bearing retainer from the inner piston.
20 Check the outer surfaces of the inner and outer pistons for scoring, nicks, rust or other damage. If light rust or scoring is present it can be removed by using No 600 grid emery cloth. If damage is deep the piston must be replaced.
21 Check the threads on the push rod. Make sure they are in good condition and replace the rod if necessary.
22 Inspect the push rod spring for any cracks or other damage and replace it if necessary.
23 Inspect the inner surface of the caliper bore for any nicks, scoring, rust or other damage. Again, if light rust or scoring is present it can be removed by using No 600 grid emery cloth. If damage is more serious the caliper housing will have to be replaced.
24 Inspect the needle bearing inside the outer piston for freedom of movement. If any of the rollers are binding the bearing will have to be replaced by prying it out.
25 Apply a coat of silicone-based grease to the needle bearings.
26 Install the seal and bearing retainer by gently tapping it into place with a plastic-head hammer.
27 Install a new lip seal onto the retainer.
28 Carefully insert the toggle lever and cam assembly into the outer piston.
29 Lubricate both ends of the strut with silicone-based rubber grease and insert it in the push rod.
30 Lightly lubricate the push rod O-ring with silicone-based grease and install it into its groove on the push rod.
31 Insert the strut and push rod into the piston.
32 Install the key plate over the push rod. Be sure that the push rod is aligned so that the locating pin in the key plate is properly fitted into its hole in the piston.
33 Install the inner snap-ring into its groove in the piston.
34 Install the spring seat, spring and spring cover over the push rod.
35 Place the outer snap-ring into position over the spring cover then place an appropriately sized socket over the push rod so that it sits on the spring cover. Place the assembly in a vise and tighten the vise until the spring is compressed enough for the outer snap-ring to be installed in its groove. Be careful that the spring cover is properly centered in the bore so that the tangs do not get damagged.
36 Install a new lip seal onto the adjusting screw. Be sure the lip is facing in the direction shown in Fig. 9.7. Lubricate the lip seal lightly with rubber grease.
37 Place the adjusting screw into the outer piston bore.
38 Place the bearing spacer, wave washer and spacer, in that order, over the adjusting nut.
39 Install the snap-ring into the outer piston.
40 Install the outer piston onto the push rod.
41 Apply a light coat of silicone-based rubber grease to the cylinder bore.
42 Install the new pistons seals into their grooves inside the bore. Lightly lubricate the seals with rubber grease.
43 Apply a light coat of sealing grease into the seal groove on the inner piston. Wipe off any residual grease that may have gotten onto the exterior surface of the piston.
44 Install a new dust seal into position on the inner piston.

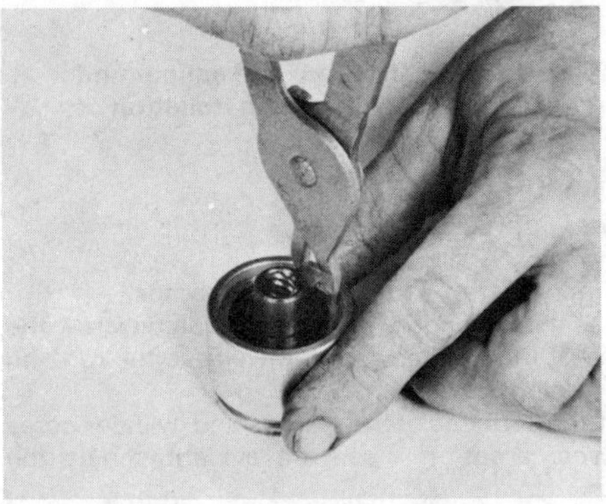
11.10a Removing the snap-ring from the outer piston

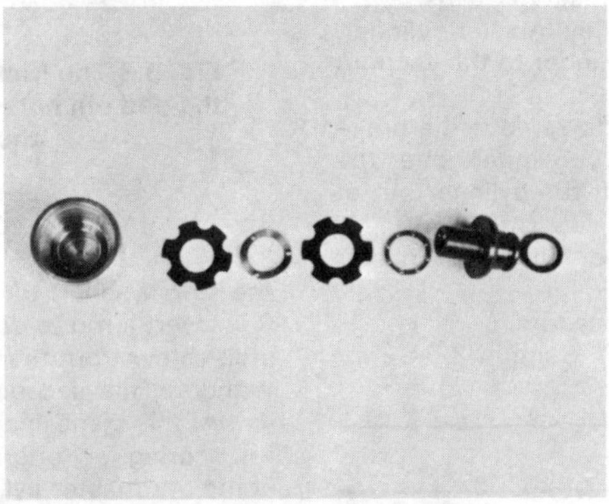
11.10b The outer piston components should be installed in the order shown above

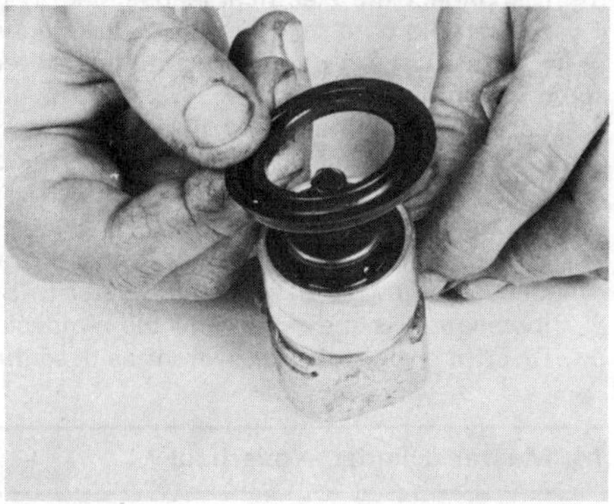
11.11 Removing the dust seal from the inner piston

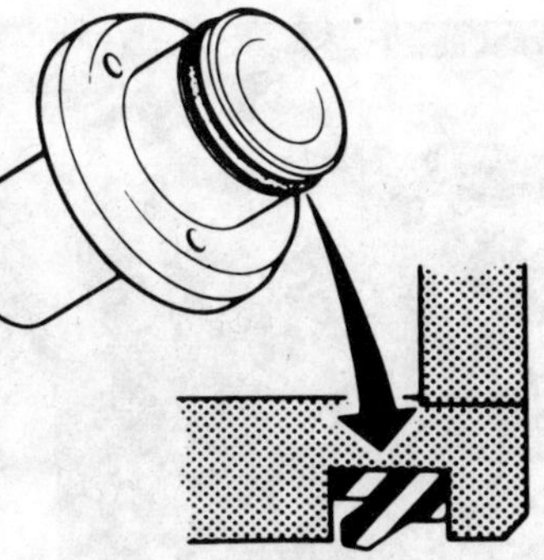
Fig. 9.7 The oil seal on the rear brake's outer piston adjusting nut should be installed as shown (Sec 11)

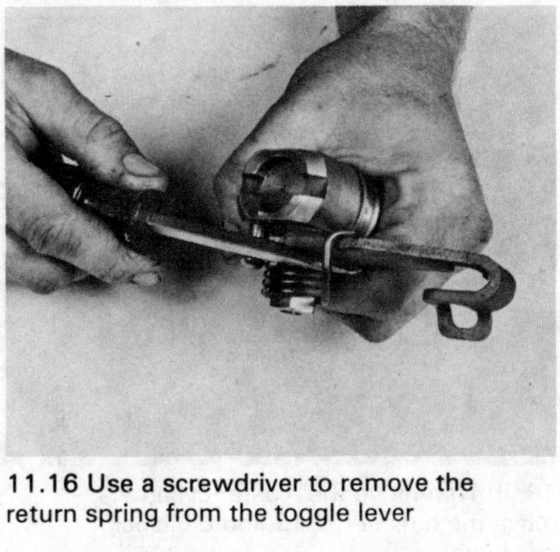
11.16 Use a screwdriver to remove the return spring from the toggle lever

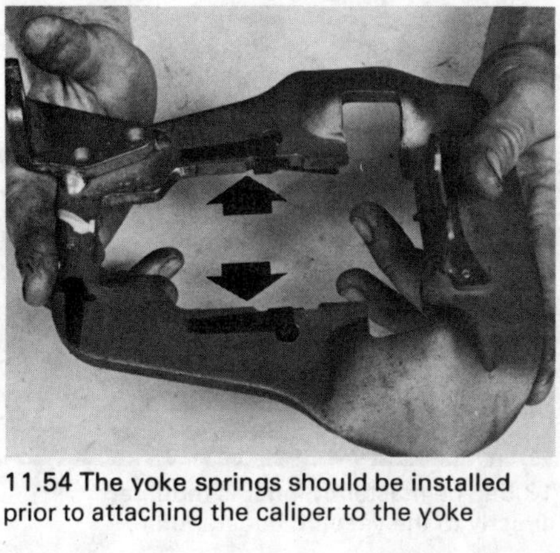
11.54 The yoke springs should be installed prior to attaching the caliper to the yoke

45 Install the dust seal retaining ring on the inner piston.
46 Apply a light coat of silicone-based rubber grease to the outer surfaces of both pistons.
47 Apply a light coat of seal grease into the two dust seal grooves on either side of the caliper housing.
48 Carefully insert the pistons into the caliper bore.
49 Align the inner piston so the inner edge of its seal groove is in line with the inner edge of the caliper seal groove, and pull the seal into position on the caliper.
50 Align the outer piston in a similar fashion to the inner piston so that the inner edge of the seal groove is in line with the inner edge of the caliper seal groove (Fig. 9.8).
51 Install the outer piston dust seal.
52 Install the dust seal retaining ring onto the outer piston.
53 Place the caliper retainer in its groove.
54 Install the yoke springs into position on the yoke (photo).
55 Apply a light coat of grease to the surfaces shown in Fig. 9.9.
56 Install the caliper into the yoke.
57 Install the anti-squeak clamps onto the yoke.

12 Rear disc rotor – removal and installation

1 Remove the rear disc caliper as described in Section 10.
2 Remove the rotor by sliding it off the hub and wheel studs. If the rotor will not separate easily from the hub, apply penetrating oil where the hub and rotor meet, and tap on the rotor with a plastic-head hammer.
3 Installation is the reverse of the removal procedure.

13 Master cylinder – removal and installation

1 Disconnect the negative battery cable.
2 Place newspaper or rags under the master cylinder to catch any leaking brake fluid. **Note:** *Be sure not to let brake fluid touch the painted surfaces of the car.*
3 Disconnect the electrical leads going to the reservoir caps.
4 Loosen the nuts securing the 2 brake lines to the master cylinder.
5 Remove the 2 nuts that secure the master cylinder to the vacuum servo unit (photo).
6 Carefully lift the cylinder off its mounting studs, remove the brake lines from the cylinder, and immediately place your fingers over the holes to prevent leakage of fluid (photo). Then lift the cylinder out of the engine compartment.
7 Plug the fluid lines to prevent further leakage of fluid. If the master cylinder needs to be disassembled, refer to Section 14.
8 Installation is the reverse of the removal procedure.
9 Bleed the entire brake system as described in Section 3.

14 Master cylinder – overhaul

1 Clean away external dirt and then remove the reservoir caps and filters and empty out the fluid.
2 From the end of the master cylinder pry out the snap-ring, extract the stop washer, the primary piston and the spring (photos).
3 Insert a rod to depress the secondary piston and then unscrew the stop screw from the base of the master cylinder. Release the rod and withdraw the secondary piston (photos).
4 At this stage, inspect the surfaces of the pistons and cylinder bores for scoring or 'bright' wear areas. If these are evident, renew the complete master cylinder.
5 If the components are in good condition, discard the seals and obtain a repair kit which will contain all the necessary renewable items. Make sure that the kit is for the Tokico master cylinder.

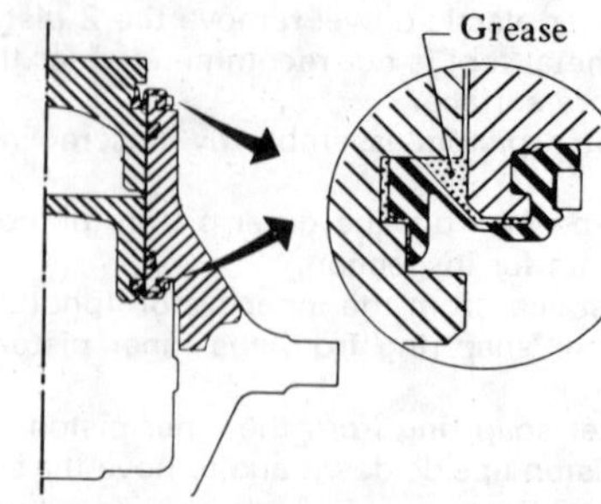

Fig. 9.8 The rear brake's pistons should be positioned as shown when installing the dust seals. Apply grease to the seal grooves before installing (Sec 11)

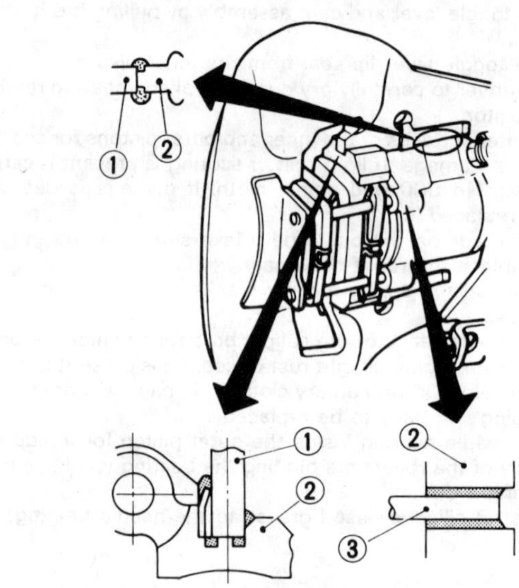

Fig. 9.9 The frictional surfaces of the yoke and caliper and the pad pin holes should be greased prior to installation of the caliper to the yoke (Sec 11)

1 Yoke
2 Caliper body
3 Pad pin

13.5a The master cylinder is mounted directly to the vacuum booster unit

13.5b To remove the master cylinder, remove the nuts at the 12 and 6 o'clock positions

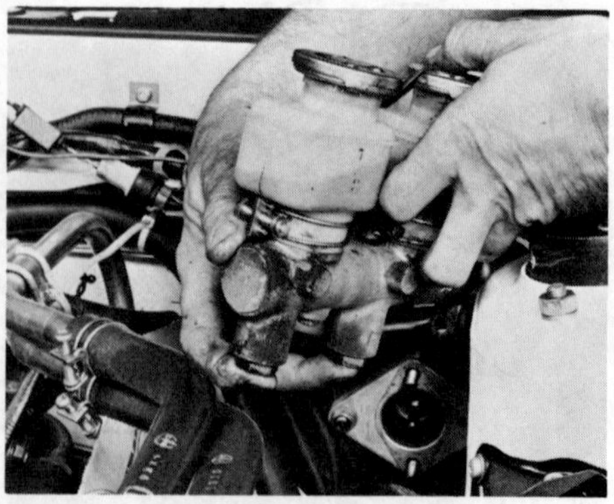

13.6 While lifting out the master cylinder, hold your fingers over the brake line connection holes

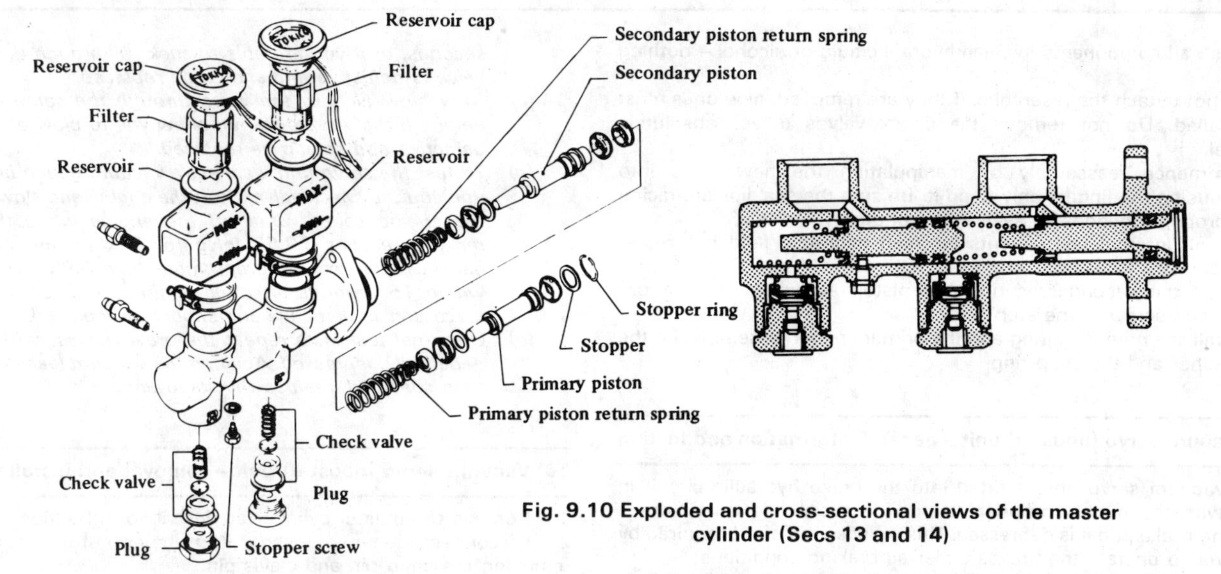

Fig. 9.10 Exploded and cross-sectional views of the master cylinder (Secs 13 and 14)

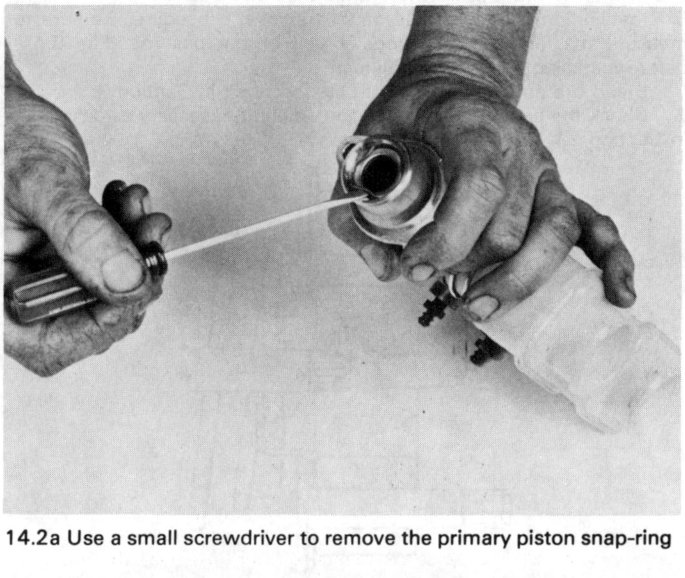

14.2a Use a small screwdriver to remove the primary piston snap-ring

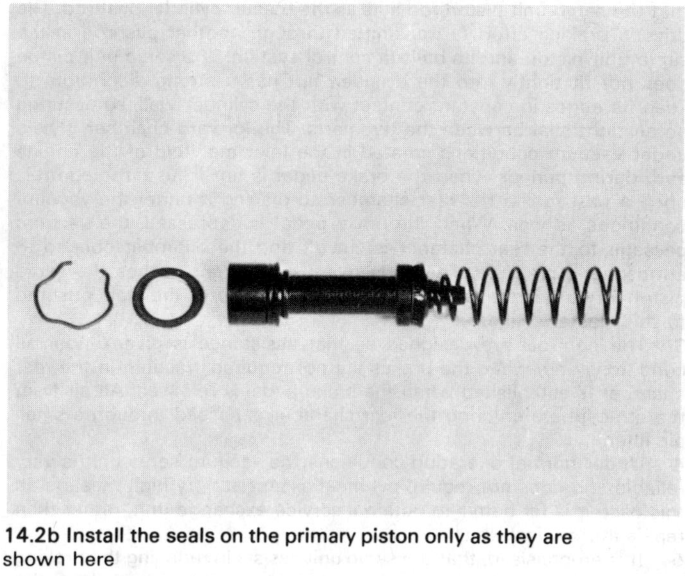

14.2b Install the seals on the primary piston only as they are shown here

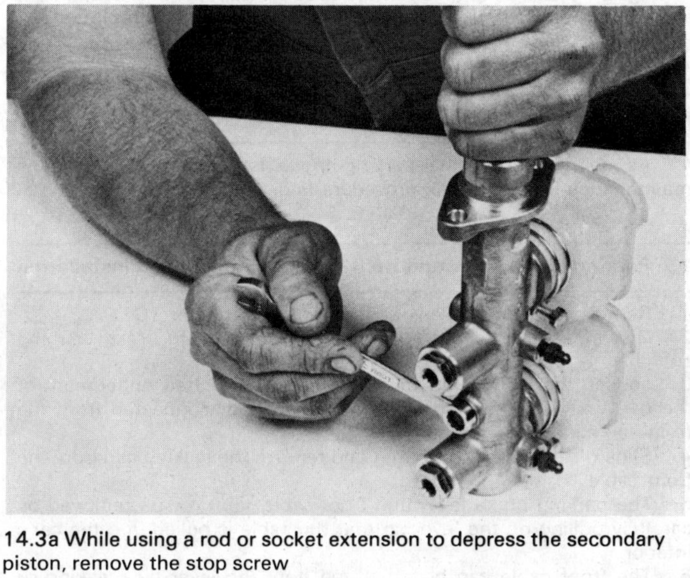

14.3a While using a rod or socket extension to depress the secondary piston, remove the stop screw

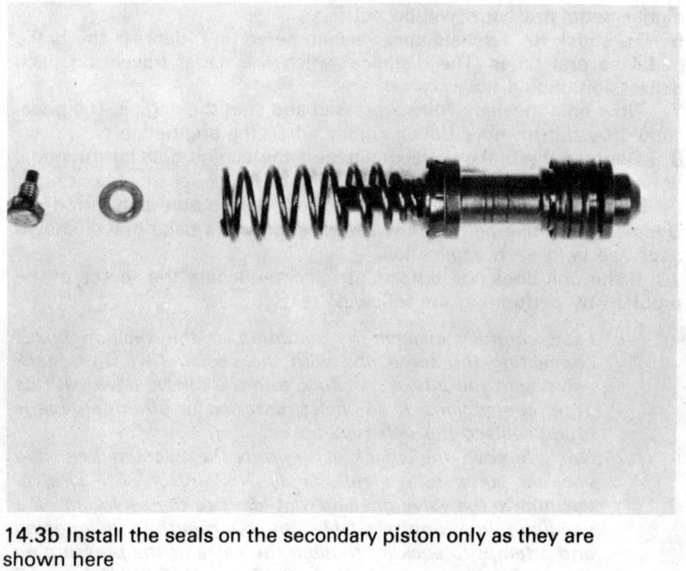

14.3b Install the seals on the secondary piston only as they are shown here

6 Wash all components in clean hydraulic fluid or alcohol – nothing else.
7 Do not detach the reservoirs. If they are removed, new ones must be installed. Do not remove the check valves unless absolutely essential.
8 Commence reassembly by manipulating the new seals into position using the fingers only to do it. Be sure the seal lips are facing in the proper directions as seen in the photos.
9 Dip all internal components in clean hydraulic fluid before re-assembly.
10 Install the secondary spring and piston assembly. Hold it depressed and screw in the stop screw.
11 Install the primary spring and the primary piston assembly. Fit the stop washer and the snap-ring.

15 Vacuum servo (booster) unit – general information and testing

1 A vacuum servo unit is fitted into the brake hydraulic circuit in series with the master cylinder, to provide assistance to the driver when the brake pedal is depressed. This reduces the effort required by the driver to operate the brakes under all braking conditions.
2 The unit operates by vacuum obtained from the induction manifold and comprises basically a booster diaphragm and check valve. The servo unit and hydraulic master cylinder are connected together so that the servo unit piston rod acts as the master cylinder pushrod. The driver's braking effort is transmitted through another pushrod in the servo unit piston and its built-in control system. The servo unit piston does not fit tightly into the cylinder, but has a strong diaphragm to keep its edges in constant contact with the cylinder wall, so assuring an air tight seal between the two parts. The forward chamber is held under vacuum conditions created in the inlet manifold of the engine and, during periods when the brake pedal is not in use, the controls open a passage to the rear chamber so placing it under the vacuum conditions as well. When the brake pedal is depressed, the vacuum passage to the rear chamber is cut off and the chamber opened to atmospheric pressure. The consequent rush of air pushes the servo piston forward in the vacuum chamber and operates the main pushrod to the master cylinder.
3 The controls are designed so that assistance is given under all conditions and, when the brakes are not required, vacuum in the rear chamber is established when the brake pedal is released. All air from the atmosphere entering the rear chamber is passed through a small air filter.
4 Under normal operating conditions the vacuum servo unit is very reliable and does not require overhaul except at very high mileage. In this case it is far better to obtain a service exchange unit, rather than repair the original unit.
5 It is emphasised, that the servo unit assists in reducing the braking effort required at the foot pedal and in the event of its failure, the hydraulic braking system is in no way affected except that the need for higher pedal pressures will be noticed.
6 To check for a satisfactory vacuum servo unit, depress the brake pedal several times. The distance which the pedal travels on each depression should not vary.
7 Now hold the pedal fully depressed and start the engine. The pedal should be felt to move down slightly when the engine starts.
8 Depress the brake pedal, switch off the engine holding the pedal down for about 30 seconds. The position of the pedal should not alter.
9 Restart the engine, run it for a minute or two and then turn it off. Depress the brake pedal firmly several times. The pedal travel should decrease with each application.
10 If the unit does not perform as indicated locate the source of the problem by performing the following tests:

(a) *First, carefully inspect the condition of the vacuum hoses connecting the servo unit with the check valve, the check valve with the intake manifold, and the check valve with its other connections. If any holes, cracking or other damage is found replace the defective hoses.*
(b) *Next, remove the check valve from the vacuum line. If a vacuum pump is available, apply 7.87 inHg (26.7 kPa) of vacuum to the valve opening that leads to the servo unit. If a vacuum pump is not available, put your mouth to the opening and attempt to suck air through the valve. If the pressure on the pump drops more than 0.39 inHg (1.3 kPa) in 15 seconds, or if you are able to suck air through the valve, the valve is defective and should be replaced.*
(c) *Now blow air into the valve through the same opening as before. If the valve does not allow you to blow air into it, it is defective and should be replaced.*
(d) *To test the servo unit, connect a vacuum gauge between the unit and the check valve. Start the engine and slowly increase the engine speed. Shut off the engine when the vacuum reading reaches 19.69 inHg (66.7 kPa) and observe the gauge. If the reading drops more than 0.98 inHg (3.3 kPa) within 15 seconds after the engine has been shut off, the servo unit is defective and should be replaced.*
(e) *One final test is to repeat the previous test with the brake pedal fully depressed. Again, if the vacuum leakage is greater than specified, replace the servo unit.*

16 Vacuum servo (booster) unit – removal and installation

1 Remove the master cylinder as described in Section 13.
2 Disconnect the servo pushrod from the arm of the brake pedal by removing the snap pin and clevis pin.
3 Disconnect the vacuum line from the servo unit.
4 Remove the 4 retaining nuts from the servo unit's mounting studs, and withdraw the unit from the engine compartment.
5 Installation is the reverse of the removal procedure. Be sure to measure the length of the booster unit output pushrod (Fig. 9.11) before installing the master cylinder.
6 Bleed the entire brake system as described in Section 3.
7 Check the brake pedal height and adjust if necessary as described in Section 21.

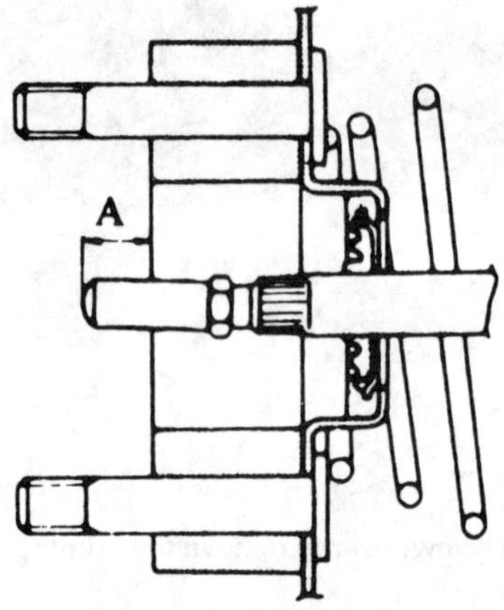

Fig. 9.11 The output rod of the vacuum booster unit is non-adjustable and if not within specs, the unit must be replaced (Sec 16)

17 Parking brake – adjustment

1 As adjustment of the parking brake is a part of the routine maintenance schedule, this procedure is described in Chapter 1.

18 Parking brake lever and front cable – removal and installation

1 Remove the console box as described in Chapter 10.
2 Disconnect the wiring lead going to the parking brake warning switch.
3 Loosen the locknut on the cable adjuster located underneath of the car, and turn the adjuster until it can be disconnected from the front cable.
4 Slide off the rubber grommet and remove the locking clip from the front cable.
5 The parking brake lever and front cable can now be removed by carefully pulling on the lever so that the cable is pulled into the car's interior.
6 The front cable can be separated from the lever by breaking or

19.3 The rear parking brake cables are retained to the rear brakes with cotter pins and locking clips

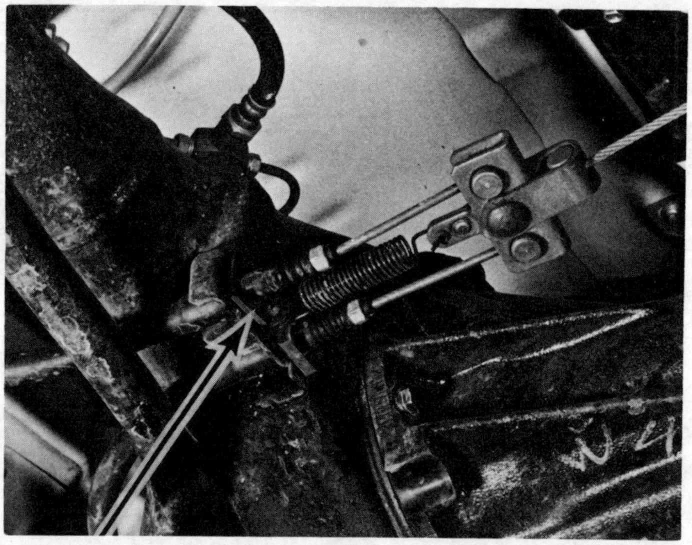

19.4 The rear parking brake cable assembly is secured to the equalizer bracket with 2 locking clips

cutting the retaining pin. A replacement clevis pin and cotter pin are available for mounting the new front cable to the lever.

7 Installation is the reverse of the removal procedure.

8 Following installation, adjust the parking brake as described in Chapter 1.

19 Parking brake rear cables – removal and installation

1 Loosen the locknut on the parking brake cable adjuster and turn the adjuster to disconnect it from the front cable.

2 Remove the 2 bolts that retain the cable clamp to the differential housing.

3 Disconnect both rear cables from their respective toggle levers at the rear brakes by removing the cotter pins and locking clips that retain them (photo).

4 Remove the locking clips that retain the cables to the equalizer assembly bracket (photo). Then withdraw and remove the entire rear cable assembly.

5 Installation is the reverse of the removal procedure.

6 Apply a coat of grease to all sliding contact surfaces.

7 Adjust the parking brake as described in Chapter 1.

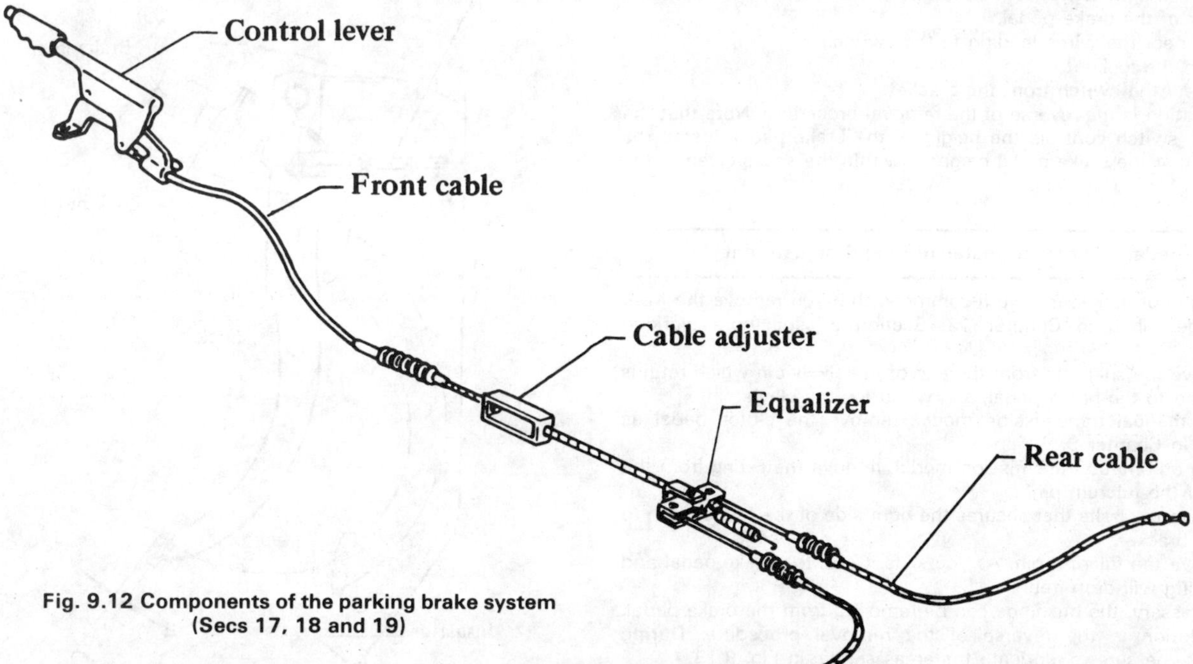

Fig. 9.12 Components of the parking brake system (Secs 17, 18 and 19)

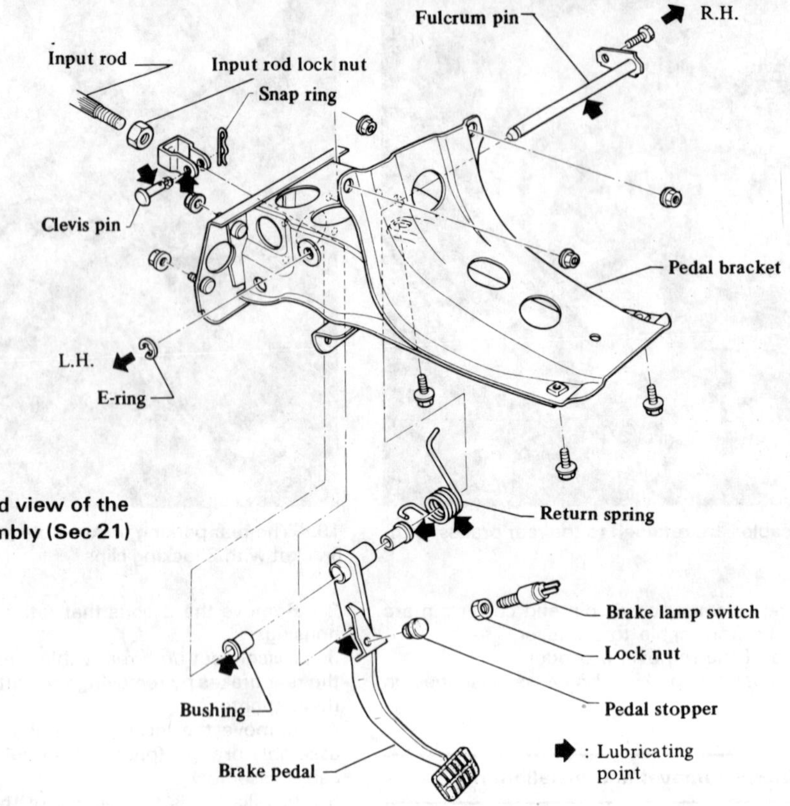

Fig. 9.13 Exploded view of the brake pedal assembly (Sec 21)

20 Brake light switch – removal and installation

1 The brake light switch is mounted to the brake pedal bracket just to the rear of the brake pedal.
2 Disconnect the wires leading to the switch.
3 Loosen the locknut.
4 Unscrew the switch from the bracket.
5 Installation is the reverse of the removal procedure. Note that the brake light switch controls the height of the brake pedal. Install the switch so that the brake pedal height is within the specs given at the beginning of this Chapter.

21 Brake pedal – removal, installation and adjustment

1 Though not necessary, we recommend that you remove the front seat as described in Chapter 12, Section 27 for more working clearance.
2 Remove the snap pin from the end of the clevis pin which retains the pushrod to the brake pedal, and withdraw the clevis pin.
3 On a manual transmission model, remove the clutch pedal as described in Chapter 8.
4 On an automatic transmission model, remove the E-ring from the left end of the fulcrum pin.
5 Remove the bolts that secures the right side of the fulcrum pin to the pedal bracket.
6 Remove the fulcrum pin. As you slide it out, the brake pedal and return spring will drop free.
7 If necessary, the bushings can be removed from the brake pedal.
8 Installation is the reverse of the removal procedure. During installation, be sure to lubricate the areas shown in Fig. 9.13.
9 Following installation, measure the height of the brake pedal (dimension h in Fig. 9.14). If this measurement is not within the specs as given at the beginning of this Chapter, loosen the lock nut on the brake light switch and turn the brake light switch as required to obtain the correct brake pedal height.
10 Next measure the free play of the brake pedal and compare this measurement with the specs. If this is not correct, loosen the lock nut on the vacuum servo unit's pushrod and turn the rod to obtain the correct free play.

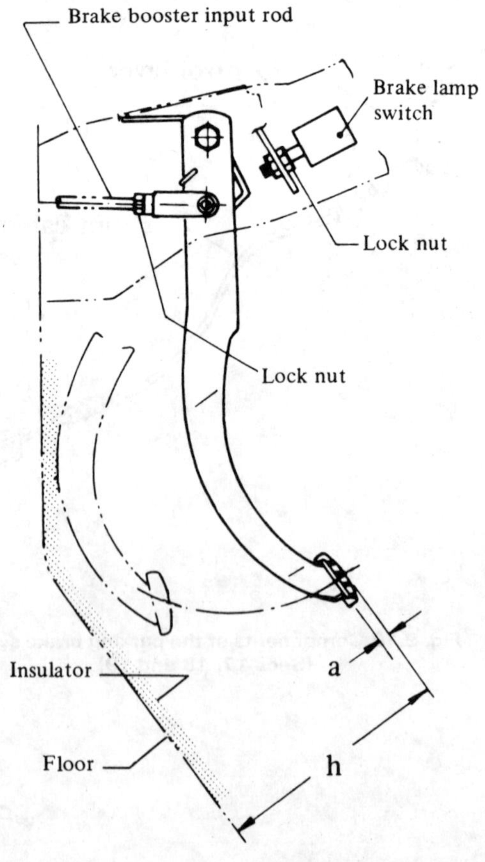

Fig. 9.14 Dimensions to be measured when adjusting the brake pedal: h – pedal height, a – free play (Sec 21)

Chapter 10 Chassis electrical system

Refer to Chapter 13 for Specifications and information related to 1982 and 1983 models

Contents

Automatic speed control device (ASCD) – general information 36
Backup lamp – bulb and lens replacement 13
Center console cluster – removal and installation 23
Cigar lighter – removal and installation 27
Clock – removal and installation 20
Console box – removal and installation 22
Door mirror switch (electric remote control) – removal and installation 30
Electrical troubleshooting – general information 2
Fan switch – removal and installation 25
Fuses – general information 3
Fusible links – general information 4
Gauges and indicators – removal and installation 19
General information 1
Glove box – removal and installation 32
Headlight – adjustment 8
Headlight – removal and installation 9
Heater/air conditioning control assembly – removal and installation 24
Horn – fault testing 7
Ignition switch – removal and installation 17
Illumination rheostat control – removal and installation 31
Instrument cluster – removal and installation 18
Instrument panel – removal and installation 33
Interior lamp – bulb and lens replacement 14
Power antenna switch – removal and installation 26
Power radio antenna – removal and installation 38
Printed circuit board – removal and installation 21
Radio – removal and installation 28
Rear defogger (electric grid type) – testing and repair 37
Relays – general information 5
Side marker lamp (front and rear) – bulb and lens replacement .. 12
Sound balancer – removal and installation (1980 models only) .. 29
Speakers (front and rear) – removal and installation 35
Speedometer cable – inspection and replacement 34
Steering column combination switch – removal and installation . 16
Taillight – bulb and lens replacement 10
Turn signal parking lamp (front) – bulb and lens replacement 11
Turn signals and hazard flashers – general information 6
Windshield wiper system 15

Specifications

Bulbs

Application	Wattage	Type
Headlight (sealed beam)		
Inner (type 1) - high	50	4651
Outer (type 2) - high/low	40/60	4652
Front combination light		
Turn signal/clearance	27/8	1157
Front side marker light	3.4	158
Rear side marker light	3.4	158
Rear combination light		
Stop/tail	27/8	1157
Turn signal	27	1156
Backup	27	1156
License plate light	8 or 10	–
Interior light	10	–
Spot light	8	–
Step light	5	–
Rear (luggage) compartment light		
Hardtop	3.4	158
Hatchback	5	–
Combination meter		
Illumination light	3.4	158
Brake warning light	3.4	158
Warning (others)/monitoring light	2	–
High beam indicator light	3.4	158
Cruise control switch		
Illumination/indicator light	1.4	–
Heater (A/C) control panel		
Illumination/A/C indicator light	3.4	158
Glove box light	3.4	158
A/T selector lever illumination light	3.4	158
Cigarette lighter/ashtray illumination light	1.4	–

Fuses

Circuit	Ampere rating
Headlamp	20
Heater, A/C	20
Rear defogger	20
Stop lamp	15
Clearance, tail lamp	15
Wiper, washer	15
Coil, injector	15
Hazard lamp	10
Horn	10
Cigarette lighter, clock	10
Room, step lamp	10
Audio	10
Engine control	10
Turn signal, meter	10

Fusible links

Circuit	Color
Ignition switch	Green
Power supply to the fuse box	Red
Electronic fuel injection circuit	Green
Electronic fuel injection circuit	Brown

Wiring harness color coding

Circuit	Base color
Starting and ignition systems	Black (B)
Charging system	White (W)
Lighting system	Red (R)
Turn signal and horn	Green (G)
Instrument system	Yellow (Y)
Others	Blue (L), Brown (Br) and Light green (Lg)
Grounding system	Black (B)

1 General information

This Chapter covers the repair and service procedures for the various lighting and electrical components not associated with the engine, as well as general information on troubleshooting the car's various electrical circuits. Information on the battery, generator, distributor and starter motor can be found in Chapter 5.

The electrical system is of the 12-volt, negative ground type with power supplied by a lead/acid-type battery which is charged by the generator.

Electrical components located in the dashboard do not use ground wires or straps, but rather use grounding provisions which are integrated in the printed circuit mounted behind the instrument cluster.

It should be noted that whenever portions of the electrical system are worked on, the negative battery cable should be disconnected to prevent electrical shorts and/or fires.

2 Electrical troubleshooting – general information

A typical electrical circuit consists of an electrical component, any switches, relays, motors, etc. relevant to that component and the wiring and connectors that connect the component to both the battery and the chassis. To aid in locating a problem in any electrical circuit, complete wiring diagrams of each model are included at the end of this Chapter. Also of benefit in locating specific circuits on the car are wiring connector illustrations which identify all connectors used on the car. There are also found at the end of this Chapter.

Before tackling any troublesome electrical circuit, first thoroughly study the appropriate diagrams to get a complete understanding of what makes up that individual circuit. Trouble spots, for instance, can often be narrowed down by noting if other components related to that circuit are operating properly or not. If several components or circuits fail at one time, chances are the fault lies in the fuse or ground connection, as several circuits often are routed through the same fuse and ground connections. This can be confirmed by referring to the fuse box and ground distribution diagrams in this Chapter.

Often, electrical problems stem from simple causes, such as loose or corroded connections, a blown fuse or melted fusible link. Prior to any electrical trouble shooting, always visually check the condition of the fuse, wires and connections or the problem circuit.

If testing instruments are going to be utilized, use the diagrams to plan ahead of time where you will make the necessary connections in order to accurately pinpoint the trouble spot.

The basic tools needed for electrical troubleshooting include a circuit tester or voltmeter (a 12-volt bulb with a set of test leads can also be used), a continuity tester (which includes a bulb, battery and set of test leads) and a jumper wire, preferably with a circuit breaker incorporated, which can be used to bypass electrical components.

Voltage checks should be performed if a circuit is not functioning properly. Connect one lead of a circuit tester to either the negative battery terminal or a known good ground. Connect the other lead to a connector in the circuit being tested, preferably nearest to the battery or fuse. If the bulb of the tester goes on voltage is reaching that point, which means the part of the circuit between that connector and the battery is problem-free. Continue checking along the circuit in the same fashion. When you reach a point where no voltage is present, the problem lies between there and the last good test point. Most of the time the problem is due to a loose connection. *Keep in mind that some circuits only receive voltage when the ignition key is in the 'Accessory' or 'Run' position.*

A method of finding shorts in a circuit is to remove the fuse and connect a test light or voltmeter in its place to the fuse terminals. There should be no load in the circuit. Move the wiring harness from side to side while watching the test light. If the bulb goes on, there is a short to ground somewhere in that area, probably where insulation has rubbed off of a wire. The same test can be performed on other components of the circuit, including the switch.

A ground check should be done to see if a component is grounded properly. Disconnect the battery and connect one lead of a self-powered test light such as a continuity tester to a known good ground. Connect the other lead to the wire or ground connection being tested. If the bulb goes on, the ground is good. If the bulb does not go on, the ground is not good.

A continuity check is performed to see if a circuit, section of circuit or individual component is passing electricity through it properly.

Disconnect the battery, and connect one lead of a self-powered test light such as a continuity tester to one end of the circuit being tested and the other lead to the other end of the circuit. If the bulb goes on, there is continuity, which means the circuit is passing electricity through it properly. Switches can be checked in the same way.

Remember that all electrical circuits are composed basically of electricity running from the battery, through the wires, switches, relays, etc. to the electrical component (light bulb, motor, etc). From there it is run to the car body (ground) where it is passed back to the battery. Any electrical problem is basically an interruption in the flow of electricity from the battery and back.

3 Fuses – general information

The electrical circuits of the car are protected by a combination of fuses and fusible links.

The fuse box is located underneath the dash on the right side of the car. Access to the fuses is achieved by simply pulling down on the fuse cover.

Each of the fuses is designed to protect a specific circuit, as identified on the fuse cover.

If an electrical component has failed, your first check should be the fuse. A fuse which has "blown" can be readily identified by inspecting the curved metal element inside the plastic housing. If this element is broken the fuse is inoperable and should be replaced with a new one.

Fuses are replaced by simply pulling out the old one and pushing in the new one.

It is important that the correct fuse be installled. The different electrical circuits need varying amounts of protection, indicated by the amperage rating on the fuse. A fuse with too low a rating will blow prematurely, while a fuse with too high a rating may not blow soon enough to avoid serious damage.

At no time should the fuse be bypassed by using metal or foil. Serious damage to the electrical system could result.

If the replacement fuse immediately fails, do not replace it with another until the cause of the problem is isolated and corrected. In most cases this will be a short circuit in the wiring system caused by a broken or deteriorated wire.

4 Fusible links – general information

In addition to fuses, the wiring system incorporates fusible links for overload protection. These links are used in circuits which are not ordinarily fused, such as the ignition circuit and the Electronic Fuel Injection circuit.

The fusible links are located near the positive battery terminal, and are easily removed by unplugging the connectors at either end.

If an electrical failure occurs in one of the circuits covered by a fusible link, these should be the first check. If the link is melted, the entire fusible link harness should be replaced, but only after checking and correcting the electrical fault that caused it.

5 Relays – general information

The various electrical relays are grouped together either in the engine compartment or under the dash for convenience in the event of needed replacement.

The main relay bracket in the engine compartment is located on the right side, and has the windshield washer reservoir attached to its outer mounting case.

If a faulty relay is suspected, it can be removed and tested by a Datsun dealer or other qualified shop. Defective relays must be replaced as a unit.

6 Turn signals and hazard flashers – general information

Small canister-shaped flasher units are incorporated into the electrical circuits for the directional signals and hazard warning lights.

When the units are functioning properly an audible check can be heard with the circuit in operation. If the turn signals fail on one side only and the flasher unit cannot be heard, a faulty bulb is indicated. If the flasher unit can be heard, a short in the wiring is indicated.

If the turn signal fails on both sides, the fault may be due to a blown fuse, faulty flasher unit or switch, or a broken or loose connection. If the fuse has blown, check the wiring for a short before installing a new fuse.

The hazard warning lamps are checked in the same manner as paragraph 3 above.

Both the turn signal and hazard warning flasher units are located on a single bracket underneath the dash on the driver's side (see accompanying figure).

When replacing either of these flasher units it is important to buy a replacement of the same capacity. Check the new flasher against the old one to be assured of the proper replacement.

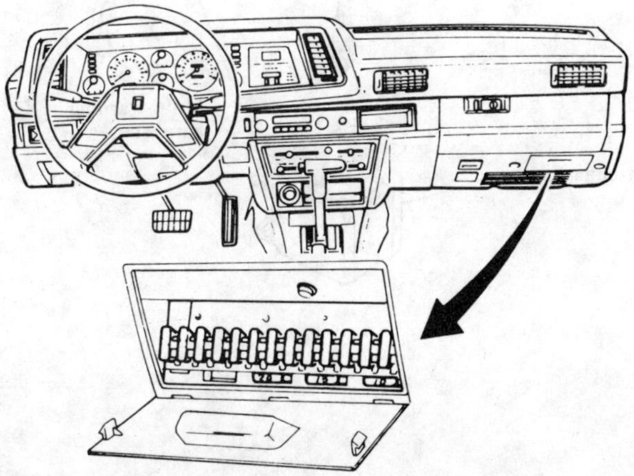

Fig. 10.1 Location of the fuse box (Sec 3)

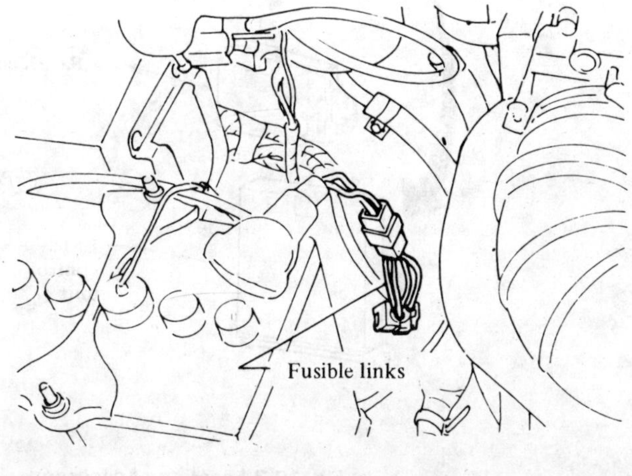

Fig. 10.2 Location of the fusible links (Sec 4)

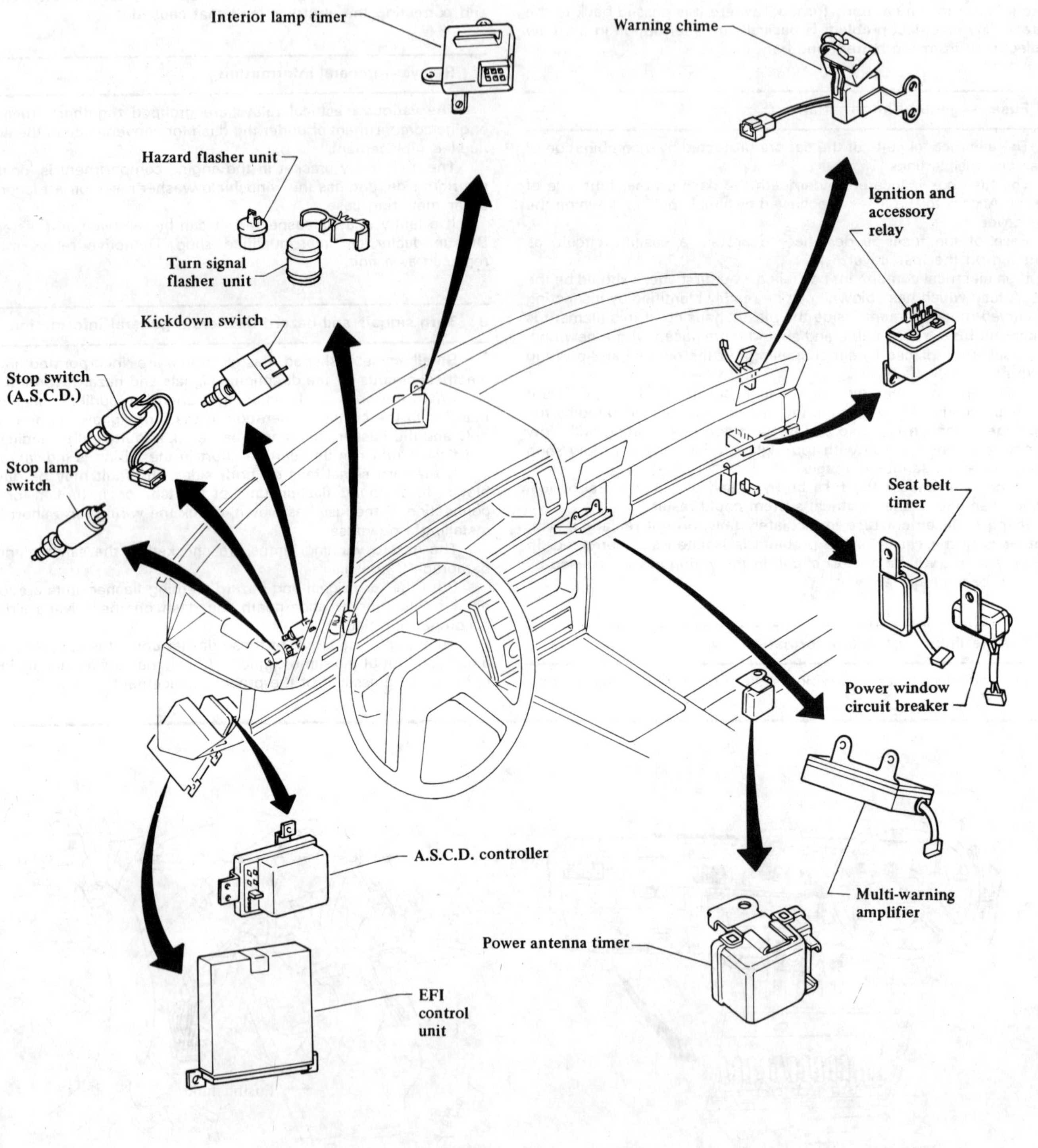

Fig. 10.3 Location of accessory electrical components in the dash area

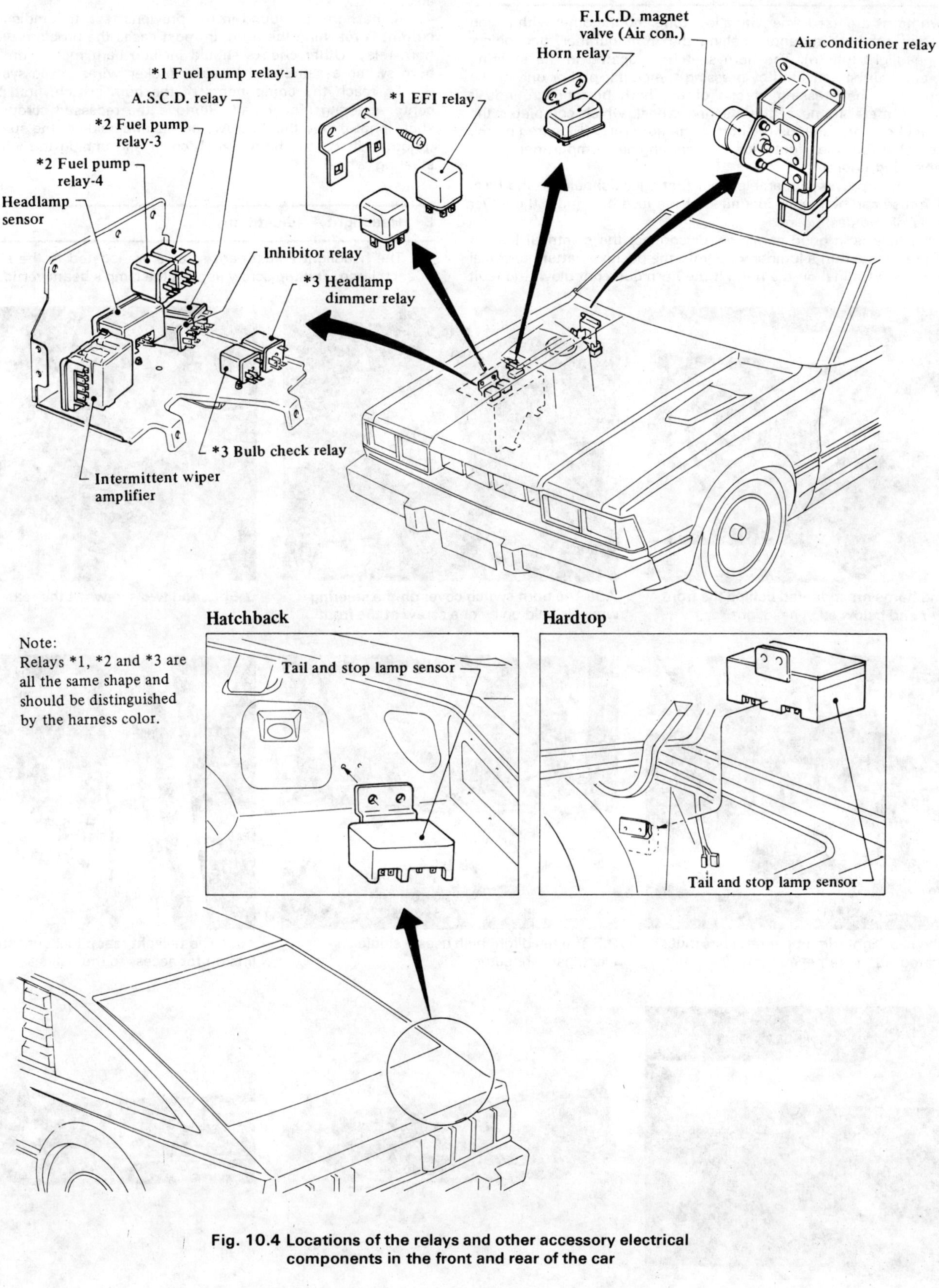

Note:
Relays *1, *2 and *3 are all the same shape and should be distinguished by the harness color.

Fig. 10.4 Locations of the relays and other accessory electrical components in the front and rear of the car

7 Horn – fault testing

1 Two horns are used, one with a low tone and the other with a high tone. They are both mounted behind the front bumper, one below either headlight (photo). The horn switch is located in the steering wheel, and can be activated by pressing the center pad or one of the side buttons. The pressing of one of the horn buttons grounds it against the metal frame of the steering wheel, which completes the electrical circuit and sounds the horns. The horn relay is located on the relay bracket on the right side of the engine compartment (see accompanying figure).

2 If the horn proves inoperable, your first check should be the fuse. A blown fuse can be readily identified at the fuse box under the lower right side of the dashboard.

3 If the fuse is in good condition, disconnect the electrical lead at one of the horns. Run a jumper wire from the positive battery terminal to the wiring terminal on the horn. If the horn does not blow, the fault lies in the grounding of the horn or the horn itself. Test the other horn also.

4 If the horn did sound in the previous test, this indicates that no current is reaching the horn. In most cases the problem will be in the horn relay. Other checks should include bent metal contacts in the horn switch assembly, or loose or broken wires in the system.

5 To reach the components of the horn switch, first pull off the center steering wheel pad. Remove the recessed screw above the shaft (photo), and the 2 screws on the underside of the steering wheel (photo). Lift off the horn switch cover and unplug the wire from the steering wheel.

8 Headlight – adjustment

1 The headlight adjustment screws are located to the side and top of each lamp. The top screw adjusts the lamp's beam vertically and the

7.1 The horns are mounted behind the front bumper and below each headlight

7.5a The horn switch cover on the steering wheel is held on by one screw at the front ...

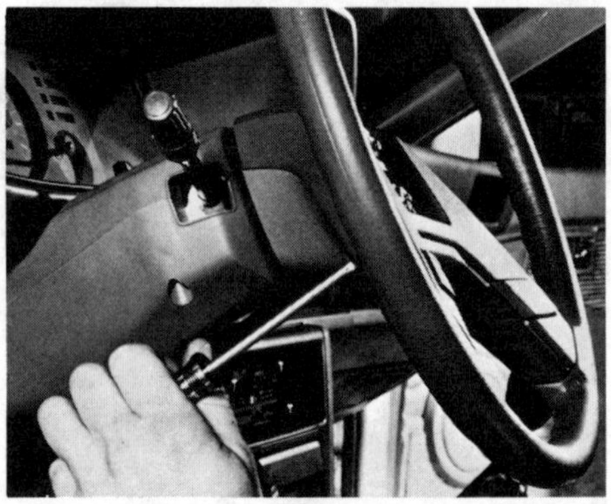

7.5b ... and two screws at the rear

9.2 The headlight trim upper retainers must be rotated 45° to remove them

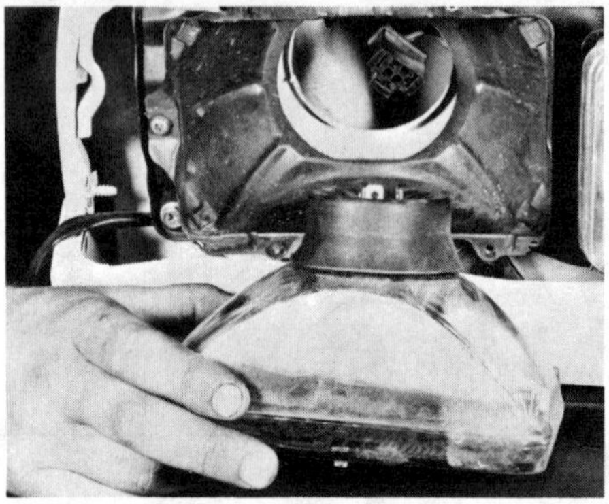

9.5 The headlight bulb uses a single electrical connector

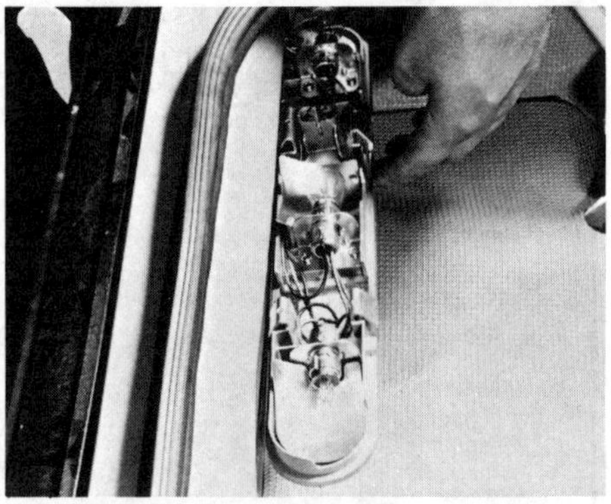

10.2 The taillight rear panel unsnaps and lifts off for access to the bulbs

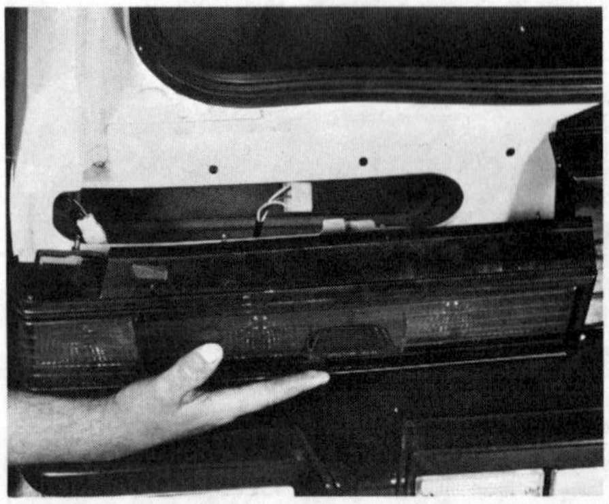

10.8 The taillight assembly is held to the body by 8 nuts

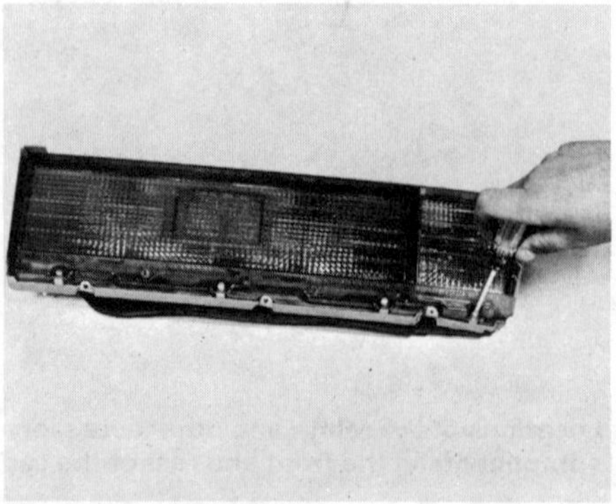

10.10 The taillight lens is held to the assembly by 8 screws

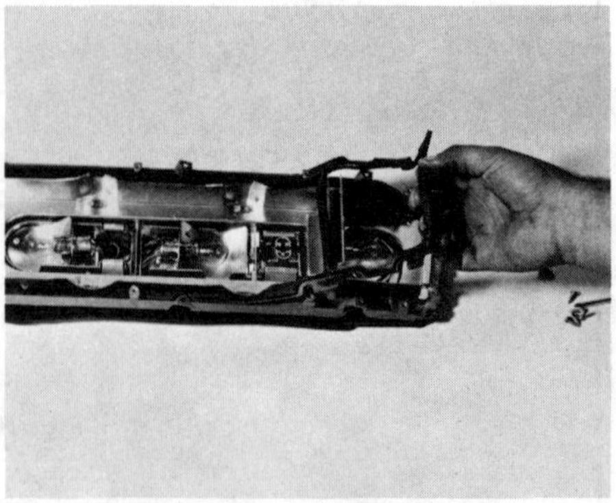

10.11 The taillight gasket should be replaced if hardened, cracked or torn

side screw adjusts the beam horizontally. Although due to legal specifications, proper adjustment of the headlights should be done using appropriate beam setting equipment, the following procedure will get them very close. Final adjustment should be done by a qualified mechanic with the proper equipment.
2 Position the car on level ground, facing and at right angles to a wall, and at a distance of approximately 30 feet.
3 Measure the height of the centers of the headlights from the ground and mark these measurements on the wall.
4 Measure the distance from the centerline of the car and the center of each headlight and mark these measurements on the wall, so that you have intersecting lines even with the center of each headlight.
5 Turn on the regular beam of the headlights and turn the horizontal adjusting screws until each beam is centered with their corresponding marks on the wall. Then, turn the vertical adjusting screw until the top of each beam is level with the horizontal centerline mark on the wall.
6 Bounce the car on its suspension and check that the beams return to their correct positions.

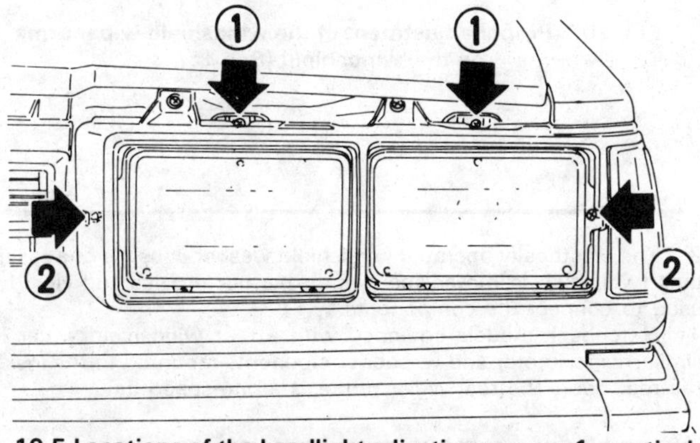

Fig. 10.5 Locations of the headlight adjusting screws: 1 - vertical adjustment, 2 - horizontal adjustment (Sec 8)

9 Headlight – removal and installation

1 Open the hood.
2 The headlight trim piece is secured to the body by 2 retainers along the upper edge and 1 screw on the side next to the turn signal lamp. Remove the screw, then with a flat-blade screwdriver, simply turn the retainers until they line up with the trim piece mounting holes (photo), and pull the top of the trim piece free. Finally, use the screwdriver again to pry loose the 2 locking clips along the lower edge.
3 Lift the trim piece off, and disconnect the wires leading to the turn signal lamp.
4 Remove the headlight retaining ring.
5 Lift the headlight out and disconnect the wiring connector (photo).
6 Installation is the reverse of the removal procedure. Prior to installing the trim piece, remove the 2 upper retainers from the body and fit them into the trim piece mounting holes. Then simply snap the trim piece into place and install the side mounting screw.

10 Taillight – bulb and lens replacement

Bulb replacement

1 On hatchback models, remove the rear trim panel to gain access to the rear of the taillight assembly.
2 The rear panel of the taillight assembly simply unsnaps from the rest of the assembly and can be lifted off to gain access to the bulbs (photo).
3 Replace bulbs as required.
4 Installation is the reverse of the removal procedure.

Lens replacement

5 Remove the rear trim panel.
6 Disconnect the wiring harness from the back of the taillight assembly.
7 Unsnap the rear panel of the taillight assembly and lift it off, complete with bulbs.
8 Remove the 8 nuts that retain the taillight assembly to the body, and lift off the taillight.
9 Remove the taillight trim piece from the assembly.
10 Remove the 8 screws that retain the lens to the assembly and lift off the lens (photo).
11 Inspect the gasket for tears, cracking, hardness or other damage and replace it if necessary. A defective gasket will allow moisture to get inside the taillight, which will result in corrosion.
12 Installation is the reverse of the removal procedure.

11 Turn signal parking lamp (front) – bulb and lens replacement

1 Remove the 2 screws that retain the turn signal lamp lens.
2 Either of the 2 bulbs can be removed by twisting counterclockwise and pulling it out of its socket.
3 Installation is the reverse of the removal procedure.

12 Side marker lamp (front and rear) – bulb and lens replacement

1 Remove the 2 screws that retain the lamp lens.
2 Remove the bulb by pulling it straight out of its socket.
3 Installation is the reverse of the removal procedure.

13 Backup lamp – bulb and lens replacement

1 Remove the 2 screws that retain the lens.
2 Remove the bulb by turning it and pulling it out of its socket.
3 Installation is the reverse of the removal procedure.

14 Interior lamp – bulb and lens replacement

Without spotlight

1 The interior lamp lens is simply removed by inserting a flat-blade

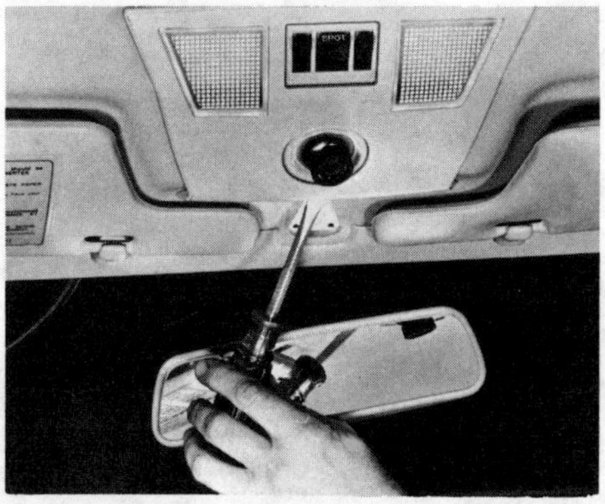

14.4 The interior lamp cover is pried off by using a flat-blade screwdriver

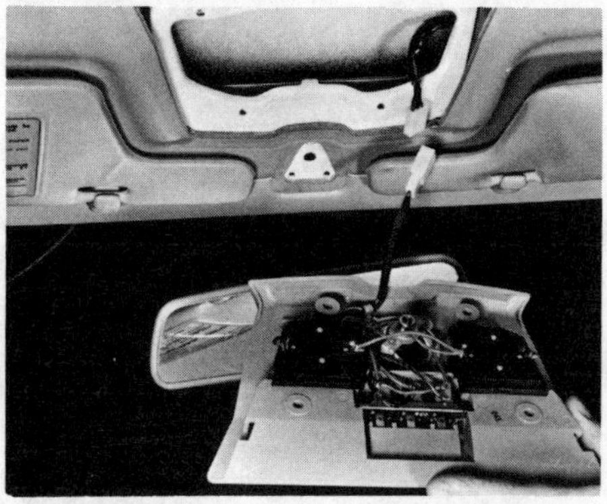

14.5 The interior lamp assembly is held to the ceiling by 4 screws

14.6 The bulb holders in the interior lamp are simply clipped onto the housing

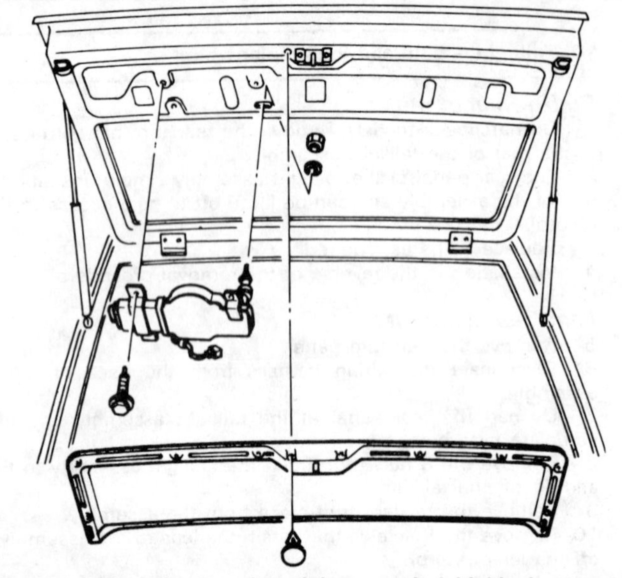

Fig. 10.6 Mounting location of the rear windshield wiper motor (Sec 15)

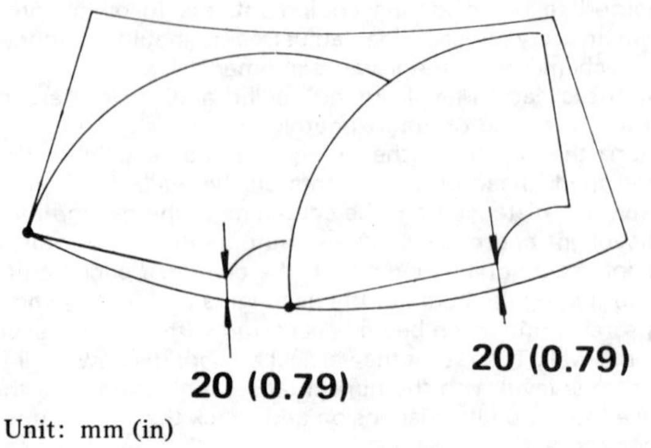

Fig. 10.7 Proper adjustment of the windshield wiper arms on the windshield (Sec 15)

screwdriver into the switch hole and carefully prying the lens off. The bulb can now be replaced.
2 To reinstall the lens, simply snap it back into place.

With spotlight

3 Remove the 2 screws that retain the small trim piece located directly over the rear view mirror.
4 Insert a flat-blade screwdriver into the front of the interior lamp cover (photo) and carefully pry the cover off.
5 Remove the 4 screws retaining the lamp assembly to the ceiling, disconnect the wiring connector and remove the assembly (photo).
6 If either of the interior lamp bulbs need replacing, simply unclip the bulb holder (photo), replace the bulb and snap the holder back into its slot.
7 If there is any problem with the spotlight, light switch or bulb connectors, the entire electrical assembly must be replaced as a unit.
8 Installation is the reverse of the removal procedure. The interior lamp cover simply snaps back into place.

15 Windshield wiper system

General description

1 The windshield wiper consists of a wiper motor unit, link mechanism, wiper arms, blades and an intermittent amplifier.
2 The motor incorporates an auto-stop device and operates the wipers in three diffferent stages: intermittent, low speed, and high speed.
3 The electrically operated windshield washer consists of a reservoir tank (with built-in motor and pump), washer nozzles and vinyl tubes used to connect the components.
4 Hatchback models equipped with a rear windshield wiper have similar wiper motor and washer components mounted to the inside of the rear door. The rear wiper motor is a one-speed unit.

Wiper blade – removal and installation

5 The wiper blade is removed by simply depressing the release tab at the end of the wiper arm (photo), and pulling the blade out from the arm.
6 If it is necessary to remove the rubber element from the blade, compress and remove the locking clip from the bottom of the wiper blade (photo) and slide the element out.

Wiper arm – removal and installation

7 Remove the nut that secures the wiper arm to the linkage (photo), and lift the arm off.
8 When installing the wiper arm, be sure it is lined up with the other arm, and check for proper positioning on the shaft.

Wiper motor – removal and installation

9 Remove the left wiper arm as described above.
10 Lift the hood.
11 Remove the 3 screws that hold the left cowl panel to the body and lift off the panel.
12 Remove the plastic cover from the top of the wiper motor and disconnect the electrical connector from the motor.

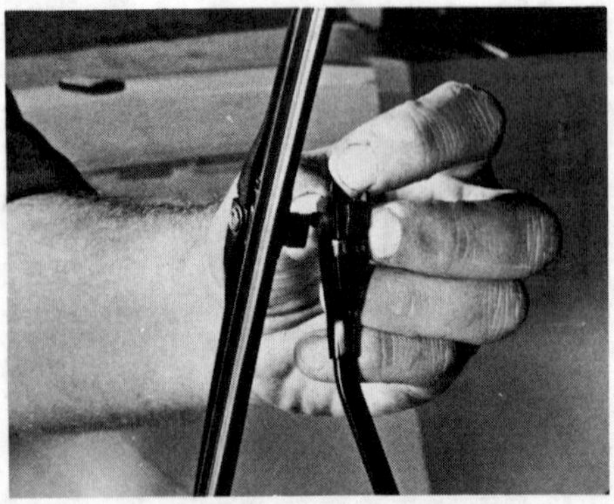

15.5 The wiper blade is released from the wiper arm by depressing the release tab

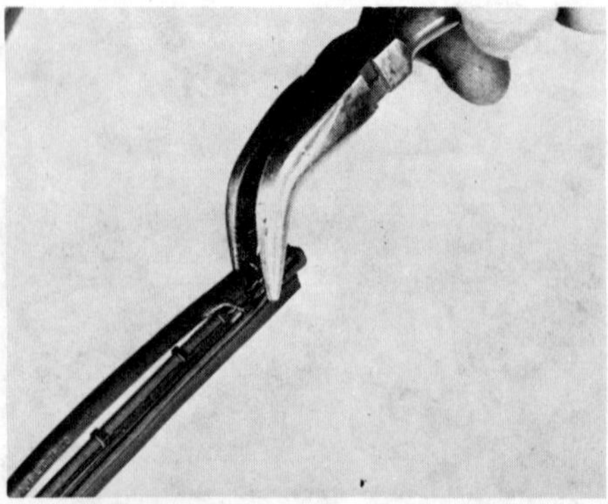

15.6 To remove the rubber element, the locking clip at the bottom of the wiper blade must be removed

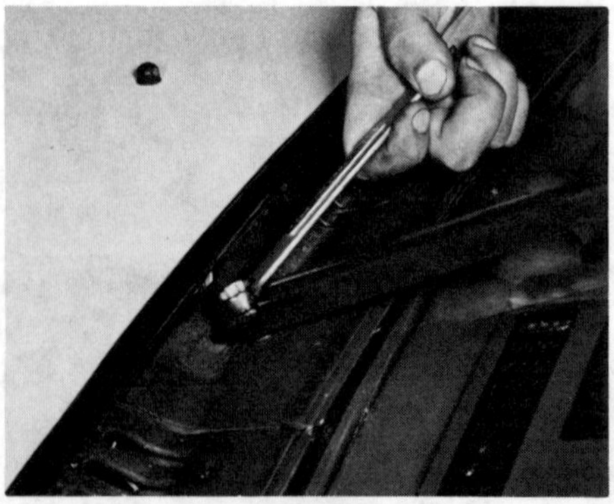

15.7 The wiper arm is attached to the linkage by one nut

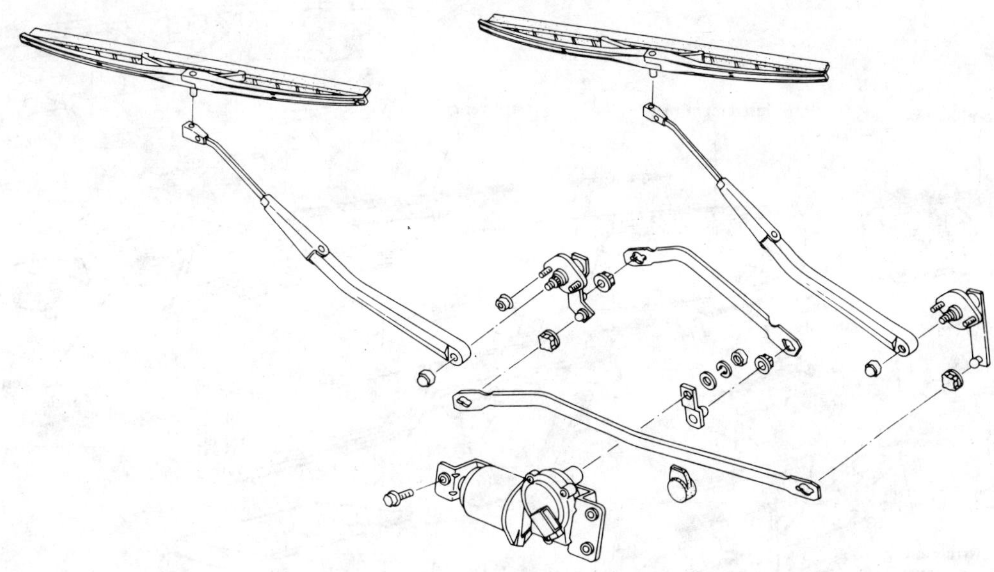

Fig. 10.8 Exploded view of the front windshield wiper system (Sec 15)

13 Remove the 3 screws that attach the motor to the body.
14 Lift the motor out of its recess far enough to remove the nut that attaches it to the linkage.
15 Remove the motor from the car.
16 Installation is the reverse of the removal procedure.

Linkage assembly – removal and installation

17 If the wiper blades strike or ride over the windshield frame this is an indication that the bushings in the linkage are worn and need replacing.
18 Remove both wiper arms as described above.
19 Remove both cowl panels.
20 Remove the wiper motor as described above.
21 The linkage is held to the body by 4 nuts. Remove these nuts and allow the linkage to drop out of its mounting holes. Withdraw the linkage through the openings in the cowl.
22 Once removed, the linkage can be disassembled as required.
23 Installation is the reverse of the removal procedure. Prior to installation, apply a little grease to the pivots and moving parts of the assembly.

Windshield washer – servicing

24 The washer fluid reservoir is located on the relay bracket within the engine compartment. The washer pump is mounted under the fluid reservoir.
25 Normally the windshield washers fitted to both the hardtop and the hatchback rear door require no maintenance other than keeping the reservoirs topped-up with water, to which a little windshield cleaning fluid has been added.
26 If the washer reservoirs or electric pump have to be renewed individually, they may be separated after disconnecting the connecting pipes and leads.
27 With regard to the front washer reservoir, when reconnecting the pump to the base of the reservoir, warm the reservoir by immersing it in hot water and use a solution of soapy water to lubricate the neck of the pump opening in the reservoir.

Rear wiper motor (hatchback) – removal and installation

28 Disconnect the battery ground cable.
29 Remove the wiper blade arm.
30 Open the rear door and carefully remove the trim panel.
31 Disconnect the wiper motor wire connectors.
32 Loosen and remove the three motor attaching bolts and lift away the motor.
33 When installing the motor, follow the reverse sequence to removal.
34 Finally, with the motor installed, position the wiper arm assembly to the motor spindle in such a manner that there is 0.390 in (10.0 mm) clearance between the bottom edge of the tailgate glass and the wiper arm.

Intermittent amplifier – general

35 The intermittent amplifier, which is located on the engine compartment relay mounting bracket, controls the intermittent operation of the wipers.
36 In the unlikely event of its failure, it is not possible to repair the amplifier and it must be renewed as an assembly.

16 Steering column combination switch – removal and installation

1 Remove the steering wheel as described in Chapter 11.
2 Unsnap the lower instrument cover, located directly below the steering column, from the dash.
3 Remove the 7 screws that retain the lower switch cover (photo).
4 Unsnap the lower cover from the upper cover and remove the fiber optic and fitting from the lower cover (photo).
5 Disconnect the electrical connector that leads to the hazard switch in the top cover and lift off the top cover.
6 If the hazard switch needs to be replaced, remove the 2 screws that retain it to the upper cover of the steering switch assembly (photo) and lift off the hazard switch.
7 Disconnect the 4 electrical connectors running to the steering column switch assembly.
8 Loosen the steering column switch clamp screw and slide the switch assembly off of the steering column shaft (photo).
9 If the headlight switch is defective, remove the 2 screws that retain it to the switch assembly and lift it off. **Note**: *Check with your local dealer as to the availability of individual components. Some dealers may require you purchase the entire switch assembly as a unit.* The headlight switch can be further disassembled, if parts are available, so the individual defective terminals can be replaced without replacing the entire switch.
10 If the windshield wiper switch or lever is defective, remove them from the assembly by removing the 4 screws that retain them and lifting them off of the assembly.
11 If the turn signal switch is defective, remove the 2 screws that retain it to the assembly and lift it out.
12 When installing the switch assembly onto the steering column shaft, be sure the tang in the retaining clamp lines up with the hole in the shaft.
13 The remainder of the installation procedure is the reverse of the removal procedure. When installing the lower switch assembly cover, route the wiring harnesses in between the center screw receivers.

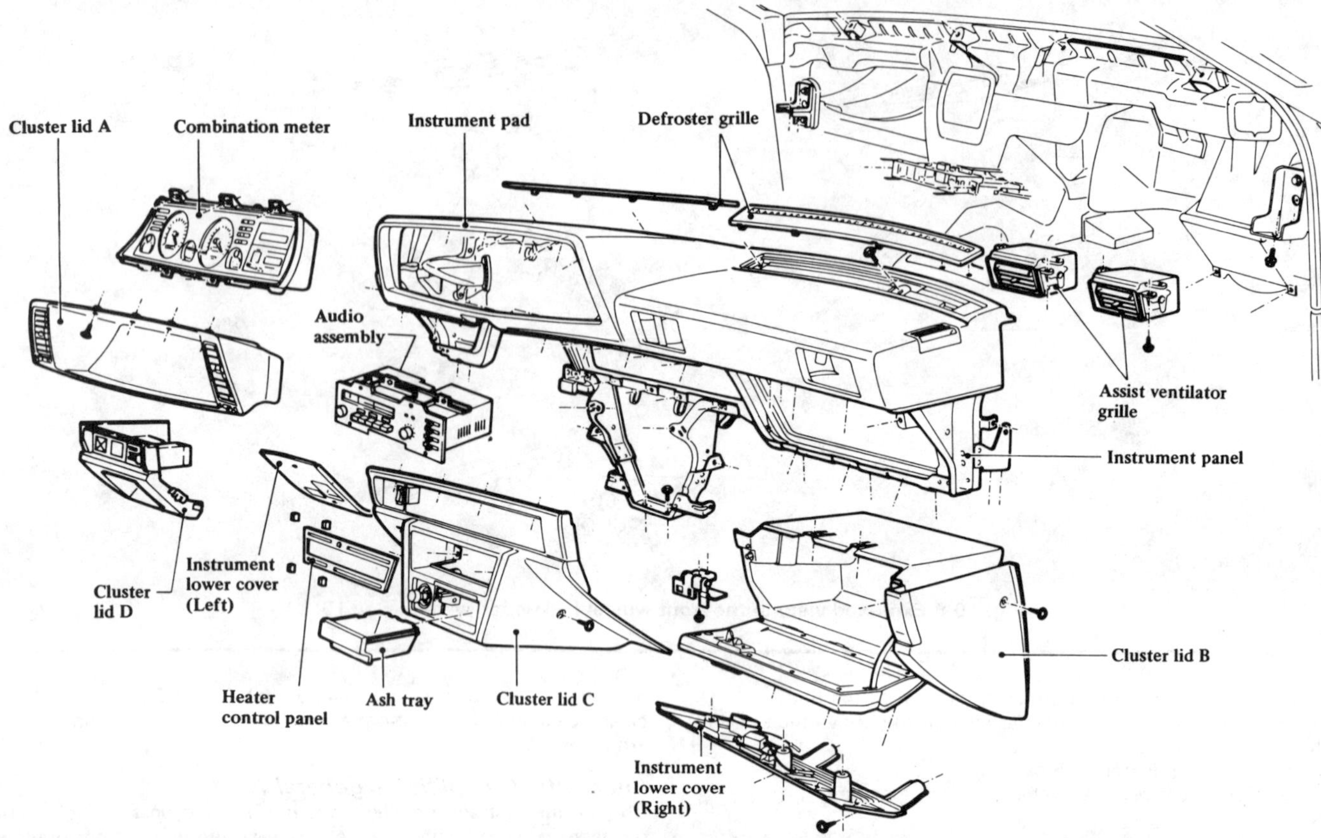

Fig. 10.9 Exploded view of the dash components

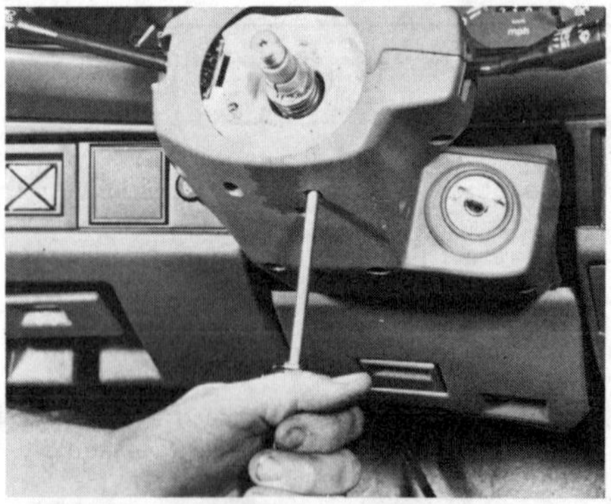

16.3 Removing the 7 screws that retain the steering column covers

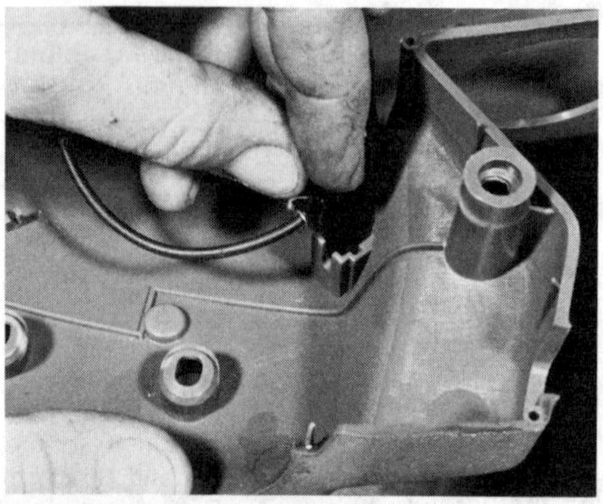

16.4 When removing the steering column covers, be careful not to damage the fiber optic fitting

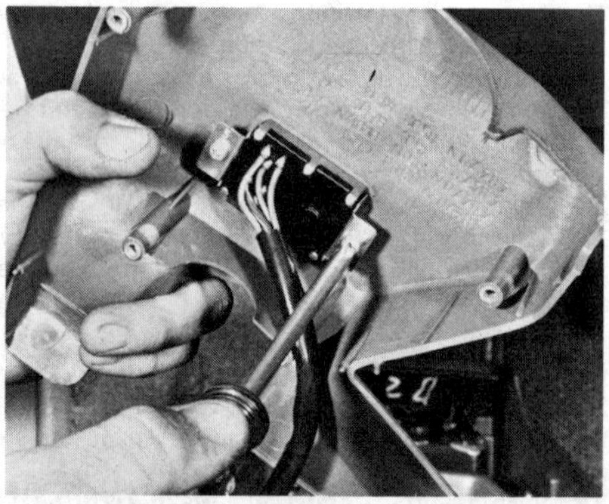

16.6 The hazard warning switch is held to the upper steering column cover by 2 screws

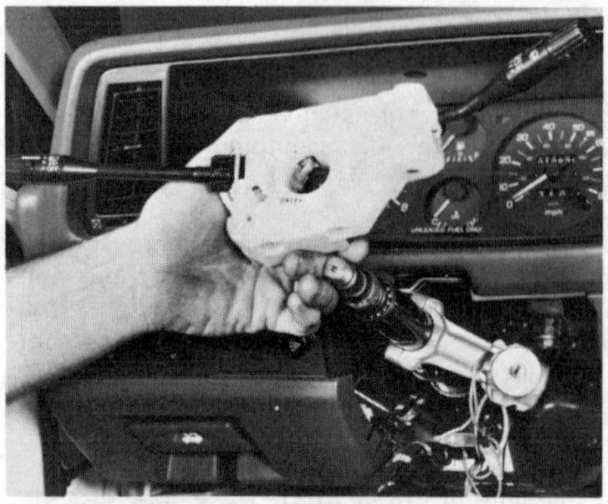

16.8 Depending upon parts availability, the combination switch may have to be replaced as one unit

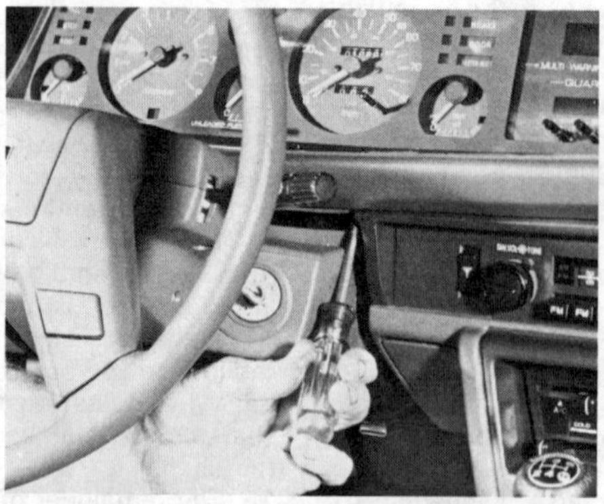

18.4 The instrument cluster is held to the dash by 5 screws

18.6 During removal, the instrument cluster should be rotated upward in order to reach the rear connections

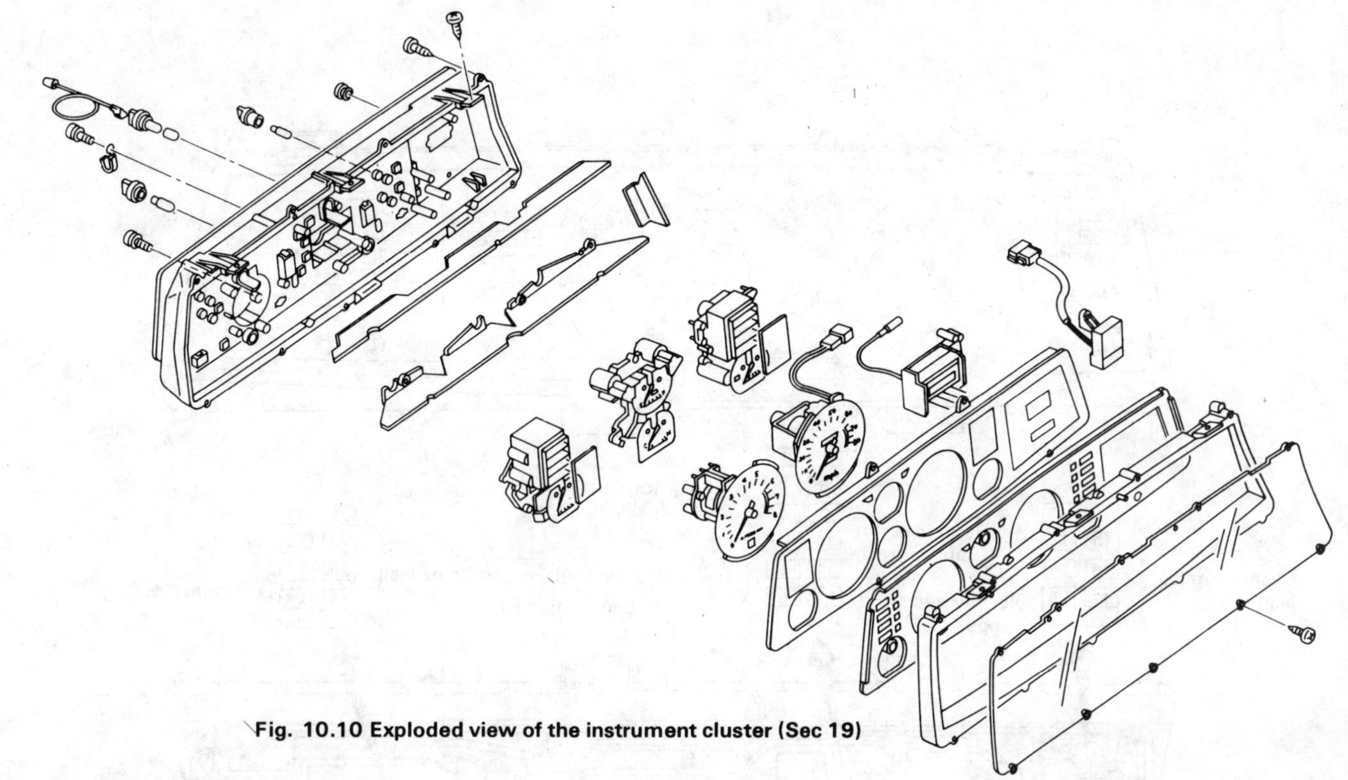

Fig. 10.10 Exploded view of the instrument cluster (Sec 19)

17 Ignition switch – removal and installation

Refer to the steering lock removal and installation procedure described in Chapter 11, Section 22.

18 Instrument cluster – removal and installation

1 Disconnect the negative battery cable.
2 Remove the 4 screws at the top of the cluster hood (photo).
3 Carefully twist the cluster hood out from the dash panel. Take note that there are 2 locating tabs at the bottom of the hood that must be disengaged. The left hand vent duct will come out with the hood. If so, remove it from the cluster and reinstall it in its position in the dash. The lower left instrument panel will have to be removed to do this.
4 Remove the 5 screws that secure the instrument cluster to the dash.
5 Reach your arm under the dash so you can disconnect the speedometer cable from the rear of the instrument cluster. The cable is disconnected by pushing in and rotating it 180° counterclockwise.
6 Carefully rotate the instrument cluster so the face is pointing directly up.
7 Carefully disconnect the 4 electrical connectors from the rear of the instrument panel. Be careful that you do not tear or damage the printed circuit.
8 Carefully remove the fiber optic receptacle by twisting it out of the rear of the instrument cluster.
9 Remove the instrument cluster from the dash.
10 Installation is the reverse of the removal procedure.

19 Gauges and indicators – removal and installation

Note: *Prior to removing any of the components from the instrument cluster, the following steps must be performed.*
1 Remove the instrument cluster as described in Section 18.
2 Remove the cluster lens.
3 Remove the cluster shield.
4 Remove the cluster trim plate.
5 Remove the front panel of the cluster.

Speedometer

6 Remove the screws that hold the speedometer to the cluster housing and lift out the speedometer.

Tachometer

7 Remove the screws that hold the tachometer to the cluster housing and lift out the tachometer (photo).

Fuel and water temperature gauges

8 The fuel and water temperature gauges are mounted together as one assembly, and if one needs replacing both must be replaced. First remove the speedometer and tachometer. Then remove the screws that attach the assembly to the cluster housing, and lift the gauges out.

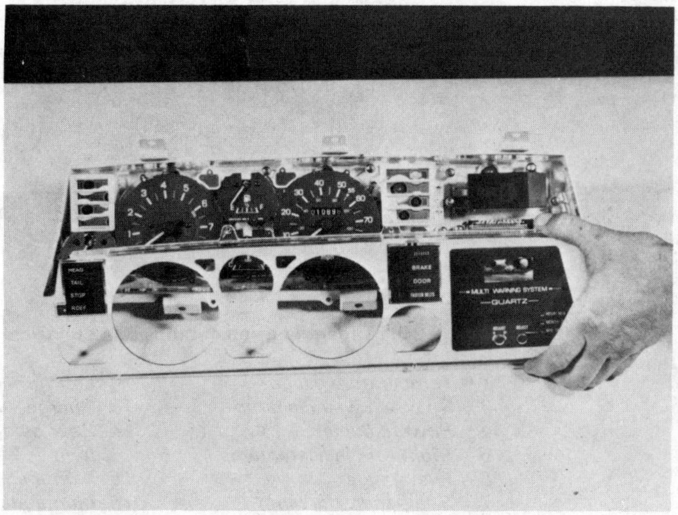

19.5 Removing the cluster front panel

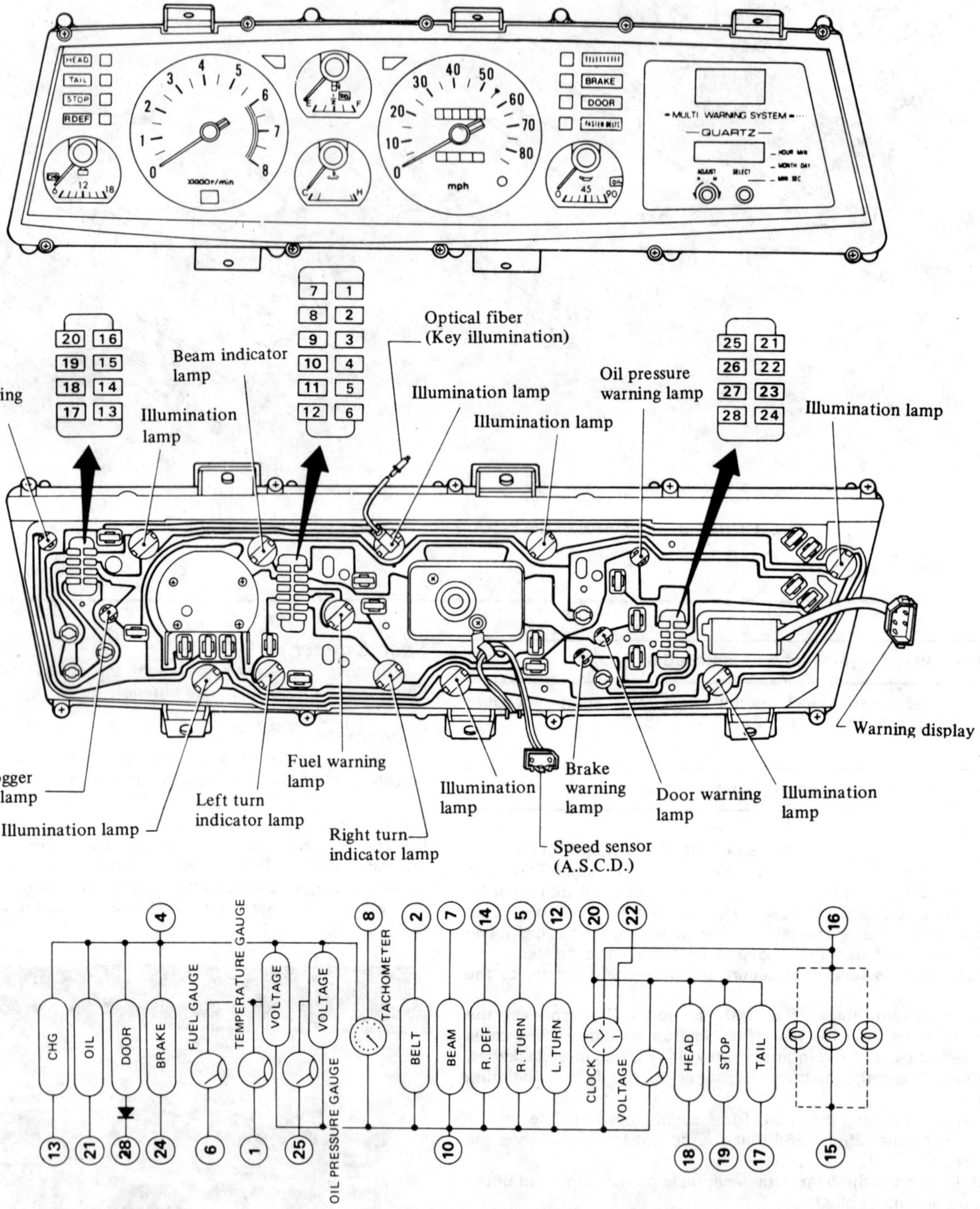

Fig. 10.11 Identification of bulbs and electrical connections in the instrument cluster (Sec 19)

1 Temperature gauge
2 Seat belt warning lamp
4 Power source
5 Right turn indicator lamp
6 Fuel gauge
7 Beam indicator lamp
8 Tachometer (signal)
10 Ground
12 Left turn indicator lamp
13 Charge warning lamp
14 Rear defogger indicator lamp
15 Illumination lamps
16 Illumination lamps
17 Tail lamp monitor lamp
18 Headlamp monitor lamp
19 Stop lamp monitor lamp
20 Clock (power source)
21 Oil pressure warning lamp
22 Clock (illumination)
24 Brake warning lamp
25 Oil pressure gauge
28 Door warning lamp

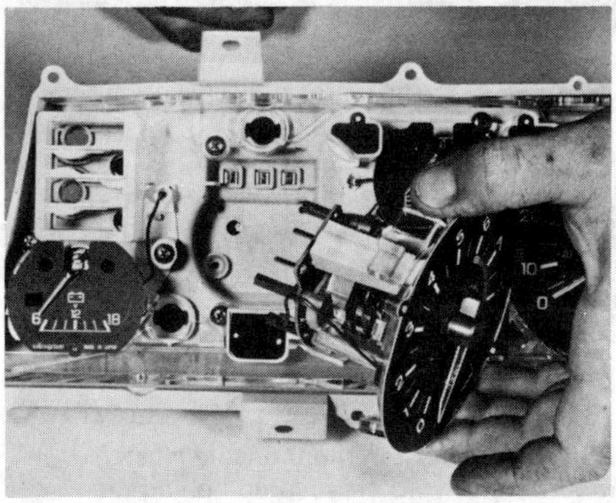

19.7 The screws that hold on the tachometer are removed from the rear of the cluster

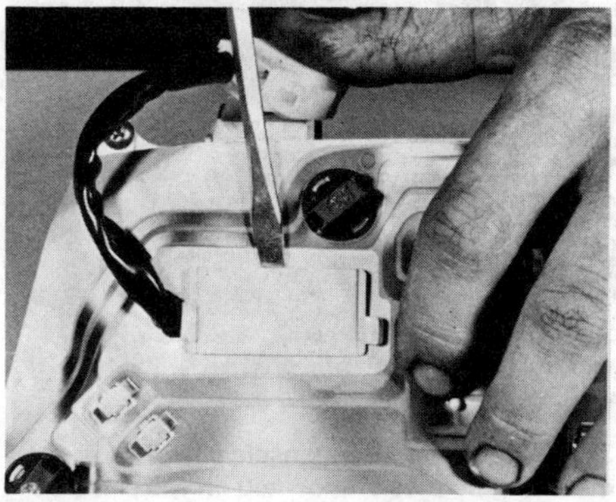

19.10 The rear cover of the multi-warning indicator compartment should be pried off with a screwdriver

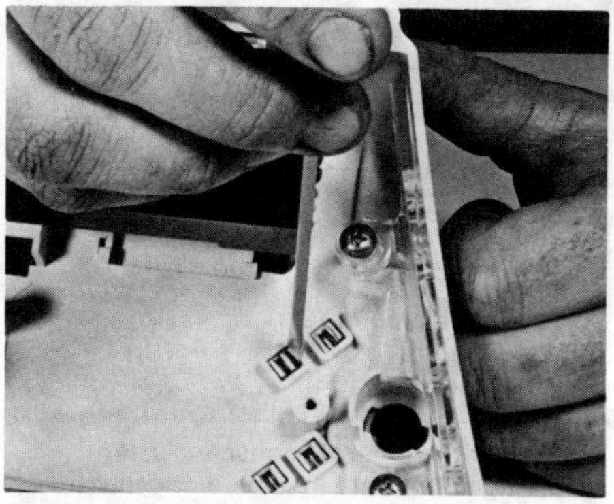

21.5 The printed circuit is secured by metal clips which can be pried out from the inside of the cluster housing

Oil pressure gauge and voltmeter

9 Both the oil pressure gauge and the voltmeter are part of assemblies that each include a bank of indicator lights. Remove the appropriate bulbs from the rear of the cluster. Then remove either the speedometer or tachometer for access to the mounting screws. Finally, remove the screws that attach the assembly to the cluster housing and lift it out.

Multi-warning indicator

10 Pry off the small cover located on the rear of the cluster housing, right behind the multi-warning indicator (photo).
11 Remove the screws that attach the indicator to the cluster housing and lift it out.

20 Clock – removal and installation

1 Remove the instrument cluster as described in Section 18.
2 Remove the cluster lens, shield, trim plate, and front panel.
3 Remove the screws that attach the clock to the cluster housing and lift the clock out.
4 Installation is the reverse of the removal procedure.

21 Printed circuit board – removal and installation

1 Remove the instrument cluster as described in Section 18.
2 Remove all of the bulbs from the instrument cluster.
3 Remove the speedometer, tachometer, multi-warning indicator, and all gauges as described in Section 19.
4 Remove the clock as described in Section 20.
5 Working from the inside of the cluster housing, use a screwdriver to pry out the metal clips which secure the printed circuit to the cluster (photo).
6 Installation is the reverse of the removal procedure. Be careful not to tear any part of the printed circuit during installation.

22 Console box – removal and installation

1 Remove the 2 forward mounting screws located on either side of the front of the console box.
2 Pull the emergency brake into the lock position and remove the access plate located at the bottom of the cavity immediately below the emergency brake handle.

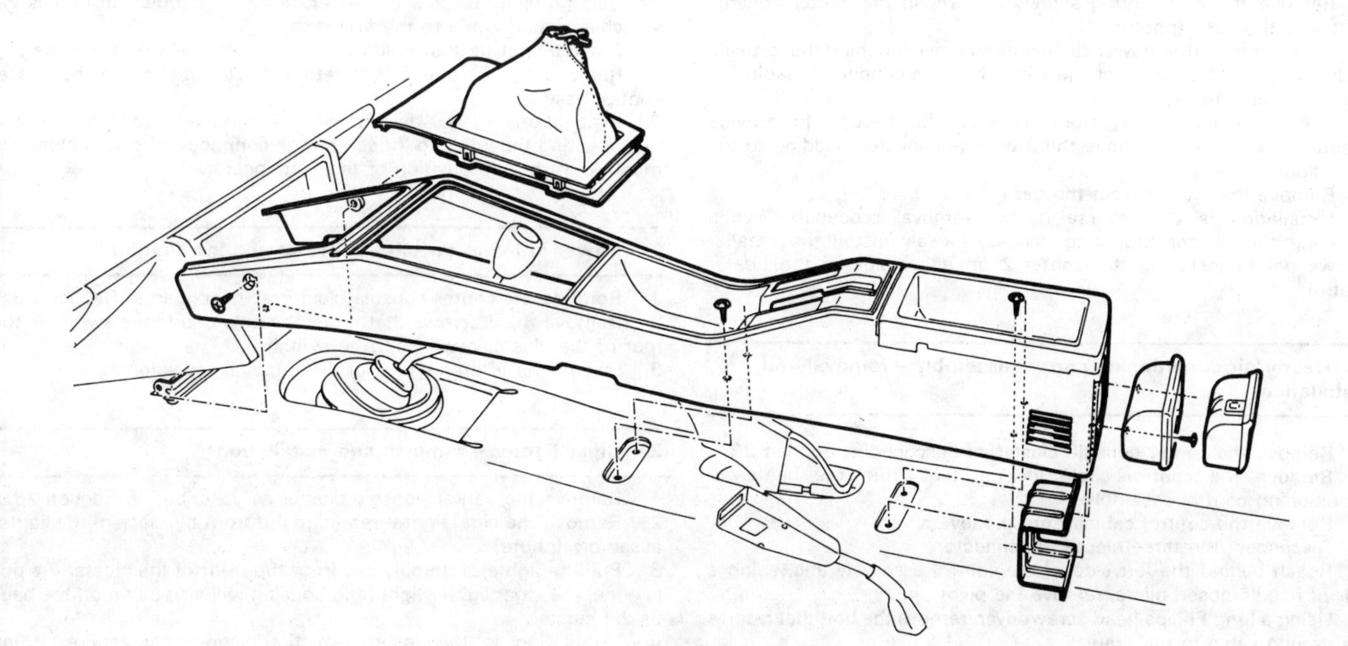

Fig. 10.12 Exploded view of the console box (Sec 22)

23.6a 4 of the 8 center console cluster mounting screws are located along the top

23.6b 2 of the center console cluster mounting screws are located on the sides

23.6c The final 2 center console cluster mounting screws are located behind the heater/AC control faceplate

3 Remove the 2 console box mounting screws located beneath the access plate.
4 Lift up the console box storage compartment lid and remove the cloth pad lining at the bottom of the storage compartment.
5 Remove the 2 console box mounting bolts located underneath the storage box pad.
6 Untie the leather cord at the top of the shifter boot.
7 Unclip and remove the shifter access panel from the console box.
8 Carefully slide the console box to the rear and lift it up so that you have access to the parking brake mounting bolt.
9 Remove the 2 emergency brake mounting bolts.
10 If equipped with a rear defroster switch or rear washer and wiper switch, disconnect the electrical connectors running to these switches.
11 Carefully lift off the console box.
12 Installation is the reverse of the removal procedure.

23 Center console cluster – removal and installation

1 Disconnect the negative battery cable.
2 Remove the ashtray from the cluster.
3 Unclip the left lower instrument panel, located directly below the steering column, and remove it from the dash.
4 Remove the 4 knobs from the heater control panel levers by pulling straight out.
5 Carefully pry out the heater/air conditioning control faceplate and remove the bulb and bulb socket from the rear of the plate.
6 Remove the 8 mounting screws that retain the center console cluster to the dash (photos).
7 If equipped with a power radio antenna, reach behind the left side of the cluster and disconnect the wiring harness connector leading to the power antenna switch.
8 Pull the cluster away from the dash far enough to provide adequate clearance to remove the 3 wiring connectors leading to the cigar lighter.
9 Remove the cluster from the dash.
10 Installation is the reverse of the removal procedure. When installing the cluster mounting screws, loosely install the smaller screws before installing the center 2 on either side of the heater control.

24 Heater/air conditioning control assembly – removal and installation

1 Remove the center console cluster as described in Section 23.
2 Remove the control cable locking clips from the heater/air conditioning control assembly.
3 Remove the control cables from the levers.
4 Disconnect the three electrical connectors.
5 Reach behind the left side of the control assembly and, using a pair of needle-nosed pliers, remove the pivot pin.
6 Using a long Philips head screwdriver, remove the bolt that retains the ground cable to the firewall.
7 Lift out the control assembly from the dash.
8 Begin the installation procedure by reversing steps 3 through 7. Prior to reinstalling the cable locking clips, the cables must be adjusted in the following manner:

a) Loosely install the mounting screws to hold the heater control assembly in place while the cables are adjusted.
b) Set the air intake lever to the recirculation (REC) position. While holding the lever in that position push the cable outer casing as far to the left as it will go (see accompanying figure). Then snap the cable retaining clip into position over the cable casing.
c) Place the temperature lever to the maximum cold position. While holding the lever in that position, pull the cable casing as far to the right as possible (see accompanying figure) and snap the retaining clip in place over the casing.
d) Set the air control lever to the defrost (DEF) position. While holding the lever in that position, push the cable casing as far to the right as possible (Fig. 10.15). Snap the locking clamp over the casing.
e) After all the cables have been secured in place, move all the levers through their full travel to make sure they are moving freely and there is no binding.
f) Remove the heater control assembly mounting screws again.

9 Reinstall the center console cluster.

25 Fan switch – removal and installation

1 Remove the center console cluster as described in Section 23.
2 Disconnect the wiring harness connector leading to the fan switch.
3 Using a long Philips screwdriver, remove the bolt that retains the switch's ground cable to the firewall.
4 Cut the spot tie that holds the heater control wiring together.
5 Remove the 2 screws that retain the fan switch to the heater control assembly.
6 Installation is the reverse of the removal procedure. When reconnecting the wires to the fan switch connector, the light blue wire must go in the top position of the T connector.

26 Power antenna switch – removal and installation

1 Remove the center console cluster as described in Section 23.
2 Remove the 2 screws that retain the power antenna switch to the rear of the cluster and lift off the switch.
3 Installation is the reverse of the removal procedure.

27 Cigar lighter – removal and installation

1 Remove the center console cluster as described in Section 23.
2 Remove the cigar lighter retaining nut from the back of the lighter assembly (photo).
3 Pull the lighter assembly out from the front of the cluster. As this is done, the cigar lighter light bulb housing will also come off the back of the cluster.
4 Installation is the reverse of the removal procedure. When installing the cigar lighter components, be sure all the components are lined up properly by engaging the locating tabs in their respective slots.

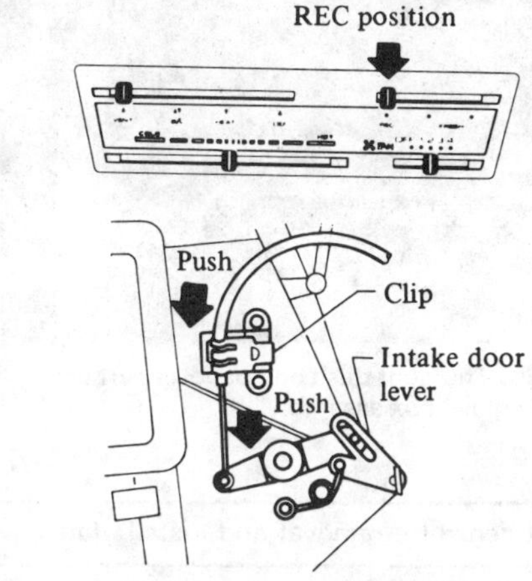

Fig. 10.13 Procedure for adjusting the air intake control cable (Sec 24)

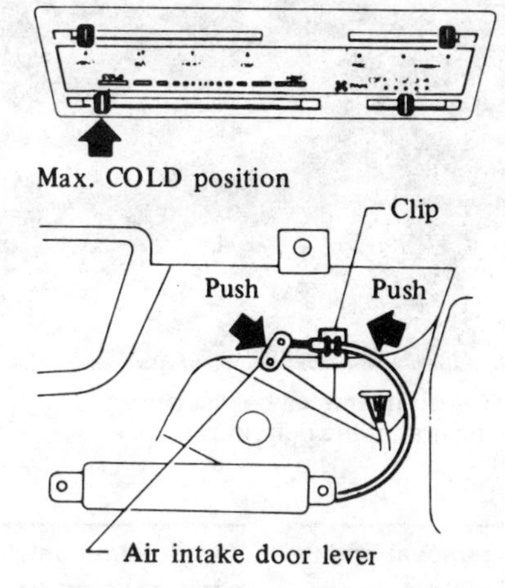

Fig. 10.14 Procedure for adjusting the temperature control cable (Sec 24)

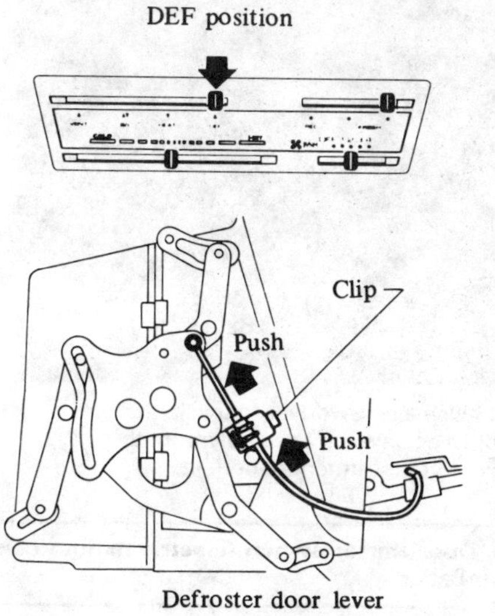

Fig. 10.15 Procedure for adjusting the air control cable (Sec 24)

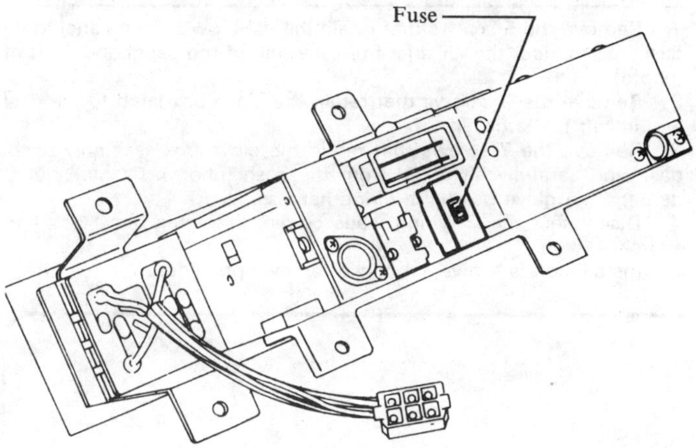

Fig. 10.16 In the event of radio failure, check the fuse in the rear of the unit (Sec 28)

28 Radio – removal and installation

1 Remove the center console cluster as described in Section 23.
2 Remove the 3 screws that retain the radio to the dash.
3 Pull the radio away from the dash and disconnect the electrical connectors and antenna plug from the rear of the radio.
4 To remove the faceplate from the front of the radio, pull off the 2 knobs and remove the 2 retaining nuts.
5 Installation is the reverse of the removal procedure.

29 Sound balancer – removal and installation (1980 models only)

1 Remove the center console cluster as described in Section 23.
2 Remove the 3 screws that retain the radio to the dash.
3 Pull the radio out from the dash to gain access to the sound balancer switch. The radio wiring does not have to be disconnected.
4 Remove the 2 screws that retain the sound balancer to the dash.
5 Lift the sound balancer off of the dash and disconnect its wiring connector.
6 Installation is a reversal of the removal procedure.

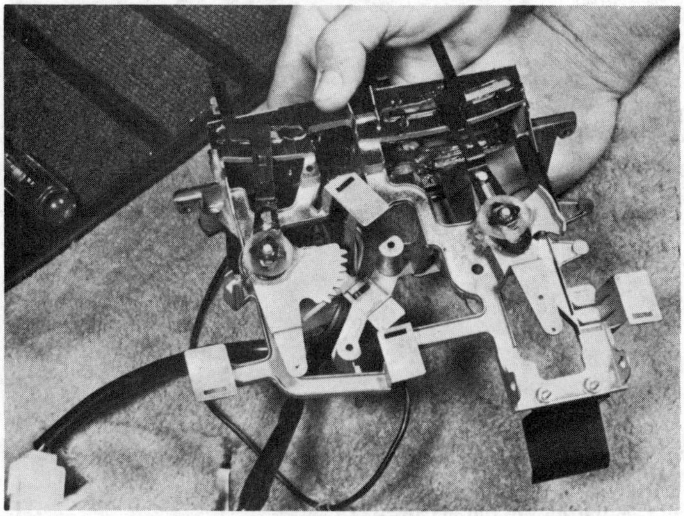

24.7 The heater/AC control assembly removed from the dash

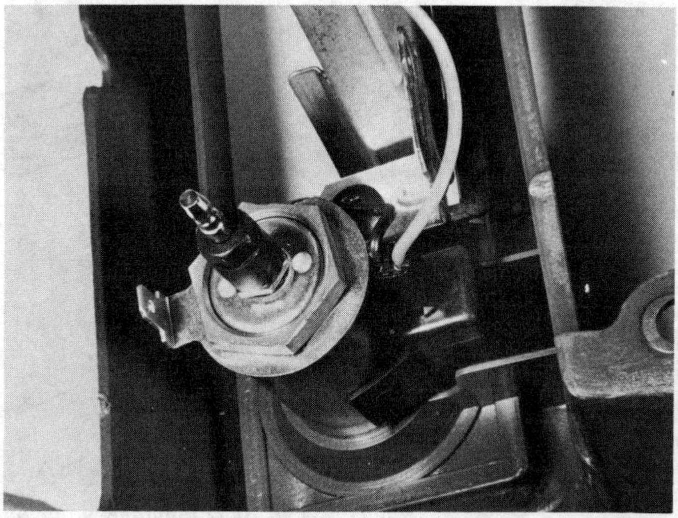

27.2 The cigar lighter is attached to the center console cluster by a retaining nut at the rear

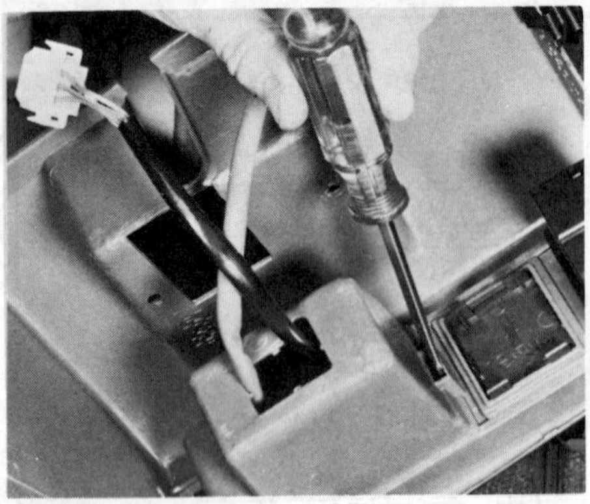

30.8 Use a screwdriver to unclip the door mirror switch assembly from the lower left instrument panel

32.1 The air duct must be disconnected from the rear of the right lower dash panel

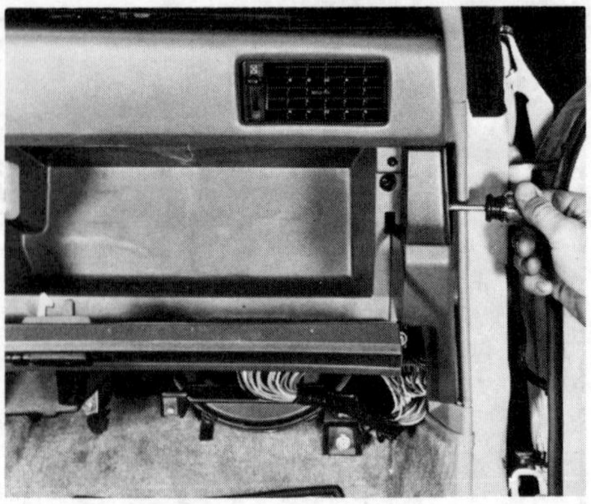

32.3 The right dash end panel is part of the glove box assembly

30 Door mirror switch (electric remote control) – removal and installation

1 Disconnect the negative battery cable.
2 Remove the lower dash panel, located directly below the steering column. It is retained by clips and simply unsnaps.
3 Remove the 5 screws that retain the lower left instrument panel to the dash.
4 Pull the hood release handle toward the rear of the car and remove the release handle bracket mounting screw that is toward the rear of the car. Then release the handle and remove the mounting screw toward the front of the car.
5 Remove the hood release cable and handle assembly from below the lower left instrument panel.
6 Pull the lower left instrument panel out from the dash so you can disconnect the 3 electrical connectors.
7 Remove the lower left instrument panel from the dash.
8 Working from the rear of the lower left instrument panel, use a screwdriver to release the locking tabs that hold the remote control door mirror to the panel (photo).
9 Installation is the reverse of removal.

31 Illumination rheostat control – removal and installation

1 Remove the lower left instrument panel by following the procedure detailed in steps 1 through 6 of Section 30.
2 Pull off the knob from the rheostat control and remove the nut that retains it to the instrument panel.
3 Installation is the reverse of the removal procedure.

32 Glove box – removal and installation

1 Remove the 5 screws that retain the right lower dash panel to the dash. Disconnect the air duct from the rear of the panel and lift it off (photo).
2 Remove the 2 screws that retain the glove box latch to the dash and lift off the latch.
3 Remove the 7 screws that retain the glove box assembly to the dash and carefully lift it out from the dash (photo). Be sure not to damage the glove box light wiring harness.
4 Disconnect the 2 wiring leads coming from the glove box light switch.
5 Installation is a reversal of the removal procedure.

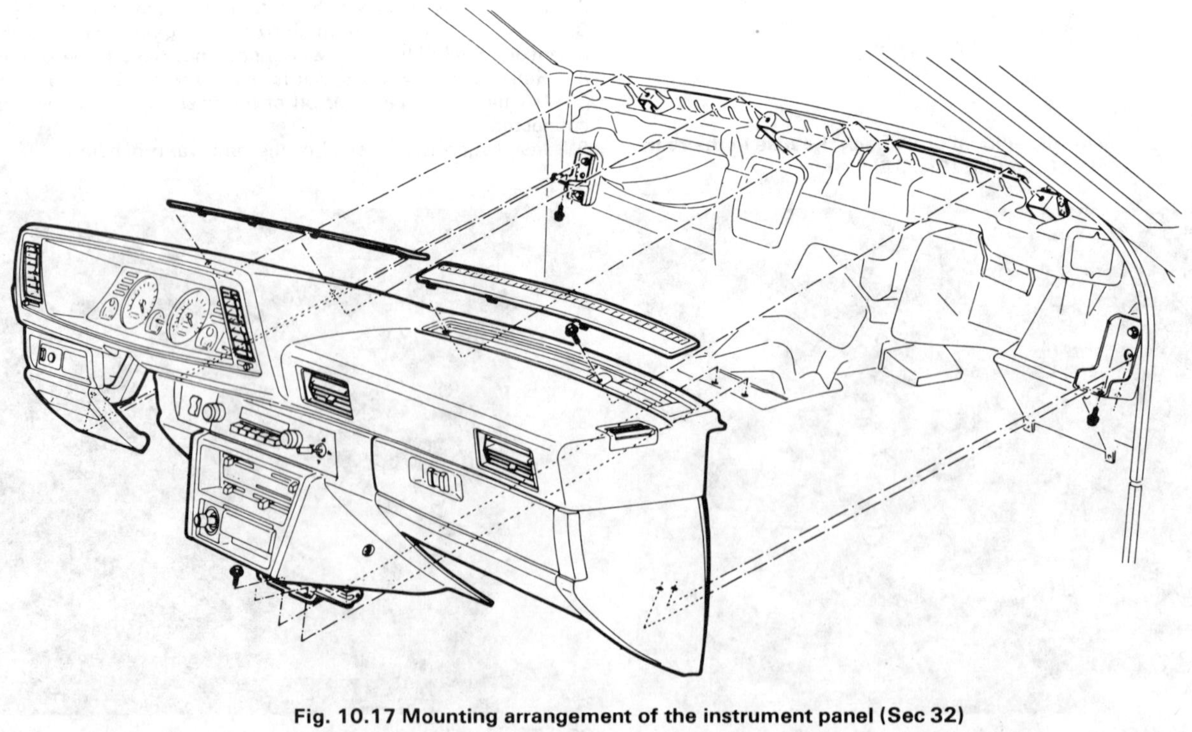

Fig. 10.17 Mounting arrangement of the instrument panel (Sec 32)

33 Instrument panel – removal and installation

1 Disconnect the negative battery cable.
2 Remove the steering wheel as described in Chapter 11.
3 Remove the steering column combination switch assembly as described in Section 16.
4 Remove the lower instrument covers located below the steering column and the glove box.
5 Remove the lower left instrument panel by following the procedure detailed in steps 1 through 6 of Section 30.
6 Remove the console box as described in Section 22.
7 Disconnect the wiring connectors from the junction box.
8 Disconnect the speedometer cable from the rear of the speedometer.
9 Disconnect all wiring harness connectors from the dash components.
10 Disconnect the antenna cable from the rear of the radio.
11 Remove the heater control attaching screws and the floor attaching bolts (see accompanying figures).

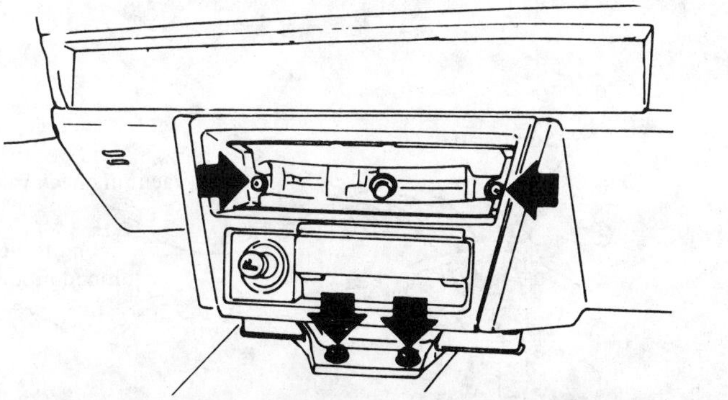

Fig. 10.18 Location of the dash mounting screws at the heater/AC control and the center floor (Sec 33)

12 Remove the defroster grille along the windshield.
13 Remove the instrument panel mounting bolts, and pull out the instrument panel.
14 Installation is the reverse of the removal procedure.

34 Speedometer cable – inspection and replacement

1 If the speedometer is noisy during operation or if the indicator needle wavers, the speedometer should be inspected for damage and alignment.
2 Visually inspect the length of the speedometer cable, checking that there are no sharp bends or other damage to the outer casing. Also check that the cable is properly installed in the speedometer.
3 If the initial inspection reveals no damage, disconnect the cable from the speedometer by pushing in and turning it 180° counterclockwise, and pull the inner cable from the casing.
4 Inspect the cable for worn spots, breaks or kinks. Any of these conditions necessitates replacement of the cable.
5 Prior to installing an inner cable, lubricate it with a suitable speedometer cable lubricant, to prevent rusting.

35 Speakers (front and rear) – removal and installation

1 Lift off the speaker grille. The front grille may have to be pryed off, but be careful not to tear the vinyl on the door trim panel.
2 Remove the speaker mounting screws.
3 Lift the speaker out of its mounting hole enough to disconnect the wires from the rear.
4 Installation is the reverse of the removal procedure.

36 Automatic Speed Control Device (ASCD) – general information

1 The ASCD is a cruise control system that allows the driver to

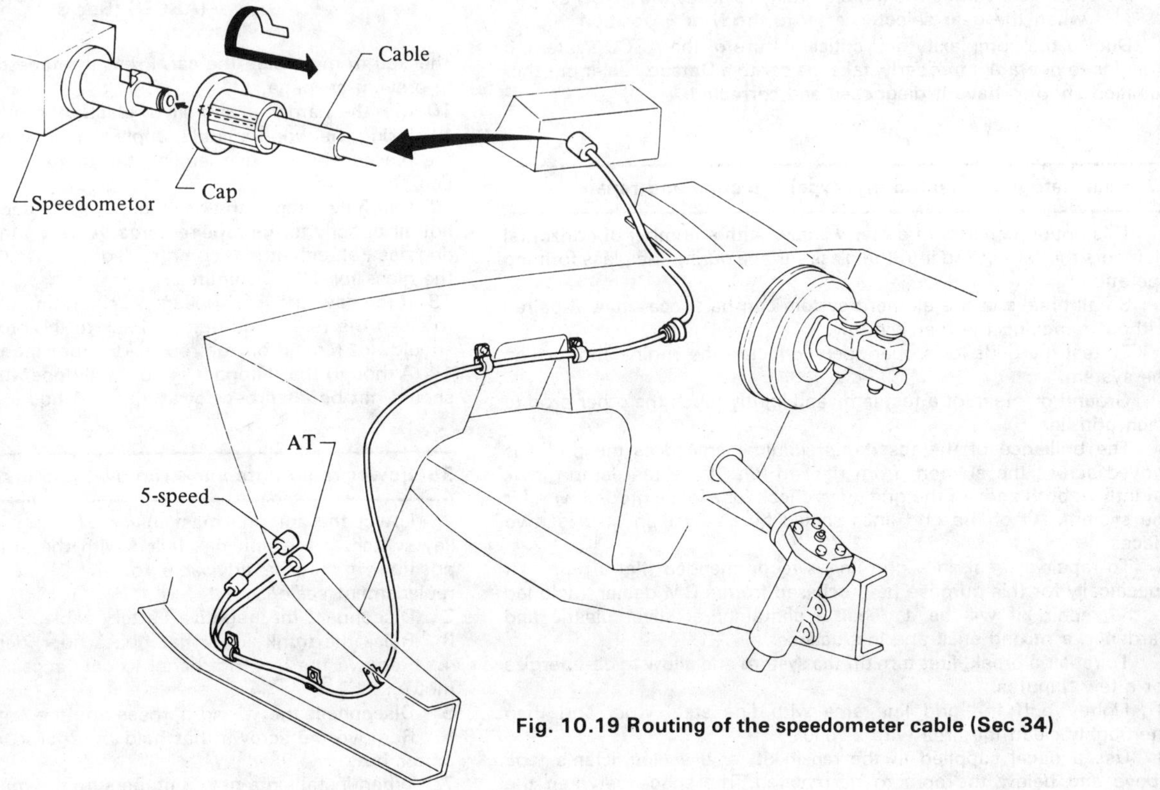

Fig. 10.19 Routing of the speedometer cable (Sec 34)

maintain a constant highway speed without the necessity of continually applying foot pressure to the accelerator pedal.
2 The system utilizes a combination of electronic and vacuum controls. Basically, the ASCD controller senses the difference between the preset speed and the actual speed picked up by the speed sensor in the speedometer, and transmits an electrical signal to the servo valve. The servo valve then adjusts the vacuum which operates the actuator, which, in turn, adjusts the throttle valve opening to maintain the speed at the desired setting.
3 See the accompanying figures for the components that comprise the ASCD system. They are:

a) **Main switch:** When the main switch is turned on (with the ignition switch on, also), the ASCD relay will become energized and will supply current to the system. The relay will turn off when the ignition switch is turned off, and will stay off until both the ignition switch and the main switch are once again turned on.
b) **Set switch:** When the set switch is depressed, the "cruise" light will illuminate and the controller will cancel the preset car speed. When the set switch is released, the controller will set the speed setting to the speed at which the car is running.
c) **Speed sensor:** The speed sensor is located in the speedometer, and signals the speed of the car by sending out two electrical pulses per revolution of the meter cable.
d) **Servo valve:** The servo valve controls the opening and closing of the vacuum valve and atmospheric valve according to the current received from the controller, and makes appropriate adjustments to the vacuum line from the intake manifold.
e) **Controller:** The controller compares the preset speed with the actual speed, and maintains the preset speed by increasing or decreasing the current flowing through the servo valve.
f) **Release valve:** This is the safety valve with shuts off the air bleed to the vacuum line when the system is activated.
g) **Actuator:** The actuator controls the opening and closing of the throttle valve, and is vacuum controlled by the servo valve.
h) **Stop switch:** When the brake pedal is depressed, the stop switch cuts off the power to the ASCD circuit and deactivates the system.
i) **Inhibitor relay:** The inhibitor relay releases the ASCD system when the gear selector is set to the N or P position.

4 Due to the complexity and critical nature of the ASCD system, if it begins to operate improperly, take the car to a Datsun dealer or other qualified shop to have it diagnosed and corrected.

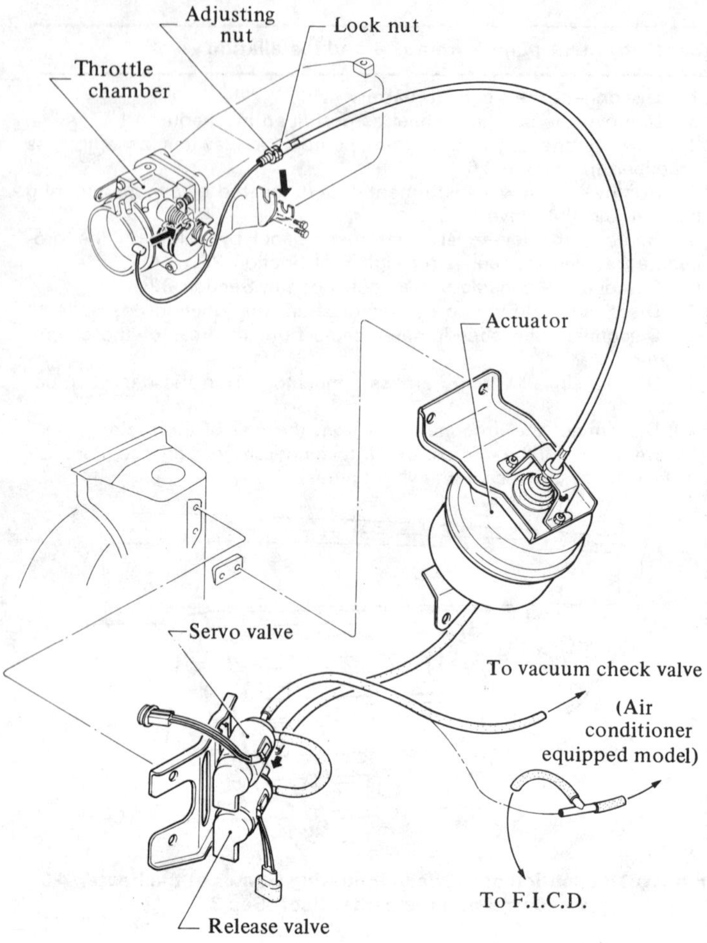

Fig. 10.20 Components of the Automatic Speed Control Device (ASCD) (Sec 36)

37 Rear defogger (electric grid-type) – testing and repair

1 This option consists of a rear window with a number of horizontal elements that are baked into the glass surface during the glass forming operation.
2 Small breaks in the element system can be successfully repaired without removing the rear window.
3 To test the grids for proper operation, start the engine and turn on the system.
4 Ground one lead of a test lamp and lightly touch the other prod to each grid line.
5 The brilliance of the test lamp should increase as the probe is moved across the element from right to left. If the test lamp glows brightly at both ends of the grid lines, check for a loose ground wire for the system. All of the grid lines should be checked in at least two places.
6 To repair a break in a grid line is recommended that a repair kit specifically for this purpose be purchased from a GM dealer. Included in the repair kit will be a decal, a container of silver plastic and hardener, a mixing stick and instructions.
7 To repair a break, first turn off the system and allow to de-energize for a few minutes.
8 Lightly buff the grid line area with fine steel wool and then thoroughly clean the area with alcohol.
9 Use a decal supplied in the repair kit, or use electrician's tape above and below the area to be repaired. The space between the pieces of tape should be the same as existing grid lines. This can be checked from outside the car. Press the tape tightly against the glass to prevent seepage.
10 Mix the hardener and silver plastic thoroughly.
11 Using the wood spatula, apply the silver plastic mixture between the pieces of tape, overlapping the damaged area slightly on either end.
12 Carefully remove the decal or tape and apply a constant stream of hot air directly to the repaired area. A heat gun gun set at 500 to 700 degrees Fahrenheit is recommended. Hold the gun about 1 inch from the glass for 1 to 2 minutes.
13 If the new grid line appears off color, tincture of iodine can be used to clean the repair and bring it back to the proper color. This mixture should not remain on the repair for more than 30 seconds.
14 Although the defogger is now fully operational, the repaired area should not be disturbed for at least 24 hours.

38 Power radio antenna – removal and installation

1 Lower the antenna mast fully by turning off the radio or ignition key switch. If the unit has failed with the antenna mast in the 'Up' position, it may be advisable to cut off the mast portion to make replacement easier.
2 Disconnect the negative battery cable.
3 Raise the trunk lid (or hatchback door, depending upon model).
4 Remove the left trim panel to gain access to the power antenna motor.
5 Disconnect the wiring harness and the antenna lead.
6 Remove the screws that hold the motor to the body and lift the motor out.
7 When installing a new unit, be sure the mast is fully retracted and that both ground screws are tight.

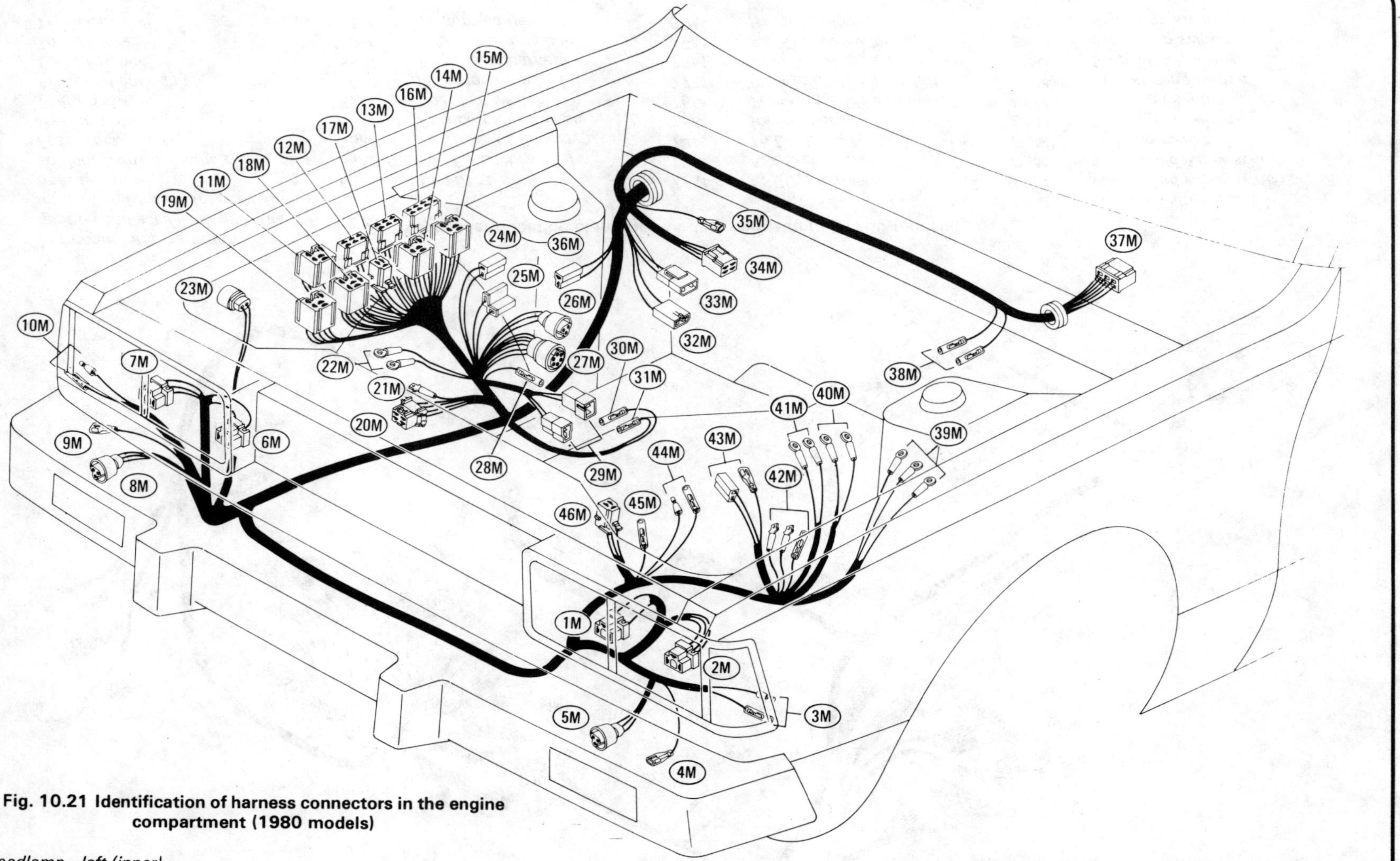

Fig. 10.21 Identification of harness connectors in the engine compartment (1980 models)

1M	*Headlamp - left (inner)*	*13M*	*Headlamp sensor*	*24M*	*Windshield washer motor*	*35M*	*Magnet air valve No. 2 (FICD)*
2M	*Headlamp - left (outer)*	*14M*	*Intermittent wiper amplifier*	*25M*	*Windshield washer sensor*	*36M*	*Rear window washer motor*
3M	*Side marker lamp - left*	*15M*	*ASCD relay*	*26M*	*To 8E*	*37M*	*Windshield wiper*
4M	*Horn*	*16M*	*Bulb check relay*	*27M*	*To 7E*	*38M*	*Brake fluid level switch*
5M	*Front combination lamp - left*	*17M*	*Horn relay*	*28M*	*To 6E*	*39M*	*Terminal block (for California models)*
6M	*Headlamp - right (inner)*	*18M*	*Inhibitor relay*	*29M*	*Alternator*	*40M*	*Ignition coil 1*
7M	*Headlamp - right (outer)*	*19M*	*Fuel pump relay - 1*	*30M*	*Thermal transmitter*	*41M*	*Ignition coil 2 (for California models)*
8M	*Front combination lamp - right*	*20M*	*Fusible link*	*31M*	*Condenser*	*42M*	*Condenser*
9M	*Horn*	*21M*	*Battery sensor*	*32M*	*Servo valve (ASCD)*	*43M*	*Distributor*
10M	*Side marker lamp - right*	*22M*	*Body earth*	*33M*	*Release valve (ASCD)*	*44M*	*Low pressure switch*
11M	*EFI relay*	*23M*	*Radiator sensor*	*34M*	*Air conditioner relay*	*45M*	*Magnet clutch*
12M	*Fuel pump relay - 2*					*46M*	*To EFI harness*

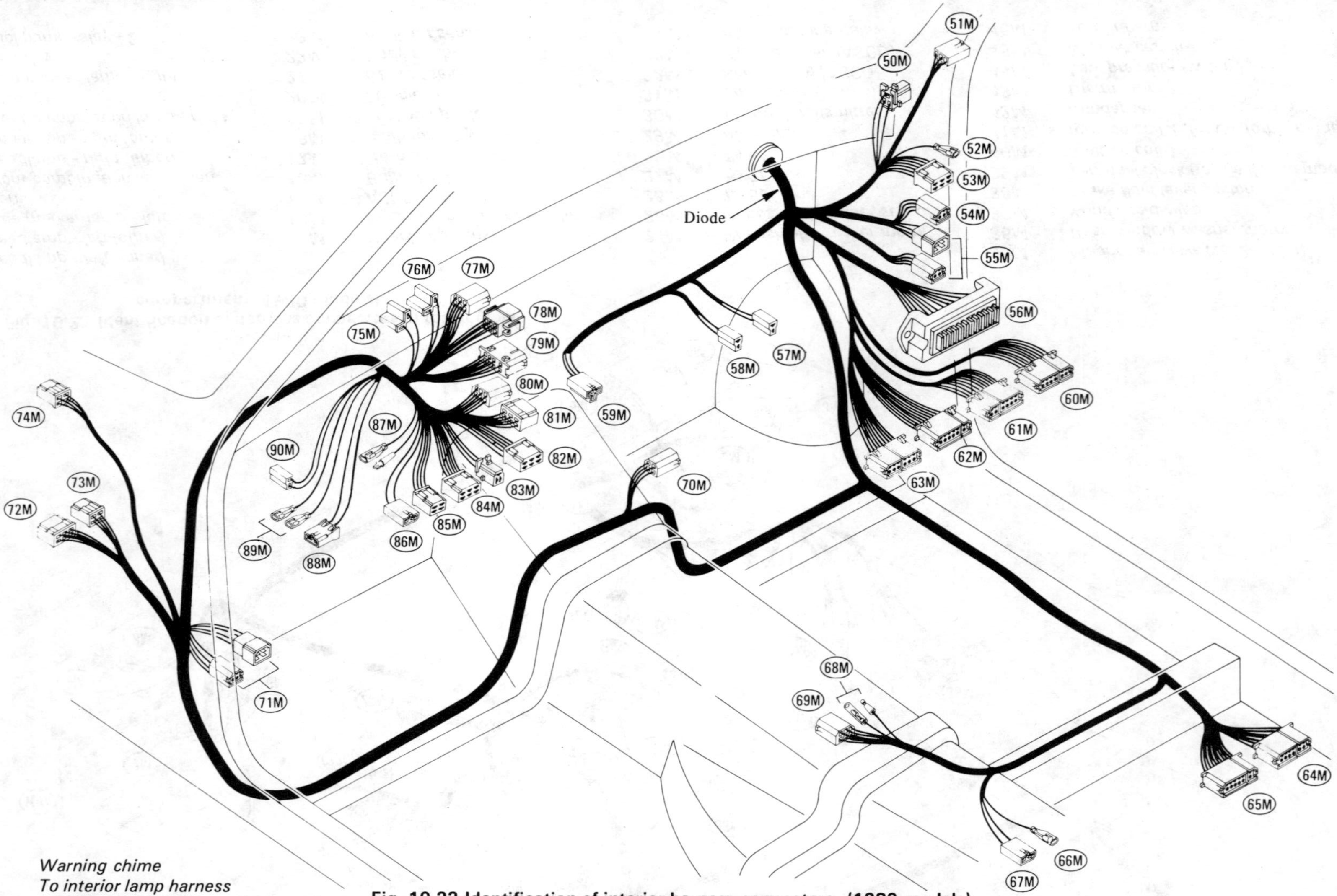

Fig. 10.22 Identification of interior harness connectors (1980 models)

50M	Warning chime
51M	To interior lamp harness
52M	Ignition and accessory relay (earth)
53M	Ignition and accessory relay
54M	Seat belt timer
55M	To door harness - right
56M	Fuse block
57M	Heater motor
58M	Thermo switch
59M	Air conditioner unit
60M	To 171 (white)
61M	To 161 (green)
62M	To 141 (black)
63M	To 151 (blue)
64M	To 1B - 51B (white)
65M	To 2B - 52B (black)
66M	Parking brake switch
67M	Seat belt switch
68M	Indicator lamp (A/T)
69M	To console harness
70M	Heater control panel
71M	To door harness - left
72M	ASCD controller
73M	ASCD controller
74M	To EFI harness
75M	Hazard flasher unit
76M	Turn signal flasher unit
77M	Door mirror switch - left
78M	Door mirror switch - right
79M	ASCD main switch
80M	Hazard switch
81M	Ignition switch
82M	Windshield wiper switch
83M	Windshield wiper switch
84M	Lighting switch
85M	Turn signal switch
86M	ASCD set switch
87M	Key warning switch
88M	Stop switch
89M	Stop lamp switch
90M	Kickdown switch

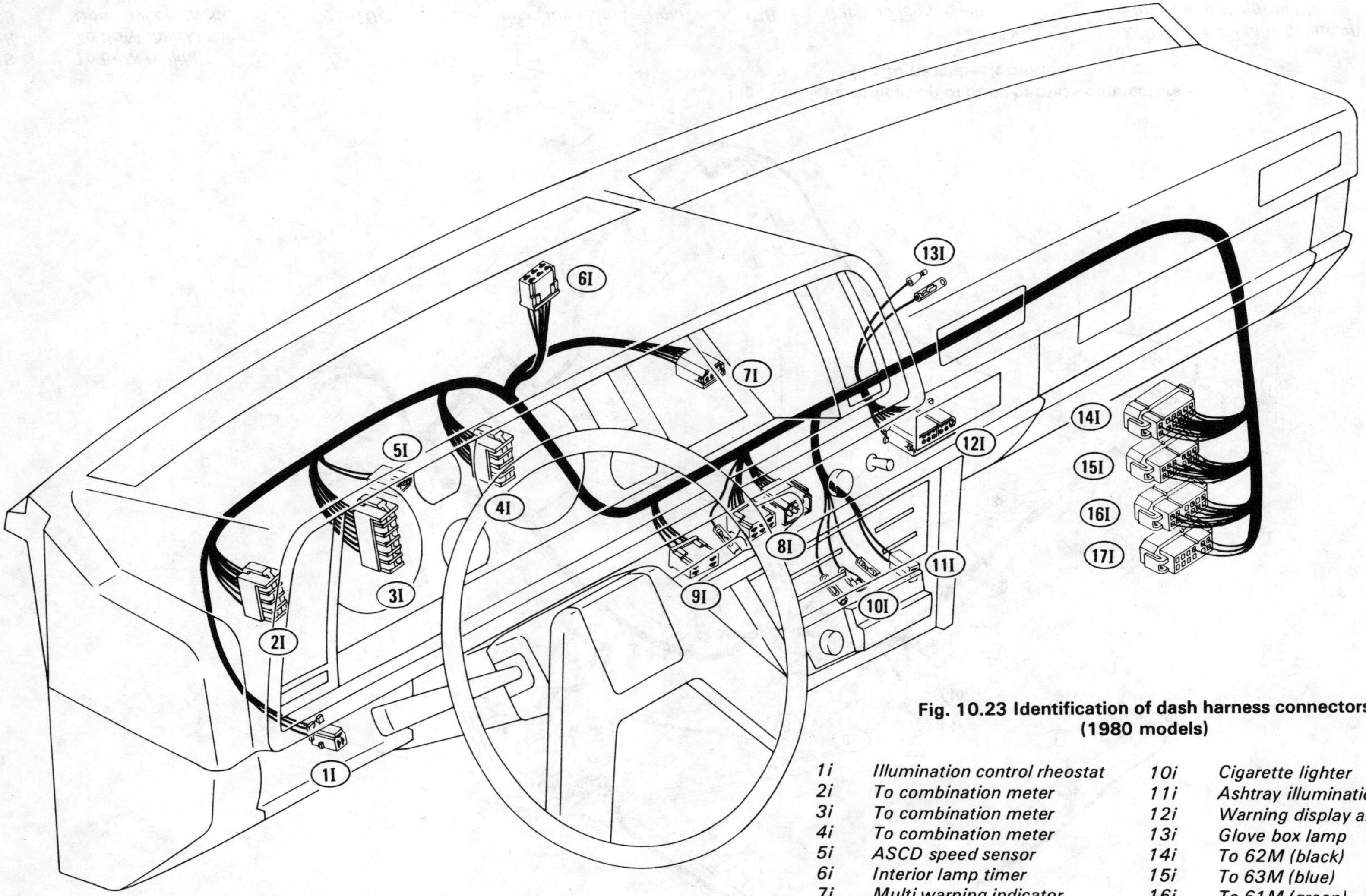

Fig. 10.23 Identification of dash harness connectors (1980 models)

1i	*Illumination control rheostat*	10i	*Cigarette lighter*
2i	*To combination meter*	11i	*Ashtray illumination*
3i	*To combination meter*	12i	*Warning display amplifier*
4i	*To combination meter*	13i	*Glove box lamp*
5i	*ASCD speed sensor*	14i	*To 62M (black)*
6i	*Interior lamp timer*	15i	*To 63M (blue)*
7i	*Multi warning indicator*	16i	*To 61M (green)*
8i	*Audio*	17i	*To 60M (white)*
9i	*Power antenna switch*		

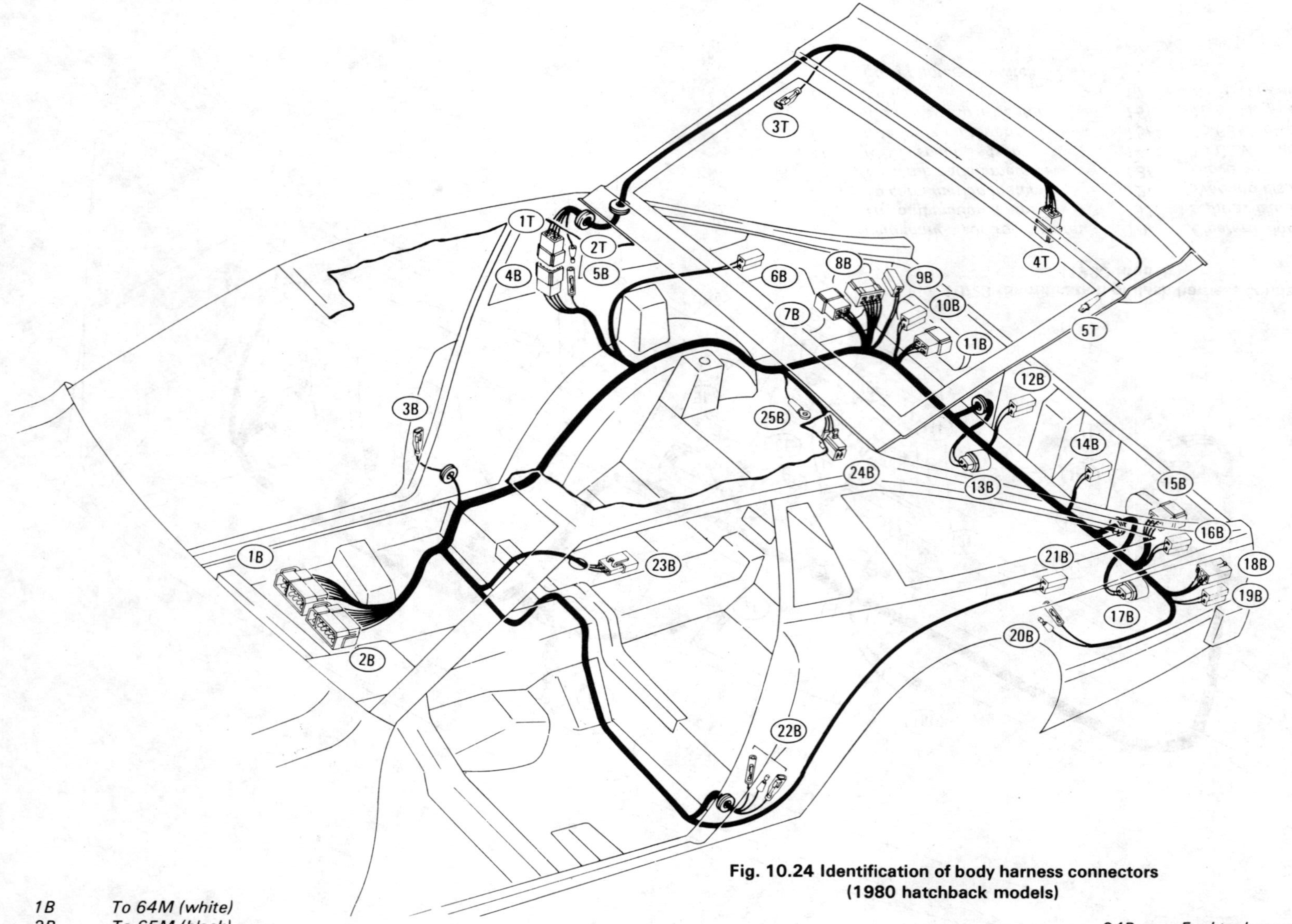

Fig. 10.24 Identification of body harness connectors (1980 hatchback models)

1B	*To 64M (white)*
2B	*To 65M (black)*
3B	*Door switch - right*
4B	*To 1T*
5B	*To 2T*
6B	*Rear speaker - right*
7B	*Tail and stop lamp sensor*
8B	*Tail and stop lamp sensor*
9B	*Side marker lamp - right*
10B	*Rear combination lamp – right*
11B	*Rear combination lamp – right*
12B	*License lamp - right*
13B	*Back-up lamp – right*
14B	*License lamp - left*
15B	*Rear combination lamp - left*
16B	*Rear combination lamp – left*
17B	*Back-up lamp – left*
18B	*Power antenna*
19B	*Side marker lamp - left*
20B	*Luggage compartment lamp*
21B	*Rear speaker - left*
22B	*Door switch - left*
23B	*To fuel pump harness*
24B	*Fuel tank gauge unit*
25B	*Body ground*
(Back door harness)	
1T	*To 4B*
2T	*To 5B*
3T	*Rear defogger*
4T	*Rear wiper motor*
5T	*Rear defogger (ground)*

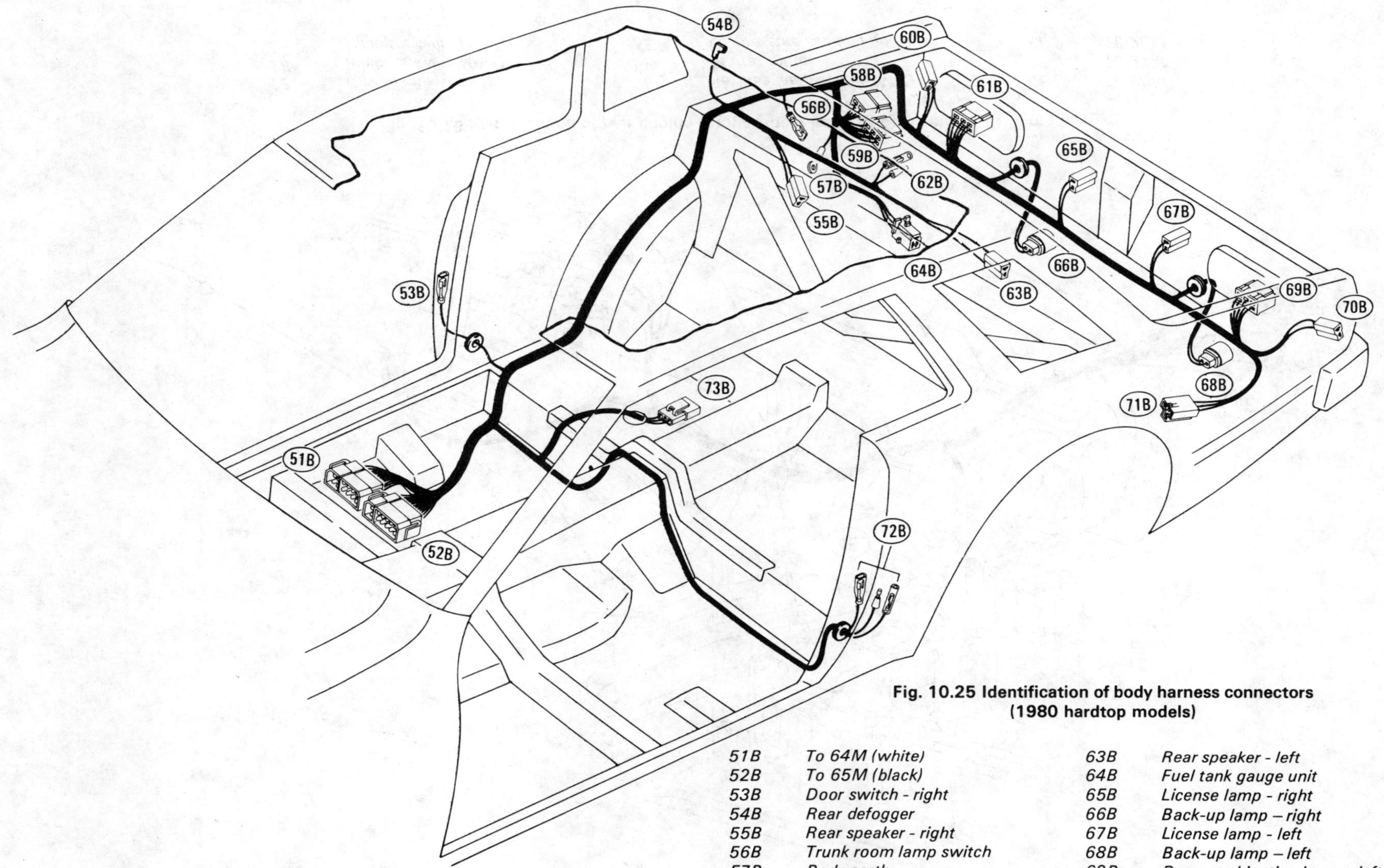

Fig. 10.25 Identification of body harness connectors (1980 hardtop models)

51B	*To 64M (white)*	63B	*Rear speaker - left*
52B	*To 65M (black)*	64B	*Fuel tank gauge unit*
53B	*Door switch - right*	65B	*License lamp - right*
54B	*Rear defogger*	66B	*Back-up lamp – right*
55B	*Rear speaker - right*	67B	*License lamp - left*
56B	*Trunk room lamp switch*	68B	*Back-up lamp – left*
57B	*Body earth*	69B	*Rear combination lamp – left*
58B	*Tail and stop lamp sensor*	70B	*Side marker lamp - left*
59B	*Tail and stop lamp sensor*	71B	*Power antenna*
60B	*Side marker lamp - right*	72B	*Door switch - left*
61B	*Rear combination lamp - right*	73B	*To fuel pump harness*
62B	*Trunk room lamp*		

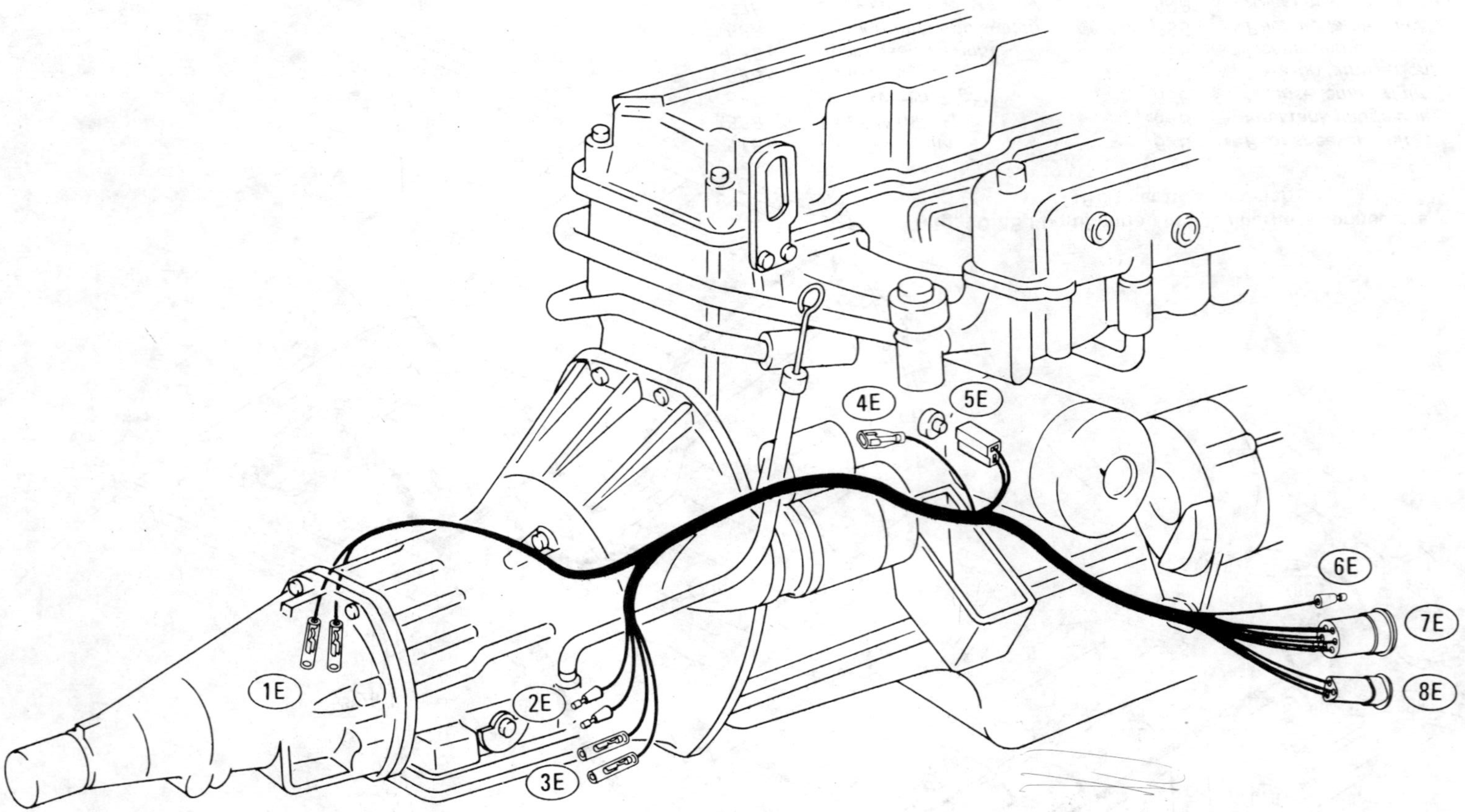

Fig. 10.26 Identification of rear engine compartment harness connectors (1980 models)

1E	*Kickdown switch (A/T)*	*2E*	*Reverse lamp switch (M/T)*	*6E*	*To 28M*
2E	*Inhibitor switch (A/T)*	*5E*	*Starter motor*	*7E*	*To 27M*
3E	*Inhibitor switch (A/T)*	*5E*	*Oil pressure sending unit*	*8E*	*To 26M*

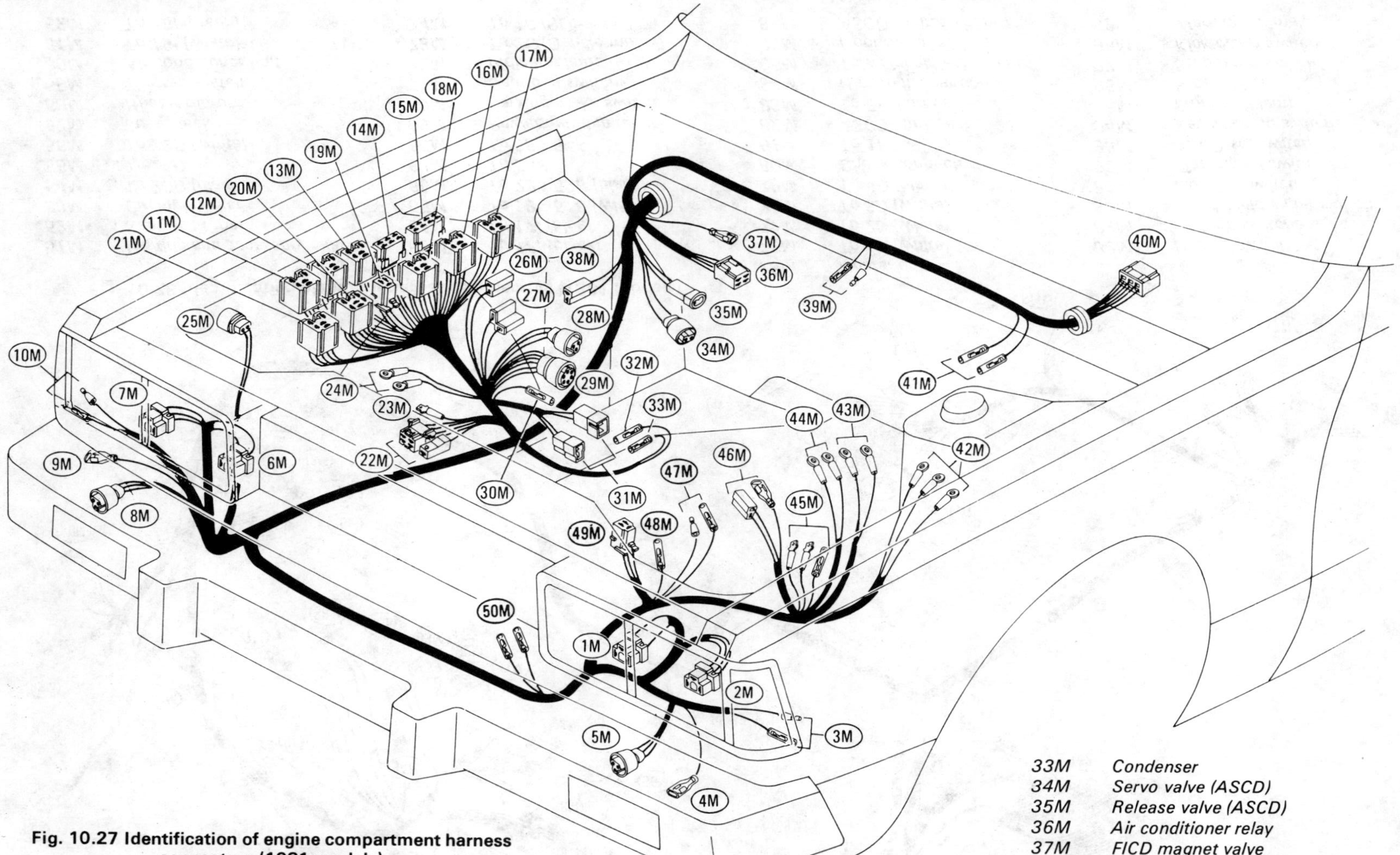

Fig. 10.27 Identification of engine compartment harness connectors (1981 models)

1M	*Headlamp - left (inner)*
2M	*Headlamp - left (outer)*
3M	*Side marker lamp - left*
4M	*Horn - right*
5M	*Front combination lamp – left*
6M	*Headlamp - right (inner)*
7M	*Headlamp - right (outer)*
8M	*Front combination lamp – right*
9M	*Horn - left*
10M	*Side marker lamp - right*
11M	*EFI relay*
12M	*Fuel pump relay - 2*
13M	*Fuel pump relay - 3*
14M	*Headlamp sensor*
15M	*Intermittent wiper amplifier*
16M	*ASCD hold relay*
17M	*Headlamp dimmer relay*
18M	*Bulb check relay*
19M	*Horn relay*
20M	*Inhibitor relay*
21M	*Fuel pump relay - 1*
22M	*Fusible link*
23M	*Battery sensor*
24M	*Body earth*
25M	*Radiator sensor*
26M	*Windshield washer motor*
27M	*Windshield washer sensor*
28M	*To 9E*
29M	*To 8E*
30M	*To 7E*
31M	*Alternator harness*
32M	*Thermal transmitter*
33M	*Condenser*
34M	*Servo valve (ASCD)*
35M	*Release valve (ASCD)*
36M	*Air conditioner relay*
37M	*FICD magnet valve*
38M	*Rear window washer motor*
39M	*Vacuum cut solenoid*
40M	*Windshield wiper motor*
41M	*Brake fluid level switch*
42M	*Terminal block (US models)*
43M	*Ignition coil 1*
44M	*Ignition coil 2 (US models)*
45M	*Condenser*
46M	*Distributor*
47M	*Low pressure switch*
48M	*Magnet clutch*
49M	*To EFI harness*
50M	*Water temperature sensor (US models)*

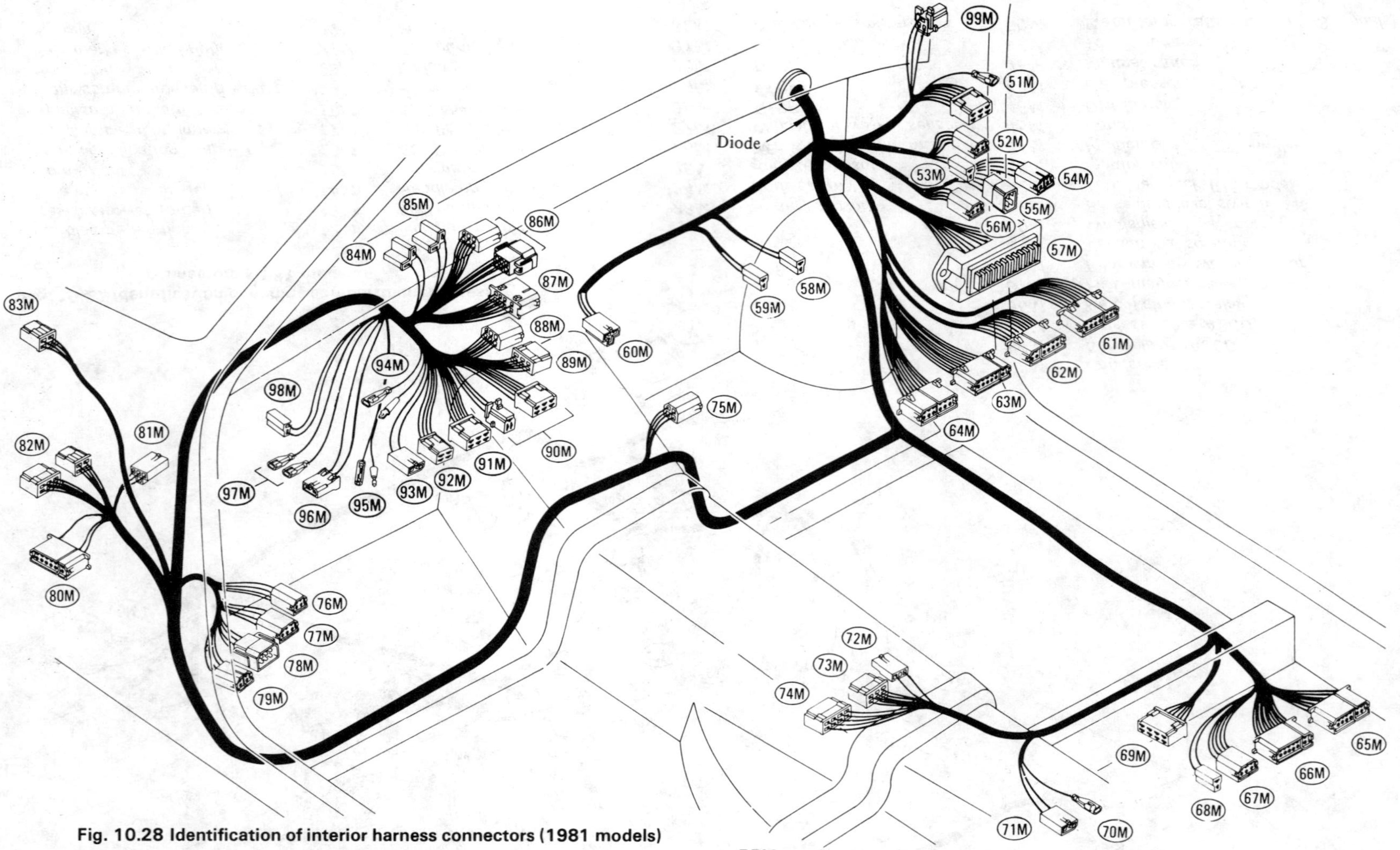

Fig. 10.28 Identification of interior harness connectors (1981 models)

				75M	Heater unit		
51M	Ignition and accessory relay	63M	To 16I (black)	76M	To 1D (white)	88M	Hazard switch
52M	Seat belt timer	64M	To 17I (blue)	77M	To 2D (white)	89M	Ignition switch
53M	Circuit breaker	65M	To 1B - 51B (white)	78M	To 3D (white)	90M	Windshield wiper switch
54M	To 20D (black)	66M	To 2B - 52B (black)	79M	To 4D (black)	91M	Lighting switch
55M	To 21D	67M	To 53B	80M	Check connector	92M	Turn signal switch
56M	To 22D (white)	68M	To 3B - 54B	81M	To 1R	93M	ASCD set switch
57M	Fuse block	69M	Power antenna timer	82M	ASCD controller	94M	Key warning switch
58M	Heater motor	70M	Parking brake switch	83M	To EFI harness	95M	Front foot lamp
59M	Thermo switch	71M	Seat belt switch	84M	Hazard flasher unit	96M	Stop switch
60M	Air conditioner unit	72M	Indicator lamp (A/T)	85M	Turn signal flasher unit	97M	Stop lamp switch
61M	To 19I (white)	73M	To 2C (Deluxe model)	86M	Door mirror switch	98M	Kick down switch
62M	To 18I (green)	74M	To 1C (SL model)	87M	ASCD main switch	99M	Warning chime

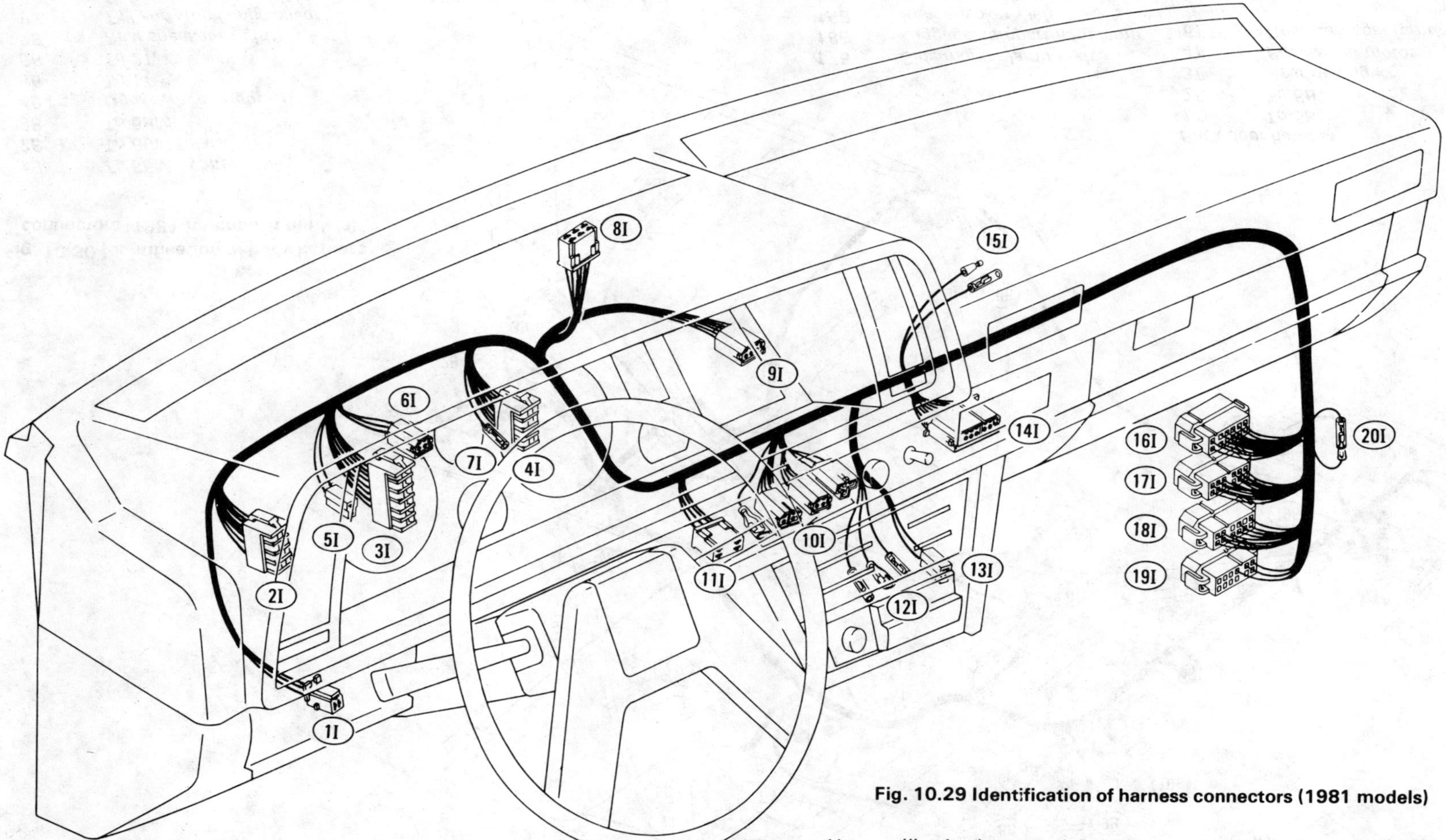

Fig. 10.29 Identification of harness connectors (1981 models)

1i	*Illumination control rheostat*
2i	*To combination meter*
3i	*To combination meter*
4i	*To combination meter*
5i	*High beam indicator*
6i	*ASCD speed sensor and odometer switch*
7i	*Clock*
8i	*Interior lamp timer*
9i	*Multi warning indicator*
10i	*Audio*
11i	*Power antenna switch*
12i	*Cigarette lighter*
13i	*Ashtray illumination*
14i	*Warning display amplifier*
15i	*Glove box lamp*
16i	*To 63M (black)*
17i	*To 64M (blue)*
18i	*To 62M (green)*
19i	*To 61M (white)*
20i	*Cut-off connector*

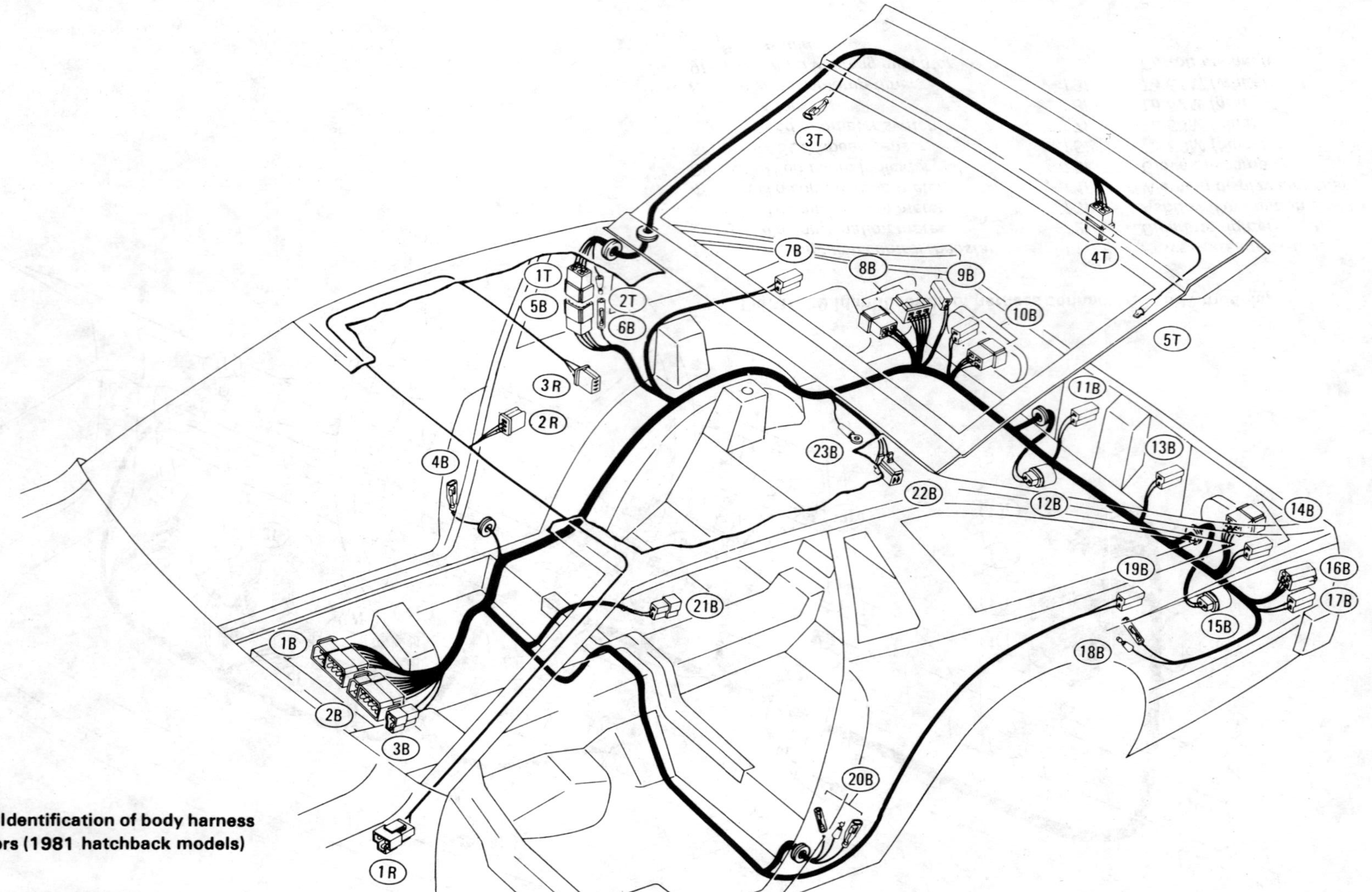

Fig. 10.30 Identification of body harness connectors (1981 hatchback models)

1B	*To 65M (white)*
2B	*To 66M (black)*
3B	*To 68M*
4B	*Door switch - right*
5B	*To 1T*
6B	*To 2T*
7B	*Rear speaker - right*
8	*Tail and stop lamp sensor*
9B	*Side marker lamp - right*
10B	*Rear combination lamp - right*
11B	*License lamp - right*
12B	*Back-up lamp - right*
13B	*License lamp - left*
14B	*Rear combination lamp - left*
15B	*Back-up lamp - left*
16B	*Power antenna*
17B	*Side marker lamp - left*
18B	*Luggage compartment lamp*
19B	*Rear speaker - left*
20B	*Door switch - left*
21B	*To fuel pump harness*
22B	*Fuel tank gauge unit*
23B	*Body earth*

Back door harness

1T	*To 5B*
2T	*To 6B*
3T	*Rear defogger*
4T	*Rear wiper motor*
5T	*Rear defogger (ground)*

Interior lamp harness

1R	*To 81M*
2R	*Interior lamp (without sun roof)*
3R	*Interior lamp (with sun roof)*

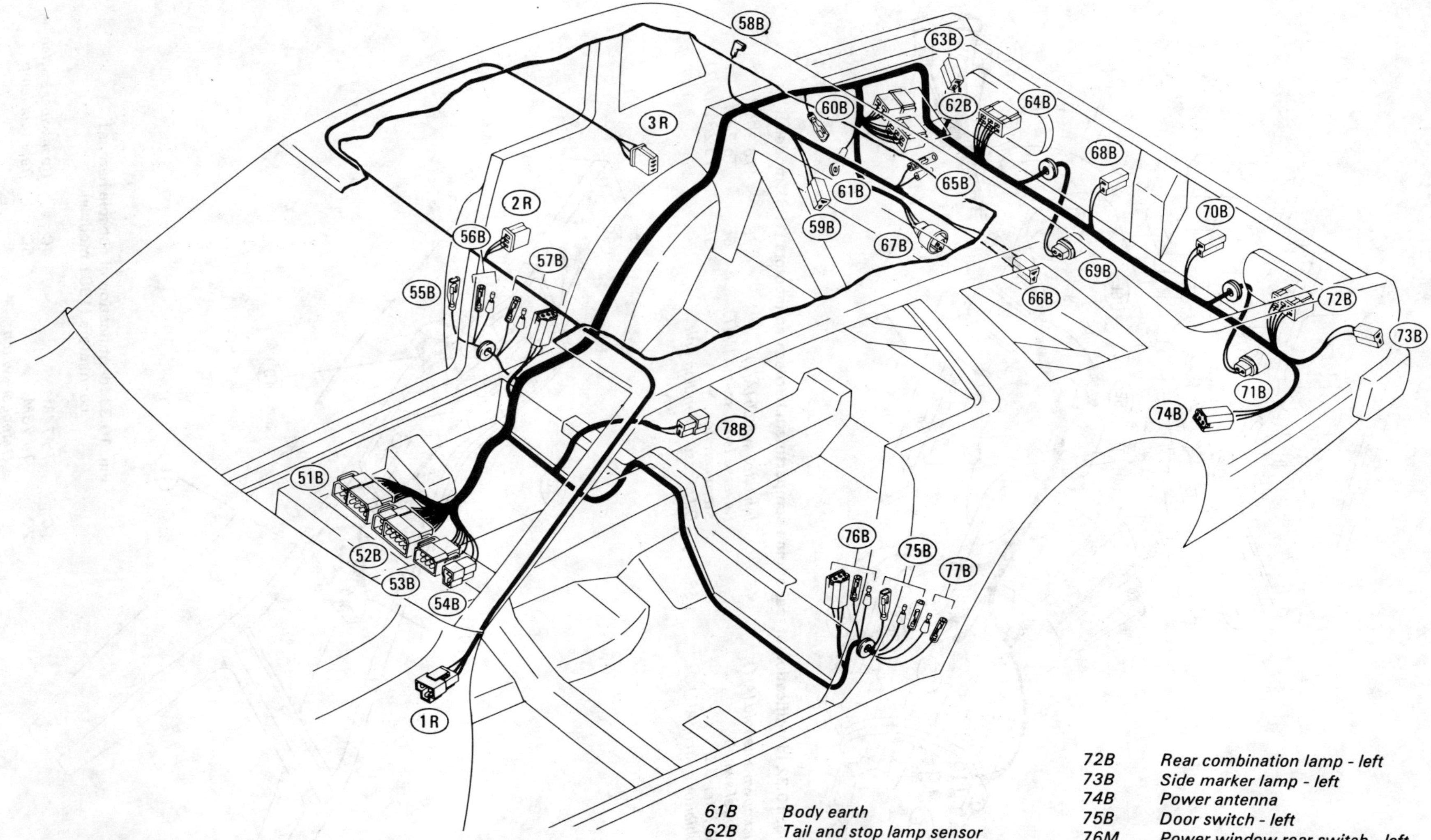

Fig. 10.31 Identification of body harness connectors (1981 hardtop models)

51B	To 65M (white)
52B	To 66M (black)
53B	To 67M
54B	To 68M
55B	Door switch - right
56B	Power window motor - right
57B	Power window rear switch - right
58B	Rear defogger
59B	Rear speaker - right
60B	Trunk room lamp switch
61B	Body earth
62B	Tail and stop lamp sensor
63B	Side marker lamp - right
64B	Rear combination lamp - right
65B	Trunk room lamp
66B	Rear speaker - left
67B	Fuel tank gauge unit
68B	License lamp - right
69B	Back-up lamp - right
70B	License lamp - left
71B	Back-up lamp - left
72B	Rear combination lamp - left
73B	Side marker lamp - left
74B	Power antenna
75B	Door switch - left
76M	Power window rear switch - left
77B	Power window motor - left
78B	To fuel pump harness

Interior lamp harness

1R	To 81M
2R	Interior lamp (without sun roof)
3R	Interior lamp (with sun roof)

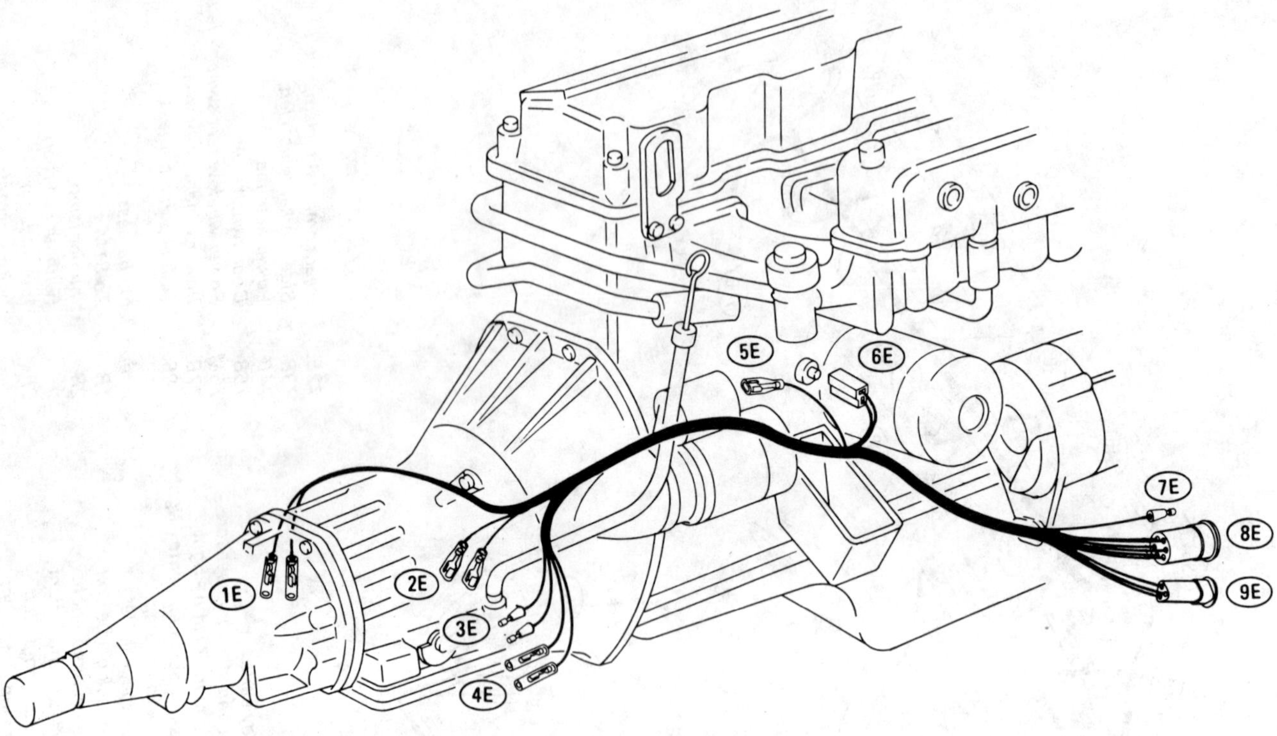

Fig. 10.32 Identification of rear engine compartment harness connectors (1981 models)

1E	*Kickdown solenoid (A/T)*	*4E*	*Inhibitor switch (A/T)*	*7E*	*To 30M*
2E	*Neutral switch (M/T for US)*		*Reverse lamp switch (M/T)*	*8E*	*To 29M*
3E	*Inhibitor switch (A/T)*	*5E*	*Starter motor*	*9E*	*To 28M (A/T)*
		6E	*Oil pressure sending unit*		

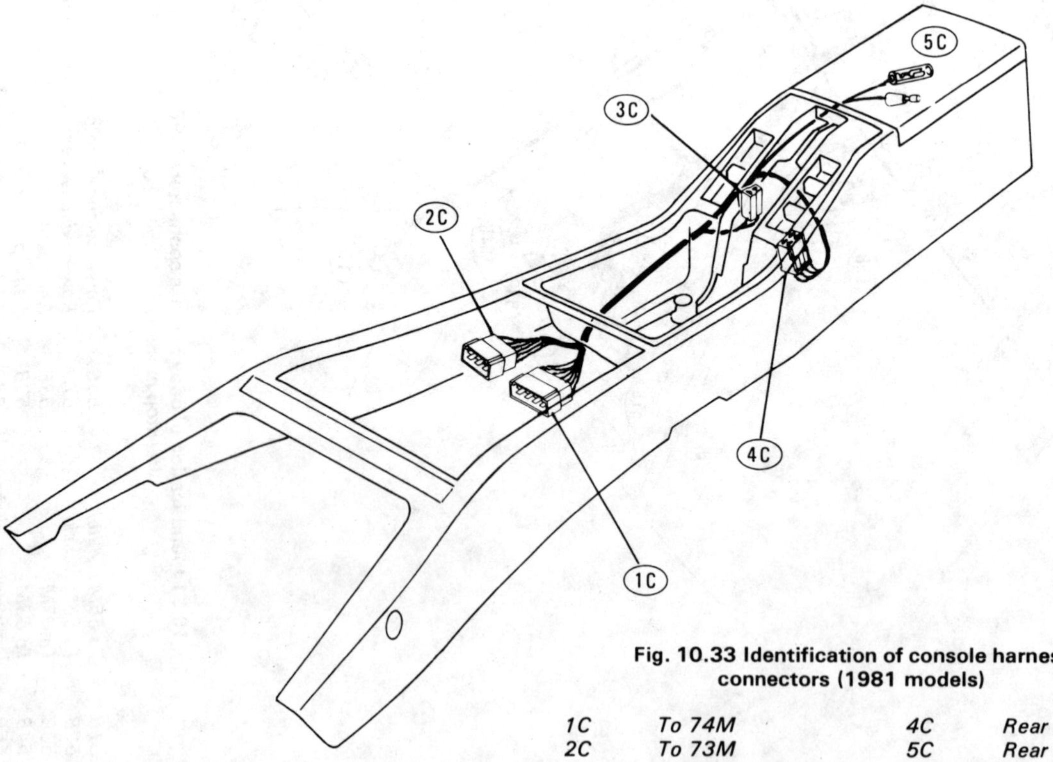

Fig. 10.33 Identification of console harness connectors (1981 models)

1C	*To 74M*	*4C*	*Rear wiper switch*
2C	*To 73M*	*5C*	*Rear foot lamp*
3C	*Defogger switch*		

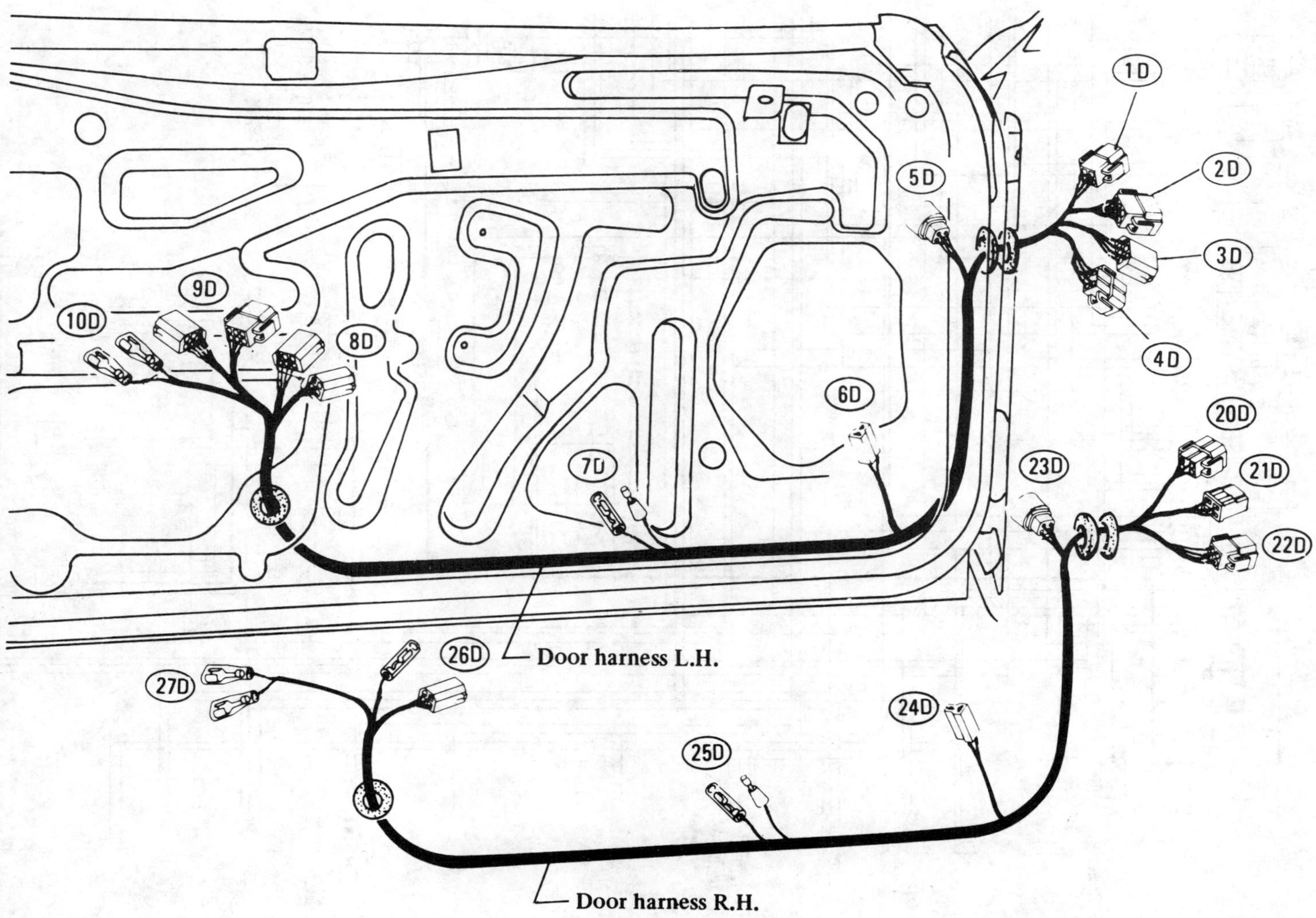

Fig. 10.34 Identification of door harness connectors (1981 models)

Door harness - left		*7D*	*Power window motor - left*	*21D*	*To 55M*
1D	*To 76M (white)*	*8D*	*Power window switch - left*	*22D*	*To 56M (white)*
2D	*To 77M (white)*	*9D*	*Mirror switch*	*23D*	*Door mirror - right*
3D	*To 78M (white)*	*10D*	*Step lamp - left*	*24D*	*Door speaker - right*
4D	*To 79M (black)*	*Door harness - right*		*25D*	*Power window motor - right*
5D	*Door mirror - left*	*20D*	*To 54M (black)*	*26D*	*Power window switch - right*
6D	*Door speaker - left*			*27D*	*Step lamp - right*

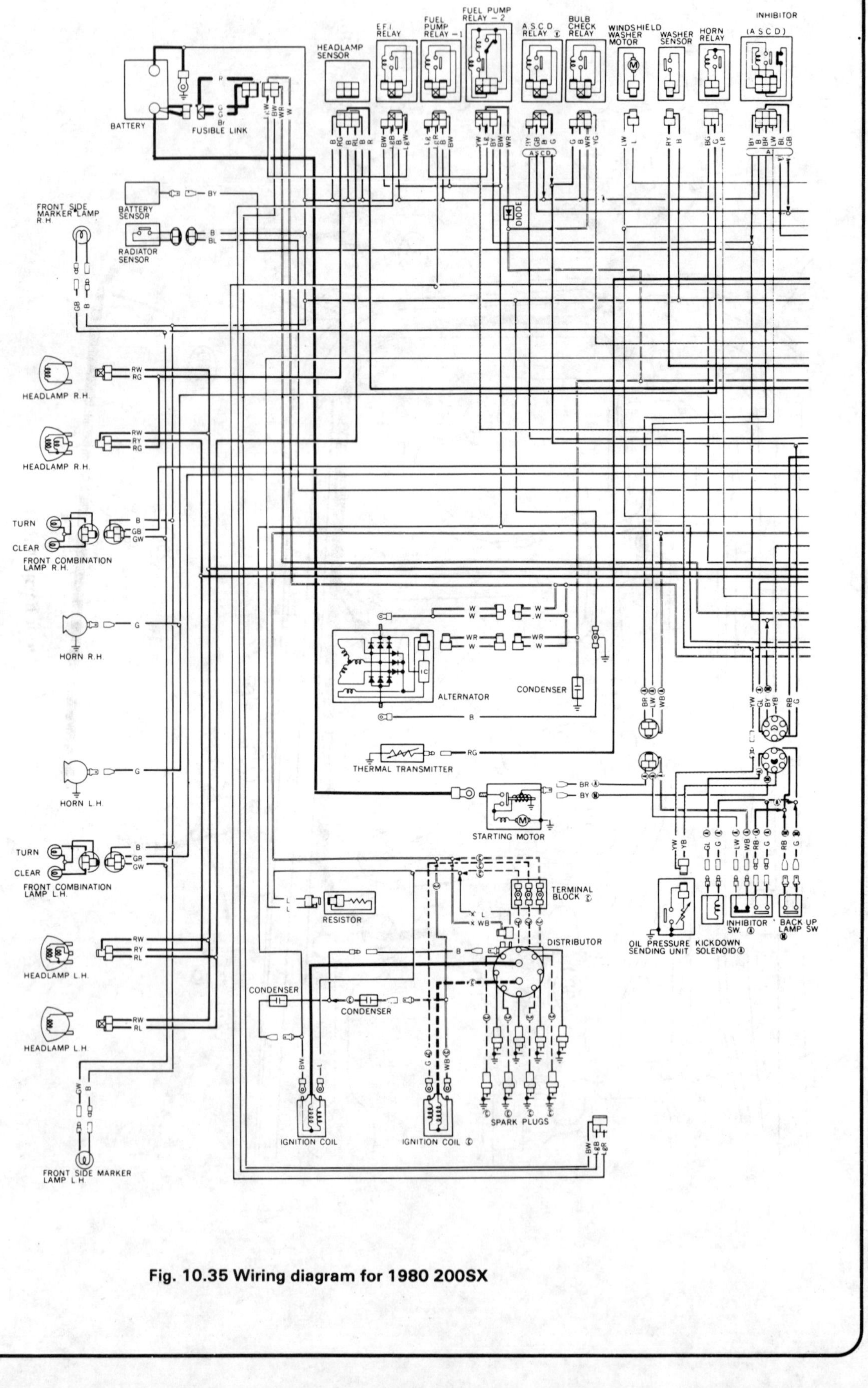

Fig. 10.35 Wiring diagram for 1980 200SX

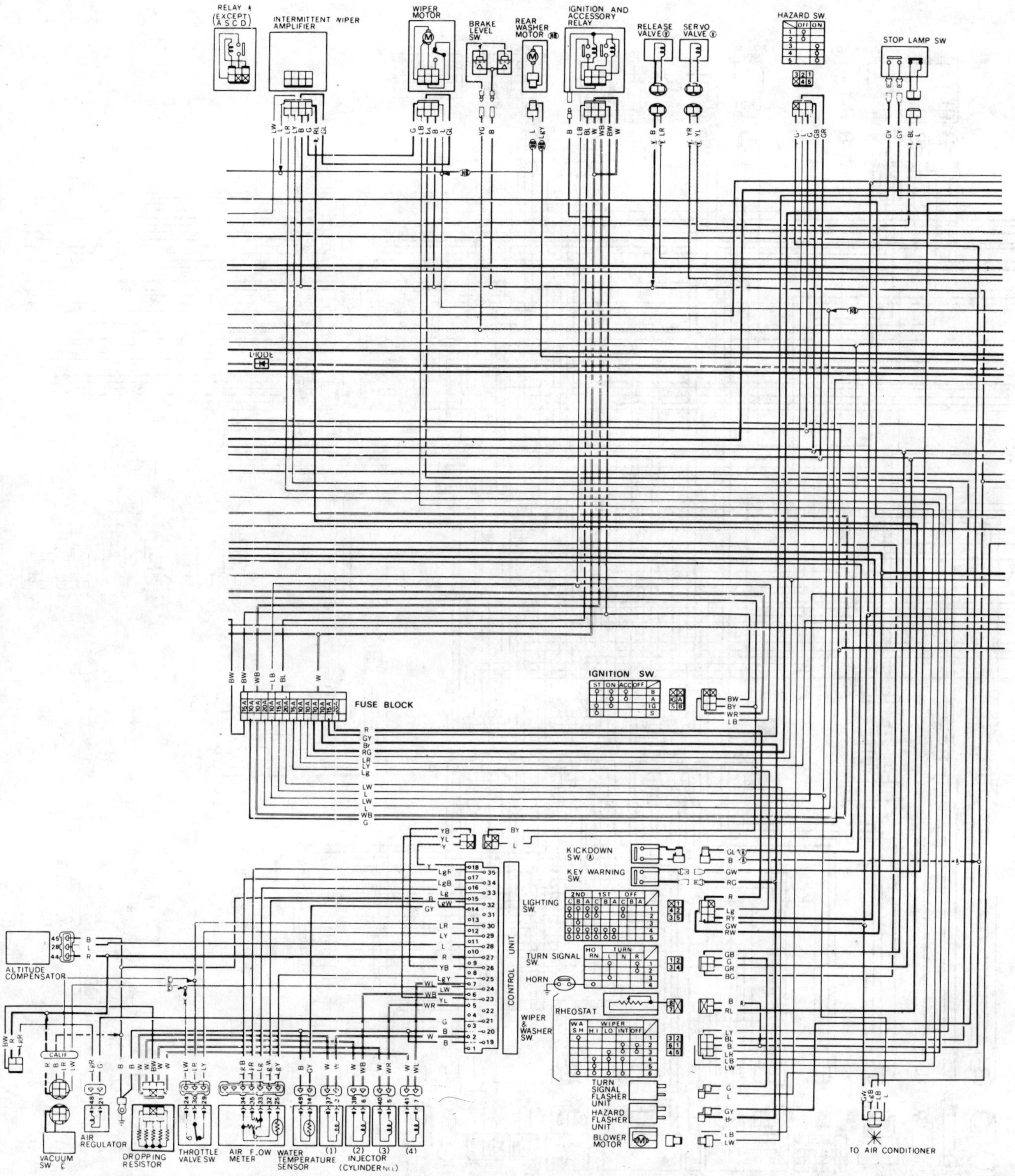

Fig. 10.36 Wiring diagram for 1980 200SX (continued)

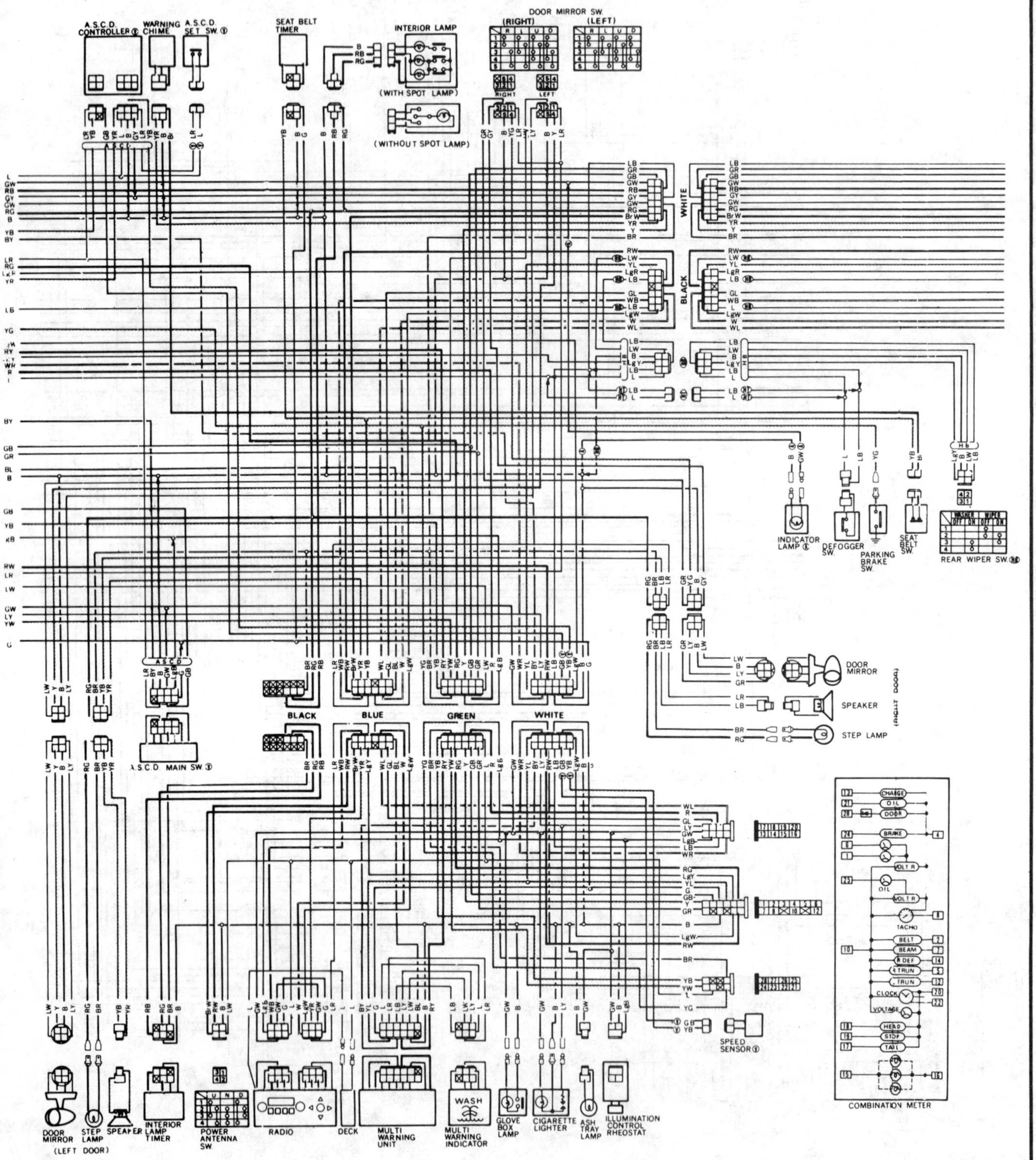

Fig. 10.37 Wiring diagram for 1980 200SX (continued)

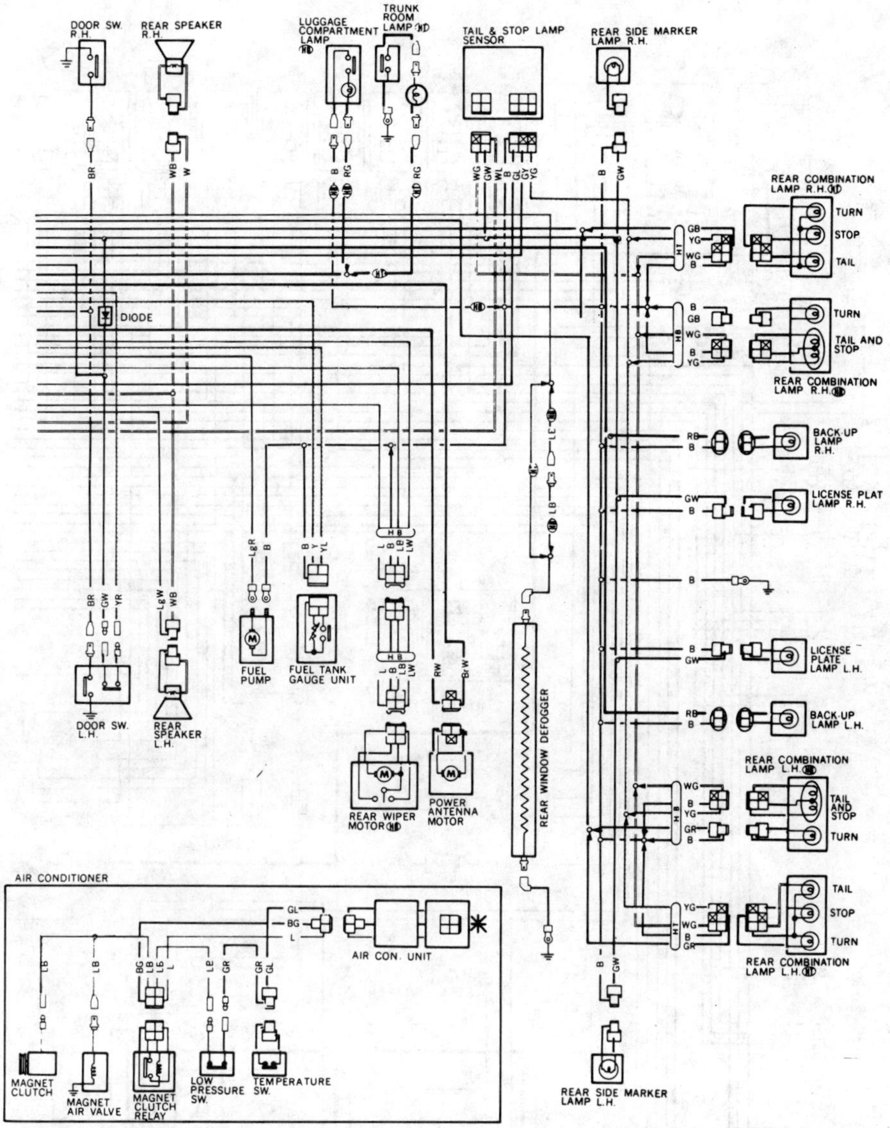

CABLE COLORS	
B	BLACK
W	WHITE
R	RED
G	GREEN
L	BLUE
Y	YELLOW
Lg	LIGHT GREEN
Br	BROWN
Gr	GREY

IN THE CASE OF TWO-TONE COLOR CABLE, CABLE COLOR IS INDICATED BY BASE COLOR ONLY AND STRIPE COLOR IS NOT SHOWN.

(Example)

GW — GREEN with WHITE Stripe

LG — BLUE with GREEN Stripe

- (A) AUTOMATIC TRANSMISSION MODELS
- (M) MANUAL TRANSMISSION MODELS
- (C) CALIFORNIA MODELS
- (X) NON-CALIFORNIA MODELS
- (V) A.S.C.D. EQUIPPED MODELS
- (HB) HATCHBACK
- (HT) HARDTOP
- (R) WITH TIME CONTROL INTERMITTENT WIPER

POSITION
- Ignition sw. in lock.
- Light sw. and wiper sw. in off.
- Door closed.
- Transmission in neutral (A/T selector lever in parking).
- Parking brake pulled.
- Driver's seat belt unlocked.

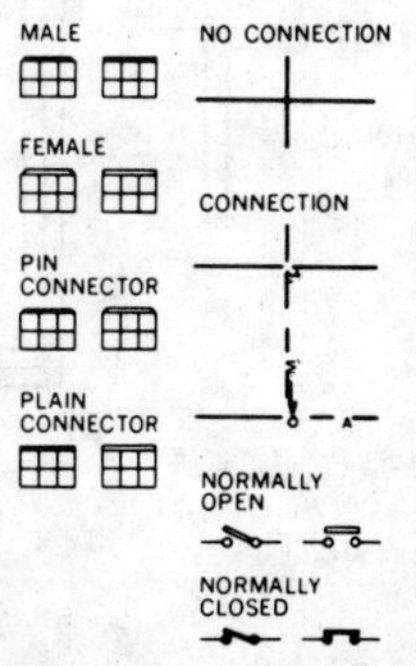

Fig. 10.38 Wiring diagram for 1980 200SX (continued)

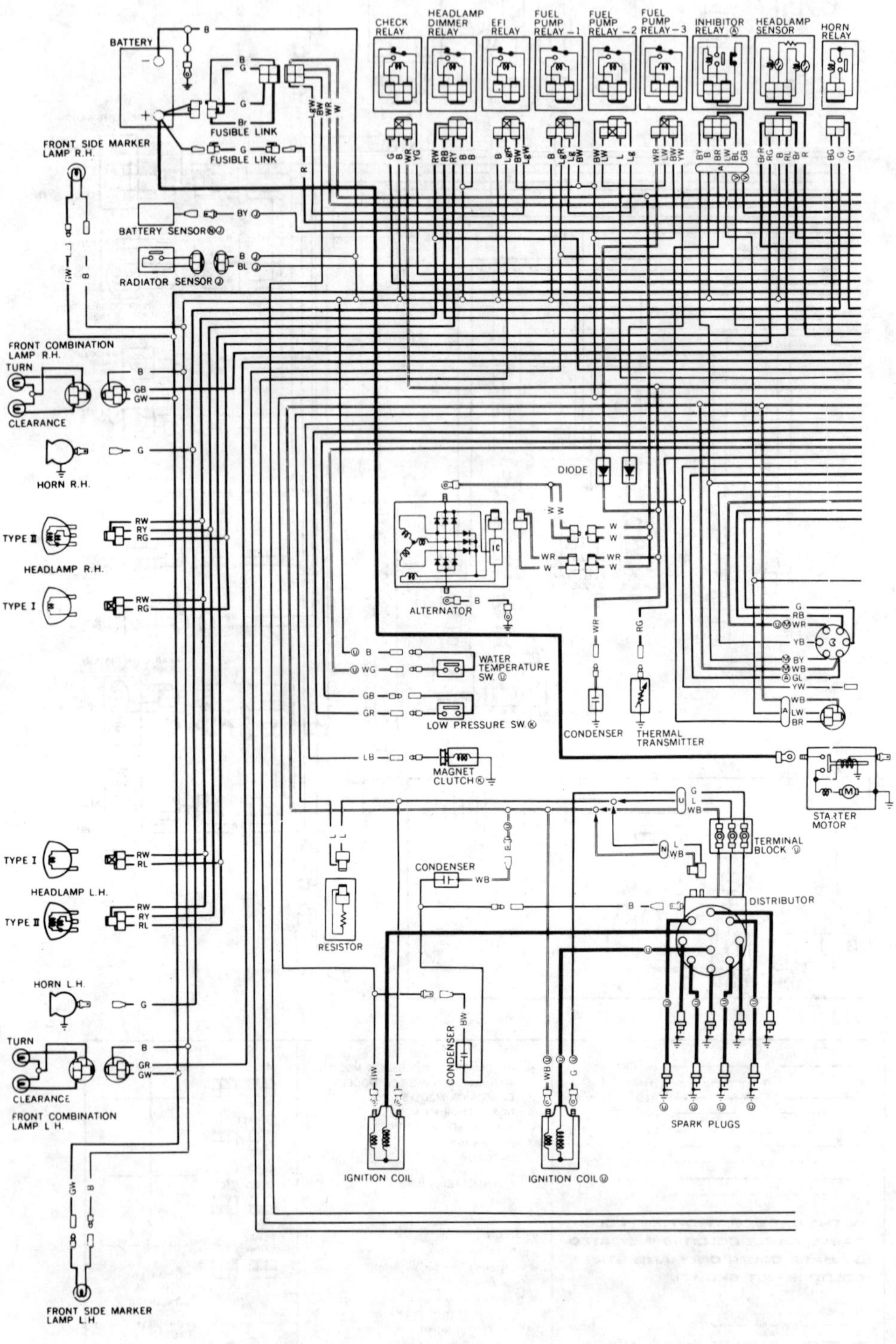

Fig. 10.39 Wiring diagram for 1981 200SX

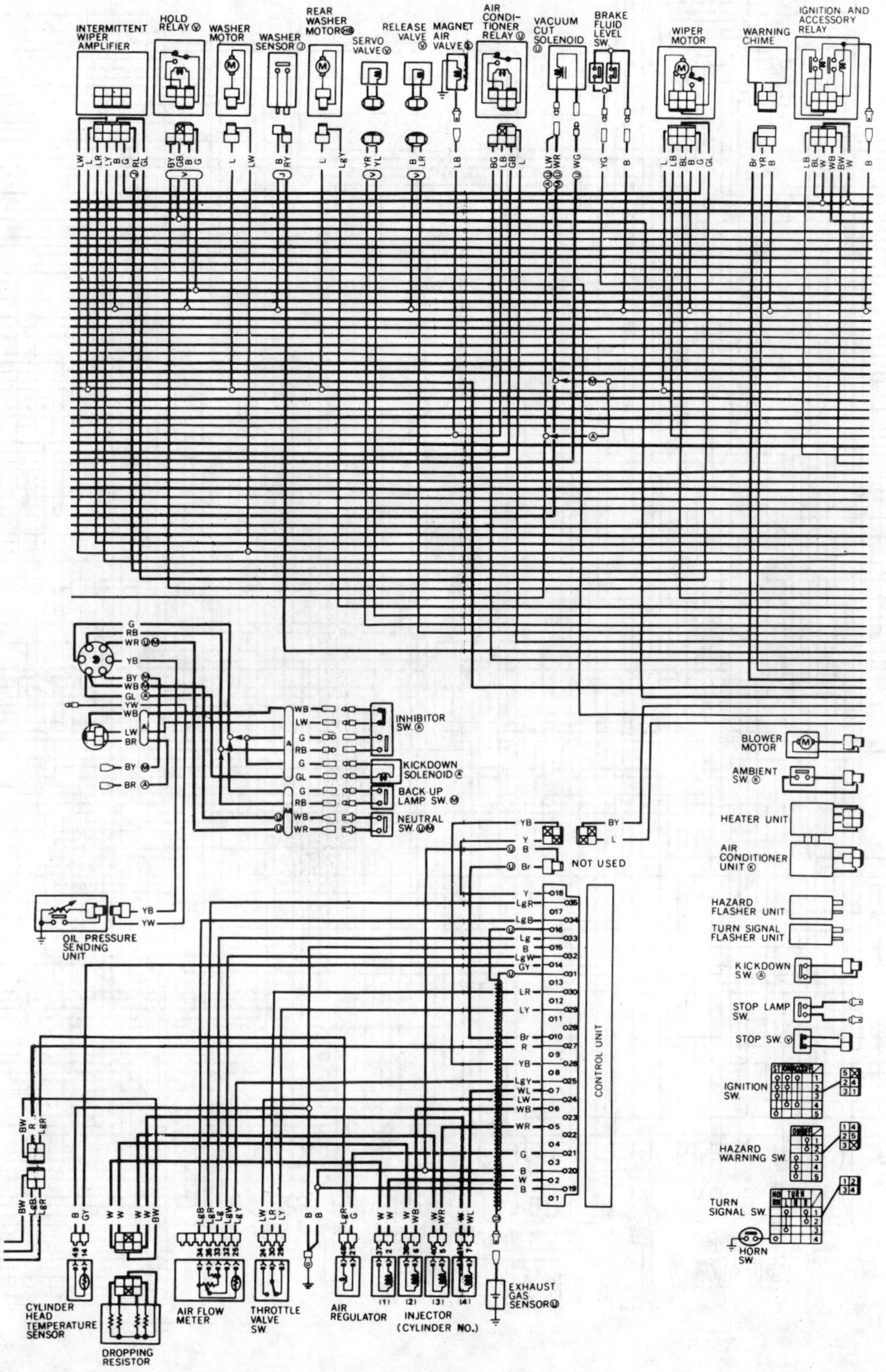

Fig. 10.40 Wiring diagram for 1981 200SX (continued)

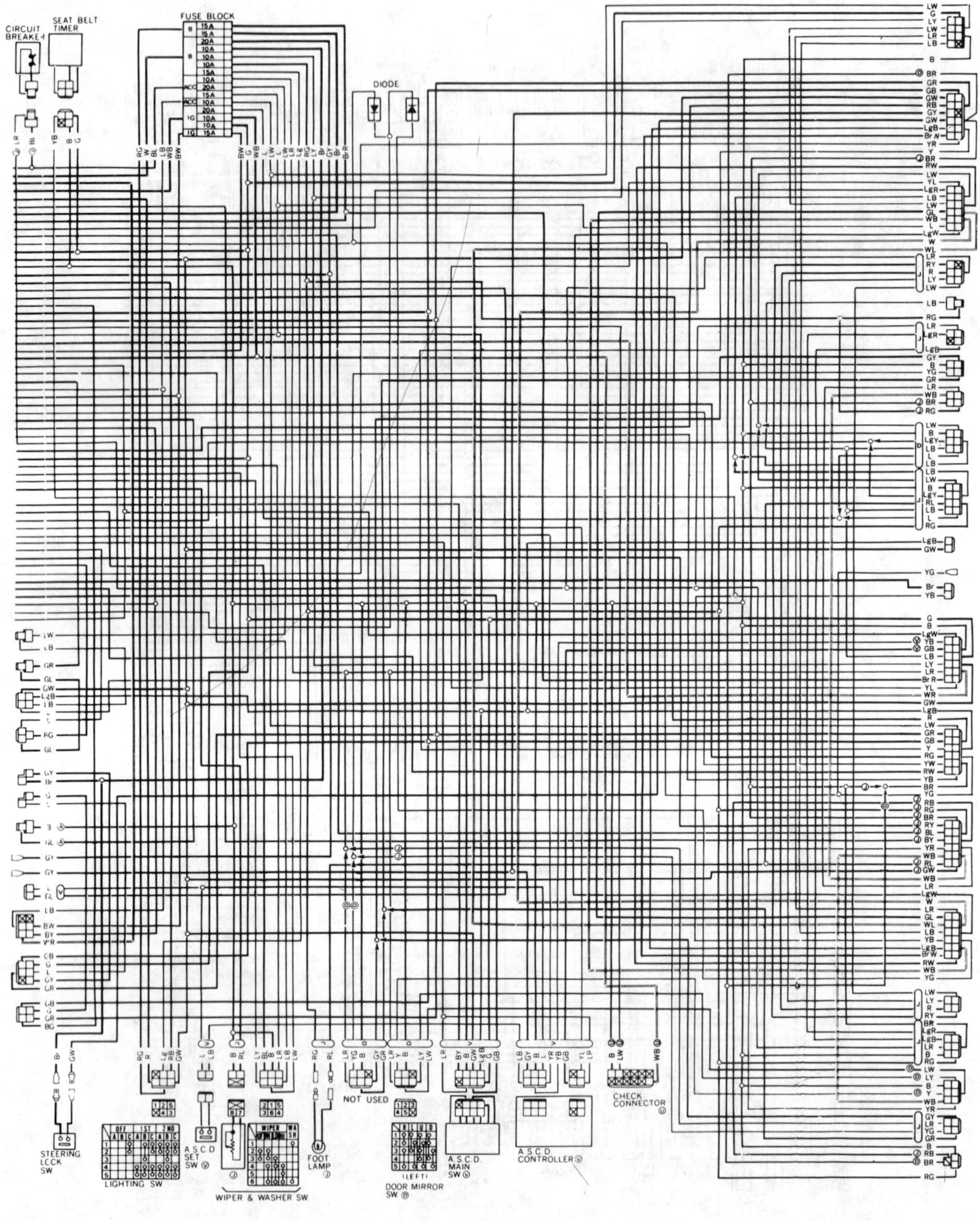

Fig. 10.41 Wiring diagram for 1981 200SX (continued)

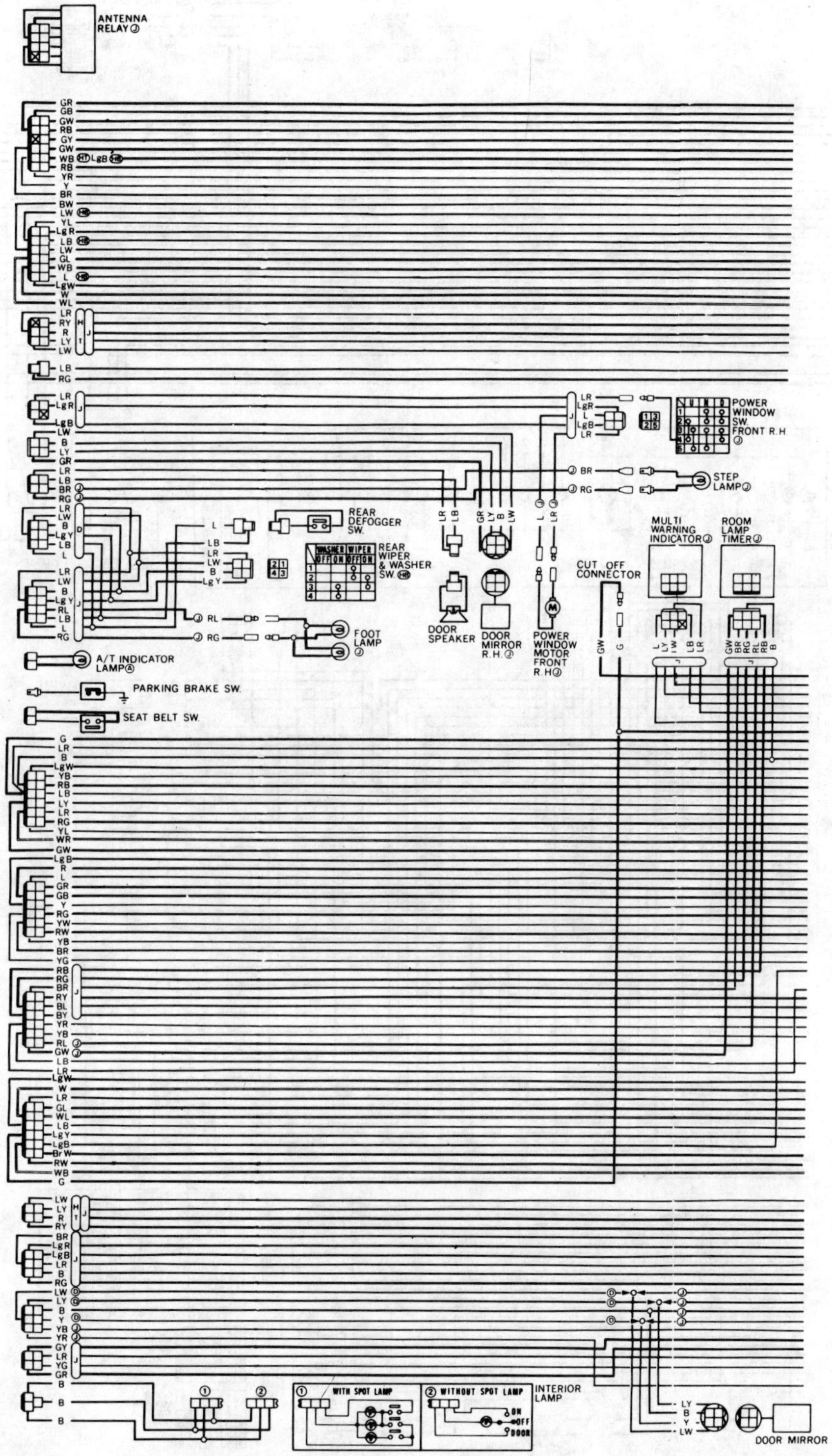

Fig. 10.42 Wiring diagram for 1981 200SX (continued)

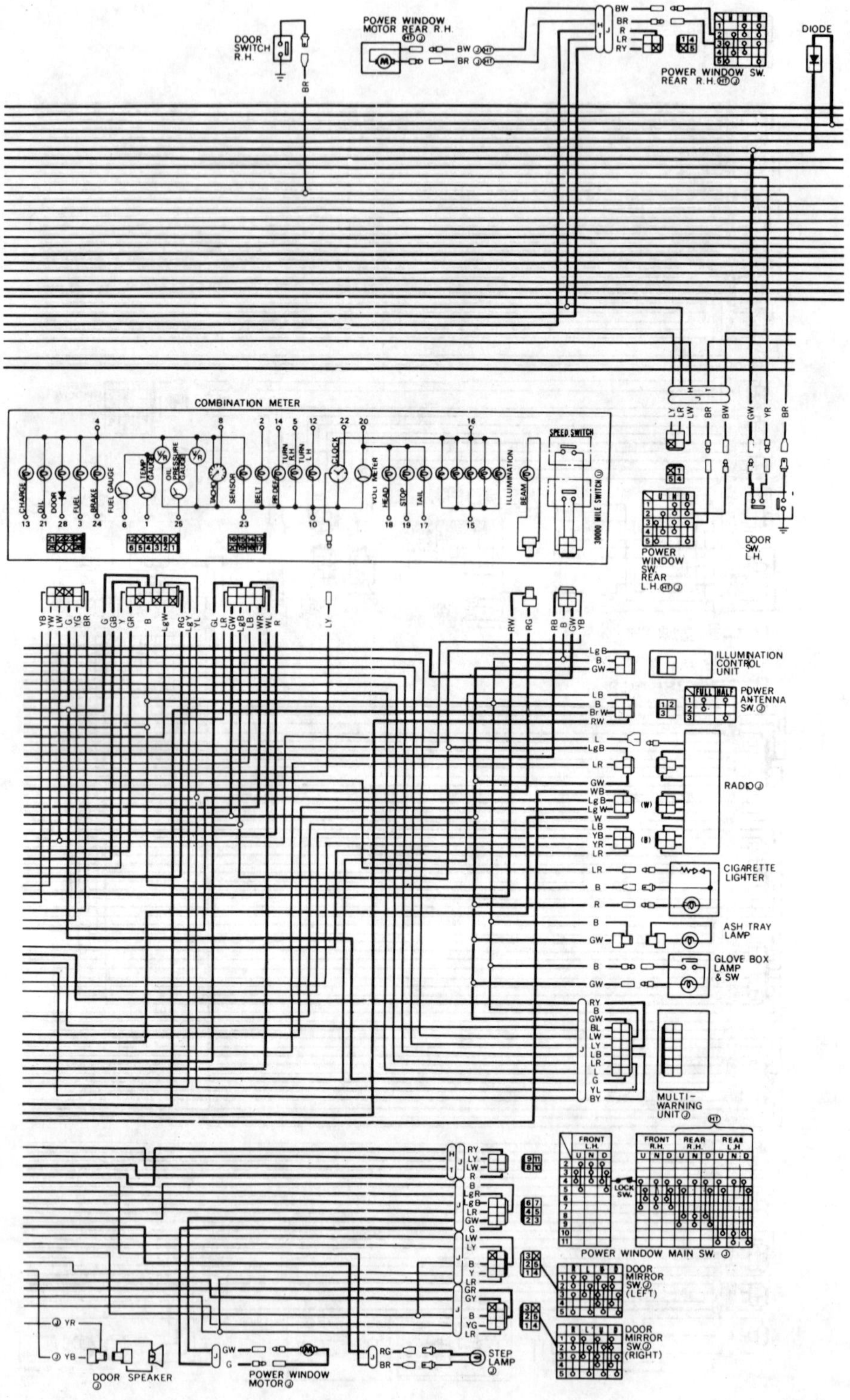

Fig. 10.43 Wiring diagram for 1981 200SX (continued)

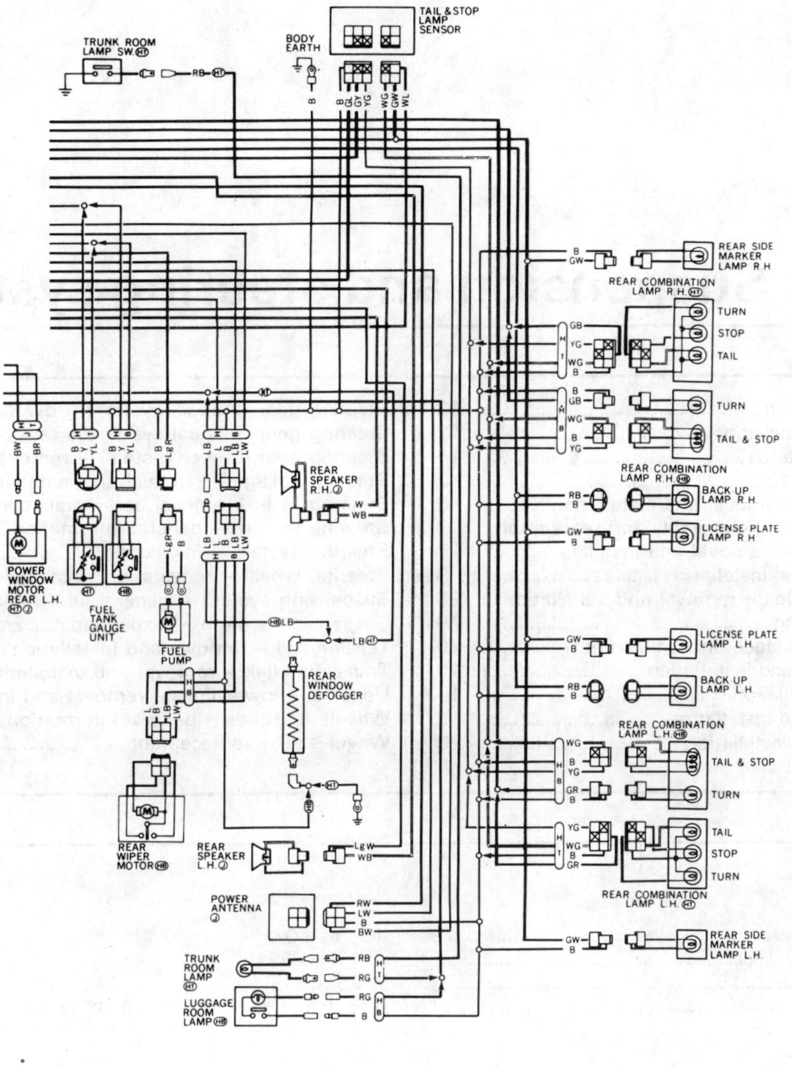

CABLE COLORS

B	BLACK
W	WHITE
R	RED
G	GREEN
L	BLUE
Y	YELLOW
Lg	LIGHT GREEN
Br	BROWN
Gr	GRAY

IN THE CASE OF TWO-TONE COLOR CABLE, CABLE COLOR IS INDICATED BY BASE COLOR ONLY AND STRIPE COLOR IS NOT SHOWN.

(Example)

GW	GREEN with WHITE Stripe
LG	BLUE with GREEN Stripe

- (A) AUTOMATIC TRANSMISSION MODELS
- (M) MANUAL TRANSMISSION MODELS
- (U) U.S.A. MODELS
- (N) CANADA MODELS
- (V) A.S.C.D. EQUIPPED MODELS
- (HT) HARDTOP
- (HB) HATCHBACK
- (J) SPORT LUXURY MODELS
- (D) DELUXE MODELS
- (K) AIR CONDITIONER EQUIPPED MODELS

POSITION

- Ignition sw. in lock.
- Light sw. and wiper sw. in off.
- Door closed.
- Transmission in neutral (A/T selector lever in parking)
- Parking brake pulled.
- Driver's seat belt unlocked.

MALE

FEMALE

PIN CONNECTOR

PLAIN CONNECTOR

NO CONNECTION

CONNECTION

NORMALLY OPEN

NORMALLY CLOSED

Fig. 10.44 Wiring diagram for 1981 200SX (continued)

Chapter 11 Suspension and steering systems

Contents

Balljoint – removal and installation 13
Crossmember – removal and installation 12
Front axle – removal and installation 14
Front end alignment 2
Front hub and wheel bearings – removal and installation 3
Front spring and strut assembly – disassembly and reassembly .. 8
Front spring and strut assembly – removal and installation 7
Front stabilizer bar – removal and installation 9
Power steering pump and reservoir – removal and installation 28
Power steering system – bleeding 29
Power steering system – maintenance and adjustment 26
Rear shock absorber – removal and installation 16
Rear spring – removal and installation 17
Rear stabilizer bar – removal and installation 15
Steering column – removal and installation 23
Steering gear (manual system) – overhaul 25
Steering gear (manual system) – removal and installation 24
Steering gear (power system) – removal and installation 27
Steering linkage – removal and installation 30
Steering lock – removal and installation 22
Steering system – general information 19
Steering system – inspection 20
Steering wheel – removal and installation 21
Suspension system – general information 5
Suspension system – inspection 6
Tension rod – removal and installation 10
Transverse link – removal and installation 11
Upper and lower links – removal and installation 18
Wheels and tires – general information 1
Wheel stud – replacement 4

Specifications

Front suspension

Front end alignment

Camber	40° to 50°
Caster	1°45′ to 3°15′
Kingpin inclination	7°25′ 8°55′
Toe-in	0 to 2 mm (0 to .08 in.) or 0° to 12′

Front wheel turning angle

Inside	33° to 35°
Outside	27° to 29°

Spring and strut assembly

Shock absorber fluid capacity	11 fl oz (325 ml)(11.4 Imp. fl oz)
Spring color identification	
Manual steering system	Cream 1, white 2
Power steering system	Cream 1, white 2 (right) pink 1, yellow 2 (left)

Rear suspension

Shock absorber

Maximum length (from center of lower eye to bottom of upper bushing)	525 mm (20.67 in)
Coil spring identification color	Yellow and purple

Steering system

Minimum turning radius	18.7 ft (5.7 m)

Standard column length (dimension L)

Manual system	179mm (7.05 in)
Power system	180mm (7.09 in)

Turns of steering wheel (lock to lock)

Manual system	3.5
Power system	3.1

Steering wheel play	Less than 1.38 in (35 mm)
Steering wheel axial play	0

Steering gear (manual system)

Type	VRB47L
Worm bearing preload	3.5 to 5.2 in-lb (4 to 6 mm)
Steering gear preload	less than 10.9 in-lb (12.5 cm-kg)
Endplay (between sector shaft and adjusting screw)	0.0004 to 0.0012 in (0.01 to 0.03 mm)
Backlash at gear arm top end (in Neutral)	0 to 0.004 in (0 to 0.1 mm)
Oil capacity	$\frac{5}{8}$ pt (0.28 liters) ($\frac{1}{2}$ Imp. pt)

Steering gear (power system)

Type	I.P.S. 56L
Fluid capacity	$1\frac{1}{4}$ qt (1.2 liters) ($1\frac{1}{8}$ Imp qt)
Fluid normal operating temperature	140 to 176°F (60 to 80°C)
Oil pump maximum pressure	782 psi (55 cm^2/kg)
Steering wheel turning force (at circumference)	6.6 to 7.7 lb (3.0 to 3.5 kg)
Steering gear turning torque (turned 360° from straight-ahead position)	less than 10 in-lb (12 cm-kg)

Steering linkage

Standard tie rod (side rod) length	2.795 in (71.0 mm)
Initial turning torque	
Balljoint	4.3 to 21.7 in-lb (5 to 25 cm-kg)
Swivel pin	less than 22 in-lb (25 cm-kg)
Idler arm	less than 69 in-lb (80 cm-kg)

Torque specifications

	ft-lb	m-kg
Wheel lugs	65	9.0
Wheel bearing nut	20	2.8
Rotor to hub bolts	33	4.6
Upper strut mounting nuts	22	3.0
Gland packing	84	11.0
Strut-to-knuckle arm bolts	63	8.5
Piston rod self-locking nut	48	6.8
Caliper-to-strut bolts	63	8.5
Knuckle arm-to-tie rod nut	55	7.5
Balljoint-to-knuckle arm bolts	82	11.0
Balljoint-to-transverse link bolts	40	5.6
Transverse link-to-crossmember bolts	50	7.0
Crossmember mounting bolt	27	3.7
Crossmember mounting nuts	48	6.7
Engine mount-to-crossmember nuts	27	3.7
Tension rod-to-tension bracket nut	36	5.0
Tension rod-to-transverse link bolts	40	5.6
Tension rod bracket-to-body bolts	27	3.7
Front stabilizer bar link nut	14	1.9
Front stabilizer bar bracket bolts and nuts	27	3.7
Upper link mounting bolts	54	7.5
Lower link mounting bolts	54	7.5
Rear hub nut	65	9.0
Shock absorber upper mounting nut	12	1.7
Shock absorber lower mounting bolt	55	7.5
Steering wheel nut	32	4.4
Jacket tube bracket-to-dash bolts	2.9	0.4
Steering column mounting bracket bolts	11	1.6
Jacket tube mounting bracket bolt	2.9	0.4
Coupling fixing bolt (manual system)	14	1.8
Idler arm mounting bolts	27	3.7
Idler arm nut	45	6.3
Tie rod locknuts	65	9.0
All ball stud and swivel pin retaining nuts (except below)	36	5.0
Tie rod ball stud and swivel pin retaining nut (power system only)	45	6.3
Manual steering gear		
Worm shaft-to-coupling bolt	33	4.5
Steering gear mounting bolts	42	5.8
Sector shaft-to-gear arm nut	100	14
Adjusting plug locknut	205	28
Sector shaft cover bolts	15	2.0
Sector shaft adjusting screw locknut	25	3.5

Power steering gear	ft-lb	m-kg
Steering gear mounting bolts	42	5.8
Stub shaft-to-joint bolt	26	3.6
Sector shaft-to-gear arm nut	100	14
Rear cover mounting screws	22	3.0
Sector shaft cover mounting screws	22	3.0
Sector shaft adjusting screw locknut	23	3.2
Oil pump-to-bracket bolts	24	3.2
Fluid hoses-to-oil pump nuts	29	4.0
Reservoir tank mounting bolts	3.0	0.4
Fluid hose-to-steering gear	44	6.0

1 Wheels and tires – general information

All Datsuns are equipped with metric-sized fiberglass or steel belted radial tires. The metric tire size code is shown in the accompanying illustration. Use of other size or type of tires may affect the ride and handling of the car. Do not mix different types of tires such as radials and bias belted on the same car, as handling may be seriously affected.

It is recommended that tires be replaced in pairs on the same axle, but if only one tire is being replaced, be sure it is of the same size, structure and tread design as the other.

Because tire pressure has a substantial effect on handling and wear, the pressure on all tires should be checked at least once a month or before any extended trips and set to the correct pressure. Tire pressure should be checked and adjusted with the tires cold.

To achieve the maximum life of your tires they should be rotated on the car at 7500 miles and then again at every 15 000 mile interval, as outlined in the car's routine maintenance schedule and detailed in Chapter 1, Section 5.

The tires should be replaced when the depth of the tread pattern is worn to a minimum of $\frac{1}{16}$-in (1.5 mm) or when the tread becomes exposed. Correct tire pressures and driving techniques have an important influence on tire life. Heavy cornering, excessively rapid acceleration and sharp braking increase tire wear. Extremely worn tires are not only very susceptible to going flat but are especially dangerous in wet weather conditions.

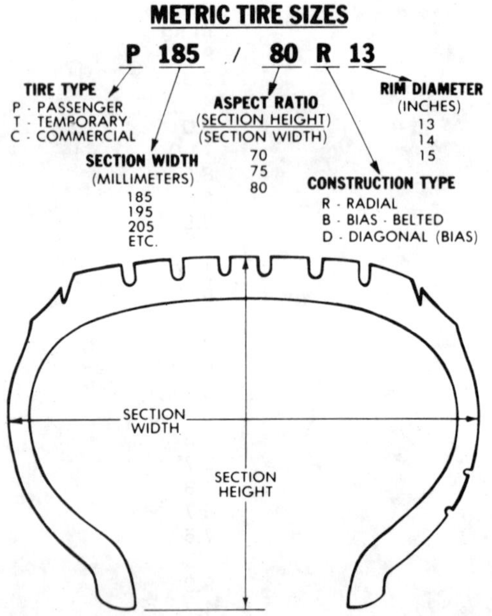

Fig. 11.1 Code used for metric tire sizes (Sec 1)

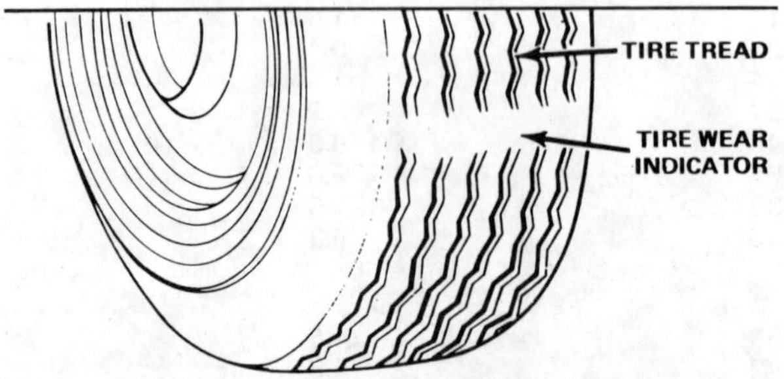

Fig. 11.2 Tire wear indicators are designed into the tread of the tires as a warning that they need replacing (Sec 1)

Condition	Probable cause	Corrective action
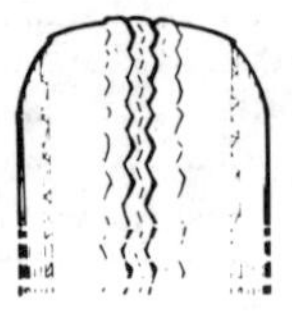 Shoulder wear	• Underinflation (both sides wear) • Incorrect wheel camber (one side wear) • Hard cornering • Lack of rotation	• Measure and adjust pressure. • Repair, or replace axle and suspension parts. • Reduce speed. • Rotate tires.
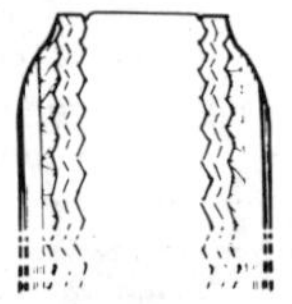 Center wear	• Overinflation • Lack of rotation	• Measure and adjust pressure. • Rotate tires.
Feathered edge 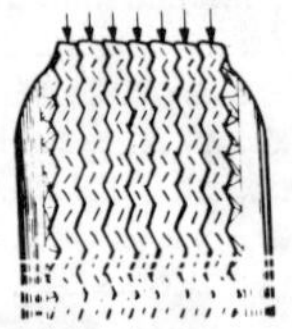 Toe-in or toe-out wear	• Incorrect toe	• Adjust toe-in.
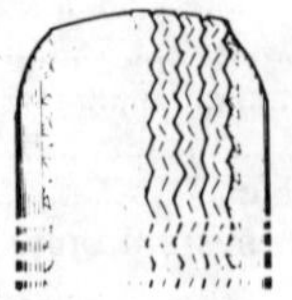 Uneven wear	• Incorrect camber or caster • Malfunctioning suspension • Unbalanced wheel • Out-of-round brake drum • Other mechanical conditions • Lack of rotation	• Repair, or replace axle and suspension parts. • Repair, replace or, if necessary, reinstall. • Balance or replace. • Correct or replace. • Correct or replace. • Rotate tires.

Fig. 11.3 The pattern of tire tread wear is indicative of various problems in the front end (Sec 1)

The tire tread pattern can give a good indication of problems in the maintenance or adjustment of tires, suspension and front end components. The accompanying illustration gives some common examples of tire wear patterns and their usual causes. If a tire exhibits a wear pattern caused by incorrect front end alignment, refer to Section 2.

Wheels must be replaced if they are bent, dented, leak air, have elongated bolt holes, are heavily rusted, ovaled, out of vertical symmetry or if the lug nuts won't stay tight. Wheel repairs that use welding or peening are not recommended, as this can weaken the metal.

Tire and wheel balance is important in the overall handling, braking and performance of the car. Unbalanced wheels can adversely affect handling and ride characteristics as well as tire life. Whenever a tire is installed on a wheel, the tire and wheel should be balanced by a qualified shop with the proper equipment.

This car is equipped with a compact T-type spare tire which is designed to save space in the trunk as well as being easier to handle due to its lighter weight. The spare tire pressure should be checked at least once a month, and maintained at 60 psi (412 kPa).

The compact spare tire and wheel are designed for use with each other only, and neither the tire nor the wheel should be coupled with other types or sizes of wheels and tires.

Because the compact spare is designed as a temporary replacement for an out-of-service standard wheel and tire, the compact spare should be used on the car only until the standard wheel and tire are repaired or replaced. Continuous use of the compact spare at speeds of over 50 mph (80 kph) is not recommended. In addition, the expected tread life of the compact spare is only about 3000 miles (4800 kilometers).

CAUTION: Be sure to use lug nuts designed for steel wheels only with this spare.

The proper procedure for removing and installing the wheel and tire is described in the front of this manual.

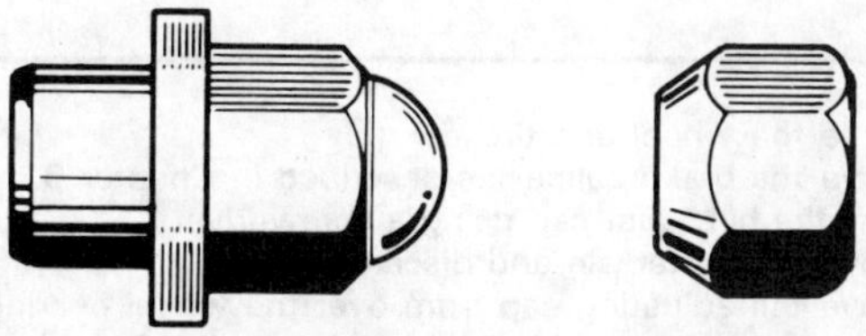

Fig. 11.4 Different wheel lugs are used for aluminum and steel wheels and should not be interchanged (Sec 1)

2 Front end alignment

1 A front end alignment refers to the adjustments made to the front wheels so that they are in proper angular relationship to the suspension and the ground. Front wheels that are out of proper alignment not only affect steering control but also increase tire wear. On Datsuns, all of the front end adjustments (except toe-in) are preset at the factory and cannot be adjusted. If the camber, castor or steering axis (kingpin) inclination is found to be incorrect, this indicates wear of the related components.

2 Getting the proper front wheel alignment is a very tedious exacting process and one in which complicated and expensive machines are necessary to perform the job properly. Because of this, it is advisable to have a specialist with the proper equipment perform these tasks.

3 We will, however, use this space to give you a basic idea of what is involved with front end alignment so you can better understand the process and deal intelligently with shops which do this work.

4 *Toe in* is the turning in of the front wheels. The purpose of a toe specification is to ensure parallel rolling of the front wheels. In a car with zero toe in the distance between the front edges of the wheels will be the same as the distance between the rear edges of the wheels. The actual amount of toe in is normally only a fraction of an inch. The 200 SX has a maximum static toe in of approximately 2 mm per wheel. Thus the distance between the front edges of the wheels should be about 4 mm less than the distance of the rear edges of the wheels when the car is standing. This is because even when the wheels are set to toe in slightly when the vehicle is standing still, they tend to roll parallel on the road when the car is moving.

5 Toe in is controlled by the adjustment of the tie rod. Incorrect toe in will cause the tires to wear improperly by making them 'scrub' against the road surface.

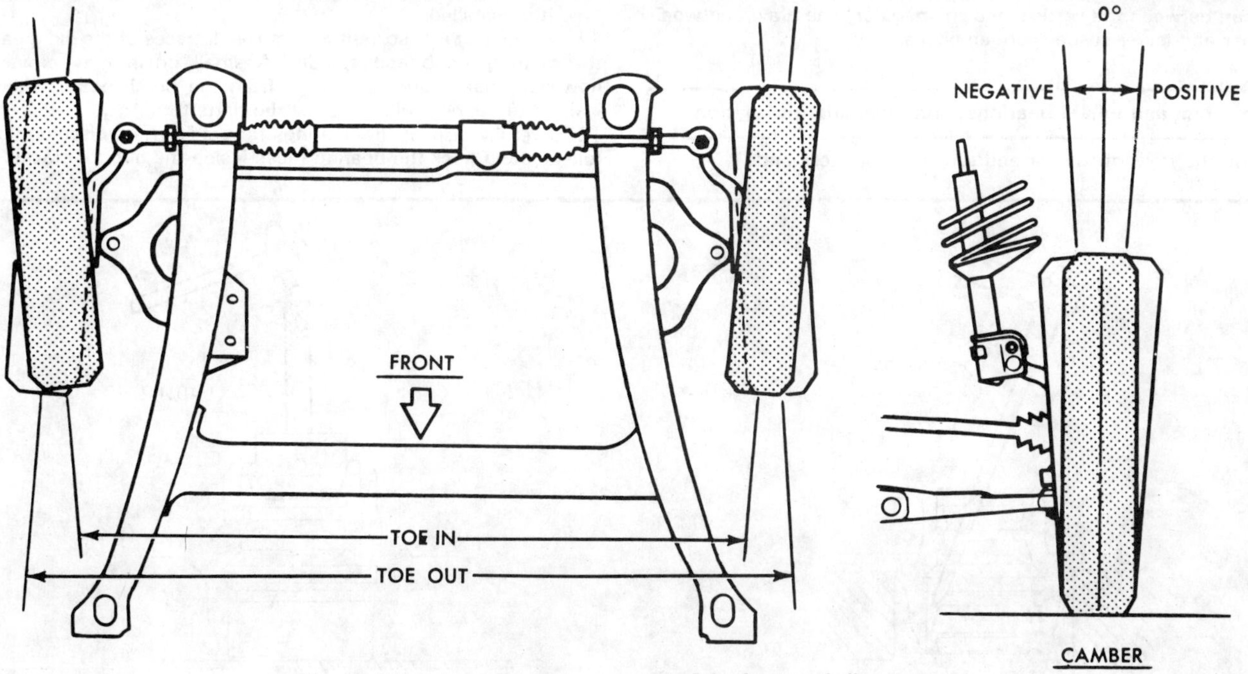

Fig. 11.5 Toe-in and camber are part of the front end alignment adjustments (Sec 2)

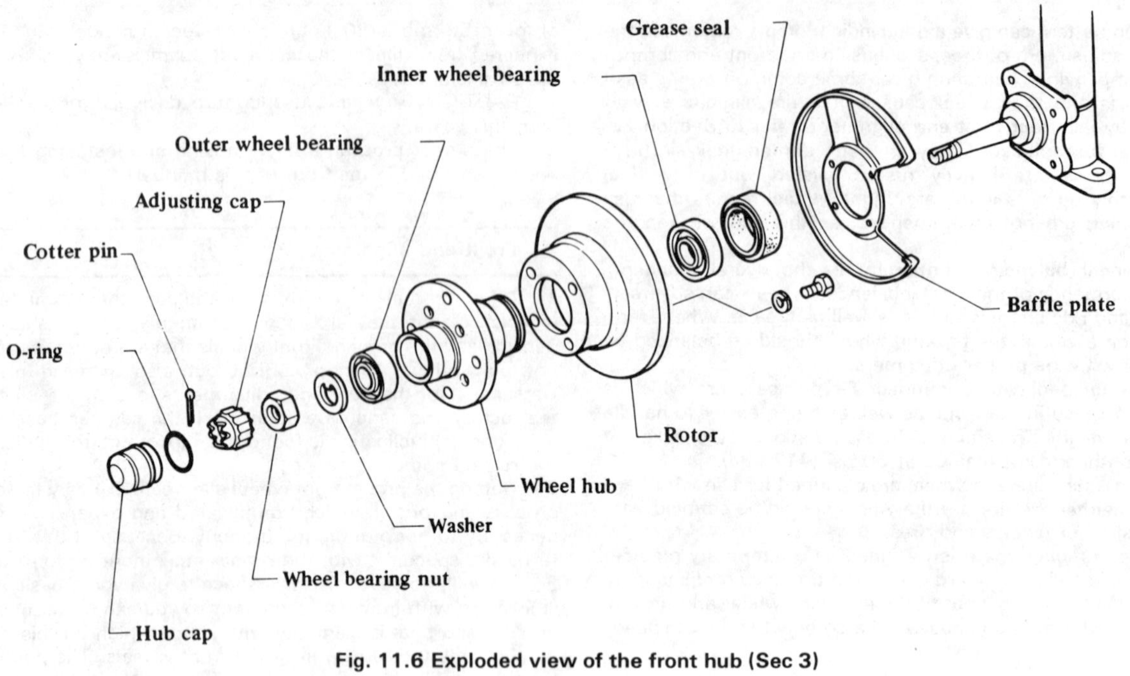

Fig. 11.6 Exploded view of the front hub (Sec 3)

6 *Camber* is the tilting of the front wheels from the vertical when viewed from the front of the vehicle. When the wheels tilt outward at the top, the camber is said to be positive (+). When the wheels tilt inward at the top the camber is negative (-). The amount of tilt is measured in degrees from the vertical and this measurement is called the camber angle. This angle affects the amount of tire tread which contacts the road and compensates for changes in the suspension geometry when the car is cornering or travelling over undulating surfaces.
7 *Castor* is the angle between the steering axis and a vertical line when viewed from each side of the car. Positive castor is when the steering axis is inclined rearward.
8 *Steering axis inclination* is the angle, when viewed from the front of the car, between the vertical and an imaginary line drawn between the upper and lower suspension leg pivots.

3 Front hub and wheel bearings – removal and installation

1 Raise the front of the car and support it on jackstands.
2 Remove the wheel and tire.
3 Remove the brake caliper as described in Chapter 9.
4 Pry off the hub dust cap using a screwdriver.
5 Remove the cotter pin and discard it.
6 Remove the adjusting cap from over the wheel bearing nut.
7 Remove the wheel bearing nut and its washer from the end of the spindle.
8 Remove the hub and rotor assembly from the spindle, catching the outer bearing as it comes out.
9 On the rear side of the hub, use a screwdriver to pry out the inner bearing grease seal. As this is done, note the direction in which the seal is installed.
10 The inner bearing can now be removed from the hub, again noting how it is installed.
11 Use clean parts solvent to remove all traces of the old grease from the bearings, hub and spindle. A small brush may prove useful; however, make sure no bristles from the brush embed themselves inside the bearing rollers. Allow the parts to air dry.
12 Carefully inspect the bearings for cracks, heat discoloration, bent rollers, etc. Check the bearing races inside the hub for cracks, scoring

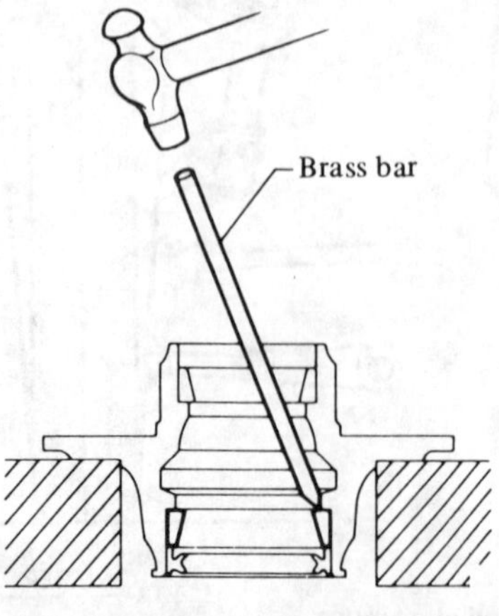

Fig. 11.7 The bearing races inside the front hub can be removed by tapping them with a brass bar or drift (Sec 3)

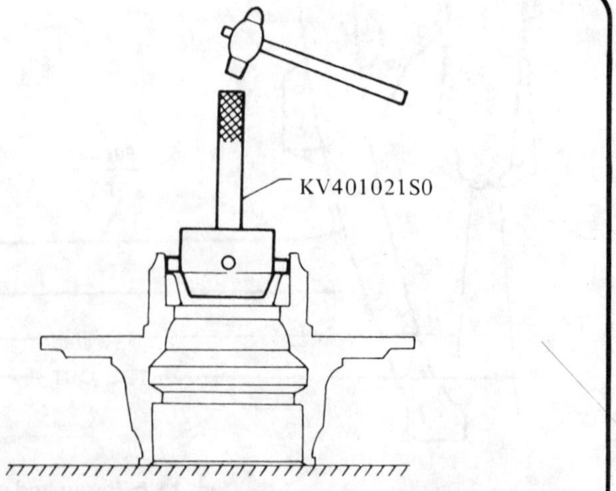

Fig. 11.8 An installing tool or large socket can be used to install the bearing races into the fork hub (Sec 3)

or uneven surfaces. If the bearing races are in need of replacement, use a drift or brass bar to carefully drive them out of the hub, as shown in the accompanying illustration. To install the new races, use an approved installing tool. These can usually be rented. If a large enough socket is available, that can also be used.
13 Use an approved high temperature front wheel bearing grease to pack the bearings. Work the grease fully into the bearings, forcing the grease between the rollers, cone and cage.
14 Apply a thin coat of grease to the spindle at the outer bearing seat, inner bearing seat, shoulder and seal seat.
15 Put a small quantity of grease inboard of each bearing race inside the hub. Using your finger, form a dam at these points to provide extra grease availability and to keep thinned grease from flowing out of the bearing.
16 Place the grease-packed inner bearing into the rear of the hub and put a little more grease outboard of the bearing.
17 Place a new seal over the inner bearing and tap the seal with a flat plate or socket and a hammer until it is flush with the hub.
18 Carefully place the hub assembly onto the spindle and push the grease-packed outer bearing into position.
19 Install the washer and spindle nut. Tighten the nut to the specified torque.
20 In a forward direction, spin the hub to seat the bearings and remove any grease or burrs which could cause excessive bearing play later.
21 After torqueing the wheel bearing nut, turn it counterclockwise about 60°.
22 At this point the wheel bearing preload must be adjusted. Place a torque wrench over the wheel bearing nut and slowly begin to rotate the hub in the forward direction, taking note of how much torque is needed to start the hub turning. With new parts installed, the torque should be 1.5 to 3.3 ft-lb (0.7 to 1.5 m-kg), while with old parts installed, the torque should be 0.4 to 1.8 ft-lb (0.2 to 0.8 m-kg). If the measured torque is not within these specs, tighten or loosen the wheel bearing nut until the proper bearing preload is obtained.
23 Install a new cotter pin through the hole in the spindle and spindle nut. If the nut slits do not line up, loosen the nut slightly until they do. From the proper preload position the nut should not be loosened any more than one-half flat to install the cotter pin.
24 Bend the ends of the new cotter pin until they are flat against the nut. Cut off any extra length which could interfere with the dust cap.
25 Install the dust cap complete with new O-ring, tapping it into place with a rubber mallet.
26 The remainder of the installation is the reverse of the removal procedure.

4 Wheel stud – replacement

1 Jack up the wheel to be worked on and support it on jackstands.
2 Remove the wheel and tire.
3 Remove the brake caliper as described in Chapter 9.
4 Remove the rotor as described in Chapter 9.
5 On front wheels, the hub will have to be separated from the rotor as described in Chapter 9.
6 Position the stud to be replaced at either the 5 or 7 o'clock position. Install a lug nut onto the end of the stud and, using an appropriate wheel stud puller, press the stud from its seat.
7 Remove the lug nut, and then the stud.
8 With the stud hole at either the 5 or 7 o'clock position, insert the

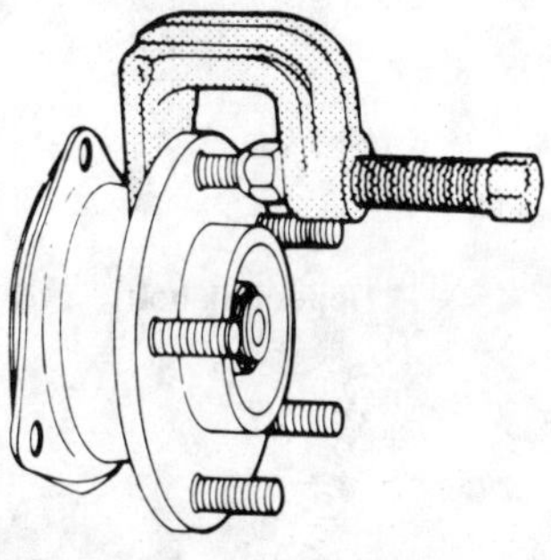

Fig. 11.9 A wheel stud removing tool can be used to press the studs from the hub (Sec 4)

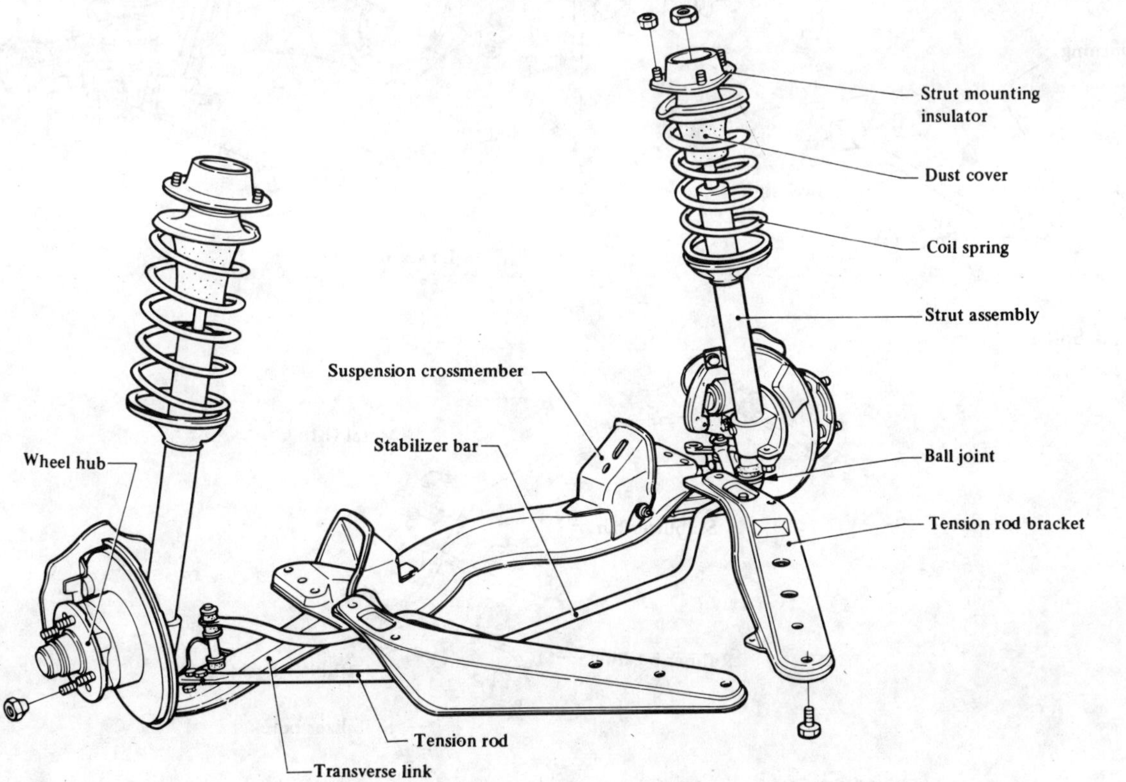

Fig. 11.10 Components of the front suspension system (Sec 5)

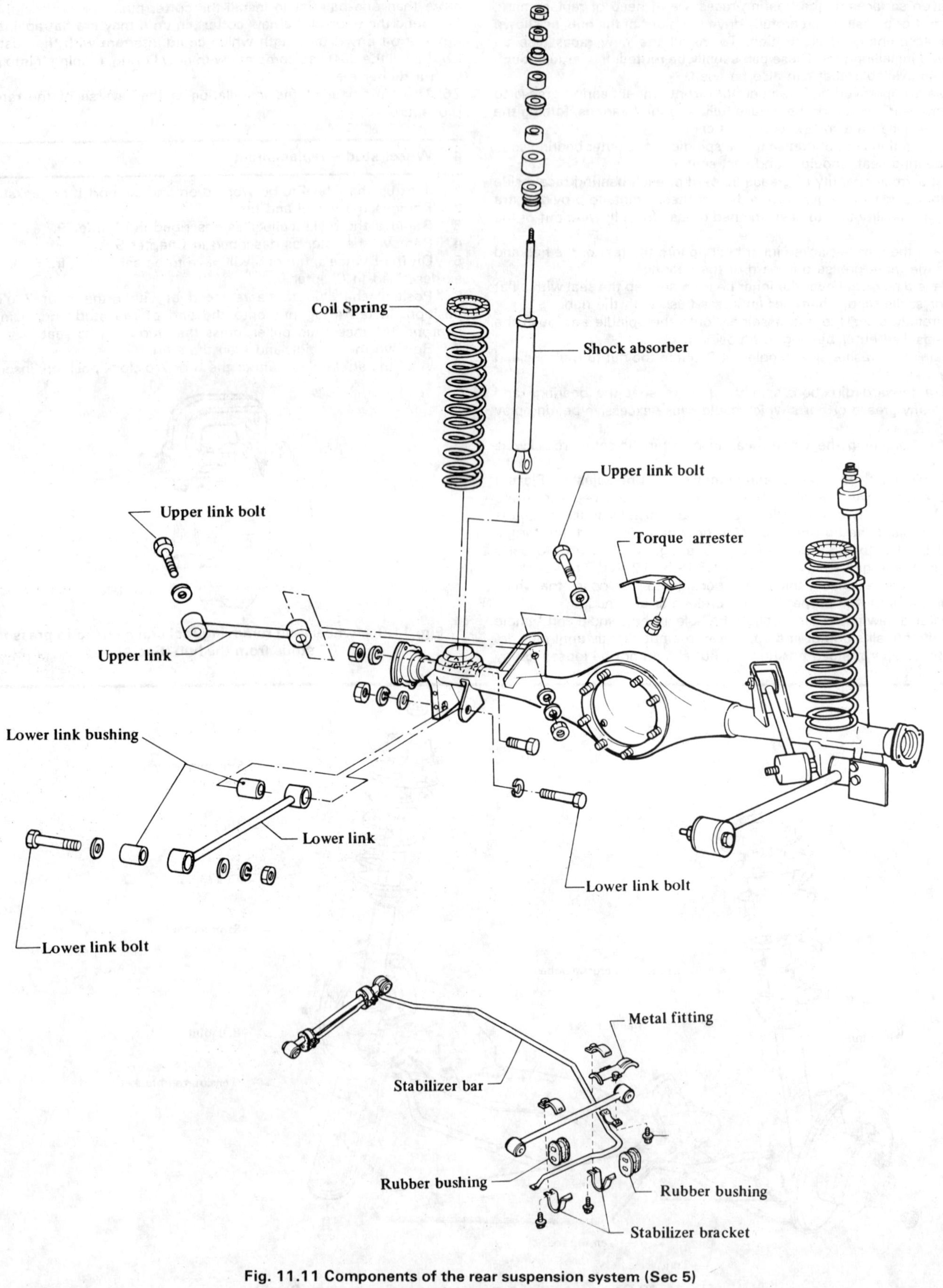

Fig. 11.11 Components of the rear suspension system (Sec 5)

new stud in the hole, making sure the serrations are aligned with those made by the original bolt.
9 Place four flat washers over the outside end of the stud, and then thread a lug onto the stud.
10 Tighten the lug nut until the stud head seats against the rear of the hub. Then remove the lug nut and washer.
11 Reinstall the components in the reverse order they were removed.
12 Mount the wheel and lower the car to the ground.

5 Suspension system – general information

This car features an independent front suspension of the MacPherson Strut design. This design uses a combination shock absorber and spring assembly which is mounted to the steering knuckle. The front axle spindles, on which the front hubs are mounted, are also part of the strut assembly.

A lower control arm (transverse link) which pivots on the front axle crossmember is also attached to the steering knuckle by way of a ball joint. The ball joint allows for free movement between the transverse link and the front wheel when the strut assembly compresses during normal driving.

Front and rear forces are controlled by tension rods, and a front stabilizer bar is installed to control body roll in corners.

All front suspension angles are set during the production of the car and cannot be adjusted.

The rear suspension consists of two coil springs, two shock absorbers, a rear stabilizer bar and two sets of upper and lower links.

These links are used to attach the rear axle to the body and, together with the shock absorbers and stabilizer bar, maintain the proper geometric relationship of the axle assembly to the body under the forces created by accelerating, braking and cornering.

The shock absorbers are conventional sealed hydraulic units. They are non-adjustable, non-refillable and cannot be disassembled. They are mounted at the bottom to a bracket on the axle housing and at the top to the body.

The two coil springs support the weight of the car in the rear and are retained between seats in the underbody and rear axle housing. A rubber insulator is used to isolate the spring from the underbody seat.

Never attempt to heat or straighten any suspension part, as this can weaken the metal or in other ways damage the part.

6 Suspension system – inspection

Since regular inspection of the suspension system is part of the routine maintenance of the car, these procedures are described in Chapter 1.

7 Front spring and strut assembly – removal and installation

1 Raise the front of the car and support it on jackstands.
2 Remove the wheel and tire.
3 Disconnect the brake line from the bracket on the strut, and plug the line to prevent fluid leaking.
4 Remove the caliper as described in Chapter 9.
5 Remove the hub and rotor assembly as described in Chapter 9.
6 Remove the deflector plate (photo).
7 Remove the 2 bolts that hold the strut assembly to the steering knuckle arm (photo).
8 Remove the 3 upper strut mounting nuts, located in the shock well under the hood (photo).
9 While supporting the strut, use a lever or large screwdriver to separate the steering knuckle arm from the base of the strut, (photo), and lift out the strut assembly.
10 If the strut assembly needs to be disassembled, refer to Section 8.
11 Installation is the reverse of the removal procedure. **Note:** *Prior to installing the strut assembly, apply a bead of silicone sealant to the steering knuckle mating surface as shown in the accompanying illustration. Also be sure the brake hose is not twisted and will not rub on any other parts.*
12 Bleed the brake system as described in Chapter 9.

7.6 The deflector shield is mounted to the front hub with 4 screws

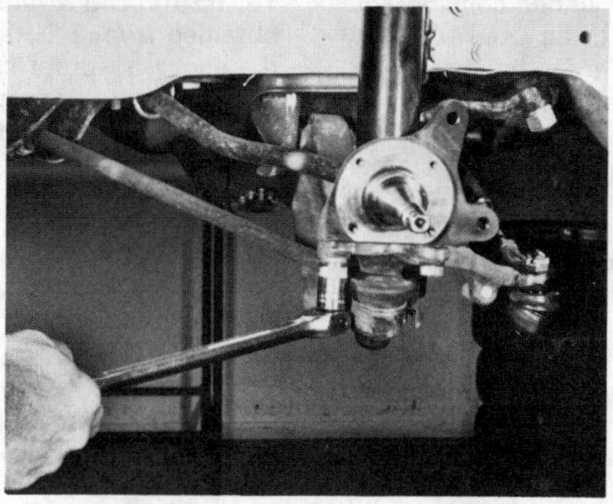

7.7 Removing the 2 bolts that retain the steering knuckle to the strut assembly

7.8 The strut assembly upper mounting nuts are located on the shock well under the hood

7.9 A screwdriver can be used to pry the steering knuckle down from the strut assembly

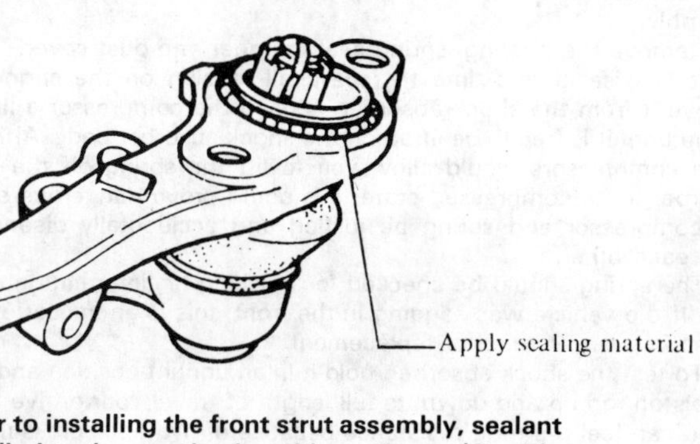

Fig. 11.12 Prior to installing the front strut assembly, sealant should be applied to the steering knuckle as shown (Sec 7)

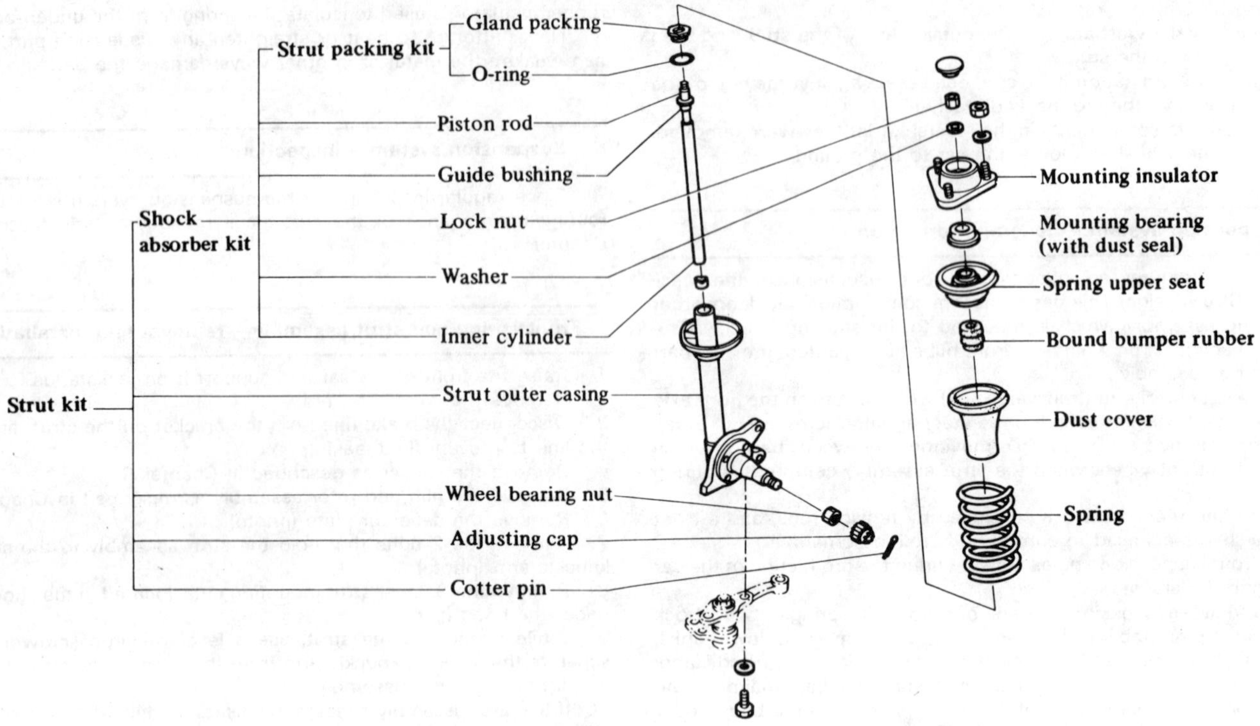

Fig. 11.13 Components of the front spring and strut assembly (Sec 8)

8 Front spring and strut assembly – disassembly and reassembly

1 The spring on the front shock absorber is under considerable pressure, requiring a special spring compressor to be used to safely compress the spring and disengage its components. Do not attempt to disassemble the spring without the proper compressor, as serious injury can occr.
2 A strut spring compressor can either be purchased through Datsun dealers or through most auto parts stores. Compressors can be rented on a daily basis from rental agencies and some auto parts stores.
3 Hold the shock absorber in a vise using wood blocks to cushion the jaws to prevent damage to the shock.
4 Following the manufacturer's instructions for the particular spring compressor being used, slightly compress the spring, making sure that the jaws of the compressor are firmly seated around the coils and cannot slip off.
5 Tighten the compressor from side to side, a little at a time, until the spring seal is clear of the uppermost coil.
6 With the spring firmly compressed and clear of its seat, reinstall the nuts onto the upper studs to protect the threads. Hold the mounting insulator stationery by placing a bar between the mounting studs, and remove the top locknut and washer.
7 Pull the mounting insulator off the top of the shock absorber assembly.
8 Remove the bearing, spring seat, bumper and dust cover.
9 It is wise at this time to relieve all tension on the spring and remove it from the shock absorber. Loosen the compressor a little at a time until it is free to be lifted off the shock absorber body. Although some compressors would allow you to lift the spring off the shock absorber in its compressed state, this could prove dangerous should the compressor and spring be jostled and accidentally disengaged from each other.
10 The spring should be checked for cracking or deformation of any kind. If the vehicle was sagging in the front, this is an indication that the springs are in need of replacement.
11 To test the shock absorber, hold it in an upright position and work the piston rod up and down its full length of travel, four or five times. If you can feel a strong resistance because of hydraulic pressure, the shock absorber is functioning properly. If you feel no marked resistance or there is a sudden free movement in travel, the shock absorber should be repaired or replaced.
12 If there are excessive amounts of fluid evident on the outside of the shock absorber, the shock absorber should be repaired or replaced.
13 If the shock absorber is defective, a new sealed unit can be obtained from a Datsun dealer, or, if the outer casing is not damaged, the shock absorber can be overhauled. If oil is leaking from the gland packing, replacement of that component may be all that's required. If an overhaul is to be done, first obtain a shock absorber rebuild kit from a Datsun dealer. One special tool will also be needed as described in the following procedure.
14 Push the piston rod in until it bottoms, then remove the gland packing.
15 Remove the O-ring from the top of the outer casing and draw out the guide bushing.
16 Lift out the piston rod together with the inner cylinder.
17 Drain the fluid from the inner cylinder and the outer casing.
18 Wash all of the metal parts in solvent.
19 Prior to reassembly, make sure that all parts are completely free of dirt.
20 With the outer casing supported in a vise between wood blocks, insert the complete shock absorber kit into the casing.
21 Pour in exactly 11 fl. oz. (325 ml) of Nissan strut fluid or equivalent shock fluid.
22 Install the guide bushing over the piston rod and into the outer casing.
23 Lubricate the inner sealing lip of the gland packing. Install a new O-ring into the top of the outer casing.
24 Lubricate the inner sealing lip of the gland packing with multi-purpose grease.
25 Wrap the threads on the end of the piston rod with electrical tape, and carefully slide the gland packing over the top of the piston rod.
26 Thread the gland packing into the outer casing and, using a special torque wrench adapter as shown in the accompanying illustration, tighten it to the specified torque.
27 Remove the shock absorber from the vise, hold it in an upright position and stroke the piston out its full length. Then invert the shock absorber and push the piston in until it bottoms. Do this several times to remove all air from the shock absorber.
28 Using the spring compressor, compress the spring approximately 2 in (50.7 mm). Then with the shock absorber main body mounted in a vise with protective wood blocks, install the spring over the shock

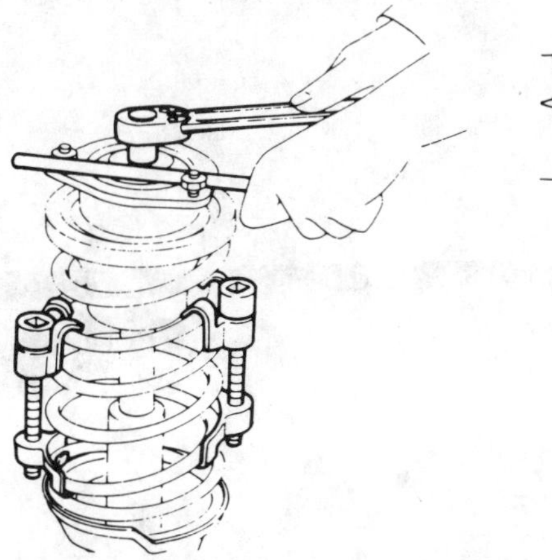

Fig. 11.14 When removing the upper retaining nut from the strut assembly, use a bar to keep the mounting insulator from turning (Sec 8)

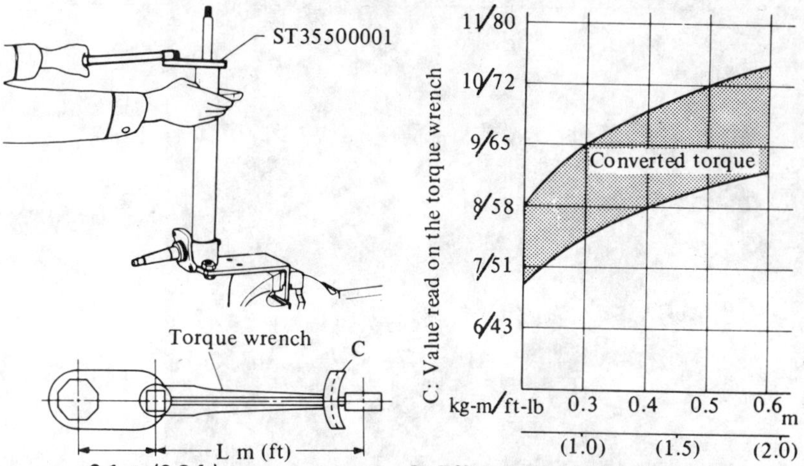

Fig. 11.15 To properly torque the gland packing a special adapter must be used with a torque wrench, and the torque indicated on the wrench must be converted using the chart above (Sec 8)

absorber body. Make sure the lower coil conforms to the spring seat.
29 Install the dust cover and bumper to the shock body.
30 Install the spring seat and mounting bearing.
31 Install the mounting insulator.
32 Install the lock washer and locknut to the top of the piston rod. Tighten this nut to its proper torque setting.
33 Carefully relieve tension on the coil spring by loosening the compressor from side to side, a little at a time. Check to be sure the top of the spring is raised properly into its seat.

9 Front stabilizer bar – removal and installation

1 Raise the front of the car and support it on jackstands.
2 Remove the undercover.
3 Remove the lower nuts from both of the stabilizer links located at each end of the stabilizer bar (photo).
4 Remove the stabilizer links from the transverse links. Remove the bushings, washers and spacers being sure to keep them in their installed order, and then remove the stabilizer links from the stabilizer bar.
5 Loosen the rear bolt of both stabilizer support brackets so that there is approximately 1 inch of clearance (photo).
6 Remove the stabilizer support nuts and washers.
7 Disengage the stabilizer supports from the rear nuts. They are

9.3 Removing the stabilizer bar link

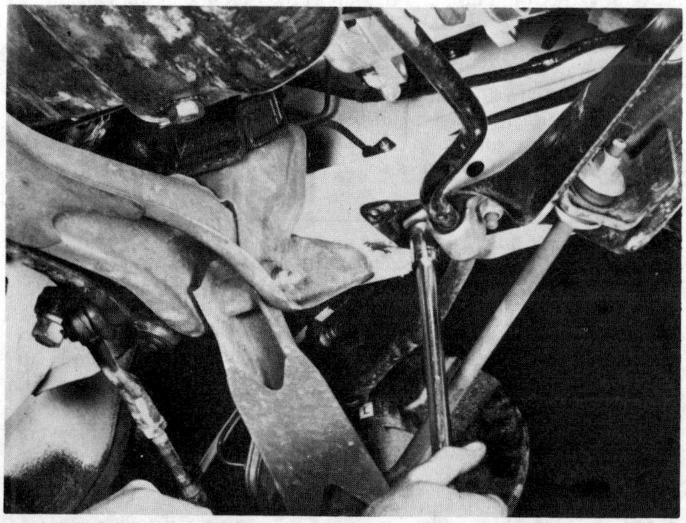

9.5 The front stabilizer bar rear bracket bolts do not have to be removed because the bracket is slotted

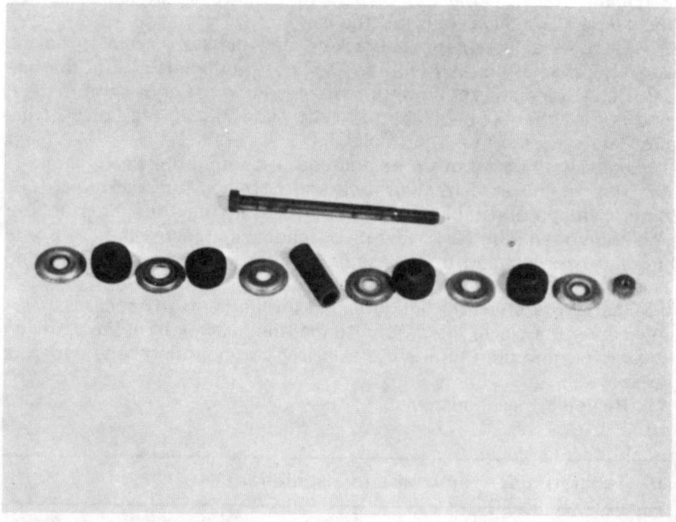

9.12 Proper order of the stabilizer bar link components

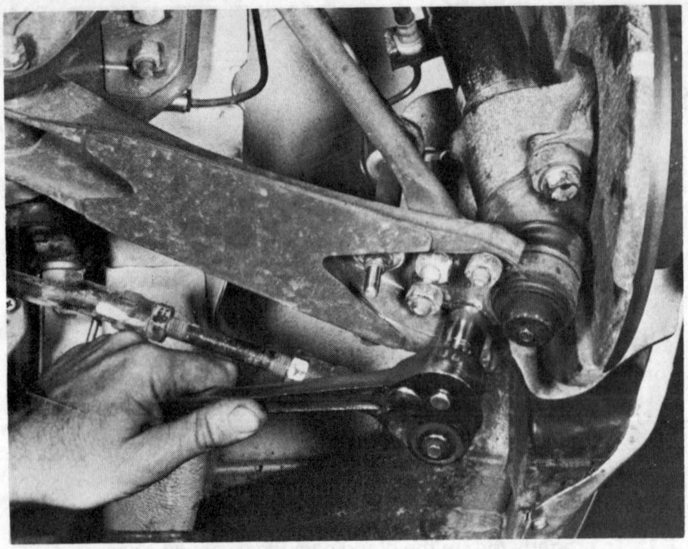

10.2a Removing the nut from the front end of the tension rod

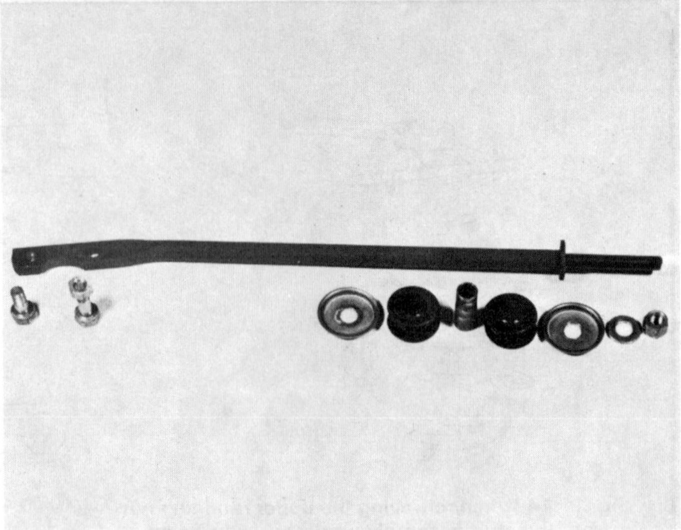

10.2b Components used to mount the tension rod

10.3 The tension rod is attached to the transverse link by 2 bolts

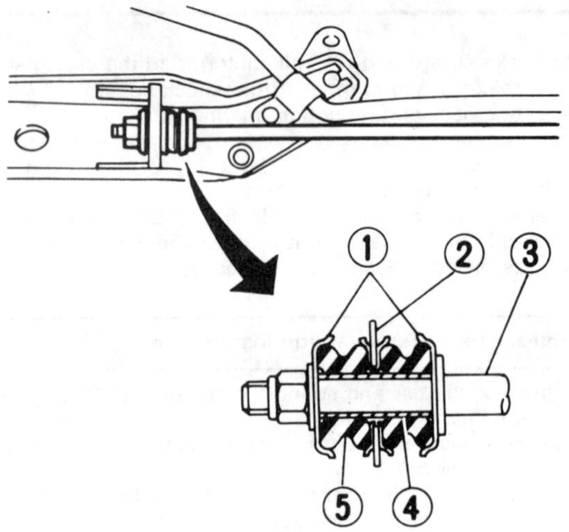

Fig. 11.16 Correct mounting arrangement of the tension rod to the tension rod bracket: (1) thrust washer, (2) tension rod bracket, (3) tension rod, (4) collar, (5) bushing (Sec 10)

slotted and will just slide out. Then lift out the stabilizer bar.

8 If the stabilizer bar bushings need to be replaced simply spread them apart and slide them off the bar.

9 Fit the stabilizer support brackets onto the stabilizer bar, making sure the bracket marked with an "L" goes on the left side of the bar.

10 Raise the stabilizer bar into position so that the light paint mark at one end of the bar is on the left side. Slide the slotted holes of the brackets onto the mounting bolts.

11 Loosely tighten both nuts and both mounting bolts.

12 Inspect the stabilizer link bolt and bushings for cracking or any other damage and replace them as necessary. Lay out the stabilizer link components in the proper order (photo) and install the links onto the stabilizer bar and transverse link, as shown in the accompanying illustration.

13 Install the stabilizer link nuts and torque them to specs.

14 Lower the car to the ground so that the full weight of the car is on the wheels and then torque the stabilizer bar mounting bolts and nuts to specs.

15 Reinstall the undercover.

10 Tension rod – removal and installation

1 Raise the front of the car and support it on jackstands for clearance.

2 Remove the nut from the forward end of the tension rod (photo) and lift off the bushings and washer plates (photo).

3 Remove both the bolt and the nut at the rear end of the tension rod (photo).

4 Remove the tension rod from the car.

5 If both tension rods are being removed at once be sure to note the marks referring to left and right for installation.

6 Installation is the reverse of the removal procedure. **Note:** *Do not torque tighten the mounting bolts until the car has been lowered to the ground and the full weight is on the wheels.*

11 Transverse links – removal and installation

1 Raise the front of the car and support it on jackstands.

2 Remove the wheel and tire.

3 Remove the stabilizer bar link.

4 Remove the bolts that attach the tension rod to the transverse link.

5 Remove the bolts (photo) that attach the steering knuckle to the transverse link, and separate the two components.

6 Remove the pivot bolt that holds the inner end of the transverse link to the crossmember (photo).

7 If necessary, turn the wheel outward for clearance, and remove the transverse link.

8 If the transverse link bushing needs to be replaced, it must be pressed out and a new bushing pressed in. Be sure that the outer end of the new bushing is flush with the end of the transverse link.

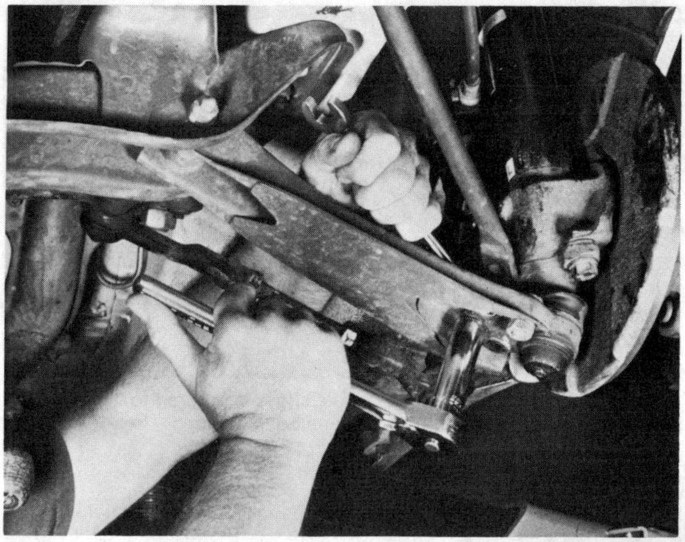

11.5 Removing the bolts that retain the balljoint to the transverse link

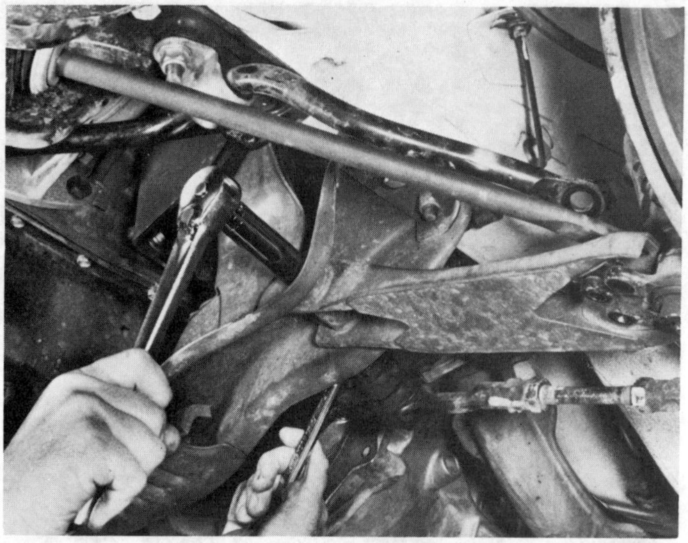

11.6 Removing the pivot bolt that attaches the transverse link to the crossmember

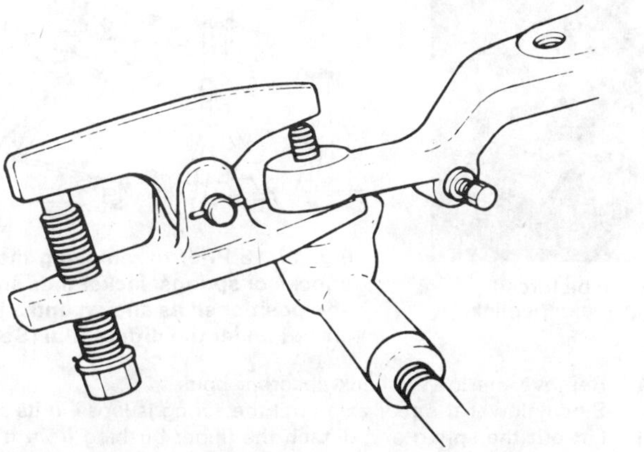

Fig. 11.17 A special separating tool must be used to separate the ball stud and swivel joints used in the steering linkage (Sec 13)

9 Installation is the reverse of the removal procedure. **Note:** *Do not tigten the pivot bolt at the inner end of the transverse link until the car has been lowered to the ground.*

12 Crossmember – removal and installation

1 Raise the front of the car and support it safely on stands placed under the body side members. The car should be high enough for the front wheels to hang free.
2 Remove the engine undershield.
3 Remove the transverse link as described in the preceding Section.
4 Support the weight of the engine either on a jack and wooden insulating block placed under the oil pan or by attaching an overhead hoist to it.
5 Disconnect the engine mountings from the crossmember.
6 Support the crossmember on a jack and unbolt it from the body sidemembers.
7 Installation is a reversal of removal, tighten all nuts and bolts to specified torque.

13 Balljoint – removal and installation

1 Raise the front of the car and support it securely on jackstands.
2 Remove the wheel and tire.
3 Remove the nut that secures the tie rod to the steering knuckle and using a suitable separating tool disengage the tie rod from the steering knuckle.
4 Remove the two bolts and one nut that hold the tension rod to the transverse link.

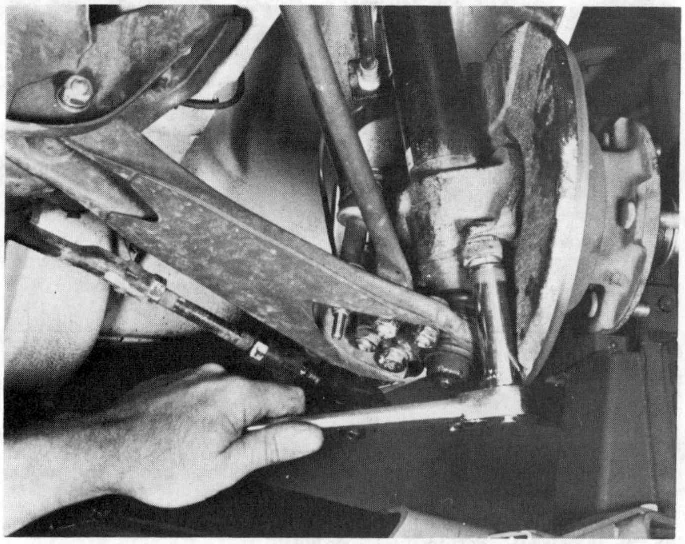

13.4 Removing the bolts that attach the steering knuckle/balljoint assembly to the strut

5 Break loose the bolts that hold the steering knuckle to the suspension strut (photo), but do not yet remove them. Break loose the bolts that hold the tension rod to the transverse link and the transverse link to the balljoint.
6 Remove the bolts that hold the steering knuckle to the strut.
7 Remove the bolts that hold the tension rod to the transverse link.
8 Remove the bolts that hold the transverse link to the balljoint and lower the balljoint and steering knuckle assembly off the car.
9 To replace the balljoint, remove the nut that holds the balljoint to the steering knuckle and press the balljoint from the knuckle using a hydraulic press.
10 Installation is the reverse of the removal procedure. **Note:** *When installing the balljoint and steering knuckle assembly, first engage it with the tie rod then install the bolts that hold the steering knuckle to the strut assembly and the bolts that hold the transverse link to the balljoint, before installing the two bolts and nut that hold the tension rod to the transverse link.*

14 Front axle – removal and installation

The front axle, which consists of the crossmember and the two transverse links can be removed as one piece by following the crossmember removal procedure described in Section 12, but without disconnecting the transverse links from the crossmember.

15.2 The rear stabilizer bar is secured to the lower links by 4 brackets

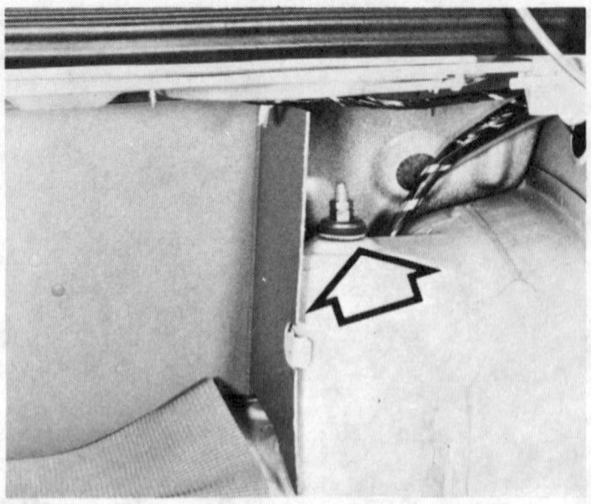

16.2 On hardtop models, a trim panel in the trunk must be removed to reach the upper shock mounting nuts

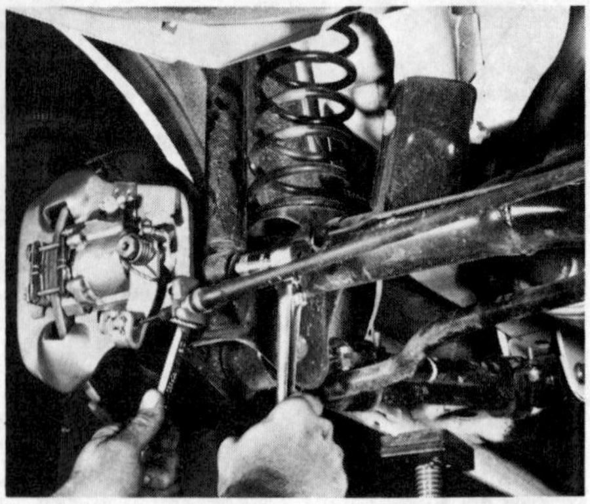

16.7 The rear shock is secured to its lower bracket by one bolt and nut

18.2 Removing the upper link mounting bolts

18.5 The rear axle may have to be forced forward or rearward to align the upper link with its bracket

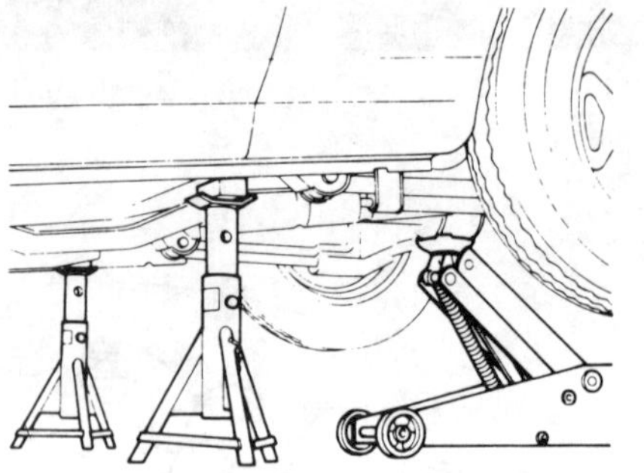

Fig. 11.18 Prior to removing the rear shocks or springs, jackstands should be positioned as shown and a jack placed under the differential (Sec 16)

15 Rear stabilizer bar – removal and installation

1 Jack up the rear of the car and support it on jackstands.
2 Remove the 4 stabilizer bar retaining bolts, two on each side (photo).
3 Remove the brackets that hold the stabilizer bar to the rubber bushings.
4 Carefully remove the stabilizer bar from the four bushings leaving the bushings attached to the lower links.
5 Inspect the bushings and if they exhibit any hardening or cracking replace them.
6 Installation is the reverse of the removal procedure.

16 Rear shock absorber – removal and installation

1 Open the trunk (hardtop) or rear door (hatchback).
2 Remove the trim panel covering the upper shock absorber nuts (photo).
3 Loosen the upper shock absorber nuts but do not yet remove them.
4 Raise the rear of the car and support it with 2 jackstands placed at the rear body support points.
5 Place a jack under the differential at the center of the rear axle.
6 Remove the upper shock absorber nuts.
7 Remove the lower shock absorber bolts (photo).
8 Carefully lower the rear axle slightly so the shock absorber can be removed from the car.
9 Installation is the reverse of the removal procedure.

17 Rear spring – removal and installation

1 Raise the rear of the car and support it on 2 jackstands placed at the rear body support points.
2 Remove both rear tires.
3 Place a jack under the differential case at the center of the rear axle.
4 Remove the lower shock absorber bolts.
5 Slowly lower the rear axle until the spring is loose in its supports.
6 Lift out the spring and detach the upper bushing from it.
7 When installing the spring be sure the bottom of the spring fits properly into its support.
8 Carefully raise the axle until the lower shock absorber bolt can be installed.
9 The remainder of the installation procedure is the reverse of the removal procedure.

18 Upper and lower links – removal and installation

Note: *If both the upper and lower links are removed at the same time, keep the mounting bolts separate as they are slightly different lengths.*

Upper link

1 Raise the rear of the car and support it on jackstands.
2 Remove the nuts and bolts at both ends of the link and lift the link out (photo).
3 If the bushings are cracked or distorted, or the link is damaged, replace the link. The bushings in the upper link cannot be replaced separate from the link.
4 To install, position one end of the link in its bracket on the body, and insert the mounting bolt to hole it there.
5 If the other end of the link will not align properly with the axle bracket, using a long adjustable or locking-type wrench, grip a secure point on the rear axle near the bracket and apply force in the direction needed to align the bracket with the end of the link (photo). As this is done, insert the other mounting bolt.
6 Once both mounting bolts are installed, torque the upper bolt to specifications.
7 Lower the car to the ground, and only then tighten the lower bolt to its proper torque.

Lower link

8 Raise the rear of the car and support it on jackstands.
9 Remove the rear stabilizer bar as described in Section 15.
10 Remove the mounting bolts and nuts at both ends of the link and lift it out (photo).

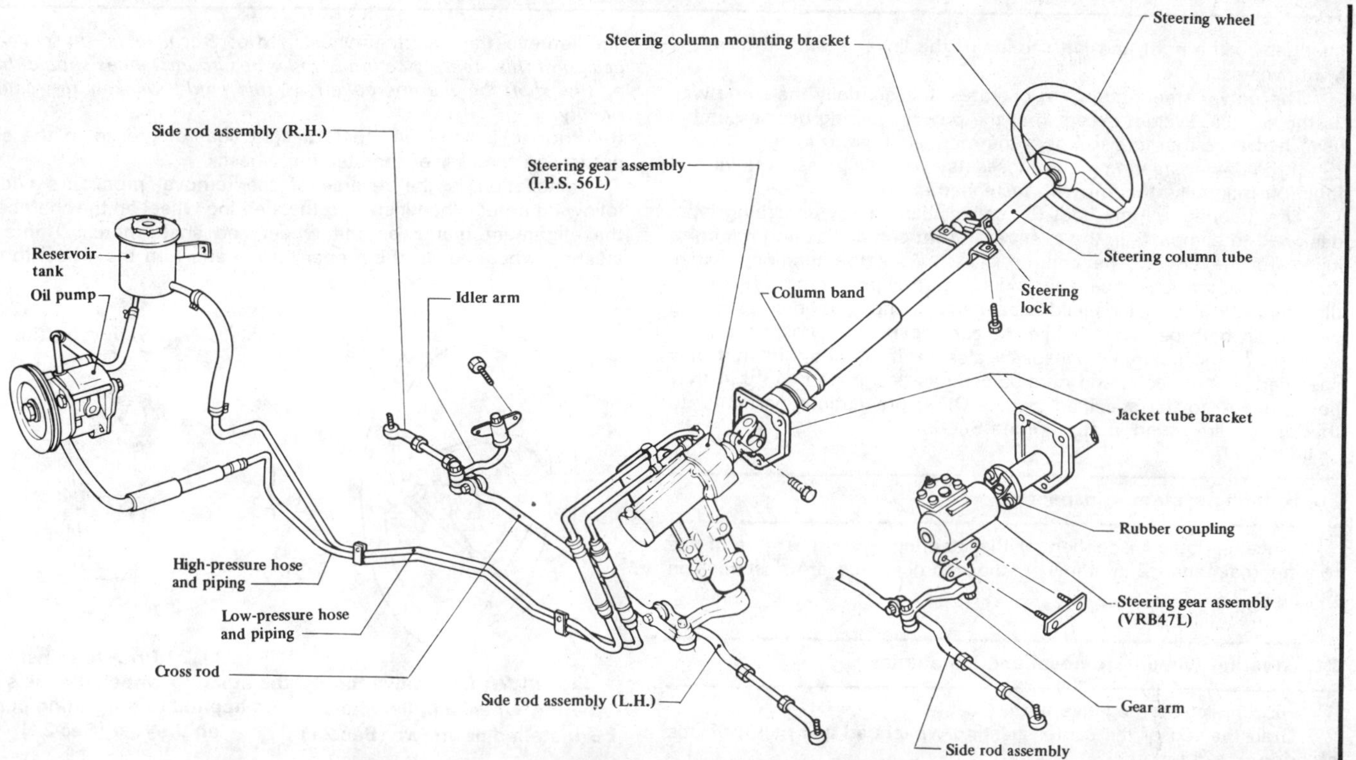

Fig. 11.19 Components of the steering system (Sec 19)

11 If necessary, remove the rubber stabilizer bar supports from the link.
12 If the bushings are cracked or deformed, a hydraulic press must be used to press the old bushings out and the new bushings in.
13 If the link itself is damaged, replace the entire unit.
14 To install, position one end of the link in its bracket on the body, and insert the mounting bolt to hold it there.
15 If the other end of the link will not align properly with the axle bracket, using a long adjustable or locking-type wrench, grip a secure point on the rear axle near the bracket and apply force in the direction needed to align the bracket with the end of the link (photo). As this is done, insert the other mounting bolt. Do not tighten the bolts yet.
16 Reinstall the stabilizer bar.
17 Lower the car to the ground, and only then the link mounting bolts to their proper torque.

19 Steering system – general information

The steering system is of the worm and nut recirculating ball type. The components that make up the manual system are the steering wheel, steering column, steering gear (steering box), and steering linkage assembly. In addition to these the power steering system also used a belt-driven oil pump with separate reservoir tank to provide hydraulic pressure.

In a manual system, the motion of turning the steering wheel is transferred through the column to the wormshaft of the steering gear. Fitted to the wormshaft is a free moving ball nut. Gear teeth on the ball nut are meshed with the teeth on the steering gear's sector shaft, which is directly connected to the linkage. It is through this ball nut and sector shaft that the circular motion of the steering wheel gets

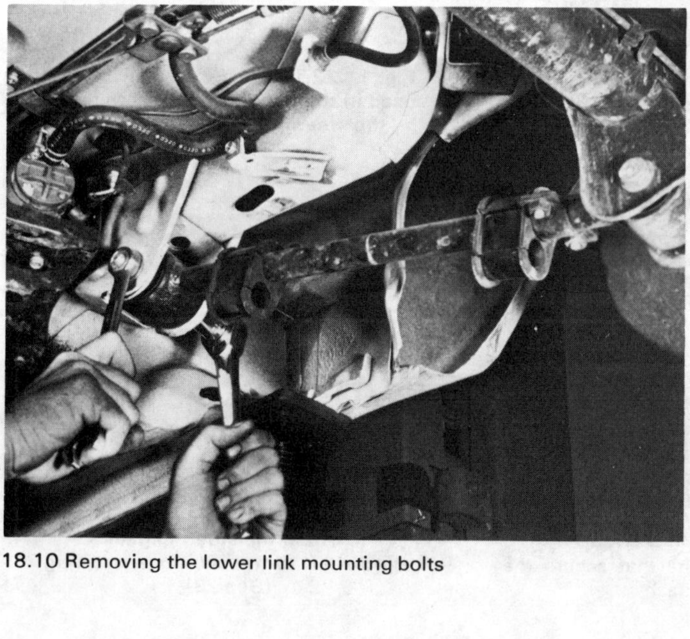

18.10 Removing the lower link mounting bolts

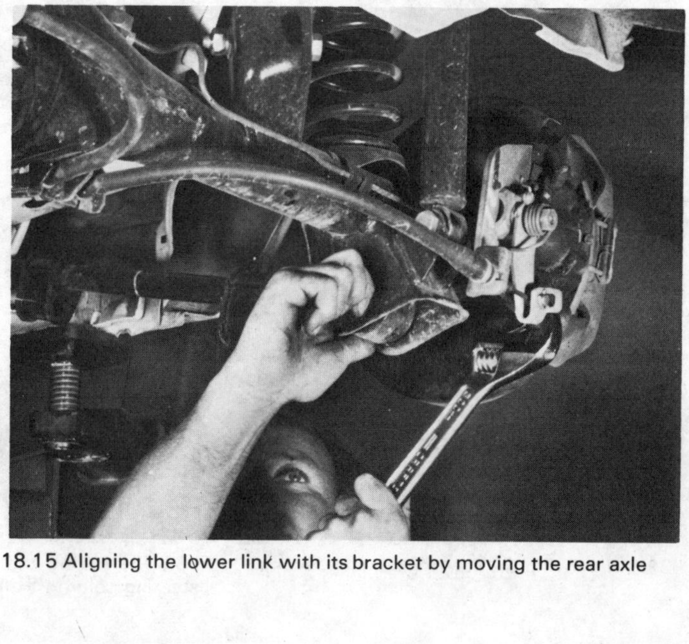

18.15 Aligning the lower link with its bracket by moving the rear axle

changed to the right and left motion of the linkage, and, in turn, the front wheels.

The power steering system operates in essentially the same way as the manual system except that the power steering gear assembly used hydraulic pressure to boost the manual steering force.

If the power steering system loses its hydraulic pressure it will still function manually, though with increased effort.

The steering column is of the collapsible, energy-absorbing type, designed to compress in the event of a front end collision to minimize injury to the driver. The column also houses the ignition switch, steering column lock, headlight switch, turn signal control, headlight dimmer switch and windshield wiper control. The ignition and steering wheel can both be locked while the car is parked to inhibit theft.

Due to the column's collapsible design, it is important that only specified screws, bolts and nuts be used as designated and that they be tightened to the specified torque. Other precautions particular to this design are noted in appropriate Sections.

20 Steering system – inspection

Since periodic inspection of the steering system is part of the routine maintenance of the car, these procedures are described in Chapter 1.

21 Steering wheel – removal and installation

1 Disconnect the negative battery cable.
2 Grab the top of the center steering wheel pad and pull it off the steering wheel (photo).
3 Be sure the steering wheel is in the unlocked position, and then remove the steering wheel nut (photo).
4 Mark the position of the steering wheel in relation to the steering shaft.
5 Note the 2 threaded holes in the steering wheel on either side of the shaft. Install an appropriate steering wheel puller into these holes, and remove the steering wheel. **Note:** *Because of the collapsible design of this steering column, under no circumstances should the end of the shaft be hammered on as this could weaken the column's rigidity.*
6 Prior to installation, apply a light coat of grease to the sliding portion on the rear of the steering wheel.
7 Installation is the reverse of the removal procedure with the following note: When installing the steering wheel on the shaft be sure the alignment marks on the wheel and shaft match. Tighten the steering wheel nut to the proper torque and turn the wheel to check for drag.

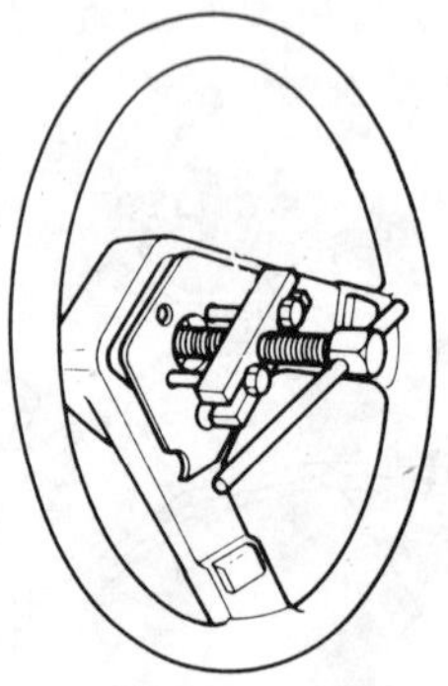

Fig. 11.20 To remove the steering wheel a puller should be installed as shown (Sec 21)

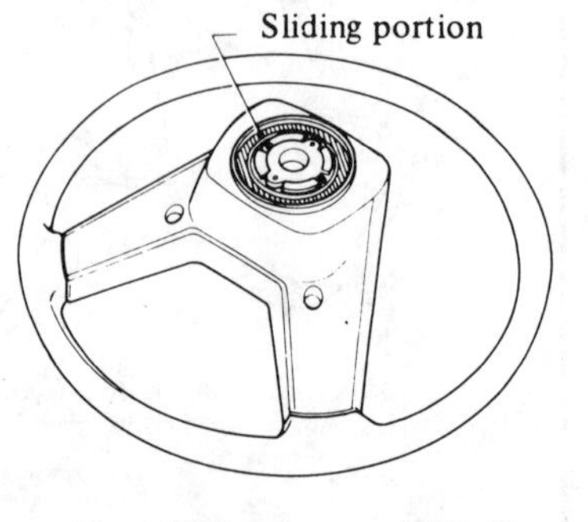

Fig. 11.21 Prior to reinstalling the steering wheel, grease should be applied to the sliding portion on the rear (Sec 21)

22 Steering lock – removal and installation

1 Obtain 2 self-shear screws from your Datsun dealer, needed to reinstall the steering lock.
2 Remove the steering wheel as described in Section 21.

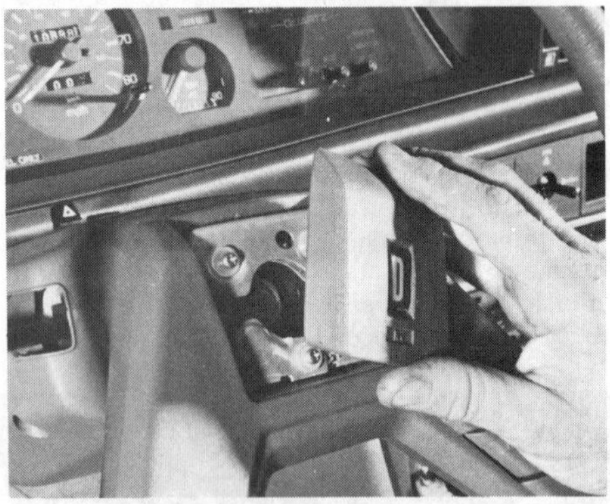

21.2 The center pad of the steering wheel simply pulls off

21.3 Removing the steering wheel nut

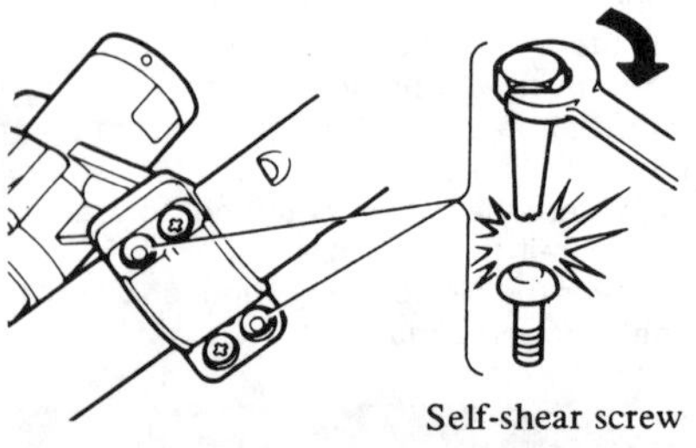

Fig. 11.22 Two self-shear screws are used in the positions shown to retain the steering lock to the column (Sec 22)

22.3 Removing the steering column cover

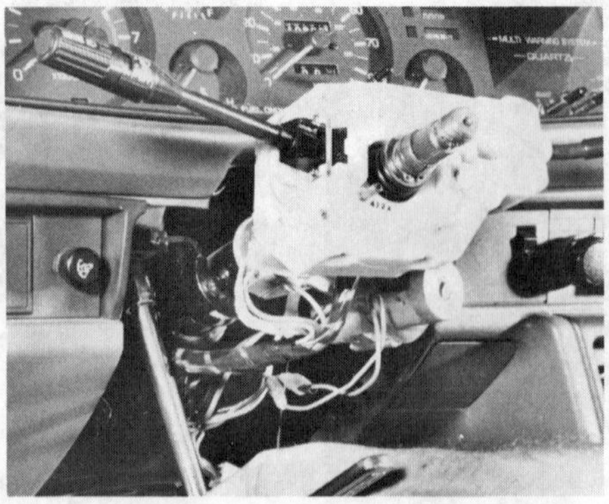

23.9 Removing the bolts that secure the steering column to the dash

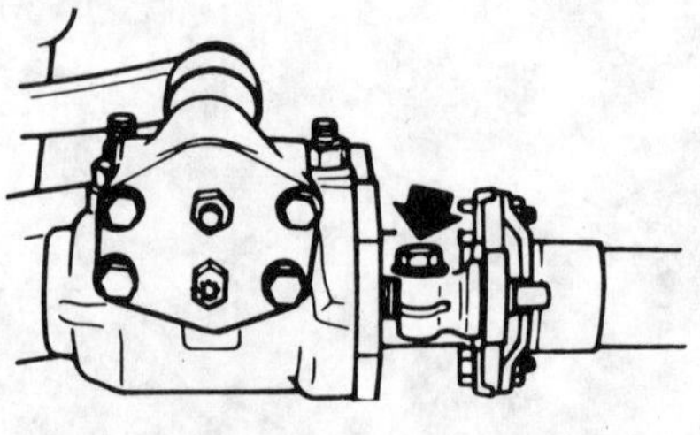

Fig. 11.24 A single pinch bolt is used to retain the steering gear's wormshaft to the column's coupling (Sec 23)

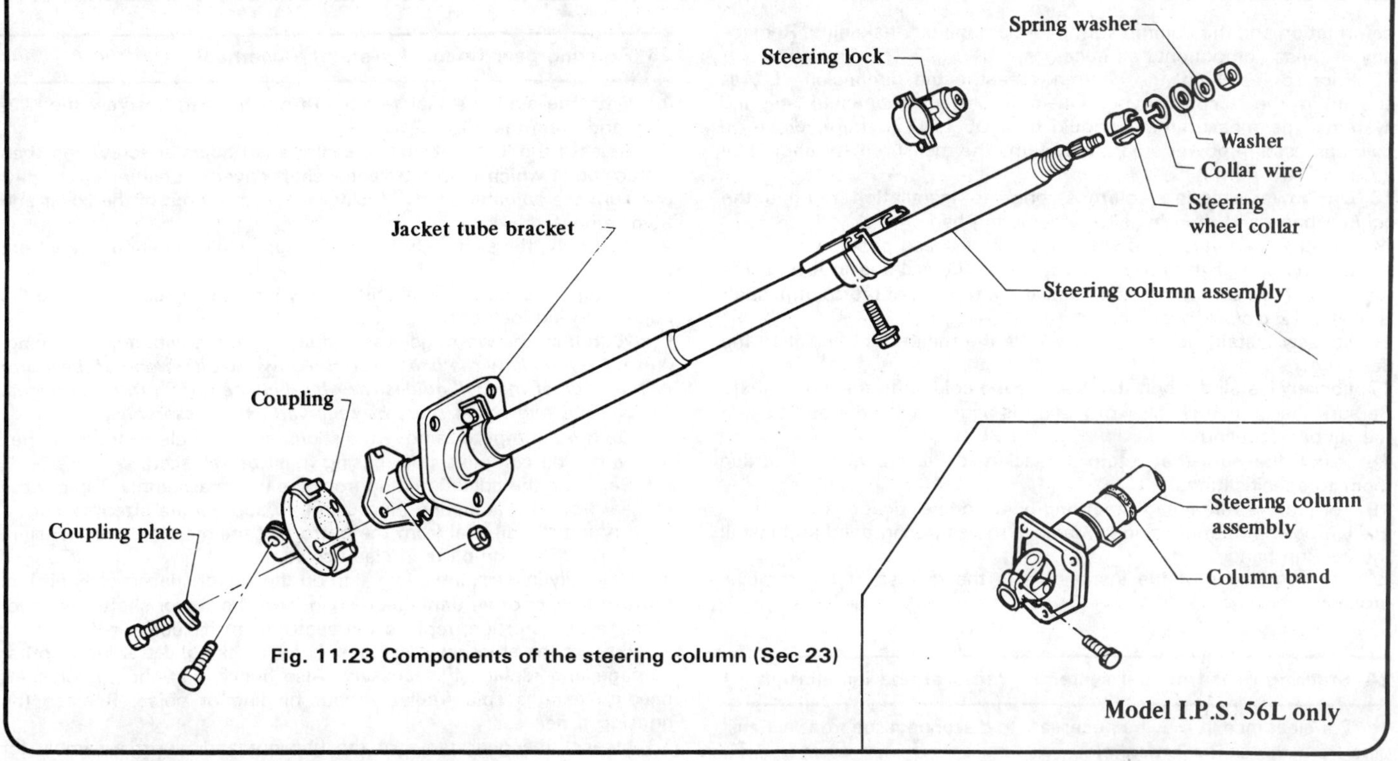

Fig. 11.23 Components of the steering column (Sec 23)

3 Remove the steering column cover (photo).
4 The steering lock is secured to the steering shaft with 2 regular screws and 2 self-shear screws. Removing the shear screws will involve very careful drilling of the screws. Start by center punching a dot in the center of the screw. Select a drill that is about the diameter of the root of the thread. Very carefully, ensuring that the drill is square to the screw, drill out the center of the screw until a screw extractor can be used to remove the screw.
5 Remove the 2 regular attaching screws and disengage the steering lock from the shaft. Disconnect the ignition switch wires.
6 To install, align the mating surface of the steering lock with the hole in the steering column tube. Then loosely install the 2 regular attaching screws. Once the operation of the lock is checked using the key, these screws can be tightened.
7 Install the two self-shearing screws in their appropriate holes, making sure the top snaps off as shown in the accompanying illustration.
8 The remainder of the installation is the reverse of the removal procedure.

23 Steering column – removal and installation

1 For clearance, remove the front seat as described in Chapter 12.
2 Open the hood and locate the steering gear. Remove the bolt that secures the stud shaft at the end of the steering column to the worm shaft at the steering gear.
3 Disconnect the negative battery cable.
4 Remove the steering wheel as described in Section 21.
5 Remove the steering column combination switch assembly as described in Chapter 10.
6 Remove the lower left instrument cover, located directly below the steering column.
7 Remove the heater duct located below the steering column.
8 Remove the 3 screws that attach the jacket tube bracket to the firewall.
9 While supporting the column, remove the 2 bolts that secure the column mounting bracket to the dash (photo) and lift out the column. **Note:** *Because of its collapsible design, the steering column is very susceptible to damage when removed from the car. Be careful not to lean on or drop the column, as this could weaken the column's structure and impair its performance.*
10 If the car has been in an accident which resulted in frame damage, major body damage or in which the steering column was impacted, the column could be damaged or misaligned and should be checked by a qualified mechanic.
11 If the steering wheel has not been turning smoothly, check the column bearings for wear or damage, the jacket tube for breakage or

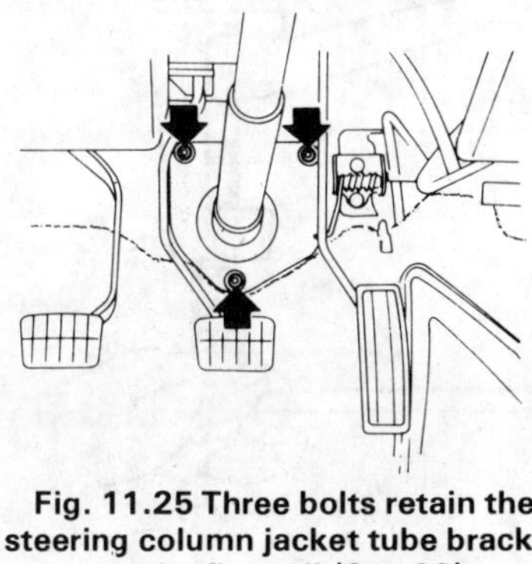

Fig. 11.25 Three bolts retain the steering column jacket tube bracket to the firewall (Sec 23)

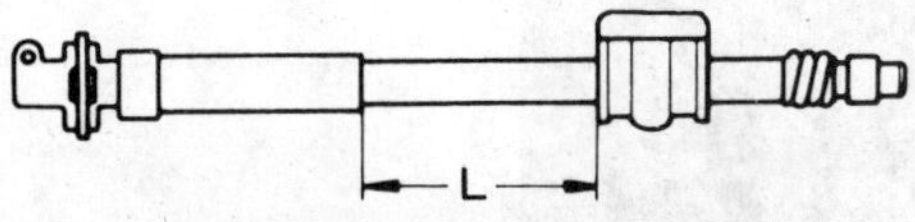

Fig. 11.26 Prior to installing the steering column, the dimension L, above, should be measured to check for column compression (Sec 23)

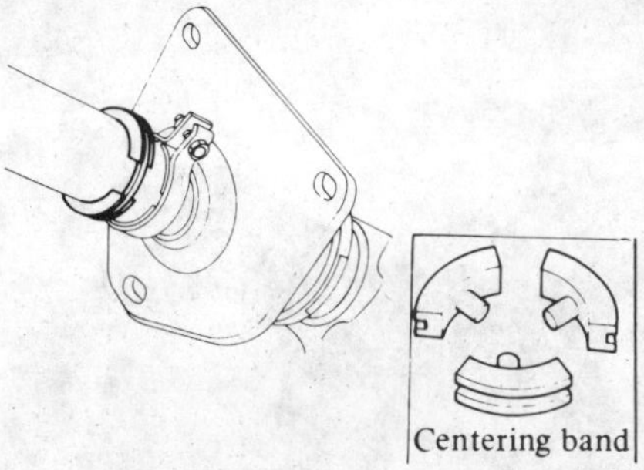

Fig. 11.27 On power steering columns, a centering band must be installed for correct installation (Sec 23)

deformation and the column spring for damage or weakening. Replace any of these components as necessary.
12 Prior to installing the column, measure the dimension "L", as shown in the accompanying illustration used in manual steering systems, the measurement should be 7.05 in (179 mm), while on columns used in power steering systems the measurement should be 7.09 in (180 mm).
13 On power steering columns, prior to installation remove the column band and then install the centering band.
14 Be sure the wheels are set in a straight-ahead position.
15 Lift the end of the column through the firewall and fit it onto the worm shaft. Be sure the punch mark at the top end of the column shaft is in the 12 o'clock position.
16 Loosely install the bolts that secure the mounting bracket to the dash.
17 Loosely install the bolt that secures the column to the worm shaft. Be sure the groove in the worm shaft is aligned with the bolt hole in the rubber coupling.
18 Install the nuts that retain the jacket to the firewall and torque them to specifications.
19 Torque the remaining mounting bolts to specifications.
20 On power steering models, remove the centering band and install the column band.
21 The remainder of the installation is the reverse of the removal procedure.

24 Steering gear (manual system) – removal and installation

1 For clearance, it may be necessary to disconnect the front exhaust pipe from the exhaust manifold.
2 Unscrew and remove the pinch bolt from the flexible coupling.
3 Unscrew the nut from the bottom of the steering sector shaft (photo), remove the washer and then using a heavy duty extractor pull off the gear arm.
4 Unscrew and remove the three steering gear mounting bolts and withdraw the gear first downward to clear the flexible coupling and then upwards out of the engine compartment.
5 Installation is a reversal of removal but observe the following points:

a) Before installing the pinch bolt that secures the coupling to the worm shaft, be sure the front wheels are in the straight-ahead position. Also be sure the steering wheel is properly positioned. The groove in the wormshaft should be aligned with the pinch bolt hole in the flexible coupling, and the pinch bolt should pass easily through. Torque the bolt to specs.
b) When installing the gear arm to the sector shaft make sure that the four master splines and grooves are aligned. Tighten the nut to the specified torque.

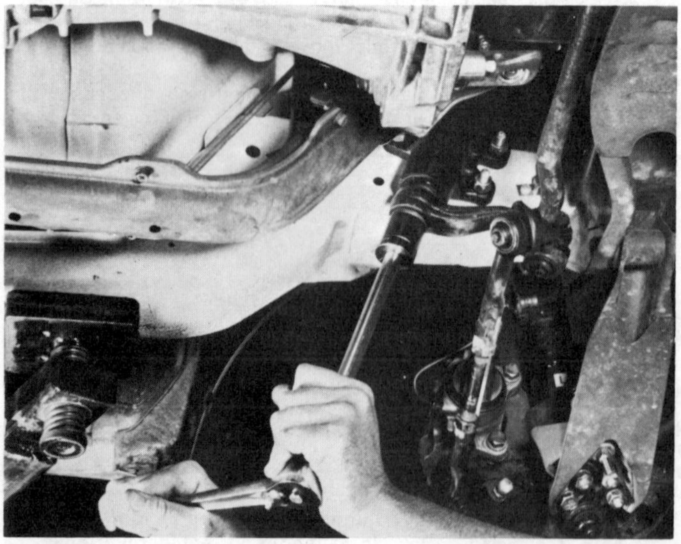

24.3 Removing the nut that retains the gear arm to the steering gear's sector shaft

25 Steering gear (manual system) – overhaul

1 With the steering gear removed from the car, unscrew the filler plug and drain the oil.
2 Release the lock nut on the sector shaft adjuster screw and then extract bolts which hold the sector shaft cover in position.
3 Turn the adjuster screw clockwise to wind it out of the cover and then remove the cover.
4 Withdraw the sector shaft and disengage the adjusting screw from it.
5 Using a special tool available from your Datsun dealer, remove the adjusting plug lock nut.
6 Withdraw the worm gear assembly, complete with adjusting plug.
Note: *Do not allow the ball nut to run down to either end of the worm or the ends of the ball guides may be damaged. If worn or damaged, the ball nut and worm must be renewed as an assembly.*
7 Do not attempt to remove the sector shaft needle bearings. If they are worn, the complete gear casing must be replaced.
8 Separate the adjusting plug from the worm assembly. Tap out the oil seal from the adjusting plug using an appropriate sized socket.
9 Pry out the oil seal from the bottom of the steering gear housing.
10 Wash all of the parts in clean solvent.
11 Carefully inspect the gear teeth on the sector shaft for any pitting, burrs, cracks or other damage. Also inspect the sector shaft splines for damage or distortion, replace the sector shaft if necessary.
12 Inspect the steering gear housing for cracking, distortion or other damage and replace if necessary. Also check that the sector shaft needle bearings spin freely without binding or noise. Replace the housing if necessary.
13 Inspect the gear teeth of the ball nut and worm assembly for pitting, burrs, wear or other damage. Check also that the ball nut rotates freely and smoothly on the worm gear. Check this by moving the ball nut to one end of the worm gear upright until the ball nut moves downward under its own weight. If the ball nut does not move freely over the entire stroke, replace the assembly.
Note: *Be careful that you do not allow the ball nut to run down to the extreme ends of the worm gear teeth.*
14 Check that the worm bearing moves freely without any binding or noise. If necessary, replace the bearing and the outer race as a set.
15 During installation, lubricate all parts with oil prior to installing them. Also, use all new oil seals, installed so that the lettering on them is visible when viewed from the outside. Fill in the space between the seal lips with multi-purpose grease.
16 Install a new oil seal in the adjusting plug.
17 Fit the adjusting plug onto the worm gear and install the assembly into the housing. Start the adjusting plug into its mating threads in the housing.
18 The worm bearing preload should now be adjusted. To do this, an adjusting plug tool and an in-lb torque wrench will be needed. Tighten the adjusting plug a little at a time until the torque required to start the worm rotating is 3.5 to 5.2 in-lb (4.0 to 6.0 cm-kg). To measure the torque, first turn the worm shaft a few turns in either direction to settle

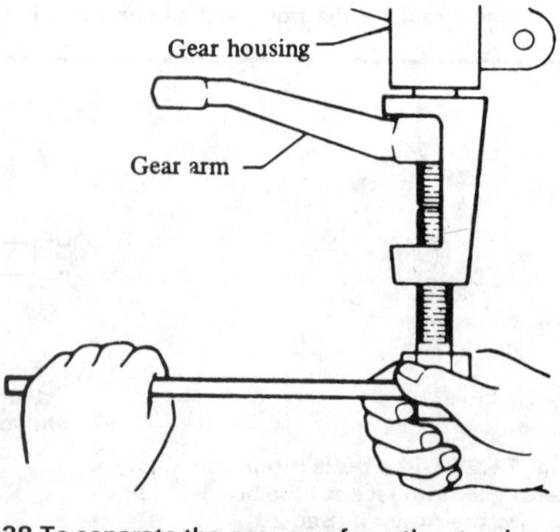

Fig. 11.28 To separate the gear arm from the steering gear's sector shaft, a puller must be used (Sec 24)

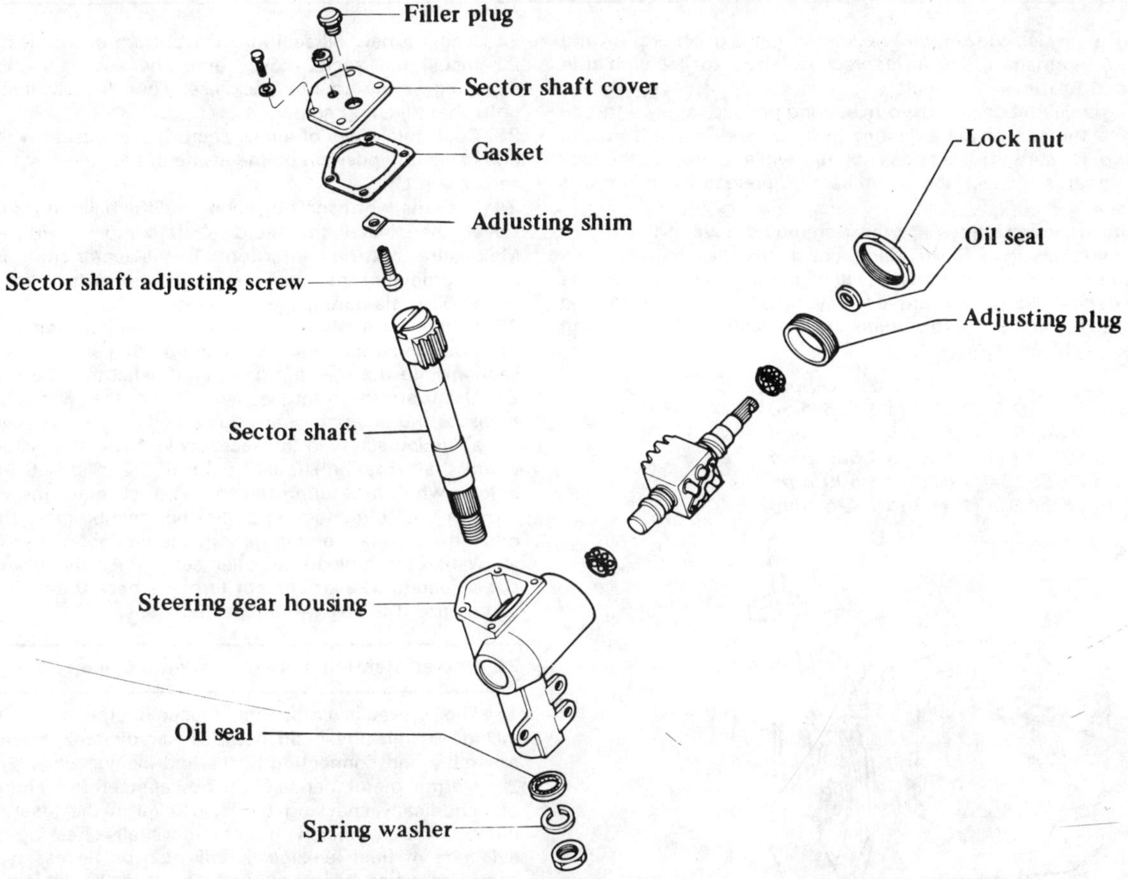

Fig. 11.29 Components of the steering gear assembly used in the manual steering system (Sec 25)

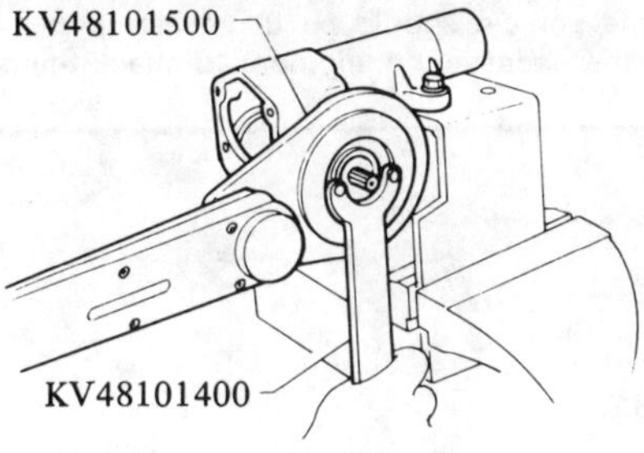

Fig. 11.30 The adjusting plug and nut are most easily removed and installed using Datsun special tools (Sec 25)

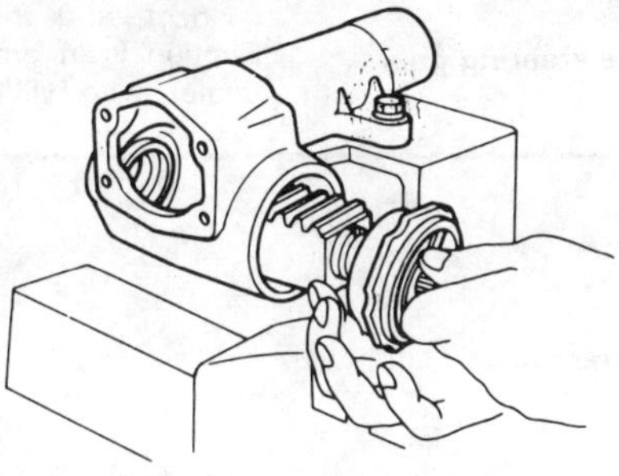

Fig. 11.31 The worm gear should be removed and installed with the adjusting plug mounted on the shaft (Sec 25)

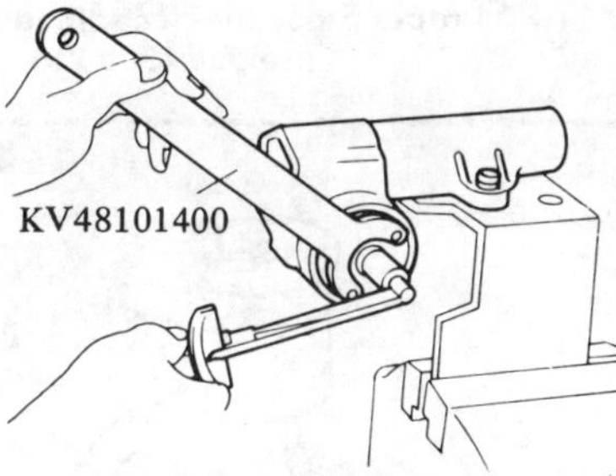

Fig. 11.32 Correct procedure for measuring and adjusting the worm bearing preload (Sec 25)

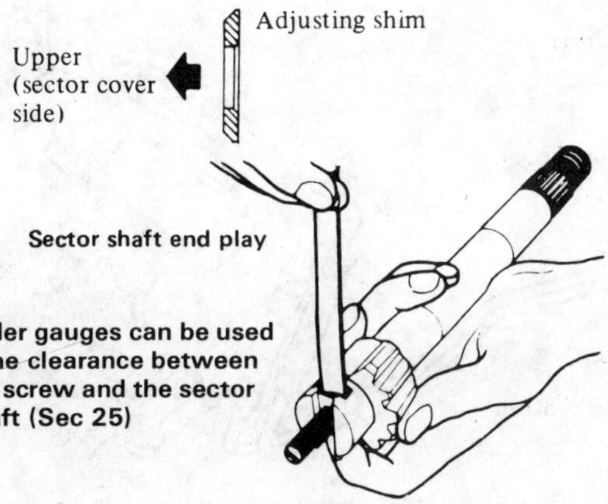

Fig. 11.33 Feeler gauges can be used to measure the clearance between the adjusting screw and the sector shaft (Sec 25)

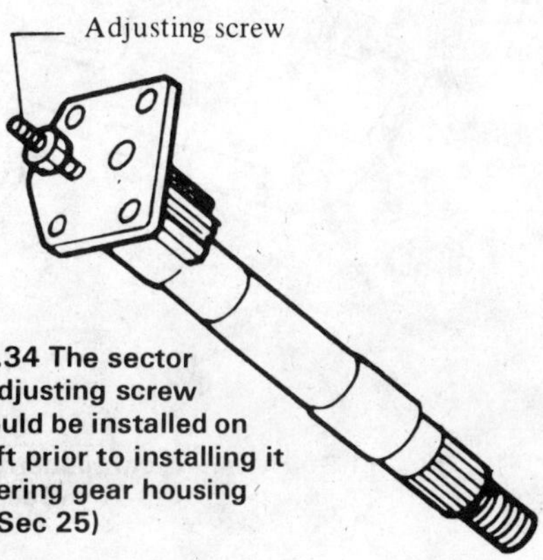

Fig. 11.34 The sector cover, adjusting screw and nut should be installed on the sector shaft prior to installing it into the steering gear housing (Sec 25)

the bearings, then use the torque wrench. To get a good grip on the splines of the wormshaft, line an appropriate-sized socket with thin cardboard, and fit it over the shaft.
19 Following adjustment of the worm bearing preload, apply a thread sealant to the threads of the adjusting lock nut and install it on the adjusting plug. Be sure the plug does not turn while tightening the lock nut, and afterwards recheck the worm bearing preload to ensure it is still within specs.
20 Insert the adjusting screw into the T-shaped groove in the end of the sector shaft. Using a feeler blade, check the play between the bottom of the groove and the lower face of the adjusting screw. Use shims if necessary to provide an endplay of between 0.0004 and 0.0012 in (0.01 and 0.03 mm). Shims are available in the following thicknesses:

0.0620 to 0.0630 in (1.575 to 1.600 mm)
0.0610 to 0.0620 in (1.550 to 1.575 mm)
0.0600 to 0.0610 in (1.525 to 1.550 mm)
0.0591 to 0.0600 in (1.500 to 1.525 mm)
0.0581 to 0.0591 in (1.475 to 1.500 mm)
0.0571 to 0.0581 in (1.450 to 1.475 mm)

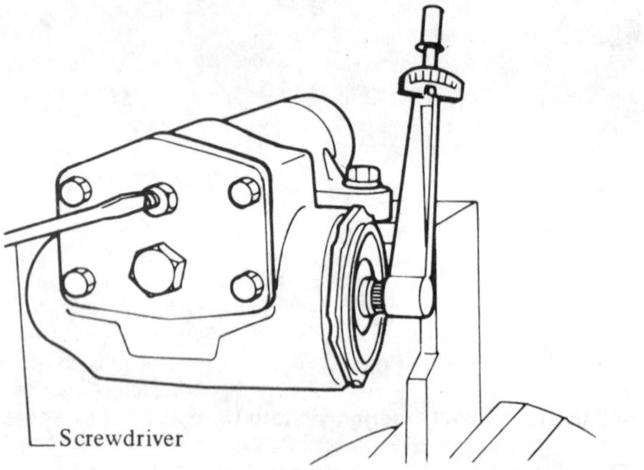

Fig. 11.35 Proper procedure for adjusting the steering gear preload (Sec 25)

21 Install a new oil seal into the bottom of the gear housing.
22 Install the sector cover onto the sector shaft by turning the adjusting screw counterclockwise. Then loosely install the lock nut onto the adjusting screw.
23 Coat both sides of a new sector cover gasket with gasket cement and place it in position on the inside of the cover by passing it over the sector shaft.
24 Turn the wormshaft by hand until the ball nut is in the center of its travel, then install the sector shaft complete with adjusting screw. Make sure that the center tooth of the sector shaft engages with the center groove of the nut. Take great care not to cut or damage the lips of the oil seals during these operations.
25 Install the 4 sector cover bolts, torquing them to specifications.
26 Pour the recommended amount of gear oil (see specifications section) into the steering gear, and install the filler plug.
27 Using an in-lb torque wrench on the wormshaft, as before, measure the steering gear reload, and adjust as necessary by turning the adjusting screw in the sector cover. The proper torque to start the worm shaft rotating should be 3.5 to 5.2 in-lb (4.0 to 5.0 cm-kg). As before, when measuring the torque, first rotate the wormshaft a few turns in both directions to settle the steering gear, then measure the preload with the steering gear in the straight-ahead position.
28 When the preload has been set, tighten the lock nut, making sure the adjusting screw does not turn. Recheck the preload one last time to be sure it is still within specifications.

26 Power steering system – maintenance and adjustment

1 The hydraulic components used in the power steering system include a belt-driven oil pump, reservoir tank, power steering gear assembly and connecting hoses and piping.
2 Normal maintenance of the power steering system consists mainly of periodically checking the fluid level in the reservoir, keeping the pump drivebelt tension correct and visually checking the hoses for any evidence of fluid leakage. It will also be necessary, after a system component has been removed, to bleed the system as described in Section 29.
3 If the operational characteristics of the system appear to be suspect, and the maintenance and adjustment mentioned in this Section is in order, the vehicle should be taken along to a Datsun dealer, who will have the necessary equipment to check the pressure

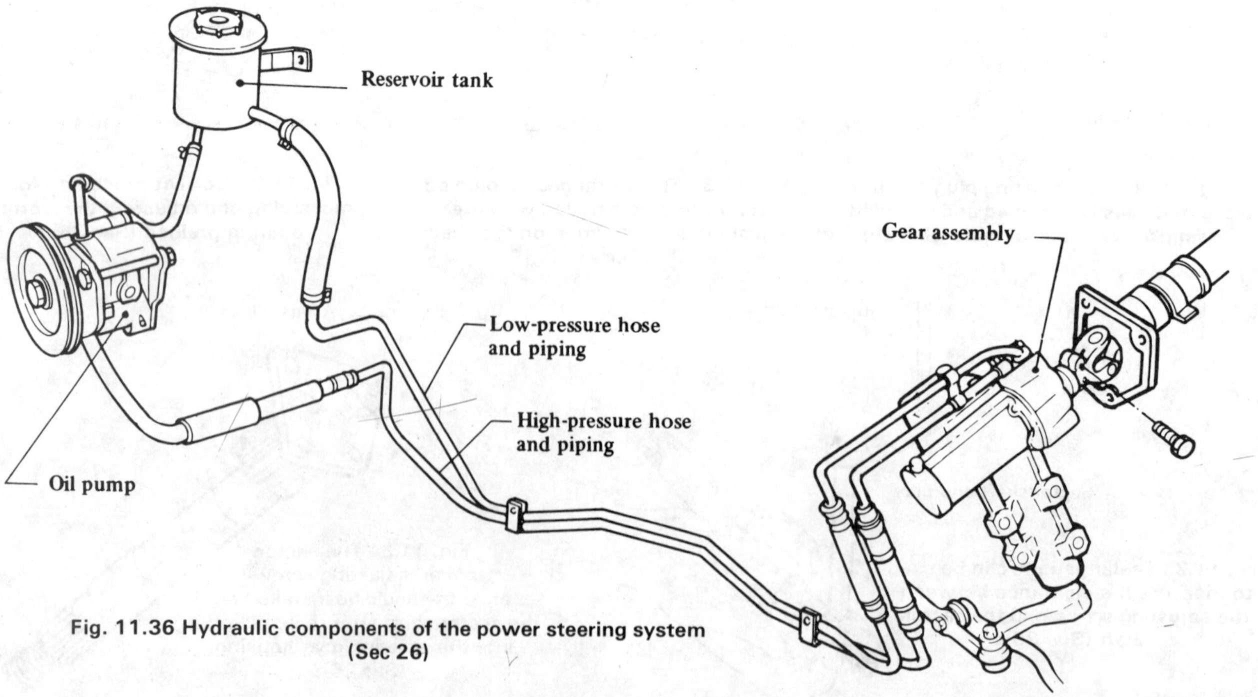

Fig. 11.36 Hydraulic components of the power steering system (Sec 26)

in the system and the operational torque needed to turn the steering wheel. These two operations are considered beyond the scope of the home mechanic, in view of the high working pressure of the system and the special tools required.

4 If the checks mentioned in paragraph 2 prove that either the oil pump assembly or the steering gear assembly are at fault, a new pump or steering gear assembly will have to be purchased as it is not possible to overhaul them.

5 If there are oil leaks from the power steering gear assembly, individual oil seals can be replaced without replacing the entire assembly. But, once again, due to the critical nature of the assembly, this job should be done by a Datsun dealer or other qualified repair shop.

6 With regard to the oil pump drivebelt tension, this is adjusted by loosening the idler pulley locknut and turning the adjustment bolt as necessary. Refer to Chapter 1, for the proper procedure.

7 Excluding the oil pump, power steering gear and its associated pressure hoses, the rest of the steering system components are identical to those used on the manual steering models. Servicing these components can be carried out by following the operations described in the relevant Sections of this Chapter.

27 Steering gear (power system) – removal and installation

1 To aid reassembly, place the front wheels in the straight-ahead position. Loosen and remove the bolt securing the universal joint to the wormshaft at the steering box.

2 Place a suitable drain pan beneath the steering box hose connections, disconnect the hoses and allow the oil to drain from the hoses and the steering box into the pan. Plug the open ends of the hoses and the open ports at the steering box.

3 Unscrew the nut and remove the washer securing the gear arm to the sector shaft.

4 Scribe a line across the sector shaft and the gear arm to ensure correct installation.

5 Withdraw the gear arm from the sector shaft using an appropriate puller.

6 Loosen and remove the bolts securing the steering box to the body sideframe and remove the unit from the vehicle.

7 Installation of the steering box assembly is a reversal of removal but observe the alignment marks on the sector shaft and gear arm. Screw in the universal joint-to-wormshaft bolt finger-tight. Tighten the steering box to side-frame bolts to the specified torque, then tighten the universal joint-to-wormshaft bolt to its proper torque.

8 When installation is complete, refill the oil pump reservoir with new oil of the correct grade and quantity. Bleed the air from the system, as described in Section 29.

28 Power steering pump and reservoir – removal and installation

1 If the power steering oil pump is found to be defective, both the oil pump and the reservoir tank should be replaced together.

2 Remove the air inlet duct as described in Chapter 4.

3 Loosen the locknut on the idler pulley and turn the belt adjusting bolt counterclockwise to loosen the belt.

4 Remove the drivebelt from the power steering pump.

5 Loosen, but do not remove the hoses where they attach to the pump.

6 Remove the pump and reservoir tank mounting bolts and lift these components up as much as the hoses will allow. Place them in a shallow drain pan and disconnect the hoses, allowing the oil to drain into the pan.

7 Securely plug the ends of the hoses to prevent oil loss or dirt from entering the hose system.

8 If necessary, the drive pulley can be removed by unscrewing the retaining nut, and using a standard puller to withdraw the pulley from the shaft.

9 Installation of the oil pump assembly is a reversal of removal but before tightening the mounting bolts ensure that the correct drivebelt tension exists, as described in Chapter 1.

10 Once installation is complete, refill the pump reservoir with the correct grade and quantity of oil. If necessary, bleed the system as described in Section 29.

29 Power steering system – bleeding

Note: *Whenever a hose in the power steering hydraulic system has been disconnected, it is quite probable, no matter how much care was taken to prevent air entering the system, that the system will need bleeding. To do this, proceed as described in the following paragraphs.*

1 First, ensure that the reservoir level is correct; if necessary, add fluid to bring the level to the mark on the dipstick. If necessary, refer to Chapter 1. If the car has not just been driven, the power steering oil should be brought up to operating temperature. This can be done either by idling the engine and turning the steering wheel from left to right for about 2 minutes, or by driving the car for several miles.

2 Raise the front end of the vehicle until the front wheels are just clear of the ground.

3 Quickly turn the steering wheel all the way to the right lock and then the left lock. Do not allow the lock stoppers to be struck with a bang. Try to gauge the end of the lock and only lightly touch the lock stoppers. This operation should be repeated several times.

4 Now check the reservoir fluid level again, as detailed in paragraph 1.

Fig. 11.37 Locations of the power steering pump mounting bolts (Sec 27)

Fig. 11.38 Location of the bleeder nipple on the steering gear used in the power system (Sec 29)

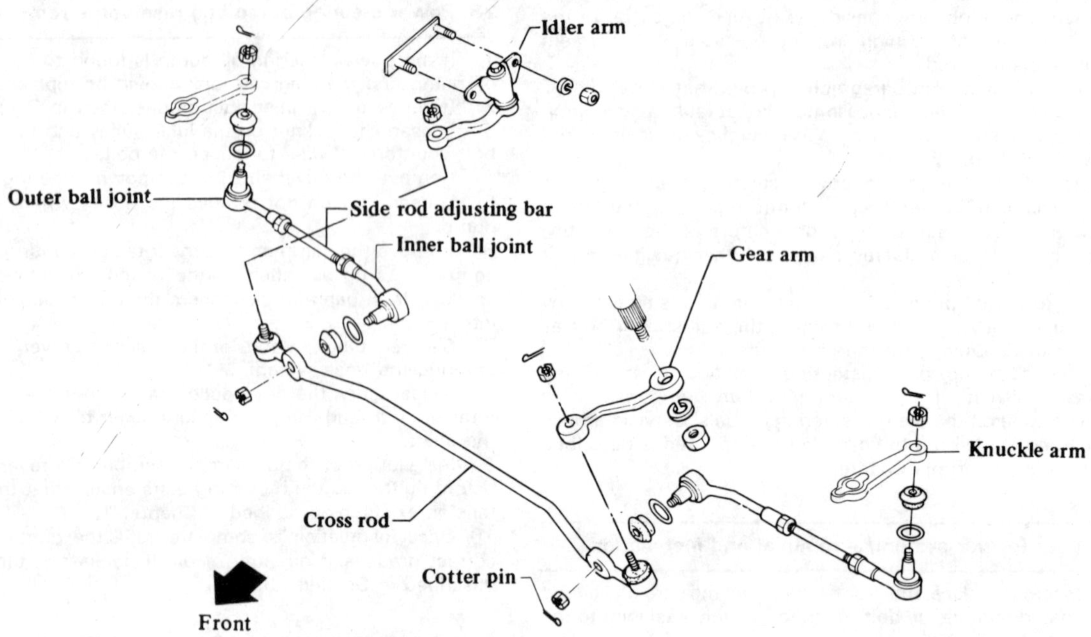

Fig. 11.39 Components of the steering linkage system (Sec 30)

5 Start the engine and allow it to idle.

6 Repeat the operations described in paragraph 3. With the steering wheel in a full lock position, quickly open the bleed nipple at the oil pump and allow a little fluid to escape. **CAUTION:** *Do not hold steering wheel at lock position for more than fifteen seconds at a time.* This operation should be repeated several times on both locks, until the fluid escaping from the bleed nipple is free from air bubbles. The bleed nipple should only be opened for a few seconds and then shut again. Check the oil in the reservoir frequently to make sure it stays at the correct level.

7 If the air bleeding is insufficient, the oil reservoir will be extremely foamy and the pump will be noisy. In this case, allow the foam in the reservoir to disperse, recheck the level again and repeat the entire bleeding process.

8 If it becomes obvious, after several attempts, that the system cannot be satisfactorily bled, there is quite probably a leak in the system. Visually check the hoses and their connections for leaks. If no leaks are evident, the problem could be in the steering box itself and the only solution is to have the entire system checked by a Datsun dealer.

30 Steering linkage – removal and installation

1 The steering linkage is basically a system of rods that is designed to transmit the steering motion in the steering gear to the front wheels.

2 Included in this system is a cross rod, two tie rods, an idler arm, a gear arm and two steering knuckle arms. The gear arm connects the steering gear to one end of the cross rod. The other end of the cross rod is connected to the idler arm, which is in turn bolted directly to the body. Each end of the cross rod is also connected to the front wheels by way of the knuckle arms.

3 The individual components of the steering linkage can be removed as a whole. Following any dismantling of the steering linkage, the front end alignment should be checked and adjusted, if necessary. **Note:** *For each of the following procedures, the front of the car should be raised and supported on jackstands. Following reinstallation of the component all nuts that are coupled with bushings should be left only finger tight until after the car has been lowered to the ground. Only when the full weight of the car is on the wheels should these nuts be tightened to their specified torque.*

Tie rod

4 Remove the cotter pins and locknuts on both ends of the tie rod.

5 Using a special separator tool, as illustrated in Fig. 11.17, disengage the tie rod from the knuckle arm and cross rod and lift it out.

6 Inspect the bushings and if they are hardened or cracked, replace them.

7 If the tie rod needs to be disassembled, first mark the points of adjustment by applying a dab of white paint on the locknuts and threads. Then loosen the locknuts, and unscrew the ends from the center rod.

8 Reassembly and installation is the reverse of the removal procedure. If the old tie rod has been disassembled, be sure the adjustment is reset at the marks made during disassembly. If a new tie rod is being installed, prior to installation, set the adjustment so the distance between the lock nuts is as specified (photo). Torque the securing nuts at either end of the tie rod to specs.

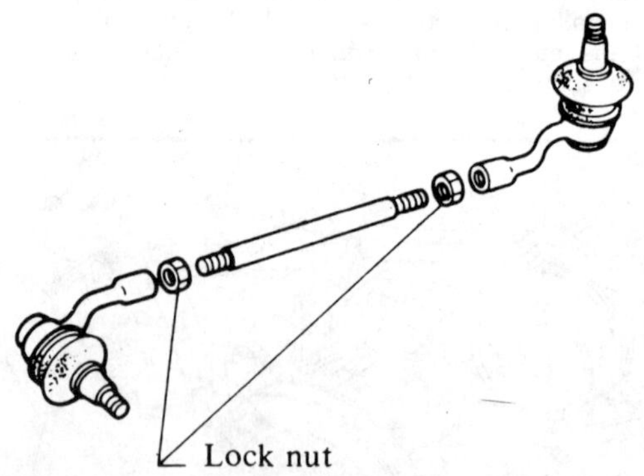

Fig. 11.40 Prior to disassembling the tie rod, mark the position of the locknuts on the threads to retain proper toe in adjustment (Sec 30)

Idler arm

9 Play with the idler arm assembly can be remedied by replacing the bushings.

10 Remove the 2 nuts and bolts that secure the idler arm to the body (photo).

11 Swing the idler arm around into an accessible position. If the idler arm needs to be removed, remove the cotter pin and locknut that retain it to the cross rod. Then using an appropriate separating tool disengage the idler arm from the cross rod.

12 If only the bushings in the idler arm have to be replaced, first remove the upper nut and washer (photo). Then lift the idler arm

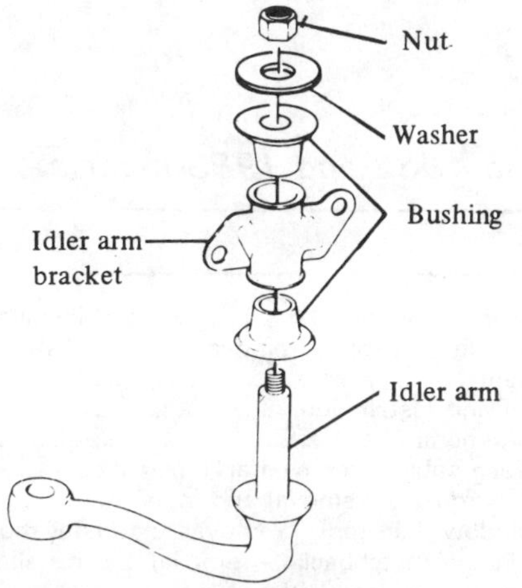

Fig. 11.41 Components of the idler arm assembly (Sec 30)

bracket off (photo) and remove the 2 bushings from it. Install new ones. Reassemble the idler arm.

13 Installation is the reverse of the removal procedure. Be sure to torque all attaching nuts to specs.

Cross rod

14 Remove the 4 sets of cotter pins and locknuts that retain the cross bar to the idler arm, gear arm and both tie rods.

15 Using an appropriate separating tool, disengage the cross bar from each of these other components, and lift out the cross rod.

16 Inspect the bushings at each end of the rod for hardening or cracking and replace them if necessary.

17 Installation is the reverse of the removal procedure.

Complete linkage

18 To remove the steering linkage as a complete assembly, first remove the nut that retains the gear arm to the steering gear. The using an appropriate puller as shown in the accompanying illustration, disengage the gear arm from the steering gear shaft.

19 Remove the 2 nuts and bolts that retain the idler arm to the body, and lift the idler arm off.

20 Remove the cotter pins and locking nuts that retain the tie rods to the steering knuckle arms. Then using an appropriate separating tool, disengage the tie rods from the knuckle arms.

21 The entire steering linkage assembly can now be lowered from the car.

22 Installation is the reverse of the removal procedure.

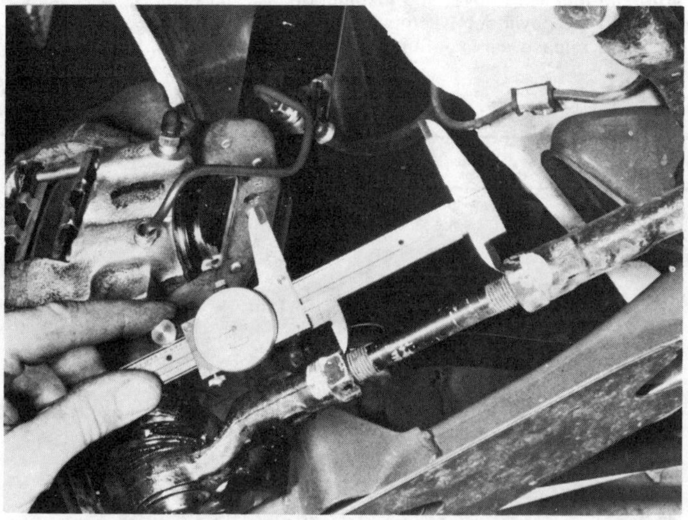

30.8 After installing the tie rod, it should be measured as shown to check for proper adjustment

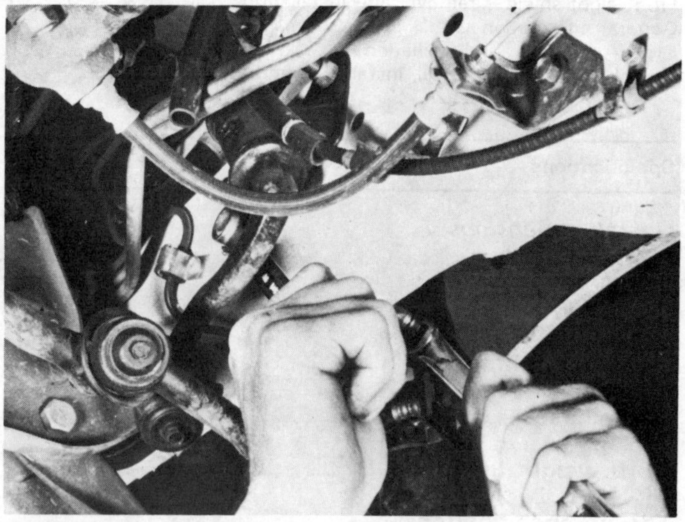

30.10 The idler arm is secured to the body by 2 bolts and nuts

30.12a After removal from the body, the idler arm can be swung into an accessible position for disassembly

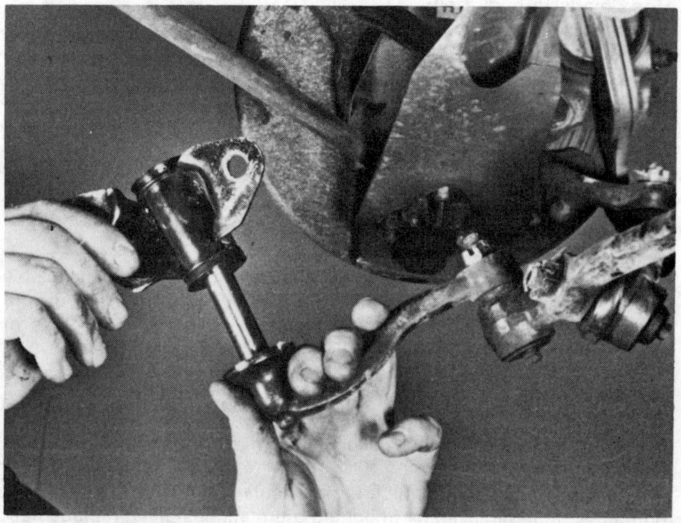

30.12b Once the upper nut is removed, the idler arm bracket can be lifted off

Chapter 12 Bodywork

Refer to Chapter 13 for Specifications and information related to 1982 and 1983 models

Contents

Body – general maintenance ... 2
Body damage – major repair ... 4
Body damage – minor repair ... 3
Bumpers – removal and installation ... 13
Bumpers and energy absorbers – general ... 12
Door lock and lock control – removal and installation ... 25
Door trim panel – removal and installation ... 23
Energy absorbers – removal and installation ... 14
Front apron – removal and installation ... 6
Front door – removal and installation ... 26
Front door window – removal and installation ... 24
Front fender – removal and installation ... 15
Front seats – removal and installation ... 27
Front sight shield – removal and installation ... 7
General information ... 1
Grille – removal and installation ... 5
Hatchback door – removal, installation and adjustment ... 22
Hatchback door lock and cylinder – removal and installation ... 20
Hatchback door release cable – removal and installation ... 21
Hood – alignment ... 9
Hood – removal and installation ... 8
Hood latches – general ... 10
Hood latch release cable – removal and installation ... 11
Opera window (hardtop) – removal and installation ... 32
Rear quarter window (hardtop) – removal and installation ... 30
Rear quarter window (hatchback) – removal and installation ... 31
Rear seat – removal and installation ... 28
Rear side trim panel – removal and installation ... 29
Seat belts – removal and installation ... 33
Trunk lid – removal, installation and adjustment ... 19
Trunk lid lock – removal and installation ... 16
Trunk lid lock cylinder – removal and installation ... 17
Trunk lid release cable – removal and installation ... 18

Specifications

Overall dimensions	**Hardtop**	**Hatchback**
Overall length	176.4 in	176.4 in
Overall width	66.1 in	66.1 in
Overall height	51.6 in	51.6 in
Wheelbase	94.5 in	94.5 in
Curb weight (approx)	2611 lb	2637 lb

Torque specifications	**ft-lb**	**kg-m**
Bumper-to-energy absorber bolts	43 to 48	6.0 to 8.0
Energy absorber mounting bolts	23 to 31	3.2 to 4.3
Hood-to-hinge bolts	12 to 15	1.6 to 2.1
Hood-hinge-to-body bolts	2 to 3.5	0.4 to 0.5
Hood lock mounting bolts	12 to 15	1.6 to 2.1
Door hinge mounting bolts	12 to 16	1.6 to 2.2
Trunk lid-to-hinge bolts	3.0 to 3.5	0.4 to 0.5
Trunk lid lock mounting bolts	3.0 to 3.5	0.4 to 0.5
Front seat mounting bolts	12 to 16	1.6 to 2.2
Seat belt anchor bolts	17 to 23	2.4 to 3.2

1 General information

During the years covered by this manual, the 200SX was available in two basic body styles: the 2-door hardtop, and the 3-door hatchback. In addition, each was offered with either the Deluxe or Sport Luxury package, which included various convenience and trim items. Differences between the various styles are noted when appropriate in the service procedures within this Chapter.

The 200SX used a unitized body construction in which the body is designed to provide vehicle rigidity so that a separate frame is not necessary.

Certain body panels which are particularly vulnerable to accident damage can be replaced by unbolting them and installing replacement items. These panels include the fenders, inner fender skirts, grille, front apron, sight shield, bumpers, hood and trunk.

2 Body – general maintenance

1 The condition of your vehicle's bodywork is of considerable importance as it is on this that the resale value will mainly depend. It is much more difficult to repair neglected bodywork than to renew mechanical assemblies. The hidden portions of the body, such as the wheel arches, fender skirts, the underframe and the engine compartment, are equally important, although obviously not requiring such frequent attention as the immediately visible paint.

2 Once a year or every 12 000 miles it is a sound idea to visit your local dealer and have the underside of the body steam cleaned. All traces of dirt and oil will be removed and the underside can then be inspected carefully for rust, damaged hydraulic pipes, frayed electrical wiring and similar trouble areas. The front suspension should be greased on completion of this job.

3 At the same time, clean the engine and the engine compartment either using a steam cleaner or a water-soluble cleaner.
4 The wheel arches and fender skirts should be given particular attention as undercoating can easily come away here and stones and dirt thrown up from the wheels can soon cause the paint to chip and flake, and so allow rust to set in. If rust is found, clean down to the bare metal and apply an anti-rust paint.
5 Use a mild detergent and soft sponge to wash the exterior of the car and rinse immediately with clear water. Owners who live in coastal regions and where salt or chemicals are used on the roads should wash the finish religiously to prevent damage to the finish. Do not wash the car in direct sunlight or when the metal is warm. To remove road tar, insects or tree sap use a tar remover rather than a knife or sharp objects which could scratch the surface.
6 A good coat of wax or polish may be your best protection against the elements. Use a good grade of polish or wax suitable for a high-quality synthetic finish. Do not use a wax or polish which contains large amounts of abrasives as these will scratch the finish.
7 Bright metal parts can be protected with wax or a chrome preservative. During winter months or in coastal regions apply a heavier coating or, if necessary, use a non-corrosive compound like petroleum jelly for protection. Do not use abrasive cleaners, strong detergents or materials like steel wool on chrome or anodized aluminium parts as these may damage the protective coating and cause discoloration or deterioration.
8 Interior surfaces can be wiped clean with a damp cloth or with cleaners specifically designed for car interior fabrics. Carefully read the manufacturer's instructions and test any commercial cleaners on an inconspicuous area first. The carpet should be vacuumed regularly and can be covered with mats.
9 Cleaning the mechanical parts of the car serves two useful functions. First it focuses your attention on parts which may be starting to fail, allowing you to fix or replace them before they cause problems. Second, it is much more pleasant to work on parts which are relatively clean. You will still get dirty on major repair jobs, but it will be less extreme. Large areas like the firewall and inner fender panels should be brushed with detergent, allowed to soak for about 15 minutes and then carefully rinsed clean. Cover ignition and carburetor parts with plastic to prevent moisture from penetrating these critical components.

3 Body damage – repair

The photographic sequences on pages 226 and 227 illustrate the operations detailed in the following sub-sections.

Repair of minor scratches in the vehicle's bodywork

If the scratch is very superficial, and does not penetrate to the metal of the bodywork, repair is very simple. Lightly rub the area of the scratch with a paintwork renovator, or a very fine cutting paste, to remove loose paint from the scratch and to clear the surrounding bodywork of wax polish. Rinse the area with clean water.

Apply touch-up paint to the scratch using a thin paint brush; continue to apply thin layers of paint until the surface of the paint in the scratch is level with the surrounding paintwork. Allow the new paint at least two weeks to harden: then blend it into the surrounding paintwork by rubbing the paintwork, in the scratch area, with a paintwork renovator or a very fine cutting paste. Finally, apply wax polish.

Where the scratch has penetrated right through to the metal of the bodywork, causing the metal to rust, a different repair technique is required. Remove any loose rust from the bottom of the scratch with a penknife, then apply rust inhibiting paint to prevent the formation of rust in the future. Using a rubber or nylon applicator fill the scratch with bodystopper paste. If required, this paste can be mixed with cellulose thinners to provide a very thin paste which is ideal for filling narrow scratches. Before the stopper-paste in the scratch hardens, wrap a piece of smooth cotton rag around the top of a finger. Dip the finger in cellulose thinners and then quickly sweep it across the surface of the stopper-paste in the scratch; this will ensure that the surface of the stopper-paste is slightly hollowed. The scratch can now be painted over as described earlier in this Section.

Repair of dents in the vehicle's bodywork

When deep denting of the vehicle's bodywork has taken place, the first task is to pull the dent out, until the affected bodywork almost attains its original shape. There is little point in trying to restore the original shape completely, as the metal in the damaged area will have stretched on impact and cannot be reshaped fully to its original contour. It is better to bring the level of the dent up to a point which is about $\frac{1}{8}$ in (3 mm) below the level of the surrounding bodywork. In cases where the dent is very shallow anyway, it is not worth trying to pull it out at all. If the underside of the dent is accessible, it can be hammered out gently from behind, using a mallet with a wooden or plastic head. Whilst doing this, hold a suitable block of wood firmly against the outside of the panel to absorb the impact from the hammer blows and thus prevent a large area of the bodywork from being 'belled-out'.

Should the dent be in a section of the bodywork which has double skin or some other factor making it inaccessible from behind, a different technique is called for. Drill several small holes through the metal inside the area – particularly in the deeper section. Then screw long self-tapping screws into the holes just sufficiently for them to gain a good purchase in the metal. Now the dent can be pulled out by pulling on the protruding heads of the screws with a pair of pliers.

The next stage of the repair is the removal of the paint from the damaged area, and from an inch or so of the surrounding 'sound' bodywork. This is accomplished most easily by using a wire brush or abrasive pad on a power drill, although it can be done just as effectively by hand using sheets of abrasive paper. To complete the preparation for filling, score the surface of the bare metal with a screwdriver or the tang of a file, or alternatively, drill small holes in the affected area. This will provide a really good 'key' for the filler paste.

To complete the repair see the Section on filling and re-spraying.

Repair of rust holes or gashes in the vehicle's bodywork

Remove all paint from the affected area and from an inch or so of the surrounding 'sound' bodywork, using an abrasive pad or a wire brush on a power drill. If these are not available a few sheets of abrasive paper will do the job just as effectively. With the paint removed you will be able to gauge the severity of the corrosion and therefore decide whether to renew the whole panel (if this is possible) or to repair the affected area. New body panels are not as expensive as most people think and it is often quicker and more satisfactory to fit a new panel than to attempt to repair large areas of corrosion.

Remove all fittings from the affected area except those which will act as a guide to the original shape of the damaged bodywork (eg headlamp shells etc). Then, using tin snips or a hacksaw blade, remove all loose metal and any other metal badly affected by corrosion. Hammer the edges of the hole inwards in order to create a slight depression for the filler paste.

Wire brush the affected area to remove the powdery rust from the surface of the remaining metal. Paint the affected area with rust inhibiting paint; if the back of the rusted area is accessible treat this also.

Before filling can take place it will be necessary to block the hole in some way. This can be achieved by the use of Zinc gauze or Aluminum tape.

Zinc gauze is probably the best material to use for a large hole. Cut a piece to the approximate size and shape of the hole to be filled, then position it in the hole so that its edges are below the level of the surrounding bodywork. It can be retained in position by several blobs of filler paste around its periphery.

Aluminum tape should be used for small or very narrow holes. Pull a piece off the roll and trim it to the approximate size and shape required, then pull off the backing paper (if used) and stick the tape over the hole; it can be overlapped if the thickness of one piece is insufficient. Burnish down the edges of the tape with the handle of a screwdriver or similar, to ensure that the tape is securely attached to the metal underneath.

Bodywork repairs – filling and re-spraying

Before using this Section, see the Sections on dent, deep scratch, rust holes and gash repairs.

Many types of bodyfiller are available, but generally speaking those proprietary kits which contain a tin of filler paste and a tube of resin hardener are best for this type of repair. A wide, flexible plastic or nylon applicator will be found invaluable for imparting a smooth and well contoured finish to the surface of the filler.

Mix up a little filler on a clean piece of card or board – measure the hardener carefully (follow the maker's instructions on the pack) otherwise the filler will set too rapidly or too slowly.

Using the applicator apply the filler paste to the prepared area; draw the applicator across the surface of the filler to achieve the correct contour and to level the filler surface. As soon as a contour that approximates the correct one is achieved, stop working the paste – if you carry on too long the paste will become sticky and begin to 'pick up' on the applicator. Continue to add thin layers of filler paste at twenty-minute intervals until the level of the filler is just proud of the surrounding bodywork.

Once the filler has hardened, excess can be removed using a metal plane or file. From then on, progressively finer grades of sandpaper should be used, starting with a 40 grade production paper and finishing with 400 grade wet-and-dry paper. Always wrap the abrasive paper around a flat rubber, cork, or wooden block – otherwise the surface of the filler will not be completely flat. During the smoothing of the filler surface the wet-and-dry paper should be periodically rinsed in water. This will ensure that a very smooth finish is imparted to the filler at the final stage.

At this stage the 'repair area' should be surrounded by a ring of bare metal, which in turn should be encircled by the finely 'feathered' edge of the good paintwork. Rinse the repair area with clean water, until all of the dust produced by the rubbing-down operation has gone.

Spray the whole repair area with a light coat of primer – this will show up any imperfections in the surface of the filler. Repair these imperfections with fresh filler paste or bodystopper, and once more smooth the surface with abrasive paper. If bodystopper is used, it can be mixed with cellulose thinners to form a really thin paste which is ideal for filling small holes. Repeat this spray and repair procedure until you are satisfied that the surface of the filler, and the feathered edge of the paintwork are perfect. Clean the repair area with clean water and allow to dry fully.

The repair area is now ready for final spraying. Paint spraying must be carried out in warm, dry, windless and dust free atmosphere. This condition can be created artificially if you have access to a large indoor working area, but if you are forced to work in the open, you will have to pick your day very carefully. If you are working indoors, dousing the floor in the work area with water will help to settle the dust which would otherwise be in the atmosphere. If the repair area is confined to one body panel, mask off the surrounding panels; this will help to minimise the effects of a slight mis-match in paint colours. Bodywork fittings (eg chrome strips, door handles etc) will also need to be masked off. Use genuine masking tape and several thicknesses of newspaper for the masking operations.

Before commencing to spray, agitate the aerosol can thoroughly, then spray a test area (an old tin, or similar) until the technique is mastered. Cover the repair area with a thick coat of primer; the thickness should be built up using several thin layers of paint rather than one thick one. Using 400 grade wet-and-dry paper, rub down the surface of the primer until it is really smooth. While doing this, the work area should be thoroughly doused with water, and the wet-and-dry paper periodically rinsed in water. Allow to dry before spraying on more paint.

Spray on the top coat, again building up the thickness by using several thin layers of paint. Start spraying in the centre of the repair area and then, using a circular motion, work outwards until the whole repair area and about 2 inches of the surrounding original paintwork is covered. Remove all masking material 10 to 15 minutes after spraying on the final coat of paint.

Allow the new paint at least two weeks to harden, then, using a paintwork renovator or a very fine cutting paste, blend the edges of the paint into the existing paintwork. Finally, apply wax polish.

4 Body damage – major repair

1 Major damage must be repaired by competent mechanics with the necessary welding and hydraulic straightening equipment.

2 If the damage has been serious it is vital that the body is checked for correct alignment as otherwise the handling of the vehicle will suffer and many other faults – such as excessive tire wear, and wear in the transmission and steering – may occur.

3 There is a special body jig which most body repair shops have and to ensure that all is correct it is important that this jig be used for all major repair work.

5 Grille – removal and installation

1 Open the hood.

2 The grille is secured to the body by 2 retainers located at the upper corners. With a screwdriver, simply turn the retainers until they line up with the grille mounting holes, and pull the top of the grille free. Then lift the grille straight up and out of its lower locating holes.

3 Prior to installing the grille, remove the 2 upper retainers from the body (photo) and fit them into the grille mounting holes. Then simply insert the lower locating tabs on the grille into their holes and press the upper retainers into place until they lock into place.

4 Close the hood.

6 Front apron – removal and installation

1 Remove the front bumper as described in Section 13.

2 Remove the 7 apron mounting bolts and lift off the front apron.

3 Installation is the reverse of the removal procedure.

5.3 When installing the grille, the 2 upper retainers must be removed from the body and installed in the grille.

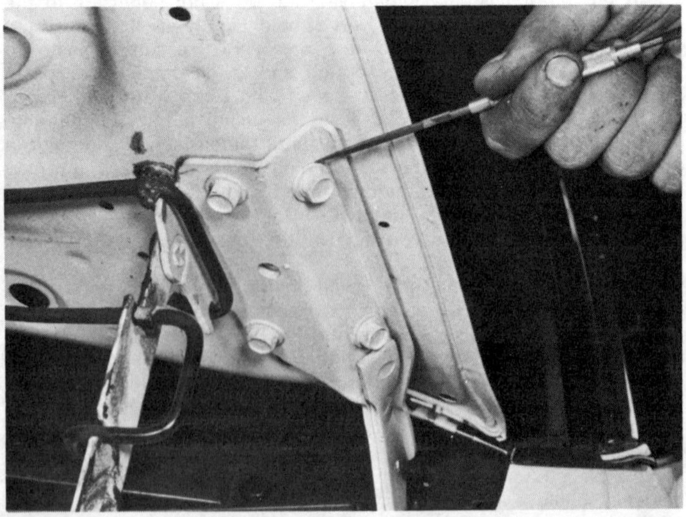

8.3 To mark the location of the hood, draw around the hinge before removing the bolts

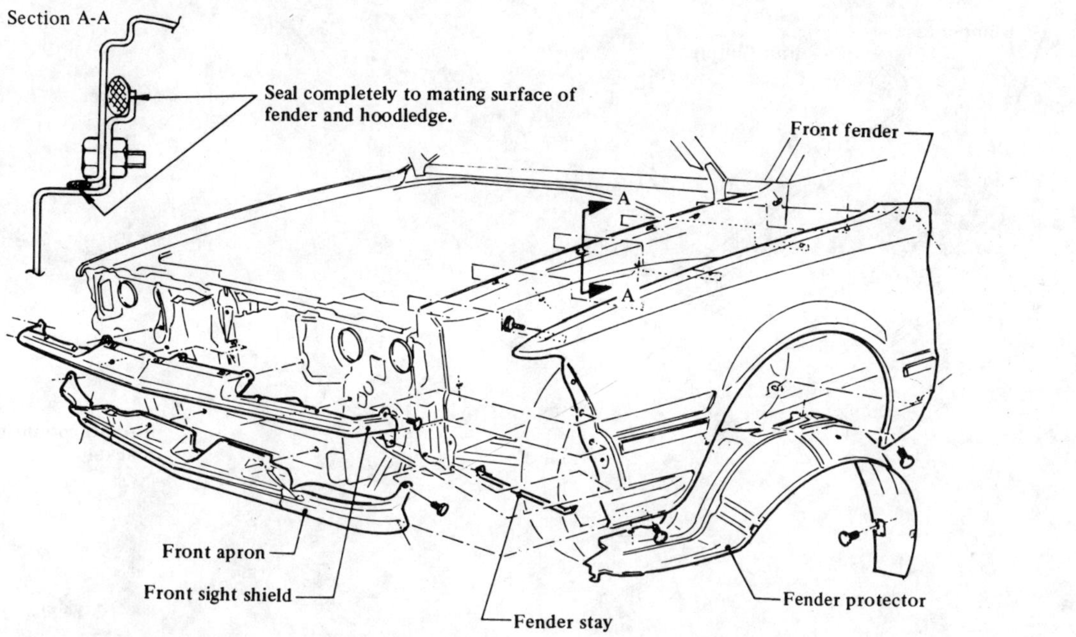

Fig. 12.1 Mounting arrangement of the front fender, apron, sight shield and related components (Sec 6/Sec 7)

7 Front sight shield – removal and installation

1 Remove the headlights as described in Chapter 10.
2 Remove the grille as described in Section 5.
3 Remove the front bumper as described in Section 13.
4 Remove the 9 front sight shield mounting bolts and lift off the shield.
5 Installation is the reverse of the removal procedure.

8 Hood – removal and installation

1 Raise the hood.
2 Use blankets or cloths to cover the cowl area of the body and the fenders. This will protect the body and paint as the hood is lifted free of the car.
3 Mark the position of the hood on its hinges by outlining the hinge plate (photo). This will greatly aid alignment when reinstalling.

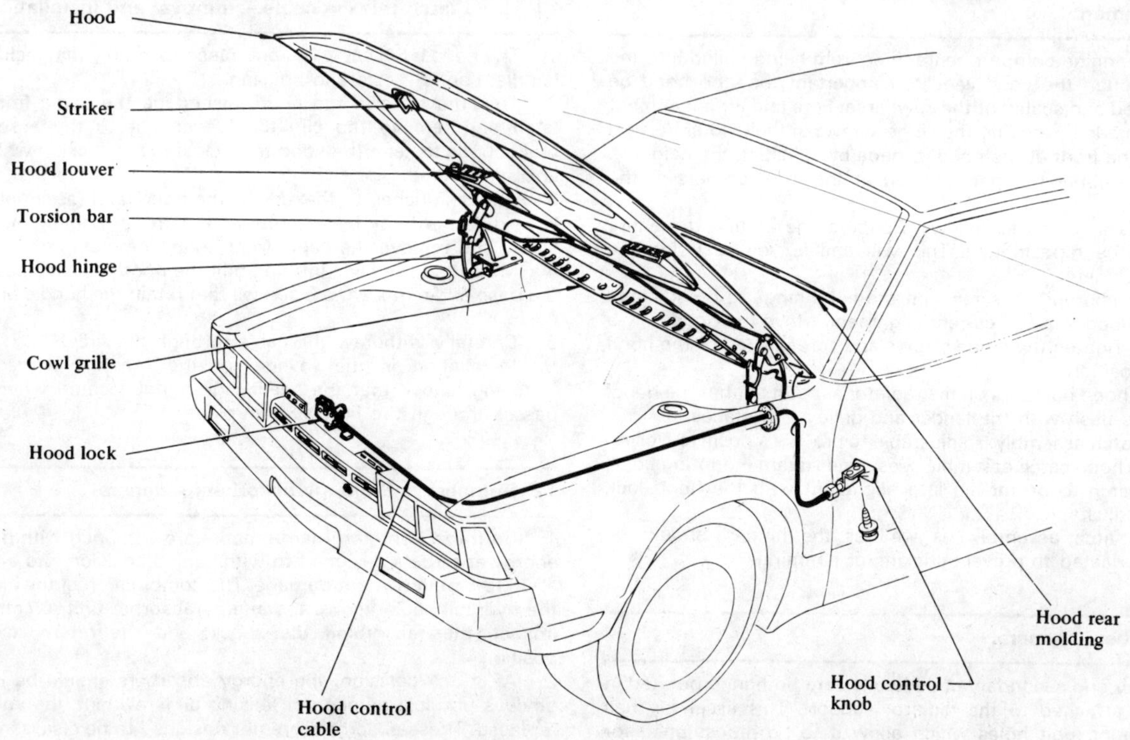

Fig. 12.2 Hood and related components (Sec 8)

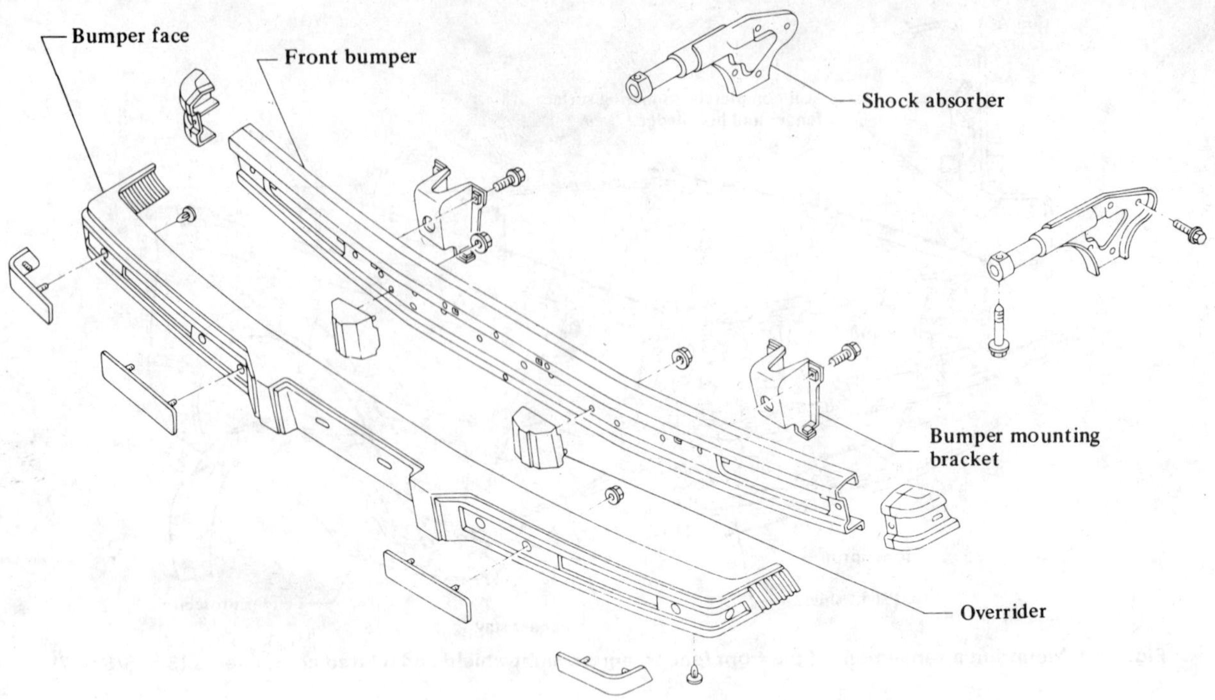

Fig. 12.3 Exploded view of the front bumper and energy absorbers (Sec 13)

4 While an assistant supports the hood, remove the hinge-to-hood screws on both sides.
5 Lift off the hood.
6 Installation is the reverse of the removal procedure.
7 Check the hood alignment and adjust if necessary as described in Section 9.

9 Hood alignment

1 To prevent engine compartment fumes from being pulled into the car interior through the cowl vent it is important that the hood be properly adjusted and sealed at the cowl area. Fore and aft adjustment of the hood is made by moving the hinge screws in their slots. Vertical adjustment of the front of the hood is made by adjusting the height of the screw-type rubber bumpers located at the front corners of the radiator support.
2 The hood is adjusted as follows: Scribe a line around the entire hinge plate to be repositioned. This will enable you to judge the amount of movement.
3 Loosen the appropriate screws on the hood hinge to be adjusted and move the hood into the current alignment. Move the hood only a little at a time. Tighten the hinge screws and carefully lower the hood to check the position.
4 Adjust the hood bumpers on the radiator support so that the hood, when closed, is flush with the fender and grille top surfaces.
5 The hood latch assembly is adjustable to provide a positive closing of the hood. To hood catch assembly uses large square mounting holes to allow the catch to be moved into alignment with the hood lock which is non-adjustable.
7 The hood latch assembly, as well as the hinges, should be periodically lubricated to prevent sticking or jamming.

10 Hood latches – general

1 The primary and secondary hood latches are both incorporated in one assembly attached to the radiator support. This assembly has widened mounting bolt holes which allow it to be repositioned for alignment purposes.
2 To remove the hood latch assembly, first mark the position of the mounting bolts by scribing a circle around them (photo). This will simplify alignment during installation. Then simply remove the 3 mounting bolts (photo) and disconnect the hood release cable from the latch.
3 To install the assembly, reverse the removal procedure, being sure to match the mounting screws up with their original positions.
4 The hood latch assembly should be lubricated periodically.

11 Hood latch release cable – removal and installation

1 The hood latch cable is a one-piece assembly that includes the pull handle, control cable and housing.
2 To remove, raise the hood, disengage the cable from the hood latch and remove the clip that secures it to the assembly. Take precautions to keep the hood from closing and locking while the cable is disconnected.
3 About 7 inches to the side of the hood latch assembly, the cable is held to the body by a screw and clamp arrangement. Loosen the screw and remove the cable from under the clamp.
4 Moving to the car's interior, pull the hood release handle out from the dash and remove the 2 screws that retain the handle bracket to the dash.
5 Carefully withdraw the cable through the firewall.
6 Installation is the reverse of the removal procedure. When installing, check that the sealing grommet located where the cable passes through the firewall is in place.

12 Bumpers and energy absorbers – general

1 Both the front and rear bumpers are equipped with gas/hydraulic energy absorbers designed to withstand a collision into a fixed barrier at up to 5 mph without damage. The combination of the insert gas and the hydraulic fluid allows the energy absorber unit to compress upon impact, thus absorbing the shock, and the return to its original position.
2 After any collision, the energy absorbers should be inspected. If obvious physical damage or leaking oil is evident, the unit should be replaced. These absorbers are not designed to be disassembled and, if defective, should be replaced as a unit.
3 Due to the gas contained in the units, never apply heat to an absorber or weld in its vicinity.

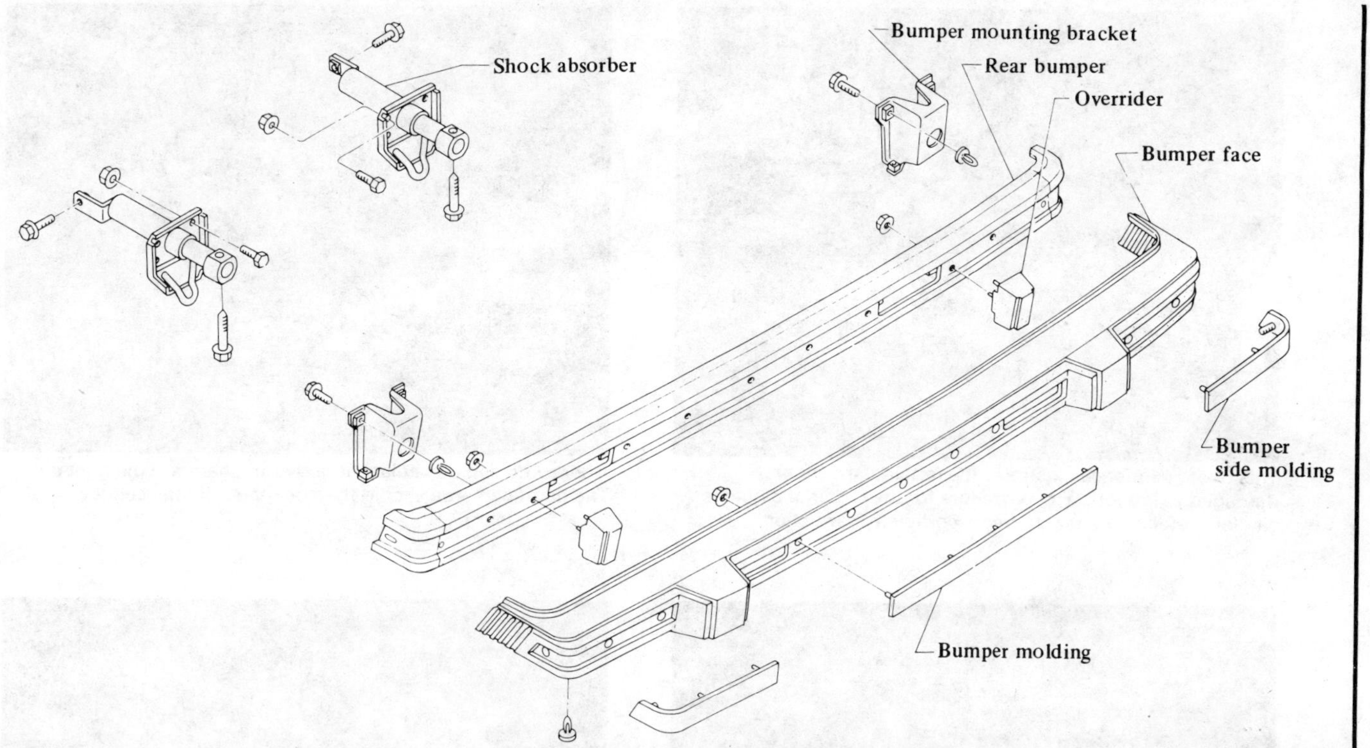

Fig. 12.4 Exploded view of the rear bumper and energy absorbers (Sec 13)

4 A method of testing the condition of the energy absorbers is as follows:

a) Position the vehicle in front of a solid, fixed barrier such as a wall, post, etc. The ignition should be off, the shifter should be in Park or 1st gear (depending upon the transmission) and the parking brake should be on.
b) Position a hydraulic or mechanical jack between the barrier and the bumper, so that the jack is in direct line with the absorber being checked. A folded rag between the jack and the bumper is recommended to protect the bumper's finish.
c) Operate the jack so that it applies pressure to and compresses the bumper at least $\frac{3}{8}$-in.
d) Release the pressure and the bumper should return to its original position. If it doesn't, the absorber needs replacing.
e) Repeat the same procedure on all absorbers to be checked. If, following a collision, the absorbers seize in their compressed position and the bumper does not return to its original position, care must be taken in replacing the absorbers. An unexpected spring-back while they're being repaired could cause serious injury. Due to this, it is recommended that a Datsun dealer or other qualified mechanic perform these repairs.

13 Bumpers – removal and installation

1 Disconnect the negative battery cable.
2 Disconnect any wiring connectors running to the bumper.
3 Using a hex wrench, remove the two bolts (1 on each side) that secure the bumper to the energy absorbers (photo).
4 Lift off the bumper. The bumper face and molding can be removed from the bumper if necessary by simply removing the bolts that secure them to the bumper.
5 Installation is the reverse of the removal procedure.

14 Energy absorbers – removal and installation

1 Remove the bumper as described in Section 13.
2 Remove the bolts that retain the energy absorbers to the body (photo) and lift off the absorber.
3 Installation is the reverse of the removal procedure.

15 Front fender – removal and installation

1 Disconnect the negative battery cable.

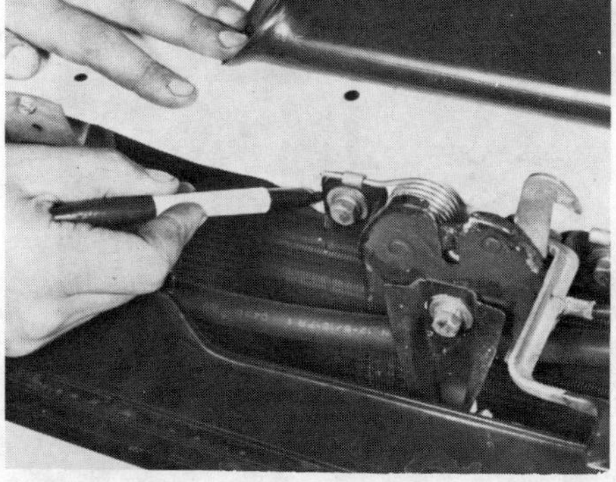

10.2a Prior to removing or adjusting the hood latch mechanism, mark the location of the mounting bolts by outlining them

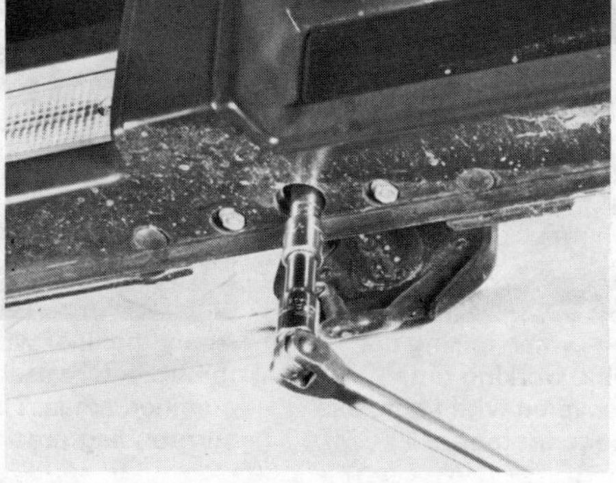

13.3 A hex wrench, shown here on a breaker bar, is needed to remove the 2 bumper mounting bolts.

13.4 The bumpers are mounted directly to the 2 energy absorbers that extend from the body

This photo sequence illustrates the repair of a dent and damaged paintwork. The procedure for the repair of a hole is similar. Refer to the text for more complete instructions

After removing any adjacent body trim, hammer the dent out. The damaged area should then be made slightly concave

Use coarse sandpaper or a sanding disc on a drill motor to remove all paint from the damaged area. Feather the sanded area into the edges of the surrounding paint, using progressively finer grades of sandpaper

The damaged area should be treated with rust remover prior to application of the body filler. In the case of a rust hole, all rusted sheet metal should be cut away

Carefully follow manufacturer's instructions when mixing the body filler so as to have the longest possible working time during application. Rust holes should be covered with fiberglass screen held in place with dabs of body filler prior to repair

Apply the filler with a flexible applicator in thin layers at 20 minute intervals. Use an applicator such as a wood spatula for confined areas. The filler should protrude slightly above the surrounding area

Shape the filler with a surform-type plane. Then, use water and progressively finer grades of sandpaper and a sanding block to wet-sand the area until it is smooth. Feather the edges of the repair area into the surrounding paint.

Use spray or brush applied primer to cover the entire repair area so that slight imperfections in the surface will be filled in. Prime at least one inch into the area surrounding the repair. Be careful of over-spray when using spray-type primer

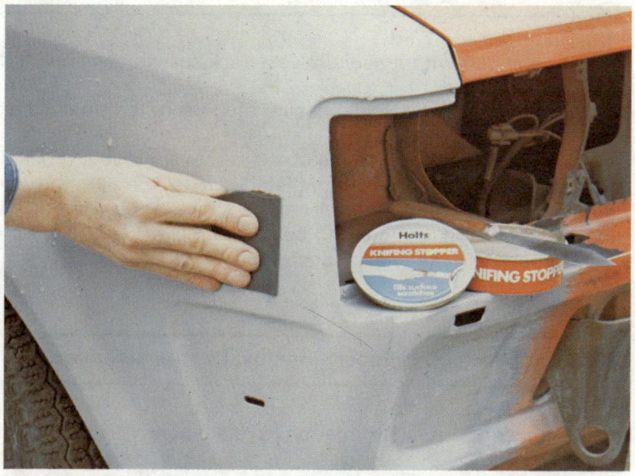

Wet-sand the primer with fine (approximately 400 grade) sandpaper until the area is smooth to the touch and blended into the surrounding paint. Use filler paste on minor imperfections

After the filler paste has dried, use rubbing compound to ensure that the surface of the primer is smooth. Prior to painting, the surface should be wiped down with a tack rag or lint-free cloth soaked in lacquer thinner

Choose a dry, warm, breeze-free area in which to paint and make sure that adjacent areas are protected from over-spray. Shake the spray paint can thoroughly and apply the top coat to the repair area, building it up by applying several coats, working from the center

After allowing at least two weeks for the paint to harden, use fine rubbing compound to blend the area into the original paint. Wax can now be applied

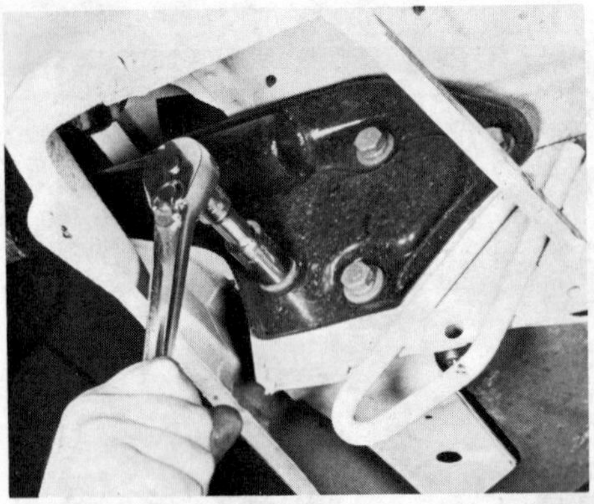

14.2a Locations of the 4 front energy absorber mounting bolts

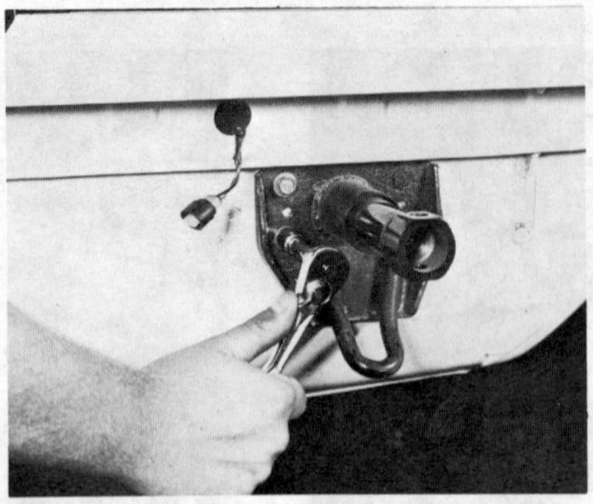

14.2b The rear energy absorbers are retained by 2 bolts in the front ...

14.2c ... and 2 nuts and 1 bolt in the rear

2 Remove the front bumper as described in Section 13.
3 Remove the 7 bolts that secure the front apron to the body and lift off the apron.
4 Remove the front sight shield as described in Section 7.
5 Remove the fender stay which connects the front of the fender to the body.
6 Remove the splash shield or fender protector.
7 Remove the fender mounting bolts.
8 Remove the sealant between the fender panel and the hood ledge (Fig. 12.1), and lift off the fender.

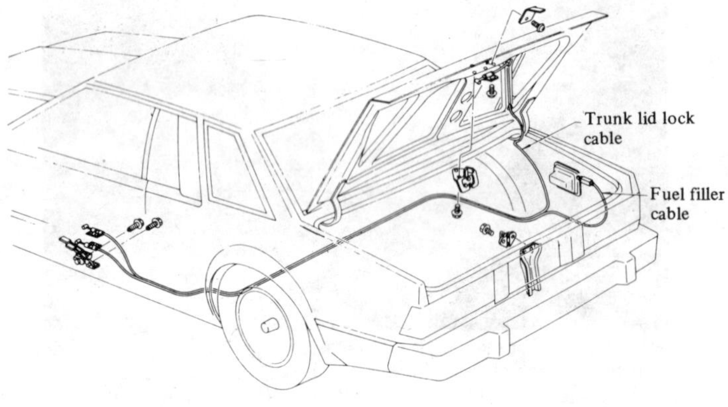

Fig. 12.5 Routing of the trunk lid and fuel filler release cables (hardtop) (Sec 16)

9 Installation is the reverse of the removal procedure. **Note:** *Be sure to use new sealant between the fender panel and hood ledge during installation.*

16 Trunk lid lock – removal and installation

1 Open the trunk lid.
2 If equipped with a cable release lock set-up, disconnect the cable from the lock.
3 Remove the 3 bolts that secure the lock to the trunk lid and lift off the lock.
4 Installation is the reverse of the removal procedure.
5 When installation is completed, close the lid and check the engagement of the lock with its striker. If any adjustment is necessary, loosen the 2 striker mounting bolts and move the striker up or down until proper engagement is achieved.

17 Trunk lid lock cylinder – removal and installation

1 Open the trunk lid.
2 Remove the lock cylinder cover plate screw and lift off the cover plate.
3 Using needle-nosed pliers, remove the lock cylinder retaining clip (photo).
4 Remove the cylinder from the lid.
5 Installation is the reverse of the removal procedure. Be sure that the lock cylinder tang engages with the lock, and check its operation with the key before reinstalling the cover plate and screw.

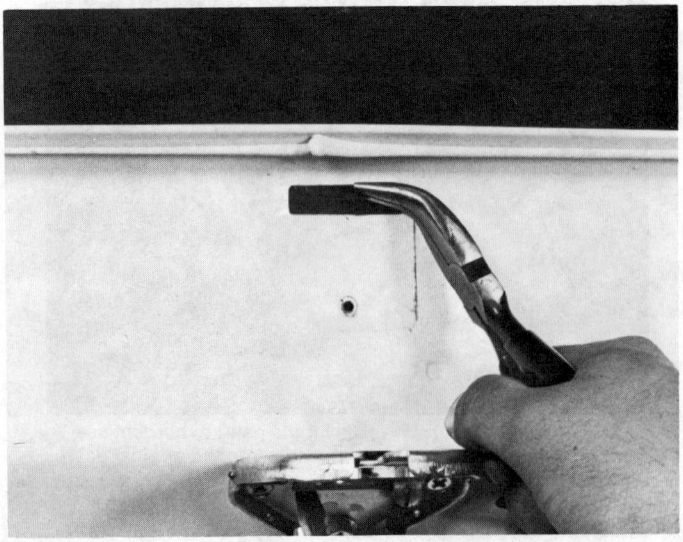

17.3 After removing the trunk lid lock cylinder cover plate, the retaining clip can be pulled straight out of the lid

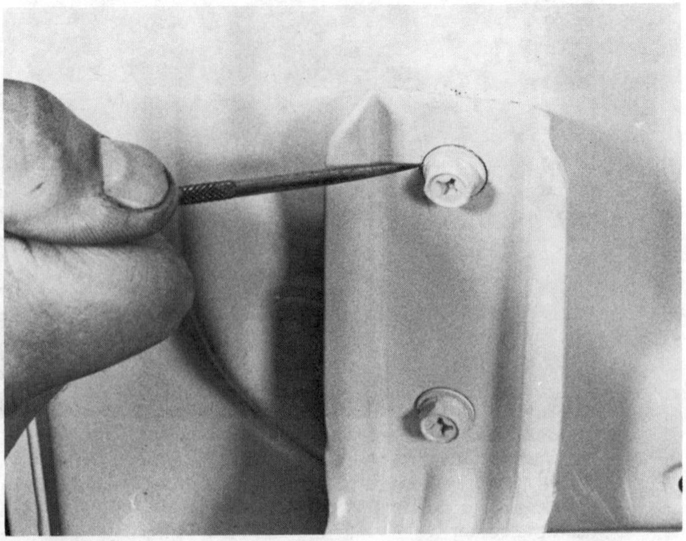

19.4 The position of the trunk lid-to-hinge bolts should be marked prior to loosening for removal or alignment

18 Trunk lid release cable – removal and installation

1 Remove the rear seat as described in Section 28.
2 Remove the metal kick plate along the bottom of the driver's door.
3 Disconnect the release cable from the trunk lid and remove it from its retaining clamp.
4 Turn up the carpet around the trunk lid release handle.
5 Remove the release handle and disconnect the release cable from the handle.
6 Remove the release cable from the car.
7 Installation is the reverse of the removal procedure. Be sure the release cable is sufficiently secured along its routing.

19 Trunk lid – removal and installation

1 Open the trunk lid.
2 Cover the edges of the trunk compartment with pads or cloths to protect the painted surfaces when the lid is removed.
3 If equipped with a cable release lock set-up, disconnect the cable from the latch, loosen the cable retaining screw enough so the cable can be removed from behind the retaining clamp and pull the cable out from the trunk lid.
4 Mark the location of the trunk lid mounting bolts in the hinges by circling the bolts with a scribe or marker (photo).
5 While an assistant supports the lid, remove the lid-to-hinge bolts on both sides and lift off the lid.
6 Installation is the reverse of the removal procedure. **Note**: *When reinstalling the trunk lid, align the lid-to-hinge bolts with the marks made during removal.*
7 When installation is completed, close the lid and check that it is in proper alignment with the surrounding panels. Fore and aft adjustments of the trunk lid are controlled by the position of the hinge bolts in their slots. To adjust, loosen the hinge bolts, reposition the lid the desired amount and retighten the bolts.
8 Check also the engagement of the trunk lid lock in its striker. If any adjustment is necessary, refer to Section 16.

20 Hatchback door lock and cylinder – removal and installation

1 Open the hatchback door.
2 Remove the rear interior trim panel to expose the hatchback door lock.
3 If equipped with a cable release lock set-up, disconnect the cable from the lock.
4 Using a marker, mark the position of the lock on the body by outlining the lock.
5 Remove the 4 door lock mounting bolts.
6 If the lock cylinder needs to be removed, first remove the left rear taillight assembly as described in Chapter 10. Then remove the 2 lock cylinder mounting screws and remove the cylinder.
7 Installation is the reverse of the removal procedure. **Note**: *Before reinstalling the rear trim panel, close the hatchback door and check the engagement of the lock with its striker. If any adjustment is necessary, loosen the 4 door lock mounting bolts and reposition the lock as necessary. The lock should be aligned with the marks made during removal.*

21 Hatchback door release cable – removal and installation

1 Open the hatchback door.
2 Remove the hatchback door lock as described in Section 20 and disconnect the cable from the lock.
3 Remove the rear seat as described in Section 28.
4 Remove the metal kick plate along the bottom of the drivers door.
5 Turn up the carpet around the hatchback door release handle and remove the release handle.
6 Disconnect the release cable from the handle.
7 Turn up the luggage room carpet enough so the release cable can be removed from the car.
8 Installation is the reverse of the removal procedure. Be sure the release cable is sufficiently secured along its routing.

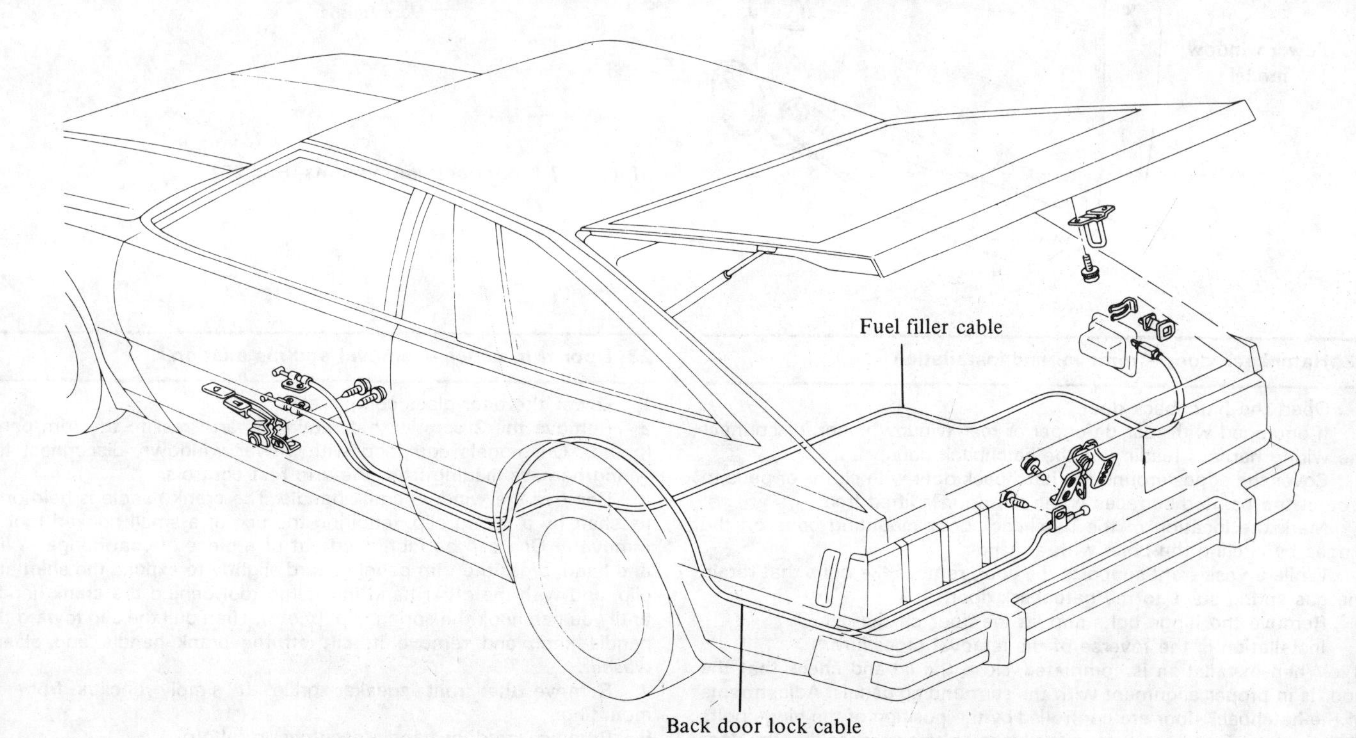

Fig. 12.6 Routing of the hatchback door and fuel filler release cables (Sec 20)

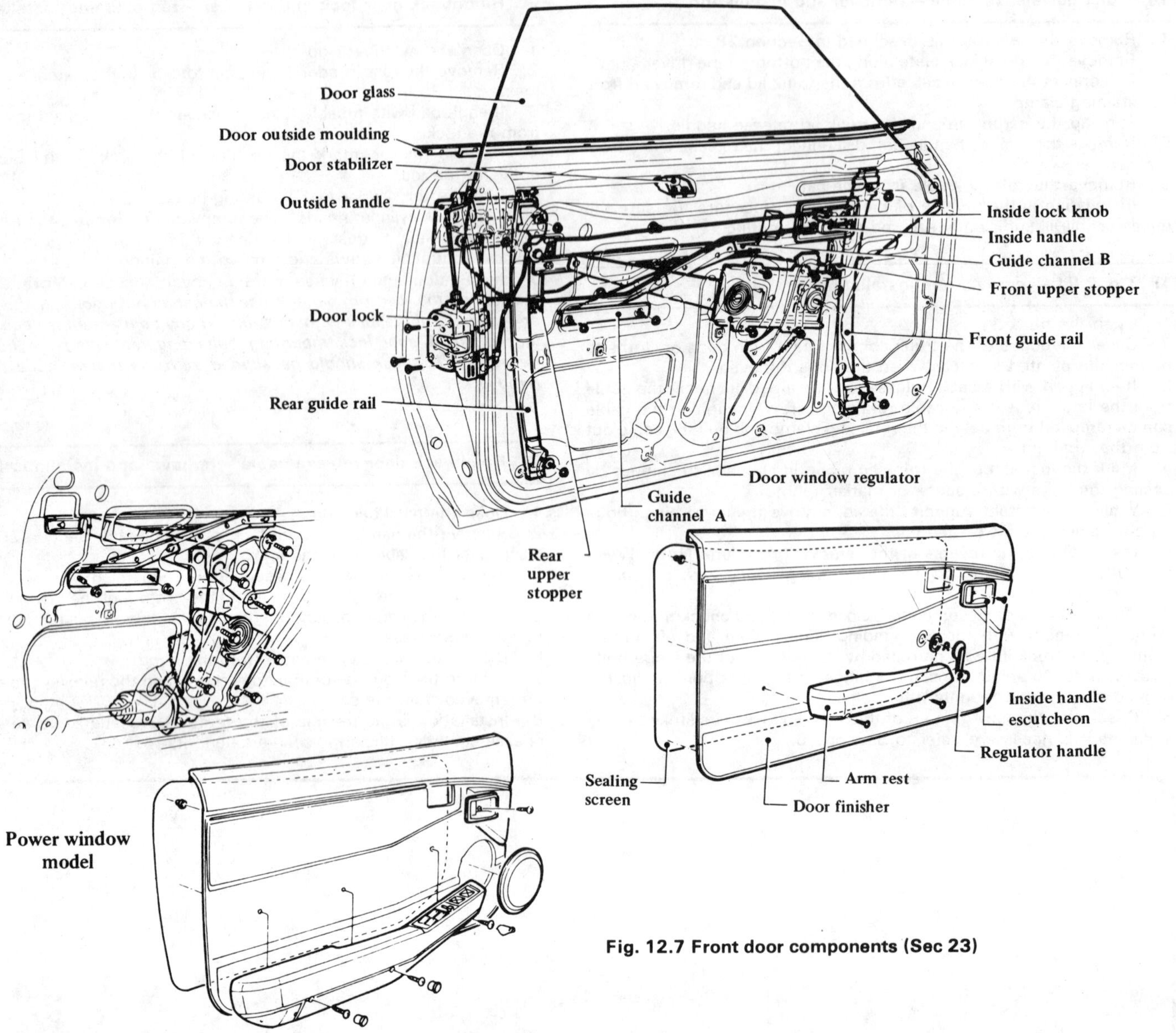

Fig. 12.7 Front door components (Sec 23)

22 Hatchback door – removal and installation

1 Open the hatchback door.
2 If equipped with rear defogger or rear window wiper, disconnect the wiring harness leading to the hatchback door.
3 Cover the edges around the hatchback door with cloths or pads to protect the painted surfaces when the door is lifted free.
4 Mark the location of the hatchback door mounting bolts on the hinges by circling the bolts with a marker.
5 While an assistant supports the door, remove the bolts that retain the gas spring stays to the hatchback door.
6 Remove the hinge bolts and lift the door off the car.
7 Installation is the reverse of the removal procedure.
8 When installation is completed, close the lid and check that the door is in proper alignment with the surrounding panels. Adjustments of the hatchback door are controlled by the position of the hinge bolts in their slots. To adjust, loosen the hinge bolts and reposition the door either side-to-side or fore-and-aft the desired amount and retighten the bolts.
9 Check also the engagement of the hatchback door lock with its striker. If any adjustment is necessary, refer to Section 20.

23 Door trim panel – removal and installation

1 Lower the door glass completely.
2 Remove the 2 screws that retain the arm rest to the trim panel (photo). On models equipped with power windows, disconnect the wiring harness leading from the arm rest controls.
3 Remove the window crank handle. The crank handle is held onto its shaft by a spring clip, requiring the use of a small hooked tool to remove it. One can be fabricated out of a piece of coat hanger. With one hand, press the trim panel inward slightly to expose the shaft and clip, and with the other hand insert the tool behind the crank handle until you can hook the spring clip (photo). Then pull the clip toward the handle knob and remove it. Lift off the crank handle and plastic washer.
4 Remove the front speaker grille. It simply unclips from its mounting.
5 Remove the door handle escutcheon (photo).
6 The trim panel is attached to the door with plastic retaining clips (photo). To disengage these clips, insert a flat, blunt tool (like a screwdriver wrapped with tape) between the metal door skin and the trim panel. Carefully pry the door panel away from the door, keeping

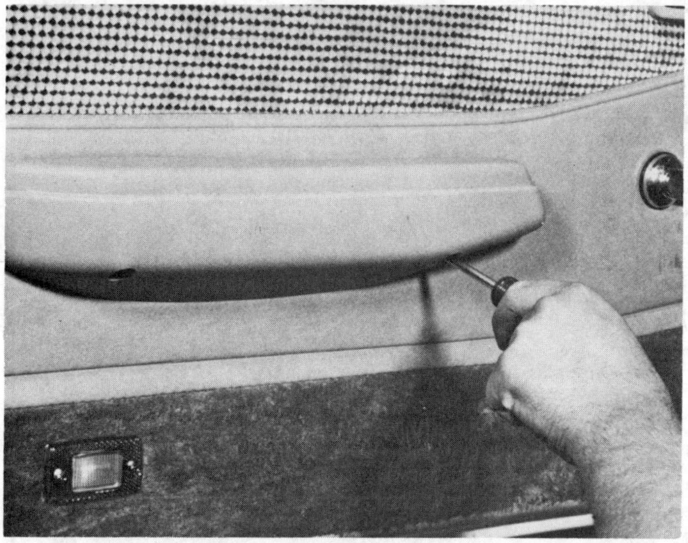

23.2 The arm rest is retained to the door trim panel by 2 screws.

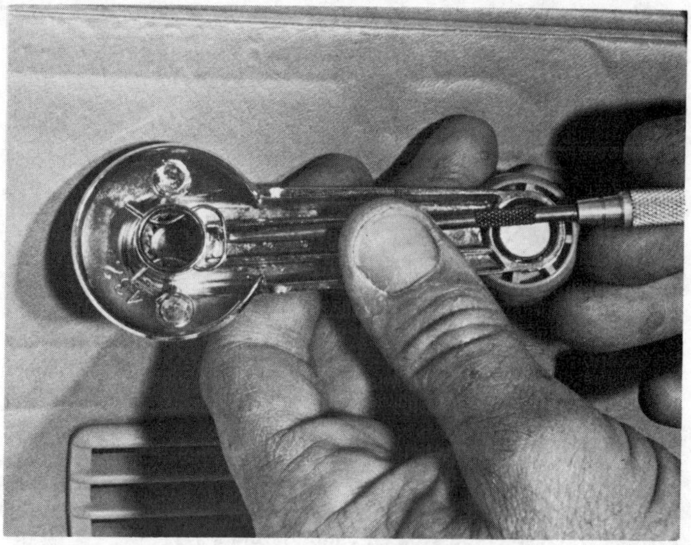

23.3 The window crank handle is retained on its shaft by a spring clip which must be removed with a hooked tool as shown

23.5 The interior door handle escutcheon is secured to the trim panel with 1 screw.

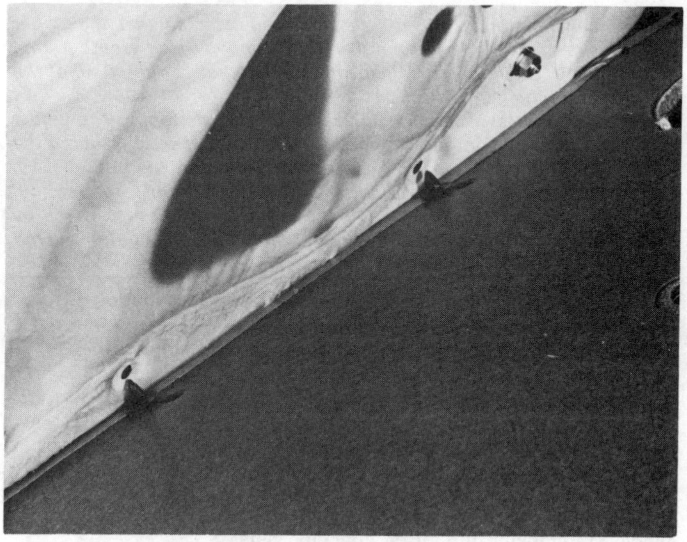

23.6 The door trim panel is attached to the door by plastic retaining clips

the tool close to the clips to prevent damage to the panel. Start at the bottom and work around the door toward the top. The top section is secured at the window channel. Once the retaining clips are pried free, lift the trim panel upward and away from the door.

7 On styles with a courtesy lamp mounted in the lower trim panel, disconnect the wire harness from the lamp.

8 Before installing the trim panel, check that all the trim retaining clips are in good condition and the sealing screen is correctly applied to the door.

9 If equipped, reconnect the courtesy lamp wiring connector.

10 Engage the top of the trim panel first and then position the panel correctly on the door. The shaft for the window winder can be used as a rough guide.

11 Press the retaining clips into their respective cups or holes in the door. Pressure can be applied with the palm of your hand or with a clean rubber mallet.

12 Complete the installation by reversing the removal procedure. To install the crank handle, first install the spring clip into its groove on the handle with the closed end facing the handle knob, align the handle with the one on the opposite door and push it onto its shaft until the spring clip clicks into place.

24 Front door window – removal and installation

1 Remove the front door trim panel as described in Section 23.

2 Using a flathead screwdriver, rotate the exterior door molding retaining clips 90 degrees and lift off and remove the molding.

3 Remove the plastic sealing screen.

4 Remove the front and rear upper stoppers.

5 Remove the bolts that attach the window to the guide channel.

6 Remove the door stabilizer.

7 Remove the glass from the door by pulling it upwards and away from the door.

8 If necessary, remove the regulator mounting bolts and remove the regulator through the large access hole.

9 Prior to installing the regulator and guide channel apply a light coat of lithium grease to all their sliding surfaces.

10 Installation is the reverse of the removal procedure. Following installation of the window, roll it up completely and use the following procedure to bring it into correct alignment.

(a) *Loosen the nuts that secure the upper ends of both the front and rear guide rails. Then raise the window completely and turn the upper adjusting bolts until the distance between the glass and the door waist molding rubber seal is 0.441 in (11.2 mm). Refer to Fig. 12.9*

(b) *Loosen the nuts securing the lower ends of both guide rails and turn the adjusting bolts until the glass is 0.55 – 0.67 in (14 – 17 mm) from the outer edge of the side roof rail. Refer to Fig. 12.10*

(c) *With the front and rear guide rail securing nuts already loosened, now loosen the front and rear upper stopper*

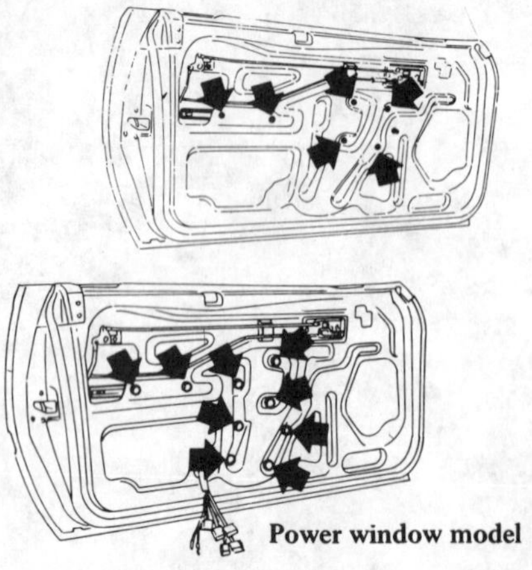

Fig. 12.8 Locations of the front door window regulator mounting bolts (Sec 24)

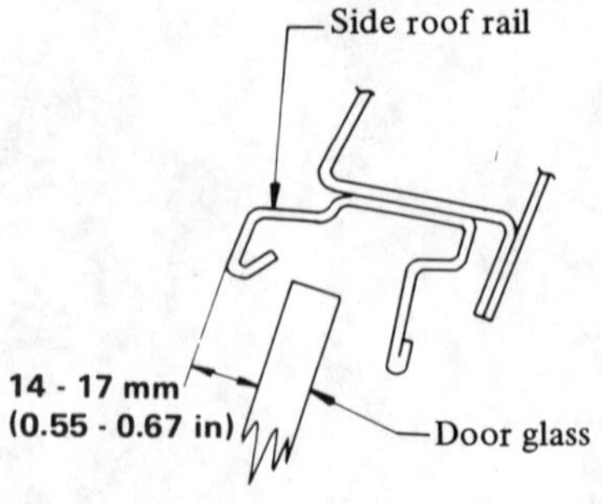

Fig. 12.9 Proper adjustment between the window and the door waist molding rubber seal (Sec 24)

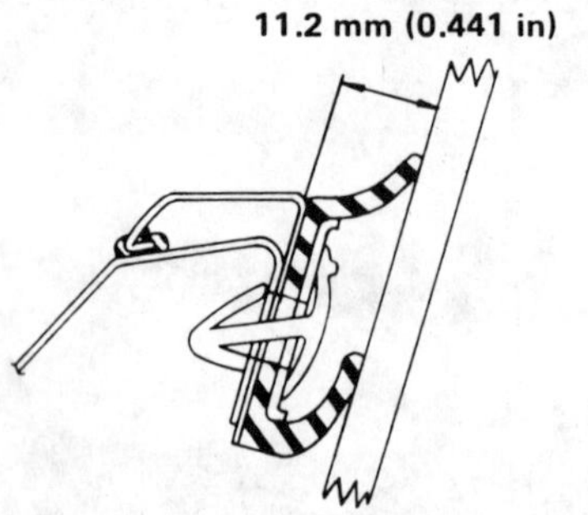

Fig. 12.10 Proper adjustment between the window and the side roof rail (Sec 24)

securing bolts. Adjust the door regulator so that the upper side of the glass is parallel with the body side weatherstrip. Refer to Fig. 12.11. Following adjustment, retighten all of the loosened nuts and bolts

(d) Loosen the nut that secures the upper rear stopper and adjust the rear height of the glass to the proper specs by sliding the stopper up or down (Fig. 12.12). Retighten the nut

(e) Loosen the nut that secures the upper front stopper and adjust the front height of the glass to the proper specs by sliding the stopper up or down (Fig. 12.12). Retighten the nut

25 Door lock and lock control – removal and installation

1 Remove the door trim panel as described in Section 23.
2 Remove the front door window as described in Section 25.
3 Remove the screws that retain the inside handle assembly.
4 Remove the screws that retain the door lock assembly to the door.
5 Remove the bellcrank attaching screw.
6 Disconnect the key rod from the key cylinder.
7 Remove the door lock and lock control from the door.
8 If the key cylinder needs to be removed, remove the exterior door handle by removing the inside attaching nuts.
9 Installation is the reverse of the removal procedure.

26 Front door – removal and installation

1 Either place a jack or stand under the door or have an assistant on hand to support it when the hinge bolts are removed. **Note**: *To protect the door's painted surfaces, place a rag between the door and stand or jack, if used.*
2 Remove the door trim panel as described in Section 23.
3 Remove the plastic sealing screen.
4 Disconnect the door wiring harness connector.
5 Remove the hinge-to-door bolts and lift off the door.
6 Installation is the reverse of the removal procedure.
7 Following installation of the door, check that it is in proper alignment and adjust if necessary as follows:

(a) Up-and-down and forward-and-backward adjustments are made by loosening the hinge-to-body bolts and moving the door as necessary

(b) Side-to-side adjustments are made by loosening the hinge-to-door bolts and moving the door as necessary

27 Front seat – removal and installation

1 Slide the seat all the way forward and remove the plastic trim covers over the 2 rear seat mounts.
2 Remove the 2 rear mounting bolts.
3 Slide the seat all the way to the rear and remove the 2 forward mounting bolts (photo).
4 Lift out the seat.
5 Installation is the reverse of the removal procedure.

28 Rear seat – removal and installation

Hardtop

1 With a small flathead screwdriver, pry out the plugs from the rear

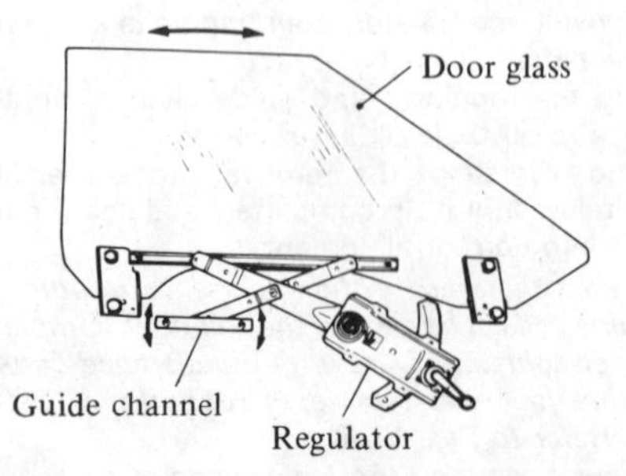

Fig. 12.11 The regulator must be adjusted as shown to ensure the front door window is parallel with the body side weatherstrip (Sec 24)

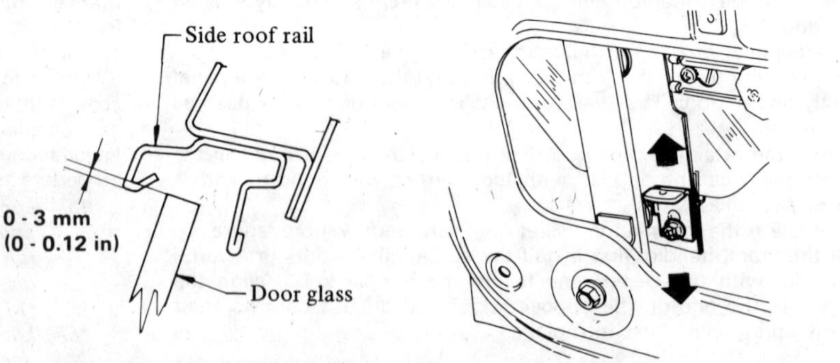

Fig. 12.12 The height of the front door window is adjusted by moving the front and rear upper stoppers up or down as required (Sec 24)

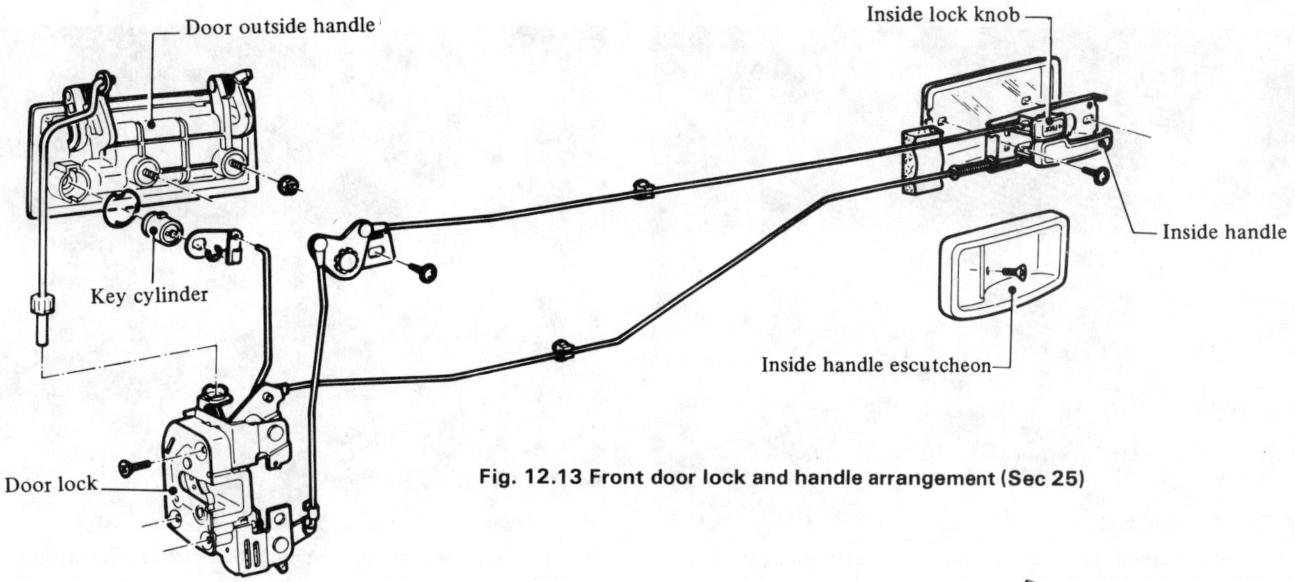

Fig. 12.13 Front door lock and handle arrangement (Sec 25)

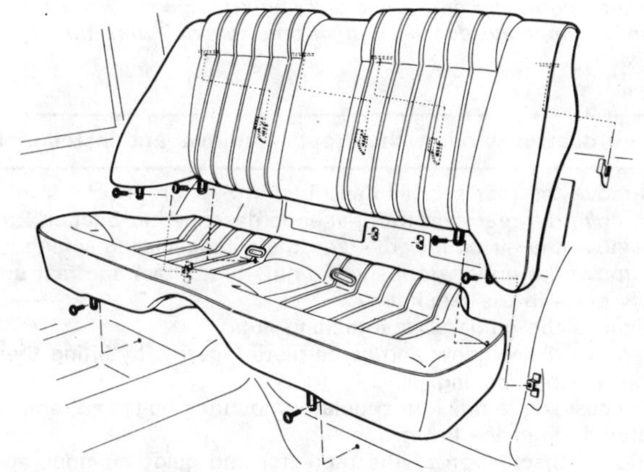

Fig. 12.14 Mounting arrangement of the rear seat (hardtop) (Sec 28)

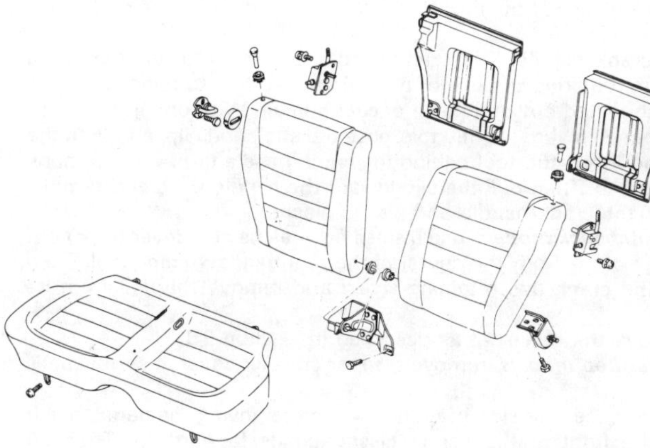

Fig. 12.15 Mounting arrangement of the rear seat (hatchback) (Sec 28)

arm rest. Then remove the 2 arm rest mounting screws and lift off the arm rest.

2 Remove the 2 screws that secure the rear seat cushion. Then pull the cushion forward and simultaneously guide the center seat belts through the holes in the seat cushion. Remove the cushion.

3 Remove the 4 lower screws that secure the rear seat back (photo). Then push up on the seat back about an inch to disengage it from its retaining hooks near the top. Then pull forward and lift the seat back out of the car.

4 Installation is the reverse of the removal procedure.

Hatchback

5 Remove the rear seat cushion as described in paragraph 2 above.

6 Remove the rear seat backs by removing the mounting bolts shown in Fig. 12.15.

7 Installation is the reverse of the removal procedure.

29 Rear side trim panel – removal and installation

1 Remove the metal kick plate along side of the front door.

2 *On hardtop models,* pry out the plugs from the rear arm rest with a small flat-head screwdriver (photo). Then remove the 2 arm rest mounting screws and lift off the arm rest.

3 *On a hardtop,* with manually operated windows remove the rear

27.3 To remove the front mounting bolts of the front seat, slide the seat all the way back and use a ratchet with an extension

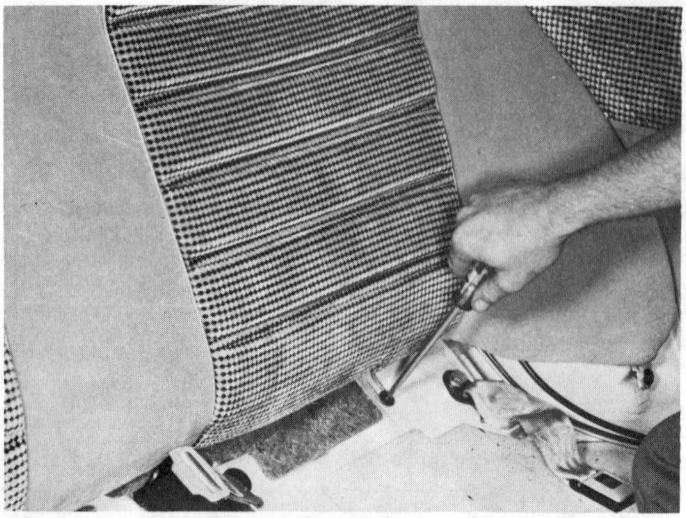

28.3 The rear seat back is secured by mounting bolts along the bottom and retaining clips at the top

29.2 To reach the rear arm rest mounting screws, first pry out the plastic filler plugs

window crank handle. The crank handle is held onto its shaft by a spring clip, requiring the use of a small hooked tool to remove it. One can be fabricated out of a piece of coat hanger. With one hand, press the trim panel inward slightly to expose the shaft and clip, and with the other hand insert the tool behind the crank handle until you can hook the spring clip. Then pull the clip toward the handle knob and remove it. Lift off the crank handle and plastic washer.

4 *On hatchback models,* use a small flat-head screwdriver to pry out the plastic cover from the center of the rear window crank dial. Then remove the crank dial retaining screw and remove the dial from its shaft.

5 Remove the rear seat as described in Section 28.

6 *On hardtop models,* remove the rear speaker cover. It simply pulls off.

7 Remove the rear side trim panel. When removing the panel, pull it toward the front of the car to disengage its forward lip. Then lift upwards to disengage its upper retainers and lift the panel out.

8 If equipped with power operated windows, disconnect the wiring connector leading to the power window switch. If the switch needs to be removed, simply remove the clip that retains it to the panel.

9 Installation is the reverse of the removal procedure. **Note:** *On hardtop models, when installing the rear window crank handle simply install the spring clip onto the crank handle, align the handle with the one on the opposite door and push onto its shaft until the clip clicks into place.*

30 Rear quarter window (hardtop) – removal and installation

1 Remove the rear seat as described in Section 28.

2 Remove the rear side trim panel as described in Section 29.

3 Remove the air outlet grille and the plastic sealing screen.

4 Remove the upper stoppers and nuts that attach the rear quarter window glass to the regulator.

5 Remove the guide plate attaching nuts.

6 Remove the window and guide plate together by lifting them up through the top opening.

7 If necessary, remove the regulator mounting bolts and remove the regulator through the lower opening.

8 Prior to installation of the regulator and guide channel, apply a light coat of lithium grease to their sliding surfaces.

9 Installation is the reverse of the removal procedure. Following

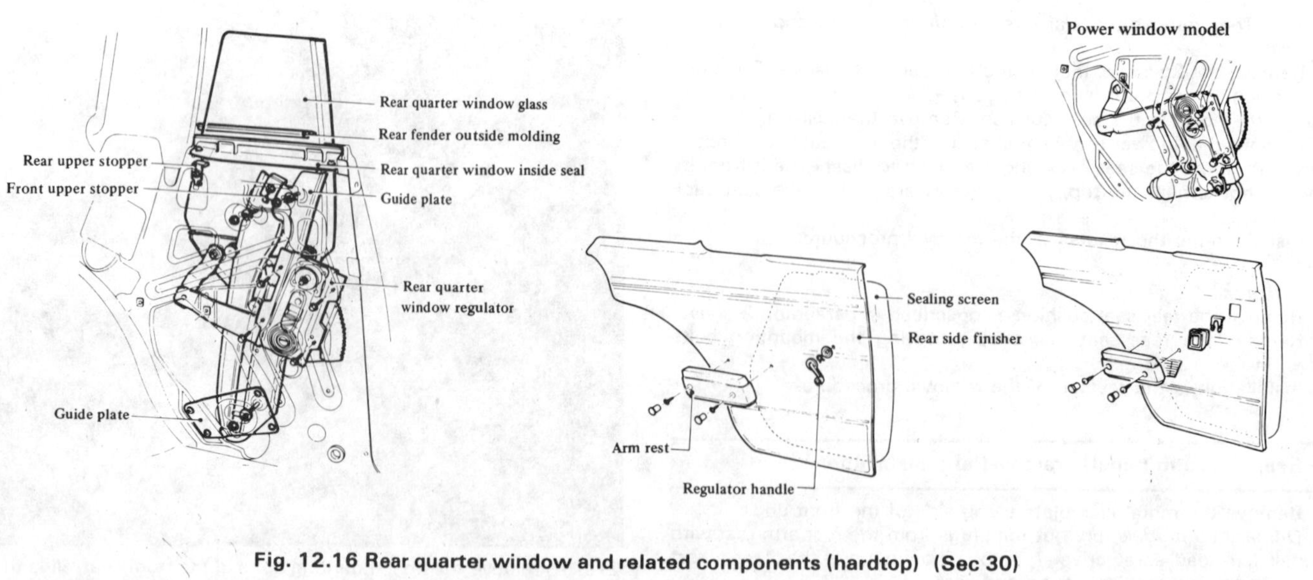

Fig. 12.16 Rear quarter window and related components (hardtop) (Sec 30)

installation of the window, it should be adjusted for proper alignment as described below.

(a) Close the rear quarter window completely
(b) Turn the adjusting bolt, which secures the upper end of the guide plate, until the distance between the glass and the rear quarter waist molding rubber seal in 0.441 in (11.2 mm). Refer to Fig. 12.9
(c) Next turn the adjusting bolt located on the lower end of the guide plate to adjust the distance between the door glass and the side roof rail. Refer to Fig. 12.10
(d) Close both the rear quarter window and the front door windows completely and check that they are properly aligned with each other. Refer to Fig. 12.18
(e) Finally adjust the 3 upper stoppers so that the top of the glass is 0.12 in (3 mm) above the bottom of the side roof rail. Refer to Fig. 12.19

31 Rear quarter window (hatchback) – removal and installation

1 Remove the rear seat as described in Section 28.
2 Remove the rear side trim panel as described in Section 29.
3 Remove the top luggage side finishing panel.
4 Remove the plastic sealing screen.
5 Remove the bolts that attach the window glass to the regulator.
6 Remove the regulator mounting bolts and lift out the regulator.
7 Remove the rear outlet grille and rear fender molding.
8 Remove the rear body side retainer (Fig. 12.21).
9 Remove the rear quarter window mounting screws and lift out the window.
10 Installation is the reverse of the removal procedure.

32 Opera window (hardtop) – removal and installation

1 Remove the rear side trim panel as described in Section 29.
2 Remove the mounting screws along the lower edge of the rear corner trim panel.
3 Remove the screws that retain the assist grip, and lift out the assist grip and rear corner trim panel.
4 Remove the opera window attaching nuts and lift out the window.
5 Installation is the reverse of the removal procedure.

33 Seat belts – removal and installation

Front harness

1 Remove the rear side trim panel as described in Section 29.
2 Remove the mounting screws along the lower edge of the rear corner trim panel.
3 Remove the screws that retain the assist grip (hardtop) (photo) or

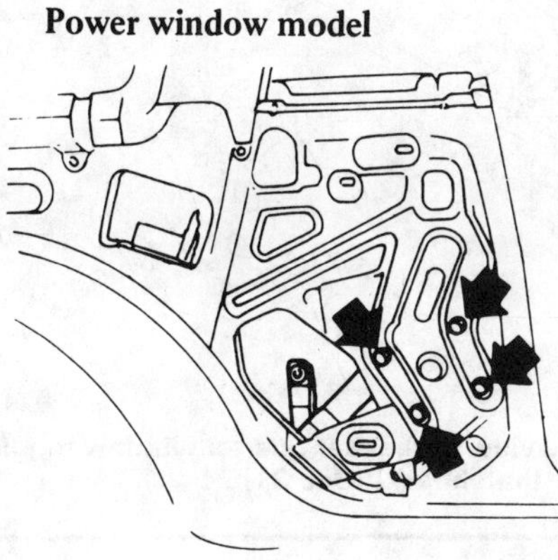

Fig. 12.17 Locations of the power operated rear quarter window regulator mounting bolts (hardtop) (Sec 30)

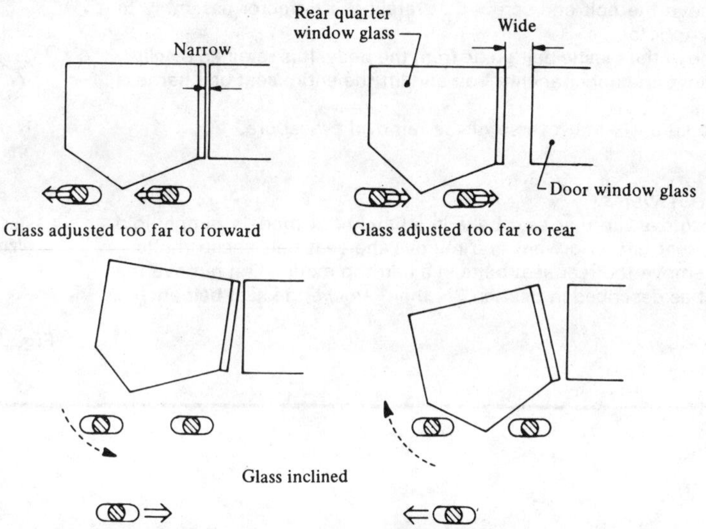

Fig. 12.18 The alignment between the rear quarter window and the front door window is adjusted as shown (hardtop) (Sec 30)

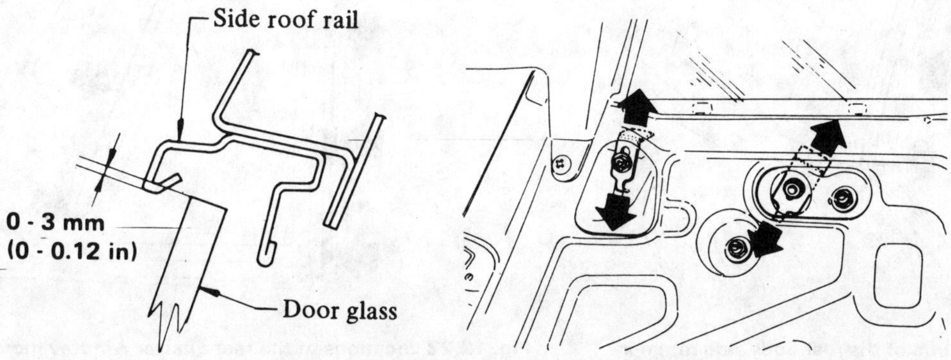

Fig. 12.19 The height of the rear quarter window is adjusted by sliding the front and rear upper stoppers up or down as necessary (hardtop) (Sec 30)

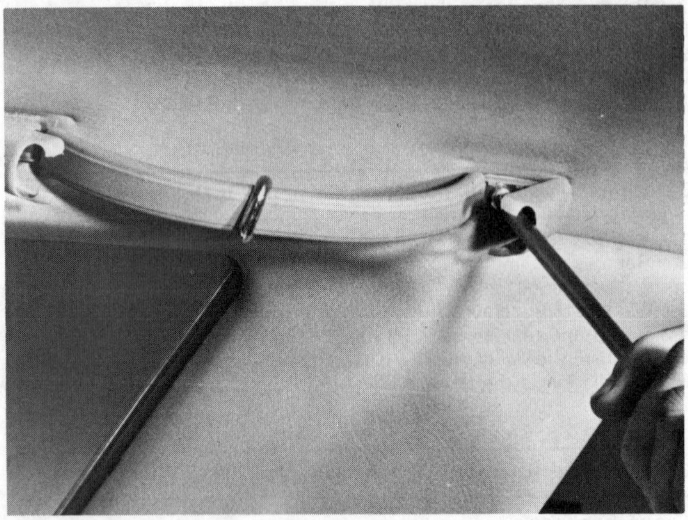

33.3 To remove the rear assist grip, unsnap the plastic trim covers and remove the 2 mounting screws

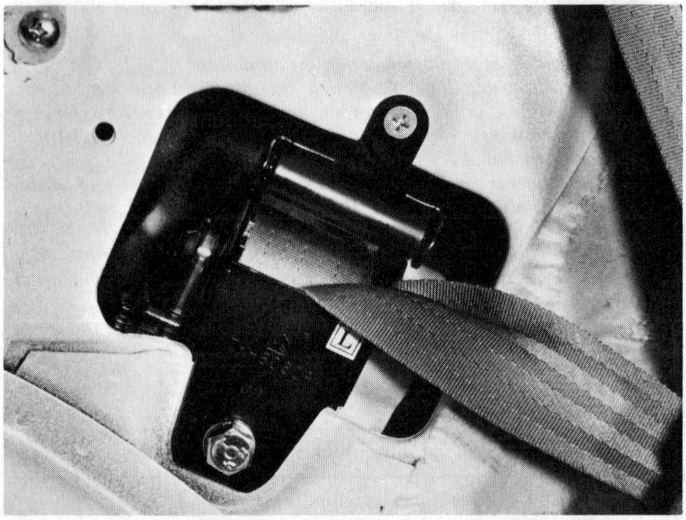

33.5 The front seat belt harness retractor assembly is held to the body by a screw and a bolt

coathanger (hatchback) and lift out the assist grip and rear corner trim panel.

4 Remove the plastic cover from the lower seat belt harness anchor bolt and remove the bolt.

5 Remove the bolt and screw that retain the retractor assembly to the body (photo).

6 Remove the plastic belt guide from the body. It is retained by clips.

7 Remove the upper anchor bolt and lift the entire seat belt harness free.

8 Installation is the reverse of the removal procedure.

Rear seat belts

9 To remove the rear seat belts in a hatchback models, simply fold the rear seat backs forward and remove the seat belt anchor bolts.

10 To remove the rear seat belts in a hardtop model, first remove the rear seat as described in Section 28, then remove the seat belt anchor bolts.

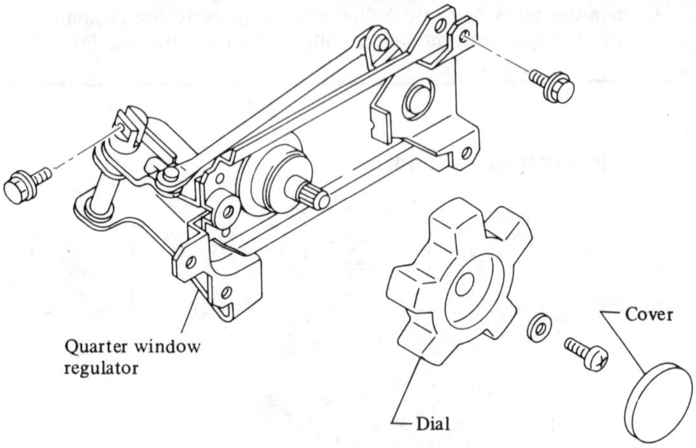

Fig. .12.20 Exploded view of the rear quarter window regulator (hatchback) (Sec 31)

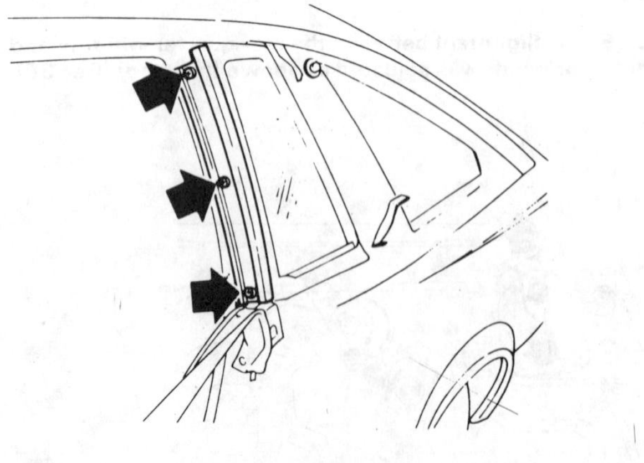

Fig. 12.21 Location of the rear body side retainer (hatchback) (Sec 31)

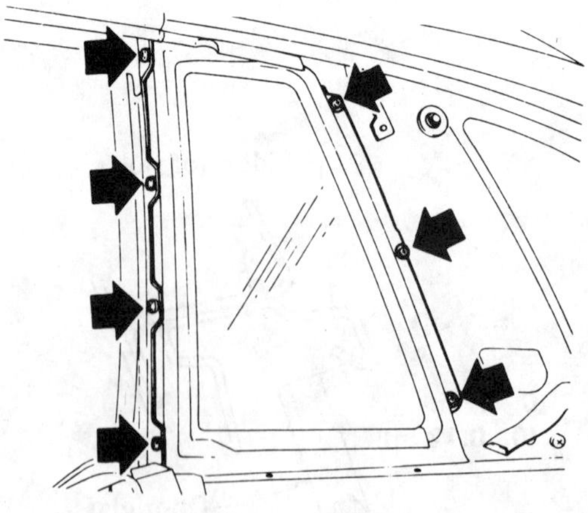

Fig. 12.22 Locations of the rear quarter window mounting screws (hatchback) (Sec 31)

Chapter 13 Supplement: Revisions and information on 1982 and 1983 models

Contents

Introduction 1
Specifications 2
Tune-up and routine maintenance 3
Routine maintenance intervals
Power steering fluid level check
Drivebelt check and adjustment
Fuel filter replacement
Valve clearance adjustment (1983 only)
Idle speed adjustment
Engine 4
General information
Oil pump installation (1983 only)
Fuel and exhaust systems 5
Throttle valve switch adjustment
Engine electrical systems 6
General information
Spark plug switching control system
Emissions control systems 7
Crankcase emission control system
Air Induction System (AIS)
Exhaust Gas Recirculation (EGR) system
Spark timing control system
Automatic transmission 8
Inhibitor switch adjustment
Removal and installation
Braking system 9
Front disc brake pad replacement
Rear disc brake pad replacement
Rear disc brake caliper removal and installation
Rear disc brake caliper overhaul
Master cylinder overhaul
Chassis electrical system 10
Voice warning system
Wiring diagrams
Bodywork 11
Front bumper removal and installation
Rear bumper removal and installation

1 Introduction

This supplement contains specifications and service procedure changes that apply exclusively to 1982 and 1983 Datsun 200SX models. In most cases, there are no differences (or very minor differences) between 1981 and later models, and the information contained in Chapters 1 through 12 will apply.

We recommend that before beginning a service procedure, you check this supplement for any new specifications or procedure changes. Make note of this supplementary information and be sure to include it while following the original procedure in Chapters 1 through 12.

2 Specifications

Note: *The following specifications are revisions of or supplementary to those listed at the beginning of each Chapter of this manual. The original specifications apply unless alternative figures are included here.*

Quick reference capacities

Engine oil	
with oil filter change	4-1/2 qts (4.2 liters — 3-3/4 Imperial qts)
without oil filter change	3-7/8 qts (3.7 liters — 3-1/4 Imperial qts)
Automatic transmission fluid	6-1/2 qts (6.1 liters — 5-3/8 Imperial qts)
Differential oil	2-1/8 pts (1.0 liter — 1-3/4 Imperial pts)

Tune-up and routine maintenance

Spark plug type	
standard	
intake	BPR6ES
exhaust	BPR5ES
hotter	
intake	BPR5ES
exhaust	BPR5ES
colder	
intake	BPR7ES
exhaust	BPR6ES or BPR7ES
Ignition timing	
manual transmission	8° BTDC ± 2° @ 750 rpm ± 100 rpm
automatic transmission	8° BTDC ± 2° @ 700 rpm ± 100 rpm

Tune-up and routine maintenance (continued)

Drivebelt deflection	
cooling fan drivebelt	
used	0.47 to 0.59 in (12 to 15 mm)
new	0.31 to 0.43 in (8 to 11 mm)
A/C compressor drivebelt	
used	0.39 to 0.51 in (10 to 13 mm)
new	0.28 to 0.39 in (7 to 10 mm)
Power steering pump drivebelt	
used	0.59 to 0.71 in (15 to 18 mm)
new	0.47 to 0.59 in (12 to 15 mm)
Clutch pedal height (1983 only)	6.38 to 6.77 in (162 to 172 mm)

Engine

Model	Z22E
Displacement	2188 cc
Valve diameter	
intake	1.654 in (42.0 mm)
exhaust	1.496 in (38.0 mm)
Valve length	
intake	4.90 to 4.91 in (124.38 to 124.68 mm)
exhaust	4.62 to 4.63 in (117.35 to 117.65 mm)
Cylinder bore	3.4252 to 3.4272 in (87.000 to 87.050 mm)
Piston diameter	
standard	3.4238 to 3.4258 in (86.965 to 87.015 mm)
1st oversize	3.4246 to 3.4266 in (86.985 to 87.035 mm)
2nd oversize	3.4435 to 3.4455 in (87.465 to 87.515 mm)
3rd oversize	3.4632 to 3.4652 in (87.965 to 88.015 mm)
Piston pin-to-piston clearance	0.0003 to 0.0005 in (0.008 to 0.012 mm)
Crankshaft	
taper and out-of-round	0.0002 in (0.006 mm) maximum
bend	0.001 in (0.025 mm) maximum
Connecting rod bearing clearance	0.0005 to 0.0021 in (0.012 to 0.054 mm)

Drivetrain

Automatic transmission type	L3N71B
Differential	
type	H190-ML
drive pinion preload with seal	9.5 to 13.9 in-lbs (11 to 16 M-kg)

Brake system

Brake pedal height	
1982	6.50 to 6.73 in (165 to 171 mm)
1983	
manual transmission	6.24 to 6.63 in (158.5 to 168.5 mm)
automatic transmission	6.32 to 6.71 in (160.5 to 170.5 mm)
Brake pedal depressed height (engine running)	2.76 in (70 mm) minimum
Rear disc brake	
type	CL11H
cylinder inner diameter	1.5 in (38.18 mm)
pad size (width x thickness x length)	1.57 x 0.31 x 2.95 in (40 x 8 x 75 mm)
rotor diameter	10.16 in (258 mm)
rotor thickness	0.354 in (9.0 mm) minimum
pad wear limit	0.079 in (2.0 mm)
Brake rotors	
runout	
front (N22)	0.0024 in (0.06 mm) maximum
rear (CL11H)	0.0028 in (0.07 mm) maximum
parallelism	0.0012 in (0.03 mm) maximum
Booster (vacuum servo unit)	
type	M20 or G20
output rod length	0.4045 to 0.4144 in (10.275 to 10.525 mm)
input rod length	5.24 in (133 mm)

Electrical system

Headlight bulbs	
type	4656
wattage	35/35
Front turn signal bulb	
type	1073
wattage	27

Front side combination bulbs

type	67
wattage	8

Torque specifications	**Ft-lbs**	**M-kg**
Cylinder head bolts	58 to 65	8.0 to 9.0
Steering pump-to-bracket	20 to 27	2.7 to 3.7
Engine mounting member-to-body	23 to 31	3.2 to 4.3
Exhaust manifold-to-exhaust tube	20 to 27	2.7 to 3.7
Rear brake caliper mounting bolts	28 to 38	3.0 to 5.3
Bumper shock absorber mounting bolts	23 to 31	3.2 to 4.3

Destination	Class	Model	Engine	Transmission	Differential carrier	Road wheel Size .... Offset mm (in)	Tire size
U.S.A.	Hardtop	RLS110FEU	Z22E	FS5W71B	H190		
		RLS110AEU		L3N71B		5J-14 .... 25 (0.98)	185/70-SR14
	Hatchback	KRLS110FEU		FS5W71B			
		KRLS110AEU		L3N71B		*1 5-1/2JJ-14 .... 25 (0.98)	185/70-SR14
Canada	Hardtop	RLS110FEN		FS5W71B			
		RLS110AEN		L3N71B		*2 4-T x 16 ...... 35 (1.38)	T135/70D16*2
	Hatchback	KRLS110FEN		FS5W71B			
		KRLS110AEN		L3N71B			

*1: Aluminum wheel (Option)
*2: Spare tire

Prefix and suffix designations:

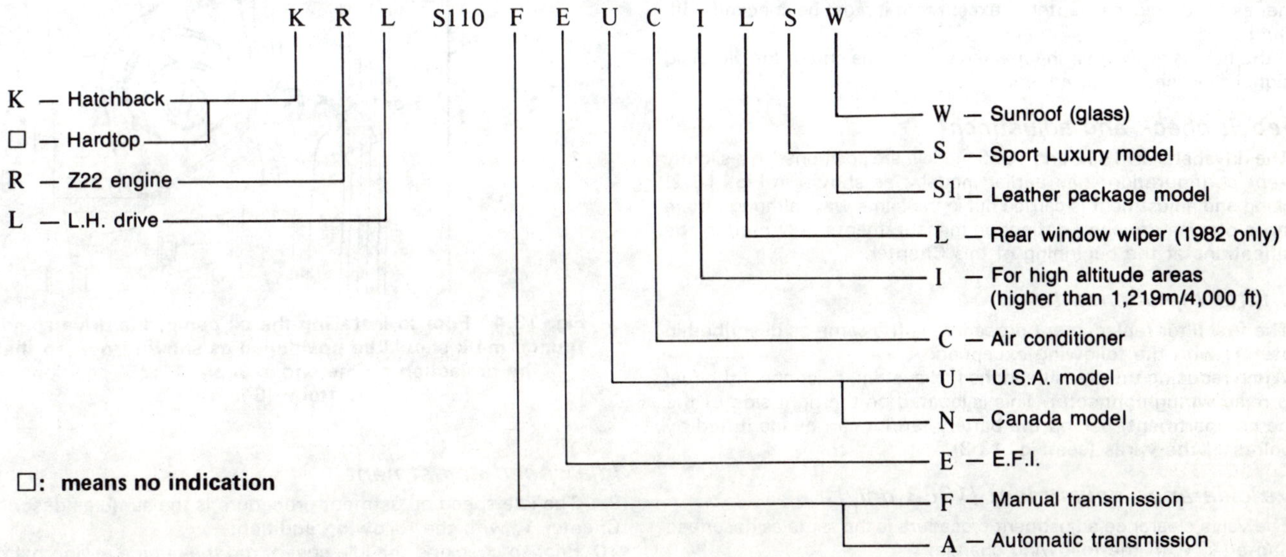

□: **means no indication**

Fig 13.1 1982 and 1983 Datsun 200SX model variations and vehicle identification code chart

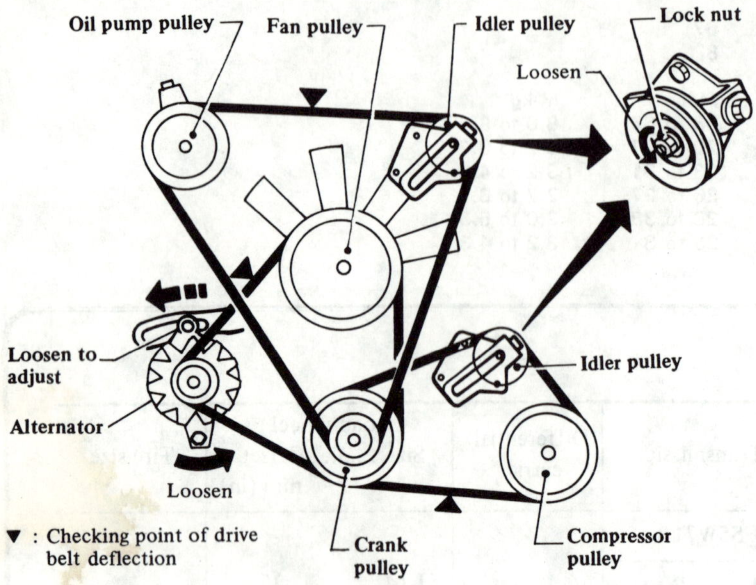

Fig. 13.2 Later model drivebelt check and adjustment details (Sec 3)

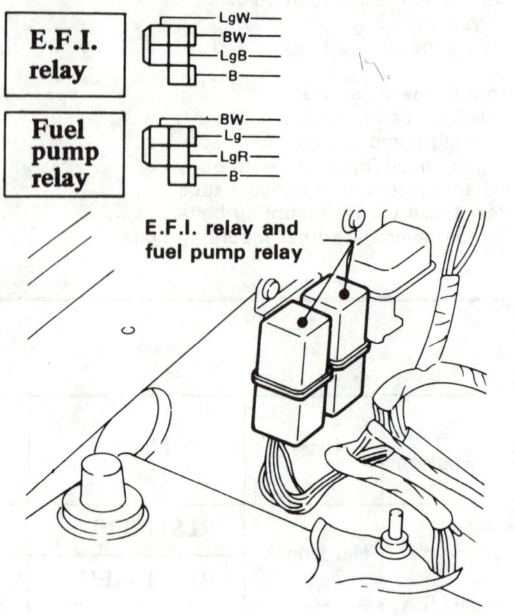

Fig. 13.3 EFI and fuel pump relay locations (Sec 3)

3 Tune-up and routine maintenance

Routine maintenance intervals

The following maintenance procedure should be done on the specified model.

Every 30,000 miles or 24 months — whichever comes first

Replace the air induction valve filter on Canada models (Chapter 1)

Power steering fluid level check

1 The fluid in the power steering reservoir is checked in the same manner as described in Chapter 1, except that it must be checked with the fluid *cold*.

2 If the fluid is not within the marked area on the end of the dipstick, additional fluid should be added.

Drivebelt check and adjustment

3 The drivebelts on 1982 and 1983 models are positioned in a slightly different configuration than earlier models, as shown in Fig. 13.2. Checking and adjustment is carried out in the same way, although there are more precise drivebelt deflection measurements, as noted in the Specifications at the beginning of this Chapter.

Fuel filter replacement

4 The fuel filter replacement procedure is the same as described in Chapter 1, with the following exception:

5 When reducing the pressure in the fuel system, disconnect the fuel pump relay wiring connector. This is located on the right side of the engine compartment, behind the battery, and it can be identified by the colors of the wires (see Fig. 13.3).

Valve clearance adjustment (1983 only)

6 The valve clearance adjustment procedure is the same as described in Chapter 1, with the following change:

7 Prior to checking or adjusting valves 1, 2, 4 and 6, turn the crankshaft until the number 1 piston is at top dead center on the compression stroke (see Chapter 5, Section 7, for more information).

8 Prior to checking or adjusting valves 3, 5, 7 and 8, turn the crankshaft until the number 4 piston is at top dead center on the compression stroke.

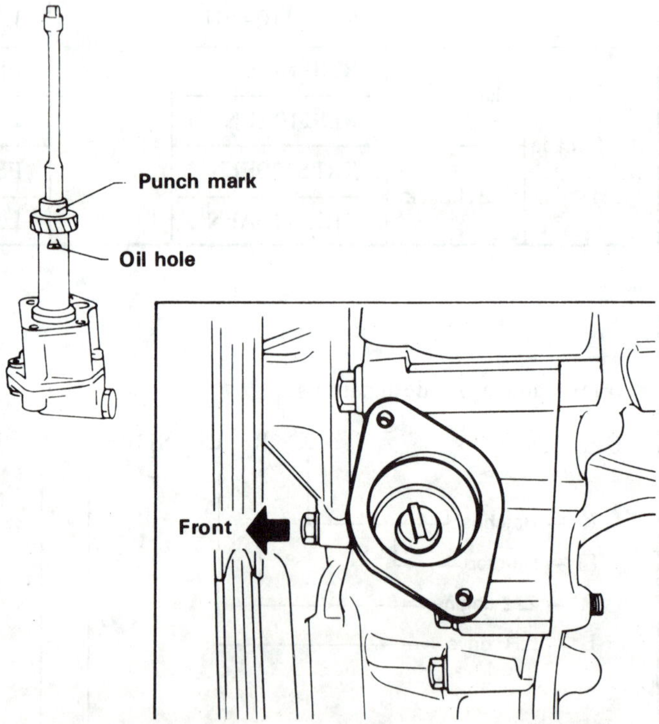

Fig. 13.4 Prior to installing the oil pump, the drive spindle punch mark should be positioned as shown (top), so that the projection on the end is in an '11:25' position (bottom) (Sec 4)

Idle speed adjustment

9 The idle speed adjustment procedure is the same as described in Chapter 1, with the following addition:

10 Prior to checking the idle speed, run the engine at approximately 2000 rpm for 5 minutes, then allow it to return to idle and adjust the rpm as necessary.

11 For 1983 Canada models only, disconnect the hose from the air induction pipe and cap the pipe.

12 Accelerate the engine to 2000 rpm two or three times, then allow the engine to idle for one minute before adjusting the idle speed.

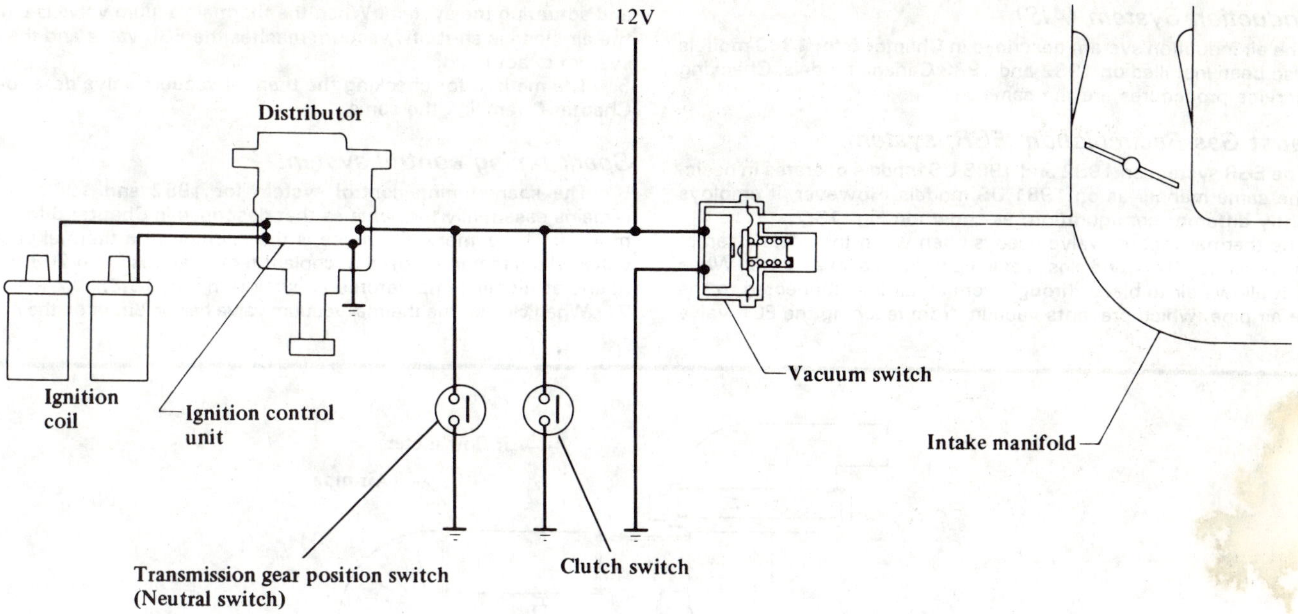

Fig. 13.5 The spark plug switching control system (Sec 6)

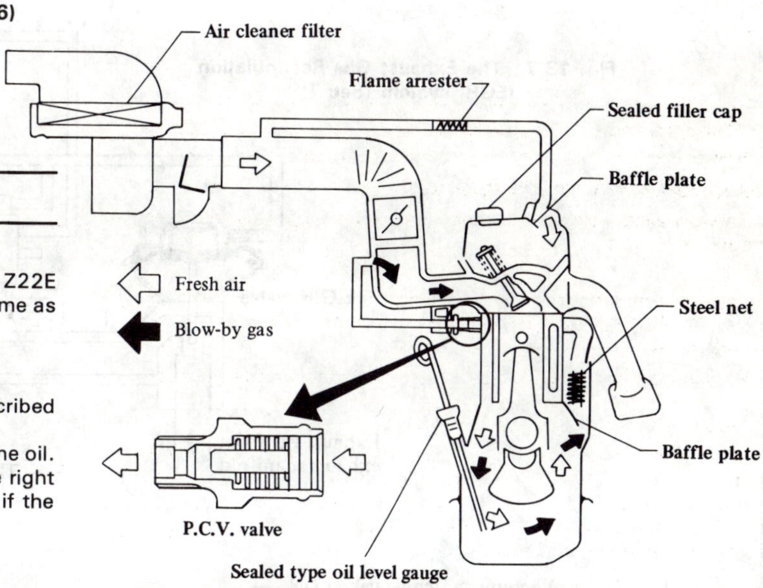

Fig. 13.6 The crankcase emission control system (Sec 7)

4 Engine

General information

1 Other than an increase in displacement to 2188 cc, the Z22E engine used in 1982 and 1983 models remains basically the same as the Z20E engine in terms of design and servicing.

Oil pump installation (1983 only)

2 Removal and installation of the oil pump is the same as described in Chapter 2, with the following change:
3 Prior to installing the pump, fill the pump housing with engine oil.
4 Position the punch mark in the drive spindle slightly to the right of the oil hole in the pump (Fig. 13.4). The position is correct if the projection on the end of the spindle is in an *11:25* position.

5 Fuel and exhaust systems

Throttle valve switch adjustment

The adjustment procedure is the same as described in Chapter 4, except that the point at which the throttle valve switch turns off (showing no continuity on the ohmmeter) is at about 900 rpm for 1982 models and 150 rpm over the standard idle speed for 1983 models.

6 Engine electrical systems

General information

1 All 1982 and 1983 models use the dual ignition system installed on 1981 US models. Follow the procedures for those models when troubleshooting and servicing the system.

Spark plug switching control system

2 This system was introduced on 1982 models and retained for the 1983 model year. The basic function is to switch the ignition system from two-plug operation to single-plug operation during periods of heavy engine load, in order to reduce engine noise. It simultaneously advances the ignition timing when single-plug operation is in effect.
3 The system consists of an ignition control unit, located in the distributor, which is controlled by a vacuum switch connected to the intake manifold (Fig. 13.5). The control unit also receives an operation signal from the clutch switch (manual transmission) or Neutral switch (automatic transmission).
4 The system switches to single-plug ignition only while the vehicle is being driven (clutch is engaged or automatic transmission is in a gear other than N or P) and when intake manifold vacuum is low.
5 Inspection and troubleshooting of the spark plug switching control system requires special tools and expertise and should be left to a trained Datsun mechanic.

7 Emissions control systems

Crankcase emission control system

1 The crankcase emission control system is basically the same as described in Chapter 6, except for a slightly different layout, as shown in the accompanying illustration (Fig. 13.6).

Air Induction System (AIS)

2 The air induction system described in Chapter 6 for 1980 models has also been installed on 1982 and 1983 Canada models. Checking and service procedures are the same.

Exhaust Gas Recirculation (EGR) system

3 The EGR system on 1982 and 1983 US models operates in basically the same manner as on 1981 US models. However, it employs a slightly different configuration, as shown in Fig. 13.7.

4 The thermal vacuum valve used is open when the coolant temperature is below 104 °F and closes at temperatures above 104 °F. When open, it allows air to bleed through from an air line connected to the intake air pipe, which prevents vacuum from reaching the EGR valve and actuating the system. When the thermal vacuum valve is closed, the air bleed is shut off, vacuum reaches the EGR valve and the EGR system is actuated.

5 The method for checking the thermal vacuum valve described in Chapter 6 remains the same.

Spark timing control system

6 The spark timing control system for 1982 and 1983 models remains essentially the same as that described in Chapter 6 for 1981 models. The primary difference is the addition of a thermal vacuum valve which remains closed at coolant temperatures up to 203 °F, and opens at higher temperatures as shown in Fig. 13.8.

7 When closed, the thermal vacuum valve has no effect on the normal

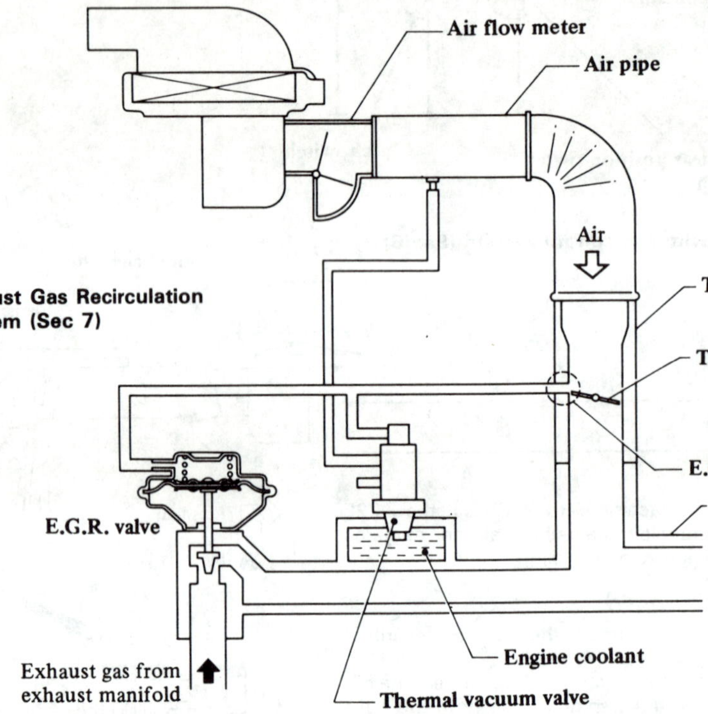

Fig. 13.7 The Exhaust Gas Recirculation (EGR) system (Sec 7)

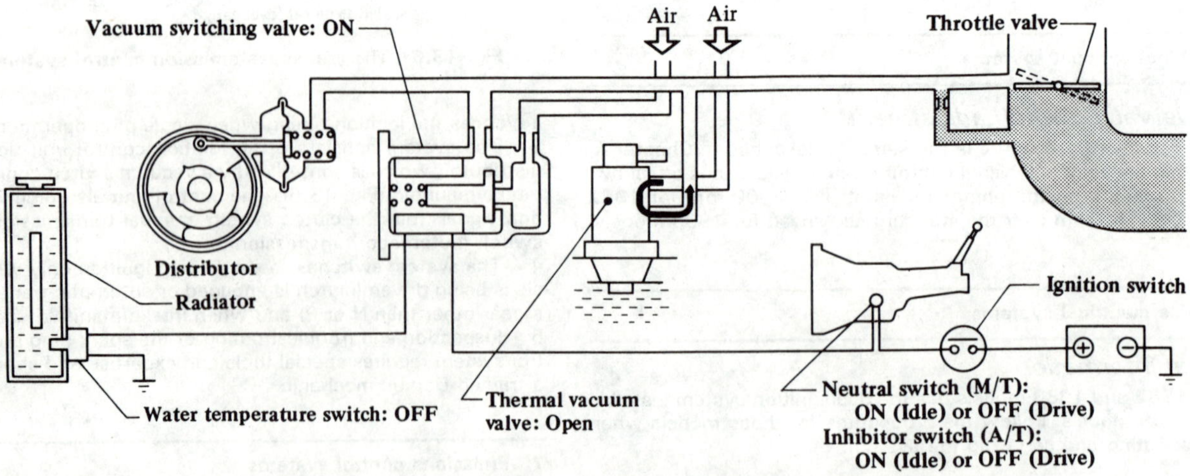

Fig. 13.8 The spark timing control system (shown with engine coolant above 203°F) (Sec 7)

operation of the system. When opened, however, it allows an air bleed in the system which cuts off the vacuum signal to the vacuum advance mechanism, thus deactivating the spark timing control system. In this way the thermal vacuum valve prevents the timing from being advanced at extremely hot engine temperatures.
8 If you suspect the thermal vacuum valve is not operating properly, it must be removed for testing.
9 Drain the engine coolant (Chapter 1).
10 Leave the hoses connected to the thermal vacuum valve, but disconnect them from the other components.
11 Using a wrench, unscrew the thermal vacuum valve.
12 Attempt to suck air through the lower hose. If you can, the thermal vacuum valve is defective and must be replaced.
13 Submerge the thermal vacuum valve in a container of cold water, making sure the ends of the hoses are kept well above the surface of the water.
14 Slowly heat the water. The thermal vacuum valve should remain closed (no suction possible) until the water temperature reaches 203°F. Above this temperature the valve should open, and you should now be able to suck air through the lower hose. If not, the valve is defective and must be replaced.
15 When installing the thermal vacuum valve, apply thread sealer to the threads, being careful not to allow the sealer to contaminate the bottom sensor.

8 Automatic transmission

Inhibitor switch adjustment

1 The inhibitor switch adjustment procedure is the same as described in Chapter 7, Part B, with the following exception:
2 When the transmission is in the P or N positions, the *blue/white* and *white/black* wires should show continuity.

Removal and installation

3 The procedure described in Chapter 7, Part B, remains basically the same except for the following addition:
4 If installing the torque converter onto the main assembly, be sure that dimension *A*, shown in Fig. 7.18, is greater than 1.378-inch (35 mm).

9 Braking system

Front disc brake pad replacement

1 This procedure is the same as the one described in Chapter 9, except that disc pad shims are now installed on the backsides of both disc pads. These shims are removed and installed along with the pads.

Rear disc brake pad replacement

2 Raise the rear of the vehicle and support it securely on jackstands, then block the front wheels. Remove the wheel and tire.
3 Disconnect the parking brake cable.
4 Remove the spring retainer (Fig. 13.9).
5 Remove the pin bolts.
6 Remove the pad springs, pads and pad shim.
7 Prior to installing new pads, retract the piston into the cylinder body by turning it clockwise with a pair of pliers as shown in Fig. 13.10. Be careful not to damage the piston boot.
8 Coat the pad contact area on the mounting support with PBC grease or a silicone-based grease.
9 The remainder of the installation procedure is the reverse of the removal procedure.
10 Bleed the brakes as described in Chapter 9.

Rear disc brake caliper removal and installation

11 Disconnect the parking brake cable.
12 Disconnect the brake hose from the caliper. Immediately plug the brake line to prevent leakage of fluid and to keep foreign material from entering the line.
13 Remove the caliper mounting bolts and lift off the caliper assembly.
14 Installation is the reverse of the removal procedure.
15 Bleed the brakes as described in Chapter 9.
16 Following installation, depress the brake pedal a few times to adjust the clearance between the brake pads and the rotor. Also check for any leakage of brake fluid.

Rear disc brake caliper overhaul

Note: *Prior to overhauling the brake caliper, purchase the appropriate rear brake overhaul kit for your particular model.*
17 Remove the caliper as described above.
18 Drain any remaining brake fluid from the caliper body.
19 Remove the spring retainer.
20 Remove the two pin bolts and separate the caliper body from the mounting support.
21 Remove the brake pad springs, pads and shim from the mounting support.
22 Remove the piston from the caliper body, using a pair of needle-nose pliers to rotate the piston *counterclockwise*.
23 Once the piston is removed, refer to Fig. 13.11 and disassemble the piston as follows:

a) Use a small screwdriver to pry out the ring.
b) Remove the spacers, wave washer, ball bearing and adjust nut

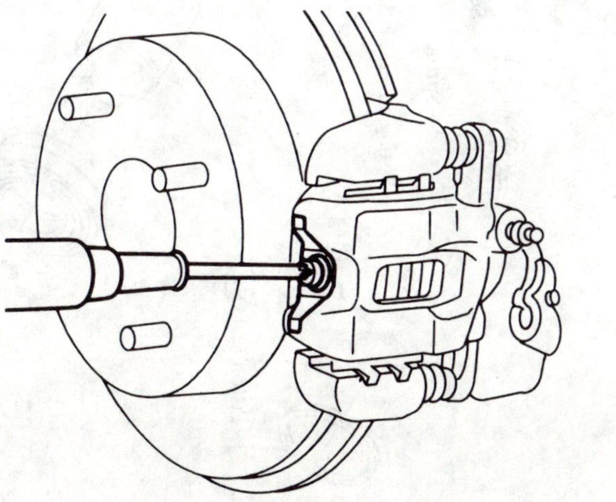

Fig. 13.9 Removing the rear disc brake spring retainer (Sec 9)

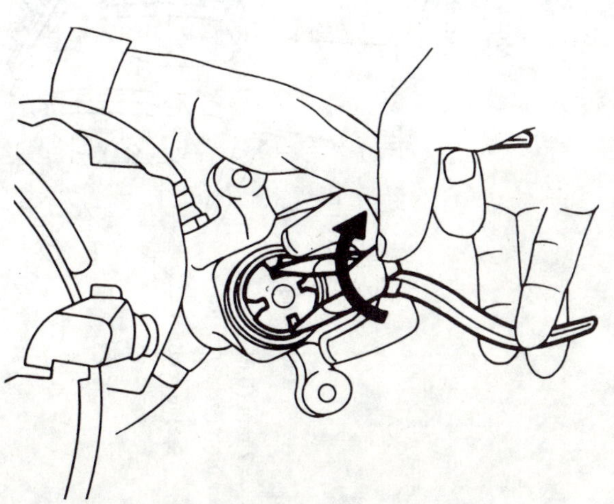

Fig. 13.10 Prior to installing new pads, the piston must be retracted by turning it clockwise with a pair of pliers (Sec 9)

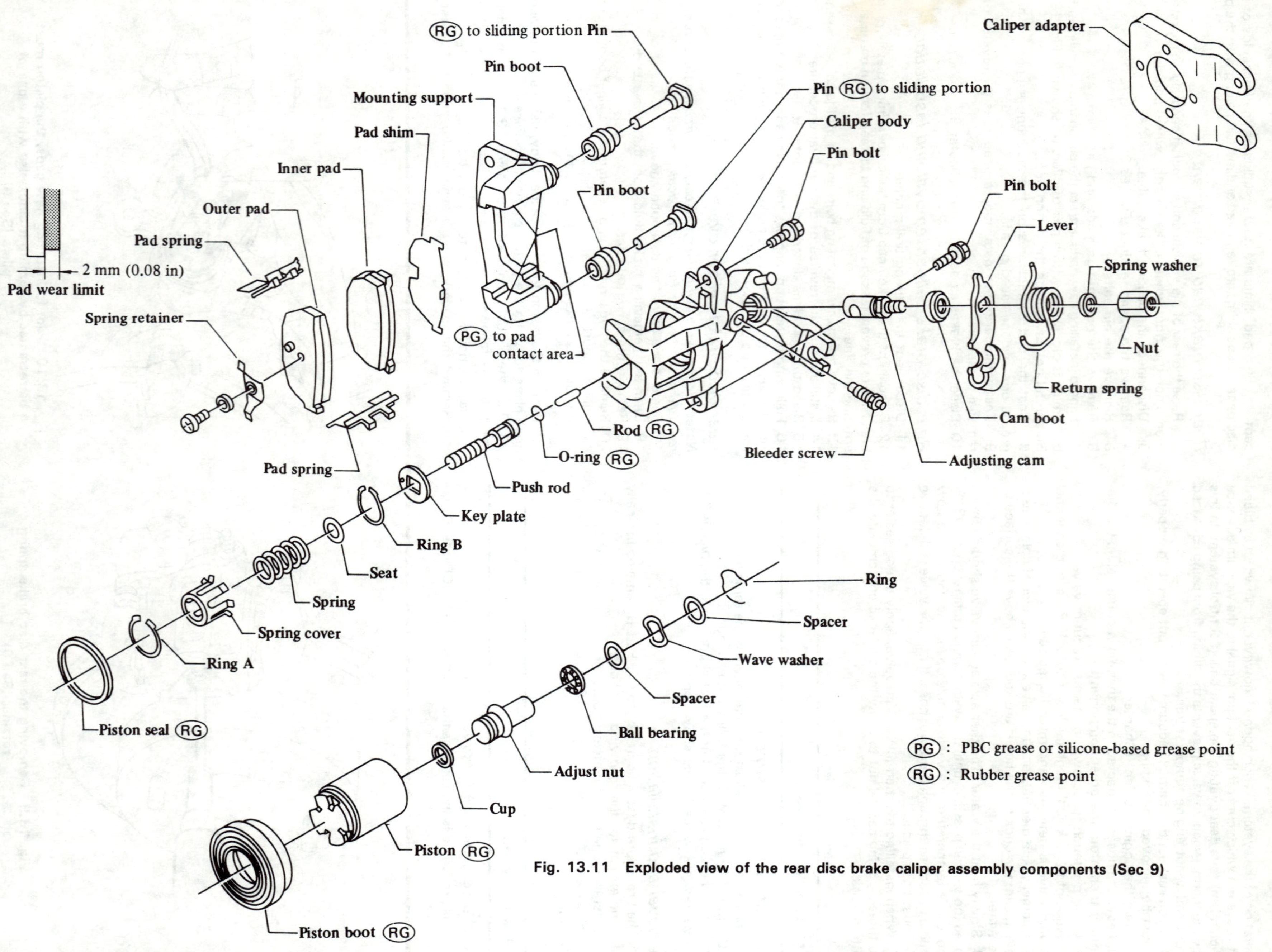

Fig. 13.11 Exploded view of the rear disc brake caliper assembly components (Sec 9)

Fig. 13.12 When assembling the rear brake caliper, the rubber cup must be installed on the adjust nut so the seal lip points in the direction shown (Sec 9)

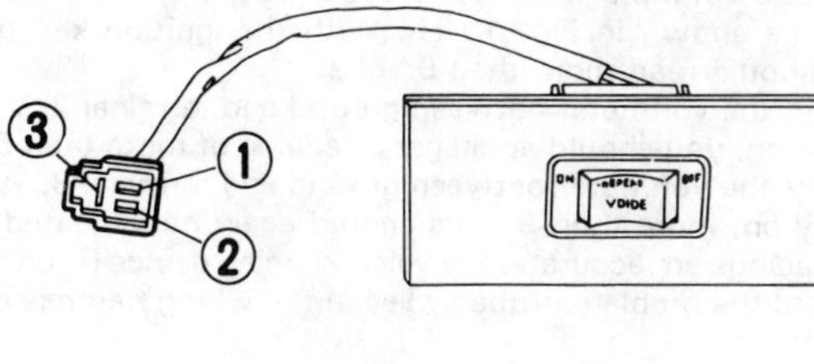

	OFF	ON	REPEAT
1		O	O
2		O	O
3			O

Fig. 13.13 When testing the voice warning switch, make sure continuity exists between the terminals indicated with the switch in each position (the solid line indicates continuity should exist) (Sec 10)

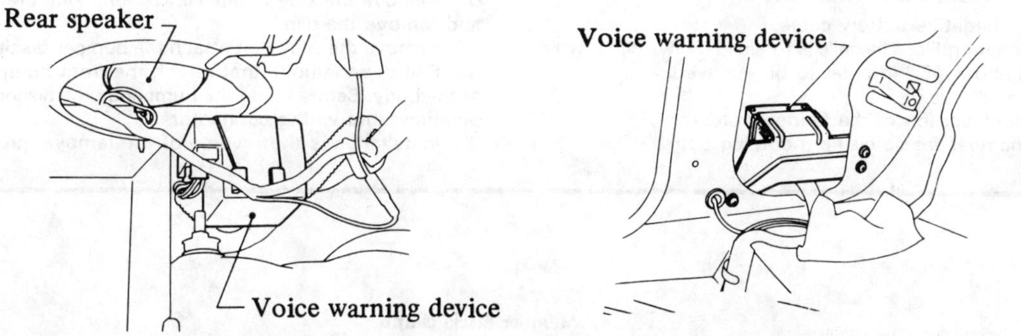

Fig. 13.14 Location of the voice warning device on hardtop models (left) and hatchback models (right) (Sec 10)

from the piston.

c) Remove the rubber cup from the adjust nut.

d) Separate the piston boot from the piston.

24 Disassemble the caliper body by referring to the illustration and using the following procedure:

a) Using snap-ring pliers, pry out ring A, then remove the spring cover, spring and seat.

b) Pry out ring B, then remove the key plate, push rod and rod.

c) Remove the O-ring from the push rod.

25 Using a wood or plastic tool, pry out the piston seal from the caliper body, being careful not to scratch the bore.
26 Disengage and remove the return spring from the lever, then remove the nut, spring washer, adjusting cam and cam boot.
27 Remove the pins and pin boots from the mounting support.
28 Clean all of the metal parts in brake fluid or denatured alcohol.
Warning: *Never use petroleum-based solvents to clean brake system parts.*
29 Check the inside surface of the cylinder bore for any scoring, rust, nicks or other damage. If light scoring or rust is present it can be removed by polishing the bore with fine emery cloth. If the damage is deep the entire body will have to be replaced.
30 Check the yoke for cracks, excessive wear and other damage and replace it if necessary.
31 Inspect the piston for scoring, rust, nicks and other damage. The sliding surface of the piston is plated and cannot be polished. If any defects are found, the piston must be replaced.
32 All rubber seals should be replaced with new ones during the overhaul process.
33 Prior to reassembly, apply a thin coat of rubber grease to the push rod groove and O-ring, the adjust nut groove and rubber cup, the piston seal, the inside of the piston boot and the sliding surfaces of the piston and pins.
34 Install the rubber cup on the adjust nut so the lip faces in the direction shown in Fig. 13.12.
35 Assembly and installation are the reverse of the removal and disassembly procedures with the following note:
36 When assembling the caliper body components, fit the push rod into the square hole of the key plate and fit the convex point of the key plate so it engages with the concave point of the cylinder.

Master cylinder overhaul

37 1982 and 1983 models use either a Tokico or Nabco master cylinder. Although the overhaul procedure is basically the same, the parts and rebuild kits are not interchangable. Be sure you obtain the correct kit for the type of master cylinder you have.
38 The torque for the check valve plugs on these master cylinders is 33 to 40 Ft-lb (4.5 to 5.5 M-kg).

10 Chassis electrical system

Voice warning system

1 Both 1982 and 1983 models are equipped with a voice warning system, which alerts the driver to certain abnormal conditions.
2 Due to the complexity of the system and the number of components tied into it, accurate troubleshooting should be left to a qualified Datsun mechanic.
3 However, if the system is not operating at all, there are a few quick checks the home mechanic can make to pinpoint the problem area.
4 Check that the speaker in the driver's door produces sound when the radio is turned On. If not, inspect the wiring and connector attached to the speaker.
5 If the speaker is working normally, use a continuity tester to check the voice warning switch (see Fig. 13.13). If the switch does not test accurately, it must be replaced.
6 If the switch is working properly, unplug the connector running to the voice warning device. On hardtop models, the device is located below the right side rear speaker. On hatchback models, it is located below the rear side box.

7 Connect a voltmeter between a body ground and the connector terminal 1 as shown in Fig. 13.15. With the ignition key off, the voltmeter should read more than 9 volts.
8 Connect the voltmeter between ground and terminal 2. With the light switch on, you should again get a reading of more than 9 volts.
9 Connect the voltmeter between ground and terminal 3. With the ignition key on, more than 9 volts should again be indicated.
10 If all readings are accurate, the voice warning device is functioning correctly and the problem probably lies in the wiring harness running to the device.
11 If the correct voltage readings are not obtained, replace the voice warning device.

Wiring diagrams

Since very few changes were made to the later models, the wiring diagrams for 1981 models included in Chapter 10 can be used for later models as well.

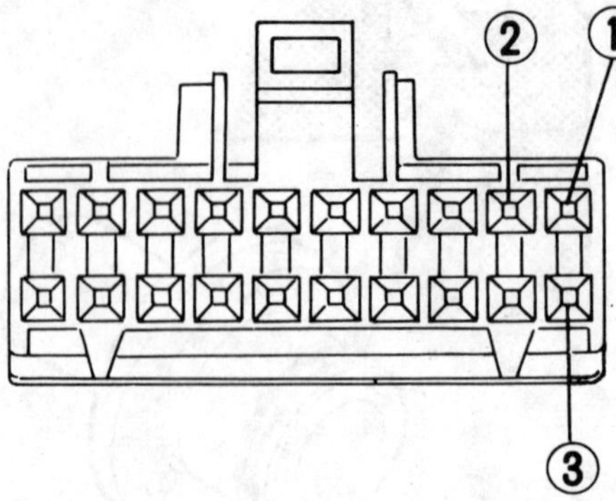

Fig. 13.15 Location of terminals 1, 2 and 3 in the voice warning device connector (Sec 10)

11 Bodywork

Front bumper removal and installation

1 Disconnect the negative battery cable.
2 Remove the radiator grille. The grille is retained by five clips, which need to be turned about 45° in order to be removed.
3 Remove the headlights.
4 Remove the front portion of the fender protector.
5 Remove the member fascia clamp mounting bolts.
6 Remove the side retainer lower and side bracket mounting bolts and remove the clip.
7 Remove the clips that attach the bumper fascia to the apron guide.
8 Remove the bolts that attach the front bumper shock absorbers to the body. Before lifting the bumper away, disconnect the front combination lamp wiring connectors.
9 Installation is the reverse of the removal procedure.

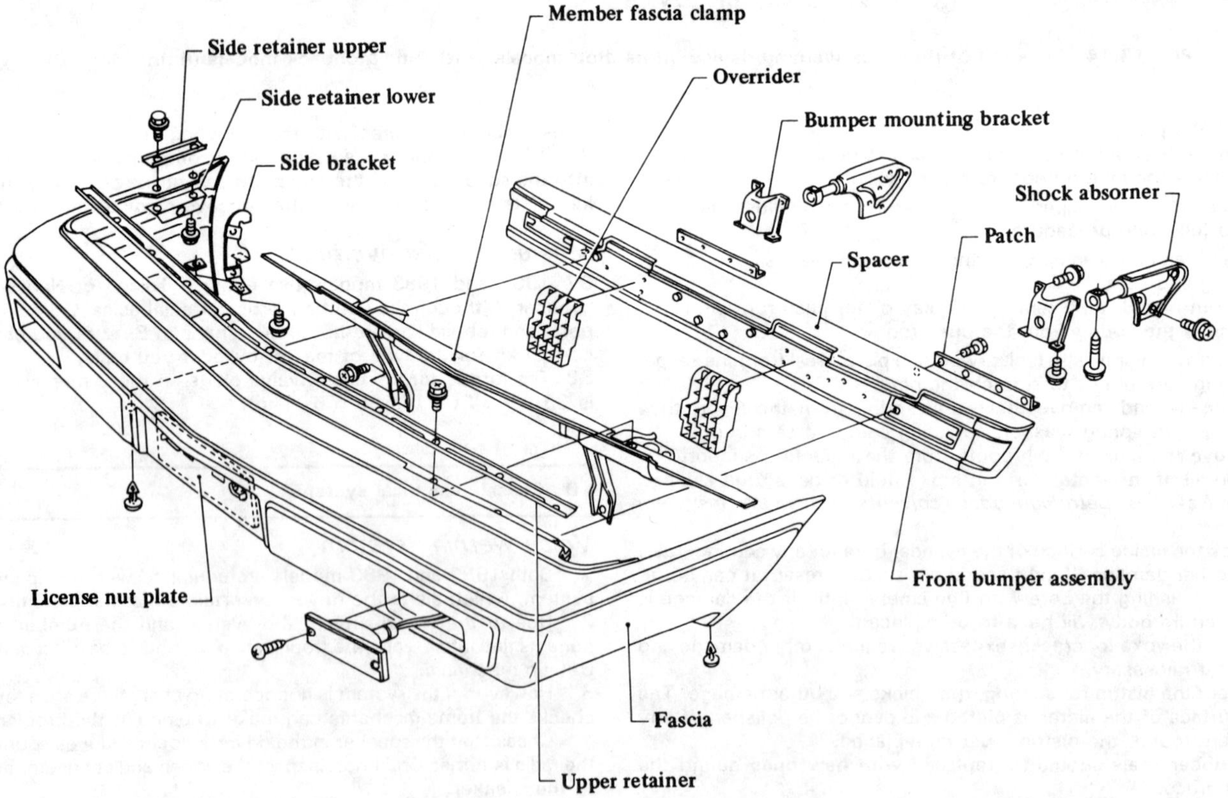

Fig. 13.16 Exploded view of the front bumper and related components (Sec 11)

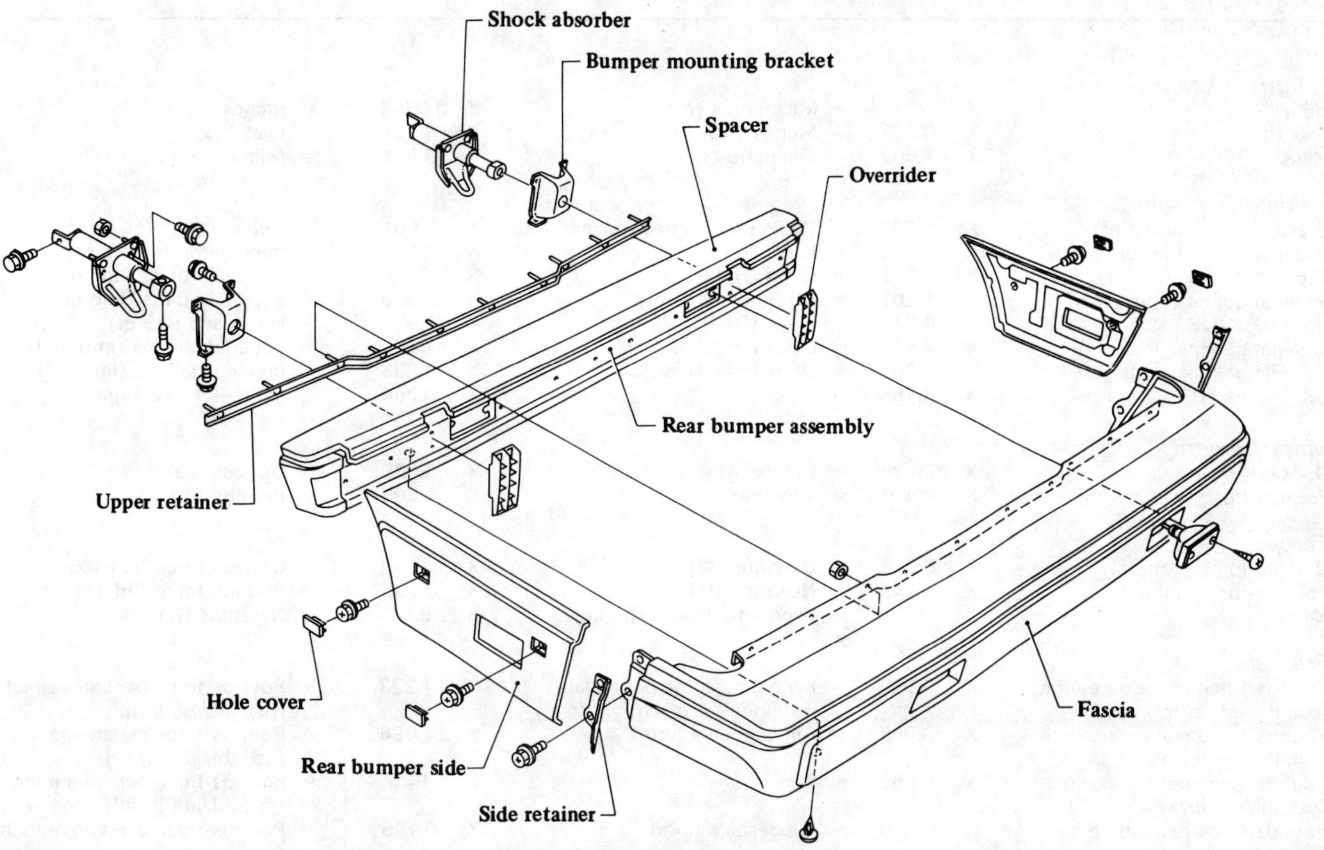

Fig. 13.17 Exploded view of the rear bumper (Sec 11)

Rear bumper removal and installation

10 Disconnect the negative battery cable.

11 Carefully pry out the hole covers on the rear bumper side and remove the bolts behind them. Lift off the rear bumper side.

12 Remove the side retainer mounting bolts.

13 Remove the nuts and screws attaching the rear finish panel inside the rear of the car.

14 Remove the nuts that secure the bumper to the rear panel.

15 Remove the bolts and nuts that attach the rear bumper shock absorbers to the body and carefully lift the bumper away.

16 Installation is the reverse of the removal procedure.

Conversion factors

Length (distance)

Inches (in)	X 25.4	= Millimetres (mm)	X 0.0394	= Inches (in)
Feet (ft)	X 0.305	= Metres (m)	X 3.281	= Feet (ft)
Miles	X 1.609	= Kilometres (km)	X 0.621	= Miles

Volume (capacity)

Cubic inches (cu in; in^3)	X 16.387	= Cubic centimetres (cc; cm^3)	X 0.061	= Cubic inches (cu in; in^3)
Imperial pints (Imp pt)	X 0.568	= Litres (l)	X 1.76	= Imperial pints (Imp pt)
Imperial quarts (Imp qt)	X 1.137	= Litres (l)	X 0.88	= Imperial quarts (Imp qt)
Imperial quarts (Imp qt)	X 1.201	= US quarts (US qt)	X 0.833	= Imperial quarts (Imp qt)
US quarts (US qt)	X 0.946	= Litres (l)	X 1.057	= US quarts (US qt)
Imperial gallons (Imp gal)	X 4.546	= Litres (l)	X 0.22	= Imperial gallons (Imp gal)
Imperial gallons (Imp gal)	X 1.201	= US gallons (US gal)	X 0.833	= Imperial gallons (Imp gal)
US gallons (US gal)	X 3.785	= Litres (l)	X 0.264	= US gallons (US gal)

Mass (weight)

Ounces (oz)	X 28.35	= Grams (g)	X 0.035	= Ounces (oz)
Pounds (lb)	X 0.454	= Kilograms (kg)	X 2.205	= Pounds (lb)

Force

Ounces-force (ozf; oz)	X 0.278	= Newtons (N)	X 3.6	= Ounces-force (ozf; oz)
Pounds-force (lbf; lb)	X 4.448	= Newtons (N)	X 0.225	= Pounds-force (lbf; lb)
Newtons (N)	X 0.1	= Kilograms-force (kgf; kg)	X 9.81	= Newtons (N)

Pressure

Pounds-force per square inch (psi; lbf/in^2; lb/in^2)	X 0.070	= Kilograms-force per square centimetre (kgf/cm^2; kg/cm^2)	X 14.223	= Pounds-force per square inch (psi; lbf/in^2; lb/in^2)
Pounds-force per square inch (psi; lbf/in^2; lb/in^2)	X 0.068	= Atmospheres (atm)	X 14.696	= Pounds-force per square inch (psi; lbf/in^2; lb/in^2)
Pounds-force per square inch (psi; lbf/in^2; lb/in^2)	X 0.069	= Bars	X 14.5	= Pounds-force per square inch (psi; lbf/in^2; lb/in^2)
Pounds-force per square inch (psi; lbf/in^2; lb/in^2)	X 6.895	= Kilopascals (kPa)	X 0.145	= Pounds-force per square inch (psi; lbf/in^2; lb/in^2)
Kilopascals (kPa)	X 0.01	= Kilograms-force per square centimetre (kgf/cm^2; kg/cm^2)	X 98.1	= Kilopascals (kPa)
Millibar (mbar)	X 100	= Pascals (Pa)	X 0.01	= Millibar (mbar)
Millibar (mbar)	X 0.0145	= Pounds-force per square inch (psi; lbf/in^2; lb/in^2)	X 68.947	= Millibar (mbar)
Millibar (mbar)	X 0.75	= Millimetres of mercury (mmHg)	X 1.333	= Millibar (mbar)
Millibar (mbar)	X 0.401	= Inches of water (inH_2O)	X 2.491	= Millibar (mbar)
Millimetres of mercury (mmHg)	X 0.535	= Inches of water (inH_2O)	X 1.868	= Millimetres of mercury (mmHg)
Inches of water (inH_2O)	X 0.036	= Pounds-force per square inch (psi; lbf/in^2; lb/in^2)	X 27.68	= Inches of water (inH_2O)

Torque (moment of force)

Pounds-force inches (lbf in; lb in)	X 1.152	= Kilograms-force centimetre (kgf cm; kg cm)	X 0.868	= Pounds-force inches (lbf in; lb in)
Pounds-force inches (lbf in; lb in)	X 0.113	= Newton metres (Nm)	X 8.85	= Pounds-force inches (lbf in; lb in)
Pounds-force inches (lbf in; lb in)	X 0.083	= Pounds-force feet (lbf ft; lb ft)	X 12	= Pounds-force inches (lbf in; lb in)
Pounds-force feet (lbf ft; lb ft)	X 0.138	= Kilograms-force metres (kgf m; kg m)	X 7.233	= Pounds-force feet (lbf ft; lb ft)
Pounds-force feet (lbf ft; lb ft)	X 1.356	= Newton metres (Nm)	X 0.738	= Pounds-force feet (lbf ft; lb ft)
Newton metres (Nm)	X 0.102	= Kilograms-force metres (kgf m; kg m)	X 9.804	= Newton metres (Nm)

Power

Horsepower (hp)	X 745.7	= Watts (W)	X 0.0013	= Horsepower (hp)

Velocity (speed)

Miles per hour (miles/hr; mph)	X 1.609	= Kilometres per hour (km/hr; kph)	X 0.621	= Miles per hour (miles/hr; mph)

*Fuel consumption**

Miles per gallon, Imperial (mpg)	X 0.354	= Kilometres per litre (km/l)	X 2.825	= Miles per gallon, Imperial (mpg)
Miles per gallon, US (mpg)	X 0.425	= Kilometres per litre (km/l)	X 2.352	= Miles per gallon, US (mpg)

Temperature

Degrees Fahrenheit = (°C x 1.8) + 32

Degrees Celsius (Degrees Centigrade; °C) = (°F - 32) x 0.56

**It is common practice to convert from miles per gallon (mpg) to litres/100 kilometres (l/100km), where mpg (Imperial) x l/100 km = 282 and mpg (US) x l/100 km = 235*

Index

A

About this manual — 2
Accelerator pedal and linkage
check and adjustment — 43
removal and installation — 88
Acknowledgements — 2
Air conditioning system
check and maintenance — 77
compressor
removal and installation — 77
compressor drivebelt
adjustment — 38
condensor
removal and installation — 78
general information — 76
specifications — 71
Air filter replacement — 39
Air flow meter
removal and installation — 89
Air gap adjustment — 103
Air induction system
checking — 121
EAI tubes
removal and installation — 121
filter replacement — 42
general description — 120
valve removal and installation — 121
valve case
removal and installation — 121
Air regulator
removal and installation — 91
Altitude sensor
removal and installation — 92
Antenna (power)
removal and installation — 178
Antenna switch (power)
removal and installation — 174
Antifreeze — 72
Apron (front)
removal and installation — 228
Alternator
drivebelt adjustment — 38
maintenance and special precautions — 109
removal and installation — 109
specifications — 99
Automatic Speed Control Device (ASCD)
general — 177
Automatic transmission
fluid change — 46
fluid level check — 31
general information — 132
inhibitor switch adjustment — 134, 247
kickdown switch adjustment — 134
rear oil seal replacement — 134
removal and installation — 135, 247
shift linkage adjustment — 134
specifications — 132
troubleshooting — 21
vacuum diaphragm rod adjustment — 134
Axleshaft
removal and installation — 143

B

BPT (Back Pressure Transducer) valve
checking — 114
removal and installation — 116
Balljoint
removal and installation — 213
Battery
charging — 35
emergency jump start — 35
fluid level check — 31
maintenance — 34
removal and installation — 35
troubleshooting — 16
Bearings (main and rod)
checking clearance — 69
Blower (heater) unit
removal and installation — 76
Bodywork
color charts — 230, 231
damage
major repairs — 226
minor repairs — 225
general information — 224
maintenance — 224
specifications — 224
Braking system
bleeding — 148
brake lines
general inspection and replacement — 149
disc brake inspection — 44
fluid level check — 31

front disc brakes
caliper removal, overhaul and installation — 150
pad replacement — 149, 247
rotor removal and installation — 153
general information — 147
master cylinder
overhaul — 156, 249
removal and installation — 156
parking brake
adjustment — 43
lever and front cable, removal and installation — 158
rear cables, removal and installation — 159
rear disc brakes
caliper removal, overhaul and installation — 154, 247
pad replacement — 153, 247
rotor, removal and installation — 156
specifications — 146, 242
troubleshooting — 22
vacuum servo (booster) unit
general information and testing — 158
removal and installation — 158
Bumpers
general — 228
removal and installation — 229, 250, 251
Buying parts — 8

C

Camshaft
removal and installation — 54
inspection and servicing — 55
Catalytic converter
general — 97
removal and installation — 97
Center console cluster
removal and installation — 174
Chapter 13 Supplement: Revisions and information on 1982 and 1983 models — 241
Charcoal canister
see EEC (Evaporative Emissions Control) system
Charging system (also see Alternator)
general information — 109
specifications — 99
testing — 109
Chassis lubrication — 43
Chemicals — 12
Cigar lighter
removal and installation — 174
Clock
removal and installation — 173
Clutch system
bleeding — 137
disc and pressure plate assembly
removal and installation — 140
fluid level check — 31
general information — 137
master cylinder
overhaul — 138
removal and installation — 138
operating cylinder
overhaul — 140
removal and installation — 139
pedal
adjustments — 43
removal and installation — 137
release bearing replacement — 141
specifications — 136
troubleshooting — 20
Color charts
bodywork — 226 and 227
spark plugs — 36
Combination switch
removal and installation — 164
Compressor
drivebelt adjustment — 38
removal and installation — 77
Connecting rods (see also Pistons, connecting rods and bearings)
checking bearing clearance — 68
Console box
removal and installation — 173
Control unit (EFI)
removal and installation — 89
Cooling system
check and servicing — 42
fluid level check — 30
general information — 71
specifications — 71
troubleshooting — 19
Crankshaft and main bearings
checking bearing clearance — 69
inspection and servicing — 66
installation — 68
removal — 65
Crossmember
removal and installation — 213
Crossrod
removal and installation — 213
Cruise control (see Automatic Speed Control Device)
Cylinder block inspection — 66
Cylinder compression testing — 40
Cylinder head
assembly — 58
cleaning — 58
disassembly — 57
inspection — 58
installation — 59
removal — 57

D

Dashpot
removal and installation — 90
Deceleration control system
general description — 119
vacuum control valve
checking — 119
removal and installation — 120
Defogger (rear)
testing and repair — 178
Differential
general information — 142
oil change — 46
oil level check — 32
pinion oil seal replacement — 145
removal and installation — 145
troubleshooting — 22
Disc brakes (see Braking system)
Distributor
checking — 39
installation — 104
removal — 104
specifications — 98
Dome lamp — see Lights
Door
lock and lock control
removal and installation — 236
mirror switch (electric remote control)
removal and installation — 176
removal and installation — 236
trim panel
removal and installation — 234
window
removal and installation — 235
Driveshaft
disassembly and reassembly — 142
inspection — 45
general information — 142

removal and installation — 142
troubleshooting — 21
Drivebelts
checking and adjusting — 38, 244
Dropping resistor
removal and installation — 89

E

EEC (Evaporative Emissions Control) System
checking — 117
filter replacement — 46
general description — 116
purge control valve
diaphragm replacement — 117
EFI (Electronic Fuel Injection) System
air flow meter and air temperature sensor
removal and installation — 89
air regulator
removal and installation — 91
altitude sensor
removal and installation — 92
component description — 81
component testing — 84
control unit
removal and installation — 89
dashpot
removal and installation — 90
dropping resistor
removal and installation — 89
exhaust gas sensor
removal and installation — 92
idle adjusting unit
removal and installation — 89
injectors and fuel pipe assembly
removal and installation — 91
general description — 81
pressure regulator
removal and installation — 91
throttle valve switch
removal, installation and adjustment — 89, 245
vacuum switch
removal and installation — 92
water temperature sensor
removal and installation — 91
EGR (Exhaust Gas Recirculation) system
BPT (Back Pressure Transducer) valve
checking — 114
removal and installation — 116
EGR valve
checking — 114
removal and installation — 116
general description — 111
thermal vacuum valve (TVV)
checking — 115
replacement — 116
VVT (Venturi Vacuum Transducer) valve
checking — 114
removal and installation — 116
Electrical system (also see Lights and Gauges and indicators)
door mirror switch (electric remote control)
removal and installation — 176
fan switch
removal and installation — 174
fuses — 162, 163
fusible links — 162, 163
general information — 162
horn fault testing — 166
illumination rheostat control
removal and installation — 176
power antenna switch
removal and installation — 174
printed circuit board
removal and installation — 173
rear defogger
testing and repair — 178
relays — 163
specifications — 161, 242, 243
steering column comination switch
removal and installation — 169
troubleshooting, general — 162
turn signals and hazard flashers — 163
voice warning system — 249
wiring diagrams — 192 to 201
wiring harness connectors — 179 to 191
Emissions control systems
Air induction system — 120, 246
Decelerating control system — 119
EEC (Evaporative Emissions Control) system — 116
EGR (Exhaust Gas Recirculation) system — 111, 246
general information — 110
Mixture ratio feedback system — 121
PCV (Positive Crankcase Ventilation) system — 110, 245
Spark timing control system — 117, 246
torque specifications — 110
Energy absorbers
general — 228
removal and installation — 229
Engine
coolant level check — 30
drivebelt check and adjustment — 38, 244
electrical systems — 98, 245
engine mounts replacement — 63
general information — 51, 245
installation — 69
oil and filter change — 33
oil level check — 30
overhaul
general disassembly information — 64
general assembly information — 66
rebuilding alternatives — 66
removal — 63
specifications — 48, 242, 243
start-up (following overhaul) — 70
troubleshooting — 17
Exhaust gas sensor
removal and installation — 92
servicing — 46
Exhaust manifold
removal and installation — 57
Exhaust system
checking — 45
catalytic converter
removal and installation — 97
front exhaust pipe
removal and installation — 97
general information — 95
muffler/tailpipe
removal and installation — 97

F

Fan (radiator)
removal and installation — 74
Fan switch (heater)
removal and installation — 174
Fender (front)
removal and installation — 229
Filter and oil change — 33
Fluids
capacities — 25
levels check — 30
recommended types — 25
Flywheel
removal and installation — 62
Front axle, removal and installation — 213
Front cover
removal and installation — 60
Front end alignment — 205

Front hub
removal and installation — 206
Front spring and strut assembly
disassembly and reassembly — 210
removal and installation — 209
Fuel gauge
removal and installation — 171
Fuel pipe assembly
removal and installation — 91
Fuel system
checking — 45
check valve
removal and installation — 95
cleaning — 87
filter replacement — 41, 244
general information — 81
line repair and replacement — 87
pump and damper
removal and installation — 88
specifications — 79
Fuel tank
removal and installation — 92
cleaning and purging — 95
gauge unit
removal and installation — 95
Fuses — 162, 163
Fusible links — 162, 163

G

Gauges and indicators
removal and installation — 171
Glove box
removal and installation — 32
Grille
removal and installation — 226

H

Hatchback door
lock and cylinder
removal and installation — 233
release cable
removal and installation — 233
removal and installation — 234
Hazard flashers, general — 163
Headlight
adjustment — 166
removal and installation — 167
Heating system
blower unit — 76
general information — 74
heater unit
removal and installation — 75
Heater/A/C control assembly
removal and installation — 174
Hood
alignment — 228
latches, general — 228
latch release cable
removal and installation — 228
removal and installation — 227
Horn
fault testing — 166

I

Idle adjusting unit
removal and installation — 89
Idle speed adjustments — 40, 244
Idler arm
removal and installation — 222
Ignition system (see also Distributor)
air gap adjustment — 103
coil removal and installation — 104
IC ignition unit
removal and installation — 103
general information — 99
specifications — 98
stator and magnet (pick-up assembly)
removal and installation — 104
testing — 101
timing — 40
Inhibitor switch
adjustment — 134
Injectors
removal and installation — 71
Instrument cluster
removal and installation — 171
Instrument panel
removal and installation — 177
Intake manifold
removal and installation — 177
Introduction to the Datsun 200SX — 2

J

Jacking and towing — 13

K

Kickdown switch
adjustment — 134

L

Lights
back-up lamp
bulb and lens replacement — 167
headlight
adjustment — 166
removal and installation — 167
interior lamp
bulb and lens replacement — 167
side marker lamps
bulb and lens replacement — 178
taillight
bulb and lens replacement — 167
turn signal/parking lamp (front)
bulb and lens replacement — 167
Links (upper and lower)
removal and installation — 214
Lubricants — 12

M

Main bearings (also see Crankshaft)
checking clearance — 69
Maintenance
routine maintenance intervals — 27
techniques — 8
Manual transmission
general information — 124
oil level check — 31
overhaul — 125
rear oil seal replacement — 124
removal and installation — 124
specifications — 122
troubleshooting — 20
Master cylinder (see Brake system, or Clutch system)
Muffler
removal and installation — 97
Multi-warning indicator
removal and installation — 173

N

Noises (see Troubleshooting)

O

Oil
change — 33
filter change — 33
fluid level check — 30
pan removal and installation — 61
pump
overhaul — 59
removal and installation — 59, 245
seals
front cover seal replacement — 61
rear seal replacement — 62

P

Parking brake (see Braking system)
PCV (Positive Crankcase Ventilation) system
checking — 111
general description — 110
PCV valve replacement — 41
Pilot bushing replacement — 62
Pinion oil seal replacement — 145
Pistons, connecting rods and bearings
cleaning and inspection — 65
installation — 68
pistons and piston rings assembly — 67
removal — 64
Power brakes (see Braking system)
Power radio antenna (see Antenna)
Power steering system
bleeding — 221
fluid level check — 32, 244
gear removal and installation — 221
maintenance and adjustment — 220
pump
removal and installation — 221
drivebelt adjustment — 38
Pressure plate (clutch)
removal and installation — 140
Pressure regulator
removal and installation — 91
Printed circuit board
removal and installation — 173

R

Radiator
removal and installation — 73
Radio
power antenna
removal and installation — 178
power antenna switch
removal and installation — 174
removal and installation — 175
sound balancer
removal and installation — 175
speakers
removal and installation — 177
Rear axle
general information — 142
removal and installation — 145
troubleshooting — 22
Rear defogger
testing and repair — 178
Relays
general information — 163
Release bearing (clutch)
replacement — 141
Reservoir tank (coolant)
removal and installation — 73
Reservoir tank (fuel)
removal and installation — 93
Rocker arm cover
removal and installation — 51
Routine maintenance intervals — 27, 244

S

Safety first — 15
Seats
front, removal and installation — 236
rear, removal and installation — 236
Seat belts
removal and installation — 239
Shock absorber (rear) (For front, see Front spring and strut assembly)
removal and installation — 214
testing — 276
Sight shield (front)
removal and installation — 229
Spark plugs
color chart — 36
replacement — 35
wires check — 37
Spark plug switching control system — 245
Spark timing control system
1980 — 117
1981 on — 118, 246
Speakers
removal and installation — 177
Speedometer
removal and installation — 171
Speedometer cable
removal and installation — 177
Spring (rear)
removal and installation — 214
Stabilizer bar
front, removal and installation — 211
rear, removal and installation — 214
Starting system
general information — 105
specifications — 99
testing — 105
Starter motor
brush replacement — 108
removal and installation — 108
solenoid
removal and installation — 108
specifications — 99
troubleshooting — 17
Stator and magnet (pick-up assembly)
removal and installation — 104
Steering column combination switch
removal and installation — 169
Steering system (see also Power steering system)
checking — 44
column removal and installation — 217
gearbox removal and installation — 216
general information — 215
linkage removal and installation — 222
lock removal and installation — 216
specifications — 202
troubleshooting — 23
wheel removal and installation — 216
Strut and spring assembly (see Suspension system)
Suspension system
checking — 44
front spring and strut assembly
disassembly and reassembly — 210
removal and installation — 209
general information — 209

rear shock absorber
removal and installation — 214
rear spring
removal and installation — 214
specifications — 202
troubleshooting — 23

T

Tachometer
removal and installation — 171
Taillights
bulb and lens replacement — 167
Tension rod
removal and installation — 212
Thermostat
removal and installation — 72
Throttle chamber
removal and installation — 90
Throttle valve switch
removal, installation and adjustment — 89
Tie rod
removal and installation — 222
Timing gear
removal and installation — 60
Tires
general information — 33, 204
pressure checks — 33
replacement — 14
rotation — 33
wear patterns — 24
Tools and working facilities — 8
Towing — 13
Transmission (see Manual transmission, or Automatic transmission)
Transverse links
removal and installation — 212
Trim panel
front door, removal and installation — 234
rear side, removal and installation — 237
Trunk lid
lock removal and installation — 232
lock cylinder
removal and installation — 232
release cable
removal and installation — 233
removal and installation — 233
Troubleshooting — 16
Tune-up
general information — 29
specifications — 26, 241
Turn signals and hazard flashers, general — 163

V

VVT (Venturi Transducer) valve
checking — 114
removal and installation — 116
Vacuum advance system (see Spark timing control system)
Vacuum control valve
checking — 119
removal and installation — 119
Vacuum diaphragm rod adjustment — 134
Vacuum switch
removal and installation — 92
Valve clearance adjustment — 40, 244
Valve rocker assembly
disassembly and reassembly — 51
removal and installation — 51
Valve spring and seal
removal and installation — 55, 58
Valves and valve seats
inspection and valve grinding — 58
Vehicle identification numbers — 6
Voltmeter
removal and installation — 173

W

Water pump
drivebelt adjustment — 38
removal and installation — 74
testing — 74
Water temperature gauge
removal and installation — 171
Water temperature sensor
removal and installation — 91
Wheels
front end alignment — 205
general information — 204
replacement — 14
stud replacement — 207
Wheel bearings
checking — 43
front bearings
removal and installation — 206
rear bearings
removal and installation — 143
Windows
Front door
removal and installation — 235
Opera (hardtop)
removal and installation — 239
rear quarter
removal and installation — 239
Windshield wiper system
general description — 168
intermittent amplifier
removal and installation — 169
linkage assembly
removal and installation — 169
rear wiper motor
removal and installation — 169
windshield washer
fluid level check — 30
servicing — 169
wiper arm
removal and installation — 168
wiper blade
removal and installation — 168
wiper motor
removal and installation — 168
Wiring diagrams — 192 to 201
Wiring harness connectors — 179 to 191
Working conditions — 8

HAYNES AUTOMOTIVE MANUALS

NOTE: New manuals are added to this list on a periodic basis. If you do not see a listing for your vehicle, consult your local Haynes dealer for the latest product information.

ALFA ROMEO
531 **Alfa Romeo** Sedan & Coupe '73 thru '80

AMC
Jeep CJ — *see JEEP (412)*
694 **Mid-size models,** Concord, Hornet, Gremlin & Spirit '70 thru '83
*934 **(Renault) Alliance & Encore** all models '83 thru '87

AUDI
162 **100** all models '69 thru '77
615 **4000** all models '80 thru '87
428 **5000** all models '77 thru '83
*1117 **5000** all models '84 thru '88
207 **Fox** all models '73 thru '79

AUSTIN
049 **Healey 100/6 & 3000** Roadster '56 thru '68
Healey Sprite — *see MG Midget Roadster (265)*

BLMC
260 **1100, 1300 & Austin America** '62 thru '74
527 **Mini** all models '59 thru '69
*646 **Mini** all models '69 thru '88

BMW
276 **320i** all 4 cyl models '75 thru '83
*632 **528i & 530i** all models '75 thru '80
240 **1500 thru 2002** all models except Turbo '59 thru '77
348 **2500, 2800, 3.0 & Bavaria** all models '69 thru '76

BUICK
Century (Front wheel drive) — *see GENERAL MOTORS A-Cars (829)*
*1551 **Buick, Oldsmobile and Pontiac Full-size** All rear-wheel drive models '70 thru '88
*627 **Mid-size** all rear-drive **Regal & Century** models with V6, V8 and Turbo '74 thru '87
Skyhawk — *see GENERAL MOTORS J-Cars (766)*
552 **Skylark** all X-car models '80 thru '85

CADILLAC
Cimarron — *see GENERAL MOTORS J-Cars (766)*

CAPRI
296 **2000 MK I** Coupe all models '71 thru '75
283 **2300 MK II** Coupe all models '74 thru '78
205 **2600 & 2800** V6 Coupe all models '71 thru '75
375 **2800 Mk II** V6 Coupe all models '75 thru '78
Mercury (in-line engines) — *see FORD Mustang (654)*
Mercury (V6 & V8 engines) — *see FORD Mustang (558)*

CHEVROLET
*1477 **Astro & GMC Safari Mini-vans** all models '85 thru '88
554 **Camaro** V8 all models '70 thru '81
*866 **Camaro** all models '82 thru '89
Cavalier — *see GENERAL MOTORS J-Cars (766)*
Celebrity — *see GENERAL MOTORS A-Cars (829)*
*625 **Chevelle, Malibu & El Camino** all V6 & V8 models '69 thru '87
449 **Chevette & Pontiac T1000** all models '76 thru '87
550 **Citation** all models '80 thru '85
274 **Corvette** all V8 models '68 thru '82
*1336 **Corvette** all models '84 thru '87
*704 **Full-size Sedans** Caprice, Impala, Biscayne, Bel Air & Wagons, all V6 & V8 models '69 thru '88
319 **Luv Pick-up** all 2WD & 4WD models '72 thru '82
*626 **Monte Carlo** all V6, V8 & Turbo models '70 thru '88
241 **Nova** all V8 models '69 thru '79
420 **Pick-ups — Chevrolet & GMC,** all V8 & in-line 6 cyl 2WD & 4WD models '67 thru '87
*831 **S-10 & GMC S-15 Pick-ups** all models '82 thru '87
*345 **Vans — Chevrolet & GMC,** V8 & in-line 6 cyl models '68 thru '87
208 **Vega** all models except Cosworth '70 thru '77

CHRYSLER
*1337 **Chrysler & Plymouth Mid-size front wheel drive** '82 thru '88
K-Cars — *see DODGE Aries/Plymouth Reliant (723)*
Laser — *see DODGE Daytona & Chrysler Laser (1140)*

DATSUN
402 **200SX** all models '77 thru '79
*647 **200SX** all models '80 thru '83
228 **B-210** all models '73 thru '78
525 **210** all models '79 thru '82
206 **240Z, 260Z & 280Z** Coupe & 2+2 '70 thru '78
563 **280ZX** Coupe & 2+2 '79 thru '83
300ZX — *see NISSAN (1137)*
679 **310** all models '78 thru '82
123 **510 & PL521 Pick-up** '68 thru '73
430 **510** all models '78 thru '81
372 **610** all models '72 thru '76
277 **620 Series Pick-up** all models '73 thru '79
235 **710** all models '73 thru '77
720 Series Pick-up *see Nissan (771)*
*376 **810/Maxima** all gasoline models '77 thru '84
124 **1200** all models '70 thru '73
368 **F10** all models '76 thru '79
Pulsar — *see NISSAN (876)*
Sentra — *see NISSAN (982)*
Stanza — *see NISSAN (981)*

DODGE
*723 **Aries & Plymouth Reliant** all models '81 thru '88
*1231 **Caravan & Plymouth Voyager Mini-Vans** all models '84 thru '88
699 **Challenger & Plymouth Sapporo** all models '78 thru '83
236 **Colt** all models '71 thru '77
419 **Colt (rear wheel drive)** all models '77 thru '80
*610 **Colt & Plymouth Champ (front wheel drive)** all models '78 thru '87
*556 **D50 & Plymouth Arrow Pick-ups** '79 thru '88
234 **Dart & Plymouth Valiant** all 6 cyl models '67 thru '76
*1140 **Daytona & Chrysler Laser** all models '84 thru '88
*545 **Omni & Plymouth Horizon** all models '78 thru '84
*912 **Pick-ups** all full-size models '74 thru '88
*349 **Vans — Dodge & Plymouth** V8 & 6 cyl models '71 thru '86

FIAT
080 **124 Sedan & Wagon** all ohv & dohc models '66 thru '75
094 **124 Sport Coupe & Spider** '68 thru '78
087 **128** all models '72 thru '79
310 **131 & Brava** all models '75 thru '81
038 **850 Sedan, Coupe & Spider** '64 thru '74
479 **Strada** all models '79 thru '82
*273 **X1/9** all models '74 thru '80

(continued on next page)

FORD
*1476 **Aerostar Mini-vans** all models '85 thru '88
788 **Bronco and Pick-ups** '73 thru '79
*880 **Bronco and Pick-ups** '80 thru '88
014 **Cortina MKII** 1300, 1500, 1500GT & 1600 GT '66 thru '70
295 **Cortina MK III** 1600 & 2000 ohc '70 thru '76
268 **Courier Pick-up** all models '72 thru '82
*789 **Escort & Mercury Lynx** all models '81 thru '88
560 **Fairmont & Mercury Zephyr** all in-line & V8 models '78 thru '83
334 **Fiesta** all models '77 thru '80
359 **Granada & Mercury Monarch** all in-line, 6 cyl & V8 models '75 thru '80
*754 **Ford & Mercury Full-size,** FORD: LTD ('75 thru '82); Custom 500; Country Squire; Crown Victoria, MERCURY: Marquis ('75 thru '82); Gran Marquis; Colony Park, all V8 models '75 thru '87
773 **Ford & Mercury Mid-size** FORD: Torino; Gran Torino; Elite; Ranchero; LTD II; LTD ('83 thru '84); Thunderbird ('75 thru '82), MERCURY: Montego; Comet; Marquis ('83 thru '86); Cougar ('75 thru '82); LINCOLN: Versailles, all 4 cyl, in-line 6 cyl, V6 & V8 models '75 thru '80
*654 **Mustang & Mercury Capri** all in-line models & Turbo '79 thru '88
*558 **Mustang & Mercury Capri** all V6 & V8 models '79 thru '87
357 **Mustang V8** all models '64½ thru '73
231 **Mustang II** all 4 cyl, V6 & V8 models '74 thru '78
204 **Pinto** all models '70 thru '74
649 **Pinto & Mercury Bobcat** all models '75 thru '80
*1026 **Ranger & Bronco II** all gasoline models '83 thru '89
*1421 **Taurus & Mercury Sable** all models '86 thru '88
*1418 **Tempo & Mercury Topaz** all gasoline models '84 thru '87
*1338 **Thunderbird and Mercury Cougar** all models '83 thru '88
*344 **Vans** all V8 Econoline models '69 thru '88

GENERAL MOTORS
*829 **A-Cars** — Chevrolet Celebrity, Buick Century, Pontiac 6000 & Oldsmobile Cutlass Ciera all models '82 thru '87
*766 **J-Cars** — Chevrolet Cavalier, Pontiac J-2000, Oldsmobile Firenza, Buick Skyhawk & Cadillac Cimarron all models '82 thru '87
*1420 **N-Cars** — Pontiac Grand Am, Buick Somerset & Oldsmobile Calais '85 thru '87; Buick Skylark '86 thru '87

GMC
Safari — *see CHEVROLET Astro Mini-vans (1476)*
Vans & Pick-ups — *see CHEVROLET (420, 831, 345)*

HONDA
138 **360, 600 & Z Coupe** all models '67 thru '75
351 **Accord CVCC** all models '76 thru '83
*1221 **Accord** all models '84 thru '85
160 **Civic 1200** all models '73 thru '79
633 **Civic 1300 & 1500 CVCC** all models '80 thru '83
297 **Civic 1500 CVCC** all models '75 thru '79
*1227 **Civic** all models except 16-valve CRX & 4 WD Wagon '84 thru '86
*601 **Prelude CVCC** all models '79 thru '82

** Listings shown with an asterisk (*) indicate model coverage as of this printing. These titles will be periodically updated to include later model years — consult your Haynes dealer for more information.*

HAYNES AUTOMOTIVE MANUALS

(continued from previous page)

NOTE: New manuals are added to this list on a periodic basis. If you do not see a listing for your vehicle, consult your local Haynes dealer for the latest product information.

HYUNDAI
- *1552 **Excel** all models '86 thru '89

JAGUAR
- 098 **MK I & II,** 240 & 340 Sedans '55 thru '69
- *242 **XJ6** all 6 cyl models '68 thru '86
- *478 **XJ12 & XJS** all 12 cyl models '72 thru '85
- 140 **XK-E** 3.8 & 4.2 all 6 cyl models '61 thru '72

JEEP
- *1553 **Cherokee, Comanche & Wagoneer Limited** all models '84 thru '89
- 412 **CJ** all models '49 thru '86

LADA
- *413 **1200, 1300, 1500 & 1600** all models including Riva '74 thru '86

LANCIA
- 533 **Lancia Beta** Sedan, Coupe & HPE all models '76 thru '80

LAND ROVER
- 314 **Series II, IIA, & III** all 4 cyl gasoline models '58 thru '86
- 529 **Diesel** all models '58 thru '80

MAZDA
- 648 **626** Sedan & Coupe (rear wheel drive) all models '79 thru '82
- *1082 **626 (front wheel drive)** all gas models '83 thru '87
- *267 **B1600, B1800, B2000, B2200 & B2600 Pick-ups** '72 thru '88
- 370 **GLC Hatchback (rear wheel drive)** all models '77 thru '83
- 757 **GLC (front wheel drive)** all models '81 thru '85
- 109 **RX2** all models '71 thru '75
- 096 **RX3** all models '72 thru '76
- 460 **RX-7** all models '79 thru '85

MERCEDES-BENZ
- 346 **230, 250 & 280** Sedan, Coupe & Roadster all 6 cyl sohc models '68 thru '72
- 983 **280 123 Series** all gasoline models '77 thru '81
- 698 **350 & 450** Sedan, Coupe & Roadster all models '71 thru '80
- 697 **Diesel 123 Series** 200D, 220D, 240D, 240TD, 300D, 300CD, 300TD, 4- & 5-cyl incl. Turbo '76 thru '85

MERCURY
- **See FORD Listing**

MG
- 475 **MGA** all models '56 thru '62
- 111 **MGB** Roadster & GT Coupe all models '62 thru '80
- 265 **MG Midget & Austin Healey Sprite** Roadster '58 thru '80

MITSUBISHI
- **Pick-up** — *see Dodge D-50 (556)*

MORRIS
- 074 **(Austin) Marina 1.8** all models '71 thru '75
- 024 **Minor 1000** sedan & wagon '56 thru '71

NISSAN
- *1137 **300ZX** all models '84 thru '86
- *771 **Pick-ups & Pathfinder** all gasoline models '80 thru '88
- *876 **Pulsar** all models '83 thru '86
- *982 **Sentra** all models '82 thru '86
- *981 **Stanza** all models '82 thru '86

OLDSMOBILE
- **Custom Cruiser** — *see Buick Full-size (1551)*
- *658 **Cutlass** all standard gasoline V6 & V8 models '74 thru '87
- **Cutlass Ciera** — *see GENERAL MOTORS A-Cars (829)*
- **Delta 88, Delta 88 Brougham & Delta 88 Royale** — *see Buick Full-size (1551)*
- **Firenza** — *see GENERAL MOTORS J-Cars (766)*
- **Ninety-eight Luxury, Ninety-eight Regency & Ninety-eight Regency Brougham** — *see Buick Full-size (1551)*
- **Omega** — *see PONTIAC Phoenix & Omega (551)*

OPEL
- 157 **(Buick) Manta Coupe 1900** all models '70 thru '74

PEUGEOT
- 161 **504** all gasoline models '68 thru '79
- 663 **504** all diesel models '74 thru '83

PLYMOUTH
- 425 **Arrow** all models '76 thru '80
- **Arrow Pick-up** — *see DODGE D50 & Arrow Pickups (556)*
- **Champ** — *see DODGE Colt & Champ (610)*
- **Horizon** — *see DODGE Omni & Horizon (545)*
- **Reliant** — *see DODGE Aries & Reliant (723)*
- **Sapporo** — *see DODGE Challenger & Sapporo (699)*
- **Valiant & Barracuda** — *see DODGE Dart (234)*
- **Vans** — *see DODGE & Plymouth Vans (349)*
- **Voyager** — *see DODGE Caravan & Voyager (1231)*

PONTIAC
- **T1000** — *see CHEVROLET Chevette (449)*
- **J-2000** — *see GENERAL MOTORS J-Cars (766)*
- **6000** — *see GENERAL MOTORS A-Cars (829)*
- **Bonneville, Bonneville Brougham & Catalina** — *see Buick Full-size (1551)*
- *1232 **Fiero** all models '84 thru '87
- 555 **Firebird** all V8 models except Turbo '70 thru '81
- *867 **Firebird** all models '82 thru '89
- **Grandville & Parisienne** *see Buick Full-size (1551)*
- 551 **Phoenix & Oldsmobile Omega** all X-car models '80 thru '84

PORSCHE
- *264 **911** all Coupe & Targa models except Turbo '65 thru '87
- 239 **914** all 4 cyl models '69 thru '76
- 397 **924** all models including Turbo '76 thru '82
- *1027 **944** all models including Turbo '83 thru '86

RENAULT
- 141 **5 Le Car** all models '76 thru '83
- 079 **8 & 10** all models with 58.4 cu in engines '62 thru '72
- 097 **12 Saloon & Estate** all models 1289 cc engines '70 thru '80
- 768 **15 & 17** all models '73 thru '79
- 081 **16** all models 89.7 cu in & 95.5 cu in engines '65 thru '72
- 598 **18i & Sportwagon** all models '81 thru '86
- **Alliance & Encore** — *see AMC (934)*
- 984 **Fuego** all models '82 thru '85

ROVER
- 085 **3500 & 3500S Sedan** 215 cu in engines '68 thru '76
- *365 **3500 SDI** V8 all models '76 thru '85

SAAB
- 198 **95 & 96** V4 all models '66 thru '75
- 247 **99** all models including Turbo '69 thru '80
- *980 **900** all models including Turbo '79 thru '88

SUBARU
- 237 **1100, 1300, 1400 & 1600** all models '71 thru '79
- *681 **1600 & 1800** 2WD & 4WD all models '80 thru '88

TOYOTA
- *1023 **Camry** all models '83 thru '88
- 150 **Carina** Sedan all models '71 thru '74
- 229 **Celica** ST, GT & liftback all models '71 thru '77
- 437 **Celica** all models '78 thru '81
- *935 **Celica** all models except front wheel drive and Supra '82 thru '85
- 680 **Celica Supra** all models '79 thru '81
- 1139 **Celica Supra** all models '82 thru '86
- 201 **Corolla 1100, 1200 & 1600** all models '67 thru '74
- 361 **Corolla** all models '75 thru '79
- *961 **Corolla** all models (rear wheel drive) '80 thru '82
- *1025 **Corolla** all models (front wheel drive) '84 thru '88
- *636 **Corolla Tercel** all models '80 thru '82
- 230 **Corona & MK II** all 4 cyl sohc models '69 thru '74
- 360 **Corona** all models '74 thru '82
- *532 **Cressida** all models '78 thru '82
- 313 **Land Cruiser** all models '68 thru '82
- 200 **MK II** all 6 cyl models '72 thru '76
- *1339 **MR2** all models '85 thru '87
- 304 **Pick-up** all models '69 thru '78
- *656 **Pick-up** all models '79 thru '88
- 787 **Starlet** all models '81 thru '84

TRIUMPH
- 112 **GT6 & Vitesse** all models '62 thru '74
- 113 **Spitfire** all models '62 thru '81
- 028 **TR2, 3, 3A, 4 & 4A** Roadsters '52 thru '67
- 031 **TR250 & TR6** Roadsters '67 thru '76
- 322 **TR7** all models '75 thru '81

VW
- 091 **411 & 412** all 103 cu in models '68 thru '73
- 036 **Bug 1200** all models '54 thru '66
- 039 **Bug 1300 & 1500** '65 thru '70
- 159 **Bug 1600** all basic, sport & super (curved windshield) models '70 thru '74
- 110 **Bug 1600 Super** all models (flat windshield) '70 thru '72
- 238 **Dasher** all gasoline models '74 thru '81
- *884 **Rabbit, Jetta, Scirocco, & Pick-up** all gasoline models '74 thru '84 **& Convertible** '80 thru '85
- 451 **Rabbit, Jetta & Pick-up** all diesel models '77 thru '84
- 082 **Transporter 1600** all models '68 thru '79
- 226 **Transporter 1700, 1800 & 2000** all models '72 thru '79
- 084 **Type 3 1500 & 1600** all models '63 thru '73
- *1029 **Vanagon** all air-cooled models '80 thru '83

VOLVO
- 203 **120, 130 Series & 1800 Sports** '61 thru '73
- 129 **140 Series** all models '66 thru '74
- 244 **164** all models '68 thru '75
- *270 **240 Series** all models '74 thru '86
- 400 **260 Series** all models '75 thru '82
- *1550 **740 & 760 Series** all models '82 thru '88

SPECIALTY MANUALS
- 1479 **Automotive Body Repair & Painting Manual**
- 1480 **Automotive Heating & Air Conditioning Manual**
- 482 **Fuel Injection Manual** Covers Bosch, Chrysler, Ford and General Motors

See your dealer for other available titles

9/89

** Listings shown with an asterisk (*) indicate model coverage as of this printing. These titles will be periodically updated to include later model years — consult your Haynes dealer for more information.*

Over 100 Haynes motorcycle manuals also available

Haynes Publications Inc., P.O. Box 978, Newbury Park, CA 91320 • (818) 889-5400 • (805) 498-6703

Printed by
J H Haynes & Co Ltd
Sparkford Nr Yeovil
Somerset BA22 7JJ England